"WHAT A STORY HE HAS TO TELL! . . .

A LIFE ON THE ROAD is much more than the story of how an ambitious young man made it to the top in the highly competitive world of television journalism. It's also full of engaging stories about the extraordinary people he met and interviewed, and it's told with warmth and humor and wonderfully crafted prose."
The Houston Post

"America. It's a big country and someone's got to explore it. As A LIFE ON THE ROAD makes clear, armchair travelers should be grateful that for 33 years, their pioneer has been someone with the discipline, intelligence and compassion of Charles Kuralt."
The Washington Post

"[A] candid and affecting biography . . . Charles Kuralt's prose is clean, flexible and incisive, its context his own generous humanity."
Chicago Tribune

"A LIFE ON THE ROAD is as warm, amusing, optimistic and low-key as its author."
Newsday

"WONDERFUL . . .

A LIFE ON THE ROAD is a beautifully written account of the American spirit."
Congressional Affairs Press

"Clearly Kuralt enjoyed his life on the road in this chatty, anecdotal book. So will you."
John Barkham Reviews

"America's favorite wandering minstrel drives right into the heart in this warm, laid-back autobiography .... A happy memoir with good words for almost everyone and a wealth of funny anecdotes."
The Kirkus Reviews

"A charmer ... The book is comic and poignant by turns."
Publishers Weekly

Also by Charles Kuralt:

ON THE ROAD WITH CHARLES KURALT
NORTH CAROLINA IS MY HOME
DATELINE: AMERICA
TO THE TOP OF THE WORLD

A LIFE ON THE ROAD

Charles Kuralt

IVY BOOKS • NEW YORK

For
Ina Bishop Kuralt
and
Wallace Hamilton Kuralt,
my mother and father

Ivy Books
Published by Ballantine Books
Copyright © 1990 by Charles Kuralt

Library of Congress Catalog Card Number: 90-39461

ISBN 0-8041-0869-2

This edition published by arrangement with G. P. Putnam's Sons, a division of the Putnam Publishing Group, Inc.

Manufactured in the United States of America

First Ballantine Books Edition: November 1991

Cover photo courtesy of Tech Photo, Inc. (Lester Lefkowitz)

Contents

Foreword

ROAD, *n*. A strip of land along which one may pass from where it is too tiresome to be to where it is futile to go.

—Ambrose Bierce

There is no contentment on the road, and little enough fulfillment. I know that now. I am acquainted with people who live settled lives and find deep gratification in family and home. I know what I have missed, the birthdays and anniversaries, the generations together at the table, the pleasures of kinship, the rituals of the hearth.

And still I wander, seeking compensation in unforeseen encounters and unexpected sights, in sunsets, storms and passing fancies. I long ago exasperated those closest to me. I beg their forgiveness for all the experiences we didn't have at home together. It's too late for me to put down roots and join the Rotary.

I come from wandering tribes, Norse and Celtic on my mother's side it seems, nomad Bavarians on my father's, ancestors become Scots–Irish and Slovenian by the time of their immigration to America. As far as I can tell, none of them stayed anywhere for long. My brother, Wallace, overcame these vagabond genes to settle happily for life in Chapel Hill, North Carolina, and raise a large and loving family. My sister, Catherine, a beautiful woman, wife and mother of two, is an ornament of domesticity on Bainbridge Island, Washington. All the itinerant impulses of our lineage seem to have concentrated in me. They still goad me. No train leaves the station that I do not want to catch.

I have not set out to write an autobiography. That book would have to refer in detail to many mentors—Ransom Gurganus, who interested me in journalism when I was seven or eight years old; Anne Batten of Alexander Graham Junior High School in Charlotte, North Carolina, who gave me encouragement; Professor William Geer of the University of North Carolina, who opened my eyes and heart; Rolfe Neill, who taught me to make up a page—and to many friends and colleagues of CBS News, Tom Spain, Irv Drasnin, Shad Northshield, Hughes Rudd, Russ Bensley, Burton Benjamin, Bill Leonard, Bill Small and Gordon Manning among them, who are mentioned here in passing or not at all. An autobiography would be about those who have touched and changed me and about those I love. This book isn't that one.

This one is simply an incomplete remembrance of roads taken, breakdowns, misdirections, potholes and detours. If the traveler expects the highway to be safe and well graded, he might as well stay home. The little roads without numbers are the ones I have liked the best, the bumpy ones that lead over the hills toward vicinities unknown.

I started traveling as the youngest CBS News Correspondent, only twenty-three. Thirty-three years later, I look around the newsroom and find no other reporter in the place who was there then. I find to my surprise that in terms of consecutive years of employment, I am the old geezer of the on-the-air staff. I knew I was growing older out in the byways, and shorter of breath. I have noticed my thoughts turning to former companions and foregone pleasures. But I am not tempted to give up my seat in the "On The Road" bus for a rocking chair, not yet. Bierce was right about the futility of the destination, but he did not take into account the joy of the trip. I keep thinking I will find something wonderful just around the next bend.

The bookshelf of my grandmother's house contained a set of books, *The Complete Works of Robert Louis Stevenson*. I took down one of the books, *Songs of Travel*, when I was a little boy, and learned a poem in it:

> *Wealth I ask not, hope nor love,*
> *Nor a friend to know me;*
> *All I ask, the heaven above*
> *And the road below me.*

Acknowledgments

I am grateful to Karen Beckers for helping me open up old cornerstones and dig up time capsules from my CBS News past; to Isadore Bleckman for reading the manuscript and correcting some of my recollections, and for poring through shoe boxes of memory to find photographic souvenirs of our travels together; to Bernard Birnbaum for discovering other evidence of my life on the road and spending much of his own time in the sorting and printing of pictures; to the CBS Photographic Department for generously opening its files; to Joseph Bellon for his dependable representation of me as literary agent; and to Neil Nyren, publisher of G. P. Putnam's Sons, editor and friend, who did not *really* begin to lose patience with me until the manuscript of this book was three years overdue.

1
WANDERLUST

Before I was born, I went on the road. The road was U.S. 17, south from Jacksonville, North Carolina, through the Holly Shelter Swamp to Wilmington, where the hospital was. My father backed the Chevrolet out of its place in the hay barn next to the farm cart and helped my mother into the front seat on the afternoon of September 9, 1934. He made the trip in little more than an hour, barely slowing down for the stop signs in Dixon, Folkstone and Holly Ridge. I was born the next morning with rambling in my blood and fifty miles already under my belt.

We lived on my grandparents' farm off and on for a while there during the Depression. A sandy road passed in front of the house and a logging path through the pine woods behind it. I always wondered where the roads went, and after I learned that the one in front went to another farm a mile away, I wondered where it went from there. Once, playing in the woods, I surprised a flock of wild turkeys, which went flying down the logging road and out of sight. I remember wanting to go with them. Whenever I hear the Judy Garland lyric "Birds fly over the rainbow—Why then, oh why can't I?" it's those turkeys I see flying.

My mother was a schoolteacher and my father was getting started in what seemed to him the right job for the times, helping out poor people. There was no shortage of poor people to help out in the thirties, of course. My father, who had earned a Phi Beta Kappa key at the University of North Carolina and had planned to become a big businessman, became a social worker instead. He found employment in several of President Roosevelt's alphabet agencies, the CCC, the ERA, the WPA, then went back to the University at Chapel Hill, took some graduate courses in social work, and accepted a job with the state Department of Public Welfare. We moved from one town to another in eastern North Carolina, and I loved every move. I began to find out where the roads went.

My father's job as field supervisor for the state required him to travel to the small-town county seats to visit the local welfare offices. Since my mother was busy teaching school, somebody had to take care of me. The solution—a little troublesome for my father, I imagine, but perfect for me—was for him to take me with him on his trips.

We rolled along the country roads to the old tidewater towns, Edenton and Plymouth and New Bern and Swanquarter, my father smoking Tampa Nuggets and spinning yarns for my amusement. He tried a little history on me, thinking to improve my mind: "The people here didn't like the British governor, and had a fight with the British at this bridge." He filled me with local lore: "At Harkers Island over there, they make wonderful strong boats and go to sea in them." He taught me to read the Burma-Shave signs:

" 'Twould Be More Fun . . . to Go by Air . . . But
We Couldn't Put . . . These Signs Up There. Burma-
Shave.'' We stopped in the afternoons to fish for a
few minutes in roadside creeks turned black by the
tannin of cypress trees, my father casting a red-and-
white plug expertly with the old bait-casting rod he
carried in the trunk, and patiently picking out the
backlashes that snarled the reel when I tried it. We
stopped for suppers of pork chops, sweet potatoes
and collard greens at roadside cafes, and rolled on
into the night, bound for some tourist home down the
road, my father telling tales and I listening in rapture,
just the two of us, rolling on, wrapped in a cloud of
companionship and smoke from his five-cent cigar.

I wanted never to go home from these trips, and
when we did go home, I contrived longer trips to
farther-away places, trips of the mind. In a field within
walking distance of our farm, a small detachment of
U.S. Marines was setting up a tent camp, forerunner
of what was to become Camp LeJeune, the sprawling
Marine base that eventually changed Jacksonville forever. On hot summer mornings, I used to walk barefoot down the sandy road to the tent camp towing a
red wagon filled with quart jars of milk from our cows
and sugar cookies my grandmother had baked and
wrapped in wax paper. It never took more than a few
minutes to sell out my stock of milk and cookies to
the Marines. If they didn't have money, I accepted
souvenirs. Somewhere in my folks' attic, there must
still be a cigar box containing sharpshooter medals,
uniform buttons and globe-and-anchor emblems from
the pith helmets of those Marines. Most of them were

young enlistees, I suppose, who had never traveled farther than a few miles from home, but the cadre was composed of old sergeants who told me casual tales of service in places I had trouble imagining, places where the people spoke other languages entirely, they told me, places with names like the Philippines and Nicaragua and the Canal Zone. I learned to seek out the three-stripers when I wanted to hear good traveling stories. I learned the words of their song, "From the halls of Montezuma to the shores of Tripoli . . ." More than anything else, I wanted to wear a Marine pith helmet and go to the halls of Montezuma. I asked a jolly fat sergeant named Carpenter if he had ever been there. He always called me "Charlie, my boy." "Charlie, my boy," he said, "I'll tell you the truth. I've never even figured out where Montezuma might be. But if the United States Marines decide to send me there, I'll send you a penny postcard." I asked Sergeant Carpenter how old he was when he joined the Marines. "Charlie, my boy," he said, "I was a grand old man of sixteen." You had to be sixteen, he said. I was only six.

In school, I proved to be a below-average student in all forms of mathematics, and later in such subjects as chemistry and biology, but I was good at reading— I had started early on the Burma-Shave signs—and I was fascinated by history and geography, subjects that were still taught in public school in those days. Indiscriminately, I read the works of writers who had traveled, including everything I could find of Richard Halliburton's. I knew the capitals of all the states. The ones I most wanted to go to were Montpelier, Vermont, and Olympia, Washington, for they were the ones that sounded most distant and wondrous.

I entered contests that promised travel as a prize. In 1947, when I was twelve, to my surprise, I won one of these competitions—or rather, finished second for the second straight year, which proved to be just as good as winning. We lived in Charlotte, North Carolina, then, where my father had become the county welfare superintendent. *The Charlotte News* sponsored an annual baseball writing contest for students on the subject "My Favorite Hornet." The prize was a road trip with the Charlotte Hornets, our Washington Senators' farm team. Baseball was my passion and regularly I spent my Saturdays in the old green grandstand watching the Hornets play, but it was the trip I was after. My essay on "bouncing" Bobby Beal, the third baseman, was judged good enough that I was invited to accompany the winner, an older boy named Buddy Carrier. We were to ride in the bus with the team and take turns covering six games in Asheville, North Carolina, and Knoxville, Tennessee. I loved it. I loved the easy chaperoneship of manager Cal Ermer, who assigned Buddy and me the same curfew that applied to the team—one A.M.! I loved listening to the banter of the players on the bus, sitting in the dugout during the games and hanging around the hotel lobbies with my heroes. I loved being away from home, in places I had only heard about. Asheville! Knoxville! A good-natured country pitcher named Sonny Dixon played catch with me on the field before each game began and took to introducing me to players on the other teams as "Flash Kuralt, our traveling big-time sports writer.'' I loved that, too. But best of all was climbing up to the press box as the game was about to end and pecking out my story on the battered portable typewriter I had borrowed for the trip from a caseworker in my father's office, then, downtown after the game, swaggering into the Western Union office, tossing the copy across the counter and saying to the clerk the words I had been instructed to say by Ray Howe, the *Charlotte News* sports editor. They are words that still give me a little thrill of importance all these years later. I did my twelve-year-old best to growl them like a veteran.

The words were:

"*The Charlotte News*. Press rate collect."

After that summer, in my imagination, I was an experienced traveling reporter. I covered junior high school basketball and football for the newspaper, frustrated by the state law and the parental discretion that agreed I wasn't yet old enough to drive a car to the games. Not that I had a car to drive, of course. My parents wouldn't even give me permission to own a motorbike. I rode the crosstown bus with my notebook showing out of my pocket and my typewriter prominent by my side, or yielded with embarrassment to a ride to the gyms or football fields in the backseat of my parents' car, where the *children* always sat. I made this humiliation tolerable by imagining, there in the backseat, that I was flying across an ocean in a DC-3, checking over my notes for a big story while on the way to Constantinople or Khartoum.

At fourteen, I won another contest and got another trip. It was a speaking contest this time, called the "Voice of Democracy." Not very many kids entered; not very many had a wanderlust like mine. As one of four national winners, I got to give my speech in the House of Burgesses in colonial Williamsburg, Virginia, at the spot where Patrick Henry said, "If this be treason, make the most of it!" My speech, as I remember, was along the same oratorical lines. From Williamsburg, I went to Washington with the other winners to meet President Truman in the Oval Office of the White House. I was gratified to notice that the double-breasted blue suit the President was wearing was just like the one I had bought for the occasion back home at Belk's Department Store. As we took notes, the President gave us his broad Missouri smile, and treated us like grown-ups, which I appreciated. But I knew I really wasn't a White House correspondent yet, because the woman holding my arm and smiling nervously back at Mr. Truman was my mother. I couldn't wait to be sixteen and off on my own, without any parent tagging along, to the halls of Montezuma. Or at least, on my sports assignments, to the Piedmont Junior High School gym.

On the dirt roads out in the country near our house, I learned to drive—with my father sitting beside me again, in the passenger's seat this time—and I started nagging my parents to lie about my age so that I could get a driver's license early.

"We could go to jail for that," my father said.

"Nobody would ever find out," I said.

Eventually, to end these daily arguments, and with

what must have been a sigh of defeat, my father gave me a notarized statement in which he swore that my birthday was June 1. It was really September 10.

With that precious, fraudulent document in my hands, the only palpable lie my father ever told, I hastened to the courthouse to apply for a driving test. For years afterward, because of the spurious date of birth on my driver's license, I was listed in employment, military draft and bank records as three months older than I actually was.

At the time, all that mattered was that I was sixteen in the eyes of the Department of Motor Vehicles of the State of North Carolina and fit to drive a car alone. Naturally, the first thing I did was plan a trip.

My friend Landon Smith and I acquired a twelve-year-old motorcar, originally a 1938 Chevy, I think, but patched up during World War II by somebody who had access to parts from various other makes, a kind of Pontiacrolet or Chevifordmobile. We salvaged a working radio from a wrecked Olds in a junkyard, and when we found it wouldn't fit in the dashboard of our car, hung it *under* the dash where it swung from coat-hanger wire, banging the shins of the front-seat passenger. That summer, with gears clashing, chassis squeaking and radio swinging, and with my lying license in my pocket, we headed for California.

Our vague idea was to explore the Rockies and the Golden West, make a great loop north, perhaps to Canada, and end up at midsummer in Evanston, Illinois, where I had a scholarship to attend a writing program for high school students at Northwestern University. We nursed the car along slowly to save fuel and because we had promised our worried parents not to drive fast. We breakfasted on nickel Cokes and peanut butter crackers and supped on cold cans of pork and beans. We slept in the car, beside the road or in truck stops or abandoned drive-in movie lots after the last movie had ended.

We had badly overestimated nearly everything: the soundness of our vehicle, the distance we could travel in a day on country roads, the adequacy of the supply of dollars we kept hidden under the floor mat in case of holdup, and our own immunity to homesickness. We saw we'd never make it to California. We crossed the Mississippi with the car coughing noticeably on the upgrades and our money and our spirits running low. We were having arguments about trivial things, like whether it was legal to turn right on red lights. Landon said yes. I said no. Neither of us had the slightest idea. Was it harmful to the transmission to keep the car from rolling backward when stopped on a hill by manipulating the clutch and accelerator instead of using the brakes? I said no. Landon said he was going to get out of the car if I kept doing it. We were having crises of inexperience. At Jefferson City, Missouri, we turned sharp right onto U.S. 54 and steered for Chicago. There, my pal Landon found a room on the North Side and a job selling hot dogs on the street to make enough money for his trip home alone. I checked into the YMCA Hotel on Wabash Avenue to await the start of my summer classes in Evanston.

I was given a room that would have had a beautiful view of Lake Michigan but for the intervening mass

of the Stevens Hotel. The joy of the tourist returned
to me. I happily wandered the streets of my first big
city, peeking through the open doors of the strip joints
at night, reading the *Tribune* with my fifty-five-cent
breakfasts in the morning. (This was the *Tribune* of
Colonel Robert McCormick, and I had read and
laughed at the *New Yorker* magazine "brightener"
quoting a *Trib* news story on a giant excavation: "The
hole will be so great that the Tribune Tower would fit
into it," to which *The New Yorker* replied, "How
about Thursday?") I discovered that jazz musicians,
returning to their rooms at the Y after their gigs, often
gathered in the basement recreation room of the hotel
for jam sessions in the predawn hours. If the musicians noticed the fifteen-year-old white kid sitting on
a folding chair off to one side, soaking up their sounds
at three o'clock in the morning, they never said anything.

At last came the day when I took the el to Evanston, "Home," announced a big sign on the station
platform, "of the Women's Christian Temperance
Union." I remember not one thing I might have
learned in the next six weeks at the Northwestern High
School Institute. I remember walking on the mani-
cured campus and watching sailboats in the distance
on the blue lake. I remember The Huddle, an upscale
coffee shop where college students laughed and chatted. I remember girls, the most desirable and unap-
proachable creatures imaginable, many driving
convertibles. Northwestern's streets and walks and
lawns and dormitories seemed to me a Hollywood
version of a college campus, and I seemed to myself

a big-boned country boy from the South, a hick kid
after all. I wanted to acquire at least a thin veneer of
the sophistication I saw all around me, but I didn't
know where to begin. And then the summer ran out
and it was too late. I caught the train to Gary, Indiana, lugged my big Samsonite suitcase to the side of
a highway and started hitchhiking home, relieved to
have cultivation and refinement behind me and the
romance of the road ahead.

A friendly elderly couple took me as far as Fort
Wayne, driving at a stately pace in their big De Soto,
questioning me about my family and background. A
truck driver drove me through the night so as to have
somebody to talk to, dropping me off south of Lou-
isville as the sun came up.

Of the rides I got after that, the one I remember
was a long one through the Kentucky hill country
with a kindly and demented evangelist in a pickup
truck with a loudspeaker mounted atop the cab. He
slowed down as we passed through each hamlet so
that he could exhort the citizens to come to God lest
sulfur and flame overtake them right there on the main
street of Roxanna or Redbush or Rockhouse, Kentucky. There was no room in the passenger seat for
me, for that was where he kept his microphone and
amplifier between villages, so I rode contentedly in
the back of the pickup with my feet propped up on
my suitcase, watching the mountain curves recede behind the truck, feeling free.

All these years later, I wonder if I haven't patterned
my life after that of the daft old man in the pickup
truck, who wandered where the back roads took him,

the means of amplification close at hand. My job at
CBS has turned out just the same, though the preacher
had a more confident message.

Riding along that day in the back of his truck, near
the end of my first trip away from home alone, I returned the wave of a man who stood up from his work
in his vegetable patch to watch us pass. I saw a barefoot young woman in a calico dress pinning sheets to
a clothesline. I saw a cluster of old men studying the
moves in a game of checkers on the front porch of a
one-pump gas station. The road retreated, mile after
mile. I was perfectly happy.

When we paused for a few minutes at a sleepy
county seat for the old preacher to pass out religious
leaflets, I went into the courthouse to find a bathroom. Walking down the halls, I looked into offices
and saw people at work at typewriters and adding
machines. I felt terribly sorry for them. They were
going to work there at their desks all that day, and the
next, and the next, and half a day on Saturday, and
return to those same desks and office machines on
Monday morning.

I walked out and found the preacher at the wheel
waiting for me. I climbed into the back of the truck
and we pulled away and picked up speed and left that
town behind us. The sun was shining, and I could
feel the wind in my hair.

2

RADIO DAYS

"I'm going down to the Texan on Lex. Anybody want anything?"

It was my first night on the job for CBS News. I was a writer on the radio overnight shift, midnight 'til eight A.M. A desk assistant—copyboy in newspaper language—made his inquiry to the newsroom at large.

"Sure," said the writer at the next desk, digging into his pocket for money. "Bring me a prune danish and a large light."

"What about you?" the kid asked. The kid was older than I was. He was looking impatiently straight at me. I did not understand anything that had been said. "Texan," "Lex," "danish" and "light" were all New York words I had never heard before.

"Sure. Same thing," I said.

What came back, from an all-night diner called The Texan on Lexington Avenue, was a sweet roll and a big cardboard cup of coffee with cream. After a few nights of listening to the three A.M. food orders given by the other writers, I learned that what I really wanted was a twisted chunk of sweet fried dough and coffee with sugar and cream (more cream than in a "dark" coffee, but not as much as in a "light").

In other words, "a cruller and a regular."

I had a lot of catching on to do.

This was May 1957. I was twenty-two years old and not exactly a man of the world. I had spent four years at the University of North Carolina, my father's old school at Chapel Hill, studying history and working at *The Daily Tar Heel*, the student-owned newspaper. In the spring of my junior year, I printed up some posters and ran for editor on a pro-integration (the state's schools were still segregated then, including the university), anti–Joe McCarthy, anti–big-time sports platform. On election day, I beat the sports editor for the job by a handful of votes. The first thing I did was call my old high school girlfriend, Sory Guthery, on the telephone. She was in school at Greensboro down the road.

"I won!" I said.

"Great!" she said.

"The job pays thirty dollars a week," I said.

"So?"

"So that's enough to live on. Let's get married!"

We were married in Charlotte in August, in a big church wedding. She was twenty, and I was almost twenty myself.

We moved into a cabin, a former tenant house, beside a cornfield a few miles out of Chapel Hill on the road to Raleigh. Our senior year I remember as pure joy. We studied history and read poetry together in the mornings; in the afternoons, I wrote my editorials, often trying them out on Sory by telephone before sending them to the printer.

I flailed about at tradition, in the best tradition of

student editors. Racial integration was the theme I adopted as a crusade. The Supreme Court's "Brown vs. Board of Education" decision had come out mandating an end to school segregation and I kept urging the North Carolina legislature to get on with it, starting with the university. "We see no reason in human history or in the human heart why this state school should not belong to all the state's citizens," that kind of thing. The all-white legislature, of course, was trying to figure out ways around the court decision at the time. I was afraid nobody was paying any attention to *The Daily Tar Heel*, so I had copies shipped over to the capital every day. Finally, I had the satisfaction of being called a "pawn of the Communists" on the legislature floor.

At night, Sory sometimes stood over the composing stone with me to watch the editorial page take shape. Always, with two or three other sleepy members of the newspaper staff, I waited until the old flatbed printing machinery cranked up at one A.M. or so and the first copies of that morning's *Tar Heel* came off the press. Then we usually went out to the cabin to admire the paper and drink coffee and talk about the next day's issue until late into the night, Sory sometimes excusing herself to get some studying done. As for me, the newspaper used up so much of my time that I started dropping courses. By the time the spring quarter arrived, I had dropped them all; I was editor of the student newspaper, but—nobody in the administration building seemed to notice—no longer a student. Graduation proceeded without me. I didn't care. I had found my career.

We moved back to Charlotte and I took a job on the afternoon newspaper, *The Charlotte News*, the paper whose sportswriting contest I had entered years before. The *News* was a wonderful place to work, with a heritage of reporters that included such famous ones as Harry Ashmore, Burke Davis, Marion Hargrove and W. J. Cash, who had gone on to write the greatest of books about the region, *The Mind of the South*. I became a general assignment reporter and after a few months, Tom Fesperman, the managing editor, gave me a daily column to write, "People," about the ordinary folk of the city, cops or kids or cabdrivers. I worked hard on all my assignments, but especially hard to make the "People" column interesting and readable. I thought *The Charlotte News* was the best paper in the state, and I assumed I'd work my way up there, perhaps becoming the star reporter or an editorial writer someday.

One Sunday afternoon in March 1957, however, the phone rang at the house. It called me in from the backyard, where I was walking around looking for signs of early blooming daffodils. The man on the line said he was John Day, calling from New York. He said he was director of news at CBS. He said he had read about my winning a prize for newspaper reporting, the Ernie Pyle award, and wondered whether I had any interest in writing for radio.

"Well, sir," I said, "I've always admired you people at CBS, but I don't think there's enough going on down here in Charlotte to write about for radio."

"I don't mean there," the man said. "I mean here.

Would you like to come to New York to talk about a job?''

I couldn't believe what I was hearing. "Well," I said, "I suppose I would, yes."

"Can you come tomorrow?" he asked.

"No," I said, "I have to go to work tomorrow. I have to work on the state edition tomorrow, see, which means they'll be expecting me at six-thirty. You understand *The Charlotte News* isn't a real big paper and they'll be shorthanded if I don't show up."

The man on the other end of the line chuckled and said, "Sure, I understand. How about later in the week?"

"Well, I'll ask for a day off," I said. "Could I call you tomorrow or Tuesday?"

"Sure," he said. "The number is PLaza 1-2345. Ask for me."

I was very much impressed by the phone number. I thought CBS must be the big time, all right, to have a telephone number like that.

My wife came in from outside to see who had called. I told her it was CBS News in New York, maybe offering a job. She said, "I bet it was Emery Wister kidding you about having the big head over that Ernie Pyle award."

Emery Wister sat at the desk next to mine in the newspaper office down on Fourth Street. He was a good reporter, but fun-loving. He was capable of a trick like this. I could just hear him the next morning telling everybody how I'd said I couldn't come to New York right away because I had to work on the state edition. I picked up the phone and asked for New

York information. When the operator came on the line, I said, "What's the number for the Columbia Broadcasting System, please?"

After a pause, she said, "PLaza 1-2345."

At least that much checked out, and the next morning Emery Wister didn't say a thing. I asked Tom Fesperman if I could have Friday off.

Sory and I had a one-year-old daughter by this time. Sory asked, "Do we want Lisa to grow up in New York City?" It was a pretty good question. But I thought of Irving Berlin escaping the squalor of the Lower East Side to become the toast of Broadway. I thought of Fred Astaire dancing on a penthouse terrace. I said, "Kids do grow up there, I guess." My wife said, "Well, you decide."

That Thursday afternoon, I flew to New York on an Eastern Airlines Constellation and took a taxi to the Blackstone Hotel. "That's where we put up our people who come in from abroad," John Day had said. I was to see him at nine o'clock Friday morning.

The Blackstone was a shabby-genteel old institution somewhere in midtown. My room for the night was on a high floor, the fifteenth or so, a higher floor than I had ever been on in my life. When I stepped over to the window and looked down at the street below, full of tiny pedestrians and toy cars, it made me dizzy. I knew New Yorkers lived at such altitudes, but I couldn't even get to sleep up there. I lay awake listening to the sirens that seemed never to stop, police cars, fire trucks and ambulances, sirens close by and far away. It seemed to me that some terrible calamity must have struck Manhattan for there to be so much loud urgency down in the streets. I wondered if it could be a Russian air raid. I lay there worrying about the sirens until the sun came up. When I got dressed and left the hotel, none of the fast-walking people on the sidewalk seemed to be aware of all the trouble their city had been in during the night. I walked down the street, talked with John Day for a few minutes, and accepted a job as a writer at CBS News in New York for $135 a week.

Then I bought a copy of *The New York Times* and turned to the real-estate ads to see if there was any such thing in the city of New York as a ground-floor apartment.

I found the next best thing eventually, a second-story walk-up in an old wooden house on Middagh Street in Brooklyn. The paint was peeling off the walls a little bit, but the kitchen window afforded a partial view of the Brooklyn Bridge and the Manhattan towers. Downstairs lived a dour modern artist named Charles Duback. Upstairs lived a jovial folk singer, Lee Hays of The Weavers quartet, blacklisted and unable to find employment at the time because of alleged left-wing associations in his peripatetic past. Duback worked below, creating vast geometric canvases nobody wanted to buy. Lee Hays worked above, composing songs on his guitar that nobody wanted to listen to. I was the only person in the house who ever put on a necktie and went to work, which sort of ruined the Bohemian style of the place.

Often, I left for the office a few hours early and walked all the way, across the great bridge ("How

could mere toil align thy choiring strings!'' asked Hart
Crane) and through the crowded streets of Chinatown
or Little Italy (''I hear America singing, the varied
carols I hear,'' sang Whitman) and up one of the
great avenues. Everywhere, I heard poetry. New York,
which was, I suppose, nearly as squalid and rude then
as it is now, seemed saucy and inviting to me. On
those long walks, I consumed the city hungrily, in-
haling the foreign smells and listening to the music
of the streets until I arrived at work almost delirious
from what I had smelled and heard and seen.

The newsroom where I labored was on the seven-
teenth floor of the CBS Building, 485 Madison Avenue, at the corner of 52nd Street. On higher floors
were the offices of Dr. Frank Stanton, the longtime
President of CBS, and of William S. Paley himself,
the founder of the company and Chairman of the
Board. The only floor I ever saw was 17, which was
exciting enough, even in the stillness of the late hour
when I arrived for work. On the way from the elevator
to the newsroom was a closed blue door on which
was lettered in gold: ''MR. MURROW.''

Of course, all these notables were out on the town
or at home in bed during my working hours. I rarely
even laid eyes on any of the important people at CBS,
and the first time I did, I was sorry. I came to the
building during daylight hours to attend some sort of
staff meeting and followed a distinguished white-
haired gentleman into an open elevator. A uniformed
doorman came rushing over, pressed the button for
the twentieth floor and stepped respectfully out of the
car. I pressed 17. The doorman looked at me aghast.

He leapt back into the elevator, turned a key that cancelled the floor selections, pressed 20 again and hustled me out by the arm. The door closed. I could hear the elevator starting up.

"What's wrong?" I asked.

"That was Dr. Stanton, buddy," the doorman said. "He goes up alone, and he don't stop on the way."

I felt bad that I didn't know Dr. Stanton. On the other hand, I felt good that he didn't know me.

My job, a task for the good of the company which no doubt escaped Dr. Stanton's attention, was to roll through reams of wire copy from the AP, UP and Reuters machines, read the night's cables from CBS News's foreign bureaus, rewrite all this into a five-minute newscast for an announcer, Bob Hall, to read on the air at two A.M.—and then do it all over again for the newscasts of three, four, five and six A.M. This did not require much thinking, but it required very fast typing. As soon as I ripped a script out of my typewriter, I tossed it onto the desk of a fierce, eagle-eyed editor named Maggie who sat like a schoolmarm at the head of the class, dying to find the slightest factual or grammatical error in the copy so she could sing out a correction as she blue-penciled the page. Maggie's corrections were so loud they made everybody jump. I dreaded them, partly because I didn't have time to anticipate them. While she was reading over my two o'clock copy, I was already rattling away at the typewriter again, desperately getting a head start on the three o'clock show.

"*Clarke!*" Maggie roared one night. "*Clarke!* With an *e!*"

A truck driver named Clarke had been killed by a freight train at a railroad crossing in Indiana. This sort of local misfortune would be ignored by CBS News during the daytime when things were happening, but on the overnight we might make it a lead. I had rendered the name of the victim "Clark."

I said, "What the . . ." and stopped. What I was going to say was, "What the hell difference does it make on the radio?" but thought better of getting into an argument with the infallible Maggie.

A couple of hours later, three bells rang on one of the wire machines. You learned to listen for the bells—one bell for a routine story; three for a bulletin or correction; five for a flash, an event of earthshaking significance. We never heard five bells on the overnight. This time it was a correction. The correct spelling of Clarke's name, it said, was "Clark."

Maggie was looking at the machine over my shoulder. I turned around and smiled at her. She said, "Don't smile at me, you smart-ass kid!" and walked back to her desk. The importance of the story really didn't justify it, but I put Clark into all the rest of my newscasts that night just for the pleasure of typing his name.

I really didn't feel like a smart-ass kid. I felt like a North Carolina boy a long way from home. The other writers on the overnight were all older and experienced, most of them jaded newspaper rewrite men between jobs. They came and went. I was just starting out, eager to make a good impression on my bosses and learn how to be a sophisticated New Yorker all at once. One of my coworkers, a man with tired

eyes who studied the *Racing Form* at night and spent
his afternoons at Belmont Park, persuaded me that
inasmuch as we finished work at eight A.M., that was
our cocktail hour. For a few mornings there, I went
with Eddie to a dark Irish bar on West 52nd Street
that opened its doors at eight in the morning. Since
he ordered martinis, very cold, straight up with a twist
of lemon, that's what I ordered, too. I loved the feeling of amity and urbanity these morning martinis induced, but I hated what followed, the tipsy walk in
the bright sun to the IND station at Madison and 53rd,
the scruffy, unwashed and unshaven descent into the
underground against a tide of freshly dressed and
beautiful young women hurrying up the escalator on
their way to work, and the struggle to stay awake on
the rattan subway seat on the bumpy trip home to
Brooklyn.

"Tough night?" Sory would inquire sympatheti-
cally. She was usually still in her bathrobe, feeding
the baby at the kitchen table.

"Yep," I'd reply, "tough night," and head for the
front bedroom of the old house, already taking off my
coat and tie. We had no air-conditioning and the room
was always hot that summer. I slept a few sweaty
hours and woke up with a hangover in midafternoon.
It wasn't long before I realized I was going to have
to find some other way to become a cosmopolitan
New Yorker. The nights at work were not so tough
as I pretended to my wife, but the mornings were
murder. I wasn't man enough to drink breakfast with
Eddie.

Instead, I started hanging around the office after

my work was done to watch them put together the
"World News Roundup." This was real journalism.
In those days in this country, anybody who wanted to
hear a serious news report in the morning had to tune
in to that one fifteen-minute radio program. On television, the news was quick and skimpy, sandwiched
in among puppets and pet monkeys and cute weather
reports. The other radio networks did their best to
compete, but none of them could call on the roster of
great reporters who worked for CBS News. Eric Sevareid, Charles Collingwood or Alexander Kendrick
reported to the "Roundup" from London each morning, David Schoenbrun from Paris, Richard C. Hot-
telet from Bonn, Winston Burdett from Rome, Daniel
Schorr from Moscow. There might be contributions
from Robert Trout, Ned Calmer or Larry LeSueur.
Never before or since has any broadcast news organization assembled a staff approaching the style and
expertise of that one. In the decades that followed,
network news staffs doubled and redoubled, the glit-
ter of television put radio in the shade, new technol-
ogies revolutionized broadcasting—but after the
"World News Roundup" of the fifties, news on the
air only went downhill.

The program was moderated by calm Dallas
Townsend, seated at a heavy table of polished wood
in a small square room known as Studio 9, with one
window looking into the newsroom and another into
the control room. Townsend wore a cumbersome
headset and spoke into a large black microphone, the
same mike Edward R. Murrow used in the evenings.
Tape recording had been invented, but nobody at CBS

News trusted it yet, so all the reports on the "World News Roundup" came in live, the ones from abroad via shortwave radio. The correspondents checked in minutes before the program started—"Schoenbrun, you'll be first up this morning, are you there?" "Schoenbrun here"—and their reports were juggled into the broadcast by an engineer with patch cords hung around his neck and his hands on the dials and switches of a giant control board known as the "piano."

There was an old Western Union clock on the wall of the control room, the kind that automatically reset itself to a time signal that came in on the hour. At eight A.M. straight up, a red light came on, the director threw a cue and an announcer said:

"This is the CBS 'World News Roundup,' with reports from our correspondents at home and overseas. From our newsroom in New York, here is CBS News Correspondent Dallas Townsend."

I wasn't experienced enough to be invited to work on the "World News Roundup," of course, but nobody minded if I sat in a corner of the control room and watched the engineer play his flawless concert on the piano, and listened to the director calling in these heroes of mine from the ends of the earth. I was dazzled by them. They seemed to me giants among men. I ached to become one of them someday, but I knew that even if I lived to be—well, fifty!—I could never attain their worldly experience or finesse. It was enough just to think that now I worked at the same place Sevareid and Collingwood and Burdett worked, the same place Murrow worked! I didn't have a single thing to do with the "World News Roundup," but I never left the control room after the program ended without a glow of secret pride. It was better than martinis in the morning.

The other thing I was proud of—I didn't see any contradiction in this—was my union card. On the newspaper back home, I had become the twenty-year-old President of the Charlotte local of the Newspaper Guild. Nobody else much wanted the job. The union was weak (it has entirely disappeared from newspapers in North Carolina now) and the local president had the onerous duty of sassing the publisher from time to time, which was considered hazardous to career advancement. But I was steeped in labor union lore, knew a few old union songs and had read the column Heywood Broun wrote in the *New York World-Telegram* before founding the Newspaper Guild in 1933:

"There should be a newspaper writers' union. Beginning at nine o'clock on the morning of October 1, I am going to do the best I can to help in getting one up. I think I could die happy on the opening day of the general strike if I had the privilege of watching Walter Lippmann heave half a brick through a *Tribune* window."

I even went to night school to take a course in collective bargaining, only to discover that collective bargaining at the *News* went this way:

I: "We think starting pay for reporters ought to be raised from fifty-five dollars a week to sixty."

Brodie Griffith, executive editor: "Starting pay is

going to remain fifty-five dollars a week. Is that clear?''

I: "Yes, sir. But it is not enough."

Mr. Griffith: "Probably not. What else would you like to discuss?"

Not having much luck at my own paper, I went down the street to the other one, *The Charlotte Observer*, which suffered no unions at all outside the pressroom. I secretly organized a disgruntled group of circulation employees, signed them right up in the Newspaper Guild and then wrote a letter to the *Observer*'s management to break the news and ask for a union representation election at the paper. The *Observer* called the circulation employees in and told them they were fired. I figured I needed some help. I called the Newspaper Guild's national office in New York and told them what I had done. "You have done *what*?" exclaimed the man on the other end of the line. The national office flew a professional organizer down the next day to apologize to the *Observer* bosses and get all those circulation guys their jobs back. I was relieved, of course, but also disillusioned. I didn't think that was the way unions were supposed to work.

In New York, I assumed, unions would be different, full of camaraderie and resolution. I looked forward to attending the monthly meetings of my new union, the Writers Guild of America. I knew it had been founded not long before, a spin-off from the national Screen Writers Guild, with whose left-wing leadership many New York writers had quarreled. I was going to become an active union member, I was sure of that. We paid one percent of our take-home

pay in union dues. At my first meeting, there was
only one topic of discussion: After a member's dues
assessment reached $1,000 in a single year, shouldn't
there be a cutoff? Some said yes, some said no. I did
the arithmetic and realized that this union was wran-
gling over the union dues of members who made more
than *one hundred thousand dollars a year*! What kind
of union was that? It was, of course, a union which
represented famous writers like Paddy Chayefsky, J. P.
Miller and Reginald Rose. I left there thinking of my
fights with Brodie Griffith over five dollars a week. I
never went to another meeting of the Writers Guild.
I figured all those rich guys didn't need any help from
me.

I worked the radio overnight through the summer,
except for a wonderful week in August. Edward R.
Murrow ordinarily composed his own nightly radio
commentary, but Ed Bliss, a gentle and scholarly
man, wrote the summary of the day's news that Murrow read to open the broadcast. When Ed Bliss took
a short vacation, I was drafted to replace him for a
week as Murrow's writer.

I worried about it all weekend, arrived early on
Monday morning and spent the day writing and rewriting the news as it clattered in on the press service
machines, hearing Murrow's voice in my head as I
worked. The great man wandered into the newsroom
from his office in late afternoon with his commentary
in hand and looked about inquisitively. I was ready.
I jumped up, my heart pounding a little, and introduced myself.

"Good," he said in that famous deep voice. We

entered the studio and swapped scripts. Murrow started timing and editing my copy. I was supposed to copyread what *he* had written, but I knew I wasn't going to suggest any changes, not in the copy of Edward R. Murrow, not to his face! I kept sneaking peeks to see how much of my work he was changing. Not very much, a word here and there. I turned my attention back to his commentary. It was about the French war in Algeria, well reasoned as always, tightly written. I read with interest—and then, in the middle of the second page, I found a grammatical error. It was a small error of the sort people make in conversation, a subject that didn't strictly agree with its predicate or some such thing. I can't remember, but I *can* remember thinking, all right, what the hell do I do now?

What I did was circle the offending word lightly in pencil and wait for Murrow to finish timing what I had written for him. When he looked up, I handed him his commentary. Trying to keep my voice from breaking, I pointed to the mistake.

"It's wonderful, Mr. Murrow," I said. Then, casually, "I just wondered about this one word."

He glanced down. He fixed it with a few strokes of his pen. He looked up at me and nodded.

He said, "Good catch."

I exhaled. No veteran ever said two kinder words to a beginner.

After the same copyreading ritual the next evening, in the few minutes before Murrow went on the air, he questioned me about my background. I told him I was from North Carolina, knowing it was the state where he was also born. He brightened and spoke a bit about his memories of Polecat Creek in Guilford County and about his Quaker forebears. He asked me about my experience in journalism. Of course, that led only to a very short conversation, but it was the beginning of an amiable interest in my career that was typical of Murrow's generosity toward all the younger staffers. Frequently at the end of the day, he'd say, "Well, we've done as much damage as we can do for one day. Shall we have a drink?" It was a general invitation to all within the sound of his voice, and we all accepted when we could, because we knew we were going to have more than a drink. We were going to have a seminar on broadcast journalism, how things were done and how they ought to be done, with the greatest broadcast journalist of all as moderator.

I couldn't resist telling Murrow that he had appraised my writing once before, when he was a judge of the "Voice of Democracy" contest and I was a schoolboy winner. He seemed delighted by this news and repeated it around the office. For the rest of his years at CBS and even afterward, Murrow made a habit of sending me, as he sent others, notes of encouragement and brief praise.

After his death, Janet Murrow told me she thought her husband had been interested in me because I was from North Carolina, from a place not unlike Polecat Creek. Whatever the reason, and in spite of all his preoccupations, I felt that he never lost his benevolent concern for me. One night that first week, a wartime friend from Europe met him at his office as I was passing on the way to the elevator. Murrow introduced me.

"This," he said, "is my colleague Charles Kuralt."

After that, going back to the radio overnight wasn't so bad.

At the end of my shift one Friday morning in early September, I waved good-bye to one of the good writers and part-time editors on the staff, John Merriman. "See you Sunday night, John," I said. "No, you won't," he said. "You'd better check the assignment schedule." They posted writers' days and hours on a bulletin board in the corner. I never looked at it because, except for the five days with Murrow, my days and hours had remained the same—twelve midnight 'til eight A.M. Monday through Friday. I walked over there and looked, thinking it was John who had been reassigned. It said "Kuralt: Monday–Friday, 11 A.M.–7 P.M., 70 E. 45."

"What's this?" I asked John.

"It's television," he said.

Television. I didn't know anything about television. Television was in another building, and another world. It occurred to me that I had irritated Maggie once too often and was being sent down to the minor leagues. But John Merriman said I should think of this as a promotion. He said they were going to try me out on the television network's big news program, the *CBS Evening News* with Douglas Edwards. One of Doug Edwards's writers, Bill Crawford, was taking a one-year sabbatical to accept a fellowship to Columbia University. I was to be his replacement.

I stood there wondering how any of the daytime bosses knew about me. Later I learned that the management had canvassed all the editors for suggestions, and that John Merriman, after checking with Murrow, had told them a young prospect was buried on the radio overnight. That morning, all he said was, "Look at it this way. Now you get to sleep at night."

3

THE GREENHORN KID

If commuters hurrying through Grand Central Station to catch the six-thirty to Scarsdale on weekday evenings in the late 1950s had ever looked up at the great arched windows of the terminal, they would have seen an odd sight—a line of people running along a catwalk high up in the arches. It might have been a chase scene in an Alfred Hitchcock thriller. What it was was merely the *CBS Evening News* staff trying to get the show on the air on time.

The program was prepared on the 45th Street side of Grand Central in an office building of heroic proportions with high ceilings and echoing marble halls, a structure meant by Commodore Vanderbilt, who put it there, to last for the ages. (Lesser mortals tore it down later and built a mediocre skyscraper on the spot.) The broadcast went on the air from the 42nd Street side of the terminal nearly three blocks away, in a cavernous space the Commodore must have intended to be a ballroom. CBS turned it into a television studio. (I believe it's a tennis court today.) The fast route from the office to the studio was along the catwalk several stories above Grand Central. We hardly ever finished preparing the show on time, so we had to run.

Don Hewitt, the director, who later became famous as the impresario of *60 Minutes*, led the race, shouting instructions to his assistants, Fred Stollmack and Dave Dewey, as he ran. Next came Doug Edwards, the star, with Kleenex tissues flapping from his collar to keep his makeup off his shirt. Doug's secretary, Petie Baird, sprinted behind him, putting his script in order on the run. Bill Porter, the editor, huffed and puffed along in front of Alice Weel, one of the writers, and I gamely brought up the rear with the film editors, Tom Micklas and Len Raff, who were carrying reels of film to the projectionist. This was the entire staff of the biggest news program in television, all in a footrace against the clock. Douglas Edwards frequently delivered the evening's lead story in an urgent pant. People thought he was trying to make the news sound important. Really, he was just trying to catch his breath.

I loved working on the show. The hours were good—nobody showed up until ten or eleven in the morning—and there was so little writing to be done for a fifteen-minute broadcast that Alice and I could discuss our approach to the news and then rewrite and polish our few paragraphs right down to the immutable deadline of six twenty-five P.M. Alice Weel chewed pencils while she was thinking. If she was thinking hard, she could go through a dozen pencils a day. She was a good, methodical writer and her desk was always littered with the remains of Eberhard Faber #2s. She taught me how to write to film.

Where *she* learned, I don't know, but, "Don't write captions," she'd say, "don't point out what people are seeing. They can see what they're seeing. Just write the story to flow along with the film. And don't ever let your words fight the pictures. Pictures are so strong that in a fight, they always win."

Don Hewitt was restless, excitable, impatient. He kept urging the motorcycle couriers who brought film in from the airport to figure out ways of making the trip faster. One day, in reaction, one of the messengers brought his Harley-Davidson up in the elevator and roared down the hall right into Don's office to dump a film shipment on his desk. Live coverage of events was rare in those pre-satellite days, but Hewitt bought land-lines to bring the news in live whenever possible. In the studio, he was forever tinkering with camera angles, trying to work out the perfect size ratio of Doug's on-screen face to the pictures that appeared behind him. He invented the "super," the little sign on the screen that identifies people and places without breaking the flow of the news. He invented the "double-projector" story, a technique of on-the-air editing; it permitted the director to choose picture from one film projector and synchronized sound from the other and to create dissolves and other effects that would have taken a week to achieve in a film lab. Hewitt was not a writer, but he knew what he liked, and what he liked were snappy beginnings and amusing endings. Hewitt's innovations became conventions of television news programs everywhere. The evening news was being invented, and Don Hewitt was its Edison.

From my working place on the Edwards show, I could look across the wide hall into the television newsroom where the assignment desk was located. On quiet days, I wandered over there to see how this desk worked. It was staffed by "reporter-contacts," a title that went back to the movie newsreel days when the lordly cameramen were accompanied by underlings who went about collecting facts and getting names spelled right. A reporter-contact at CBS was not a correspondent by a long shot. His main duty was to assign free-lance cameramen to cover fires, train wrecks and beauty contests. Occasionally, if no correspondent was available, a desk reporter might be lucky enough to go out on a story himself. On the assignment desk, people were always quitting or being fired, rarely promoted. But I made friends over there, Phil Scheffler and Harry Reasoner and Bob Schakne. They were the new generation. They did not owe their jobs to Murrow or any of the other titans of CBS News. Their interest was the new medium, television, which the great correspondents disdained. Most of the desk men had lately come from newspaper jobs as I had, and from my safe haven across the hall, I began to envy them the uncertainty and commotion of their lives.

Reporting was what I really wanted to do, and they, at least, had a chance once in a while to cover the news. Reasoner was even sent on a big story, President Eisenhower's dispatch of federal troops to Little Rock to enforce school integration there. Day after day, he sent back magnificently reported stories. Sitting in the peaceful office writing the lead-ins to his reports, I realized I'd rather be in turbulent Little Rock with Reasoner.

"You're crazy," Hewitt said when I told him I was thinking of applying for a job on the assignment desk. "That's a dead-end job." Ralph Paskman, the crusty taskmaster of the desk who always said everything at the top of his voice, said, at the top of his voice, "You're a greenhorn kid, you're lucky to have a job, and you should stay where you are!" He warned that if I moved to the desk, I'd have to take a cut in pay.

But I think Paskman was touched that I wanted to work for him. He was so tough and unforgiving that nobody else wanted to. When the next vacancy came along, he called me aside. "The job's yours if you still want it," he growled. "Come to work at midnight Sunday." I was back on the overnight, and starting all over again.

Paskman didn't want to be awakened at home unless the world was coming to an end, so for a while there, between midnight and eight A.M., all the decisions about national news coverage for the CBS Television Network were in the hands of a twenty-three-year-old ex-cub reporter from *The Charlotte News*. "God help you if you screw this up," Paskman had said, so I kept a scrupulous typewritten log: "2:36 A.M. Woman calls to say drunks making a racket outside saloon on W. 43rd St. Passed. Suggested she call NYPD." CBS had no bureaus outside New York and Washington in those days, so if a dam broke somewhere or a grain silo exploded, we had to hope it happened within range of a stringer cameraman whose name could be found in a thumb-worn

Rolodex file along with comments on his past performance: "Caution against panning" and "Give us close-ups for a change" and even "Do not hire if *anybody* else available." I kept an eagle eye on the wire machines for postmidnight calamities that justified leaping to the Rolodex and assigning a cameraman before NBC could get to him. To Paskman, wasting money on cameramen was a sin—after all, CBS paid these guys $25 per assignment and replaced their film free—but getting shut out on a story was a *cardinal* sin.

After a few weeks, Paskman called me at home one afternoon to give me my own first assignment, that night's Chinese New Year celebration. "You can do it on your way in to work," he said. Somehow, I had thought I'd have more time to prepare for my big moment. I hurried to the Brooklyn library, read everything I could about the Chinese way of counting time, and scribbled notes to myself on the subway. I met a staff cameraman named Al Gretz on Mott Street. Gretz set up his heavy, 1,200-foot Auricon sound camera in the middle of all the horns and firecrackers, and with a knot in my stomach and a battery-powered light in my eyes, in my best imitation of the way I thought Murrow would have done it, I delivered into the microphone a sober lecture on the traditions of the Chinese New Year.

I finished and Al turned off the light. I asked him, "What do you think?" He said, "I couldn't hear what you were saying in all this racket, but you sure looked grim. I think this is supposed to be fun."

I said, "Maybe I'd better think of something else

to say." We stood there in the middle of the street while I thought.

After a while, Gretz said, "If you will watch the camera and keep anybody from knocking it over, I think I will just have a quick drink in that bar over there."

Paper lions went dancing by, blaring bands passed, confetti fell from the rooftops, strings of firecrackers exploded. The minutes ticked away. I stood in the street alone, trying, and failing, to write a script in my head. I was blowing my first assignment. I might never have another one. I needed a typewriter and a little peace and quiet.

Gretz came back from the bar. "Ready?" he said. "Sure," I said. The light came back on. As I looked toward the camera and opened my mouth to say something, anything, a cherry bomb exploded at my feet with a deafening bang. I jumped and exclaimed, "Wow, that one nearly got me, Al!"

They used thirty seconds of film of the Chinese New Year celebration on the late local news that night, including this much from the reporter on the scene:

"Wow, that one nearly got me, Al!"

They were my first words on the air for CBS News.

My next appearance was even shorter and even sillier. Marilyn Monroe came to town with her husband, Arthur Miller, to promote a new movie. A camera crew and I elbowed our way through a mob of other reporters in a hotel ballroom until I made it to her side. She was wearing a low-cut gown with sequins all over it. She was gorgeous and perspiring. The camera rolled. A surge of the crowd pushed us tightly together.

I said, "Good afternoon, Miss Monroe."

She smiled and said huskily, "Oh, isn't it *hot* in here?"

Grinning foolishly, I wiped my forehead and said, "It sure is!"

She turned away, looking for a way out of the crush, and I couldn't reach her again. That was my interview with Marilyn Monroe. It went on the air in its entirety.

I covered a "cleanup" of Times Square, with Radio City Music Hall Rockettes wielding brooms, a press agent's idea of a compelling story. Even in those innocent days, the film was judged too hokey to inflict on CBS's audience. It was discarded. Nobody but me even remembers that the event took place.

The Brooklyn Dodgers announced plans to move to Los Angeles. In retaliation, a longtime Brooklyn congressman named Emanuel Celler started promoting a third major league for baseball, the Continental League, with a team that would play in Ebbets Field. I went to his office, drew him out on this subject at great length, and watched back in the editing room as they cut my precious interview down to a sentence or two.

I covered the opening of the Ringling Brothers Circus and made a lyrical, carefully memorized speech to the camera with acrobats performing over my shoulder; but then a lion escaped from his cage and sauntered briefly through the lobby of Madison Square Garden before being recaptured. They put the lion on the air, naturally, instead of me. I was beginning to get discouraged.

One night, just at the change of shifts on the assignment desk, Bob Schakne and I were shooting the breeze beside the teletype machines when the bells rang and a short notice moved on the city wire. It said: "Editors: An aircraft is reported down in the East River. Staffing. Will advise." We both reached for phones and called Idlewild and LaGuardia airports. Nobody claimed to know anything, but I could hear a commotion in the background at the LaGuardia tower. Schakne said, "Might be a Piper Cub. Might be nothing. But maybe one of us better get out there just in case." He called a cameraman named Pat Kinghan who lived near LaGuardia and sent him on his way. Then he turned to me.

"You want to go?" he asked.

I said, "Sure, I guess so."

Schakne said, "Well, I do, too, but one of us has to stay here on the desk." He pondered this problem for a couple of seconds and said, "I'll flip you for it."

He took a quarter out of his pocket. "Call it," he said.

"Heads," I said.

He slapped the coin on the back of his hand. It came up heads. Schakne turned back to the phones. I grabbed my coat and hat and a windup Kudelski tape recorder and ran out the door.

About five minutes past the Midtown Tunnel, the taxi I was riding in bogged down in traffic. Radio stations had broadcast the news of a plane crash and half the population of Queens was trying to get to the airport to see it. The cabdriver said, "Nothing I can do for you, pal. We're in it, that's all." I paid him off, jumped out of the cab and started waving my press pass, hitching rides with cars in whichever lane of traffic seemed to be moving.

After a couple of minutes of this, getting nowhere, I saw a motorcycle coming up from behind, working its way between the lanes. I stepped in front of its headlight. The rider was a tough-looking guy in a studded leather jacket. I said, "Look, I'm a reporter. I have to get to LaGuardia in a hurry, and it looks like you're my only hope." He jerked his thumb toward the saddle behind him. "Hold on," he said. I climbed aboard, clutching my tape recorder and holding my knees in tight to keep from banging them into the cars on either side. He gunned the bike forward. He drove that thing like a stunt rider, squeezing through impossibly narrow spaces at full speed, and in no time, he banked hard right onto the LaGuardia Airport grounds.

"Where do you want to go?" he hollered back at me. Off in the distance, I could see a cluster of lights at the end of a runway, the revolving red lights of police cars and a searchlight aimed into the darkness of the river.

"I want to go there," I said, "but . . ."

Behind us, a fire truck gave us a blast of its horn and headed for an open gate onto the field. The motorcycle driver slowed to let the fire truck pass, then fell in behind the truck and roared right through the gate and across the taxiways and runways to the cluster of emergency vehicles at the water's edge.

"Jesus," I said, "that was a hell of a ride."

I reached into my pocket. All I had left was a five-dollar bill and some loose change. I handed him the five. "It's all I have," I said. He handed it back.

"Forget it," he said.

"By the way," he said, "what's going on?"

I said, "A plane crash, I think."

A New York cop came over to us from the crowd around the trucks and police cars. "What do you think you're doing here?" he snarled. I showed him my press card. He turned to the motorcycle rider. "And what about you?" he asked. The bike rider nodded to me and said, "I'm with him." The cop said, "Don't get in the way," and walked off.

I didn't see the motorcycle rider again. I never even got to thank him. A big portable generator was roaring to power the searchlight. People were hollering to one another in confusion. More emergency trucks kept arriving. I looked around and realized I was the only person on the scene who wasn't wearing a uniform. I turned on the tape recorder, walked up to a police sergeant, waited until he finished shouting into a radio and then asked him what he could tell me.

"American Airlines," he said. "One of their new planes, four-engine turboprop coming in from Chicago. Hit the water. There are survivors. That's all I know."

"How do you know there are survivors?" I asked him.

He stared at me.

He said, "Just walk over there and listen."

I walked away from the sound of the generator into the darkness along the shore. When I was far enough away, I could hear occasional faint shouts coming from out in the river and see the searchlight lingering on floating bits of debris. Some of the passengers were alive in the water and calling for help, but the searchlight couldn't seem to find them. A couple of police launches inched through the darkness in the middle of the river, fanning the water with their own tiny spotlights, and I could see what looked like a small fishing trawler tacking back and forth. Everything seemed to be happening in slow motion. The muffled cries from the river became less frequent.

I stood there alone in the dark. I didn't know what to do. I felt like crying.

Finally, I remembered the tape recorder. I turned it on and aimed the microphone at the river, wondering if it would pick up the distant calls for help. Then I spoke into it, trying to describe the sound of the voices in the darkness, the deliberate movement of the boats, the frustration of the would-be rescuers on shore. I remembered to mention that there was a tugboat strike in New York at the time, otherwise many more harbor craft would be out there on a night like this looking for survivors.

After I had said everything I could think of into the machine, I realized I had failed to get the name of the police sergeant I'd talked to a few minutes before. I walked back toward the crowd of emergency vehicles to try to find him and ran into Pat Kinghan, our cameraman, just arriving. He was out of breath from carrying his heavy equipment across the field.

"They're not letting anybody out here," he said. "I had to climb a fence. How the hell did you get here so fast?"

"I got a ride," I said.

Kinghan shot a fast hundred feet of film of the lights and the fire trucks and said, "We'd better get out of here before they throw us out." I shouldered his tripod and one of his batteries and we headed back across the maze of runways for the terminal. It took a long time to get there. On the way, Kinghan said, "We better go in and talk to people who were waiting for the plane." I hadn't thought of that. I didn't want to do it. What could I say to people who knew their relatives might be dead out there in the river? But when we reached the terminal building, Kinghan ran right up the stairs into the American Airlines waiting room and I followed.

It was worse than I imagined it would be. Twenty or thirty people stood in shock or sat on benches with their heads in their hands. Some of them were sobbing uncontrollably. When they saw Kinghan setting up the camera, several turned away. I whispered, "I'm not going to try to talk to them, Pat. I just can't."

But two or three, then half a dozen of the people crowded around us. They *wanted* to talk, to ask what we knew, to tell me how long they'd been waiting and how they heard the news of the crash. An airline official came over to try gently to intervene but they ignored him. They wanted to share their fears with somebody.

"I am Mr. Warren from Flatbush," one man said with dignity. "It's my wife. She only went to Chicago for two days to visit her mother. You haven't heard, have you, anything about a Mrs. Warren?"

I felt awkward. I wanted to leave and give these people back their privacy.

"I'm sorry," I said. "I do think there are going to be some survivors."

"Let us pray you are right," Mr. Warren said.

Other reporters and camera crews were showing up. A CBS motorcycle messenger came running through the door. He came up to me and said quietly, so nobody else could hear, "Don Hewitt has lined up a big tugboat and a tape crew, and they're on the way to the scene. We're way ahead of everybody else. Paskman says for you to break off right now and get into the office with whatever you've got."

Pat Kinghan ripped the film magazine from his camera and handed it to me. He said, "Take good care of that, kid." I grabbed the magazine of unprocessed film and followed the courier out to his motorcycle for my second wild ride of the night. We reached the office in fifteen minutes, and half an hour later, I went on the air with the first pictures and description of the crash scene, an incomplete story of the accident, but—I was only beginning to understand how important this was in television news—the *first*.

After that, working with a film editor who matched my tape recording to Pat Kinghan's pictures, I put together a more coherent version of the story for the morning news program. There were the lights on the river and the indistinct cries for help. There was Mr.

Warren asking about his wife. I was relieved that the pictures and sound were all there, but when we projected the finished story, I felt like crying again. I had to look away from the screen.

"Go home," Ralph Paskman said gruffly. "You did okay."

It was the middle of the morning. I walked down into the Grand Central subway station to wait for the shuttle to Times Square and the Seventh Avenue Express to Brooklyn. I bought an early edition of an afternoon newspaper with the plane crash splashed all over the front page. Inside, the paper listed the names of a few survivors the police boats had picked up. Mrs. Warren's name wasn't in there.

My head ached and my chest felt full. I wondered if I might be having a heart attack. I knew that real reporters were aggressive while covering a big story, and exhilarated afterward. I had been reluctant and meek, only going on the story because I won a coin toss, only getting to the scene because a nameless motorcycle rider took me onto the airfield without asking, only doing the interviews at the terminal because Pat Kinghan told me I had to. And now that it was over, I didn't feel exhilarated. I felt sad.

Well, it was all my secret. I went home and went to bed.

A few days later, the President of CBS News, Sig Mickelson, called me into his office.

"We'd like to offer you a job as a correspondent," he said.

CBS News Correspondent was the title held by Murrow, Sevareid and Collingwood. Only one correspondent had ever been promoted from the assignment desk, and that was Harry Reasoner just a few weeks before. But Reasoner was a seasoned reporter in his thirties. I was not yet twenty-four years old. I had just proved to myself that I didn't have what it took to cover a big story. As I opened my mouth to speak, Sig Mickelson held up his hand.

"Think about it," he said. "Talk it over with your wife. You'd be based in New York, but the job would involve an awful lot of traveling."

I don't know how I'd have answered him if he hadn't said that last word.

"Traveling."

I took the job on the spot.

4
=

GLOBE-TROTTING

I already had a New York City press shield. It said "Bearer is entitled to pass police and fire lines wherever formed." Now, CBS News issued me a green air travel card, good for ticket purchases to any destination on earth. I regarded these credentials as icons, the confirmation of worldly attainment. I didn't have much time to indulge my newfound self-importance, however. The Eisenhower era was ending, the world was changing out there, and CBS News was woefully short of legmen. I was sent running.

My first assignment was to cover the beginning of something—the opening of the new St. Lawrence Seaway, which permitted seagoing vessels twice the length of a football field to sail right into the middle of the continent. I was the first person to enter the seaway, standing in the bow of the first ship. At Chicago, that ship unloaded steel bars from Japan almost in the shadow of the Gary, Indiana, steel mills. In my story, I said something about coals to Newcastle, making much of a ship bringing Japanese steel up the seaway for sale in Gary. I did not imagine that other ships would someday bring Japanese automobiles for sale in Detroit.

Then I was sent off to cover the end of something—one of the last lynchings in the deep South. A twenty-three-year-old black man, Mack Charles Parker, accused of raping a white woman, was taken from his jail cell in Poplarville, Mississippi, on the eve of his trial. A mob of masked white men dragged him by his feet down the steps of the county jail, leaving a trail of blood from his head on the stairs.

Ten days later, Mack Charles Parker's body was found floating in the Pearl River. By that time, I knew the names of every man in the lynch mob and had even been to see a couple of them, my first experience at looking murderers in the face. It had taken the FBI about a day to solve the crime and provide a complete report to the county prosecuter. Working together, a UPI reporter and I managed to "borrow" the FBI report for a few hours one night and copy it in longhand. The killers named were ignorant backwoods tung tree growers, a former lawman, a fundamentalist preacher. The whole county knew them. The all-white county grand jury refused to indict any of them. Those still living are probably walking around free to this day in Pearl River County, Mississippi.

I left Poplarville feeling sick. I haven't been back there. When crossing southern Mississippi, you can avoid that one county seat by swinging up through Hattiesburg or going south along the coast by way of Biloxi, and all these years later, one way or the other around Poplarville is the way I always feel like going.

Most of the rest of that summer I spent among empty farmhouses, screen doors banging in the wind, weeds growing in the corn stubble. I was in the Great Plains for the first time, wandering through Nebraska, Kansas and Oklahoma to chronicle the death of family farms.

My cameraman and guide was Wendell Hoffman, a rangy, grown-up farm boy who had taught himself how to use a Bell & Howell Filmo and the big, awkward Auricon sound camera. Wendell had rambled all over the world for CBS News as a free-lance cameraman, but he insisted on making his home in Manhattan, Kansas, where he lived with his wife, Doretta, dean of the Department of Home Economics at Kansas State, and a houseful of growing sons. When he wasn't shooting film for CBS, Wendell was out on the land, trying to make a farm of his own pay off, changing his crop from corn to hogs to Christmas trees depending on his mood and his calculations of national demand. He was a wonderful cameraman, but I don't think he ever made it as a farmer. It was Wendell who had suggested a series on the spreading failures among small farmers, and it was from Wendell that I learned much in my first summer as a CBS News Correspondent about hard work, pain and disappointment in rural America. I also discovered the satisfying camaraderie that can develop between a cameraman and a correspondent working together toward a common goal. In Wendell's battered station wagon, we drove thousands of miles together in the summer of 1959, stopping at small-town grocery stores for supplies of baloney, mayonnaise and white bread from which to make our lunches, spending stories back to New York every few days, driving on, soaking up the feelings of vast, rolling land under the big sky.

Next thing I knew, I was chatting with Nikita Khrushchev in a silage pit on a farm outside Coon Rapids, Iowa.

"You look a little tired," I said to Nikita Khrushchev.

"No, no," he said. He put a beefy hand on my shoulder. "I do not sleep eight hours a night," he said. "If you sleep eight hours and live sixty years, that's twenty years of sleep!" He waited for this remark to be translated. He shook a finger at me and repeated reprovingly, "Yes, twenty years of sleep!"

Krushchev was on the final leg of a grumpy tour of America. In New York, he was needled by the crowds. In California, he complained that they showed him the backsides of dancers doing the can-can on a movie lot when what he really wanted to do was go to Disneyland. In Des Moines when they gave him his first hot dog he said it would have gone down a lot better with a cold beer.

But now on Roswell Garst's hog farm, wearing a fedora with the brim turned up and a suit with sleeves that were too long for him, the Premier of the Union of Soviet Socialist Republics was having a roaring good time at last, traipsing in the silage pit, reaching down for handfuls of corn shucks to throw at the news photographers when they crowded too close, bawling insults at the big mob of reporters. My job was to stay at Khrushchev's elbow come what may, holding a radio transmitter with a great long whip antenna, so that no remark could go unrecorded.

Farmer Garst said, "Well now, Mr. Premier, you should know that Iowa produced something above 700 million bushels of corn this year. . . ."

Krushchev said, "The Ukraine, you know, is the most fertile land on the earth."

Garst said, "Well, we could produce even more corn in Iowa if the government didn't pay us to produce less."

Krushchev said, "The big American corporations don't want to see farmers get too rich, isn't that it?"

"Well, not exactly," Garst said. "You see . . ."

Nikita Khrushchev wasn't listening. He was waving his arms, shouting at the reporters again and cutting up for the cameras. In the maelstrom, I lost my place at his side, slipped in the wet silage and fell down. When I looked up, all I could see was the rump of the Soviet Premier as he climbed out of the pit and headed toward the Garst farmhouse for lunch. I thought, this is the man the whole free world is afraid of? He's a clown, that's what he is. And we, I reflected, brushing corn silks off my pants as the horde of my fellow reporters and photographers thundered away after Khrushchev and Garst, we're clowns, too.

The only trouble was, I was beginning to enjoy life in the center ring. The political primaries of 1960 were coming on and I was enlisted in the ragtag band of reporters who crisscrossed the country as political camp followers. I didn't let my prejudices show through in my reports, but I found myself pulling hard for the joyful liberal, Hubert Humphrey, against the rich young interloper, John F. Kennedy. I felt personally forsaken when Kennedy, pouring his father's money into the race, ended Humphrey's presidential hopes for that year with a victory in the grimy cities and lonely hollows of West Virginia. Harry Reasoner got to cover that one. After the voting, Robert Kennedy came over to Humphrey headquarters in Charleston to escort the loser to Kennedy headquarters a few blocks away where Humphrey was to publicly congratulate the winner. Up on the stage, a country singer, refusing to give up, whanged away at his guitar and loudly sang a Humphrey anthem we had all heard a hundred times: "I'm for Huburt Humphrey, he's for you and me . . ." Bob Kennedy put his arm around Humphrey's shoulder. They walked out into the night, Humphrey still smiling bravely. I always thought he would have been a great President.

CBS News did not yet have bureaus all over the country, not even in Los Angeles or Chicago. The correspondents whose names everybody knew covered London or Paris or stuck to their radio essays from Washington. That left the whole United States of America to Harry Reasoner and me. We were pals, Harry and Charlie, CBS's good soldiers, willing to go anywhere and cover anything. It didn't matter if one of us outworked the other on a story so long as between us we made NBC and ABC look bad. Reasoner and I listened to John F. Kennedy's ringing acceptance speech at the end of the Democratic convention in Los Angeles that July and then drove straight through to Chicago without stopping to sleep, in order to be ready for the Republican convention which was about to begin. Afterward, I trailed Richard Nixon through Texas, Wyoming, Washington and California, then went off to cover Kennedy in Ohio, Illinois and Michigan.

We watched the campaign transform the campaigners. Richard Nixon, Eisenhower's vice president, started out projecting an image of calm and maturity, trying to play both experienced statesman and regular fellow, telling homey stories about his boyhood employment in a general store, about a toy train his family couldn't afford to buy him for Christmas; by the end of the campaign, rattled by Kennedy's attacks on the Republican Party, he seemed grim and angry. His speeches became defensive and indignant and sometimes a little out of control.

Kennedy, on the other hand, was stiff and businesslike at the outset of the campaign, hacking the air awkwardly with his right arm as he punched his points across in speeches; but as the summer ended and fall came on, the impatient, over-serious candidate gave way to a relaxed and smiling one who could joke with his staff and then go out and respond to the cheers of the crowds. Moreover, he became easily accessible to reporters. If we needed a moment alone with Kennedy to fill out a story we were working on, all it took was a word to Pierre Salinger, his press aide. Kennedy gave dozens of these private interviews; Nixon avoided them. Kennedy seemed to enjoy the give-and-take with the reporters; Nixon suspected us and kept us at arm's length. After Richard Nixon's narrow defeat in November, he accused the press of being secretly on Kennedy's side. By that time, I am sure, he was right. I always have believed that the outcome of that election might have been different had Nixon been able to put his feet up at the end of the day and relax with the reporters, explaining his positions over a glass of scotch and a cigar. But he was not the drinking, smoking, explaining sort, or the relaxing sort either. I think it cost him the Presidency in 1960.

In the middle of the Presidential campaign, CBS

News started a new Friday night program, *Eyewitness to History*, with the avowed intention of covering the big news story of the week wherever in the world it occurred. I was pulled off the campaign and installed as the youthful anchorman. I bought a trench coat and waited for the phone to ring.

"The Congo," Les Midgley, the *Eyewitness* producer, said on the phone, and I was off to the Congo. A more experienced globe-trotter, Ernest Leiser, and I played gin rummy for seventeen hours as we throbbed across the Atlantic toward west Africa in a DC-7, then flew eight more hours down the coast into the Heart of Darkness. But even Joseph Conrad's story, even the dying Kurtz crying out "The horror! The horror!" had not prepared me for the chaos and danger of the place. The Belgians, under world pressure, had suddenly given up their dominion over a land of 14 million, leaving behind not one doctor, not one judge, not one engineer or economist. In a sovereign nation newly "free," there were no courts, no lawyers and no law. Terror ruled the streets of the old Belgian capital and tribal rivalries erupted into warfare in the bush. Soldiers of the former Force Publique raced about in jeeps, frenzied, armed and belligerent. There was no safety anywhere. The Congo was a bad dream.

The first night I spent in Léopoldville, now Kinshasa, all the reporters in the hotel were rounded up by soldiers banging on doors with rifle butts. We were forced into the lobby and required at gunpoint to prove we were not Belgians by presenting our documents to noncommissioned officers who could not read. One reporter showed the only identification he had—his Italian driver's license, which had also served to get him into the country after a trip across the Congo River from Brazzaville in a dugout canoe. The next day, as a group of reporters gathered in the street outside the house of Premier Patrice Lumumba to wait for a promised interview, guards pointed excitedly to one of those waiting, grabbed him, took him aside and began clubbing him. There was nothing the other reporters could do to help. The victim was an Algerian journalist friendly to Lumumba who had made the mistake that morning of putting on a web belt and brass buckle to hold up his pants. Spotting the belt, which was similar to those worn by Belgian officers, the guards had taken the poor man for a spy. Without asking any questions, they beat him to death with their rifle butts and left him lying there in the street. When this was reported to Lumumba an hour later, he shook his head and laughed.

Capricious death overtook others, too. One morning, I watched a young American reporter, Henry J. Taylor, Jr., leave the hotel in a jeep to join a column of troops out in the countryside who were said to be loyal to Joseph Kasavubu, the President of the country. That night, we heard that the column had been ambushed and that Taylor had been killed—victim of a poisoned arrow in the chest. I was deeply shaken. I wanted to go home.

Instead, I let myself be talked into going to Matadi, the port city on the Congo River a day's drive away. It was John Tiffin, a dashing English cameraman for CBS, who talked me into it.

"Nobody's been there, you know," he said. "Rumors of a massacre. Abandoned streets and all that. Hell of a story.'' He produced a taxi driver willing to make the trip and a big American flag to stretch across the hood of the car. "Who'd do harm,'' he asked with a smile, "to two nice fellows under the protection of the Stars and Stripes?''

He got his answer in the first village we came to. A barefoot man with a rifle stepped in front of the car and signaled us to pull over.

"We better stop!'' I shouted to the driver.

"Step on it!'' Tiffin shouted louder. *"Allez-y! En avant!"*

The driver accelerated straight toward the man with the gun, who leapt aside as we ducked to the floor of the car. We looked aback to see him squeezing off wild shots in our direction. The bullets all missed and the car careened around a corner and back to the open road.

I sat up slowly. I said, "What if he radios ahead?''

Tiffin said, "The bloke doesn't even have shoes. It's a safe bet he doesn't have a radio.''

In Matadi, we didn't find any evidence of a massacre. What we found instead were Congolese randomly strolling about in their neighborhoods as if on holiday, and in the former white district, sepulchral silence. I still see Matadi sometimes at night in my dreams of the world after Armageddon. The business section held only broken, looted stores. In the residential districts where 1,800 Europeans had lived, the houses were empty. It took the Belgians eighty years to construct Matadi—and a few panic-stricken hours to clear out and leave the city to the river and to the

Congolese. We walked about among artifacts of the white man's civilization, curious relics now—a swing for the children, an outdoor theater for amusement, a tennis court for exercise, all empty and irrelevant. The Congo, about to become Zaire, had no use for swings, theaters and tennis courts at the moment. A mailbox sign said "Dr. von Dreesche." The doctor, whoever he may have been, had abandoned his car on the dock with those of his neighbors and sailed for Antwerp.

I didn't feel sorry for the Belgians. I knew their record of cruel colonialism; the penalty for petty thievery once had been loss of the thieving hand, and hundreds of Congolese now walked around handless. But I felt terribly sorry for the country the Belgians had left behind. In Matadi, I had a vision of the future of black Africa, and it was a gloomy vision, silent and despairing.

Tiffin and I found lodging for ourselves and the cabdriver at the Metropole Hotel above the river, an old building with rooms arranged around an open courtyard. The French owner of the hotel had sent his family to safety and stayed on to try to protect his property. He helped carry our bags up to the rooms in the otherwise nearly empty building, wryly apologizing for the absence of the hotel staff, and let us borrow his shortwave radio receiver.

"Now," Tiffin said, fiddling with the tuner, "the ace trick is to dial the Beeb."

It took him only a few minutes to find a BBC newsreader dryly reciting the day's developments in the Congo. Lumumba and Kasavubu were still feuding.

There was a report of fighting in Katanga Province. "And in the vacated port city of Matadi, officials of the Force Publique have threatened to direct their artillery against a hotel, the Metropole, which they describe as a hiding place for Belgian saboteurs."

We looked at each other in shock. "Time for a word with the management," Tiffin said. We ran down the stairs to the Frenchman's office to tell him what we had heard.

"Oh, yes," he said wearily. "They have been saying this for several days now. What can one do?"

What Tiffin and I did was stay awake the rest of the night. Sometime after midnight, a truculent squad of obviously drunken soldiers stormed into the hotel courtyard shouting for the Frenchman to come out. When he did, the soldiers surrounded him menacingly, poking him with the barrels of their rifles. Tiffin and I looked down at this frightening scene from a dark balcony above. My impulse was to get out of there somehow and hide. Tiffin's was to grab his camera and a portable light.

"What the hell are you doing?" I whispered.

" 'The heart of danger,' " he said, " 'is where we shall find safety.' It's a Chinese proverb." He handed me the light. "Turn it on when I say. Let's go."

He led the way calmly down the stairs and addressed the sergeant who seemed to be in charge. "*Bon soir, Monsieur le Commandant. Je suis journaliste Américain.* Light, please!" I pressed a button and flooded the courtyard with light. The soldiers looked about uncertainly as Tiffin proceeded to film them as if they were a winning Liverpool soccer team—wide shot, close-up, with special attention to the sergeant, captain of the team. The soldiers assumed something like military bearing. One or two of them grinned self-consciously. After a couple minutes of this, the sergeant said a word to the French hotel owner and led his squad smartly out of the hotel and down the street. "Kill the light, please," Tiffin said to me.

Often afterward, I have heard the argument that television news can never quite be true to life because the camera's presence alters events. Well, it did that time, thank God.

We headed back to the capital with our film of Matadi, the deserted port and the midnight callers. On the way, we stopped at roadside grocery stores looking for Players cigarettes, Tiffin's brand, which were unavailable in the ransacked stores of Léopoldville. We finally were able to find two precious tins of Players in the rural grocery of a woman who kept a shiny long-barreled six-shooter on the counter to guard her stock from looters. She agreed to part with the cigarettes if we would also buy a chicken. We struck the deal. She went out back and caught the chicken, which the taxi driver placed, untrussed and cackling, in the trunk. Tiffin tossed the Players in his shoulder bag. Cash, smiles and handshakes were exchanged, and we departed in an air of satisfaction all around. The driver, for all his bravado on the trip down, took a long detour on dirt roads on the way back to avoid the village of the barefoot rifleman. We arrived in Léopoldville feeling smug and successful with a chicken in the trunk.

The next morning, I hired an illegal launch to take me across the river and out of the country. Weeks later, when I saw John Tiffin again, he told me that a few nights after we left Matadi, the Metropole Hotel had been shelled to the ground.

He also told me he had rationed the priceless Players so that only one cigarette was left on the morning of his own departure. He took it out as he was being ferried across the river, lighted it, and tossed the empty tin into the Congo. A crocodile rose from the depths, crushed the tin in its jaws and disappeared into the brown water.

I knew I would need a stopover on the way back to New York. I flew from Brazzaville to Paris, arriving in the midst of the morning rush hour with the dust of the Congo still on my clothes. I had never been to Paris before. I took a taxi to the Hotel Raphael, where David Schoenbrun, the Paris bureau chief, had reserved a room for me. The hotel proved to be small and extremely elegant. I was shown to a room with a crystal chandelier hanging from the ceiling and a rich Bokhara rug on the floor. The white sheets of a canopied feather bed were turned down and waiting for me.

I drew back the heavy draperies, opened the French doors and stepped out onto a balcony that overlooked the Avenue Kleber. I was dirty, unshaven and exhausted. I looked to my right and saw a beautiful woman dressed in a terry-cloth robe standing on the balcony of the room next door. It was Leslie Caron.

"Good morning, Miss Caron," I said. Without a

word she turned, swept back into her room and closed the doors.

I laughed to myself. I had been to Africa and been shot at. I was alive. I was in Paris. There was a movie star in the room next door. It was a beautiful, clear, cool morning. It was my twenty-sixth birthday.

I left the balcony, took a long, hot shower and slept the day away.

"Cuba," Les Midgley said on the phone, and I went off to Havana with Wendell Hoffman. In the days when Fidel Castro was still a guerrilla in the Sierra Maestra, Wendell had undertaken a long, dangerous journey into the mountains on foot to secure the first film interview with him. Now that Castro was in command of the country, Wendell thought CBS might have a certain *entrée* to the centers of power. We wasted a lot of time hanging out in designated bars in the small hours of the morning waiting for a promised rendezvous with Fidel. To Wendell's disgust, this meeting never materialized. As booby prize, I was awarded an interview with Che Guevara. He was going to become a martyr and a legend, but in the second year of the Cuban Revolution, Che struck me as a pompous braggart.

"New Orleans," Midgley said, and a few hours later I was in the midst of a screaming mob of white parents trying to prevent a six-year-old black girl named Ruth Nell Bridges from entering a public school. The little girl wore a pretty yellow dress and held the hands of two strapping U.S. marshals as she walked up the steps of the William Frantz School with the cruel, loud insults of all those white people in her ears. When she came out after school, the crowd was even larger and louder. Wendell Hoffman and I walked down the steps with her, with the camera aimed, not at the little girl, but at the howling throng on the sidewalk. "This," I said, as the camera moved through the crowd, "is what the only Negro student in the only truly integrated school in the deep South sees and hears every afternoon." It was a forceful and appalling bit of film. Shooting it cost Wendell a rotten egg on his jacket.

The Frantz school was "truly integrated" only because a handful of white parents refused to join the boycott that kept all the other white youngsters at home. One of these was a man named James Gabrielle who accompanied his six-year-old daughter Yolanda to her first-grade class every day through the jeering, threatening gauntlet. "Hold your head up," he told his daughter. "They can't keep you from going to school." After school one day, Wendell Hoffman and I followed James Gabrielle and Yolanda back to the public housing project where they lived. The little girl was crying.

"Don't cry," her father said. "You have to do this again tomorrow."

"I know, Daddy," she said.

James Gabrielle's shirt was torn and he was steaming. I told him what he was doing seemed courageous. He said, "Well, I wouldn't say courageous. I am just not going to have a goddamn mob tell me what to do with my child."

I wonder whether Ruth Nell Bridges and Yolanda Gabrielle, first-grade classmates, became friends. I wonder whether they remember each other. They should, because they did something important together. Deep South school integration had to start somewhere. It started with two brave little girls in New Orleans.

A few days later, Midgley said, "Laos." I left on a Friday night, flew twenty-seven hours on Pan Am and Royal Air Lao, and stepped out into a country just emerging into the thirteenth century—except for all the guns and airplanes. King Savang Vatthana's troops were fighting Communist rebels in the Plain of Jars, gingerly, at a distance, with artillery. Unmarked transport planes flew all over the country, Russian planes bringing guns and rice to the rebels and American planes bringing guns and rice to the Royal Lao Army, a few thousand loyal Meo and Hmong tribesmen. Neither army seemed to want to hurt anybody, and neither needed more guns, but the United States had solemnly committed $50 million a year to guns for our Laotians and the Russians probably that much or more for theirs, so the guns kept coming in.

On the outskirts of Vientiane, I saw a neat little cinderblock building with a sign that said "Indiana Telephone Company." I knocked on the door. The man who answered said, "Yep, we're under contract to improve the phone service in the country. If you'll excuse me, we're awfully busy right now." But there wasn't any phone service in the country. I figured I had just met the CIA station chief.

At night, the Indiana Telephone Company employees congregated in a bar downtown to drink beer and dance with the local girls. In the distance, the sound of the artillery went on all night. I thought it would make a great sequence on film if I stood outside in the street and listened to the guns and then walked into the Lido Nightclub where the music was playing and everybody was dancing, ignoring the war. But when I tried it, it didn't work. The minute I walked into the place with the camera rolling, all those "telephone workers" covered their faces, dived under the tables or ran out the back door, and the band stopped playing. Even the musicians worked for the CIA.

I visited a couple of *boun*s at rural temples, Buddhist church socials with dancing on the grounds. I drove to the royal capital, Luang Prabang, on a highway being built with millions of American dollars, passing at the place where the paving ran out a sign warning travelers to turn around, Communists ahead. I made this trip in a Mercedes-Benz. I don't know what they were doing there, but there were hundreds of Mercedes-Benzes in Vientiane, some of them for hire, so I hired one.

A few other Western reporters trickled into the country while I was there. We met nightly on the veranda of the Continental Hotel and talked about our illnesses. We all had taken care to drink only the bottled water provided in the rooms, but still we all felt sick. A *Time* magazine reporter had to be evacuated to Bangkok with a severe case of dysentery. Finally one morning, Keyes Beech of the *Chicago Daily*

News, an old Asia hand, solved the mystery. He caught the room boy from the hotel filling the bottles at the filthy town well. When Beech remonstrated with him, the young man shrugged and smiled an innocent Laotian smile. "The Europeans like their water in bottles," he said.

"If Laos fell to the Communist Pathet Lao," I said on the air, "pro-Western Thailand and South Vietnam could no longer be considered safe, so the stakes in this secret war are high: the future of Southeast Asia." In truth, I thought the "secret war" had all the elements of a comic opera. But I wasn't sure enough of my judgment to report it that way. It was the first war I had ever attended. For all I knew, all of them were like this.

When I reached Hong Kong on the way home, I reported to Les Midgley by telephone.

"Well, chum," he said, "I'm sorry to tell you, but you've been bumped out of the sled."

"What does that mean?" I asked.

"You're not the anchorman of *Eyewitness* anymore," he said.

"What have I done wrong?" I asked.

"Not a thing as far as I'm concerned," he said. "It seems to be Aubrey's decision." Jim Aubrey was the head of CBS Television "across town," a man known to underlings as the Smiling Cobra. I had never even met him.

"Aubrey thinks our ratings might go up if somebody more mature anchors the show," Midgley said. "Mickelson argued for you, I think, but he lost. We're going to have a new anchorman."

"Who's it going to be?" I asked.

"Fellow named Cronkite," Midgley said.

So that is how Walter Cronkite got his first big break in television.

Cronkite was a solid, experienced wire service reporter who had distinguished himself as a combat correspondent in World War II and decided during the Korean War to try his hand at broadcasting. I liked and admired him, and figured he was a lot more logical choice than I had been to anchor *Eyewitness* in the first place.

I said this to Midgley and then asked, "What's going to happen to me?"

"You'll still be in the field," Midgley said. "We want you on every story. Nothing's going to happen to you, except that you won't ever have to come home anymore."

"Okay," I said. "Now let me tell you what we got in Luang Prabang."

I found that I didn't mind being kicked out of the studio—which was just as well, because it was good practice for all the studios I was going to be kicked out of in the future. I knew I could get along fine without makeup, lights and camera, even without fame and fortune, as long as they didn't take away my air travel card, the green one, the one that lets you go everywhere in the world.

5

THE RUNAWAY
CRUISE SHIP

The new President, John F. Kennedy, sent his Secretary of State, Dean Rusk, to a SEATO meeting in Thailand; I went along. There was a steel strike in Pennsylvania; I covered it. Ambassador Adlai Stevenson made a tour of South America; I traveled with him, discovering a new country every day. I woke up those mornings staring at hotel room ceilings and trying to remember whether I was in Bangkok, Bethlehem or Bogotá. Wherever I was, it wasn't Brooklyn, where I was supposed to live.

My wife had another baby. We talked by phone and agreed to name her Susan. I stopped by the hospital to admire Susan and then caught another flight to somewhere else. I was drunk with travel, dizzy with the import of it all, and indifferent to thoughts of home and family. Pretty soon, I no longer had a home or family. Sory and I agreed to separate. We did that by phone, too. She moved back to North Carolina with Lisa and Susan. I gave up the apartment, put my few possessions into storage, and flew off to the Dominican Republic with a camera crew to cover the final fall of the Trujillo dynasty. This was callous and unfeeling behavior, of course. The thought of missing

a breaking story had become more intolerable to me
than the thought of letting our lives fly apart. It was
much later that the burden of guilt settled upon me,
and much too late.

My passport, fattening with fanfold inserts, grew
to the thickness of a paperback novel. I still listed my
residence as "New York, N.Y." on the visa appli-
cations and airline landing cards, but for a long time,
I had no residence at all except for whatever room I
happened to be staying in for the night. I didn't want
a place to live; I had nothing to do there. I didn't
want days off; I had no way to fill empty days. All I
wanted was stories, the wilder the better.

A wild one came along. A luxurious Portuguese
cruise ship, the *Santa Maria*, with 600 souls aboard,
including about forty American vacationers, was hi-
jacked in the Caribbean by a band of Portuguese rebels. Their leader, a stouthearted old crackpot named
Henrique Galvao, put a boat ashore in Venezuela with
members of the ship's crew who were wounded when
the pirates stormed the bridge, then steered the *Santa
Maria* for the open sea.

My assignment—and that of dozens of other reporters from all over the world—was to get to that
ship somehow. But first we had to find it. The *Santa
Maria* just vanished into the South Atlantic. For several days, U.S. Navy reconnaissance planes criss-
crossing the ocean and U.S. Navy destroyers steaming
in search patterns turned up nothing. It began to be
a little embarrassing. I interviewed an admiral. "It's
a big ocean out there," he said.

I flew to Caracas, found the ship's purser who had

just been put ashore, and persuaded him to give me his first interview:

"Did you talk to Galvao yourself?"

"Yes, before I leave the ship, I talk to him."

"What did he tell you?"

"He told me you go ashore but during four or five days, you don't speak about this."

"He told you not to talk to anybody?"

"No, not talk about this. He said if you talk and come ships or planes to catch me, I sink the ship together with passengers."

"Do you think he meant it?"

"Yes, he's serious. It's not a joke."

The U.S. State Department protested to CBS News that this interview should not have been broadcast because it might have "upset" the rebel captain Galvao. I wondered how the old pirate could be upset by something he couldn't see aboard a ship the U.S. Navy couldn't find.

Frustrated reporters gathered in cities all over the rim of the South Atlantic. Some went to Africa on the theory that the *Santa Maria* was headed for one of the Portuguese colonies. Others collected in Caracas and Trinidad.

When a search plane finally spotted the *Santa Maria* one morning, she was discovered to be about 400 miles north of the big bulge in the South American continent. By fabulous good luck, a CBS News cameraman, Herb Schwartz, happened to be aboard the Navy Constellation that made the sighting. He persuaded the crew to remove the door and hang on to his belt to keep him from falling out as he made the first pictures of the runaway cruise ship, footage every news organization in the world was dying for.

Back on the ground, as the plane refueled and Herb reloaded his camera for the next flight over the ship, an envious cameraman from UPI Movietone, an old friend of Herb's, admitted defeat on the story and offered to ship Herb's film to CBS for him. Herb gave him the film cannister with many thanks and took off on another run with the Navy. The film was purloined by UPI Movietone, which offered it to its worldwide clients the next day. CBS News had to buy a copy like everybody else.

"THROW YOUR FILM IN THE WATER BEFORE GIVING IT TO UPI FOR SHIPPING," Ralph Paskman cabled.

Herb's feelings were hurt. He cabled back, "EYE FLY 48 HOURS WITHOUT SLEEP, RISK LIFE HANGING OUT PLANE DOOR, OBTAIN EXCLUSIVE FIRST FOOTAGE OF SANTA MARIA, SHIP FILM BEST WAY EYE KNOW HOW, AND THIS IS ALL THANKS EYE GET."

Paskman cabled, "NEXT TIME DON'T RISK YOUR LIFE FOR UPI."

I took a look at a map of the Santa Maria's position and headed for Recife, Brazil, on the chance that when the ship finally stopped running, it might be in that Portuguese-speaking port. When I got there, I found the waterfront hotel filling up with reporters from many countries who had made the same guess. Ernest Leiser, my old traveling companion to the Congo, came down from New York to join me, but we still felt shorthanded.

"SCHEFFLER ON WAY FROM GUATEMALA," Paskman cabled.

Phil Scheffler had switched over from the assignment desk where I first met him to join our little band on *Eyewitness* as reporter-producer-bon vivant. He had been in Guatemala City doing spadework for a future story, but he was a whiz with the airline schedules and I knew he and his camera crew would make it to Brazil in no time.

A day passed. News reports speculated the *Santa Maria* was Recife-bound, all right.

"WHERE SCHEFFLER?" I asked Paskman.

"ON WAY FROM MIAMI," he replied.

Phil had calculated that the fastest way south to Recife was north to Miami, the hub of South American airlines. This was the long way around, but it made sense.

Leiser boarded an American warship, USS *Gearing*, which called in Recife for provisioning before heading out to sea, to try to intercept the *Santa Maria* and escort the cruise ship into port. I felt awfully alone on shore.

"WHERE SCHEFFLER?" I cabled.

"BUENOS AIRES," Paskman replied.

Buenos Aires was 2,500 miles *south* of Recife! But Scheffler was good. He had those airline schedules down cold, I knew that. It had to be that the fastest connections to Recife that day were through Buenos Aires, that's all.

Another day passed. By now, the *Santa Maria* was dead in the water a few miles offshore while the renegade captain, Galvao, negotiated with the U.S. Navy and the Brazilian government. Up on the hotel roof with a pair of strong binoculars, I thought I could actually *see* the ship on the distant horizon. Any hour now, the impasse might be resolved, the passengers might be freed, and I'd have to cover the whole complicated event by myself.

"WHERE SCHEFFLER?" This time I was agitated.

"MADRID," Paskman replied.

Madrid?

What had happened was that Phil and his camera crew had made a tight connection in Buenos Aires to an international flight of Aerolíneas Argentinas. In the rush to get them aboard, the airline had neglected to check their documents. When the plane landed in Rio de Janeiro, they had stayed aboard. When the plane landed in Recife and they headed impatiently through Brazilian Immigration, an official asked them politely for their disembarkation cards.

"What disembarkation cards?" Scheffler asked.

"Carteira verde," the man said. "Green card. The airline gave it to you in Buenos Aires."

"Oh, well," Phil said, "they must have forgotten. Here, we'll fill out the cards now."

"No," the man said. "You must have green cards upon arriving in Brazil."

"Or what?" Phil asked.

"Or you may not enter this country," the man said firmly.

Phil had been traveling two days from Guatemala. He was tired. He hit the ceiling. He screamed at the immigration officers, he screamed at the airline clerks. He threatened to call the U.S. Consulate, and would have done so except that the telephones were all just on the other side of the immigration barrier, inside the country, and he wasn't allowed inside the country. Phil shouted, cajoled, harangued, spoke of the urgency of his mission, pointed out the absurdity of the situation. He banged on the table, he showed his passport, he showed his press credentials. The immigration officer was interested only in seeing a little green card.

The Aerolíneas plane was about to leave. Brazilian law stated that anyone lacking proper documents for entering the country must depart on the same aircraft that brought him. Phil refused to board. Soldiers were summoned. They pointed their rifles. Phil boarded.

The plane's next stop was Dakar, West Africa. Phil and the crew didn't have documents to get off there, either. They flew on thousands of miles to the next stop—Madrid.

Phil called Midgley by telephone to explain the situation and ask for instructions.

"Come home," Midgley said.

But the plane to New York encountered a blizzard and was diverted to Montreal. Having traveled from Miami to Buenos Aires to Rio to Recife to Dakar to Madrid to Montreal, Phil took the train home to New York in a February snowstorm, still wearing the Palm Beach suit he had put on four days before in Guatemala City. In the annals of fruitless journalistic travel, Phil's 17,000-mile expedition to three continents is writ large, but to this day, he changes the subject when anybody brings up the *Santa Maria*.

The reporters on land began a hectic scramble to reach the ship, but Galvao's armed pirates repelled all boarders from the sea. Two plucky French photographers, demented by competitiveness, decided to board from the sky. They hired light planes to fly them over the ship and bailed out by parachute, aiming for the *Santa Maria*'s deck. Both missed and landed in the sea. Some humanitarian instinct stirred in Captain Galvao's breast; he ordered them fished out and taken aboard.

I went down to the Recife waterfront and chartered a forty-foot sailboat owned by an elderly Argentine couple who were on the last leg of a circumnavigation of the world. At a stately five knots, Herb Schwartz and I were conducted to sea under sail aboard the yawl *Gaucho*. It took forever to reach the *Santa Maria*. When we did, I used a megaphone to shout questions to the passengers as our sailboat tacked back and forth under the ship's stern. They yelled back that the ship was running low on food and water and that they had been told they would be freed the next day at Recife. I had a big international scoop—and no way to send it from the sailboat.

One of the French parachutists aboard the *Santa Maria* had the same problem. He decided to use me to get his story out. We played a seagoing game of pitch and catch out there. He threw me a knotted handkerchief with a weight and a note inside. It asked in several languages, "Who are you?" I held up a big yellow CBS News film bag for identification. On our next pass under the stern, he dropped a bag of his own. I leaned overboard and caught the bag one-handed just before it dropped into the sea. It contained several cassettes of 35mm color film, the exclusive pictures aboard the *Santa Maria* he had leapt from the sky to get, and two rolls of unprocessed motion picture footage. There was another note, this one written in red ink, in capital letters.

It said: "GOD WILL PUNISH YOU IF YOU DO NOT DELIVER THIS FILM IMMEDIATELY TO *AGENCE DALMAS*, PARIS."

When the good ship *Gaucho* finally returned to the dock in Recife, I sped to the airport and faithfully shipped the man's film to his French picture agency. By way of CBS News, New York. The pictures were sold by Dalmas to magazines and television networks all over the world. But first, they showed up on CBS.

The old UPI trick.

6

LIEUTENANT SON

That spring, Les Midgley said something that came within an inch or two of costing me my life. He said, "Vietnam."

It was April 1961. My notes on the trip say "Approx. 500 U.S. military advisers here." No U.S. news organization yet considered the Vietnam War important enough to open a permanent bureau in the country. A visit by an American television crew was so unusual that when Los Angeles cameraman Fred Dieterich and I arrived at the Saigon airport, the South Vietnamese government sent a chauffeured Citroën to pick us up and take us comfortably into the city. The government arranged a palace interview with President Ngo Dinh Diem for the next morning.

Diem was an elected President who had turned into an autocrat, ordering mass arrests of his opponents and censoring the press in the name of victory over the Communists. His army was fighting a brutal war in the jungles and rice fields, and was slowly being worn down. In the interview, Diem discussed the plight of his country in plain language, without any of the diplomatic obfuscation I had expected. He made a frank pitch for U.S. military aid.

When Vietnam was partitioned in 1954, he said, 900,000 people fled to the South. Most of these were anti-Communist refugees, he said, but among them were about 10,000 *Việt Nam cong-san*, trained Communist troops under orders to hide out among the people and terrorize them.

"Kill the village chief," he said, "kill his deputy, frighten the people, control the village. That is their tactic. And now the Vietcong are being reinforced directly by uniformed cadres from Hanoi. This is a stealthy invasion, supported by China and the Soviet Union. To combat it, our government needs much military aid from the United States."

I suggested that as a former French colony, South Vietnam might expect help from France.

"France has no will," Diem said bluntly. "Only your country has the will to defend freedom in the world. If the United States also loses its will, there will be no freedom in Vietnam."

Ngo Dinh Diem gave me pretty good history that day. Pretty good prophecy, too.

I found Saigon the most seductive of cities. The war in the countryside had not yet had any effect on the capital. All the people I met, teachers, newspapermen, waiters and cabdrivers, were friendly and considerate. The women were beautiful, I thought, gliding along in their diaphanous costumes, and the spring weather was lovely, and the sidewalk cafes delightful. I walked along the tree-shaded avenues during the day and, lying in bed under the lazy ceiling fan in my room in the old Majestic Hotel, listened to the sounds of the river traffic at night. As hordes of

Western reporters were to do in years to come, I fell in love with Saigon. This is worth defending, I thought. If this sunny, beguiling city ever falls to the Communists and becomes gray and regimented, there just isn't any hope for civilization.

Every day, I dropped by the government press office to badger an official there for permission to go out into the country on a military operation. "Too dangerous," he said at first; then, "Maybe"; then when he saw I wasn't going away, finally one day, "Tomorrow. Lieutenant Son will pick you up at your hotel at noon. Be prepared to be gone for several days."

Fred Dieterich placed his gear in the back of a Vietnamese Army jeep the next day and climbed into the backseat. I sat up front with the driver, Lieutenant Son, a neatly turned out young Ranger officer who had spent a few months in training in the United States. My poor French and his poor English were enough to permit us to talk to each other as we drove north out of town. Young as he was, Lieutenant Son turned out to be a veteran of warfare. He came from a nationalist family, he said. He and two brothers had been members of the Viet Minh army that expelled the French, and Son himself had taken part as a teenaged foot soldier in the final siege of Dien Bien Phu in 1954. "But we want a free country," he said. "My family did not fight the French in order to be ruled by Ho Chi Minh." He shrugged and smiled. "So now, we fight on. You will find many like me in the Rangers."

We spent the night in an abandoned warehouse in

the provincial town of Bencat with Lieutenant Son and his outfit, the 150th Ranger Company. Son introduced us to the men in his platoon. We shook hands formally with each of them and then he made a speech to them. "I tell them to take care of you tomorrow," he said with a grin.

As night came on, Son brought us food, rice and meat in a pungent sauce. "What is it?" I asked. "I don't know how to say it," he said, and laughed. "Anyway, don't ask." He gave Fred and me cots to sleep on while he and his men rolled out bedding on the floor. "I don't like this," I said. "We are prepared to live exactly as you do." He held up his hand. "You are our guests," he said.

The officers met in a corner of the building to study a map under the glare of a bare light bulb hanging from the ceiling. The next morning, three platoons of Rangers were to move south into a pocket of land between the Saigon River and a canal, hoping to trap what they thought was a small group of Vietcong at a place called An Dien. Lieutenant Son's platoon was to be the center column. "We don't go on trail," Son said to me apologetically. "I am sorry, but you will get muddy feet."

We set out in trucks before dawn. After a short trip, the trucks stopped beside a patch of thick woods. The men quietly put on their helmets and hoisted rifles and cartridge belts in the dark. Artillery opened up somewhere behind us, firing 155-millimeter shells over our heads as we walked into the woods toward—what? I had no idea. Toward whatever was in there.

When the sun came up, I could see that we were

passing occasional clusters of empty houses in the forest. "Nobody home," Son said. "Afraid of us, afraid of enemy. Always run away."

The artillery fire stopped. The morning became silent, except for the sound of about thirty pairs of boots moving over the ground. We emerged from the woods, climbed a barbed-wire fence and slogged through a mile of rice fields. Freddy Dieterich and I walked a few steps ahead of the point man, turning to film the platoon advancing toward us. The day was beginning to get hot. I thought, well, nothing's going to happen. At least, we're getting some good film of troops in the field.

Just as we reached the high ground of an earthen dike, a sudden rattle of automatic weapons burst from a tree line on the other side of a small stream, about half a mile away. The firing grew and grew in volume and intensity until it sounded like one long sustained explosion. We could see men running at the edge of the trees and hear their shouts.

Lieutenant Son shouted orders to his troops. "Ambush!" he said to me. "Other platoon fall into a trap. They need us now." He drew his .45 pistol and, waving it overhead, led his men toward the battle. The soldiers followed him at a run, waded the stream and rushed to the edge of the trees. Fred Dieterich and I had everything we could do to film the running soldiers and record the sound of the fighting without being left behind.

By the time we reached the tree line, the shooting had stopped, except for isolated bursts of fire from deep inside the forest. I saw bodies of dead men sprawled everywhere at the edge of the woods, most of them Rangers but two wearing the loose black pajamas of the Vietcong. One of the dead VC had a heavy Browning automatic rifle lying beside him. The other was armed only with a sword.

Lieutenant Son stopped his platoon at the tree line. On his orders, each of the men took out a pocket handkerchief and tied it around his left arm. Son produced handkerchiefs for Fred and me. "So we don't shoot at each other in there," he explained. "We go in slow now. You stay with me."

The soldiers fanned out along the tree line and on Son's signal, we entered the forest. We crept fifty yards in, a hundred yards, each soldier alert for the slightest movement ahead. We came upon more bodies. We passed a wounded Ranger trying to stop the bleeding in his more seriously wounded buddy's chest; Son stopped for an instant to speak to him and then led us on, slowly, wordlessly. Fred Dieterich whispered to me, "This is scary as hell."

We came at last to a dirt road leading to a large clearing in the forest. In the clearing were a small, run-down temple and a roofless house. Son motioned to four of his soldiers to search the buildings. They banged open the door of the temple with their rifle butts and barged in. Empty. They cautiously surrounded the house and then entered it. Empty. The searchers rejoined the rest of us in the center of the clearing. We formed a rough circle, each man peering into the silent woods.

And then all hell broke loose. The forest around us just detonated. We were surrounded by a clatter of

gunfire, deafeningly loud. It took me a second or two
to realize that all the shooting was taking place only
a few yards away, and was aimed at us. I looked
around for cover, but there wasn't any except for a
shallow depression in the center of the clearing. Fred
Dieterich and I fell into this slight hollow together.
We could see figures in the trees taking aim and firing
at us. Incredibly, Fred flipped his camera turret to the
long lens, raised himself to his elbows, aimed and
fired back at them.

"Stop that!" I hollered. "Get your head down!"

Fred Dieterich said calmly, "Charlie, I figure this
is it. We might as well take pictures to show what
happened to us."

"The hell with that!" I shouted. "This is *not* it!
Keep your head down!"

Seeking to rescue the first platoon from an ambush,
we had walked into an ambush ourselves. Even with
my own head down, I could look around and see that
we were in terrible trouble. Several of the Rangers
had been shot down in the initial volley and lay surrounding us in the clearing, dead or wounded. Those
still on their feet were fighting back bravely, however.
One rushed straight into the woods with his weapon
firing until he was dropped by enemy fire. He fell
with his finger still tight on the trigger, his gun pump-
ing bullets into the sky. Others formed a perimeter
and poured a steady volley of return fire into the
woods. Lieutenant Son had taken a bullet in the arm,
but he was still in action, kneeling on the ground
beside his radio operator, cranking the handle of the
magneto-operated radio, trying to call battalion head-

quarters for reinforcements. Fred Dieterich and I crawled the few yards over to him to film the attempt. Bullets spattered the ground around us. Son ignored them and kept cranking. But it was useless. No answer came. We were out of radio range.

Then the radio operator, a kid no more than seventeen or eighteen years old, performed the most astounding act of courage I have ever seen. Without a word, he reached into his pack, found a coil of wire and attached one end of it to the radio antenna. He ran to a tree, uncoiling the wire as he ran. Holding the other end of the wire in his mouth, he climbed the tree with bullets whizzing around him, tied the wire to a high branch, shinnied back down the tree and made it back to his radio unscratched. He cranked the handle furiously. Lieutenant Son, lying beside the radio, spoke into the microphone, reached battalion headquarters and started reading coordinates from a map. He handed the mike back to the radio operator. "Stay down," he said to Fred and me. "It's okay. They send the paratroopers."

The firing eased off. I could no longer see any VC in the woods, although occasional shots still crisscrossed the clearing from somewhere. Two of Son's men bandaged his arm and then the three of them crawled about with a medical pack to see whether they could do anything to help the other wounded. They dragged several wounded men to the cover of the temple wall, where most of them went into shock and died while we waited for the promised paratroopers.

Son was up and walking around the clearing now,

encouraging his surviving soldiers. He came over and knelt beside Freddy and me. "We are nearly out of ammunition," he said. "You should know this. I don't think we will be attacked again, but if we are . . ."

A single shot was fired from the woods. It hit Son's helmet in the back center and exited the front. He pitched forward into me and fell to the ground.

The wound looked so small at first. I cradled his head on my chest. I picked up a handful of leaves from the ground and tried to stuff them into the wound to stop the bleeding.

The shot that killed Son was the last one I remember being fired that day. The paratroopers arrived, riding in trucks. The VC disappeared into the woods, carrying their dead and wounded with them. We went a few miles down the road to a rural schoolhouse to regroup. There was a poster on the floor, which I picked up and later had translated. It said: "Do not give Communists rice. Do not give Communists information. Do not let Communists into your house." The poster was on the floor because the Communists had wrecked the schoolhouse the night before.

A Colonel, the commander of the Rangers, arrived at the schoolhouse in a jeep. He lined up the 150th and told them, "You are a courageous company. You held off an enemy force five times greater than you. Don't think about the dead. You fight for a great cause and you will prevail."

But nineteen members of the company were not there to hear him. They were killed that day. Among them were two officers, Lieutenant Son and his company commander. I saw at least eleven wounded; there may have been others.

The Colonel assigned an armored car to drive Fred Dieterich and me back to Saigon. We reached the safety of the graceful city in little more than an hour. We clattered down the broad avenues. Bicyclists pedaled here and there. The sidewalk cafes were crowded. We arrived at the front door of the Majestic Hotel before dark and walked through the lobby toward the elevators, carrying our gear. People turned to look at us because we were so dirty and out of place. I had Lieutenant Son's blood all over my shirt.

I never was able to get Son out of my mind. Through all the years of the Vietnam War, I thought of him. I returned to Vietnam several times, went out into the countryside with troops again—they were American troops by then—and was present when other good men were killed in jungle clearings. As the war dragged on inconclusively and American casualties mounted, it became the fashion in the United States to say that those American boys were dying for nothing. All my friends agreed it was an immoral war, imperialist America against "the Vietnamese people."

I never thought so. The Vietnamese people I met wanted nothing to do with warfare. They wanted to be left alone to live peacefully. But they weren't being left alone. They were being invaded by an army from the North, sent by a government they hated. I thought of Son, who wanted so much for Vietnam to be free that he was willing to go on fighting for the idea long after his fighting days should have been over. I thought of the men of the 150th, the one who charged into the woods firing his rifle, the one who climbed the tree with the radio antenna in his teeth. I thought, I still think, that justice and virtue resided with those brave men. I hated going back there later and hearing them called "gooks" by my own countrymen.

The ones who lived through it—not many of the Rangers did—have presumably been "re-educated" now. Lovely, languid Saigon has become Ho Chi Minh City. The wound of the Vietnam War is healing in America. In America, most people don't remember the war very well or take into account any longer the wishes of "the Vietnamese people."

I go to the Vietnam War Memorial sometimes when I am in Washington. There are names of some men I knew carved on the black marble. I think of them. Son isn't up there, of course, but I think of him, too.

I only knew him for a day.

I never even learned the rest of his name.

7
RIO

I came back to New York for a few days when the *Eyewitness* season ended in the spring of 1961, and one of my bosses, Blair Clark, took me to lunch. He asked, "What do you think is going to be the big story of the next few years?"

"Latin America," I said.

It was the wrong answer, as things turned out, but Blair Clark said, "Right! Fidel Castro is going to try to communize the hemisphere, with plenty of help from the Russians and Chinese. I know that Jack Kennedy is determined to stop them by pouring billions into the Alliance for Progress."

"How do you know?"

"Jack told me."

Blair Clark moved in impressive circles.

He sketched a scenario of coming Cold War confrontations in the Central American jungles and the valleys of the Andes. It sounded like a CIA briefing, which may have been where Blair got it.

"You know who's covering Latin America for us?" he asked.

"Nobody," I said.

"Wrong," he said. "You are."

"I've forgotten my high school Spanish," I said.

"It'll come back to you," he said. "I want to start a Latin American bureau right away and get on this story fast. You can open the office anywhere you want to, as long as you do it within thirty days. What do you say?"

What could I say? I was CBS's good soldier, willing to go anywhere and do anything. I was getting divorced, I had no ties to New York anymore, I liked the idea of taking on twenty countries in one gulp, and I was sure my boss was right when he said the U.S.–Cuban face-off was going to spread all over the hemisphere. I chose Brazil, the "sleeping giant" of South America, as the logical base for reporting this coming struggle, and it didn't take me thirty days to get there. I filled one suitcase with my clothes, another one with volumes of Latin American history and diplomacy, and went off to Rio studying Spanish and Portuguese phrase books on the plane. I found a hotel room on Copacabana Beach, rented an office downtown on Rua Mexico across the street from the U.S. Embassy, had business cards and stationery printed up identifying myself as "Chief Latin American Correspondent" (if you're going to be the *only* Latin American Correspondent, I figured, why not be chief?) and sent Blair Clark a cable ten days after our lunch in New York: "COLNEWS RIO OPEN FOR BUSINESS."

But it was pretty primitive business. The office had a cameraman, Mario Biasetti, who had come down from Boston to join me, and a secretary, a Lebanese emigré named Mireille, who had answered my ad in *Jornal do Brasil*.

But the office didn't have a telephone; there was a two-year wait for telephones in Rio. I hired a telephone expediter to try to speed things up.

The office didn't have a business license. When an inspector came by one afternoon demanding my business license, I tried to explain that CBS News was not a business: We manufactured nothing, we sold nothing. We were an organization of the highest principles. We did not make money; we only spent money. He smiled, unpersuaded, and said I must close the doors of my business until I obtained a business license. I hired a lawyer to try to straighten this out.

The office also didn't have any camera gear. In spite of arrangements carefully made with the Brazilian Consulate in New York, our lights, cameras and sound equipment resided in the Rio airport customs shed awaiting the payment of $40,000 duty. But we have an import permit, I said, displaying this document. We are not going to sell the equipment, I explained, merely use it in the free exercise of our newsgathering responsibility, don't you see? The customs officials did not see. I remembered the intransigence of the immigration officers who had put Phil Scheffler on that plane bound for Africa. I hired a customs broker to try to cut the red tape.

If you really want to learn about a country, work there. Slowly, I learned. Things could not be speeded up or straightened out in Brazil, and red tape could not be cut. Everything, however, could be, with patience, sidestepped. Brazilians have a word, *jeito*, untranslatable into English, which has no such word or concept. *Jeito* combines the meanings of a favor, a boon, a detour around difficulty, a solution for the insoluble. A *jeito* may involve a bribe, but is more likely to consist of a kindness. The telephone expediter, the lawyer, the customs broker, all came to my office and explained that they were seeking, and would surely find, a *jeito*. I grumbled that they seemed to be taking their own sweet time.

"We are being rude, Charles," said Mireille, the secretary. "You talk too fast when people come to the office, you press too hard, and you do not offer them coffee."

We bought a coffeepot. I learned to offer office guests, even guests who made me impatient, several small, sweet *cafèzinhos* before getting around to whatever we were to talk about. And whatever it was, I forced myself to talk slower. Mireille had a mastery of Arabic, which was useless to me, and only a fair knowledge of Portuguese, Spanish and English, the languages I'd hired her for, but she knew the conventions of the country. I learned to ask her questions, sometimes before making a fool of myself.

When a telephone finally was installed, it proved to be useless, except for calling around the city. Long distance calls often took hours to complete, and calls out of the country were out of the question. To talk to my bosses in New York, I had to book a radio transmission with the RCA office down the street and around the corner, enter a broom closet in the back of the building, put on a headset and shout into an ancient microphone. I wondered why I had ever wanted a telephone in the first place.

When at last we were able to spring the camera gear from customs and shoot our first story, a report on the building of Brasília, the new capital in the middle of nowhere, we found we were unable to ship our film. Brazilian law required that motion picture film be processed and viewed by censors before it could be forwarded legally. So I forwarded it illegally. Every time we finished shooting a story in Rio, I caught a taxi to the airport before a Pan Am flight was scheduled to depart for Miami, wandered innocently among the passengers until I found one with an honest face, and asked if he'd mind carrying a package for me. "It's a present for my cousin in Florida," I'd say. "Just hand it to the first U.S. Customs agent you see and my cousin will pick it up." Then I'd go back to town and send a cable to the CBS News traffic desk: "PACKAGE FOR COUSIN ARRIVING MIAMI PAN AM 301 0830 THURS." Not one shipment ever was lost.

I learned that everything could be done in Rio, though not today, and probably not tomorrow, and perhaps not according to the letter of the law. The lawyer came by to report, after a few cups of coffee, that we wouldn't be having any more trouble with the business license inspector.

"Did it cost you a trip to court?" I asked.

"No, Senhor," he said, "it cost me a trip to the liquor store."

I learned that I, who had lectured the government inspector on the lofty ethical principles of the organization I represented, had just bought him off with a case of Chivas Regal.

Not that the whisky cost very much. Great luxuries could be had in Brazil in those days for a few cents, provided only that one's income was paid in U.S. dollars. Brazil was suffering through one of the prodigious inflations in the history of the world, amounting to several hundred percent per year. Every day, the cruzeiro was worth considerably less than the day before. No matter how fast prices and wages were raised, they could not keep pace with the shrinking value of the currency. I felt profoundly sorry for people with savings accounts, some of whom did not understand what was happening until they withdrew their deposits and discovered that the money they had been counting on for retirement was now hardly enough to buy a good meal. All notions of the virtues of thrift were turned upside down; children were urged *not* to save, not even for a day, but to go out and *buy* something. I bought a used MG motorcar. The seller wanted cash. I filled a big suitcase with 1,000-cruzeiro notes, the largest denomination, and threw in the suitcase as part of the deal. He riffled through the contents to make sure there was nothing but currency in there and handed over the keys without bothering to count it. The day I bought the car, it cost the equivalent of $800. A few months later, that suitcase full of money wouldn't have paid for an oil change.

Newsgathering in Rio provided a puzzle almost as mind-bending as currency transactions. Where was I to find out what was going on? The newsstand on the corner sold about thirty daily newspapers, which I could read only with the greatest difficulty, and even after I succeeded in understanding what was printed on their front pages, I found I couldn't believe much of it. Nearly every paper represented a different shade of the arching rainbow of Brazilian political opinion, from the Communist daily on the left (actually, I think there were one or two papers to the *left* of the Communists) to the raving imaginings of the fascist right. If the police shot someone at a land reform demonstration in the northeast, the event became a screaming example of police brutality in one newspaper, and a triumph of law over terrorism in another.

To conquer my handicap with the language, I studied Portuguese every night after dinner in the dimly lighted sitting room of a penurious retired professor. This instruction was in the classical language of Lisbon, not in the colorful Carioca idiom I heard in the streets, but the professor's scholarly ministrations helped me cipher out the prejudices of the newspapers. To overcome my failures of understanding, I relied on the few resident American reporters, especially Juan de Onis of *The New York Times* and his deputy, Henry Johnston, who were generous with explanations of the arcane politics of Brazil. Hank Johnston took me under his wing, introducing me to all the most interesting politicians, tycoons, spies, models, musicians, money-changers, barflies and fellow expatriates of the city. Rio de Janeiro so intrigued Hank Johnston that when he was mustered out of the U.S. Navy in Rio in 1945, he never bothered to go home again.

I wandered out into the vast country to report stories. I traveled up to the northeast coast and inland to the Amazon headwaters and down to São Paulo, a bustling, overgrown Chicago. Brazil is larger than the mainland United States, and was a lot harder to get around in.

I reported trouble, or rumors of trouble, in Chile, Argentina, Ecuador, Bolivia, Peru, traveling on perilous mountain roads, sometimes even on horseback. I was on hand when President Kennedy, carrying the torch for the Alliance for Progress, showed up in Mexico, Costa Rica and Colombia. I "lived" in Brazil, but I never bothered to get a visa to live there; the airlines issued thirty-day tourist cards, and I was so steadily on the move around the continent that I never overstayed the thirty days.

But it was always lovely to come back to Rio for a week or so, to return to my room in the Excelsior Hotel with its view of the soft curve of Copacabana Beach, and to the cramped office on Rua Mexico, with windows on Guanabara Bay. Nearly every person who lives in Rio enjoys an expansive view of water, and the poor people of the *favelas*, the wretched slums high in the hills, have one thing, at least—the best views of all. It was easy to decide that Rio de Janeiro, clinging to the narrow littoral between the mountains and the bay, was the world's most beautiful city.

The people were beautiful, too, I thought, a cheerful mixture of races and religions (around many a Carioca neck, a voodoo fetish and a Catholic cross hang on the same chain) with an agreeable mixture of tolerance and impartiality. When I sought to ask

them, in earnest man-on-the-street interviews, about
the struggle between the United States and Fidel Castro, they merely shrugged. A grinning shoeshine man
tried a locution on me, delivering it in heavily ac-
cented English: "Make love," he said, "not war."
In Rio, people were geographically thousands of miles
below the fight, and geopolitically, far above it. About
Cold War confrontation, most Cariocas gave not a
damn.

They cared about music. As the time approached
for *Carnaval*, the samba beat was everywhere in the
streets. Bands hired by competing composers walked
about in every block playing songs that were contend-
ing for official *Carnaval* theme song. During January
and February, you could close all your windows and
all your doors, and go into the innermost room of
your house, and enter the closet, and stand there and
hear that beat from the street. The sound of the drums
and horns intensified for weeks until finally, in the
days of *Carnaval*, it became a ceaseless din, a pan-
demonium. Mardi Gras days in Rio are not merely,
as in New Orleans or Mobile, a lot of parades and
parties. *Carnaval* is like nothing else on earth, an
explosion of joy.

The other great passion of the city was soccer. *Carnaval* came once a year, but soccer went on forever.
Every midafternoon when the sun dropped behind the
tall buildings of Copacabana and the sunbathers on
the beach went in, the soccer players came out. The
beach was the scene of dozens of games, played by
boys as young as five or six who could do to a round
ball uncanny things with their heads and feet. Soccer

was played all day and year-round in all the play-
grounds and vacant lots of the city, and when the
young Pelé and his team from Santos came to Rio to
play an ordinary club match, it was routine for
200,000 spectators to crowd into Maracanha Sta-
dium, standing and shouting the whole game through.

Brazil's national team dominated international
competition in those days, and I could see why: The
team had nearly the entire male population of the
country from which to choose its players. During
the World Cup matches of 1962, the rest of the country might as well have been on the team, too. That's
how great the fervor was.

During a Brazilian game against Argentina during
the Cup finals, with all of Rio indoors listening on
the radio, I walked past the American Embassy on
some errand. It was a Sunday afternoon. Only the
U.S. Marine guard was on duty.

"How's the game going?" he asked, with a worried look.

I said, "Brazil was ahead by a goal last I heard."

He said, "I sure hope they win."

"You a big soccer fan?" I asked.

"Not really," he said. "But you know how everything bad gets blamed on the United States. If Argentina beats Brazil, I'm afraid everybody will come
down here and break all the windows."

The guard needn't have worried. Nobody beat Brazil that year. When Brazil won the Cup, I happened
to be in a downtown bank. Clerks shouted for joy and
threw handfuls of money in the air. Elsewhere in the
city at that moment, a man incautiously leapt through

the window of a skyscraper, and out in the country somewhere, another man jumped into the air, forgetting that he was on the platform of a moving train. Both died in paroxysms of ecstasy. After experiencing the World Cup of 1962, the Super Bowl and the World Series have always seemed a little tame to me.

Not even rainstorms stopped the soccer games on Copacabana Beach. And on the day when the army tanks came rolling down the beach, the soccer players didn't even stop their games to notice.

The tanks were sent by the Minister of War to make a political point. I was having a drink at a beachfront bar when I looked up and saw them rumbling along, trying to avoid the soccer games. I was getting used to Brazilian incongruity by this time but I thought, *now* what the hell? I made a phone call and found out President Jânio Quadros had resigned.

Quadros, a slight man with a great bushy moustache, had been elected only a few months before with more votes than had ever before been cast for a Presidential candidate in Brazil. His election was hailed as the start of a new era, a break with the dictatorial past. But he proved an odd, quixotic man, ill at ease amid the trappings of power. He tried to avoid the gleaming new Presidential Palace in faraway Brasília, preferring to drive himself around Rio in his old Volkswagen. He had a few ideas for reforming the country and reducing inflation, but the Congress wouldn't go along with any of them. So Quadros decided one morning that he had had enough. He quit, and he disappeared. One moment, he was President.

The next moment, he wasn't, and he was gone, nobody knew where.

Quadros's constitutional successor was his sworn enemy, Vice President João Goulart, a leftist hack who was at the moment on a state visit to China. The tanks on Copacabana were the Army's way of saying it had no intention of letting Goulart return to rule the country. But already, I was told on the telephone, there were reports that military units away to the south in Rio Grande do Sul Province, where Goulart came from and had his power base, were disobeying orders and preparing to defend his claim to the Presidency.

This was Brazil. Make love, not war. I was pretty sure there wasn't going to be a civil war, not with the sun shining and the soccer players ignoring the tanks. But I paid for my drink, grabbed a taxi for the airport and caught the first plane to Pôrto Alegre, Goulart's hometown. It was good I didn't stop to pack a bag. That was the last plane into Pôrto Alegre for days, except for the one that brought João Goulart—President Goulart, he now called himself—home from China. The local army and air force commanders, rebelling against headquarters in Brasília, had barrels rolled out onto the runways at the airport, sank a scow at the entrance of the harbor to prevent entrance from the sea and barricaded themselves behind sandbags in the Governor's Palace in Pôrto Alegre. I found myself inside a blockaded city without even a toothbrush, and more important, without any means of getting the story out, since cable and wireless connections to Pôrto Alegre had been cut from the other side.

Not wishing a most un-Brazilian shooting war, both

sides commenced a war of nerves. Back in Brasília, the War Minister demanded that Congress declare the office of vice president vacant and arrange for new elections. The Congress refused. The Congress demanded that the War Minister read the constitution, especially the part about legal succession, and permit Goulart to take office. The War Minister refused. The War Minister sent tanks toward the border of Rio Grande do Sul. The commanders in Rio Grande hauled artillery up toward the border to meet them.

In the basement of the sandbagged Governor's Palace in Pôrto Alegre, the pro-Goulart forces set up a shortwave radio station to try to broadcast their message to the rest of the country. They gave it an important-sounding name, Radio Legalidade, but the transmitter was an ancient model with glowing vacuum tubes and the antenna was a copper wire leading to the chimney on the roof. I regarded this rig with grave doubt, but it was the only link with the outside world. I made myself presentable and paid a call on the Colonel who had command of the building.

"The world press is in Rio reporting the news from the other side," I said.

The Colonel agreed, gloomily.

"But I am here," I said. "I would like to report the news from this side."

"What do you want?" he asked.

"Ten minutes on your radio station every morning," I said, "and another ten minutes in the evening."

The Colonel, who had no idea whether his radio

station was getting out past the city limits, thought about this for a minute and then nodded his assent.

I had my air time. I could broadcast to the world. The only problem was that nobody in the world would be listening.

I scribbled a cable to Ralph Paskman in New York, giving the frequency of Radio Legalidade and telling him I'd be up on that frequency every day at ten A.M. and six P.M. New York time. I could see Paskman rolling his eyes and muttering about that kid Kuralt wasting CBS's money again. Then I really wasted some of his money. I found a cabdriver in the street, presented him a thick wad of cash, handed him the cable and instructed him to send it from the nearest possible place—Uruguay, 200 miles away.

"Give it to the first telegraph office you come to, and stay there until it is sent," I said. "Can I trust you?"

"You can trust me," he said.

"It is very important," I said.

"I am a gaucho," he said.

All the men of Rio Grande do Sul call themselves gauchos, after the gallant cowboys of the pampas. Gauchos have a well-known code of honor. A gaucho's word is his bond, and there are stories about gauchos drawing their daggers and killing those who question their integrity. So I didn't question my gaucho, whose steed was an old but polished Packard. I watched him ride off into the sunset toward the Uruguayan frontier.

I saw him again two days later. The Packard was covered with dust. He said simply, "Your message has been sent.'' But he asked for a little more money for fuel. He had crossed into Uruguay with no difficulty, but found there were no cable offices in any of the border towns. So after his 200-mile journey, he kept going. He kept going *another* 200 miles. He had sent my cable from Montevideo. The man standing before me had just returned from an 800-mile round trip to send a telegram! I felt like hugging him, but something told me you don't hug gauchos.

I had already discovered that I didn't like the competitive pressure of being CBS's only correspondent in South America. NBC always had at least three good reporters working against me, Richard Valeriani and the husband-wife team of Wilson and Lee Hall, and the chances were good that one of them would beat me to any given breaking story. I was forever getting cables from Paskman: ''NBC HAD SIX HOUR BEAT ON CHILE EARTHQUAKE. WHERE YOU?''

But the only other American reporter I ran into in Pôrto Alegre was Morris Rosenberg of the Associated Press, who had made his way across the river from Uruguay. NBC wasn't there and probably couldn't get there, so for once I had a page-one story to myself— if, that is, Radio Legalidade had a strong enough shortwave signal to reach New York.

Each evening, the makeshift station interrupted its routine of propaganda and martial music for a few minutes. An announcer shouted into the microphone in impassioned Portuguese, ''And now, Radio Legality pauses in its regular transmissions of candor and veracity to permit the truth to be broadcast to the world in the English language!'' Whereupon, I would

slide into the chair and say, "Hello, New York, hello,
New York. This is Kuralt talking up for CBS News,
New York. I will begin in sixty seconds. . . . " And
so on, to a countdown, "Five . . . four . . . three
. . . two . . . " Then, I'd deliver my report on the
political declarations and troop movements of the day
in the cutoff and beleaguered provincial capital, re-
peating the reading a couple of times and signing off,
"Charles Kuralt, CBS News, Pôrto Alegre, Brazil."
I felt frustrated after each of these exercises, unsure
whether I was triumphing over the opposition with
reports they couldn't possibly have or making an ass
of myself by talking into thin air.

At length, the opposing forces in the political impasse reached a compromise, found a *jeito*: The army
would permit Goulart to assume the Presidency, but,
at least for the time being, without most of the Presidential powers. In Pôrto Alegre, cheers went up,
barriers came down, and a couple of ancient airliners
showed up at the airport to conduct Goulart and
the press to Brasília for the swearing-in.

"Pistola, pistola?" inquired a functionary at the
door of the press plane, collecting the pistols of the
reporters, all of them Goulart partisans in a celebra-
tory mood. Each man dropped his pistol into a basket
after inserting a rolled-up business card in the barrel
to facilitate the weapon's return upon landing. Morris
Rosenberg and I, the only unarmed reporters on the
plane, were glad to see the pistols locked away in the
cockpit, since the *cachaça* was *not* confiscated. Each
man brought aboard a bottle or two of the potent Brazilian white lightning with labels like "Black Cat"

and "Bad Saturday Night" and all through the long night on the way to Brasília, the reporters argued, laughed, sang old campaign songs and rolled empties down the aisle. The press was poured out of the plane at the end of the trip, collected its weaponry and went weaving off into the city, a small army of drunks with pistols in their pockets.

I covered Goulart's inauguration and flew home to Rio to find a stack of cables from the radio editors in New York. They said things like "ALL YOUR PORTO ALEGRE TRANSMISSIONS RECEIVED" and "YOU WERE WORLD NEWS ROUNDUP LEAD FOUR DAYS IN ROW" and "CONGRATULATIONS YOUR INITIATIVE." There was also a cable from Ralph Paskman: "NBC HAD GOOD COVERAGE ARMY SIDE OF CONFLICT. WHERE YOU?"

I tried and tried to think of a response to this incredible message, but the words wouldn't come. I had a souvenir in my baggage, a gaucho dagger. I wrapped it carefully, addressed it to Paskman, went down to the post office and sent it off, airmail. Then I went to my hotel room and slept the sleep of the just.

8
═

EQUATOR CROSSINGS

Ralph Paskman, my friend, my boss, my nemesis in faraway New York, thought it ought to be easy to commute back and forth between Pôrto Alegre and Rio, something like catching the air shuttle from New York to Washington. He never understood the distances in Latin America. He dashed off cables saying "THINK YOU BETTER HOP OVER TO MEXICO CITY" without the slightest idea that he was speaking of a 5,000-mile hop. He thought—for all I know, the CBS News Foreign Editor still thinks—that Rio de Janeiro is down there near Tegucigalpa somewhere, that Latin Americans all wear sombreros and take siestas under palm trees, that the countries are all pretty much alike. I began to appreciate the differences, as great as among the countries of Europe, and to find favorites among the cities.

I liked Buenos Aires for its tree-lined boulevards and good wine and European flair—if not for its people, who struck me as often cold and intolerant; Punta del Este, Uruguay, for its *dolce vita* sophistication; Quito, Ecuador, and La Paz, Bolivia, for the opposite of sophistication, an appealing Andean simplicity. In spite of an aura of violence which was even then in

the air, I liked Bogotá, Colombia, for its intellectu-
ality and fine use of language; most of the statues in
Bogotá are of poets, not generals. I liked San José,
Costa Rica, for its air of freedom, its dislike of
dictators and its painted oxcarts.

I did not much like Asunción, Paraguay; the people
were cautiously friendly but meek under the authori-
tarian thumb, as if they remembered Francisco So-
lano López. He was the nineteenth-century dictator
who came unhinged and insanely declared war on
Brazil, Uruguay and Argentina all at once, resulting
in the death by warfare, famine and disease of
225,000 Paraguayans, more than half the population
of the country. Ninety years had passed since then,
and the current dictator was named Stroessner. He
seemed never to be criticized, not even in whispers.
Paraguayans had heard from their grandparents what
a dictator could do to them when vexed.

I never could bring myself to like Lima, Peru, city
of vile poverty, bad smells and colonial relics, chief
among the latter cruel Pizarro himself, a shrinking
mummy under glass in the cathedral. I usually went
to Lima during times of trouble in the streets; three
times I was caught in tear gas attacks in the Plaza
Bolívar. I associate Lima with choking and gasping
for breath.

Rural Chile was beautiful and invigorating, but I
could not love the capital, Santiago, all cold stones,
dark clothing, goose-stepping soldiers and scowling
faces. Once, leaving a cafe after lunch with a Chilean
newspaperman whom I regarded as friendly, I
dropped a coin into the cup of an old man in Indian

garb who was standing on the sidewalk. "No!" shouted the newspaperman. He rushed over, retrieved the coin and gave the beggar a furious shove into the street. *"¡No es chileno!"* he exclaimed, "He's not a Chilean!" Meaning, I suppose, that Chileans are too proud to beg. My own thought was that maybe Chileans were too proud, period.

I dreaded my trips to Managua, Nicaragua, a hot, brutal place, tubercular and corrupt. Lake Nicaragua is the only freshwater lake I've ever heard of that is full of sharks, and Managua was full of sharks, too, Somozas, father and sons, nephews and cousins, all feeding on the people.

It didn't do anything for my Yankee self-respect to reflect that many of Nicaragua's woes were the fault of my own country. Starting back in the 1850s when a mountebank from Tennessee named William Walker actually established himself as President of Nicaragua for a couple of years, the United States has treated Nicaraguans as wayward children in need of frequent chastising. President William Howard Taft chastised them with the United States Marines, and the Marines stayed on right into the 1930s. I remembered the old-time sergeants at the tent camp down the road from my grandparents' farm in North Carolina who had earlier known, and presumably hated, Managua. The Marines didn't leave until they found somebody they could trust to run the country their way, Anastasio Somoza García. "He's a bastard," they used to say of Somoza in Washington, "but he's *our* bastard." After twenty years, having learned all the tricks of fraud and torture, one of Somoza's sons took over.

With Washington's approval, this younger Anastasio Somoza set out to screw the lid on the country even tighter. I went to Nicaragua for the first time in 1961, nosed around for a few days and sent a series of stories back to New York warning that the Somoza lid might be about to blow off. Who cared? Most of the stories never even made it to the air. The Sandinista guerrilla movement started in 1962.

I was always uneasy in Managua, worried about something that hadn't happened yet. Little earthquakes would come in the night and I would lie awake waiting for the big one. (I wasn't there when the big one came. It killed 6,000 people in 1972 and left the city in rubble.) Little incidents in the street had a way of flaring unexpectedly into violence.

There was a bell tower overlooking a plaza in Managua. During one of Somoza's staged "elections," I wanted to start a story with a picture of the clock in the tower and the sound of the bells ringing out the hour of twelve—probably to be accompanied by a line of narration about "high noon in Nicaraguan politics" or some such trite expression. I was working with Wendell Hoffman again. We arrived at eleven-thirty A.M. or so and set up the camera in the empty plaza to wait for noon. As we stood there, a couple of people walked across the plaza to see what was going on.

"¿Qué pasa?" one of them asked.

"Nada," I said. "Nothing's going on. We're just waiting to take a picture of the tower."

Curious, these two people waited with us. Seeing

them there, several other people strolled over with the same question, *"¿Qué pasa?"*

"Nada," I said. *"Esperamos el mediodía."* These people, too, decided to stick around to see what was going to happen at noon. Still others arrived. By eleven forty-five, we had a pretty good-sized crowd standing around us.

I felt silly. I made a little speech in my most plaintive Spanish. "Look, *nothing* is going to happen. We are going to take a picture of the tower at twelve o'clock, that's all!" But nobody left.

A van full of anti-Somoza youths happened to pass by the plaza just then. Seeing the crowd and the camera, they stopped, jumped out of the van and came running over to us unfurling a banner and chanting political slogans.

I said to Wendell, "Well, let's forget it. They're making such a racket we'll never be able to hear the bells anyway." He removed the camera from the tripod and we started packing to leave. Twelve o'clock came and went. We had missed our shot, and we weren't about to film a demonstration that was being put on just for us.

The demonstrators had lost the camera, but they still had the crowd; they chanted louder and began a march around the square with most of the throng following. Wendell and I, disgusted, were walking back toward our hotel when we heard sirens approaching. Police cars roared into the plaza. Cops got out and waded into the marchers, swinging clubs. An NBC camera crew came huffing and puffing around a corner. Tear gas was fired and rose from the scene in thick clouds. A couple of the demonstrators, fighting back, were clubbed to the ground. A shotgun went off and a man, wounded in the legs, was hurried away to the hospital in the back of a panel truck.

Wendell and I watched all this in amazement. The next day, of course, one of Paskman's cables arrived: "NBC HAD GOOD COVERAGE RIOT. WHERE YOU?"

I was always glad to get out of Managua. Many years later, when the Sandinistas chased the Somozas into exile in Florida, I rejoiced inwardly that relief had come to Nicaragua at last. But the Sandinista leaders turned out to be swaggering young incompetents, more interested in power than in reform. Most of the non-Communists among the revolutionaries defected. And the United States, as always, was ready with a machination. President Ronald Reagan, vividly imagining an army of Red Nicaraguans marching into Brownsville, Texas, organized a huge armed band of Contras to bring the Sandinistas down. What the marauding Contras couldn't accomplish, the Nicaraguan voters finally did in 1990, thirty hellish years after my first visit to the country. Maybe the people there will have a taste of peace now, and a taste of liberty. I hope so, but since they live in Nicaragua, I would never bet on it. "Nicaragua needs our help," Ronald Reagan used to say, meaning the sort of "help" we have been giving that forlorn little country for most of the century. What Nicaragua needs are our prayers.

Eric Sevareid, the best of the thinkers and writers among the CBS News Correspondents, said on the air one time, "Modern revolutions do not make people freer. Revolutions always make them less free."

I thought at the time that it was an odd and reactionary remark, but then I thought of the outcome of the Bolshevik Revolution, of the one in China, and of the two Latin American upheavals of my own experience that qualify as genuine revolutions, the Nicaraguan one, and before that, Fidel Castro's Cuban Revolution, and I realized that Sevareid was on to something there. One trip to Cuba is enough to break your heart. I made a lot of trips to Cuba.

I didn't like Havana. I didn't like the depraved Havana of the dictator Fulgencio Batista, which was Miami but more so, swarming with prostitutes and high rollers, American mobsters and the rich relatives of Batista generals on the make. It took me a while—having seen plenty of right-wing regimes in Latin America, I thought maybe a left-wing revolutionary ought to be given the benefit of the doubt—but finally I came to be even more appalled by what Havana was becoming under Fidel Castro, the capital of a preposterous, regimented police state, a kind of tropical Bulgaria.

My disillusionment became complete in the spring of 1962 when the Castro revolution was three and a half years old. A year had gone by since the American-sponsored invasion at the Bay of Pigs had ended in debacle. During that year, U.S. reporters were effectively barred from Cuba. I applied for visas, I wrote to officials in Havana asking them to intercede, I stopped at Cuban embassies in other countries to appeal for entry, I even became friendly with the Soviet *chargé d'affaires* in Rio, thinking he might be able to help. Nobody ever said no, but nothing happened. I was beginning to think I'd never get into Cuba again.

One day in April 1962, a clerk at the Cuban Consulate in Rio called on the telephone.

"When would you like to pick up your visa?" he asked.

"What visa?"

"Your name is Kuralt?"

"Yep."

"I have instructions from Havana to issue you a onetime admission to Cuba. You may enter from Mexico."

I didn't ask any questions. The next morning, I was on a plane to Mexico City with a thirty-day Cuban visa stamped on a page of my passport. The immigration officer at the Havana airport looked doubtful and checked my face against the passport photo a couple of times, but finally waved me into the country. At the airport curb, I recognized an old acquaintance among the cabdrivers and fell into the front seat of his rattling '52 Cadillac.

"How's it going?" I asked him on the way into town.

"Horriblemente," he said. *"A más no podemos.* There's nothing we can do about it."

We drove straight to the Foreign Ministry, where visiting reporters had to be accredited. On the stairway, I ran into Carlos Rafael Rodríguez, an old Communist intellectual in the underground days, now a bureaucrat wrestling with Castro's agricultural reform.

"What the hell are you doing here?" he asked.

"Special invitation from the first Socialist Republic in the Western Hemisphere," I said cheerfully.

"Come with me," he said. He led me into the press office.

"Give me your passport," he said. "Sit there." He disappeared into a back room. Functionaries unused to visits from a government minister bustled in behind him.

After a few minutes, he emerged laughing and shaking his head. "You are not supposed to be here," he said. "They thought you were a goddamn Brazilian. You must leave on the next plane that has space for you."

My heart sank.

"However," he added, giving me back my passport, "there is no space on any planes for at least three weeks."

I walked down the stairs with him. "Don't get smart and try to leave the capital without permission," he said. "I will send one of my guys with you if you want to see the countryside. We will show you some of the good things we've done."

"I want to see the bad things you've done," I said.

"I know," he said. "That's why you must have an escort."

"How about lining me up an interview with the Maximum Leader?" I asked.

"Go to hell," Carlos Rafael Rodríguez said.

In the streets, martial music played from loudspeakers. Giant portraits of Fidel Castro towered over the city. "This is Radio Havana, Cuba," the radio announced every half hour, "Free Territory of the Americas."

The next day was May Day and there was a workers' and peasants' parade. Since I was working without a camera crew, I enlisted a teenager from the crowd on the curb to carry my tape recorder and point the microphone at the parade while I did the filming. Through the viewfinder, I watched lines of cane cutters march by with their machetes at right shoulderarms, columns of children in uniform holding up their schoolbooks, marching nurses with stethoscopes. Banners said "¡VENCEREMOS!" "We Will Win!" and "Remember the Bay of Pigs!" and "Do Your Fisminutos!"—daily exercises beside your desk or machine—and "Forward, Comrades of the Defense Committees!" The Defense Committees were block-by-block organizations which had been set up for the purpose of spying on the neighbors. The May Day parade was earnest and humorless, a bad dream out of Orwell. The Defense Committee members marched past holding up hundreds of pictures of Big Brother, Fidel Castro. They sang "The Internationale" in Spanish.

When the parade was over, the marchers stuck around to hear a speech by Castro, who appeared on a bandstand in the late afternoon. "¡Viva nuestra revolución socialista!" he shouted, and the crowd answered, a little mechanically, I thought, "¡Viva!" Dusk came on, and dark of night, and still Fidel went on, blustering at the top of his voice, drunk, so he seemed to me, on his own rhetoric. "¡Cuba sí, Yanqui no!" he thundered, and the crowd took up the refrain, *"¡Cuba sí, Yanqui no!"* so vehemently that I began to get edgy. A man waving a big Cuban flag stopped long enough to grin at me and say in English, "Don't worry. We don't mean you."

The next day, I went for a walk with the camera. On a corner where a Chevrolet agency had stood, I found the House of Czechoslovakian Culture. On a former shopping street, there were few shops and no shoppers, but there was a Hungarian exposition featuring a display of machine tools. The Soviet flag hung beside the Cuban one all over town. The American Embassy was boarded up and empty, with a Swiss flag flying over it for protection.

I stopped in a poor residential neighborhood to take pictures of a food store with almost no food in it. The ration in the cities was down to five eggs per person per month and three-quarters of a pound of meat per week. Even rice and beans were in short supply. As I aimed the camera at the food store, a woman came running out of a house across the street shouting, *"¡No puede filmar!* You can't take pictures here!" She held up her hand to block the camera lens. I had run afoul of a comrade of the Defense Committees.

I was polite. I showed her my credentials from the Foreign Ministry. She said the Foreign Ministry didn't decide things on this block, the Defense Committee did. She shouted for a cop at the top of her voice. I smiled, nodded good-bye and made a fast getaway, leaving her there shouting on the sidewalk.

At night when I returned to my hotel room, I found my belongings slightly rearranged, papers in my briefcase in a different order than I had left them, even the drawer in which I'd put my socks and underwear freshly disheveled. Somebody had searched the room, without bothering very hard to hide the fact. This became routine. I left a note in the underwear drawer: "No secrets here, just underwear." Whoever it was made off with the note. Clicks were heard on the telephone when I tried to use it. It was surveillance, but of a particularly clumsy sort. I thought the Cubans were going to have to get better at this if they aspired to a world-class despotism.

They were more successful at teaching children, some of whom had never before been to school. All over Havana, I found school kids wearing neat uniforms and living in luxurious buildings that had been yacht clubs a couple of years before, or the mansions of the rich. The gaudy old Hotel Nacional, in whose casino I had once lost a few dollars at roulette, was being put to a more constructive use: it housed 1,200 former domestic servants studying mathematics, grammar, penmanship, shorthand, typing and "revolutionary instruction"—how to overcome the servant mentality. Education in the new Cuba was pervasive, and touching, even inspiring, to witness.

But nearly everything else was in a terrible muddle. By 1962, Che Guevara had told me two years before, Cuba would be producing steel and starting a shipbuilding industry. Cuba would manufacture its own radios, sewing machines and typewriters. A $250 million nickel plant was in the works, he had said. Now it was 1962, and the only new undertakings I could discover were a cement works, a tomato canning plant and a pencil factory. (There were also missile launching pads under construction, but I didn't find out about those. The world found out about them a few months later when the Cuban missile crisis occurred. The first thing I thought of then was Carlos Rafael Rodríguez's warning to me not to go poking around in the countryside.) Che Guevara had boasted that Cuba would be manufacturing trucks and buses by 1962. In vacant lots all over Havana, I saw collections of broken-down American buses. Cuba didn't even make spark plugs or fuel pumps to keep them on the road.

There was plenty of aid from the Soviets. I counted 750 big Zovod trucks on a Havana dock. A dockworker told me they had been sitting there for seven months. The Cubans couldn't think of any use for them. The warehouses at the docks also held thousands of cases of lathes and drills and electronic instruments from China, Czechoslovakia and East Germany, equipment hardly anybody in Cuba was trained to use. I counted boxes containing 200 electron microscopes; Cuba might have needed eight or ten. The same building held 50,000 Chinese voltmeters; the order had been for 500, I was told, but somebody had misread it. I took a certain satisfaction in noting the awful mess the Communist world was making of aid to Cuba. I had been traveling all over Latin America finding examples of waste and inefficiency in the U.S. Alliance for Progress program. But not even the United States would have shipped a country 750 useless heavy trucks or 49,500 too many voltmeters.

Even more conspicuous than the failure of industry

was the failure of collectivized agriculture. One of Rodríguez's land reformers took me out to see an exhibition dairy farm. Canadian milk cows, purchased with scarce dollars, were milked by former sugarcane cutters, *guajiros*, the impoverished field hands of the old Cuban society, now earning three times their former pay, with free housing and paid vacations. The cattle were beautiful and the workers were happy, but the manager of the collective farm admitted the farm didn't produce enough milk to pay the workers' wages, let alone to become profitable.

With the cane cutters promoted to other jobs in Castro's classless society, somebody had to harvest the sugarcane upon which everything else in the Cuban economy depended. That became the job of "volunteers" from the city. I found schoolteachers swinging machetes, sweating and grousing in the cane fields of Las Villas Province while a brigade of workers loaded the cane into trucks. One man's straw hat proclaimed him a "distinguished worker." I stopped to talk to him and found that he was a distinguished *electrical* worker. The amateurs in the fields were bringing in a harvest down 25 percent from the year before. They were subsidizing with their labor the new houses and schools that Castro aimed to provide for 300,000 rural families, formerly the poorest of the Cuban poor, now the core of support for the revolution. But after listening to the grumbling among the teachers and electrical workers in the cane fields, I thought I saw some counterrevolutionaries being created, too.

"*Gusanos,*" they were called, "worms," who complained too much about the way things were going. They included almost all of the former shopkeepers, professionals and small business people, the old middle classes of the country. By the hundreds every day, the *gusanos* were leaving Cuba, leaving everything they owned behind. At last, the day came for me to join a planeload of them for the flight to Miami. A dentist was stationed at the airport to remove gold inlays. An old woman, weeping, was forced to give up her wedding ring. A guard opened my camera case and confiscated all my film. I put up a big argument, but it was just for show. The film was blank; I had talked an acquaintance at the Mexican embassy into shipping my precious exposed film, the first American views of Cuba in more than a year, by diplomatic pouch to Mexico City.

The Pan Am flight taxied to the end of the runway—then was called back. It was a bit of spiteful theater, preplanned vengefulness. Policemen came aboard, seized a passenger who had thought he was safely away, handcuffed him and marched him off the plane while everyone else sat frozen in silence. The silence continued as the plane left the gate again, reached the end of the runway again, took off and climbed away from the island, the passengers united in mute tension.

The silence was not broken until the voice of the pilot was heard. He said in Spanish, "We have left Cuban airspace and will be landing in twenty-five minutes."

A great cheer went up. People broke into tears and clapped one another on the back. The plane began to descend, and the passengers, all talking excitedly at once, peered through the windows for the first glimpse of land.

"Welcome to Miami, Florida," the pilot said, "*Free* Territory of the Americas." They cheered again, even louder than before.

To my surprise, I felt like cheering, too. I had been in Cuba only twenty-three days and unaware of any great pressure, but what lifted from my shoulders in that moment was a very heavy weight. The busybody comrades of the Defense Committees, the dresser drawer-rifling secret police, the marches blaring from loudspeakers, the Big Brother slogans, the sense of menace were all behind me, and America was just ahead.

I was to have the same feeling again in years to come—on taking off from Saigon and escaping the war in Vietnam, and on getting out of pre-*glasnost* Russia, and on leaving brutal China behind me in the midst of the Tiananmen Square uprising. The peace of the twenty-third Psalm settled upon me, the part about still waters and green pastures and the soul restored.

I felt released. I felt light as air.

HOLLYWOOD

Sory and I were divorced in a courtroom in Hillsborough, North Carolina. I didn't have to be there, for which I was grateful. She was planning to remarry, Lisa and Susan were doing well, so Sory and I both had what we had wanted. She had a close family, and I had a thick passport.

But now I found I was lonely. My old pal Reasoner was becoming a television star on a daily morning program called *Calendar* (with Andy Rooney as chief writer and Mary Fickett as costar, perhaps the best series CBS News ever put on the air). My old pal Phil Scheffler was becoming an important producer. And I was thousands of miles away in Rio, working on stories nobody much cared about but me. I needed somebody to have a drink with once in a while, and tell my troubles to.

On rare trips back to New York, I always had a drink with Petie Baird, the beautiful secretary who used to run along the Grand Central catwalk with me, arranging Doug Edwards's scripts. She was a reader of books, all books, Thurber, Steinbeck, Faulkner, Bruce Catton, Rex Stout, Alexander Pope. She was always able to tell me things I didn't know. One night, she overcooked a pork chop for me at her walk-up apartment in Greenwich Village.

"You are a terrible cook," I said. "I don't suppose you'd like to marry me?"

"Maybe, someday," she said.

I reminded her of this remark now and then in letters from Rio. When I came to New York to make a half-hour documentary of the footage from Cuba, I took her to dinner and asked, "Why not now?"

She said, "All right. Now."

"I'll be traveling all the time."

"I'm used to being alone."

"I'm not kidding. I'll never have a nine-to-five job."

"I couldn't stand having somebody always around the house from five to nine."

I called the Moore-McCormack Line, which ran steamships to Rio, and booked passage for the next week. I asked whether the ship's captain really could perform weddings at sea. Of course, I was told. Petie and I sent our bags down to the docks. She quietly resigned her job, explaining, and actually making everybody believe, that she had come into an unexpected inheritance. We knew our marriage would create a stir in the office, we had friends who ought to be invited, and we knew we didn't want to go through all that. I raced to finish the Cuba documentary before the sailing date of the SS *Argentina*.

An American in Cuba was broadcast May 25, 1962. It expressed my conviction that the Cuban Revolution was a disorganized flop and that Cuba was becoming a police state, but the program still caused a considerable fuss in Miami. The fiercely anti-Castro exiles were upset by the part about good schools and decent housing. "Lies!" they said in telegrams and phone calls. "CBS is a dupe of the Communists!" Most people, I was discovering, don't want to hear the truth of controversial subjects, they want to hear the truth as they wish it were or imagine it to be. A Florida congressman demanded that I appear before an Un-American Activities subcommittee.

I figured I couldn't be subpoenaed if I was on a ship at sea. I called the shipping line to reconfirm the reservations. I asked again, "And the captain can perform weddings, right?" The woman on the phone said, "Yes, the captain can perform weddings, but not on this particular ship. The sailing was cancelled this morning. There has been a seamen's strike."

I went down to the docks and had all our suitcases transferred to Idlewild Airport. I called Harry Reasoner and asked if he would like to be best man at a City Hall wedding. The next day happened to be the first of June. While Petie and I waited on a bench for Harry to arrive, a reporter named Tom Costigan, an old friend from the assignment desk, showed up with a camera crew. He was doing a feature on June brides.

"I thought I was assigned to this," he said.

"I am not here to do a story," I said. "I am here to get married. Kindly point that lens in another direction."

He kindly did. There was a time clock on the desk of the clerk who performed the ceremony which went "chunk" once every sixty seconds. It only chunked once while we were in there. We were married in less than two minutes. We went out to the airport and caught the Pan Am flight to Rio.

I suppose we haven't spent more than a week at a time together from that day to this. Petie has not minded this much. People ask, "And what does your wife do while you're away?" I say, "She reads, and when I come home, she tells me things I don't know."

I kept wandering around the hemisphere, trying to work Fidel Castro's name into every lead so they'd use the story on the news back home. I developed pretty good sources in most of the capitals of Latin America, set up a network of stringer reporters and cameramen who could keep me informed about stories coming up in their countries and polished my Spanish and Portuguese. Just as I was beginning to get good at my job, I was told I was being transferred back to the United States.

Naturally. Correspondents at CBS get used to being whisked away from jobs they're good at on the whim of some executive. Only the great Winston Burdett resisted successfully, by explaining calmly that if ever transferred from Rome, he would resign. He spent his whole career there, outlasting several Popes. I was no Burdett, either in ability or clout. I resisted briefly and gave in. "You'll get on the air more often if you're in the States," I was told.

I was given a choice of two assignments, the White House or the new Los Angeles bureau. I knew I'd be number two man to Bob Pierpoint at the White House and that I'd never get to travel, except as part of the pack on the press plane. I knew nothing at all about the alternative, except that the job called for keeping track of the news in places I liked, California, Oregon, Washington and the mountain states east to the Rockies. Petie and I had acquired some furniture by now. I pasted Los Angeles stickers on the packing crates.

Before long, we were lying awake listening to that heavy furniture from humid Brazil splitting along the grain in the dry California night in sudden contractions that sounded like pistol shots. The house was in the Hollywood hills above Sunset Boulevard. About eight inches of the house was on solid ground. The rest of it was cantilevered perilously over a canyon; to stand at the edge of the sun deck was to experience the giddy sensation of the high diver at the end of the board. Eartha Kitt's backyard swimming pool was down there a couple hundred feet below.

Like the furniture, I had trouble adapting to southern California. I tried. I bought sunglasses, and a white convertible to go with them, and drove down the hill to Television City with the top down. ("Mr. Kuralt" it said at my parking place near the artists' entrance.) I got introduced around town by Bill Stout, the most knowledgeable reporter in Los Angeles, temporarily working for a rival independent television station between long stints at CBS. I nodded to Judy Garland and Sammy Davis, Jr., when I chanced to meet them in the halls. I tapped my toe in time with the music that filtered into the office from the rehearsal hall next door. I became known to the *maître d'hôtel* at Chasen's Restaurant. All the time, I was aware of playing a role, and I felt miscast—awkward country boy as Hollywood man-about-town.

The bad telephone circuits between New York and Latin America had meant I was usually free to choose my own assignments while based in Rio. Now, though I was called the West Coast Bureau Manager, I was under the thumb of the New York assignment desk whenever an important story came along, and New York had some odd ideas about what constituted an important story. As long as I was at my desk in Los Angeles, I was vulnerable to telephone calls sending me off to pointless stakeouts at the Governor's Mansion in Sacramento or to interviews with movie stars.

To escape, I found as many stories as possible in places where I could make myself hard to reach, the Willamette Valley of Oregon, the Cascades, the Sierra, small-town Nevada and the Grand Canyon country. I gloried in the landscape of the rural west, loved working alone with a camera crew out in the country, and always resented it when real news came along that demanded my presence on the scene.

It seemed to me that everything of genuine importance happened on somebody else's beat, anyway. That was all right with me. I had done a typical California bureau story, a report on Chatty Cathy, the first talking doll, a pretty good story, I thought. I had shipped it to New York, where it languished on the shelf, so before heading to the office one November morning, I called Don Hewitt in New York, thinking I'd remind him about Chatty Cathy.

"He can't come to the phone right now," said the young woman who answered. "Everybody's over at the wire machines. Something about President Kennedy being shot."

I turned on the radio in time to hear the first bulletin. After that, all I could do was watch and listen as a newly hired correspondent named Dan Rather told the story from Dallas, coolly and accurately. I was aware that I was witnessing a prodigious job of reporting. Without raising his voice, Rather scooped the world by many minutes on the fact of the President's death. I sat in my living room in West Hollywood dry-mouthed, paralyzed by the enormity of the news. I remember thinking, thank God I'm not there. I knew I could never do what Rather was doing. It took all my willpower to get myself to the corner of Hollywood and Vine for a live man-on-the-street interview as the news spread through the city.

I had a drink that night with Bill Stout. I confessed that my unprofessional shock and dismay had overwhelmed all my reportorial instincts. He put a hand on my shoulder.

"Look," he said, "there's nothing you could have done anyway. It's not exactly a Hollywood story."

When Hollywood stories did come along, I had a way of blowing them. Frank Sinatra, Jr., was kidnapped, an abduction that held the country's attention for days. I reluctantly abandoned a story about Basque sheepherders in Nevada to send daily reports to the network from Lake Tahoe, scene of the kidnapping. I was still working all the Tahoe angles when young Sinatra was released—at an exit of the San Diego Freeway back in Los Angeles. I had missed another one. Nothing to do but shrug and rejoin the Basques, whom I found far more interesting. But the feeling was growing in New York that the West Coast Bureau

Manager was not exactly a news hawk when it came to breaking stories.

Fred Friendly had become the President of CBS News. He was an active volcano. When he erupted on the telephone, hot coals and lava burned the wire from New York to California. He called me to say that he did not give a hoot in hell about Basque shepherds or Basque sheep. Would I please start covering the news?

I did the best I could, but kept getting diverted. California was a big prize in the 1964 Republican Presidential primary. Nelson Rockefeller, all reasonableness, and Barry Goldwater, all bluster, made repeated sweeps through the state. I dutifully covered them while steadily losing interest in them. When the Goldwater campaign branched out one day to Reno, Nevada, Robert MacNeil, a reporter for NBC News in those long ago pre-*MacNeil/Lehrer* days, mentioned to me that he had never visited a gambling casino. We asked some other reporter to cover for us at a luncheon at the old Riverside Hotel in case Goldwater varied the speech we both had heard a dozen times or more, and while the rest of the press corps went to the lunch, MacNeil and I went to the roulette table.

"It's a child's game, Robin," I said, out of my vast experience in Latin American gambling hells. "You just put a couple of chips on 27, the red, and wait for the little white ball to drop into the 27 on the wheel."

We both did, and I'll be damned if it didn't.

We stood there half an hour, plunging—at least as working stiffs understand the word. Neither of us could lose. By the time Goldwater had finished his speech, I had won $1,600 and MacNeil nearly $1,000. At the cashier's desk, MacNeil said, "Nothing to it! I can't wait to try this again!"

He has since told me that those thirty minutes in Reno proved expensive in later life, and that he blames me. At the time, a good deal richer, we both had to hurry to catch up with the motorcade and file our stories on Senator Goldwater's stirring speech in Reno.

Then came the earthquake.

Most people don't remember earthquakes, even the big ones, unless they were there. They don't remember the one in the Peruvian Andes that buried alive 67,000 people, some of them people I knew, in 1970. Or the one that killed more than 22,000 in Guatemala early in 1976. Even if you ask them about the earthquake in the summer of '76 in which as many as 800,000 people may have perished in China, a calamity almost beyond imagining, they look blank. The Alaska earthquake of 1964 is mostly forgotten now. Except by me.

It struck on March 27 with a force of 8.5 on the Richter scale, the most powerful earthquake ever recorded in North America. Within seconds after the bulletin appeared on the wire service machines in our Los Angeles office, I was on the phone to Alaska, only to discover, as I had feared, that suddenly there were no working telephones in Alaska. I called Seattle and found that the Navy was summoning doctors and collecting medical supplies for a relief flight which would leave for Anchorage within hours. I

wangled a space on the plane for a Seattle cameraman. Then I called New York to tell the assignment
desk I was off to Seattle to try to get aboard the Navy
plane myself.

"Don't go," I was told. "We're not even sure
there's a usable runway in Anchorage. This is going
to take days to sort out and somebody is going to have
to give us reports from Los Angeles in the meantime.
Anybody else you can send?"

I looked around the office. My eye fell on Terry
Drinkwater, a young election researcher who had
never done a television story in his life. But I knew
he wanted to be a reporter.

"Go to Seattle right now," I said. "Call me as
soon as you get there. I might be able to get you on
the first plane into Alaska."

Terry Drinkwater made the plane. So did a reporter
from NBC. Terry did his first quick report from
Alaska right at the Anchorage airport showing the
damage there. So did the reporter from NBC. Terry
alertly shipped the film back to Seattle on the plane
he'd come in on, which had been converted to a medical evacuation flight for some of those injured in the
quake. The NBC reporter got his film on the plane,
too. With no way of knowing any of this, I had a
motorcycle courier I'd relied on in the past stand by
at the Seattle airport. NBC had a courier, too. I gave
mine instructions to call me at any hour of the night
or day when he found a flight was expected from
Alaska. He called. The navy plane was returning, expected to arrive in one hour. I alerted New York and
made sure the CBS station in Seattle was ready to

feed film instantly to the network. The plane landed. The CBS film and the NBC film came off the same plane at the same time. Both motorcycle couriers, mine and NBC's, roared off toward the city.

Mine ran out of gas.

NBC went on the air with the first film of the Alaska earthquake, beating CBS by twenty-six minutes.

Fred Friendly called it his "Bay of Pigs." He convened a formal court of inquiry a few days later to discover how this humiliation could have occurred, with all of his executives in attendance in his office and I testifying by telephone. When I got to the part about the motorcycle running out of gas, I tried a euphemism to protect the courier's job, if not his life.

"He ran into logistical difficulties," I said.

The volcano rumbled and blew.

"And by the way," Friendly roared, "why didn't *you* go to Alaska?"

"The desk in New York told me not to."

There was a pause while Friendly verified this with the others in the room. Then he came back on the line.

"The next time the desk tells you not to go to Alaska," he bellowed, *"go to Alaska!"*

He slammed down the phone.

Terry Drinkwater went on to become a CBS News Correspondent on the basis of his good reporting of the Alaska earthquake.

I got recalled to New York on the basis of an empty gas tank.

10

NINETY DEGREES
NORTH

Having decided that I was a washout as a reporter of breaking stories, my bosses assigned me to work on documentaries.

I should explain to the young: We made documentaries back then, programs of thirty minutes or an hour on single subjects. We did not do this because we thought they would attract large audiences or beat the other networks in the ratings. We did it because the management thought we ought to.

The management of CBS News passed from Fred Friendly to Richard S. Salant. Fred's inner Mount Etna went off in a dispute about news coverage with the management across town. He resigned. Salant was a company lawyer with no background in journalism. Never mind his background; Salant was the best leader we ever had. Almost alone among CBS News Presidents, he represented the news staff to the CBS corporation, rather than the other way around. Salant's idea was that he would worry about sponsors and ratings and air time, leaving the rest of us to worry about telling people the news. Salant had high principles and expected us to live up to them. With the advice of two able deputies, Bill Leonard and

Gordon Manning—also the best we ever had—he cod-
ified all the unwritten ethical rules of broadcast journalism into a thick white book with a plastic cover,
CBS News Standards and Practices. He made it a
loose-leaf book so that he could add new rules as he
thought of them.

Among the first documentaries I worked on was a
one-hour study of the labor union movement, *The
State of the Unions*, produced by Joe Wershba, one
of the most gifted of Ed Murrow's former producers.
Our program was a comparison of an old, powerful
union, Walter Reuther's United Auto Workers, with
the young, weak one Cesar Chavez was organizing
among California farm workers. For the sake of a
little historical background, we filmed the opening in
Chicago at the site of the 1937 Republic Steel massacre. "The strikers were here," I said, "the police
ranks were over there . . ." A public relations man
from Republic Steel wandered out of the building to
listen to this speech. He must have reported it to his
superiors because a few days later in the interoffice
mail Joe Wershba and I received copies of some correspondence. The President of Republic Steel had
written a sharp letter to Frank Stanton, President of
CBS, saying Republic Steel did not appreciate CBS
News dredging up ancient history this way and reminding Stanton that Republic Steel was sponsoring
certain entertainment programs on the network. Stanton had passed the letter to Dick Salant for a reply.
Salant's reply said, "I assume this filming was done
for a broadcast we are preparing called *The State of
the Unions*. . . ." He went on to tell the President of

Republic Steel when and where he could see this program if he wanted to, and signed the letter, "Very truly yours. . ." Salant sent copies of these letters to Joe Wershba and me without comment. He never even asked us what we had done outside the Republic Steel property. His letter said unmistakably to this big sponsor that *whatever* we had done was going on the air just as we had done it. And it did.

The reporter is a stone skipping on a pond, taking an instant to tell one story and ricocheting to the next, covering a lot of water while only skimming the surface. But in those years of the mid-sixties, I got good and wet. I spent several weeks in one block of Harlem working on a documentary that tried to explain the grievances of people who were black and poor, *117th Street, New York, New York*. With another of Murrow's old producers, Jack Beck, I worked on an hour-long broadcast about Mexico, and with still another, David Lowe, I delved into the ugly mysteries of the Ku Klux Klan.

I spent nearly all of December 1964 in the dreary hollows of Letcher County, Kentucky, with a friend from *Eyewitness* days, Bernie Birnbaum, and a skilled cameraman, Walter Dombrow. The resulting broadcast, describing a dark and silent *Christmas in Appalachia*, shocked viewers with pictures of children thin and pale and dying of hunger in the richest country in the world. I was shocked, too. I kept returning to eastern Kentucky and West Virginia to make sure nobody missed the point that half a million of their fellow citizens were living in tar paper shacks without electricity or running water, families of six subsisting

on nothing but $56 a month in food stamps. I am not
sure those stories did any good. I'm pretty sure they
didn't. But they were stories, perhaps the only ones,
ever, I felt I had to do.

Bernie Birnbaum and I looked around again the
next year for the most miserable possible place to
spend Christmas. We settled on Vietnam. We picked
a First Division infantry squad fighting a war against
snipers and booby traps at a place called Lai Khe.
We were there long enough to get to know every man
in the squad and to take it personally when incoming
bullets and mortar rounds started picking them off
one at a time. A mine exploded in the brush one day
while two of Sergeant Ralph Bosalet's men, Bill Floyd
and José Dueñas, were creeping around in there.
Our cameraman, a brave man named Jerry Sims,
stopped filming to help the badly wounded Floyd into
a truck. His assistant cameraman wrapped a tourniquet around Floyd's leg to stop the bleeding. Then,
while I twisted the tourniquet and held it tight, Sims
filmed the wild ride to the aid station and the attempt
to save Floyd's life, muttering as he worked, "Goddamn this war, goddamn this war . . ." You can hear
him murmuring this phrase in the background of the
film's sound track. I was feeling the same way. Floyd
lost his leg. We visited him at the army hospital in
Denver when he got home, and again when he was
married. Years later, we found him still trying to adjust to his artificial leg at his home in Florida.

There was nothing we could do for Dueñas but
pay our respects to his family. Dueñas was killed
when the mine went off. *Christmas in Vietnam* ended

with a picture of the squad leader, Ralph Bosalet, a spirited and animated man, sitting on an ammunition box beside an outdoor Christmas tree, lost in grief.

I came back to America persuaded that I had had enough of death and danger. It always has been a mistake to walk around the halls of 524 West 57th Street where your bosses can see you. One day late in 1966, I ran into Bill Leonard in the hall. He was the vice president in charge of documentaries.

"Yes!" he said. "You're the one!"

"I'm the what?" I asked.

"Come into my office," he said. "Sit down."

He poured me a cup of coffee. This was more hospitable treatment than I was used to from my superiors.

"Next spring," he said, "a bunch of Minnesotans are going to try to drive snowmobiles to the North Pole."

I felt an icy premonition down my spine.

"We're going to do a one-hour documentary. Bob Clemens is going to shoot it. Dick Wiggins and Bob Mingalone are going along as soundman and assistant. Palmer Williams will be the producer in New York. I've been trying to think of a correspondent we can spare for a couple of months."

"And?"

"And you're the one. Stop looking so worried. You're going to love it." He wrote a name and telephone number on a piece of paper and handed it to me.

That's how I met Ralph Plaisted. He was not a professional explorer. He was a former door-to-door

peddler of spices, extracts, fly spray and cattle vita-
mins around Askov, Minnesota, Rutabaga Capital of
the World. Now, at thirty-eight, he had graduated to
selling insurance in White Bear Lake. He was an out-
doorsman, like so many others who live on the rim
of the Great Lakes, always seeking some new stren-
uous adventure. The winter before, he had wondered
how long it would take him to drive a snowmobile to
St. Paul from his summer cabin at Ely, 250 miles
away. It took him thirteen hours and fifty-two minutes
nonstop in thirty-below-zero temperatures. He started
looking around for some other place to go on a snowmobile. He settled on the North Pole.

The National Geographic Society disdainfully declined to sponsor him. Ralph was a little rough-hewn
for the gentleman-explorer establishment. At a luncheon in the society's inner sanctum in Washington
(''Six pieces of silverware on each side of the plate.
Real dainty food. Nothing to drink''), he was told that
he would never make it to the Pole. He told the society bigwigs they could just sit there and watch him.

He rounded up some of his pals, a doctor, a high
school geography teacher, a dentist, a computer engineer and others, and talked them into going along.
He used his flair as a salesman to collect donated
supplies—ten snowmobiles, 250 pounds of soup,
forty-five pounds of mixed nuts, tents, pickaxes,
candy bars, sleeping bags, caribou hides, medical
supplies, sleds, dried milk, canned beef, radios, nylon cable, pots and pans, thermal underwear and
cheese in wheels and tubes and boxes which came

with a flag to be raised at the North Pole emblazoned: "3110 Miles to the White Bear Lake Cheese Shop."

By mail, Ralph sent me my uniform. There was an inner parka, knee-length, made of poplin and lined with Sherpa cloth, its hood encircled by wolverine fur. This garment alone would have sent any Eskimo into raptures, and it was only the *inner* parka. The outer parka was made in layers of windproof canvas duck and quilted spun nylon with hand-stitched hem, cuffs and hood lined with arctic wolf fur and the finished article dyed a bright color for easy identification on the trail. Mine was bright red. The trousers, of matching, thickly insulated duck, were held up by gaudy suspenders and tied at the bottom between knee and ankle with rawhide thongs. The boots were most impressive of all. They were Eskimo-style *mukluks* of smoked moosehide, lined with seamless Finn boots made of raw carded wool with soles of plastic mesh and felt, designed to be removed and dried at the end of the day.

I put on all this gear in my apartment in New York and looked at myself in the mirror. My Plaisted Polar Expedition patch blazed back at me from the breast of my crimson parka. The wolverine fur bravely circled my face. I was Nanook, or Peary, or Roald Amundsen. I took all that stuff off before somebody came to the door and caught me wearing it.

Self-conscious rehearsals were staged on the ice of Mille Lacs in northern Minnesota, a smooth, glassy surface as different from the Arctic Ocean as a millpond from a rapids. Little crowds of people began showing up on the lake to see what polar explorers looked like. Bumps Woolsey, Ralph Plaisted's dentist, opened the flap of the tent out there one Saturday afternoon in February and peered back at the people.

"You know, Ralph," he said, "if we keep talking about going to the North Pole like this, we're really going to have to go."

We really went.

We assembled at the Queen Elizabeth Hotel in Montreal on Good Friday, March 24, 1967. The waitress in the coffee shop, who could hardly overlook our colorful wind jackets, asked where we were going.

"The North Pole," we answered.

"What are you running away from?" she asked.

We flew north in a Royal Canadian Air Force C-130 Hercules—also donated—with our knees rubbing against a towering twelve-ton mound of cargo. Montreal is about 2,200 miles from Canada's most northerly regions. Canada is approximately as tall as it is wide. You have to make the trip in a metal bucket seat to appreciate the fact. On the way, I read Vilhjalmur Stefansson's classic books on the Arctic and other cold-weather advice: "If your hand freezes to your ax blade at 50 below, urinate on it. If *both* hands freeze to your ax blade, you'd better have a friend along."

We made an overnight stop at Thule Air Base in Greenland and took off in the following dawn for Eureka, a nine-man U.S.–Canadian weather station on Ellesmere Island, where an unused building was to serve as the expedition's base camp. I stepped out of the aircraft into blowing snow to see three animals racing toward me with bared fangs. I thought, my

God, wolves! and took an involuntary step back toward the door before I noticed their tails were wagging. They were the weather station huskies.

The insulated tin buildings of Eureka, the only habitations ever constructed in that part of the Arctic, sit squarely on latitude 80 degrees north—100 miles down Nansen Sound from the edge of the Arctic Ocean and exactly 600 nautical miles from the Pole. The Plaisted Polar Expedition set out three days after our arrival on snowmobiles towing sleds top-heavy with spare parts, charts, chain saws, rifles, ice axes, duffel bags, radios, camera gear, tents, sleeping bags and food. One sled carried a 450-pound drum of gasoline. Never having been on a polar expedition, nobody knew exactly what to take on a polar expedition—so they took everything they could pack.

Bob Clemens rode with the lead snowmobiles. The plan was for Wiggins, Mingalone and me to shuttle back and forth to the expedition by plane. So it was Mingalone who filmed the departure in the frigid morning as Plaisted, at the head of the column, raised his arm, circled his mittened hand in the air and pointed north. One by one, the bright yellow machines followed, the overloaded sleds wobbling precariously behind. We followed them with the long lens of the camera until they disappeared into the cold mist. It was a great scene. Mingalone and I went inside to reload the camera. When we opened the camera door, thousands of little film chips spurted out at us. The film had frozen and shredded into confetti.

Bob Clemens wasn't having any better luck. His sled tipped over in the first mile; as he righted it, all he could think of were the 599 miles to go. The lens of his camera became ice-covered. The tripod head affixed to his snowmobile froze up and wouldn't move.

And the rest of the expedition was encountering even worse troubles, straying in wrong directions. Compasses are useless at that latitude, the Magnetic North Pole lying, as it does, away to the *south*, so Plaisted relied on the direction of the sun, which circled the sky above the horizon, neither rising nor setting in the early spring. Jerry Pitzl, the navigator, had a sextant for taking sun shots, but in the whiteouts, it sometimes took close study of Bob Clemens's photographic light meter to find the location of the sun. The comparatively simple trip up Nansen Sound to the edge of the Arctic Ocean took the expedition long, miserable days to accomplish.

Back at the base camp, we fought off cabin fever by playing chess, teaching one another Morse code, or walking up to the weather station to watch the weathermen send up their meteorological balloons (special fun on windy days).

The building where we slept was insulated and warm but the toilet was an unheated outhouse. Since temperatures there remained below zero, the old two-holer had to be approached with a kind of daily heroism. "The only true happiness in the Arctic," Bob Clemens said, "is pulling your pants back up."

Water for bathing and drinking came from a handy iceberg frozen into the fjord a mile or so away. Somebody had to take a Ski-Doo out there every morning, chip off a sledload of ice and haul it in to melt on the cookstove, a woodburning relic off some ancient schooner which a whimsical mechanic had converted to oil. The stove burned with a hellish roar, and there being no way to regulate the heat, it cooked capriciously. A ham came out burned to the core after a few minutes in the oven; a cheesecake, after cooking for hours, remained a flabby pudding. We all lost weight at base camp.

One day, on an ice-collecting and exploring trip, Dick Wiggins and I took snowmobiles miles across the hills of Ellesmere. The little cluster of weather buildings vanished in the distance. The impression came upon us that we were the only men who had ever ventured into this wilderness. It was a beautiful subzero day. We came across snowy fields full of arctic hares, entirely white except for the black tips of their ears, and so unafraid of human beings that they permitted us to walk almost close enough to touch them. They communicated with one another by shadowboxing, each flurry of boxing in the air followed by quick hops toward fresh patches of sparse brown grass growing up through the snow. They pawed and nibbled and boxed for two hours or more as we stood among them, fascinated.

Then we spotted a herd of musk-oxen and gave chase. At first, the great shaggy animals ran from us, but when we caught up to them, they formed their characteristic circle of defense, old bulls shoulder to shoulder on the outside of the circle, horns lowered, with cows and calves herded into the center. It is a strategy musk-oxen must have learned in the Ice Age as a defense against wolves, a tactic copied by covered wagoneers on the western prairie and by British grenadiers in battle against Zulus. We made pictures, but the fixed look of a formation of stomping, snorting musk-oxen has a certain forcefulness which restrained us from moving in for close-ups.

The Arctic Ocean ice is constantly in motion. The floes, shifted by wind and current, break apart, creating "leads" of open water, and grind together, forming jumbled pressure ridges. Both leads and ridges slowed the Plaisted Expedition, which was forced to camp frequently to wait for wide leads to freeze over or to spend hours chopping rough paths through towering barriers of ice. Sleds turned over and broke apart in the rough going, skis separated from the machines and went flying. When at last it was time to camp, sleep was hindered by condensed moisture dripping from the walls of the tents, often by loud cracks as the floes chosen as campsites began to break up, once by a fire when a catalytic heater tipped over, once by the arrival of a curious polar bear.

They knew they must reach the Pole by early May when the arctic storms begin and create huge channels in the ocean ice. Mid-April found them in a region of jumbled ice Bumps Woolsey called "the Rock Quarry," through which they had to cut a path for every inch of progress. After that came a monstrous pressure ridge which forced them to rope machines and sleds up one side and down the other. The cold and the exertion induced a profound weariness none of them had ever experienced before. The vigorous doctor of the expedition, Art Aufderheide, wrote in his diary one night: "This could turn out to be too much for a 45-year-old man."

I took a turn on the ice to spell Bob Clemens for a few days. The first morning was a fast, easy floe-hopping operation. I rode standing on Woolsey's sled. I had to bury my face in the fur lining of my parka hood to escape the icy draft our speed created. In the afternoon, we entered an area of broken ice, first jagged cracks two or three feet wide that lent themselves to thrilling snowmobile jumps, then wider leads that required us to dismount and test the thickness of the ice crusts before crossing. It was hard not to think of the ice as "land" and the cracks as "streams"—but those streams were hundreds of fathoms deep. To reach the Pole in time, we needed an average daily advance of eleven miles. That day, we made ten.

The next day, we made at least thirteen, and the next day twenty, in a bracing, exciting scramble through a gathering fog. The plane came out, guided now by a tracking beacon, landed and took me back to base camp with the film I had shot out there. As we took off from the ice, all I could see to the north was a broad, smooth expanse leading straight toward the Pole. It looked as though the Plaisted Polar Expedition had gone and got lucky.

That night, the wind came up as the men on the ice were pitching their tents. Aufderheide suggested it might be a good idea to build a snow wall around the tents and they did. Jerry Pitzl brought out his anemometer. It showed a wind speed of 1,500 feet per minute, about eighteen miles per hour. Nothing to worry about. Then he checked his other instruments.

The barometer read 29.5. It was falling fast. The thermometer read +2°F. It was the first time the mercury had risen above zero. These readings were a classic indication of the approach of an arctic spring storm. They all knew it. They just didn't want to believe it.

That night, high winds were blowing from every point of the compass over half the Arctic Basin, attracted by the vacuum effect of a monstrous low-pressure system moving across the North Pole from Siberia. As the storm approached the men on the ice, its winds, backing clockwise in a 500-mile diameter, reached a speed of sixty miles per hour. This wind hit their light tents after midnight. They heard a series of loud concussions over the roar of the flapping tent walls. That was the ice breaking up around them.

Their two tents were fifteen feet apart. In the blowing snow of the morning, they couldn't see from one tent to the other. They had no choice but to stay where they were and hope their floe outlasted the storm.

On the third day of the big blow, Ralph Plaisted realized he had stopped thinking about taking these men to the Pole. He was thinking only about keeping them alive. He decided that if they were alive when the storm ended, he would end the expedition there and take the men home.

If a tent had blown away, if the floe had cracked beneath them, they would have perished. But on the afternoon of the seventh day, the wind stopped.

It stopped. It did not slowly diminish, the way wind usually does. It dropped in fifteen minutes from a gale to a dead calm. The sky cleared, except for streaks of black cloud trailing back from the south-east, and within an hour, even they had disappeared.

It was over.

Back at the base camp, I happened to be passing the radio room. I heard a small voice coming through the static we had been monitoring for a week. I pressed the mike button and said, "Go ahead."

It was Jerry Pitzl's voice. "I have to talk fast because the generator is sputtering. Our position is 83-34 north, 89-32 west. Send out the plane."

The Plaisted Polar Expedition of 1967 ended there, in failure, 384 nautical miles short of the North Pole. The exhausted men, glad to have survived the storm, crossed their last lead on May 4 to reach a floe big enough for the plane to land on. It was a fresh crack, four feet wide. They bridged it with the slender poles of the radio antenna and drove recklessly across. The crack widened while they were crossing. The last sled across knocked the poles into the ocean.

After the plane landed, they loaded one snowmobile, one tent and their sleeping bags. All the rest of the equipment they were forced to leave on the ice. It is still floating there, I imagine. Someday, if the floe drifts down into the North Atlantic, a passing mariner may be startled by what he sees through his binoculars: bright-yellow snowmobiles and toboggans, food boxes, stoves and axes and caribou hides. More likely, the floe will break up in some future storm—as it almost did during the big blow of April and May 1967—and these last remnants of the Plaisted Polar Expedition will drop to the bottom of the sea.

When the plane landed at the Eureka airstrip, Jerry Pitzl was the first to step upon solid ground.

"It was just a shame," he said, "just a damn shame. I've got to tell you. We could have run and run and run. I climbed up on a big ridge just before the plane came in, and for miles to the north was good going, nothing but good ice as far as I could see. . . ."

He put a finger under his sunglasses to wipe tears away.

That night, we opened the champagne we had hoped to drink at the Pole and drank it all. What Plaisted, Pitzl, Aufderheide and some of the others talked about that night were the mistakes they had made, the lessons they had learned—and their next attempt to reach the Pole.

I was proud of them. There have always been a few people who, with no visible motive, background of experience or likelihood of gain, have strained for the ends of the earth. I put Ralph Plaisted and his buddies in that company.

The next year, with some of the same men, Plaisted returned to Ellesmere, set out earlier, traveled lighter, left his fears behind him and reached the North Pole. I wasn't along. I was in Cedar Rapids, Iowa, where Collins Radio had set up a shortwave link to the new expedition.

I asked, "What's your location, Ralph?"

His shout filled the room in Cedar Rapids.

"Ninety north! Ninety north!"

A U.S. Air Force plane flew over and confirmed it. Ralph Plaisted was camped at the North Pole.

Except for the officers of the National Geographic Society, which sponsored Commander Robert E. Peary's attempt to reach the Pole in 1909, hardly any modern arctic expert believes Peary made it. At about 88 degrees north latitude, Peary sent his navigator and all other scholarly members of his party back toward land, continuing toward the Pole with Matthew Henson, his black assistant, and four Eskimos. On April 6, Peary abruptly announced to Matt Henson that this was to be their final camp. He started for land the next day. At this point, his speed miraculously doubled. A close examination of Peary's diary shows that after leaving the "North Pole" he made 150 miles in two days, walking all the way. When later challenged on this distance by Congress, he was able to walk only thirty miles per day on the roads around Washington.

I reviewed the Peary diaries and the testimony of Peary and others for a month or more on returning to the United States, and what I believe is this: that Peary, who left with great fanfare on his ninth arctic expedition, which he knew must be his last (a fleet of yachts and a cheering crowd attended his departure from New York, and President Theodore Roosevelt, wringing his hand, said, "I believe in you, Peary, and I believe in your success if it is within the possibility of man") was determined not to return this time without the prize; that after thirty-seven days of hard travel northward, his observations showed that the Pole was still beyond the farthest ice ridges; that there in the wasteland of ice, his crippled feet tormenting him, his years telling on him, he was overcome by the uselessness of going on toward an abstract Pole no different from the rest of the ice pack; that he raised his flags and took his photographs, secure in the knowledge that nobody on earth could successfully dispute his claim.

In his own account, Matt Henson reported that when Peary took his last sextant observation, "I was sure that he was satisfied. Feeling that the time had come, I ungloved my right hand and went forward to congratulate him."

But Peary did not take Henson's extended hand. He only covered his eyes, murmured that he was tired and entered his igloo to sleep.

I believe Robert E. Peary did not cross the ice to the North Pole.

If he didn't, then the first who did was Ralph Plaisted, an insurance man from White Bear Lake, Minnesota.

11

BOXES ON WHEELS

In early fall 1967, Jim Wilson and I were flying to Cleveland. And drinking, the way people do on airplanes, and looking out the window. It was one of those cool, clear nights when you can see the lights of all the small towns from 30,000 feet. We had enough airline whisky in us to make us maudlin.

"Look down there," Jim Wilson said. "Every one of those lights has a story to tell."

"Yep," I agreed mushily. "Damn right."

"Here we are, flying to a story," Wilson said, "and flying right over *ten thousand* stories!"

"A *hundred* thousand!" I exclaimed. I recalled for Wilson the joy of my driving trips through the Great Plains with Wendell Hoffman years before. "By God," I said, "next time we go somewhere, we ought to drive and find out what's really going on in this country!"

The next morning, we were both perfectly sober. The tipsy idea of the night before still seemed a good one. Wilson was a temperamental cameraman with a bit of the artist in him. He was trying to get out of the lock-step routine of hard news coverage. I had known from the beginning that I was better suited to

151

feature stories than to wars, polar expeditions, politics and calamities. I had worked ten years for CBS
News, often on assignments that taxed my physique
and temperament. While I did not plan to say the word
out loud, I felt I needed a vacation. When I got back
to New York, I went to see Dick Salant.

I said, "Why don't you let me just wander for three
months to see what I can find?"

He said, "What do you *think* you'll find?"

I waxed poetic. "Farmers bringing in their crops,
first-graders starting school, county fairs, town meetings. Pulse of the country. You know."

President Salant was distracted by the pile of work
on his desk.

"Okay," he said. "Try it. Keep the budget down."

I called Jim Wilson. I said, "We'll go in a couple
of station wagons."

"No," he said, "let's go in a motor home."

I said, "What's a motor home?"

That's how long ago it was. Motor homes were still
a novelty. I had never seen one. Many times in the
next twenty years, I was to wish I *still* had never seen
one. Of all the mixed blessings and curses of my life,
I put motor homes at the top of the list.

Wilson explained that a motor home was a house
trailer with a motor and steering wheel. A neighbor
of his in Maryland, a *National Geographic* photographer, had just driven one to Alaska and back for a
photo essay on the Alcan Highway. Wilson thought
we could rent this very vehicle from the *National
Geographic*. "It's parked in this guy's driveway,"
Wilson said. "Come down tomorrow and we'll have

a look at it." Bob Funk, who volunteered to make the trip as our soundman, and Bill Lewis, who was to be our lighting man, came too.

What greeted my eyes was a tall, fiberglass box on wheels, originally painted beige, I believe, but bleached pink by the sun. I wondered whether I really wanted to traverse America in a pink box. But when Wilson showed us all the wonders inside—the refrigerator, the stove, the electric coffeepot, the combination shower room and toilet, the sofas that converted into beds, I was seized by the romance of it all. Why, we wouldn't even have to stop at motels for the night! We could pull off the road wherever we wished in all this fair land, and watch the sunset through our own picture window as we cooked our own steaks on our own broiler and washed them down with cold beer from our own electric icebox!

(We could also, I learned, sleep miserably on hard foam rubber bunks and rise grumpily, four grown men all trying to bathe and shave in cramped quarters at the same time, quarreling over whose turn it was to cook breakfast. We soon converted the convertible sofas into what we really needed, storage cabinets for the lights and cables and film supplies, and started looking for motels and cafes when the sun went down. Sleeping in the bus lasted about a week.)

We duly rented the pink box, and had a sign painter place the words "On The Road" in modest letters on the door, with the stylized CBS eye. I did not know at the time that I was making a deal with the devil: In return for the freedom of the road, I was going to have to spend the rest of my life in a motor home.

Motor home technology was primitive in the beginning and has not advanced very far since. The things are always breaking down. We've been through more than half a dozen "buses" as we call them. That first one, the one we rented, was a prototype Travco, a Dodge truck chassis perilously supporting a lofty fiberglass body. The pink box swayed alarmingly when under way, like a sailboat tacking into the wind. In the Travco, we learned to hang on to our coffee cups in the curves. When the stove stopped working, followed by the water pump and the propane system, we didn't even bother to have them fixed, figuring these were the landlord's problems, not ours.

When our allotted three months of travel were up, nobody at CBS said stop, so we pluckily kept going. We returned the rented Travco to the National Geographic Society much the worse for wear and bought a new one with CBS's money. We painted it white. Since then, we've painted all our buses white. Except for the paint job, the second Travco was not much improvement over the first. It would have been fine for family vacations, but it swooned under months of hard pounding. One day, as we labored along a dirt road near Stuttgart, Arkansas, a piston rod came flying through the roof of the engine compartment and landed greasily in Bob Funk's lap, persuading me that it was time to look around for a different model motor home.

Jim Wilson and his crew, having had enough of rusticity, now resigned to return to the comparative ease of jet airplanes and Hertz rental cars. Wilson's place was eventually taken by Isadore Bleckman, a congenial Chicago-based cameraman who had run a one-man sports car garage in his youth. Izzy prided himself on his mastery of mechanical matters. He volunteered to search out the state-of-the-art vehicle we could drive confidently into the future. His kitchen table in Evanston became heavy with brochures for this "Interstate Cruiser" and that "Land Yacht." The motor home, which I had never even heard of two or three years before, was becoming a national rage. Suddenly, there was such a thing as a Winnebago, and dozens of other makes to choose from. Izzy chose the Cortez.

Our love-hate affair with the Cortez lasted nearly a decade. Until one of those gas shortages of the '70s forced consumers to reconsider vehicles that got nine miles to the gallon on the open road, the Cortez was made, more or less by hand, in Kent, Ohio. It was better-engineered than the lumpy old Travco, but with a fatal flaw of its own: The metal body was way too heavy for the flimsy chassis and suspension system. In the Cortez, we winced at every pothole, knowing that what was a bump in the road to others was probably a blowout or broken wheel to us. From lonely crossroads stores, from the garages of baffled mechanics, from at least one farmhouse outside which our glamorous vehicle had sputtered and died, from a dozen remote and inconvenient places, and frequently from a mobile telephone we finally installed in our too-frequently-immobile bus, we called the Ohio factory for new wheels. Expressmen bearing Cortez wheels did a brisk business nationwide for a few years there.

The tires were a novel size made by Goodyear to fit only a certain obscure cattle trailer and the Cortez. Whenever we found a tire dealer with a supply of these tires, we bought them all and warehoused them in a compartment atop the bus, knowing we were going to need them. We experienced four spectacular blowouts in May 1974 alone, in California, Arizona, Missouri and finally, in Ohio, when both rear tires blew at once. The 11,000-pound Cortez descended upon its rear springs at sixty miles per hour, sending up a rooster tail of sparks for a quarter of a mile behind us before we could get the thing stopped.

Some of the troubles we had with the Cortez were our own fault. We drove it on rutted back roads where it was never meant to go, getting out to check the undersides of little country bridges before daring to drive across. Izzy pretty regularly used to knock the protruding side mirrors off on roadside signs and telephone poles. But it was the wheels and tires that drove us crazy.

Here are Izzy's notes for a four-month period in 1975:

Monday, July 7, Hannibal, Missouri, changed cracked wheel.

July 9, Topeka, repaired cracked gasket on generator.

July 12, Topeka to Wichita to Lincoln, replaced exhaust system.

July 16, Alliance, Nebraska, Sandoz ranch, replaced cracked wheel.

July 19, Des Moines, changed wheel.

Aug. 14, Grand Portage, Minnesota, new wheel.

Aug. 27, Duluth to Bismarck, changed cracked wheel.

Sept. 1, Billings, Labor Day, garages closed. Changed wheel, replaced muffler, adjusted brakes, greased suspension, changed plugs, adjusted torsion bar in motel parking lot.

Oct. 27, Detroit, Greenfield Village. Picked up two new wheels.

Nov. 8, Indianapolis. Changed two wheels, one cracked, one bent in blowout.

Nov. 13, Columbus, Ohio. Changed tires and one cracked wheel.

Nov. 17, Lower East Side, New York. Guy refused to fix air-conditioning coil, so Larry and I replaced it ourselves on the street. Guy then charged it with Freon and asked for one hundred bucks.

We never could have made it without Izzy. Driving along in the California redwood country one Sunday, I glanced into the rearview mirror to notice that we were trailing smoke and fire. I pulled off the road outside Boonville, where a kindly resident named Jack June let us prop the rear of the bus on a white oak stump in his front yard. The rear wheel bearings had welded themselves to the rear axles. Izzy chopped the bearings off the axle stubs with a cold chisel, used a thread file to reconstruct the threads and installed new bearings. It sounds easier than it was. The effort took all day, lacerated Izzy's knuckles and got grease all over his best Eddie Bauer safari shirt. When Mrs.

June cooked us supper and served it on the kitchen table, blood from Izzy's knuckles dripped on her tablecloth.

The Cortez transmission had to be replaced in Seattle when we cracked it driving over some railroad tracks, and again in Evanston, Wyoming, after the oil cooler broke in a blizzard and dumped out all the transmission fluid. I say Evanston, Wyoming, because that's where it happened. There was nobody in Evanston who wanted to tackle the job, though, so we hired a wrecker to tow us back to Salt Lake City at the rate of one dollar a mile.

We took aboard one of those wheeled dollies mechanics use to hike themselves under cars without jacking them up. Izzy spent more time under the bus than in it. One time in the middle of a week of breakdowns, we pulled into a rest stop somewhere between Bartlesville and Ponca City so Izzy could see what was wrong with the transmission case this time. Mixed with the sound of mechanical clanging and banging coming from under the bus, I heard a different sound. It was Izzy under there crying.

We liked the way the Cortez looked and liked the way it rode. It was just that so much of the time, it wouldn't ride at all. After the second Cortez broke down irreparably, we discovered that the company had gone broke and was blessedly unable to provide a third.

We bought a brand-new Revcon, an elegantly appointed product of California. This was my idea. I liked the thick carpet. I liked the swivel chair and baronial desk the factory custom-built for me. I liked the expansive view from the big curtained window on the starboard side.

Izzy, bruised by the Cortez in body and mind, had his doubts.

"What do you think?" I asked him, after his first close inspection of our gleaming new bus.

"I think every moving part is going to break down," he said.

We bought it anyway. Every moving part broke down. We found that the big signs on the outskirts of cities that say "RV Repair" don't mean anything. When we pulled into the garages under the signs, there was always a guy who took one look at the Revcon and said, "Well, I dunno . . ." When he started scratching his head, we learned, it was time to get out of there. That guy wasn't going to be any help to us.

We switched to a ten-year-old used FMC we found on a motor home lot in Wisconsin. The salesman said, "An elderly doctor used it only once a summer to take his grandchildren to the place on the lake." I do not doubt that it served the old gentleman well. It must never have rained on these annual excursions, however, for the first time we turned on the windshield wipers, one of them flew off and vanished into the storm. When we switched on the auxiliary air conditioner, it blew the electrical fuses—not only the air conditioner fuse but also all the others. The FMC company no longer makes motor homes. I think they switched to making tanks for the Army.

This vehicle also came with its own mouse, a traveling companion who revealed himself in the first day of our ownership by leaving only crumbs and scraps of paper where there had been, in a cabinet, half a box of Ritz crackers. That night, while we settled on canned chili and beans for dinner, the mouse dined in our pantry on imported macaroons. After a few days of this, Larry Gianneschi, who had settled in as our permanent soundman, also appointed himself exterminator. He set a trap with Camembert cheese. The mouse enjoyed the cheese and left the trap unsprung. You may take it from me that a mouse will unwrap and eat an entire Bit-O-Honey candy bar. This one did. We chauffeured that Wisconsin mouse through Michigan and northern Pennsylvania, catering his meals and providing him with warm lodging, while never directly making his acquaintance.

Finally, there came a cold night outside Erie when the electrical line we used to keep the camera equipment warm worked itself loose and the interior of the bus suffered a deep chill. The camera gear came through unharmed, but the mouse must have been made uncomfortable. We never saw evidence of him again. Other motor homes were parked about the motel lot that night, and we figure he chose one of those in which to continue his journey. For his sake, I hope his new conveyance had a full pantry and was headed south. For a day or two there, we sort of missed our mouse.

The FMC was never intended for cold-weather travel, either by mice or men. Over the winters, we have gradually insulated it, using foam pads, bits of carpeting, rags and old underwear to caulk its many drafty seams, but the interior still feels like a wind tunnel when the bus is up to speed on a cold day. We dress for winter trips in down jackets and wool caps, and I keep a portable electric heater under my desk to keep my toes from freezing off and rattling around in my boots.

The engine compartment could use a little insulation, too. Something is always freezing up down there. We left Moab, Utah, on a wintry Friday afternoon, bound for the airport at Grand Junction, Colorado, so that I could catch the last plane to Denver and go on to New York for the *Sunday Morning* program. The distance from Moab to Grand Junction is not great, but the road is an exceedingly lonely one, through the region of stone windows and arches and canyon lands along the Colorado River. The wind rose, the snow began falling and the bus began slowing down.

"What's the matter?" I asked Izzy, who was driving.

"Won't go," he said.

He pressed the accelerator to the floor. The bus gave one last lurch forward into the blinding snow and stopped, right there in the middle of the road in the middle of nowhere in the middle of a blizzard.

"What's the next town?" Izzy asked.

"Cisco, Utah," I said, looking at the map.

"How far?"

"Too far to walk," I said.

We put on our parkas, went out into the storm and pried open the hatch to the engine compartment. Everything in there was coated thick with ice.

"Must be water in the gas line," Izzy said. "The carburetor's frozen up. Where's the ether spray?"

"We used up the ether spray back there in Green River," Larry said.

"Let's pour in some of that Drygas," I said.

"We used that up, too," Larry said.

"We need some alcohol," Izzy said.

"Well, we don't have any," Larry said. "Except the vodka."

We looked at one another.

I went into the bus and came back with a quart bottle of vodka, unopened. Larry opened it and solemnly poured the whole quart into the gas tank. Izzy climbed in and cranked the accelerator a few times. The engine started with a roar. We closed the door and were off.

A mile or two later, on a slight hill, the bus slowed to a stop again.

"There's always the scotch," Larry said.

The scotch got us to the top of the hill, but not much farther. We stopped again in the snow.

"Not the brandy!" I exclaimed. It was a fifth of VSOP, the good Hennessey.

"It's no use," Izzy said. "We have to dry out the carburetor somehow."

I remembered that Larry carries a small hair dryer in his sound case. He uses it to remove humidity from the tape recorder and the delicate circuit boards of the camera. I suggested using it on the carburetor.

Usually, at about this point in our breakdowns, an old rancher comes along in a pickup truck, stops and offers to help. All the old ranchers must have been

home by the fire. Not a single soul passed that way
in either direction that afternoon. If one had, he would
have been treated to the sight of a motor home
stranded in the storm with only its auxiliary generator
running, and three snow-covered figures struggling to
tape a hair dryer inside the engine compartment.

It took our entire supply of electrical tape, but we
finally got the nozzle of the dryer aimed delicately at
the carburetor. We closed the door to the engine compartment. We could hear the generator roaring and
the hair dryer humming away in there. We felt foolish. Izzy waited a few minutes, then twisted the ignition key. The engine started right up.

We made it through the snow to Cisco, Utah, and
up to Interstate 70. We made it across the state line
into Colorado, running on Texaco regular, Smirnoff
90-proof, Dewar's White Label, and Clairol hair dryer
power. We made it to the Grand Junction airport, just
in time to see, above the low terminal roof, the tail
of my airplane as it turned and taxied out to the runway.

We stopped at the curb outside the United counter,
so that I could go in and ask about the first flight to
Denver the next morning. I tried to think of something to be glad about.

I was glad we hadn't poured the Hennessey into the
gas tank.

12

ON THE ROAD

I had the conceit that once under way, I would find stories at every country crossroads. We set out from New York in October in the rain and wandered aimlessly through small-town New England for a few rainy days without an idea in our heads. I began to get nervous, wondering whether an idea would ever come.

Then the sun came out and the wind came up and the bright foliage of the New Hampshire autumn shivered and began to fall. A shower of lemon and scarlet and gold washed across our windshield. In every town, people were out raking leaves and children were playing in piles of leaves. We got the camera out and did our first "On The Road" story just about how pretty it all was. An old friend, Sandy Socolow, maintains that the best story we've ever done was that first one, that they've all gone downhill from there.

"On The Road" required a change of gears for the *Evening News*, which in those days of racial violence and the Vietnam War certainly was not accustomed to spending time on autumn leaves; and for viewers, who had never seen peaceful glimpses of rural places on the Cronkite program; and for me, too. I was used

On the Desk
at CBS News,
1958. *(CBS News.)*

With Martin Plissner,
Martin Agronsky, and
Mike Wallace at the
Democratic National
Convention, 1964.
(CBS News.)

On the Léopoldville – Matadi road, 1960.

John Tiffin filming in Matadi, Congo, 1960. *(Charles Kuralt.)*

Tokyo, 1961.

In the Andes above Vicos, Peru, 1961.

Lieutenant Son. *(Charles Kuralt.)*

117th Street, New York, with cameraman Herb Schwartz.
(CBS News.)

Campaign '64. *(CBS News.)*

Bernard Birnbaum in Letcher County, Kentucky, 1964. *(Charles Kuralt.)*

Incoming sniper fire, Lai Khe, South Vietnam, 1965. From left: Sergeant William Floyd (standing), SFC Ralph Bosalet, Charles Kuralt, cameraman Jerry Sims. *(Bernard Birnbaum.)*

With the musk-oxen on Ellesmere Island, 1967. *(Dick Wiggins.)*

The Travco at Grizzle's Grocery, 1968.

Dinner at home, 1968. From left, Larry Gianneschi,
Jim Wilson, Bill Lewis. *(Charles Kuralt.)*

Mr. Norris
feeds the deer,
Colorado, 1969.

Larry and Izzy.

Breakdown: Changing tires on the Cortez. From left, Charles Kuralt,
Larry Gianneschi, Izzy Bleckman, Charlie Quinlan.

Breakdown: Izzy unclogging the fuel line. *(Charles Kuralt.)*

Tubin' on the Apple.

Morning on the road.

At work.

Kansas
wheat field.

Oregon waterfall.
(Isadore Bleckman.)

Celebrity.
(Isadore Bleckman.)

Celebrity.
(Isadore Bleckman.)

Fair warning.
(Isadore Bleckman.)

Mr. Black and his mule. *(Isadore Bleckman.)*

Mr. Black in the Oval Office.
At extreme left: Harvey J. Witherell.

I AM AN ODD FELLOW

I BELIEVE IN THE FATHERHOOD OF GOD AND THE BROTH
ERHOOD OF MAN I BELIEVE IN FRIENDSHIP LOVE AND
TRUTH AS BASIC GUIDES TO THE ULTIMATE DESTINY OF
ALL MANKIND I BELIEVE MY COMMUNITY DESERVE MY BEST WORK
E MY LODGE AND MY HOME MY CHURCH OR TEMPL
MY MODEST PR MY EARNEST FAITH AND MY DEEPEST
LOYALTY AS I RFORM MY DUTY TO VISIT THE SICK
RELIEVE THE TRESSED BURY THE DEAD AND EDUCATE
THE ORPHAN   AS I WORK WITH OTHERS TO BUILD A
BETTER WO   CAUSE IN SPIRIT AND IN TRUTH I AM
AND MUST   BE GRATEFUL TO MY CREATOR FAITH-
FUL TO MY   RY AND FRATERNAL TO MY FELLOW MAN

I   AN ODD FELLOW

Odd Fellows Hall in Kansas. *(Isadore Bleckman.)*

Calling the office
from Wahoo, Nebraska.
(Isadore Bleckman.)

With Father Ron on the slopes of Mount McKinley.
(Isadore Bleckman.)

In Andrew Wyeth's museum, Chadds Ford, Pennsylvania.

In Vladimir Horowitz's living room.
(CBS News.)

Alf Landon on his front porch,
Topeka, Kansas.
(Isadore Bleckman.)

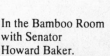

In the Bamboo Room
with Senator
Howard Baker.

Dr. Aseyev remembers.
A park bench
in Moscow, 1988.

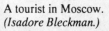

A tourist in Moscow.
(Isadore Bleckman.)

to going fast and working hard. "On The Road" seemed to work best when I went slow and took it easy. I found that while it helped to have a story in mind up the road somewhere, the world would not come to an end if I never got there; I might find something more interesting along the way. It was best to take a deep breath, mosey along and soak up the moods of the country and the changes of weather and terrain. When I finally shook off the tempo of daily journalism and fell into the rhythms of the country-side, I didn't have to worry about finding stories any longer. They found me.

I had to revise my conception of the people who lived in the country, too. To judge from the news of the day, they were bitterly divided along racial or po-litical lines, contentious and angry. But the people I actually met seemed neighborly and humane.

In Westerville, Ohio, Professor John Franklin Smith taught speech and dramatics at Otterbein College un-til he reached the mandatory retirement age of sev-enty.

"I loved my students," he said, "and I think they loved me."

He couldn't imagine leaving the students behind. So when he was forced to retire, he just kept working at the college. He had worked on for fifteen years—as janitor in the gym.

"During my years as a professor," he said, "I'd walk through here and see the man cleaning the floor. I knew what a mop was and what a bucket was. It was hard work at first, but I got on to it. It is neces-sary work, and I try to do it well."

I asked him which was more rewarding, being a professor or being a janitor.

This eighty-five-year-old man smiled and said, "Now, don't put me on the spot like that. I think I'd have to say every age in life has its own compensation."

We walked out across the campus together.

"I'm still looking ahead," he said. "I don't want to die. There's too much fun in this world, and a lot of good folks, a lot of them. And good books to read and fish to catch and pretty women to admire and good men to know. Why, life is a joy!"

At Pilottown, Louisiana, a community built on stilts near the mouth of the Mississippi River and reachable only by seaplane or boat, we met Andy Spirer, hunter and fisherman, reader of Greek in the original, and the only teacher, for ten years, in the one-room Pilottown schoolhouse. Why did he stay on in such a lonely place? "Well," he said, "they have trouble getting teachers to live out here, and somebody has to teach the kids."

On a little stream called Hunting Creek in Caroline County, Maryland, we came upon a 300-year-old gristmill still being operated by its eighty-one-year-old miller, Captain Frank Langrell. The Linchester mill ground corn for settlers in 1681, ground cornmeal for Washington's army nearly 100 years later and was grinding cornmeal yet. It must have been the oldest continually operated business in the country. But the mill didn't interest me as much as the miller. After sixty-five years beside his millstone, wasn't Frank Langrell tired of it all? "Yes," he said, "yes, I can't really say there's profit in it anymore, but these farmers count on me, you see. There's no other place to grind their corn, you see. . . ."

In Professor Smith and Andy Spirer and Frank Langrell, I saw Americans of a sort I had not known before, wedded to the places they lived and toiling not so much for themselves as for others. "It is necessary work . . ." "Somebody has to teach the kids . . ." "These farmers count on me, you see . . ." Their purposes and undertakings seemed entirely admirable to me. They had about them no delusions of superiority or motives of greed. I read the papers every day. The front pages were full of selfishness, arrogance and hostility toward others. The back roads were another country.

We wandered west. At Eagle Pass, Texas, on the Mexican border, we ran into Jo and Rumel Fuentes. They lived on a dirt street in a poor neighborhood. Every morning before dawn, Rumel Fuentes caught a bus to the nearest college, Southwest Texas Junior College in Uvalde. Uvalde is seventy miles away. It made for a long day, but three nights a week after coming home on the bus, Rumel taught American history classes for citizenship applicants. Two nights a week, he taught classes for high school dropouts. Washington had cut off funds for these courses several weeks before and most of the other teachers had left, but as long as the students kept studying, Rumel kept teaching.

Jo Fuentes had come to Eagle Pass from Ohio two years before as a Vista volunteer. During the mornings when Rumel was away in Uvalde, she, a Catholic, worked as a Planned Parenthood counselor. In the afternoons, she was the secretary at the Methodist church. Weekends, they both worked on the neighborhood center which they had persuaded the people to start building, and which was being paid for by the sale of tamales and old clothes.

They didn't see anything remarkable about their lives. Jo Fuentes said, "I think anybody who has the capability to do something about another person's sad situation should do it. It's not a matter of altruism or anything else. If you can do it, that's what you should do."

In Montana, we found a tough old rancher determined to save the wild horses of the Pryor Mountains if he had to do it all by himself. In California, we found a woman giving her life to the hummingbirds of Mojesca Canyon; she had a hundred hummingbird feeders hanging from the eaves of her porch. She said, "I know I can't save the world, but I can help out the hummingbirds."

That April, Martin Luther King, Jr., was murdered, and several American cities erupted in flames. In June, Robert Kennedy was murdered. I had known them both. I grieved for them, and for the country they had done so much to change for the better. I might have thought the country was now going mad if I hadn't been on the road. I had eyes and ears. I kept running into people who made me feel confident and reassured. In July, I ran into Pat Shannon Baker.

She was a young, white woman, the mother of three children, who lived in Reno, Nevada. The night Martin Luther King was killed, Pat Baker sat up late thinking, I have to do something about this. On her way to work, she often had passed a weedy vacant lot in a black neighborhood and wondered why the city hadn't turned it into a park. Now, she went to see her city councilman, who spoke of the strained budget and the difficulty of passing a bond issue. Pat Baker decided she couldn't wait for all that. She went to see people in the black neighborhood. She went to see garden supply houses and cement companies and surveyors and the heads of the construction unions and tough-minded contractors she had never met before. Pretty soon, her idea became everybody's idea.

At seven-thirty on a Friday morning, in a town not famous for early risers, a crowd began gathering at the vacant lot. By eight-thirty, 2,000 tons of donated topsoil was being spread by front-end loaders operated by heavy-equipment operators not used to working for free. They were working for free. I stood there and watched all this.

I watched a school custodian, an unemployed teenager, a roofer and a garage mechanic digging a ditch together. A junior high school kid assigned to saw two-by-fours to serve as cement forms sawed all day in the hot sun as if his life depended on it. A little girl carried water to the workers. Coastguardsmen, Marines and Seabees came by and pitched in. Cement was laid for a double tennis court and smoothed out by noon. A basketball court was in before the sun went down. Dozens of people worked all night.

Saturday morning, a crowd of several hundred

showed up for work, black and white, old and young. An eighty-four-year-old man who came by to watch stayed all afternoon helping to plant trees; he said he needed the exercise. They sodded the lawn Saturday night and turned on the sprinkler system Sunday morning. By Sunday afternoon, the park was finished, with walks and grass and basketball courts and trees and benches.

They named it Pat Baker Park and asked her if she would like to say something. She said, "This was a great, big, black and white thing, that's what it was."

I went back there more than twenty years later. The grass was neatly mowed. The trees were tall and leafy. In the shade of the trees, people were sitting on the benches talking. Some kids who hadn't been born in 1968 were practicing gaudy hook shots on the basketball court.

I thought back to the weekend the park was built. A black man, leaning on his shovel, looked around and said, "This is the best damn thing that has happened since I came to Reno."

He didn't mean the park. He meant building the park.

In that first year on the road, I fell in love with my native land. I rode the Wabash Cannonball through Indiana and the *Delta Queen* down the Ohio River and the cable cars up and down the San Francisco hills. (The cable car story ran seven minutes and twelve seconds on the *Evening News*, a third of the broadcast, prompting Les Midgley, by then the *Evening News* producer, to remark, "Well, there's one we don't have to do again.") I spent time among Pennsylvania Dutchmen in Kutztown, and Greek sponge fishermen in Tarpon Springs, Florida.

I came upon M. C. Pinkstaff, the roadside poet of Gordon Junction, Illinois, proprietor of Pinkstaff's Two-Pump Gas Station and Poem Factory. He sold his gasoline for thirty-nine cents a gallon and his poems on local topics for ten cents apiece. His best-selling poem was "Morose Maud, the Mule That Kicked Down the Barn Door." He said he had noted differences among Americans in their appreciation of verse: "You take folks that are from south of the Ohio, they'll buy poems a little more readily than those from north of the river. And Hoosiers will buy it before a 'Llini will. Folks from the Hawkeye State, Iowa, they love poetry and will buy it far more readily than people from Minnesota will. You pry a dime out of somebody from Minnesota and you've done something, brother! When a Minnesotan goes somewhere for a week, he puts on a clean pair of overalls and puts a ten-dollar bill in his pocket, and never changes either one!"

I heard jazz music in the streets of New Orleans and brass bands in the streets of Bristol, Rhode Island. I listened to echoes in the ghost town of Bodie, California. I saw corncob pipes being made in Washington, Missouri, and windmills being built in Broken Arrow, Oklahoma. I walked half a day down into the Red River Gorge of Kentucky to find a cave Daniel Boone once camped in.

That first year, I sent back to New York forty-seven

stories from twenty-three states, all of them my own discoveries. The biggest discovery of all was about myself: On the back roads of America, I felt at home at last. I knew I wanted to spend the rest of my life out there.

13

IZZY AND LARRY AND CHARLIE AND ME

Working with a cameraman over a period of weeks or months is like having a love affair. You have to like him, to begin with. Then you have to woo him to keep him from running off with some other reporter. Slowly, you come to trust him, admire him and learn from him. You help him out whenever you can, try to cheer him up when he's down. After a while, you notice he's doing the same for you. The two of you find you both want to keep this good thing going.

After Jim Wilson left, I worked with a number of good cameramen, but none who were crazy about the idea of spending months at a time covering blacksmiths, loggers, Mail Pouch tobacco sign painters, sand castle builders, tombstone carvers, barbed wire collectors, backwoods hermits and muleback mailmen.

Until Izzy came along.

Isadore Bleckman came out from Chicago to meet me in Colorado. He was a nervous, intense little guy with a big moustache and darting eyes. His manner said, okay, where's the story, I don't have all day, let's get on with it. When it was his turn to drive the bus, he drove it faster than anybody ever had before, putting the swaying Travco through its paces on the mountain roads as if it were a sports car.

"Hey, man, slow down a little!" I said.

Izzy grumbled, "It's not the *Queen Mary*, you know."

This guy was talking back to me, even telling me how to drive the bus. I figured this was going to be a one-story relationship.

The story was deep in the woods up the north fork of the Gunnison River. Somebody had written to me about a man who lived up there in the West Elk Mountains tending a remote power station. The wild birds knew him so well that they'd perch on his shoulder and the skittish white-tailed deer would come out of the forest to take food from his hand.

It was all true. George Norris and his wife, Ann, had been feeding the deer for many winters. "C'mon, Cutter," he'd say, "C'mon, old Cakeeater. You better come runnin', Soap, or all the food will be gone!" And the wild deer would leap the picket fence into his yard, as docile as house pets in the presence of this one man they trusted. A great antlered buck stood nose to nose with Mr. Norris and took an oatcake from his mouth.

"I was deprived of the city life and schools," Mr. Norris said. "I just got what you might call an Indian's education. But even when I was a boy, I never liked hunting deer. Now, I wouldn't think of it. I wouldn't know where to hunt, because for thirty-five miles around here, all the deer are my friends. I'll never fire a rifle again."

I saw Izzy's eyes growing wider. The big-city boy

had never had a day like this before. I figured these were probably the first deer he had ever seen close up. He shot the story from every angle, even climbing a tree to look down on the scene from above. Afterward, he couldn't resist trying to feed the deer himself, to see if they'd take morsels from a stranger. They would, as long as the stranger was in this particular backyard. Izzy was enchanted, by the remote place, by the deer, by George Norris's reverence for life.

The Norrises gave us dinner that night. Izzy enthused over the pictures he had made. I got the impression he had just shot the first story he had ever really enjoyed.

"By the way," he said, "this steak is terrific! Where do you get it?"

There was an awkward pause.

"It's venison," Mr. Norris said.

Izzy stopped chewing.

"Oh, not what you're thinking!" Mrs. Norris said. "Our son brought it to us from Wyoming."

Izzy had a little trouble finishing his meal, but afterward, on the long drive through the mountains back to our motel, all he could talk about was his first experience with deer, on the hoof and on the plate. "Where do we go next?" he asked.

We didn't know it that night, but where we were going next was to every part of every state, over and over again, for twenty years.

Izzy relaxed into the rhythms of the road, stopped looking at his watch and started driving a little slower. But he never lost his enthusiasm for new places and

new experiences. He saw the road—he still does—
through fresh eyes. He saw children swinging on a
rope tied to a tree limb and said to me, "Boy, that's
nice, isn't it? If you could think of something to say
about it, I could sure make some pretty pictures."
And the next thing the Cronkite news got from us
was a pretty story just about children swinging on a
rope.

We went to the fiddlers convention in Galax, Virginia, and Izzy, whose tastes ran more to Yehudi
Menuhin, was charmed by a great country fiddler
named Clark Kessinger. We still play Clark Kessinger
fiddle tunes on the bus as we roll along, ballads and
breakdowns we recorded in Galax on a hot day in
August 1970. Izzy tasted his first oyster aboard the
oyster-dredging skipjacks of Chesapeake Bay, and
traveled with his first carnival out of Cape Girardeau,
Missouri, (with Sunflower the Naked Lady, and
Johnny the Geek, "60 Attractions 60," "Ladies In a
Family Way Are Not Invited!") and rode his first
steam train, the Sidewinder, hauling lumber and
mixed cargo up into the hills out of Robbinsville,
North Carolina. The last thing you need on a voyage
of discovery is a jaded, worldly-wise traveling companion. Izzy was the opposite, a dazzled Odysseus,
giddy with the wonders of the world and equal to all
its perils.

I was very impressed when he climbed that tree at
the Norrises'. That was nothing. Pictures other cameramen give up on, Izzy finds a way to make. In the
course of our time together, I have watched him make
pictures while hanging from a crane, riding a Ferris

wheel, standing on the back of a circus elephant, floating on an inner tube, drifting in a hot-air balloon.

Off Maine, under way in a stiff breeze aboard *Victory Chimes*, last of the three-masted schooners, Izzy had himself hoisted to the top of the mast in a bos'n's chair; the crew on the heeling deck looked like scrambling termites from up there.

Izzy has put on roller skates to get just the dollying shot he wanted. He has shot from trains, planes, combines, tractors, racing cars, dune buggies, motorcycles, snowmobiles and countless helicopters. He has dived under the sea with an Aqua-Lung and climbed to the tip-top of the Golden Gate Bridge without a safety harness. He has shot from a one-horse open sleigh, a sailboard, a glider, a dugout canoe.

When we went out with a Coast Guard patrol boat into a wild sea off the Oregon coast, a crew member said, "The boat's designed to roll 360 degrees. Keep your lifeline hooked and watch the Chief. If the Chief keeps his cigar in his mouth, don't worry. If he spits out his cigar, take a deep breath, because we're about to roll."

Izzy said to me, "God, I hope we roll! What a picture!"

To ease his disappointment when we didn't, I said, "Do you realize if we'd gone under out there, we would have ruined a $50,000 camera?"

Izzy said, "Yeah, there is that."

On a story about a family of steeplejacks (a son swings into the picture at the top of the steeple and says, "Got a hammer, Ma?") naturally Izzy had to dangle out there with them. I stayed on the ground, afraid to look up.

When we did a story about a beer wagon drawn by forty horses, nothing would do but that Izzy ride backward on one of the lead horses so as to aim back at the driver; if he had fallen off, thirty-nine Belgian horses would have run over him.

When we did a story about an elderly farmer who flew kites for the amusement of children, Izzy wanted a shot from the *kite's* point of view; we hired a fifty-foot cherry picker to put him up in the sky with the kite in the foreground, the camera looking down the kite string to the farmer and the children far below. It was one of the loveliest pictures I've ever seen.

While working, Izzy is an acrobat. While waiting to work, he's a worried optimist. When rain interrupts a story, Izzy frets about the lost time, but always looks up into the downpour and says, "The sun's gonna come out. Just give it a minute or two." When we drove the bus off a desert road in Utah and got stuck in the sand, Izzy said, "The next guy to come along is going to be a Mormon farmer in a pickup truck. He's going to hook a chain to us and pull us out." That's just the way it happened. Izzy has kept my spirits up for twenty years.

We took on Charlie Quinlan, a former Chicago stagehand, as our electrician and traveling companion. Charlie didn't know a lot about motion picture lighting, but he was willing to work hard at stringing cables and hanging the lights where Izzy wanted them. Charlie diverted us with tales of the South Pacific, where he had spent World War II on a destroyer,

USS *Phelps*. The *Phelps* took part in all the great naval battles against the Japanese. Charlie didn't set foot on land for three years, until the *Phelps* limped home to Pearl Harbor. As the small, crippled ship was passing Battleship Row, all hands were piped on deck. Charlie, head of the "black gang" in the engine room, came blinking up into the sunlight to hear a band playing on shore. The crews of all the battleships, in dress whites, stood at present arms along the rails.

"What's this for?" Charlie asked a buddy.

The buddy was weeping.

"It's for us," he said.

Charlie told us a hundred stories about his beloved ship and took time off every summer to attend a reunion of the crew. I asked what happened to the *Phelps* after the war.

Charlie said, "They sold it to Gillette and turned it into razor blades."

But most of Charlie's yarns were not poignant; most of them were funny. And he kept us amused with puns and spoonerisms (a crushing blow became a "blushing crow" in Quinlan-speak) and misunderstandings based on his slight hardness of hearing.

"Why are they always having steak dinners at the White House?"

"They're *state* dinners, Charlie."

He was a shade disorganized. Driving the bus in Amarillo one morning, Charlie cut across four lanes of traffic to make a left turn from the right lane—with a police car right behind him. The police car stopped us, of course. Two hefty cops wearing neat uniforms came aboard and asked the first thing cops always ask in such circumstances: "May I see your driver's license, sir?"

"Sure," Charlie said. "It's in my billfold."

The policemen waited.

"And my billfold is in the back there, in my suitcase."

Charlie climbed out of the driver's seat, went back and started moving boxes of lights and camera gear. Finally, he came to his suitcase, a huge leather number with straps, almost big enough to qualify as a trunk. He opened it on the floor and delved through piles of dirty clothes with the two Amarillo policemen as bemused spectators. Charlie saved the cost of doing laundry on the road by taking all his laundry home with him.

"Gotta be here," Charlie muttered.

"Charlie," I said, "if you don't mind telling me, what is your billfold doing in your suitcase?"

"Always hide it there," Charlie said. "Don't want to get it stolen."

Long minutes passed, with Charlie still unpacking his bag furiously right there in downtown Amarillo, flinging dirty socks and underwear everywhere. Even the cops could barely suppress their laughter.

After a while, one of them said, "Tell you what, sir. We'll just take your word there's a billfold in there somewhere. Next time, will you just get into the left lane to make a left turn?"

"Sure thing," Charlie said. He started piling his laundry back into the suitcase. While he did, I thanked the cops. They got into their car and drove away.

"Okay, Charlie," I said, "where's your driver's license?"

"It's in my billfold," Charlie said, climbing back into the driver's seat.

Charlie probably saved our lives with an alert job of high-speed driving one midnight on a lonely stretch of road in Nevada. The rest of us were napping when the bus suddenly lurched left, veered right, bumped along the shoulder and careered back onto the highway.

I woke up and hollered, "What the hell was *that?*"

Charlie said, "I don't know. A lot of critters on the road."

We backed up to find that Charlie had somehow steered right through a big herd of wild burros clustered on the highway for warmth—without grazing even one of them.

Charlie was a quick thinker in times of trouble. In southern Illinois, we came upon a car that had just turned over in a ditch. Its wheels were still turning in the air and a little fire had started under the crushed hood. Other cars had stopped. Their drivers were standing around trying to figure out what to do. Charlie dashed out of the bus without a word, ran down the embankment and pulled two people out of the wreck before the fire could spread. Then he grabbed our fire extinguisher and put out the blaze.

"Fire control," he said later. "First thing you learn."

In the Navy, he meant.

Charlie helped perform another rescue on Interstate 80 in a Wyoming snowstorm. We had stopped on the shoulder to film the blowing snow and record the sound of the wind. A battered car with a broken windshield came out of the storm, slowed and stopped beside us. The face of the young woman behind the wheel was covered with blood. She said her car had been hit from behind by a speeding truck, then spun around and hit by another truck. When we opened the door to try to help her, her terrified pet Airedale leapt out and ran away into a snowy field.

"My dog, my dog!" she cried, and started after him.

Charlie took over. He grabbed her. "We'll take care of you," he said. "He"—pointing to me—"will take care of your dog."

She stood there bleeding and crying in the snow. Charlie picked her up and laid her on the floor of the bus. He cleaned her face with moist towels and held her hand while Izzy took the wheel and sped down the mountain toward the Laramie hospital. I walked around in the snow chasing the dog until I was able to calm him a little and coax him back into the wrecked car. On the way down the mountain, I met a lot of ambulances coming up with their lights flashing and their sirens wailing. The accident, we read in the papers the next day, was a seventeen-car pileup.

I made it into Laramie and found a boarding kennel for the dog. By the time I got to the hospital, they were just wheeling the young woman into an operating room. Months later, she sent a smiling picture of herself after reconstructive surgery on her face. "Just wanted you to know what I really look like," she said. She looked very pretty. In her note, she thanked us all.

But it was Charlie she addressed it to.

Soundmen came and went. We had a nervous husband who had to call home a couple times a day and soon left us because our long trips were breaking up his marriage. We had an affable Black Muslim who was lured away by one of the CBS bureaus. A moody young man with a guitar didn't pan out because he gave more attention to his music than to his work.

Izzy said, "We need a permanent soundman. Who's the best soundman in the business?"

I said, "Larry Gianneschi."

"Right," Izzy said. "Let's call Larry Gianneschi."

"Be serious," I said. For a lark, Larry Gianneschi had dropped in on "On The Road" in the early Jim Wilson days, but he was a soundman of great reputation who had worked with Murrow, was now working all over the world on important documentaries for *CBS Reports*, and was in the kind of demand that almost permitted him to choose his own assignments. It would take a lot of nerve to ask him to bring his big talent to a little project like ours.

"All it can cost us is the price of the phone call," Izzy said.

Larry Gianneschi said, "You guys are the only ones in television having any fun. When do I start?"

That was sometime in 1972. Larry has recorded the sound for nearly every "On The Road" story since.

You have to distinguish among Larry Gianneschis. Our Larry was born to the business. His father, Larry, was an old newsreel man. Our Larry's son Larry was getting started in television, as were his other sons, who must have grown up disappointed that they had to be named something else.

Larry is a man of sociable inclination, sensitive, polite and compatible. He did much more for us than aim a microphone. He thought up story ideas, helped out with the lighting, worked with Izzy on camera repairs and bus repairs and immediately stepped in to do a service for me.

The toughest moment of every story comes right at the beginning. You drive up into the yard of an old Iowa farmer who, sick and tired of farming, is building a yacht in his barnyard so he and his wife can see the world. Naturally, knowing what you're there for, the farmer takes you out back to see the yacht and starts telling you all about it. That's just what you *don't* want. Izzy is still fiddling with the camera and looking for angles. We're not quite ready yet. I have learned that we have to have the camera rolling the *first* time the farmer tells me about his unlikely project; the second time, he won't tell it as well. This is where Larry comes in. He engages the farmer in unrelated small talk. Have you had any rain this summer? How's the corn crop looking? This permits me to busy myself in the bus for the few minutes it takes Izzy to get all set up, then emerge for a spontaneous talk with our farmer. Larry and I never discussed this. It was just a job that he saw needed doing. He was a lot more than a soundman, right from the start.

Larry follows his own routine on the road. He rises earlier than everybody else, has himself a proper breakfast in the motel coffee shop while he peruses the morning paper (the rest of us usually settle for toast and coffee aboard the bus once we're under way) and prepares calmly for the day. Since Izzy is always the first each morning to take his turn at driving, and I'm up front with a map, navigating, Larry usually brews the coffee—he keeps the coffeepot going all day—and then wanders to his worktable at the back of the bus to work the crossword puzzle in peace and do a little maintenance on his sound equipment. We're so used to this that once we left a gas station in Carlsbad, New Mexico, and drove thirty miles before anybody noticed that Larry wasn't aboard. He said, ''I figured you'd come back for me when you needed another pot of coffee.''

Through most of the seventies, before I had to start finding an airport every weekend to fly back to New York for the *Sunday Morning* program, and before we switched over from film to videotape and lost Charlie Quinlan to new union rules that said we no longer needed a lighting man, "On The Road" was Izzy and Larry and Charlie and me. We covered hundreds of thousands of miles through all the states before 1976, and in that one year we revisited every state to report a moment of history from each one, our "On The Road" contribution to the Bicentennial.

We did stories about wrestlers and jugglers and

mountain climbers, traffic cops, tattoo artists, gandy dancers, sheep shearers, bagel bakers, horseshoe players, rodeo riders, sorghum makers and seashell collectors. We ran to keep up with a 104-year-old jogger in California. We spent a day with a weight guesser at the Arizona State Fair. We met a man in Death Valley who lived in a house built out of beer bottles. We cruised Denver with a trumpet-playing taxi driver; I mean he drove with one hand and played the horn with the other. We passed the time of day in a one-parking-meter town, Lookingglass, Oregon; they were thinking about getting a streetlight next.

We did stories about ferryboats and fire trucks and pawnshops and driftwood and lightning and fog. We met a Texas horse trader, a Kansas mule dealer, a Florida pig auctioneer and an old wildcatter trying to coax oil out of a dry hole in Oklahoma. In Darwin, Minnesota, we spent a day with the owner of the world's largest ball of string. He kept adding to it while we talked. That's the trouble with owning the world's largest ball of string; you live in constant fear that somebody, somewhere, is making a larger ball of string.

At the end of 1977, I got sick and had to spend a couple of weeks in the hospital. Roger Mudd came to see me. He kidded me about "On The Road." "Give it up while there's still time!" he said. "You're a reporter and there are important things going on in the world! It's time you came in from the cornfields!"

I just laughed. Roger covered Congress, the Watergate hearings, all sorts of history-making events. I covered musical saw players, church suppers and greased pig contests. I wouldn't have traded jobs with him for anything. Nobody in journalism had better jobs than Izzy and Larry and Charlie and me.

14

CELEBRITY

In the early days, before "On The Road" became a familiar part of the *Evening News*, nobody knew who we were. People would see us shooting film by the roadside and ask what was going on. Once, thinking we might somehow make a story of some farm kids flying kites in a field, we stopped and went to work, chasing those little boys and girls all over the place, Izzy lying on his back for a low angle, then jumping up and running after a kid and a kite; Larry running after him with his sound amplifier bouncing on his chest, the two of them connected by wires; Charlie Quinlan trotting along with a big silver reflector; I scribbling in a notebook. What rural parent, glancing through the kitchen window, could be prepared for such a sight? A mother finally came out of the house across the road to inquire just exactly what we thought we were doing.

"Madam," I said, "you're not going to believe this, but we are preparing a story for the *CBS Evening News* with Walter Cronkite."

Of course, she *didn't* believe it at first and tried to run us off. Izzy says in those days I started every new conversation, "Madam, you're not going to believe this . . ."

Gradually, we became better known. People commenced smiling and waving at the "On The Road" bus. This had a heady effect on us. In the first place, as veterans of stories like civil rights demonstrations, we were accustomed to being unwelcome wherever we went. I had covered the Freedom Rides in Mississippi and Alabama and found that everybody, the Freedom Riders, the Klansmen, the cops and the local population, suspected or despised the press; Izzy, Larry and Charlie had lately been dodging brickbats during protest marches in Chicago. "On The Road" was different. Patrons of small-town taverns would hail us as celebrities come to town and buy us rounds of beers. The editors of country weeklies would feature the news of our passing on page one, with photographs of us posed beside the bus. People would ask for autographs, "for the kids," they'd say. I signed bits of paper and restaurant menus and dollar bills. Once, a man asked me to sign the back of his T-shirt. Once, a man asked me to sign the blade of his chain saw. The peaceful stories of "On The Road" were making us popular; even, we fancied, making us loved!

Local boosters made us welcome everywhere. "Gee," I said to Izzy one day in Oklahoma, "a couple of months ago they made me a Kentucky Colonel, last month they made me an Arkansas Traveler, and this month I was inducted into the Kiowa tribe."

Izzy assumed the solemn expression of the rabbi at his Chicago synagogue. "My good man," he said to me sardonically, "you are slowly working your way up to Jew."

Occasionally, it got ridiculous. A producer and camera crew from the Public Broadcasting network traveled with us for a few days to make a documentary about "On The Road." As we shot a story in Leland, Michigan, about the morning coffee klatch in the firehouse, the PBS crew tagged along. The Traverse City television station heard we were nearby, and a cameraman-reporter showed up to shoot a story about us. "Hey," said the PBS producer, "a local station shooting a story! That's part of our story!" So, while we shot our story, the Traverse City newsman shot us shooting our story, and the PBS crew shot a story about him shooting us shooting our story. I felt I was a character in some sort of Kafka nightmare. The morning coffee drinkers probably were glad to see us all leave town.

In time, people stopped being surprised when we showed up in their small towns. It came to seem almost as if they were expecting us.

We went to Sopchoppy, in the Florida panhandle, to look into a story about worm grunting. Worm grunting is not practiced just everywhere. Maybe I'd better explain it:

You go out into the woods and pound a hardwood stake into the ground, preferably using a heavy truck spring to do the pounding. Then, you rub the truck spring sensually, but with a certain pressure, across the top of the stake. This sets up a vibration in the ground which you can feel in the soles of your feet. Earthworms must find the vibration disagreeable, for to escape it, they wriggle to the surface; whereupon, you pick up the worms and go fishing.

I didn't believe this when I first heard about it, but it turns out that some people around Sopchoppy make a living at it, selling their worms by the canful to Mr. M. B. Hodges's bait store. It will not surprise you to learn that if you go worm grunting in the National Forest, you have to have a federal Worm Gathering Permit displayed in the window of your pickup truck.

We parked the bus outside Mr. Hodges's store to inquire where we could find some worm grunting going on. An old man was sitting on a bench outside the store whittling—not carving anything, just making a pile of shavings the way old men do outside stores in the south. As I walked by, he looked up at me and said, in a soft, confidential drawl:

"I knew you guys would show up here sooner or later."

It was as if he had been sitting there waiting for us.

We were careful not to display our wondrous new importance to those we met, but the truth is we were beginning to feel like big shots. Therefore, it was good for us that a few days later, down the road in Fort Myers, we stopped the bus on a residential street to consult the map, and a woman came out of her house smiling.

I smiled, and she smiled, and I opened the door to accept the usual congratulations for our stories about America, or perhaps to sign another autograph.

She said, "I think I'd like a couple of loaves of rye today, please."

She thought we were the bread truck.

In the course of the years, we have also been mistaken for the library book van, and several times for the Red Cross Bloodmobile. (Izzy says the next time we are mistaken for the Bloodmobile, he is going to say,"Just step to the rear of the bus and remove your garments, ma'am. The doctor will be with you in a moment.")

Such incidents have made us wear our fame a little more lightly. In one of the after-work seminars Ed Murrow used to conduct in Colbee's bar on 52nd Street back in New York, he said, "Just remember that even though you have a loud voice, even though your voice may reach 16 million people every time you speak, that doesn't make you any *smarter* than you were when your voice only reached the end of this bar." Those who work in the celebrity-making craft of television news ought to remember Murrow's dictum. Overweening pride is an occupational hazard.

Of course, sometimes there is an advantage to being recognized. The Police Chief of Nebraska City, Nebraska, paid us a visit as we were parking the bus on the main street to film the Arbor Day parade.

The Chief: "You shouldn't park here, you'll get in the way of the parade."

I: "Well, we sure do need to, Chief."

The Chief: "Say, you're that 'On The Road' feller, aren't you? Well, hell, all right then, go ahead."

But in general, we try to slip into town quietly, do our work unobtrusively and make our getaway before the Rotary Club invites us to lunch or the mayor shows up with the key to the city. And we try to make sure the story we are working on ends up being about the subject of the story and never about ourselves.

With respect to my own appearances on camera, we have adopted the Tricycle Principle. We were somewhere in the midwest, watching the local news on the television set in the bus before going out to supper. There was a feature about a children's tricycle race, cute little toddlers pedaling away and bumping into one another, an appealing story pretty well filmed and edited.

Izzy said, "You know what? Before this is over, the reporter is going to ride a tricycle."

"Oh, no!" I said. "That would ruin the whole thing."

Sure enough, the reporter signed off in close-up with a silly grin, the camera pulled back to show that he was perched on a tricycle, and he turned and pedaled clumsily away, making inane what had, until then, been charming. The anchor couple came on laughing to sign off the show.

The Tricycle Principle is simple: "When doing a tricycle story, don't ride a tricycle." The story is about children, dummy, not about you. Keep yourself out of it. Try to control your immodesty.

Even when some guy in a bar is buying you a beer.

Even when a smiling stranger comes up to you with a grease pen wanting you to autograph his chain saw.

15

LUCK

You'll think this is a whopper, and I wouldn't believe it either if I hadn't been there. Tom Cosgrove will tell you it's the honest truth.

We were deep in the Okefenokee Swamp in an outboard motorboat run by an old man who was born and brought up on the fringes of the swamp and knew everything about it. We had left early in the morning, thinking we'd make pictures in the swamp for an hour or two, but we kept seeing more alligators, more herons and egrets and ibises, more flowering water plants and thickets of cedar each more beautiful and mysterious than the one before. In midafternoon, we were still out there filming. Every time I figured we had enough for one day, Izzy noticed some new wonder. On and on into the swamp we went.

It was hot, boiling hot, and muggy in the way that only certain places on the continent ever become, the south Georgia swamp being one of them. We were all sweaty and tired, and above all, we were thirsty. The black swamp water looked too murky to drink. Anyway, it wasn't water Cosgrove was thinking of that afternoon.

Tom Cosgrove, who was our soundman on this

swing through the south, was devoted to the healing qualities of beer. Any beer would do on a hot day, but his beverage of choice was Budweiser. Long summer rides in the bus when Cosgrove was along were punctuated by the staccato sound of pop-tops popping back where he sat, and usually there were a few empty Budweiser cans in the bus's trash bin at night when we got where we were going.

That steamy day in the Okefenokee, the rest of us could have used a beer, too, or anything at all to quench our terrible thirst, but it was Cosgrove who said finally, to nobody in particular, to all of us, to the great sweltering swamp itself:

"What I would give for a Budweiser right now!"

Not one minute later, in the middle of that watery wilderness, we noticed sunlight glinting from something bobbing in the water directly ahead of the boat. We slowed down beside whatever it was. Cosgrove leaned over the side, reached into the water and lifted out a six-pack of Budweiser beer.

The rest of us just looked at one another. Cosgrove set the dripping six-pack on the seat beside him and extracted a can from one of the plastic rings. He popped the top. He took several long, slow swallows and regarded the can thoughtfully.

He said, "Could be a little colder."

The old man who was running the boat thought the beer must have fallen out of somebody else's boat days or weeks before. Cosgrove gave as his own opinion that, considering the brand and all, it was a gift from the great spirit of the swamp to him alone, though he did bestow one can upon each of the rest of us. All I know is that every traveler needs a care-free and optimistic spirit, curiosity about his sur-roundings, powers of keen observation—and a little bit of dumb luck.

There was the time we were shooting a story com-memorating General Washington's arduous crossing of the Delaware in the winter of '76. We went down to the riverbank at the place where he had started the crossing and found some old boats tied up, boats not much different from the ones the General had used to get his ragtag army over to Trenton—just the picture we were hoping to find. But the day was bright, not wintry-looking enough. Izzy said, ''I wish to hell it would start to snow.'' We looked up at the sky. A cloud passed over the sun. It started to snow. The snow covered the boats; Izzy made his pictures, evoc-ative of the Continental army's hardships in the snow; I made my little speech to the camera with big snow-flakes falling all around me. Just as we finished shooting, the cloud passed by, the sun came out, it stopped snowing and didn't snow again for a week.

We have found, in the words of the golfer's epi-gram, that it's better to be lucky than good.

Once, looking for stories on the back roads of Ohio, we were suffering a week-long dry spell. A colorful beekeeper we'd been told about was away from home when we called on him, visiting a niece in Colorado or someplace. A promising old-time candy store had been sold and turned into a pizza joint. A venerable amusement park where we thought we might find a story had shut down for the season. We began to get a little discouraged.

We passed a farmhouse with a homemade banner stretched between two oak trees in the front yard. The banner said in huge letters: "WELCOME HOME, ROGER!" We drove on for a mile or two. Somebody said, "Wonder who Roger is?"

We turned around, went back there and knocked on the door.

Roger was a soldier on his way home from the Vietnam War. His family knew he was coming, but wasn't sure what day he was going to arrive. Roger's mother was in the kitchen baking his favorite chocolate cake. Really—she was. His wife was there with a baby son Roger hadn't seen. We asked if they'd mind if we brought the camera into the house. Roger's mother said it would be all right if we'd give her a minute to fix her hair. I am sure we weren't there more than an hour, talking to those people who were all excited about Roger coming home. We never did see Roger, of course.

At my desk in the bus as we rolled on that afternoon, I wrote a simple story letting Roger represent all the GIs coming home to their families from Vietnam. We found an airport and shipped the film to New York, and Walter Cronkite put the story on the *Evening News* the next night.

Rarely has any of our stories caused such a reaction from viewers. It was just an account of waiting for Roger, that's all, but it resonated in the country. The CBS switchboard lighted up that night with dozens of calls from people moved by it in some way, and hundreds of letters came in, some of them asking that the story be repeated. There was so much interest nation-

wide that Cronkite felt compelled to report on the air
a few nights later, "Oh, and by the way—Roger got
home!"

That hour with Roger's family made it a good trip
to Ohio, after all. I had done a fair amount of careful
planning in preparation for the week's work, but careful planning got us nowhere. Then along came a banner stretched across a farmhouse yard.

Back at the office, people asked, "How do you *find*
these stories?"

"Well," I said, "you do have to work at it."

All you really have to do is look out the window.

We stopped off in Douglas, Wyoming, to inquire
into the jackalope phenomenon. I guess you know
about the jackalope, the rare creature of the western
plains. It seems to be a cross between the jackrabbit
and the antelope. From its rabbit head sprout antelope
horns. Jackalopes breed, it is said, only during flashes
of lightning, so there aren't many of them. Cowboys
singing songs around campfires at night report hearing jackalopes joining in from the surrounding darkness, in high tenor voices that are described as
"unusual, but not unpleasing." They are timid animals unless cornered, when they have been known to
attack. A jackalope in full charge, old-timers attest,
can only be stopped with a buffalo gun.

Some people think jackalopes are creations of taxi-
dermists with time on their hands. They say the same
thing about the famous fur-bearing winter trout of
Montana. All I know is that there are plenty of Wyoming bars with mounted jackalopes looking down
inscrutably from the walls, and that in Douglas, where

history records the first sighting, they have a jackalope statue right there on Center Street.

We hung around Douglas for the first couple of
days of July 1978, and then, having absorbed as much
jackalope lore as we could stand, decided to go on to
Cheyenne to see what was doing there on Independence Day. The way to go from Douglas to Cheyenne
is straight south on Interstate 25. It's a two-hour drive
at the speed limit. But we remembered that stretch of
interstate as a shade tedious, so we took off instead
on a dirt road that goes about eighty miles over the
hills to Medicine Bow. It was a road we'd never been
on before. We planned to pick up old U.S. 30 at
Medicine Bow and still make it to Cheyenne in plenty
of time for supper.

But we never made it to Cheyenne at all. Not that
trip. A few miles out of Douglas, we started noticing
the wildflowers. There were patches of daisies and
wild geraniums, stands of mountain columbine at the
bottoms of the hills and vast fields of Indian paint-
brush on the slopes. The farther we went along that
road, the more spectacular the wildflower show became. There were thousands of flowers, millions of
them. They grew to the horizon in every direction, a
patchwork of brilliant white and blue and purple, yellow, orange and flaming red. We kept stopping the
bus to get out and look at them.

After a while, Izzy said, "Do you suppose we
ought to make some pictures?"

I said, "Sure. Do you have any film in your
Leica?"

He said, "I mean television pictures."

Sometimes I am a little slow.

We went to work. Every time we saw a different variety, we stopped for Izzy to make wide shots and close-ups. There wasn't much sound for Larry to record except the whisper of the wind and the buzz of an occasional bee, so he scouted ahead for species of flowers we hadn't seen before. The trouble was he kept finding them far from the road. "Oh, man," he'd holler from some hilltop, "come look at this one!" and Izzy and I would trudge up there with the gear. Charlie Quinlan, following us with the bus, would shout from the road, "There's a whole bunch of iris-looking things down here by the creek!" and down the hill we'd plod. I suppose we walked fifteen or twenty miles of the eighty miles to Medicine Bow that day in quest of little bits of beauty.

When the sun went down, we had two or three hours of vivid wildflower pictures on tape, dozens of memories in our heads of the wild splendor we had seen—and one big problem: how to describe it in words. I didn't even know the names of most of the flowers. I was painfully aware that the big-city cynics on the *Evening News* would be skeptical right away when a shipment came in labeled "Wyoming Wildflowers." I couldn't accompany it with a script that said only, "My, look at all the flowers! Aren't they pretty?" We had lovely pictures, but we didn't have a story yet. I needed a little knowledge.

Knowledge, a wise old city editor once advised me, consists of knowing where to look it up. We had a wildflower book in the limited library aboard the bus, but not many of the flowers in there looked like the

flowers we had on tape. Anyway, I couldn't take
chances. I knew from experience that if I made a
mistake and called a primrose a phlox, thousands of
viewers, horticultural experts in numbers never before suspected, would materialize in the hinterlands
and write identical letters calling me a blockhead.
Where could I find, anywhere in the wilds of Wyoming,
a dependable authority to save me from indignity?

I looked at the map. Nothing up ahead but Medicine Bow, Rock River, Laramie . . .

Laramie! Laramie was the seat of the University
of Wyoming, and universities have departments,
don't they? And one of the departments would be,
would it not, the Department of Botany? It was already after dark, and the next day was the Fourth of
July, when the university would be shut down, but
we drove on to Laramie and I went to bed that night
happy in the certain knowledge that somewhere in
the same city a Wyoming wildflower expert had to
be sleeping.

His name turned out to be Dennis Knight. He was
in his side yard cooking Fourth of July hamburgers
for the neighbors by the time I tracked him down. Up
his driveway into this tranquil holiday tableau rolled
the "On The Road" bus full of demanding strangers
interrupting everything.

"See, we have pictures of all these flowers," I said,
"and we don't know what they are. Could you look
at the tape and identify them for us?"

"When?" he said.

"Well—now," I said.

Dr. Dennis Knight, chairman of the Department of Botany at the University of Wyoming, who thought he was having a day off with his family, sighed a professorial sigh.

"Sure," he said. "Have a beer."

He spent most of the rest of that afternoon aboard the bus with us while his cookout went on without him.

I froze a frame on the monitor. "Daisy?" I guessed.

"Balsamroot," he said. "The bighorn sheep eat them in the spring."

"This one looks a little like a violet," I said.

"Blue flax," he said. "*Linum lewisii*. Named for Captain Meriwether Lewis. He found it out here and carried a specimen back to President Jefferson. The Indians used the stems to make fishing lines."

Dennis Knight's knowledge of those flowers was exhaustive, encyclopedic. If I had searched the world over, I could not have found anyone half so edifying on the subject. I couldn't type fast enough to record all the interesting things he knew.

"Sulphur flower," he said. "It's in the buckwheat family. Here, what do you think this one is?"

"Looks like a buttercup," I said.

"Bingo!" he said. "You got one!"

From time to time, Dr. Knight's kids, Charley and Christy, appeared at the door of the bus wondering when they could have their daddy back. But he was just warming up.

"Stonecrop. It's a *sedum*. Tough little thing. You

think it's dead and gone, then it rains and there it is again.''

I went back to the motel that night and wrote a beautiful, informed script about the wildflowers, full of nuance and understanding. There weren't any mistakes in it. The *Evening News* loved it. People who saw the story probably still think of me as some kind of naturalist. I am not, but I met a man who certainly is. He let me steal his Fourth of July and pick his brain of half a lifetime's knowledge all in one afternoon and never even murmured a complaint. I think he sort of enjoyed it.

What on earth led us to take the back road out of Douglas? What delivered Dennis Knight into our hands just when we had to find him?

I'd say the Almighty, if I didn't believe He has better things to do with His time than provide a wandering camera crew with fields of wildflowers and scholars on demand.

What it was was dumb luck.

16

DOWN BY THE
RIVERSIDE

I started out thinking of America as highways and state lines. As I got to know it better, I began to think of it as rivers. Most of what I love about the country is a gift of the rivers: birchbark canoes and cottonwood pirogues, steamboats and trading scows; Huckleberry Finn, Mike Fink and Evangeline; blue herons and bald eagles and snowy egrets; the Grand Canyon and the Hudson palisades; Warren LeRuth's fancy restaurant in Gretna, Louisiana, where people come to dine wearing their cuff links and pearls, and the Silver Dollar Cafe in Ennis, Montana, where the customers eat without taking off their cowboy hats; the walnut-brown brick houses of the rich old merchants up on the bluffs, the tar paper shacks of the fishermen down on the flats; the sound of whistles, bells and foghorns in the night; jazz and crawfish and ferryboats and covered bridges. None of them would be there, in the country or in our memories, without the rivers.

I was born not far from the New River and brought up not far from the Catawba ("And we have heard the sorrowful silence of the river in October," Thomas Wolfe wrote. "Flow on, Catawba, to the

sea.''). I learned early that the towns with character
there in North Carolina were the river towns—Elizabeth
City on the Pasquotank, Edenton on the Chowan,
New Bern on the Neuse.

The next river towns I came to know were also in
my native region. Proud old Charleston, South Carolina, (so they say in Charleston) is ''where the Ashley
and the Cooper rivers join to form the Atlantic
Ocean.'' And if there is a finer place than Charleston
in the spring, when azaleas bloom in every garden
behind every wrought-iron gate on every winding
street, I don't know it.

Unless, of course, it is Savannah (on the Savannah)
in the spring, when the yellow forsythia gives way to
the blue wisteria, which gives way to the dogwood,
dazzling white. Then the citizens feel the urge to in-
hale April while strolling the cobblestones of the
riverfront, which is crowded with shops and ships,
now as ever; or to drive out to Desposito's across the
Thunderbolt Bridge for a helping of hot, sweet, pink,
miraculous shrimp, ordered by the pound, boiled in
their shells, and served in a steaming pile.

Much of the fun and discovery of the country has
occurred for me alongside one river or another. One
day, the crew and I stopped to have our lunch on the
banks of the Buffalo in the Ozarks, the first stream
chosen by the country to be a national river. A man
in overalls came along and said, ''There's a woman
up the road here you boys ought to meet.'' That's how
we became acquainted with Violet Hensley, the whittling fiddler of Yellville, Arkansas. She sat on her
front porch playing ''Old Dan Tucker'' and ''Wild-

wood Flower'' for us on different fiddles she'd carved herself out of native maple, patting a bare foot in time with the music until the moon started to come up from down in the valley of the Buffalo.

It was the Colorado River that led us to Robert P. McCulloch. He was a millionaire with big ideas. No other river on earth has cut such a labyrinth of deep gorges as the Colorado and no river has inspired more big ideas—most of them bad ones, like damming up the Grand Canyon. The dam builders have already flooded so many of the Colorado's canyons that the mighty river is now safe for water-skiers but not much to marvel at anymore. Robert P. McCulloch's big idea was completely outrageous but comparatively benign. He started by building his own dream town beside one of the lakes that the lower Colorado has become. But after he had done it, and named the town Lake Havasu City, and filled it with streets and houses and golf courses and all, he still wasn't satisfied. The city still needed something, a kind of centerpiece. Robert P. McCulloch thought the London Bridge would be nice. So he went to London and bought it. He shipped it over from the River Thames, every stone of it, and put it up in the Arizona desert, and only then detoured the Colorado so the London Bridge would have a river to cross. More than a million people make a special trip every year to see if it's true that the London Bridge is now in Arizona. It's true. People drive across the London Bridge and look out at the desert and grin.

I owe the Apple River in Wisconsin for leading me to Jack and Alice Raleigh. At the river's edge, they ran a place called River's Edge. Their sons still run it, dealing in inner tubes and frog's legs. What you do is rent an inner tube and put it in the Apple River and lie down on it. Then you float contentedly for an hour or two through the woods and pastures, meditating on the scenery, until you reach the town of Somerset. There, the Raleighs pick you up and dry you off and drive you back to their restaurant and serve you frog's legs. They have the toughest inner tubes and the tenderest frog's legs in Wisconsin.

It wouldn't be much of a country without the rivers, and the people who have figured out a way to make a living beside them. Not that all the river towns are charming. Most of them, to tell the truth, are tumbledown and sad. At Arkansas City on the Mississippi, Mark Twain asked a steamboat passenger who belonged there what sort of place it was. " 'Well,' said he, after considering, and with the air of one who wishes to take time and be accurate, 'it's a hell of a place.' A description," Mark Twain wrote, "which was photographic for exactness."

But something draws us to the riverside and keeps us there through winter freezes and spring floods. It was so from the beginning. There would be no Bunker Hill, no Beacon Hill, no Back Bay, no Boston Red Sox, no Boston, if there were no Charles River. John Winthrop and the first Bostonians chose the Charles because it offered easy access and the possibility of a quick getaway. Virginians chose the James River for the same reasons.

Later on, when Lewis and Clark set out to find what, if anything, might lie between the Mississippi and the Pacific, they traveled by river, and the river they traveled by, the Missouri, took them a long way west, upstream all the way. When the river forked, they named all the forks and followed what looked like the main one. In this way, those great trout streams, the Jefferson, Madison and Gallatin, got their names in honor of the President, Secretary of State and Secretary of the Treasury. (President Jefferson remarked dryly, ''You went fairly far west before you found one to name for me.'') Then when the Jefferson River forked, they named the branches for the shining attributes of the President—Philosophy, Philanthropy and Wisdom. (But these names were too much for the rough trappers and prospectors who followed. Those three rivers now are called Beaverhead, Ruby and Big Hole, though the intention of Lewis and Clark to honor their fellow Virginian's sagacity is preserved in the names of two cowtowns on the Big Hole River— Wise River and Wisdom. I wonder how many people who pass through Wisdom, Montana, are aware that it is *Thomas Jefferson's* wisdom that is commemorated there.)

Finally, Lewis and Clark and their tired men trudged up a mountain to what they took to be the headwaters of the Missouri, a spot where a little spring bubbled out of the ground. This was the place, Captain Lewis wrote in his diary, ''in surch of which we have spent so many toilsome days and wristless nights.'' One of their privates, a man named Hugh McNeal, ''exultingly stood with a foot on each side of this little rivulet and thanked his God that he had lived to bestride the mighty and heretofore deemed endless Missouri.''

(If you don't mind sharp climbs on winding dirt roads, you can drive right to the same spot and step across the "Missouri" yourself. Izzy and Larry and Charlie and I did it, with Izzy driving and the rest of us pushing the bus around the steepest switchbacks. The little spring still bubbles there on the east side of the Lemhi Pass, just before you reach the Continental Divide and go plunging dangerously down into Idaho.)

Lewis and Clark thought the Salmon River might take them on to the Pacific, but they found that one too wild to ride. "The passage by canoe," Clark wrote, "is entirely impossible." It still is. The two captains had to look for a more placid passage, and found it in the Snake, which leads to the Columbia, which leads to the western sea. President Jefferson had told them he had a hunch the continent could be crossed by water, and they were able to come back and tell him he was pretty nearly right.

After Lewis and Clark returned to spread the word, Americans who were already moving west along the Ohio, the Cumberland and the Tennessee were emboldened to make the great leap "across the wide Missouri," following the North Platte, that shallow, muddy river "too thick to drink and too thin to plow." You can still see the wagon ruts of those who went west in countless places in Nebraska and Wyoming. When the North Platte gave out, they followed a little river called the Sweetwater. Climb to the top of Independence Rock in Wyoming and you'll find the names of the pioneers up there: "Milo J. Ayer, age 29." "Fox, Cincinnati." "Ryan, Indianapolis." From the rocky height where they carved their names, all you can see is parched desert to the west, with the blue Sweetwater winding through it and the tracks of the Oregon Trail along the riverside. That sight tells you all you need to know about the importance of rivers to the people who rolled west in covered wagons.

The destiny of America—that it would become one country from sea to shining sea—was finally settled one fine day in 1848, the day James W. Marshall discovered gold at John Sutter's sawmill, which stood on the American River, which flows into the Sacramento, which flows into San Francisco Bay.

And that is the complete history of the United States of America from Boston Harbor to the Golden Gate— all rivers, twenty of them.

And I've hardly mentioned the greatest of them all, the one which figures largest in the country's history, the one that has such a hold on our imagination and our topsoil. The Mississippi River carries the mud of thirty states and two provinces 2,000 miles south to the delta and deposits 500 million tons of it there every year. The business of the Mississippi, which it will accomplish in time, is methodically to transport all of Illinois to the Gulf of Mexico. I've paddled my own canoe on Minnesota's placid Pigeon River, ridden a jet boat up the Rogue in Oregon and an oil-drum raft down the Tanana in Alaska, but when I traveled on Old Man River, I went in style—on the stern-wheeler *Delta Queen*, with the big river gliding by and the sun bouncing back into my eyes from the brass trim on the pilothouse and the steam calliope hooting and wheezing a tune from the stern. Oh, that was fine! I understood how Mark Twain felt the day of *his* first steamboat ride:

"I packed my valise and took passage. . . . When we presently got underway and went poking down the broad river, I became a new being and the subject of my own admiration. I was a traveler! A word had never tasted so good in my mouth before."

Just to recite the names of the Mississippi River ports of call is to compose a poem of mid-America: St. Paul, Red Wing, Winona, Prairie du Chien, Dubuque, Clinton, Rock Island, Keokuk, Hannibal, St. Louis, Cairo, Memphis, Vicksburg, Natchez, Baton Rouge, New Orleans!

New Orleans received more from the river than any other city, and gives back more to the visitor than any other. I lie awake in my bed in Room 9 of the Maison de Ville on Toulouse Street in the French Quarter, the room where Audubon once labored at his canvases and Tennessee Williams once struggled with the words of a play. The door to the courtyard is ajar. I can hear the soft splash of the fountain outside the door, and beyond that the brassy staccato of a trumpet from a jazz joint on Bourbon Street, and beyond that the moan of a tugboat horn from away the other side of Jackson Square on the river. This is the town of the tragic Manon Lescaut and the noble Le Moyne and the pirate Lafitte and Kate Townsend, the madam whose establishment had bed hangings of lace and chamber pots of gold; the town of Buddy Bolden, the

horn player who drove himself mad with his own de-
moniacal cornet solos in the cribs of Storyville. (But
his genius survived among certain admiring young
members of his audience, young Bunk Johnson and
Joe Oliver, young Louis Armstrong.) This is the
town of L'Alouette, the suave fencing master, and
Marie Laveau, the Voodoo Queen, and of numberless
outrageous demagogues: Andy Jackson the populist-
general-savior of the city, Ben Butler the carpetbag-
ger, and the Kingfish, Huey Long. It is the town of
Rex, Lord of Misrule, and the Carnival Krewe of Co-
mus. And it is the town of a certain Mr. Moriarty,
who had his deceased wife buried in Metairie Cem-
etery in a monumental tomb with four great grieving
sculpted statues at the corners, representing, so it is
said in New Orleans, "Faith, Hope, Charity and Mrs.
Moriarty."

Once upon a time, as a young reporter from New
York, I sat at a back table of the Acme Oyster Bar
on Iberville Street through a long afternoon of oy-
sters and bourbon whisky in the company of Earl
Long, a rough-hewn, slightly demented man who
happened, at the time, to be Governor of the state,
and Blaze Starr, a kindly stripper who was his mistress. Governor Long patiently explained to me the
folkways, mores, history, culture and politics of New
Orleans. When I got up to leave, Miss Starr summa-
rized for me: "There ain't any place like it, honey."
And I have found that truly, there ain't. Every other
large American city reminds the visitor faintly of
someplace else—Seattle of San Francisco, Atlanta of

Kansas City, Chicago of New York. New Orleans refers only to itself.

If there were no Mississippi River, there would be no Galena, Illinois, with its steamboat Gothic mansions and its memories of Ulysses S. Grant, who went off to war from Galena as drillmaster of the local volunteers. There would be no Ste. Genevieve, Missouri, a French village lost in time beside the timeless river. There would be no Greenville, Mississippi, and therefore no Doe's Eat Place serving hot tamales and iced tea at tables in the kitchen, and this would be a loss to the world. The Mississippi River gives many satisfactions.

Oh, so do they all. As I sort through remembered pleasures, Madison, Indiana, comes to mind, old Madison on the Ohio, largest city of the state for a little while there, now content to be merely the most evocative, its Greek Revival houses aging gently in the sun; and Sistersville, West Virginia, where a sumptuous Victorian suite in the Wells Inn still sets you back about $35 and a rocking chair is waiting for you on the porch; and a few miles down the Ohio and across the river, Marietta, Ohio, named for Marie Antoinette in her lifetime, where you can take an eccentric corner room in the Lafayette Hotel and watch the river life go by.

Some of our greatest river cities turned away from their rivers for a while there, but now they're turning back. Pittsburgh has done so, with its inviting Point State Park right downtown on the rivers. St. Louis's Gateway Arch soars over a riverfront rebirth. Detroit has reclaimed a part of its riverside from the ram-

shackle warehouses and vacant lots and transformed
it into a stretch of graceful glass towers and plazas
and fountains fronting on the river. Even New York—
the greatest river city of them all, which has come to
ignore its greatest river—is talking about replacing the
broken-down piers along the majestic Hudson with
green parks and public walkways.

Every city lucky enough to be on a river ought to
take as its model San Antonio. Izzy and Larry and I
drove into San Antonio one time to have a bent axle
straightened, found that our rooms in a former con-
vent school now known as La Mansion Hotel came
with balconies overlooking the San Antonio River—
and stayed for a week. I have been back there often
to walk on the Paseo del Rio, the winding walk along
the river, past shops and sidewalk cafes, under the
shade trees and the arched footbridges. The San Antonio River was a forgotten storm drain until the thirties when the WPA went to work landscaping it and
building paths beside it. Now it is the most inviting
feature of the city. You can catch a water taxi to the
public library in San Antonio! Visitors take a table
beside the river, order a pitcher of sangría, and forget that this was the afternoon they were going to visit
the Alamo.

Highways are handy, ribbons of concrete, man-
made. But if you are in search of the authentic America, seek out the little river that runs under the bridge
at Concord. Pay your respects to the Suwannee, the
Shenandoah, the Appomattox. Walk in the grass beside the Little Bighorn and think about what happened there. Spend an afternoon waist-deep in the

Henrys Fork with a fly rod in your hand, in the fall when the trumpeter swans fly low over the river. Walk down to the banks of the Missouri, which used to change its course so often that farmers along it complained they never knew whether their crop was going to be corn or catfish.

America is a great story, and there is a river on every page of it.

17

MR. BLACK

George Black was a brickmaker. He turned out to be a pretty good diplomat for the State Department, too, but that part of the story comes later. George Black was a brickmaker, the craft he and his brother chose when their father died in 1889.

"We aren't going to get to go to school," his brother, fourteen, said to George, eleven. "We're going to have to work for a living. If we haul ourselves up and make men out of ourselves, even if we don't know A from B, we'll make somebody call us 'Mr. Black' someday."

Mr. Black quoted his brother with pride more than eighty years later. He was a tall, dignified old man. Everybody called him Mr. Black.

The little boys, George and his brother, setting out on their own in 1889, walked the forty miles from Randleman, North Carolina, to Winston-Salem. They apprenticed themselves to a brickmaker for a while, and after they learned the trade, they started their own business while they were still in their teens. Since well before the turn of the century, George Black had been making bricks the way I watched him do it one afternoon in his backyard.

He had a mule hitched to what he called a "mud mill." With his giant, practiced hands, Mr. Black scooped up the mud mixed by the paddles of the mill as the mule plodded in a circle, and packed the mud expertly into six-brick forms ready for the kiln.

"How many bricks do you figure you've made in your life?" I asked him.

"Oh, Lord," he said. "I don't know. I'd be most afraid to know." He handed a finished form to one of the neighborhood youngsters who were serving as stackers that day, and impatiently awaited another stack of empties.

"I made a million bricks in one year," he said. "Mr. R. J. Reynolds rode out here on a white horse. He always rode a white horse, you know. He asked me if I thought I could make a thousand thousand bricks. He said he had in mind to build a tobacco factory. I studied and said yes, I could. I did, too, and you can go downtown and see them if you want to. That building's still there. They're all my bricks. Yes sir."

I found myself filled with admiration for this man standing in a pit before me in mud up to his elbows. He had made a life of the basic elements, water and earth and fire. And he had made the building blocks of a city.

Mr. Black dressed up in his Sunday suit the next day and took me on a stroll about Winston-Salem.

"These bricks we're walking on," he said, as we passed through the restored village of Old Salem, "I made these only about forty years ago. They're holding up nice. Yeah."

He pointed with his cane. "I made the bricks for that building over there." It was a schoolhouse. "I made the bricks for the Old Home Church over there," he said. "I made the bricks for that brick wall yonder." Wherever we walked, he pointed out the work of his own hands.

When we reached the block-long R. J. Reynolds factory, he said, "I believe I told you wrong about this job. It wasn't a million bricks. It ended up being a million and a half." He leaned on his walking stick and looked up at the massive structure. "Made these bricks six at a time," he said. "Put 'em out on the board and put 'em in a kiln and burned 'em for a dollar and a half a day. You don't know it but that was good pay in those days. Yes sir."

We walked on. "Made all these bricks six at a time," Mr. Black said, "and I'm going to make some more yet!"

The morning after our story about Mr. Black went on the air, I was sitting on the edge of my bed in a motel room, rubbing my eyes and trying to figure out where to go next, when the phone rang. It was the CBS News State Department Correspondent of the time, Marvin Kalb.

Of course, that made it a red-letter day for me right there. I wasn't used to getting phone calls from Marvin Kalb.

He said, "There's a guy at the Agency for International Development who wants to talk to you. His name is Harvey J. Witherell. He's on the Guyana desk over there. I think he probably *is* the Guyana desk. I don't know what he wants with you, but he's been calling me all morning. I wish you'd give him a ring and get him off my neck.''

"Sure, Marvin," I said.

"If it turns out to be anything I can help you with, let me know," Marvin said generously, and a little wearily. The life of a State Department Correspondent must be hard. He has the whole world to worry about all the time.

When I reached Harvey J. Witherell, his voice was trembling with excitement.

"I hear you had a story about a brickmaker on television last night," he said.

"Yep," I said.

"Oh, gosh, I've been looking all over this country for a brickmaker who still does the job by hand," Harvey J. Witherell said. "I didn't think there were any left. What's he like?"

"He's a nice man," I said.

"You see," Harvey J. Witherell said, "the government of Guyana wants us to send a brickmaker down there. They have a Five Year Plan or something like that to rebuild the whole country in brick. There's no shortage of raw materials, I mean there's plenty of mud in Guyana, but they don't want to build a big brick factory. They want somebody to go village-to-village for a couple of weeks to teach people how to make bricks for themselves."

"Well," I said, "I've got just the man for you, Harvey, but he *is* ninety-two years old. . . ."

"I don't care how old he is," Harvey said. "I think he's the last brickmaker." I gave him Mr. Black's address and telephone number. "You have made my day!" said Harvey J. Witherell.

When I called Mr. Black to warn him what was coming, he said he had already had a call from Washington.

"Where is Guyana?" Mr. Black asked.

"It's a little country in South America," I said.

Mr. Black said, "My, my."

The very next day, on official government business and carrying his government briefcase, Harvey J. Witherell caught a plane from Washington to Winston-Salem. He and Mr. Black hit it off. They came to an agreement that amounted to one of the best deals in the history of American foreign aid: Mr. Black would go to Guyana for ten days. He would take his granddaughter, Evelyn Abrams, who also knew how to make bricks, and a kid from the neighborhood, Thomas Brabham, and they would go down there and teach those people how to make bricks. Mr. Black would be paid $100 per day. Not much, I thought when I heard about it, but better than the dollar and a half he got from R. J. Reynolds.

Harvey J. Witherell was awash with a feeling of accomplishment.

He said, "This is a wonderful thing you're going to do, Mr. Black. We in Washington very much appreciate it."

There was no false modesty in Mr. Black. He said, "I believe you have picked the best man to do the job for the U.S.A."

Planning commenced.

No government planning is ever done simply, of

course. Harvey J. Witherell had to formulate a detailed proposal for his own superiors and for higher-ups in the Department of State. He filled out reports in triplicate. He mapped the projected journey hour-by-hour and village-by-village. He developed plans and exigency plans. He put in travel orders and meal requisitions. There are forms for these things, and Harvey J. Witherell followed the forms.

All this planning had to be coordinated with the U.S. Embassy in Guyana, of course, and with the office of the Guyanese Prime Minister, Forbes Burnham, and the whole thing had to have a name. It was given the name "Operation Black Jack." It became a pretty big deal.

Cables began flying back and forth between Washington and Georgetown, the capital of Guyana, all of them bearing the capitalized admonition: "EXPEDITE." Later, somebody sneaked copies of those cables out of the State Department for me to read. (This did not constitute another Pentagon Papers case; they were not classified documents.) I was astonished by their number and by the baroque majesty of their prose. All this urgent intercontinental communication just to arrange for an elderly maker of bricks to show a few foreigners how it is done! A new appreciation of my government arose in my breast as I perused that tall stack of Operation Black Jack cables.

Harvey J. Witherell was thrilled; his big project was proceeding apace. George Black was thrilled; he had rarely been out of the county, and now he was about to be transported to a foreign land as an official representative of the United States of America. I was pretty excited myself; as Latin American Correspondent ten years before, I had been to Guyana a number of times on assignment. I figured I still had credit in some of the bars of Georgetown, and this would be a chance to get back there and look up some old friends.

As I awaited final word of the departure date, however, calamity struck.

Some high official of the Agency for International Development, some administrator whose job it was to review agency proposals and give them final approval, some insensible overseer, reading one of the forms Harvey J. Witherell had prepared in triplicate describing Mr. Black and the perfect match of the man to the mission, said to himself, wait a minute, this man is *ninety-two years old*! He reached for a stamp, one that said "CANCELLED," or perhaps "DENIED," stamped this stamp all over the proposal, and sent it tumbling back down through the bureaucracy, where it landed with a thud on the desk of Harvey J. Witherell.

He called me again, this time almost in tears.

"It's all off," he said. "They say he's too old."

"Well, Harvey," I said. "Way it goes. You sure tried hard."

By now, I liked Harvey J. Witherell. He was one of those bureaucrats we're always hearing about. He had spent twenty years or more in government service. Now, he was hovering on the brink of actually *doing* something. It didn't seem fair for Harvey's big idea to die this way, officially branded a bad idea. I felt the pain of his disappointment over the phone, and did my best to cheer him up.

"Too bad," I said.

"Yeah, too bad," he said. "Well, so long." And he hung up. It was over.

That is, it *would* have been over, except that right then we all got a lesson in how one branch of government doesn't always know what the other branch is doing.

Mr. Black, naturally, had been going around telling people about how he was going to Guyana. There was a good newspaper in Winston-Salem, the *Sentinel*. Somebody on the newspaper heard about Mr. Black's forthcoming trip and said, "That's a pretty good story." The *Sentinel* ran the story on page one: "Mr. Black Is Going to Guyana."

The people at the United Press wire service read the *Winston-Salem Sentinel*. Somebody there said, "That's a pretty good story." The UPI picked up the story and transmitted it nationwide: "Mr. Black Is Going to Guyana."

The Washington Post subscribes to the United Press wire service. Some editor there said, "That's a pretty good story." *The Washington Post* printed it with a wirephoto of Mr. Black and his mud mill: "Mr. Black Is Going to Guyana."

The White House reads *The Washington Post*. Somebody at the White House said, "That's a pretty good story," and showed it to somebody else who said, "Wouldn't it be wonderful if the President would see this man off?"

The timing could not have been more perfect. On precisely the same day Mr. Black's trip to Guyana was being cancelled by the State Department, the

White House was inviting Mr. Black to stop off in Washington on his way to Guyana for the State Department, to meet President Nixon in the Oval Office!

Harvey J. Witherell, sitting there amid the wreckage of his dream, let his eye fall on the President's appointment schedule for the next week as published in the Official Register.

"10 A.M. Wednesday:" one item read. "George Black, brickmaker of Winston-Salem, N.C., who is going to Guyana to teach brickmaking at the invitation of U.S. AID."

This made Harvey J. Witherell feel much better. Whistling a little tune, he tore out this item, highlighted it with a yellow marker, and confidently sent it back up through the bureaucracy to the official who had stamped his idea "CANCELLED."

Of course, all the wheels that hours before had rolled backward to a halt now started running fast forward again. The project just stamped "CANCELLED" was restamped "HIGH PRIORITY." Harvey called me to say I'd better make airplane reservations for Guyana after all. He said he didn't have time to talk. He said Mr. Black was coming to Washington to meet the President.

Naturally, nobody at the White House thought to ask Mr. Black how he was going to *get* to Washington. He got there by making the first airplane flight of his life. His granddaughter, Evelyn Abrams, sitting beside him on the plane, said it might as well have been his hundredth flight, that's how composed he was. The White House told Mr. Black, "Bring your family with you." He did. He brought about thirty-two of them, uncles, aunts, nephews, nieces and cousins from all up and down the eastern seaboard.

The guard at the White House gate said, "Oh, no, this is way too many people." They discussed it. The guard said, "I'll tell you what. I'll let half of you in."

At a White House "photo opportunity" they open the door to the President's office for three minutes, and a herd of animals comes in, pushing and shoving. These are reporters and photographers, competing for the most appealing photograph of the President and his visitor, and straining for the quotable remark. I was one of the animals that day.

"This is a very nice family you have here, Mr. Black," said President Nixon.

"This is only half of them!" Mr. Black exclaimed. "The other half are waiting out there on the street. The man wouldn't let them in!"

The reporters scribbled notes.

"Why, that won't do," President Nixon said, and soon the other half of Mr. Black's family crowded into the Oval Office, filling it nearly to overflowing.

So George Black got to meet the President, and so did his close and distant relatives. He did go to Guyana. I went along. There, Mr. Black taught brickmaking with such energy that he exhausted his official hosts, his village pupils, and a retinue of U.S. government hirelings, one of whom was probably the very official who had told Harvey J. Witherell that Mr. Black was too old for this trip.

The problem was that in their attempts at brickmaking, the villagers kept getting it wrong, and Mr.

Black wanted to stay in every village until they got it right. One day, Mrs. Forbes Burnham, wife of the Prime Minister, fashionably dressed in a riding outfit, came out to one of the villages in a limousine to be photographed for the local press with the visiting American brickmaker. Mr. Black nodded to her, extended a muddy hand, and went back to teaching brickmaking.

"He is quite a man," Mrs. Burnham said, as someone came up with a towel to wipe the mud from her hand.

He was, too.

I don't have many souvenirs from my adventures on the road, but from the story of George Black, I have two. The first is one of his bricks, solid and strong, like the man who made it. The second is a photograph of President Richard Nixon, standing awkwardly erect in the Oval Office flanked by Mr. Black and his granddaughter and some of the other family members. The head of the Agency for International Development is in the picture, too.

As for Harvey J. Witherell, the brave bureaucrat who had made this moment possible, he was in the room that day, only to find himself shoved rudely aside by a wire service photographer who said, "Excuse me, buddy, let me get through here." He stepped in front of Harvey, and so did all the other photographers. Flashbulbs were popping. Immortality in the government archives was being bestowed. In the moment of his greatest achievement, Harvey had been pushed into the shadows.

But bureaucrats are nothing if not nimble. For in a

corner of this photograph, one other white face appears at the extreme left, wearing the insouciant expression of a man who has just elbowed his way back into the picture.

It is the face of Harvey J. Witherell.

18

FLIGHT

Every December, on the anniversary of the Wright brothers' first flight, a motley fraternity of pilots, aerospace engineers and writers about aviation gathers at Kitty Hawk, North Carolina. After an all-night party, these celebrants assemble bleary-eyed on the sand dunes where Wilbur and Orville's craft of hickory sticks stuck together with Arnstein's Bicycle Cement first started forward into the wind. At the precise moment of the Wrights' lift-off in 1903, two Navy jets representing the two brothers come roaring in low from the sea, rise to clear the sand dunes, kick in their afterburners over the Wright monument, and then, in a thundering instant that rattles the earth, turn straight up into the sky and climb until they are out of sight. The day is often raw and windy, but the faithful club members are always out there for this small, moving ceremony. They style themselves the "Man Will Never Fly Society." Their motto is, "Birds fly. Men drink."

I am not a member, but when I am bouncing around up there among thunderstorms, I always recall the society's name and credo with profound appreciation.

To beat a deadline, I once flew from Montevideo to Buenos Aires in an open-cockpit biplane piloted by a Uruguayan teenager decked out, reassuringly he thought, in helmet, goggles, white scarf and gloves. I have flown up the Amazon in an ancient commercial seaplane, landing in the river at each village along the way for passengers and mail to be rowed out from shore. I have skimmed under the fog a few feet above the waves on my way to an Eskimo settlement on an island in the Bering Sea. ("Don't fly with that guy," I was told back in Nome. "He always comes back with seaweed on his struts." But there wasn't any choice.) Three times in two days, I was forced by the pressure of a story to fly with a San Francisco daredevil who was willing to land, and a little later take off again, at the North Lake Tahoe airport, which was closed to landings and takeoffs at the time by snow and ice.

I have flown in airplanes that lost engine power aloft, once in a four-engine plane that lost three of its engines, once in a twin-engine plane that lost first one and then the other, and ended up nose-down in a field of sagebrush in eastern Oregon. I have flown in a glider, which had no engines to begin with, of course, with a pilot who aimed the craft straight at the sea cliffs of La Jolla, California, counting on the updrafts to lift us to safety. They did, but I have not wished to fly in a glider since.

Like every other reporter who covered the Vietnam War, I have a number of times flown in helicopters that were being shot at. U.S. chopper pilots had conflicting theories about gunfire avoidance: fly high, out of the range of enemy bullets, or fly fast and low over the treetops to give the enemy no time to aim. Both schools of thought had fervent adherents. Advocates of both, I noticed, often came home with bullet holes in their helicopters.

I have three times been in airplanes that were struck by lightning, an Army Beaver and two commercial jets. (American Airlines captain to his stunned and silent passengers after the deafening crack and blast of white light inside the cabin: "Folks, we seem to have experienced a negative electrical discharge . . .")

"There are old pilots and there are bold pilots," goes the familiar saying around the hangars. "There are no old, bold pilots."

Oh, I don't know:

There was Weldy Phipps, who flew his Twin Otter out of Resolute in the Northwest Territories well into his seventies, using a sextant for celestial navigation and doing the calculations in his head. They say he landed once in a clearing to pick up a Tlingit Indian woman who needed a fast trip to a hospital, and found that he didn't have enough room to take off again. After he made the woman comfortable in the back of the plane, he tied the tail of the Otter to a tree with a rope, revved the engines to full power, gave the signal for somebody to cut the rope with a chain saw, and bounced the plane out of there. It was Weldy who flew the supply plane for the Plaisted Expedition. I was aboard several times when he landed on pans of ice floating far offshore in the Arctic Ocean. His method was to taxi around on skis after landing while his passenger tumbled out of the plane with an ice ax to see whether the pan was thick enough to land on.

There was Edna Gardner Whyte, who was eighty when we met her. She was giving flying lessons in Roanoke, Texas, which she felt well enough qualified to do after 30,000 hours in the air. She had 123 aviation trophies on the shelves in her living room, and to show us that she could still handle an airplane, she took Izzy up for some aerial acrobatics. After a snap roll or two, Izzy lost interest in his work. He can be heard moaning softly on the sound track of the tape he was shooting.

"That's good for your veins," said eighty-year-old Edna Gardner Whyte. "Only two and a half gs! Want another one?"

"No, ma'am," said Izzy, politely.

Then there was the old man in Kansas, an old, bold pilot if ever we met one. We never caught his name. We were doing a story about Stan Herd, an artist whose canvases are eighty-acre fields. Stan Herd plants crops—soybeans, milo, alfalfa, sunflowers—in patterns which when viewed from the air become lovely pictures, vases of flowers on checkered tablecloths, or western landscapes, or portraits of Indian chiefs. Seen from the ground, they're just a jumble of crops; you have to be in an airplane to appreciate them. A few miles from where Stan was working in a field with his tractor, we spotted an old J-2 Piper Cub parked in a barnyard. Izzy knocked on the door of the owner, an elderly farmer with a competent air about him, and explained our need.

"Sure, I'll take you up," the farmer said.

"We need to take the door off so I can make pictures," Izzy said.

"Fine!" the old man said.

Up there at 2,000 feet over Stan's field, making pictures from the Cub with the door off, Izzy remarked, "How long ago did you get your ticket?"

"Ticket?" the man asked.

"You know," Izzy said, "your pilot's license."

"Hell, I don't have any pilot's license," the old farmer said. "I just found this thing wrecked out here and patched it up and taught myself to fly it."

Of all the flyers into whose hands we have placed our lives, Don Sheldon is the one I'll always be most thankful for. We had heard of him before we met him. Everybody in south central Alaska had heard of him.

Wandering around Alaska one spring, we thought we'd make some pictures of Mount McKinley—Denali, the great mountain of the continent. On clear days, the old giant can be seen from a hundred miles or more away, but, as usual, we wanted close-ups. We drove to Talkeetna, the village that has always served as headquarters for expeditions to McKinley, and was best known as the home of Don Sheldon, the fabled mountain pilot. He turned out to be a slender, unassuming man with thinning hair. He wore a plaid shirt, army pants and work boots. Very modest-looking, I thought, for a legend. He said he was free for a couple of days and we engaged him to fly us up to the mountain. As we helped him roll his ski-equipped, single-engine Cessna out of the hangar, he made gentle jokes about the dangers of mountain flying.

"Never know what we'll run into up there," he

said, shaking his head and smiling. "You sure you boys want to do this? Well, let's fuel 'er up then."

I noticed he pumped his gas through a chamois strainer.

Light, fluffy cumulus clouds floated above the Alaska Range when we approached, Izzy riding beside Sheldon up front and a soundman named Stan Roginski strapped in behind with me. Izzy thought it would make a wonderful shot to fly through a cloud straight at the mountain with the camera rolling, so that when we came out of the cloud, the sunlit peak of McKinley would appear suddenly and dramatically.

"Let's try that cloud over there," Izzy said, and the mountain scenery tilted dizzily as Don Sheldon banked one way, then the other, to oblige. We flew toward the mountain through one cloud after another. Izzy was never satisfied that we had captured quite the desired spectacular effect. There were a lot of clouds to try, and we tried most of them. I found myself gripping the armrests and trying to keep my breakfast down each time we broke through into the sunlight, steered straight for Mount McKinley and veered sharply away at the last minute.

"Let's try that one over there," Izzy said, pointing to yet another cloud close to the peak.

"If we try that one," Don Sheldon said, "it will ruin my reputation."

"What do you mean?" Izzy asked.

Sheldon said calmly, "That one's got rocks in it."

"Look," I said, "is there someplace we can set this thing down for a while? Maybe we need a rest."

"I know just the place," the pilot said, putting the plane over on one wing again and tilting the nose sickeningly downward. "I think I even brought along a Thermos of coffee for you boys. We'll take a little coffee break." He set the plane's skis for landing, dropped the flaps and, a few minutes later, brought us to a bumpy stop in the snow in a big curved bowl, an ice field of the Ruth Glacier.

When Sheldon shut down the engine and we stepped out into the sunlight, I was nearly blinded by the brilliance of the white world around us. The glacier formed a vast, silent basin surrounded by massive slopes, a universe of ice and rock. Range upon range of mountains stretched before us into the measureless distance, and behind us, towering almost straight up from the ice field, rose Denali itself, with snow blowing from its summit thousands of feet overhead.

After a long silence, one of us said, "Good God!"

"Yep," Don Sheldon said, "I've always sort of liked this place myself."

We spent a long time just standing there before we remembered we were supposed to be making pictures. Don Sheldon tramped about thoughtfully in the snow while we worked.

When it was time to go, he had a little news for us.

"Good news and bad news," he said. "The good news is that the sun hasn't gone down yet and I can still get this plane out of here and back home before dark.

"The bad news is that the sun has made the snow

so mushy that I can't take off with all of you on board."

I gulped, "You *can't*?"

"Nope," he said. "Too much weight. Best I can do now is take one of you back to Talkeetna, and maybe some of your gear. Two of you are going to have to spend the night up here, I'm afraid. I'll come back for you in the morning."

I looked around, imagining the nighttime temperature on the glacier. Also imagining wolves and polar bears.

"Nothing up here to hurt you," Don Sheldon said. "I'll dig a couple of sleeping bags out of the plane for you."

While he was doing so, he added, "Oh, and you won't have to be alone, either." He nodded toward a rocky outcrop about a mile away at the edge of the ice field. "You can't see it from here, but there's a cozy one-room cabin on the other side of that rock. Some of the climbers use it for a base camp. There's a Catholic priest in there now on some kind of a retreat. He's a nice guy. Father Ron is what I call him. He's been up here a while. He won't mind a little company."

Sheldon held up the bedrolls. "Who wants these?" he asked.

I was still letting all this news sink in, about the necessity for two of us to spend the night in this wilderness, and then about there being a *cabin* in this unlikely place, and not only a cabin but also a *priest*. . . .

I heard Izzy say, "I'll stay." He shouldered his

camera and the tape recorder and took one of the bedrolls. Then I heard myself say, "Sure, I'll stay, too." Don Sheldon handed me the other roll of bedding and a long length of rope.

"Better rope yourselves together when you walk over there," he said. "You know. Crevasses. See you tomorrow."

He climbed into the pilot's seat with Stan beside him, started the engine, and began his takeoff run down the glacier. The plane lifted off and turned toward home. We watched until it vanished among the mountains.

Izzy tied one end of the rope around his waist and handed me the other end, regarding my 220-pound bulk doubtfully. "If one of us falls into a hole in the ice," he said, "it better be me, I guess." We started across the glacier with the setting sun casting our shadows a hundred yards ahead of us and creating imaginary hidden crevasses every few steps.

It must have taken us nearly an hour to make it off the ice and into the rocks of the mountain. When we started up, we could see a big, red-bearded man wearing a bright parka coming down toward us, carrying a coiled rope of his own over one shoulder, and in his hand, a staff. He looked like a Biblical prophet of the mountains.

"Good afternoon, Father," I said.

"Never mind the Father blather!" he boomed cheerily. "Sorry to be late in greeting you! The truth is I wasn't expecting company! Haven't seen another soul since sometime last month! Here, let me carry some of that load for you."

He talked loudly all the way up the hill, not stopping even to ask where we had come from and what we were doing there. It had been weeks, I guess, since he had heard the sound of his own voice.

"I suppose Don Sheldon dropped you off," he said, "unless you took a wrong turn on a stroll in Anchorage and hoofed it up here. Don likes to show off his shelter. He built it himself, you know. He got tired of climbers freezing in the storms. Tough work, you know, having to fly their bodies back down and all, so he flew a few loads of lumber and nails up here—and here we are. Welcome to our humble abode!"

The cabin was small, six-sided and half buried in snow. Inside, sleeping shelves were built up off the floor under a ring of windows. A wood stove squatted in the center of the room with a fire crackling inside. That's all there was to the place. It looked very good to me.

"I am pleased to offer you northern exposures with a view of the mountains," Father Ron said, dumping our bedrolls on the shelf. "All the exposures have a view of the mountains. The menu tonight is stew. That is the menu every night." He walked outside, dug around in the snow for a black iron pot full of beef and beans, came back in and set it on the stove. "Dinner will be served shortly," he said, "but first the cocktail hour." From his duffel bag on the floor under the shelf, he produced a bottle of Christian Brothers brandy. "We like to support the brothers in their good work," he said. He unscrewed the cap and passed the bottle ceremoniously to Izzy to drink first.

Over tin bowls of stew, Father Ron told us that he

had come to Alaska seeking solitude in the loneliest place he could find. Somebody in Talkeetna had told him about the Mount McKinley shelter and he had talked Don Sheldon into flying him up here. He was escaping a critical bishop in Boston or someplace. He said this sojourn in the mountains was partly for religious reflection and partly for figuring out what to do with his life.

"Well," I said, "I guess it doesn't help your solitude much for a couple of strangers to show up at dinnertime and stay all night."

"I am very glad to have your company," Father Ron said solemnly. "I've never been alone for so long before. Let me tell you what I have discovered about being alone: it is a great gift, but it is damned lonely."

I laughed.

"Solitude is hard to come by in this world," he went on. "It is a priceless luxury. Only the very rich can afford it—and paupers like me. Everybody else in the world dreams of splendid isolation, workers from their bosses, husbands from their wives, but they can only dream, you see. They are in the grip of daily life, and daily life must be lived with others."

I said I envied him his escape from daily life.

"Yes," he said, "it offers communion with God. But about this time of day, you find yourself in need of some kind of human communion, somebody to have a drink with, or a debate. God listens well, but doesn't talk much. Moses went to the mountaintop to talk with God, but you'll remember that he came right back down again. And I have found out why. The pressure is too great up here. It is not natural to human beings to talk only with God. The tension accumulates. . . ."

We all fell silent, thinking about this.

"But now," Father Ron said, "the after-dinner show! Look over your shoulder."

In the sky behind us, a faint white light was shimmering. It grew brighter, changed to a shade of purple, then pink and suddenly shot in a streak to the dome of the sky. Izzy and I stood up and stared through the window.

"*Aurora borealis*," Father Ron said. "It is Latin, meaning 'the northern dawn.' "

I had seen the northern lights before, glowing dimly on some northern horizon. This was different, a display of brilliant pastels that trembled over the silhouettes of the mountains, a big Wurlitzer jukebox in the sky. Ripples of color rose in layers from bottom to top and unexpectedly sent bright streamers flying so high that we had to draw close to the windows to see where they ended above our heads.

"Charged particles from the sun entering the atmosphere of the earth," Father Ron intoned. He was used to the show.

"If you gentlemen will excuse me, I am going to retire," he said, and soon he was snoring lightly in his sleeping bag. But Izzy and I sat there on the shelf through the short subarctic night watching those bright rivers of light transform the dark world. For one night only, we had the best seats on the planet for nature's most spectacular show. It faded away only with the rising of the sun. Both of us were left awed and exhausted. Neither of us has ever been able to describe that night adequately to others, though we did our best to tell Father Ron what he had missed as soon as he wakened.

"Very good, very good," he said, with a sort of pride of ownership. "We do our best to satisfy our guests in this inn. How do you take your coffee? Black, I hope."

We were just roping ourselves together at the edge of the ice field when Don Sheldon's silver Cessna appeared overhead, turned upwind and landed. Father Ron helped carry our gear out to the plane. He took off his mittens to shake hands. Izzy and I climbed aboard, waved once, and left the big, bearded prophet standing there on the glacier, alone again with only God to talk to. I have not seen or heard of him since. I hope he worked it all out up there in the mountains, but have no way of knowing.

"Pretty nice night?" Don Sheldon asked over the engine noise.

"It was okay," I said. "Not a very good place to sleep though, what with the lights coming in the window."

He chuckled. "I thought you might not mind it up there," he said. "I haven't seen every place, but it's the prettiest place I've ever seen."

"Well," I said, "me too. How can I ever thank you, Don?"

He said, "Don't thank me. I wanted to take you home with me last night. Thank the soft snow on that glacier."

That's what he said, but I wonder. I wonder whether

Don Sheldon sized us up as a couple of guys who thought we were in a bigger hurry than we really were and would benefit from a night to slow down and look around and think about this place where we were.

I can't ask him. Don Sheldon had cancer then, knew he had it, and died less than a year later. You can find his name on the new Geological Survey map of Mount McKinley, printed in small letters on a white patch that represents the ice field where he landed us for coffee and wouldn't take us home from until we'd spent the night, the place he said was the prettiest he'd ever seen. The beautiful big white bowl of the Ruth Glacier where the northern lights put on their show every night is forever named the Don Sheldon Amphitheater.

19

ALUMINUM TUBES WITH WINGS

These days, I am on the road during the week, but I always have to get back to New York on the weekend to work on the *Sunday Morning* program. So I spend a lot of time in the lines at the airline counters. Most people who have to go somewhere in America nowadays wait in those same lines. I can remember when people in those lines laughed and chatted, anticipating the exciting trips they were about to make up above the clouds. Now, they wait glumly and check their watches. This is because airline travel has changed, and they know they're not going to have any fun up there.

Once, you could fly from Denver, Colorado, to Elko, Nevada, on the same airliner. You could have a drink and a smoke and a hot meal served on a real plate and watch the mountains go by. It was always a little bumpy over the mountains, but the stewardesses never looked worried. They made the trip so nice that when it was over, you sort of hated to get off the plane.

Today, you can't go from Denver to Elko. You go to Salt Lake City instead. Your plane leaves Denver at the same time about sixty other planes are trying to leave, for Denver has become a hub for United and Continental, and you arrive in Salt Lake City at the same time about thirty other planes are trying to land, for Salt Lake City is a hub for Delta. When the plane finally makes it to an open gate, you step off into a swarming hell of connecting passengers, all of whom started their trips in Denver or Boise or Los Angeles in an attempt to get to Elko or Billings or Idaho Falls. All of them are in Salt Lake City, where none of them wishes to be. They crisscross in the maze, their suit bags flying behind them, running and cursing from Terminal C to Terminal A (for a master airline computer hums all day to assure that no passenger may ever depart from the same concourse at which he landed). For a distraught and agitated hour, they jam the bars, toilets and telephone booths and sprint down the endless corridors until the last gate is shut, the last jetway retracted and the last winged aluminum tube has departed with its cargo of sweaty passengers and misdirected luggage to wait in line out on the taxiway. Then an otherworldly peace descends upon Salt Lake City International Airport. A few lost souls wander dazed in the strange silence, having been left behind. And you—you who remember the old, easy days when airplanes flew from Denver to Elko—you are one of these. For the plane you were looking for in Salt Lake City, designated by Delta as Delta Flight 5857, is known to the people who actually fly it as Sky West 5857. This is a little trick played on you by the big airlines. Nobody back in Denver ever mentioned anything called Sky West, or that the airplane in question is the sort you must bend deeply to enter and double your legs under your chin to sit down in after divining its distant parking place. So you—you who still think of passenger airplanes as DC-9s or -10s, or at least -6s or -7s—watch from a window as something known as a Fairchild Swearingen Metro leaves without you. There will be another flight to Elko in two hours and thirty-two minutes. An Embraer EMB-110 Bandeirante, which is made in Brazil. I used to live in Brazil and watch them make things there. This Brazilian plane, they say, will go to Elko after a while. In the meantime, you have a big, quiet airport pretty much all to yourself in which to reflect on the improvement in North American air travel over the years.

Or you can rent a car and drive to Elko. At seventy miles per hour, which is as slow as anybody drives out here, and with a two-and-a-half-hour head start, you'll beat the Embraer to Nevada, and the road takes you over the Donner Trail through the Great Salt Flats, and through Wendover astride the Utah–Nevada line, my favorite state-line town, even more wonderful than Texarkana (Texas–Arkansas) where the courthouse was built on the state line and fugitives have to be extradited from one end of the hall to the other. For peculiarity, Wendover also beats Virgilina (Virginia–North Carolina) or Monida (Montana–Idaho) or Florala (Florida–Alabama), all places I have visited more than once, as it happens. Wendover is my state-line darling, for here in a single step you leave modest Mormon Utah Wendover, a town of tidy houses with prim lace curtains at the windows, and enter gaudy Nevada Wendover with neon signs that flash the words "Li-

quor" and "Keno" and "Casino" back into sleeping
Wendover, Utah, through the desert night. One step
in the same town takes you from Mountain time at
midnight an hour back into Pacific time where the
evening is young yet. It is the step Adam made, one
step from the garden to the fast lane. Most wanderers
through Wendover, children of Adam, prefer the Nevada side of town.

So you may not make it to Elko tonight after all.
But at least you've made it out of the Salt Lake City
hub.

Cities *want* to be airline hubs. The theory, I guess,
is that a certain number of passengers will miss their
planes and spend nights in town, dining and dancing
and spending money freely, shopping the next morning for washer-dryers, and, who knows, station wagons, before winging on to their destinations. But
regular travelers hate these wretched sprawling ter-
minals, and eventually, by extension, the cities whose
names they bear: Chicago, Atlanta, Pittsburgh, St.
Louis, Dallas, Denver, Minneapolis–St. Paul. (Old
question in the south: "If you die and go to hell, do
you have to change in Atlanta?" Answer: "If you die
in Georgia, Alabama or Mississippi, yes, you do.")

"For Your Convenience" are the words I dread.
Whenever they make an airport ghastlier, they put up
a sign that says they are doing it for my convenience.
At friendly little old Raleigh–Durham, for example,
an airport where I land often for down-home reasons
collegial and familial, I used to get off the plane, walk
across the street to the rental car lot, adjust the rearview mirror on the Cutlass, and be off to Chapel Hill.

One day I saw a sign in the airport lobby: ''For Your Convenience . . .'' Now I wait for the Hertz bus in a throng at the curb. When the bus finally arrives, after the buses of Avis, National, Budget, Alamo, Sheraton, Ramada, Holiday Inn and Airport Employees have passed, I wait for it to drive me a mile out into the piney woods and then wind through the parking lot dropping off other customers. Eventually, the driver hollers my name, points to a car, hands me my rental contract, opens the door and says, ''Have a nice day.'' But the nice days are over. American Airlines, which never even bothered to fly to Raleigh–Durham in the nice days, now deposits thousands of passengers there whether they want to be there or not, and after an hour or two, at its convenience, picks most of these same people up and flies them somewhere else. Raleigh and Durham are very proud that their airport is now a hub. So far, it's not a big enough hub to be notorious, but it's growing and may yet become nationally despised.

Most steady customers of the airlines mention Atlanta Hartsfield and Chicago O'Hare as the abattoirs of the continent, but I have more often been hacked and bloodied at Minneapolis–St. Paul. Victims attempting connections at Minneapolis must run a fiendish gauntlet, a corridor constructed in a former cornfield on the bluffs above the Minnesota River. There is plenty of room in the cornfield to add hundreds of yards to this corridor, and every couple of years, they do. When the pathetic connecting passenger finally drags his suitcase to its end with the seconds ticking away before the departure of his outgoing flight, the smile of triumph on his face suddenly vanishes. He discovers he has not reached his goal at all. What he saw in the glimmering distance was only a mirage, the main terminal, where he now must pass out of the security zone, struggle the length of the building, line up to pass through *another* security gate and then pant down *another* interminable hallway in order to miss a connection on the same airline he came in on! I have missed so many flights on this airline and dawdled away so much time in the Minneapolis airport that employees of the gift shops and newsstands there nod to me as I pass. They think I work there too. I will not mention the name of the airline. It knows which one it is.

I miss the vanished airlines whose names described the wonderful destinations to which their planes flew directly: Western, Piedmont, Allegheny, Southern, Ozark, North Central. I miss the orderly, regulated days when I knew the airline to call if I wanted to fly from, say, Los Angeles to San Francisco. In that case, the airline was United. Everybody knew this. Flights every hour on the hour. Do you know who flies from Los Angeles to San Francisco today? Delta. (Delta used to mean the *Mississippi* Delta, for heaven's sake! Delta was how you got to New Orleans.) United still flies to San Francisco, as it happens. Also Continental, USAir, American, America West, Southwest, Northwest, Westair, Pan Am and Alaska Airlines, just to list the planes that depart before ten o'clock in the morning.

This is called competition by theorists in faraway Washington, D.C., who brought it about, free market in action, good for the public. At least one miserable member of the public, trapped aboard a cramped airplane on a Los Angeles airport taxiway, calls it chaos. The country cheered when Ronald Reagan fired all those uppity air traffic controllers, and now—how many years later?—the captain is still saying on the intercom, ''Well, we're thirteenth in line to take off, folks, and we've been informed of an air traffic delay for spacing on the way up to the Bay Area, so if you'll just sit back and make yourselves comfortable for a while . . .''

You could drive to San Francisco, if they'd only let you off the plane. It is one of the great trips on the continent, up the trail of Spanish missions, San Buenaventura, Santa Barbara, Santa Maria, San Luis Obispo . . . (Then comes San Simeon, which is the most splendid of all, but should not be confused with the missions built by the Spanish padres. It was built by William Randolph Hearst, a sugar-padre, off on a mission of his own.) . . . San Carlos de Borromeo, Santa Cruz, San Jose. You could stop at Point Lobos, the country's most breathtaking meeting place of land and sea, and watch the sea otters floating around out there on their backs opening clams on their tummies. You could go shopping in Carmel, and walk around Monterey in the footsteps of the great Steinbeck, and play a quick nine holes at Pebble Beach, and buy a sack of artichokes in Castroville, Artichoke Capital of the World. California Route 1, *that's* the way to get to San Francisco.

But I know, I know. You have to meet a hot business prospect at Tadich's Grill at noon. Well, as the captain just said, sit back and make yourself comfortable. Tadich's stays open all afternoon, and this unsympathetic, unregulated corporation into whose hands you have put yourself will drop you off by the bay by and by.

I miss the fine old hand of government interference. I miss the comfortable seats and the considerate captains with gray at their temples who conducted historical tours of the landscape passing below.

"General Custer marched down from Bismarck into these Black Hills and camped at a little spot you can see down there on the right. They call it Custer now." On his flights from Denver up into the Dakotas, Captain Larry Beardsley of Frontier Airlines used to keep his passengers straining for a look at historic rivers and crumbled forts. "On up to our left about fifteen miles is the famous old western town, Deadwood City, home of Wild Bill Hickok and Calamity Jane. Wild Bill was killed in a poker game, as you no doubt recall, holding aces and eights at the time, the 'dead man's hand' . . ."

Often, when he had a few minutes to spare, Larry Beardsley would bank his Boeing 737 in a tight 360-degree turn around Mount Rushmore so that people seated on *both* sides of the plane could see the sculpted presidents; when Frontier was gobbled up by a bigger company and the new owners told him to knock it off, Captain Beardsley got so bored that he retired. Something went out of aviation that day.

They are all retired, it seems to me, the airline people who loved flying, except from the television commercials where the flight attendants still smile and bring an extra pillow. On the planes, they do not smile. They serve bad food wordlessly, pick up the empty trays mechanically and spend the rest of the flight in the galley talking about their dates and their days off. Their union representative explains that this is because they are not there to serve passengers, they are there to assure safety.

Please do not speak to me of safety. Please smile and make this trip pass as quickly and pleasantly as you can. I will do my part by smiling back, though I do not much want to be up here in the first place. Birds fly, men drink. Safety is the job of whoever's up there in the cockpit flying this thing.

I have accumulated many free miles in the airlines' frequent flyer programs. But there is a catch. To use those miles, I have to take another trip on an airline.

20

PERILS

"Thrice I have suffered shipwreck," wrote Saint Paul one day when his nerves were jangled by travel. "A night and a day I have been in the deep, in journeyings often, in perils of waters, in perils of robbers, in perils by mine own countrymen and by the heathen, in the city and the wilderness and the sea . . . in weariness and painfulness and cold."

I know. It's not all fun out there.

It helps if you make it a rule never to eat in any restaurant with kings, foxes, coaches or horses in the name. Beware of the word "gourmet." If a restaurant says it serves gourmet food, you are going to get a frozen dinner that has been warmed up in the microwave.

Do not eat in a restaurant on the top of a building. If you *must* eat in a restaurant on the top of a building, never eat in one that revolves.

Do not try to find a good restaurant in Kansas. There is much good home cooking in Kansas, but there are no good restaurants. There used to be one: the dining room of the hotel in the cowtown of Alma, but the proprietor got disgusted and moved to California, where his cooking would be appreciated.

When you cross the Missouri River headed west, pack a peanut butter sandwich, for there is nothing to eat until you get to Denver.

When you go out to dinner, leave the television set on and a "Do Not Disturb" sign on the doorknob. This may keep the maid's boyfriend from entering and stealing your suit.

Never sleep on the side of the bed next to the telephone. That is where everybody else sleeps, for the convenience of answering the morning wake-up call, and that is where beefy traveling salesmen sit during the day to call their clients. The mattress on that side of the bed is always broken down, and you will find your slumber interrupted by the need to keep grasping the uphill sheet to keep from rolling off toward the telephone.

The interstate highway system is a wonderful thing. It makes it possible to go from coast to coast without seeing anything or meeting anybody. If the United States interests you, stay off the interstates.

Carry a rubber sink stopper in your pocket. The mechanical arrangements for keeping water in motel room sinks never work.

If you rub a thin film of soap on the bathroom mirror, it will keep it from steaming up while you take your shower.

When making motel reservations, say, "Down and out, up front." They will know what you mean. A room that is downstairs with an outside entrance is easy to reach, preventing the tendonitis that afflicts the suitcase-carrying arms of travelers who convey bags down halls and up stairs. A room that is also near the front of the building will be farthest from the diesel refrigerator trucks that are invariably parked all night with their engines running. They park in back.

Always ask for dry toast at breakfast, with butter on the side, so they do not slather that greasy stuff on your toast back in the kitchen. I don't know what it is, but it isn't butter.

Pay for your breakfast with paper money only. Save all the quarters you get in change. You are going to need plenty of quarters as the day goes along, at newspaper boxes, toll booths and Coke machines. The traveler setting out without a pocketful of quarters in America today is a soldier going into battle without ammo.

If you are going from New York to Washington, avoid both the Pan Am Shuttle and the Trump Shuttle. Save time and aggravation by going on the train. Take the club car on the way down, for on the southbound Metroliner, they hook the club car right behind the engine, making for a trip smooth enough for you to read the papers and do the crossword puzzle at 100 miles per hour. Ride in an ordinary coach on the way back, however. Northbound, the club car is always the last car on the train, not the first, and it snaps around on the curves like the business end of a whip, requiring you to hold on with both hands while your complimentary seafood tidbits slide off the tray into your lap.

West of the Mississippi, travel, if possible, with your own coffeepot. The coffee gets progressively weaker from Illinois westward. My theory for this is that the pioneers ran out of coffee as they traveled west and had to re-use the grounds. Their descendants grew up liking it that way. The weakest coffee in America is served in Brookings, South Dakota. Some say Salt Lake City, but they are people who have not yet been to Brookings.

Never be without a pint of vodka. There are still dry counties in this country.

Never be without a big safety pin. The curtains of motel room windows never quite meet in the middle. They must be pinned unless you want a direct shaft of bright sunlight to fall across your eyes in the morning an hour and a half before it's time to get up.

The best suitcase—I have tried them all—is the small Lark, which expands to give you a way to bring home all the stuff you didn't have with you when you left.

You could carry a knife, scissors, tweezers, magnifying glass, can opener, corkscrew, toothpick, awl and Phillips screwdriver—or you could carry a Swiss Army knife. I find an essential use for mine nearly every day on the road.

Hotel room radios never work. If you want a little news in the morning and a little Haydn at night, as I do, you should have a fifteen-band FM/long-wave/medium-wave/shortwave/alarm clock Sony ICF-7700 in your bag. It's the size of a paperback book, weighs less than a pound, and is always there to keep you company.

If you must work at night, carry a 100-watt light bulb. Forty-watt bulbs are manufactured exclusively for the motel trade, which puts them in the lamps in the rooms. They provide enough light to find your way to the bathroom, but not enough to read by.

If you don't like loud rock music, change the settings on the rental car radio as soon as you rent the car. The guys who wash rental cars all like rock music, and the push buttons of all rental cars are set for rock stations. Sometimes *all* the buttons are set for the *same* rock station.

Whatever you order in a cafe, do not order chili. Cafe chili is invariably disappointing and potentially lethal. Red Fenwick of Denver, a western historian, told me chili was invented by a Wyoming sheepherder to keep the feet of his sheepdogs warm on cold nights. He sent some to a Texas friend, who ate it by mistake, which Texans have been doing ever since.

Gift shops are well named. There's never anything in them that you would want to keep for yourself.

Gas station attendants become more polite the farther the gas station is located from the main highway.

If you have to travel by air and connect at a hub, carry a bandage with you and wrap it around your ankle. They will call you an electric cart.

21

ANIMAL TALES

We have spent a lot of time close to the creatures of wilderness, ranch and barnyard. At the Turkey Festival in Cuero, Texas, where they herd thousands of turkeys through the streets each year, we learned they always pray for sunshine on Festival Day. If it rains, turkeys look up with their mouths open to see what's hitting them on the head. They are so dumb that they forget to look back down, and if the rain continues, the turkeys are in danger of drowning right there on Main Street.

This is what we were told. You do not pick up this sort of fact in the reading rooms of libraries, you know. You have to be out there in the field, in intimate contact with birds and animals.

We did a story about Ralphy, the remarkable swimming pig of San Marcos, Texas, for example. To tell you the truth, we got kind of sweet on the pig's trainer, a pretty young woman in a bathing suit, and probably spent a day or two longer than we should have making pictures of Ralphy in his pool. We even hired an underwater housing for the camera so we could get shots from below of that little porker paddling along. In my script, I made a big deal of the pig's accomplishment.

After the story went on the air, I got a lot of letters from farmers saying, "You idiot, *any* pig can swim!"

So now I know about turkeys and pigs. I am still finding out about horses.

I was a hell-for-leather rider back when I was Hopalong Cassidy and my horse was a broomstick, but now I dread it when we have to ride real horses to get where we are going. We put as much of our gear as we can into saddlebags and carry the rest slung about our necks. Loaded down that way, we are even gawkier on horseback than we would be riding free, which would be plenty gawky. But every ride teaches us new lessons.

After a day on horseback in the Superstition Mountains of Arizona, where we were trying to put together a story about the Lost Dutchman gold mine, I found that the insides of my legs were chafed raw and bloody from shifting in the saddle.

"Too bad," the wrangler said. "You should have wore pantyhose."

So *that's* the cowboy's secret! Under the chaps and jeans and boots—pantyhose! That's something I know about horseback riding now, but I never worked up the nerve to go into a store and ask for a pair of pantyhose in my size. Horses remain a trial.

We went on a bison roundup outside Medora, North Dakota. For television purposes, I wanted to ride my horse up to the camera, manned by Izzy on the ground, and make a short, poignant speech about the noble buffalo. I rode up to the camera all right, but the horse wouldn't stop.

"You got to pull back on the reins!" the wrangler shouted.

We tried it again. The horse and I got to the camera and I pulled back on the reins. The horse kept going.

"You got to pull back *hard* on the reins," the wrangler said.

I got the horse turned around and headed back toward Izzy. This time I practically yanked the bit down the poor animal's throat. He galloped a few yards past the camera, into just the wrong position, and stopped.

I climbed down and gave my poignant speech dismounted.

"Too bad," the wrangler said. "You got to pull back on the reins."

A while later, we were covering a mule train carrying construction material to a dam site in the California Sierra. We had to ride horses to get up there. Larry's horse kept wanting to trot on the narrow trail. Larry tried to slow him down. The horse reared, kicking at the air with his front feet. Larry fell off backward and slid down the mountainside. He got his hands and face all scratched up and bruised his ribs something terrible.

"Too bad," the wrangler said. "You shouldn't have pulled back on the reins like that."

Even when we come out of our animal episodes uninjured, we usually look back on them with a certain wry regret.

A woman wrote me a letter from Ohio. She said her parakeet could say, "And that's the way it is," like Walter Cronkite. We went there right away, of course. As soon as she opened the door, the parakeet said, "And that's the way it is!" While we set up the lights and camera there in the living room, the parakeet watched us from inside his cage and said, "And that's the way it is!" We pointed the lens at the cage and started rolling. The parakeet looked at the camera and said:

"AAAAWK!"

The parakeet's owner said, "And that's the way it is!" to give him a cue.

The parakeet said, "AAAAWK!"

"And that's the way it is!" she said patiently.

He said, "AAAAWK!"

We turned off the lights to let the parakeet calm down. We went into the kitchen and had a cup of coffee and talked about the weather and other things. Then we sauntered back into the living room, pretending to pay no attention to the parakeet in his cage. The bird's owner thought this might work. We said nothing. The parakeet said nothing. We turned on the camera again.

The parakeet said, "AAAAWK!"

After an hour or two of this, we packed up, promising to return some other time. We said good-bye to the disappointed woman who wanted to see her parakeet on Walter Cronkite's news program. We closed the front door and started down the walk to the driveway, carrying our camera and lights. Behind us in the living room, we heard the parakeet say:

"And that's the way it is!"

Then there was the lovable little shopping center

dog in Florida who carried people's packages for them in his teeth. He seemed to be owned by nobody, we were told. He was petted and fed by everybody. He was especially fond of small children.

We went to the shopping center on a day when it was raining lightly. We saw the dog. A woman had given him a small plastic bag of groceries and he was walking along beside her toward her car, carrying the bag in his teeth. His tail was wagging. It was an adorable picture. We quickly set up the camera a long distance away so as not to disturb the scene, but the darling animal spotted us. He dropped the groceries in a puddle, growled, wheeled and raced toward us, baring his fangs and snarling. We retreated. He followed us back to the bus, snapping at our heels and barking.

"For heaven's sake," said somebody passing by, "leave the poor little dog alone!"

It appears there's just something about a television camera that four-legged creatures, wild and domestic, find disconcerting. If, in Nebraska, we see a panorama of the plains with three palominos in the foreground, the sort of picture any photographer aches to capture on film, our inclination these days is to drive on by, for we know from hard experience that those ponies will probably mosey away behind a hill before Izzy can focus on the scene. For a while there, Izzy used to whistle to them to show his friendly intentions. This just made them walk away faster. He tried offering them apples and sugar cubes, which they always rejected, for the very good reason that farmers and ranchers do not give their livestock apples and sugar cubes and the animals were unfamiliar with such delicacies. In our archives are many, many pictures of the rear ends of horses. Also of moose, antelope, deer, donkeys, pigs, sheep, polar bears, squirrels, mules and chickens, some walking away disdainfully, some galloping away in fright, but all departing.

Frequently, on the road, we stop to make pictures for the nature vignettes that always close the *Sunday Morning* program. Careful viewers of these short pieces will remember that the ducks are ordinarily flying—or swimming or waddling—*away* from the camera. We have seen much of nature, but usually of nature retreating.

The shyness of animals never has been more than a time-consuming inconvenience to us—except once in west Texas, when it became a mortification. I wanted to crawl under the bed in embarrassment. As it happened, there was no bed to crawl under for many miles.

We were covering the spring cattle roundup on a big ranch in west Texas, the Kokernot spread in the rough mountain rangeland around Marfa and Alpine. The western landscape here is so rugged that the roundup can only be accomplished the old-fashioned way, by riders on horseback. The cowboys begin with a chuck wagon breakfast before dawn and then spend a hard day in the saddle, coaxing cows and calves out of the rocky ravines and down from the precipices where they have hidden themselves during the winter. Among those crags, there are wild cows that have gone unfound year after year. It is harsh, unfenced country, and it is cowboying at its hardest—sleeping on the ground at night, riding, roping and branding under the hot sun all day. A passing thunderstorm and a downpour of rain made things worse the day we were there.

As the sun finally went down, twenty or so riders, wet, miserable and exhausted, came toward camp, herding several hundred wet, miserable, loudly objecting cattle to the corral. As they neared the corral gate, at the end of their ride at last, we walked out beside the trail to make pictures of the scene. As the lead cows passed us, Izzy pressed the button and the Arriflex film camera started with a soft whir. Only long afterward did we speculate that the sound of an Arriflex camera in operation must be, to a cow, exactly the sound of a rattlesnake coiled and preparing to strike.

The first cows in the herd bolted away from the camera, nearly running down a couple of tired riders whose horses reared to escape the charge. This sudden wild commotion ran through the whole herd in an instant horrible to see. The next thing we knew, hundreds of cattle were stampeding back along the trail, headed for the hills again, with twenty cursing cowboys spurring their horses in mad pursuit.

We stood there, suddenly utterly alone. We watched the cattle thunder into the distance, the riders galloping at full speed to try to head them, until the whole chaotic horde of cattle, men and horses disappeared from our sight.

Izzy looked at me and said, "Did *I* do that?"

A couple of hours later, in the dark of night, having

finally slowed, and stopped, and turned the cattle, the cowboys had them heading back our way again. As they neared the corral for the second time, we were watching from a hundred yards away. A single rider turned and rode over to us. He stopped his horse, touched the brim of his hat politely and looked down at us from the saddle. There was mud all over his face. He said, "The foreman told me to ask you if you'd mind not taking pictures this time."

When the gate to the corral was finally shut with the cattle inside and the horses put away for the night, the cowboys came struggling over to the campfire in the dark, carrying their saddles. They threw themselves down on the ground in silence to wait for their supper.

I said, "I sure am sorry. We never imagined anything like that would happen."

They just sat there, looking into the fire. Finally, one of them said, "Oh, hell, it don't matter. Some days, that's just the way it is."

I thought of that parakeet in Ohio.

22

WHAT THEY SAY

I met a man who told me that he and his wife were too hungry to wait until they got to Waco to have their lunch, so they stopped in Mexia, Texas, for a couple of hamburgers. They knew what town they were in, but they got to speculating about how to pronounce it—me-*hee*-a, or mex-*ee*-a, or *mex*-ya. "Excuse me," the man said to the waitress, "would you tell us how you say the name of this place?"

"Sure," she said, and pronounced it for them slowly:

"*Day*-ree-*queen*."

I walked into the barbershop in Dillon, Montana, needing a haircut. The barber was alone in there, sweeping up the place.

"Are you free?" I asked him.

"Nope," he said, "I charge seven dollars."

Sign on the door of a cafe in Evansville, Indiana: "Open 24 Hours a Day, 7 Days a Week. Closed Thursdays."

West Virginia hills are so steep that people who live in the valleys say they have to look up their chimneys to see their cows come home.

Rhododendron is called "laurel" by old-timers in the Blue Ridge Mountains. Laurel is "ivy." Ivy is "vine."

Song at a girls' basketball game in Eagle, Nebraska, to the tune of "My Country 'Tis of Thee":

> *There ain't no flies on us,*
> *There ain't no flies on us,*
> *No flies on us.*
> *There may be one or two*
> *Great big green flies on you.*
> *There ain't no flies on us,*
> *No flies on us.*

Chicago cabdriver's advice to a tourist inquiring the way to Lake Michigan:
"Walk east 'til your hat floats."

New York restaurateur on why he never considered leaving Manhattan:
"Every place else is a piece of raisin cake."

Great Plainsman Roger Welsch on how hard the wind blows on the Plains:
"People don't bother with weather vanes. They just look out the window to see which way the barn is leaning."

* * *

Stranger to west Texan: "Mr. Jordan?"

West Texan, sticking out his hand: "Mr. Jordan
was my daddy. I'm Joe."

In Minnesota, the birds sing in Swedish.

A paper bag in Virginia is a paper sack in Vermont.
A burlap bag in Illinois is a tow sack in North Car-
olina is a grass sack in Arkansas is a croaker sack in
Georgia.

What is called everywhere else the beach is called
in New Jersey "the Shore."

Things learned from Mrs. Ora Watson of Deep
Gap, North Carolina:

Never kill hogs or dig potatoes in the dark of the
moon.

Never make soap or cut shingles in the light of the
moon.

You'll have good luck if you see a red-haired girl
riding a white mule.

If a rooster crows at night, there will be snow before morning.

If your nose itches, company is coming.

If the wind is from the south on March 22nd, the
summer will be dry.

If a honeybee buzzes around your head, you are
about to find some money.

If you need to stop a cut from bleeding, say the

sixth verse of the sixteenth chapter of Ezekiel while walking toward the sunrise.

Signs seen by the side of the road:
"Park Hear."
"No Trustpassing."
"No Boats Aloud."
"No Congretating On The Driveway. Vialtors Will Be Proscuated."

After a night of drinking, University of Nebraska students might wake up with the "brown bottle flu." If they are also throwing up, that's "calling dinosaurs."

North Dakota farmer on his marriage of forty years: "Kissing don't last, but good cooking does."

Breakfast in east Tennessee, described by a Jonesboro innkeeper: "Get yourself a jug of good corn liquor, a thick beefsteak and a hound dog. Then feed the beefsteak to the hound dog."

The earth is so rich in Missouri that if you plant a nail, it will grow into a spike by morning.

How to say "I don't believe it" politely:
In Iowa: "Could be."
In Maine: "I imagine."
In Wyoming: "You reckon?"
In Arkansas: "That's a new one on me!"

Graffito on toilet stall wall in a truck stop in northern Idaho:
"I hate this part of Texas."

Scrawled on the toilet seat paper cover dispenser in the Albuquerque airport:
"Free Cowboy Hats!"

Scratched on the prophylactic machine in a truck stop in Iowa:
"This gum tastes like rubber."

Jim Griffith of Tucson on the size of western mosquitoes:
"There was one, I remember it was in the papers at the time, there was one that come into Nellis Air Force Base, and they were about to fill it up with high-octane fuel until they realized it had the wrong markings on it."

Heard in the hills:
"She's as ugly as homemade soap."
"He's too blind to see through a barbed-wire fence."
"He's such a liar he has to get somebody else to call his hogs."
"She was born tired and raised lazy."
"He ain't worth the salt that goes into his bread."
"She's on the down-go. She ain't got the strength to brush the hen off the roost."

Q: How many Californians does it take to change a light bulb?

A: Six. One to change the bulb and five to share the experience.

Sign behind the bar in Laramie, Wyoming: "Don't Buy A Drink Before Seeing That Your Baby Has Shoes."

In Natchitoches, Louisiana, they say they have more morality and more immorality than any other town. There's nearly as much immorality down the road in Alexandria, they say, and no morality at all.

Pennsylvania Dutch farm wife to her husband:
"Throw the mule over the fence some hay."

Key Largo fisherman to his wife:
"I'll be home at day-down, right about the pink of the evenin'."

BRUSHES WITH THE FAMOUS

Fenwick, Connecticut, is a collection of fine old houses on the Long Island Sound, the sort of big, rambling, shingled dwellings that were called "cottages" by the wealthy Connecticut Yankees who summered there at the turn of the century. My friend Oliver Jensen, author and historian, lives in one of those houses, does his writing there at a window overlooking the Saybrook breakwater, and regales his guests in the evenings with yarns about American railroading and seafaring and the settlement of old New England. Izzy and Larry and I used to drop by to see Oliver whenever we needed a well-told historical tale.

We were filming one summer afternoon on the Jensens' spacious porch facing the sound when a ruckus arose out on the water. A boy had fallen out of the speedboat he had been driving. He was in the water about fifty yards offshore and the empty boat was roaring around him in circles, threatening on each pass to run him down—a really frightening situation for him and for the handful of people who could see his predicament from shore. Nobody was doing anything, though; nobody could figure out what to do.

Izzy, who spent part of his youth as a lifeguard on the beach at Venice, California, took one look at this scary state of affairs and sprinted for the dock of a big neighboring house where a rowboat was tied up. We watched him free the boat, jump in and start rowing as fast as he could toward the kid in the water. A few people on shore shouted encouragement. The youngster was still managing to escape the runaway boat's repeated passes by dodging away each time it came knifing by, but we could tell he was getting tired out there.

Izzy, rowing hard, planned to wait for the empty speedboat to go by, then rush in, pick up the boy and try to make a safe getaway. Just as he approached the scene, however, a couple of fast powerboats came speeding in from the sound. The driver of one of them fell in beside the runaway craft. A young passenger grasped the gunwale of the empty boat, steadied himself, then tumbled into the cockpit and shut down the engine. The other newly arrived boat stopped beside the boy in the water and plucked him to safety. Big cheers for this performance arose from the little knot of people watching.

Izzy, no longer needed, turned the rowboat around and made the long trip back to the dock where he started. When he got there, all tired out, a woman was standing on the dock wearing dark glasses and a scarf. She said, "I saw it all. You were quite magnificent. Thank you for what you did." Izzy held an oar up to her and said gruffly, "Pull me in, will you?" She did, and helped him tie up the boat.

Izzy came walking back to us from the dock of the

big house looking shaken. He sat down on the steps of Oliver's porch.

"That was great, Iz," I said.

Izzy didn't say anything.

I said, "I mean you looked like the old lifeguard out there."

He still didn't say anything. I figured he was exhausted from his effort.

After a while, Izzy said, "Do you know who I just stuck an oar at and ordered to pull me in to the dock?"

"Who?" I said.

He said, "Katharine Hepburn."

I said, "Are you sure?"

Oliver Jensen laughed. "Whose dock did you think that was?" he said. "Whose rowboat did you think you were using?"

Izzy sat in silence another minute or two. Then he said, "Do you know what Katharine Hepburn said to me? She said I was magnificent. And do you know what I said to her?"

"What?"

"I said, 'Pull me in, will you?' "

I could tell he was miserable.

"Hell, she didn't mind, Iz," I said. "She *did* it, didn't she?"

He just looked out at the water.

I remember the day as the one on which Izzy reacted to danger so quickly and behaved so heroically. He remembers it as the day he failed for one horrible moment to recognize his favorite actress of all time and treated her as if she were a dockhand.

Our brushes with the famous have almost always been by accident like that. Famous people get plenty of coverage; battalions of reporters seek them out. So we intentionally go looking for people you wouldn't expect to read about on the front pages or see on the evening news. But when we've stumbled upon a household name, we have almost always found the person behind the name to be friendly and agreeable—even willing to pull a stranger in a rowboat into a dock when ordered to. I know that some rich, famous and powerful people enjoy acting rich, famous and powerful, but the best of them don't. Maybe it's their memories of youthful struggle, or a certain discomfort with the perquisites and praise that are lavished on them all the time, but it turns out that many celebrated people are just folks when you get to know them.

We were in Haines, Alaska, one fall, making pictures of eagles. Haines is at the end of the dusty 650-mile road that comes down from Fairbanks through the Yukon. If you want to go on from Haines, you have to fly or hire a fishing boat, because Haines is where the road runs out. There's a sawmill there and the Captain's Choice Motel on the harbor and Bell's Store and a good cafe bearing the unlikely name of Bamboo Room. Most of the people in Haines are very friendly to strangers and do not ask too many questions, for the town attracts travelers who seem to be running away from something somewhere else. People reach the end of the road in Haines and collect there for a few days or weeks. Some of them just stay. Among the permanent residents are a former New

York debutante, the worldly son of a Wehrmacht officer who plotted against Hitler and an Indian woman who always walks in the middle of the street.

The eagles come in November. Bald eagles are scarce and endangered in most of the country, of course, but when the salmon run up the Chilkat River in November to spawn and die, the eagles fly in by the hundreds to feed on their carcasses. You can drive a few miles out of Haines on the road to Klukwan and see flocks of bald eagles soaring nobly in the air, posing in the trees and behaving just like vultures among the dead salmon on the riverbank.

One morning, I was in Haines with Shad Northshield, founding producer of *Sunday Morning*, naturalist and old friend, and a cameraman named Bob Dunn. We were surprised to see a man walking down the street who bore a great resemblance to Senator Howard Baker. He had a camera in his hand and a film bag over his shoulder. He was accompanied by a small retinue of aides and greeters, which, I realized, meant that undoubtedly he *was* Senator Howard Baker. He was one of the country's most important politicians at the time, Senate Minority Leader, and, it was rumored, a likely candidate for President. As we met on the sidewalk, I said, "If you don't mind my saying so, this is a hell of a place to start your Presidential campaign."

He laughed and said, "I know you from television, and I'd say I'm here for the same reason you are. Which way are the eagles?"

I pointed north up the Klukwan road. Senator Baker had been in Anchorage the night before to make a speech. He was an avid photographer of considerable ability, and it was well known that he never went anywhere without his cameras and lenses. Somebody had told him about the eagles of Haines and he had decided to detour for a couple of hours on the way back to Washington for the rare chance at some head-and-shoulder close-ups of the national bird. It was beginning to snow. Somebody handed Senator Baker a parka. He pulled it on over his coat and tie and piled into a van to be driven off in search of eagle pictures.

We had eagle pictures of our own to make that day. The snowfall grew heavier along the river, coated the blue-green limbs of the spruce trees, and made for splendid portraits of the big birds in windblown wintry settings. When we got back to town after dark and walked down the slippery street to the Bamboo Room for our nightly steak, we were surprised to find Senator Baker there having dinner with two of his young aides.

"I thought you were leaving this afternoon," I said.

"Too much snow," he said cheerfully. "Airplane can't take off. Pull up a couple of chairs and join us!"

One of his assistants said, "We have to get the Senator back to Washington tomorrow. Any ideas?"

"Can't get back to Washington if the airplane can't take off," Senator Baker said with a shrug and a smile. He spent the evening comparing notes with Shad, a splendid photographer of birds, on the fine points of shutter speeds and lens apertures when photographing eagles in a snowstorm.

He was still smiling at breakfast the next morning,

at lunch the next afternoon, and at dinner the next night. Back in Washington, the Senate was preparing to go into session with its Minority Leader snow-bound in a small town at the end of the road 3,500 miles away. The snowstorm turned into a full-blast southeastern Alaska blizzard. Drifts piled up outside the Captain's Choice, which had found rooms for the Senator and his retinue. His aides fretted on the phones. Senator Baker walked happily around town in the heavy snow, freed by an act of God from whatever crushing national responsibilities awaited him at his office back at the Capitol. I imagined these were the first days he had enjoyed for many years with absolutely nothing to do.

Still another day went by before the storm passed and they were able to clear the snow from the airstrip at Haines. So we had another breakfast, lunch and dinner with Senator Howard Baker (G.O.P.–Tenn.). While his aides looked glumly out the window at the snow piling up, he told us funny inside tales of life at the top in Washington. He told us stories on Lyndon Johnson, Richard Nixon and George Bush, with the unspoken understanding that these yarns would not be retold anywhere outside the Bamboo Room Cafe. I got the impression his assistants thought their boss was being a little reckless with his storytelling, and the equally strong impression that he was having the time of his life. He was the most agreeable big-time politician I had ever come across—certainly the funniest Republican—and he struck me as wise and humane besides. I decided that if he did run for President, I might have to vote for him.

The blizzard ended, the sun came out, and we all left Haines and the snow and the eagles behind us and went our separate ways. Howard Baker didn't run for President. He became President Ronald Reagan's chief of staff instead, at a time when the Reagan White House was beleaguered and much in need of help. I sent him a telegram: "MY GOD, LOOK WHERE YOU'RE SNOWED IN NOW!" but I never got a reply. By then, his joyful respite in a small town in Alaska, the gift of the snowflakes, was long past and Howard Baker was up to his ears in affairs of state again.

I've always been a little diffident when meeting people who are very well known, reluctant to take up too much of their time. This is not the approved attitude for reporters, I know; how far would Mike Wallace have come if he had been the least bit in awe of moguls, mobsters, presidents and kings? (To tell you the truth, after thirty years of acquaintance, I find I am still a little bit in awe of Mike Wallace!)

But the great Eudora Welty, who should have been writing that afternoon, insisted that I spend a couple of hours with her in her parlor in Jackson, Mississippi. She even opened a bottle of old bourbon so fine that it didn't have a label, only a number inscribed by pen in a fine hand, a gift, she said, from her friend Robert MacNeil of PBS. She talked about her Mississippi upbringing and her days in journalism, thoughtfully about the art of the short story, about good young writers she hoped to encourage, and when I left, walked me down her sidewalk to the curb and bestowed on me a parting smile that felt like a benediction. I knew about her genius from reading her books; that afternoon, I learned about Eudora Welty's generosity.

Andrew Wyeth and his son Jamie spent the better part of a day with Shad, Izzy, Larry and me, strolling about the splendid, small Wyeth museum in Pennsylvania. It was a day in March when the brown landscape around Chadds Ford looked like a melancholy Andrew Wyeth painting.

"Yes," he said, "I like Pennsylvania this time of year, this open country with patches of snow and the feeling of deep earth below. My father and I were great friends, but we had arguments. He said, 'Andy, you paint this country only in its severe feeling.' 'Well,' I said, 'that's what I like about it.' If you get to know these farmers here intimately, as I have, you know they have had a tough time, and you begin to realize the power of this country, and its somber mood."

He looked out across the land in silence for a while.

"I can look at that hill there. To me, it's not just a hill with snow on it. It's a hill that I know. In painting it, I can fly across the valley and land on the top of that hill and be a part of that hill. It's part of me. I've played there. I've walked over it. It's real.

"I just find the more I look, the more I see, the more I feel, and I want to go deeper. I have not exhausted the ground I stand on. . . ."

I have met a lot of men and women who seemed inseparable from their times and places, but none so much an element of the land as that one man in that one place, Andrew Wyeth in Pennsylvania in the spring.

The Wyeths take care for their privacy, as they must, but they can still make a new acquaintance feel like an old friend. Jamie and his graceful wife, Phyllis, invited Shad and me to dinner at their farmhouse that night. I was distracted from the Wyeth conversation by the Wyeths all over the walls. They were hanging there casually, wonderful pictures I had seen before only in books.

I had a note from Andrew Wyeth when I got home: "Come back and see us at the Mill again when you have more time." I know I'll never do that, not, heaven knows, because of any shortage of my time, but out of consideration for his. I'd hate to interrupt the old lion in his den on a day when he happened to have some surpassing new masterpiece half finished on his easel. There is plenty of artistic chitchat in this world, but there can never be enough Wyeths.

By another accident of timing, I spent a few days in the company of Marlon Brando. He wasn't very good company. For Brando, I guess I have to make an exception to my rule that the very famous, down deep, are just like you and me. Marlon Brando is not one bit like you and me.

I was covering a big public squabble between the state of Washington and the Puyallup Indians over fishing rights. The Indians claimed they had the right to fish for salmon out of season on their reservation; the state said that would ruin fishing everywhere in Puget Sound. The dispute dragged on for weeks, with the Puyallups catching fish and the state Fish and Game wardens issuing them citations and taking them into court.

A few days before a big Indian demonstration was planned for the state capitol steps in Olympia, Marlon Brando showed up from Hollywood and moved into a suite on the same floor of the same hotel where I was staying. I don't think anybody invited him, but Brando was eager to be known as a supporter of Indian causes, and he brought along a beautiful brunette secretary to handle his press releases. The reporters all crowded around the movie star, of course. I noticed this did not exactly thrill the Puyallup fishermen, who saw the attention the press had been giving to their struggle suddenly shift over to Brando. Hearing that he was in Olympia, Brando groupies came rushing to town from all over the northwest. One of them, a pretty, star-struck farm girl from Yakima, was more persistent than the rest. She climbed atop a soft-drink vending machine outside Brando's hotel room door, one of those low, old-fashioned boxes that gave you a Coke for a nickel, and sat there with her legs dangling down. Whatever the hour I walked down the hall, she was there. She said her name was Flo. Every time Brando entered or left the room, she was there, looking at him from atop the Coke machine. He never spoke to her. She never spoke to him. She was just there. After a couple of days, this began to irritate the gorgeous secretary who was occupying Brando's suite. I heard the two of them arguing about Flo in the coffee shop one morning.

Brando's trip was going sour in other ways, too. His aim was to catch an illegal salmon on reservation waters, get arrested and make headlines to publicize the Indian cause. Morning after morning, he went out and trolled a salmon lure from a boat with a flotilla of photographers following and the Fish and Game officers watching from a respectful distance. The problem was that Marlon Brando was a movie star, not a fisherman. He couldn't catch a fish. He worked at it, from midmorning until late afternoon, in bright sun and driving rain, but the salmon would not yield to his fame. This became a joke to everybody but Brando. The reporters and photographers started drifting away to other assignments, which made Brando moody and angry. One day, around a little bend close to shore, he found a dead salmon floating in the water. He plucked it out and went looking for the Fish and Game boat. He presented this deceased relic to the officers triumphantly, expecting to be arrested at last. The chief of the detail regarded the limp fish suspiciously, sniffed it, and handed it back.

"I'm sorry, Mr. Brando," he said. "This one won't do." Brando headed for shore in disgust.

He went out drinking with Hunter Thompson, who gained fame later as the gonzo journalist chronicler of the Hell's Angels and other misfits, like the Presidential Press Corps. At the time, Hunter was a relatively orthodox reporter for a Dow Jones weekly, *The National Observer.* I knew him from Rio, where I had once lent him bail money to get out of jail after he had slugged a guy who had kicked a dog in a bar. Hunter told Brando he suspected I was growing tired of the Indian fishing story and was about to pull out with the CBS crew. Brando went to a phone, called me at the hotel and spoke to me as seriously as a man with several double scotches under his belt can speak.

He said, "If you leave this town before I catch a fish, you scum, I will find you wherever you are and kill you with my own hands."

That night, he had another quarrel with his beautiful dark-haired companion. She went storming out of the suite carrying her suitcase and took a limousine to the Seattle–Tacoma airport. I thought about Brando's threat. I decided there was no way *Marlon Brando* was going to stalk *me* around the country. So I decided to give up, too, on the long-running saga of the Puyallups and the movie star and made plane reservations for the next morning.

I don't think Marlon Brando helped the Indian cause much, or furthered his own reputation either as Indian rights crusader or salmon fisherman. The press and the public, and maybe the fish, too, were all pretty weary of him before he left town. There weren't any winners.

Except Flo.

As I was passing Brando's suite on my way to bed that night, the door opened, and Brando himself stood in the doorway. He ignored me. He looked straight at Flo, the adoring farm girl from Yakima, who was still sitting atop the Coke machine with her legs dangling off. She looked back at him. She hopped down and walked into his room, and Marlon Brando followed her and closed the door.

Other brushes with the famous, let's see:

We keep running into Pete Seeger, who could give Brando lessons in dedication to causes. Clean rivers, racial justice, homes for the homeless, gay rights, you give the demonstration and Pete will come sing at it.

I admire him for his passion, and I like his singing.
Pete Seeger is the legitimate heir to Woody Guthrie
and all the wandering troubadours of history. Inscribed around the rim of his banjo are the words
"This Machine Surrounds Hate and Forces It to Sur-
render."

I'll always be glad I met Archibald MacLeish. I
was knocked out by his poems in college. Like a lot
of other people, I thought he must have written them
directly to me. Soon after the new satellite made it
possible, I moderated a transatlantic television discussion in which MacLeish took part from New York,
as did Prime Minister Harold Wilson from London.
This was a brand-new thing. The picture was one-
way only. Those of us in New York could see the
participants in London; they could only hear us.
Somebody said to me before the program started, "I
don't think Wilson and MacLeish have ever met.
Maybe you ought to introduce them." So I said, "Excuse me, Prime Minister . . ." On the screen, Mac-
Leish and I could see him look up at the camera.
"Before we begin," I said, "I would like to introduce Mr. Archibald MacLeish."

"Indeed, indeed," Wilson said, "I am very glad
to meet you, Mr. MacLeish!" As he spoke, the Prime
Minister of Great Britain stood up to acknowledge the
blind introduction of a man who was thousands of
miles away. Seeing this, MacLeish also stood. And
I, feeling awkward but not knowing what else to do,
stood up too.

"I very much admire your poems," Wilson said,
and started saying one of them: " 'A poem should

be palpable and mute . . . as a globed fruit . . .' ''
When he finished quoting ''Ars Poetica'' to its author, the Prime Minister sat down and presently the
program began. When we were off the air, MacLeish
said to me, ''Wasn't that the damnedest thing, Wilson
standing up that way? That's a lesson in the intimacy
of television, the power of it. We were all on the same
program, so to him it was as if we were all in the
same room.''

I saw Archibald MacLeish one or two times again
before he died, was always impressed that erudition
and humanity could come together so felicitously in
one man, and was proud of our acquaintance. I always wanted to hear him talk about poetry. He always
wanted to talk about television, about Prime Minister
Wilson standing up that time in London to acknowledge the introduction of someone in New York. ''Just
the damnedest thing,'' he said. ''It will become commonplace, I suppose.'' Whenever I see Ted Koppel's
nightly worldwide panel discussions which today's
technology have made perfectly commonplace, I always think of the great old poet who saw the future
coming.

Alf Landon was interested in communications, too.
''As Maine goes, so goes the nation'' was the truism
in Presidential elections until Alf Landon came along.
He was the progressive Republican Governor of Kansas who lost the Presidency to Franklin D. Roosevelt
in the famous landslide of 1936. Even his home state,
where Governor Landon was very popular, went for
FDR that year. Landon carried only rock-ribbed Republican Maine and Vermont—''leading,'' he never

tired of joking, "to the familiar political saying, 'As Maine goes, so goes Vermont.' "

Alf Landon was well up into his eighties when Izzy and Larry and I went to see him to ask him about the changes he had noticed in the lives of Kansas farmers over the years. He sat in a rocking chair on his big front porch in Topeka dressed in boots and jodhpurs, fresh from his daily horseback ride.

"Communications!" he said. "That's the ticket! That's the thing that's made all the difference in the farmer's life."

I told him I expected him to say improved feed and seed and fertilizer and farm machinery.

"Communications!" he repeated. "The seed question was all settled way back at the beginning when the Russian immigrants came out here on the Union Pacific Railroad with those hard, red winter wheat seeds in their pockets. That's the wheat that feeds the whole country now. Most years, it helps feed several other countries, including Russia, where it came from in the first place.

"No, the Kansas farmer always had good land and good seed. But the problem was he lived an isolated life, see? He and his family didn't know what was going on. He could be a good farmer, but he had no way to be a good citizen. And do you know what changed that? It wasn't FDR. It was . . ."

He leaned forward and confided the secret of Kansas progress:

"RFD!"

"Rural Free Delivery?"

"Correct!" Alf Landon said. "It was the idea of

the Democrats. I remember when it came in," he said, his eyes twinkling as he leaned back in his rocking chair.

I checked later and found he would have remembered the start of rural mail delivery, all right. It was an innovation of the second Cleveland administration. That's how far back Alf Landon's political memory went.

"All the bankers and merchants were against it," he said. "They thought it was a terrible waste of money. But it made all the difference to the farmers, see? It meant they didn't have to wait 'til Saturday when they came to town to find out the news. They could get a newspaper in the mailbox every day and read the news after supper and discuss it around the table. That's when farmers became as smart as everybody else."

I agreed that it is pretty hard to find a hayseed in the country anymore. The old vaudeville figure of fun, the country bumpkin, seems to have vanished from the land.

"Yes," Alf Landon said, "if you think you've found one, and ask him how his sorghum crop is coming along, he's liable to reply with some smart remark he heard on the Johnny Carson show. Everybody knows all the same news and the same jokes now. There aren't any country hicks for the politicians and the traveling salesmen to trick. That's good for the country, see?"

We never passed through Topeka after that without paying our respects to Governor Landon. He rode his horse every day until he was ninety-three, saw his daughter, Nancy Kassebaum, elected to the U.S. Senate—probably not without some advice from her old man—and lived on to be 100, never losing interest in the welfare of Kansas farmers or the beneficial effects of spreading the news around so everybody can be in on it.

I have always had heroes. Some of them became friends, people I work with who do the same things I do and outdo me: Morley Safer, Harry Reasoner, Andy Rooney, Bruce Morton, Dick Threlkeld, Charles Osgood, Tom Fenton and John Leonard, whose television essays on *Sunday Morning*, full of metaphor and allusion, always leave me dazzled.

My line of work has given me the chance to meet others I long admired from afar; not once do I remember being disappointed.

I sat next to Mickey Mantle on an airplane flight from Dallas to New York, hesitantly introduced myself and was rewarded with a guileless Oklahoma grin and a string of great yarns about those other heroes, Casey and Billy and Whitey.

I went to a dinner honoring Norman Corwin, the princely user of words who, with *On a Note of Triumph* and other masterpieces, elevated the radio documentary beyond mere craft to art. I have held Corwin in reverent respect since I first came upon a book of his radio plays when I was in high school; I can hardly believe that now I carry on a regular correspondence with him, getting more than I give.

I saw Adlai Stevenson, Hubert Humphrey and John F. Kennedy close up. I spent a day talking with Eleanor

Roosevelt, after she amiably permitted me to pin a microphone to the bra of her corset.

I met people who were better at what they did than anybody else: the sculptor, Henry Moore; the sportswriter, Red Smith; the singer, Mabel Mercer; the author, Teddy White. They were everything I'd imagined they'd be.

Plenty of reporters meet more celebrities in a month than I have met in a lifetime on the road, but I am contented with this register of congenial artists, writers and politicians—and one egomaniacal actor for spice. I have one more name to add.

Except on records, I had never heard Vladimir Horowitz play the piano until the day he played for me in his living room. He was eighty-two years old. He hadn't played much in public for many years, and when he did play a concert, tickets were notoriously hard to come by. Anyway, I thought this wasn't a bad way for me to begin my encounter with the fabled maestro—leaning on his Steinway while he sat at the keyboard pounding away mercilessly to make a musical point.

"This is what is wrong with pianists today!" he shouted over the sound of the music. "They treat the piano as if it were a percussive instrument! No, no! It is all wrong, you see." He stopped pounding and caressed the same notes of Chopin from the piano softly and slowly, with his palms below the keyboard, his long fingers arching upward to touch the keys. "More like this," he said. He played for a few more seconds. "Is better," he said, looking up for agreement.

Who was I to disagree? I was a former third-chair, third clarinet player in the high school band. He was Horowitz, the last of the Romantics, the transcendent pianist of the world. I wasn't exactly alone with him. To begin with, no stranger ever was alone with Horowitz; he was eternally guarded and attended by his formidable wife, Wanda, daughter of Toscanini. She defended him from fools, reporters and autograph-seekers—I was there that day in all three of these capacities—and she defended him from himself. The great man had human tendencies. While strolling down the street, he might have popped into a bar for a few beers with the boys had it not been for Wanda's stern hand on his elbow.

Besides, on this day, the Horowitz living room in New York was cluttered with lights, cables, cameras and TV technicians. Izzy and Larry were there, and Shad Northshield, among many others. A momentous announcement had recently rocked the world of classical music: Horowitz was going to play a concert in the land of his birth, the Soviet Union, to be telecast worldwide. By inflexible tradition, all Horowitz concerts began at four P.M. on Sunday afternoon. Four in the afternoon Moscow time is Sunday morning in New York. *Sunday Morning!* Shad quickly negotiated with Peter Gelb, Horowitz's manager, the right to broadcast the concert on CBS as an expanded version of our *Sunday Morning* program. We were all crowded into the Horowitz town house for a predeparture interview, with the great man at center stage and Wanda an unsmiling presence off camera.

"I think that is enough piano playing," she said to

her husband. "And more than enough criticism of other pianists. Do come back and sit on the sofa." He obeyed, and the cameras dutifully refocused on him as he settled into the soft cushions and took an envelope from his inside jacket pocket.

"Look," he said, "I even have a letter from my niece in Kharkov!"

I said, "Will you read it to us?"

"But it is in Russian," he said coyly. "You won't understand it."

"But you can translate," I said.

"Ahh!" he said with a playful smile. "You want it in English! It is written in Russian. But very well, I shall try:

" 'Dear Volodya, is it true you are coming? We will come to meet you at the airport. . . . We will be so happy to see you. I have always dreamed of hearing you in concert, and now my dream will come true. . . . We are waiting for you.' "

Horowitz looked up from his translation of the letter to say, "I last saw her when she was nine years old. Now she is seventy!"

Horowitz left Russia in 1925, a beautiful twenty-two-year-old boy from Kiev. He was already celebrated in his homeland for the pyrotechnics of his piano style. Even the Bolshevik border guards knew who he was. One of them, Horowitz remembered, put a hand on his shoulder and told him gravely, "While you are gone, do not forget your motherland." Horowitz was touched by this admonition, but also profoundly relieved that the guard didn't require him to remove his shoes, for in them were hidden thousands of American dollars to finance his concert tour of Germany.

His exit visa permitted him to be gone for six months. He overstayed it by sixty years. He received his United States citizenship in 1942, and often said he had no wish to return to the Soviet Union.

But with old age, he began to yield to a desire to see Russia once more before he died. When the cultural exchange agreement between the United States and the Soviet Union was reinstated in 1985, Horowitz wondered aloud to Peter Gelb if he might not return as "an ambassador of peace." Gelb knew right away, of course, that a Horowitz concert in Moscow would become, automatically, one of the musical events of the century. He dashed off to Washington to start making arrangements. When he was able to assure the finicky maestro and the doubtful Wanda that the trip could be carried off in the customary Horowitz style—comfortable apartment in Spaso House, residence of the American ambassador; the Steinway company's chief technician on hand to tend Horowitz's own piano; a supply of Dover sole flown in daily from Paris—Horowitz said yes, and the trip was announced.

Mikhail Gorbachev's policy of *glasnost*, openness, had not taken hold in Russia in the spring of 1986. Though they had agreed to it, the Soviets were not, in fact, particularly open to the return of a native who had skipped the country more than sixty years before, no matter how famous he had become in the meantime. The impending concert was big news among music lovers in the United States. In Moscow, there was nothing in the newspapers or on the radio or television. The great event was announced only on a single poster that appeared one morning on the pale yellow wall of the Moscow Conservatory of Music. The poster said a piano recital would be presented at four P.M. Sunday, April 20, by "Vladimir Horowitz (USA)." In a music-loving city like Moscow, however, one poster was all it took. The news was all over town within hours. As it turned out, 1,400 seats in the conservatory's beautiful Great Hall were reserved for government officials and members of the diplomatic corps, leaving only 400 tickets for sale to the general public. People stayed up all night in a long line to buy those precious few. Minutes after the box office opened in the morning, the concert was sold out.

Elena Dolberg, the niece who wrote to Horowitz from Kharkov, did come to the Moscow airport to meet her celebrated uncle as Horowitz and his entourage stepped off a flight from Paris. Volodya was back at last, and the two old relatives ignored our television lights and a small crowd of European reporters for a time as they sat in a corner of the airport lounge holding hands and exchanging reminiscences.

After that, we didn't see much of Horowitz. He secluded himself in Ambassador Arthur Hartman's capacious official residence under the watchful eye of Wanda, making a pilgrimage only to the house of the composer Aleksandr Scriabin, who had praised the playing of the young Horowitz once upon a time. There, on Scriabin's piano, he played Scriabin études to the delight of Scriabin's daughter Yelena and a small group of American onlookers. He seemed to want to stay and play longer, but—well, you know. Wanda. She guided him toward the door.

The Soviets weren't much help to our little band of visitors from CBS. I arrived on an Aeroflot flight from London with Al Balisky, the genial chief tape editor of *Sunday Morning*. He wasn't so genial when the immigration officials got through with him. First, a sharp-eyed officer discovered a spot of smudged ink on his visa and led Al away to a holding room for an hour and a half while this possible forgery was straightened out. Then, while minutely searching his luggage, they found a music cassette he had brought along for diversion featuring Sly and the Family Stone, and we had to wait another hour for the censor of rock music to be summoned. By the time this functionary showed up, declared Sly harmless to the Soviet state and waved us into the country, the night was getting late. We were tired and famished on the long taxi ride to the Intourist Hotel. All the hotel bars and restaurants had closed, except for a crowded roof cafe where a woman was frying beefsteaks on a grill. Around us, people were eating steaks. Al walked up to the counter and caught the cook's attention. "Two steaks," he said, holding up two fingers. "*Nyet* steaks!" she exclaimed. She scooped the steaks off the grill, put them all in a refrigerator and pointed to the only food that was left—a single bit of smoked fish on a tiny round of stale brown bread, the last of the early evening hors d'oeuvres. Al paid her for it, said, "Welcome to Moscow, Charles," and bit the morsel in half. He handed me the other half. I swallowed it, and we went to bed wondering what kind of country it is that cooks steaks and then puts them in the icebox for the night.

We had plenty to do to prepare for the concert. But if you were a foreign TV journalist in Moscow in those days, you didn't do anything without a "keeper," an official from Gostelradio who went everywhere with you, served as interpreter and censor, and undoubtedly turned in a report on your activities to the KGB each evening. Our keeper was an attractive young woman named Nona. Nona kept telling Izzy and Larry and me all the things we couldn't take pictures of and making a nuisance of herself, but we understood that was her job and kidded her along. Nona was working on improving her English. She carried a little notebook full of colloquialisms she had picked up from other camera crews, with English definitions.

"This town is giving me the heebie-jeebies," Larry said one day.

"Please, what is heebie-jeebies?" Nona said. We explained and she wrote it down.

We needed to build a small camera platform for the concert. "Maybe we can find a few two-by-fours somewhere," Izzy said.

"Please," Nona said, "what is two-by-four?"

One day when we were in a hurry, our taxi driver made a U-turn to get us into the conservatory driveway. A policeman wearing white gloves appeared from behind a post and motioned the taxi over to the curb.

"Tell him to fuck off," Izzy said.

Nona got out and talked to the cop and got the cabdriver off the hook. When she came back to the car, Izzy said, "I noticed you didn't put 'fuck off' in your notebook."

Nona said, "I've already got that one."

On the Friday afternoon before the concert, Horowitz came to the hall to rehearse. The hall was packed with music students and their professors. Horowitz paced about on the stage, meticulously checking the lighting and the placement of the piano. He sat down at the piano and played a few dissonant chords, clowning with Izzy, who was up there respectfully taping the whole thing. Then, sensing the expectations of the audience, he began to play seriously. A great silence settled on the hall. The rehearsal became a concert, prelude to the advertised one to follow. Peter Gelb stood beaming offstage. He said later that this "rehearsal" was one of the finest Horowitz performances he had ever heard.

The students cheered Horowitz for many minutes. They followed him into the conservatory courtyard and mobbed his car. In spite of the best efforts of a cordon of police, it took nearly half an hour for the limousine to make it fifty feet to the street. And after the car had escaped the crowd of young admirers and sped away, the students remained in the courtyard in small groups, discussing what they had heard.

It was raining two days later when the afternoon of the formal concert arrived. I got to the hall three hours early and had to work my way through a huge crowd standing under umbrellas in the street. These were people who knew they would not hear a note. They just wanted to be able to say they were there.

At the appointed hour, the applause began as a thunderclap from the seats at stage right as a slight old man in a dark blue suit and tidy gray bow tie appeared in the wings. The applause swept through the audience and was joined by cheers as he shambled to the center of the stage, gave the crowd a shrug and a nervous grin, patted his piano as if to reassure the instrument and himself, and sat down to wait for silence.

I was watching from a box at the back of the great hall. When that small man alone on that big stage put his fingers upon the keys to play the first notes of a Scarlatti sonata, a chill ran down my back. Vladimir Horowitz (USA), at the age of eighty-two, after an absence of more than sixty years, was playing again in the country of his birth.

He played with great subtlety and great power. He gave the crowd rainbows and thunderstorms, while looking down at his fingers with a bemused expression, as if he were as astonished as the rest of us by the remarkable, nimble things those fingers could do. It was a hell of a performance, which millions of people have heard by now. The Deutsche Grammophon recording of it became the worldwide classical best-seller for more than a year. By the time Horowitz reached the music of the Russian composers Rachmaninoff and Scriabin, many in the audience were weeping.

At intermission, a concertgoer said, "It is not human. It can only come from heaven." "He is the only pianist who can play colors," said another. A Soviet pianist in the audience told an interviewer, "His music is just bits of beauty flowing through the air." The headline on page one of *The New York Times* next day read "For Horowitz in Moscow, Bravos and Tears."

On the lofty State Department–Foreign Ministry level, relations between the United States and the Soviet Union were tense just then. The U.S. Air Force had bombed Libya, and the Soviet government had reacted angrily. The world's television screens had been full of warlike images for a week. Now, on those same screens, appeared the wistful image of a great Russian-born American pianist playing for a Russian audience Schumann's tender "Träumerei," one of the *Scenes from Childhood*. The emotional message implied by Horowitz's choice of encores was lost on nobody in the hall, and he played the piece gently, softly, as if lost in a private reverie.

Back home in New York, my friend Andy Rooney, who often plays curmudgeon on *60 Minutes*, let his private sensibilities show through in his syndicated newspaper column the next day. He wrote:

During the latter part of the concert, watching this eighty-two-year-old genius play, I found mist forming in my eyes for some mysterious reason I could not explain. I was not sad. I was exultant. It had something to do with my pride, at that very moment, in being a part of the same civilization that this great and endearing man playing the piano was part of.

Almost at the same instant I felt the suggestion

of tears in my eyes, the television camera left Horowitz's fingers on the keyboard and dissolved to the face of a Soviet citizen in the audience. He did not look like the enemy. His eyes were closed, his head tilted slightly backward so that his face was up . . . and one lone teardrop ran down his cheek.

It was the same teardrop running down mine.

24

THE DENTIST

I went back to the Soviet Union in May 1988. Sometimes—once in a great while—a story on television actually brings people together, and touches them, and helps make their lives whole. I watched this happen that spring. The man who made it happen was a retired Russian dentist.

I carry around in my head memories of hundreds of people I have met in these years of wandering. The memory of this one man haunts me. Hardly a day goes by that I don't think of Nikita Zakaravich Aseyev.

He was a stocky old bulldog of a man who barged into the hotel where I was staying in Moscow while I helped out with coverage of the Reagan–Gorbachev summit meeting. The hotel, the gigantic Rossiya which looms behind Red Square, was closed to Soviet citizens that week. All comings and goings were regulated by KGB men at the doors wearing red armbands inscribed "I am here to help you." "Pals," the wry Muscovites call these grim-faced guards. Those of us who had rooms and temporary offices in the hotel—mostly American and Western European reporters—wore credentials on chains around our necks to get us into the building past the Pals. Dr. Aseyev got in on his medals.

He wore his World War II medals on the lapels of his suit coat, as do many old soldiers in the Soviet Union. When the KGB men stopped him at the front door of the Rossiya, an acquaintance of mine happened to be there watching. He reported that the old man erupted in indignation.

He thundered, "What do you mean I cannot enter? You children, you pups! You have the gall to tell a veteran of the Great Patriotic War he cannot pass into a common hotel lobby?"

He slapped the place over his heart where his medals hung.

"Where were you?" he demanded of the young chief of the guard detail, who had come striding over to see what the shouting was about. "Where were *you* when I received these honors for helping repel the fascist hordes from our precious motherland?"

His voice rose even louder as he theatrically answered his own question. "Cowering in a safe corner, a child who never heard the guns!" he roared. "Or suckling at your mother's breast!"

The KGB men looked at one another with resignation. The chief of the detail started to speak, but the old man interrupted him.

"Where were *you* when the Gestapo gave me *this*?" he shouted, pointing dramatically to a deep scar in his skull over his right eye.

A little crowd of Western reporters was beginning to gather. The raving old man poked the KGB chief in the chest with a stubby finger.

"Where were *you*?" he roared at the top of his lungs. He jutted out his old square chin and paused for a reply.

The KGB man shrugged. Without a word, he unhooked the chain that barred the door and stood aside.

The old man marched into the lobby of the Rossiya Hotel looking satisfied, his medals swinging from his chest.

He approached the first person in his path and demanded to see a representative of American television. "CBS, third floor," he was told.

Minutes later, he showed up in the CBS News offices, a chunky, obviously unofficial character ranting in Russian, insisting that he be heard. As it happened, everybody in the place was busily preoccupied, preparing for coverage of what seemed more important at the time: the final meeting of the week between the President of the United States and the General Secretary of the Communist Party of the Soviet Union. A young assistant, a Russian-speaking foreign student at Moscow's Pushkin Institute who had been hired by CBS for the week of summit duty, took the old man into a vacant room in order to get him out of the hall, calm him down and get rid of him. The student listened to a few minutes of what seemed to be a carefully rehearsed speech, explained that everybody was too busy to hear his story at the moment, walked the old man back down to the hotel lobby and sent him home in a CBS-hired taxi—but only after making a solemn promise that a reporter from CBS News would see him next morning.

And that is how it happened that the next morning,

I went for a walk in a park with Dr. Nikita Zakaravich Aseyev.

He wore his medals. He carried a walking stick in one hand and a worn shopping bag in the other. The tail of his sport shirt hung out over his trousers, which did not match his suit coat. We were accompanied by an interpreter, but Dr. Aseyev kept forgetting to wait for his words to be put into English. He was in a great rush to say what he had to say.

"You have to help me," he said. "You are my hope. Everybody lives in hope, you know, and I am no different. For more than forty years, I have waited for this chance, and now it has come."

He shifted his cane to the hand that held the shopping bag and grasped my arm.

"You can speak to America, is this not true?" he asked, and went on before I could answer. "You must help me find some Americans I knew during the war. I have to thank them for saving my life and the lives of many other Russian soldiers."

We sat down on a park bench. He pointed to the scar in his forehead.

"A memory of the Gestapo," he said. "Not a very happy memory. I have another in the side of my body."

He cleared his throat and began:

"We were all prisoners of the Germans at a big concentration camp at Fürstenberg on the Oder River. There were eight thousand American soldiers there, captured in North Africa. The camp was laid out this way."

With his cane, he drew a map on the ground in front of the bench.

"Here the town . . . here the river and the railroad tracks . . . here the camp, Stalag 3-B. The Gestapo barracks were here, near the gate," he said, "here the French prisoners, the Polish, the Yugoslav, the partisans." He indicated each compound by drawing large rectangles in the dirt. "Here," he said, drawing the largest enclosure of all, "the Russians. And next to us," he said, finishing his map, "just across the wire fence—the Americans.

"Nearly every Friday, the Americans each received a five-kilo food parcel from the Red Cross. But the Germans gave us only one liter of turnip soup per day, and one liter of water. It wasn't enough to keep us alive. We were dying by the tens, and then by the hundreds. The Americans could see this. Twenty-five thousand men died in that concentration camp. . . ."

His eyes looked past me for a moment, into the distance.

"I could tell you many stories about those who died," he said softly. He paused, still looking away. Then, abruptly, returning to me, "But that is not what I am here to do. It's the Americans I want to talk about, you see.

"In all the camp, I was the only dentist. Every living person, can, of course get sick, and the Germans permitted me to treat the Americans. There was no dental surgery. I just accepted patients in an ordinary chair, even when I had to perform complicated operations. I treated hundreds of American soldiers, and I believe there were never any complications afterwards, even in such conditions as perhaps you can imagine. I was the only Russian permitted any contact with the Americans, and the Americans respected me. All eight thousand of them knew me, or had heard about me, and understood that I was a very good specialist, and they held me in respect.

"One day, after I had been there about a year, two American brothers named Wowczuk, Michael and Peter, and a third American whose name I forget, spoke to me about conditions in the Russian compound. These brothers I knew by now. They were from Chicago, workers in the stockyards, and I understood already that they were very good people. We were alone in the room that was the dental clinic. This was the beginning of the thing I want to tell you. The brothers Wowczuk and this other, whose name I cannot remember, proposed a plot by which the Americans would smuggle food to the Russians. They told me that not only the three of them, but many others of the Americans were willing to participate. I instantly agreed. That is how it all started."

"Wasn't this dangerous?" I asked.

Dr. Aseyev threw up his hands. "Oh, of course!" he exclaimed. "We would have been shot if they had caught us. Merely to be found outside the barracks at night was a shooting offense, and many men were executed in that camp for much less!"

"How did the Americans get the food to you?"

The old man smiled to remember. "They waited until the sentry had passed at night and threw the parcels over the fence," he said. "The fence was only eight meters high. Those Americans were strong!

They could have thrown those things a hundred meters!'' He laughed.

"I organized a group on our side to rush out to the fence and retrieve the packages. In one night, we received 1,350 parcels in this way.''

Dr. Aseyev took my arm again and gripped it tightly.

"Do you realize what I am saying?'' he asked me. "This was nearly seven thousand kilos of food in one night! Do you understand what this food meant on our side of the wire, where men were dying every night of starvation?''

He released my arm. "This went on,'' he said, "at least one night a week for many months. At least one night a week, the Americans, many different ones, risked their lives to collect food parcels and dash out at night to throw them to us. Not one parcel ever failed to make it across the wire. Not one ever was wasted.''

"Why do you think the Americans did this?'' I asked.

"Because we were allies,'' Dr. Aseyev answered. "And because they were good men.''

He reached for the old plastic shopping bag lying beside him on the bench and brought out a fuzzy photograph.

"This was a good man, too,'' he said. "This was a German corporal, one of the guard detail. He stumbled into knowledge of what we were doing almost from the first night. He turned his back and let us continue. He was a soldier of the Wehrmacht, but he did not like seeing enemy soldiers starve. After the war, I wrote to his family and they sent me this portrait of him." He handed the photograph to me. "I had a copy made yesterday," Dr. Aseyev said. "It is for you to take home to America. With perfect assurance, you may tell people that Corporal Alfred Jung was an exceptional member of the human race."

"What happened to him?" I asked, looking at the unfocused image of a young man in a German Army uniform.

"The day the plot was finally discovered," Dr. Aseyev said, "they took him out and guillotined him."

He set the shopping bag back on the bench.

"What else do you have there?" I asked.

"I will show you presently," Dr. Aseyev said. "But now I want to tell you about the behavior of the Americans when the plot was discovered.

"All eight thousand American prisoners were assembled on the parade ground in a great semicircle. This was late in May 1944. It was a hot day. Four SS officers went down the line of them saying to each one, 'Give us the name of the Russian who organized this plot.' For three hours in the sun, with nothing to drink, the Americans stood in absolute silence. They stood there with clenched lips. The German officers threatened them with severe reprisal. They stood in silence. Not one word was spoken. Not one American gave the name of the Russian Dr. Aseyev.

"Finally, to bring the thing to an end, the brothers Wowczuk, Peter and Michael, stepped forward. 'We did it,' they said. 'The whole thing was our idea.' A squad of German guards seized them, and the two brothers were driven out of the camp in a closed truck.

Later, I learned that they were taken to another camp, a place for special punishment, where they were questioned every day for four months by the Gestapo—and the Gestapo was the Gestapo, you know! I was afraid for them, but I had no fear for myself. I knew that Michael and Peter would never reveal my name, and they did not.''

Dr. Aseyev smiled and lowered his voice. "Later, we were all moved to a different camp," he said, "and do you know—I found Michael and Peter there. And within a few days, we had organized the plot all over again!''

He beamed triumphantly, and started rummaging around again in his shopping bag.

"After the war," he said, "I wrote down the names of those Americans so I could never forget them." He showed me a carbon copy of a document of several pages, typed in Cyrillic characters and dated September 1, 1949.

"This is for you," he said. "It is the only extra copy, so do not lose it. It tells the names of the Americans and what I remember about them. For now, I will tell you the names only."

Gravely, he began to read.

"Wowczuk, Michael.

"Wowczuk, Peter.

"Oh," he said, "Bennett! I just thought of Bennett. He isn't on the list. He was on his deathbed and I did an operation on him. I don't know his first name.

"Jarema, William. He was from New York.

"Harold Symmonds. He was from Mississippi. He lived on that famous river of yours.''

"Walhaug, Lloyd. He was a farmer from Illinois.

"Emil Vierling, thirty years old, also a farmer.

"Gut. He was a medic.

"Gasprich. How I loved Gasprich!"

He looked up from the paper in his hand to say emotionally, "What good men they were! What good men they all were!"

He took out a handkerchief and wiped his eyes. "I loved these guys," he said. He continued reading:

"Brockman. Doctor. Captain. I will tell you more about Brockman. . . .

"Dr. Hughes. He was a good friend.

"Dr. Amrich."

I sat on a park bench in Moscow listening to these American names pronounced in a Russian accent. I knew I was hearing a roll call of heroes.

"There were others not written down here," Dr. Aseyev said. "They all took part in smuggling food. I remember Rossbridge, Tossi, Snow—from California, I think—Mangelomani, Audeni . . ."

He leaned forward and said to me, "There were four of us Russian doctors in the camp who took an oath one night that after the war we would find a way to thank these Americans. You see, I am getting old now. This is my chance.

"Now, now because of you," he said, "if these guys are still alive they will know I remember—this dentist who loved them, and whom they did not betray."

He stopped. He exhaled deeply, handed me the list of names and slumped back on the bench. After forty-

three years, Nikita Zakaravich Aseyev had just ful-
filled an oath.

I invited him to lunch at the Rossiya Hotel. The
KGB men stood aside as we entered, not wishing to
tangle with him again. At the lunch table, where we
were joined by CBS News producer Peter Schweitzer
and others, Dr. Aseyev produced more keepsakes
from his shopping bag.

"Oh," he said, "oh . . . These are my darlings,
my treasures!"

There were photographs of the abandoned camp,
clipped from a Soviet newspaper after the war. There
were snapshots of the Russian medical doctors who
had survived the ordeal of Stalag 3-B with him. There
were more medals, wrapped in tissue. Finally, there
was a crude cigarette case made of hammered tin.

"Late in the war," said Dr. Aseyev, "Dr. Brockman, who was a gentleman, and with whom I had
many long and searching conversations, left the camp.
He and some others learned they had been exchanged
for German prisoners. Before he left, he came to me
and gave me this. It was the only thing he had to give
me."

Into the top of the case was scratched the inscrip-
tion "To N. Z. Aseyev from Sidney Brockman, Captain, U.S. Army."

After lunch, I walked Dr. Aseyev to the taxi that
would take him home.

"I know you will not fail me," he said.

I extended my hand, but he didn't take it. Instead,
he gave me a vigorous military salute, stepped into
the taxi with his cane and shopping bag, and shut the

door. As he was driven away, he looked back, and I said good-bye to him in the only way that was now possible. I stood at attention in my best imitation of the form I learned once in the Army Reserve, and returned his salute.

The next morning, June 4, I left Moscow for London by Aeroflot jet, carrying in my hand an orange CBS News shipping bag with the word "URGENT" printed on it in red capital letters. The bag contained the videotape cassettes of Dr. Aseyev's story. All our news shipments are labelled "URGENT." This one, I felt, really was. On arrival in London, I went straight to the CBS News offices in Knightsbridge, where Al Balisky was waiting for me in an editing room. As we sat with the door closed screening the cassettes, I noticed Al's eyes growing moist.

"Imagine," he said gruffly. "The old guy remembered all these years."

Then, without saying anything more, he began the hard job of editing Dr. Aseyev's story into a form that would fit the stringent time requirements of that night's *Evening News*. Once more, on tape, Dr. Aseyev recalled the names.

"Wowczuk . . . Symmonds . . . Jarema . . . Brockman . . ."

"Listen to these names back there in America," I said. "If your name is on this list, an old soldier is saying thank you."

Watching the news that night, William Jarema, retired New York City police detective, felt tears spring to his eyes. "It was a different kind of weeping," he explained a few days later, still unable to speak without choking up. "These are tears of joy. We were like brothers. I thought he was dead."

Dr. Sidney Brockman, retired from the San Antonio, Texas, Health Department, also wept that night. "We were all very close to Dr. Aseyev," he explained later. "We all had tremendous respect for the man, because we knew the Russian prisoners were having things mighty rough.

"In the wintertime, when the Russian prisoners died in their barracks, their comrades did not report their death to the Germans. They brought them out and stood them up for roll call so that their bodies would be counted for rations."

He took out a handkerchief, just as Dr. Aseyev had done on the park bench, and dabbed at his eyes.

"How could we not try to help them?" he asked.

But to risk his own life for them?

"It was part of the game," Dr. Brockman said. "We had all risked our lives to begin with or we wouldn't have been in that place. What was one more risk?"

He said, "Look, I have not believed in being a professional prisoner of war. What happened is done with. I want to forget it if I can." Against his will, he started to weep again.

"But I can't," he said. He paused for a while to collect himself.

"I appreciate Dr. Aseyev remembering me. I have never forgotten him. I will never forget him. What more can I say?"

He got up, went to a cedar chest in a hall closet, and after a time found what he was looking for. "I keep it in here where it's safe and where I don't have to look at it very often," he said. "I took it with me when I left the camp. It's about the only thing I've kept from the war."

It was a cigarette case fashioned of scrap wood, patiently handmade. He opened the case and shook a small metal plaque into his hand.

The plaque read: "To Sidney Brockman from N. Z. Aseyev."

The typewritten pages Dr. Aseyev entrusted to me on the park bench, when translated, give further details of the sacrifice and heroism that ennobled a miserable place once known as Stalag 3-B. When he wrote these notes in 1949, they were meant only as a memorandum to himself, insurance against forgetting some men he had vowed never to forget. But as I read his unadorned recital of bravery and brotherhood in a dark time, I could not help thinking of his notes as a message to the world.

AMERICAN ANTI-FASCIST PRISONERS OF WAR,
MEMBERS OF THE UNDERGROUND IN
THE CONCENTRATION CAMP 3-B
IN THE TOWN OF FURSTENBERG-ON-ODER, 1942–1945.
GERMANY.

1. Michael Wowczuk. Senior sergeant. 25–30 years old, blond, native of the town of Chicago, former worker at a slaughterhouse . . . active member of the underground . . . organizer of help to our prisoners of war and to our partisans. Continually informed me about the situation on the

Soviet–German fronts . . . In the American blocks, there were two radios under the platforms in barracks 13 and 15. Michael Wowczuk continually organized collection of food parcels . . .

2. Peter Wowczuk. Brother of Michael. 35 years. Blond. Was always with Michael. He helped Michael in all undertakings to organize more food provisions for our prisoners. He also obtained English leaflets, translated them into Russian, and passed them to me in the American medical unit. He also actively helped Michael in collecting food parcels for Soviet partisans in May, 1944. He also was imprisoned with Michael together with a third whose surname I have forgotten in a prison in Frankfurt-on-Oder. There they were convicted by a fascist tribunal. The Germans were seeking the name of the Russian Communist who helped organize food parcels for the Soviet partisans. Neither they nor the other 8,000 American POW's gave me up as the organizer, though the Gestapo sought me for four months. The brothers Wowczuk and the third person during four months in the prison were subjected to interrogations, but did not give my name and thus saved me from death at the hands of the Gestapo.

3. William Jarema. 25–30 years. Native of the town of New York. Formerly a New York courier. A remarkable and warmhearted person. Active member of the underground. Constant companion of the Wowczuk brothers. Constant organizer

amongst the Americans of collection of food parcels for Soviet prisoners of war and also for our long-suffering tormented partisans.

4. Harold Symmonds. 20–25. Blond. Senior sergeant. Medic with the American infirmary with whom I had a close friendship, especially when I worked in their infirmary where there was not even a dentist's chair for the dentist. So Harold Symmonds always stood behind an ordinary chair and held the head of the patient as if he were a headrest, and also helped me in my specialist work where necessary. . . .

He always said that such a war as the fascists had conducted against all countries would not happen again, that Marshal Stalin would come to an agreement with our President Roosevelt and that then there would be no war.

Harold Symmonds was from the town of Mississippi. His house was on the banks of the river. He studied in a technical college for three years, but since he didn't have enough money to continue studying, he was forced to take out a contract with the Army for two years. Then the war started and he was sent to Africa, either to Tunis or Algiers. I don't remember very well, but as I understand they were captured in the fortress of Tobruk, taken captive by Rommel's army, and ended up with us. . . .

Symmonds was a good antifascist underground member for more than three years, and when we were liberated from captivity in the town of

Luckenwald in April 1945 by the tanks, Symmonds came to our meeting and seeing me, ran to embrace me. He took me in both arms and wept for joy that both he and I were alive. In all my life, I can't remember such tears, especially from a young man, such as those wept by my dear friend, my American savior, and all of them, 8,000 men, were my saviors when they stood on the parade ground in May, 1944, in a semicircle before the head of the Gestapo, Krautzer, who expected that one of them would step forward and say who was the organizer of the collection of food parcels for the Russian partisans, but no one gave the name of the Russian Dr. Aseyev.

5. Lloyd Walhaug. American medic . . . Walhaug was 20–25 years old, a farmer from the state of Illinois . . . Loved to joke, very communicative, helped in every way the Soviet POW's, especially in throwing food parcels over the wire barricade . . . He continually told the Americans that the Russians were good people and that they were suffering from starvation, being driven to hard labor and being brought home dead from work. He would say, "Why, why, why? It is not their fault that the Germans don't feed them but force them to work, beat them and kill them." Lloyd Walhaug in Luckenwald in Camp 3-A obtained for our underground, I do not know how, much medication and many bandages, three liters of iodine, 500 bandages, 300 vials of 2% novocaine . . .

* * *

6. Emil Vierling. A farmer with a lettuce plantation
   from the state of Iowa. He was an active underground member, often threw materials from the
   infirmary courtyard over the wire barrier. Next
   door to the infirmary was the general camp bath
   area in which worked 17 of our Soviet doctors
   who were assigned to this wash area with great
   difficulty through the fascist Dr. Kruger who
   agreed to the doctors being taken from heavy
   work on the railway and uprooting tree stumps in
   the forest. It was necessary to save these doctors
   by feeding them and this was achieved. The bath
   area was common to all foreigners . . . The
   American medics collected food, packed it in
   bags and kept it in the infirmary stores and upon
   my direction, the American medics threw the
   bags to our doctors in the wash area under cover
   of darkness. . . .

7. Gut. Medic of the American infirmary. An
   American of Spanish origin, 20–25 years, brunet, a quiet type, rarely entered into conversation
   . . . but helped to collect food parcels in the infirmary . . . and threw food sacks to our doctors.
   I remember [Gut's parcels being picked up by]
   the surgeon from the town of Voronezh, Nikolai
   Alekseevich Petrov. . . . But in general, I remember hazily.

8. Gasprich. A huge man, 35, blond, from New
   York, one of the organizers of the collection of
   food parcels. . . . After we were moved to Con-

centration Camp 3-A, he became representative
of the American Red Cross. In Camp 3-A in February, 1945, he learned that I also had arrived
and came to visit me. Michael and Peter Wowczuk, William Jarema, Gasprich and I organized
amongst the Americans the collection of 800
5-kilogram parcels which were conveyed to our
block in the first days of April. This helped to
put a stop to the recruitment of our starving people into Vlasov's criminal plot. [A scheme by
which Russian prisoners were offered normal
food rations and release from the camp in return
for joining the German Army and fighting on the
German side.] The attempt collapsed and burst
like a soap bubble. In this way, the Americans
helped me fulfill the tasks set by the underground
group opposing fascism in Camp 3-A. The head
of the underground unit was Pilot Captain Victor
Ivanovich Yuschenko.

9. Brockman. Doctor. Captain. Blond. . . . He was
very communicative and related to me very well.
He always greeted me in the infirmary with some
chocolate and invariably opened a golden cigarette case and said, "Please, Doctor, have a
smoke." He said that he was apolitical, although
I didn't ask about that. He put questions to me
such as, "Tell me, Doctor, is it true that in Russia when a child is born it is taken from its
mother?" I asked him where he got that idea. He
said that's what they write in American newspapers. I said to him that a newspaper is just a bit

of paper and you can write any nonsense you like on it, but if you want the truth I'll tell you. This conversation took place in the presence of my convoy, Alfred Jung, who brought me to visit Brockman at his invitation, illegally, under cover of darkness. I told Brockman that we have nurseries, thousands of them, and if any mother decides to work in industry or anywhere else, then she can leave her child in a nursery and after work collect her child and take it home. We have thousands of nurseries in the USSR!

Brockman looked hard at me and listened attentively. Then raising both hands, he said loudly, "Very good, Doctor. We don't have that in America!"

As far as politics was concerned, of course, he was a gentleman with a batman like a baron. He treated me to good food that night, even omelet with sausage. Before the convoy left, having turned out the light in the corridor, Brockman entrusted to me one food parcel and another one to his batman, and having said good-bye, we left with the two parcels by the camp road and the convoy took me to the Soviet block and returned with the batman.

10. Hughes. Doctor, captain, blond, perhaps 35 years old. A fine person. He sympathized with the Soviet POW's whom the Germans treated so cruelly. "Why?" he always asked me. What could I answer to his why? Especially since I knew where I was and amongst whom. So I always answered

I don't know. Dr. Hughes gave the Soviet POW's much food from his personal supply. He would say to me, "I would like you to accept for the Russian prisoners . . ."

Dr. Hughes was killed when the town of Brandenburg was bombed by American aviation, along with the Yugoslav Doctor Rado Savlevich Manchino. He also was a fine person.

11. Amrich. Doctor, captain, brunet from New York. I did not know this person well. He always kept to himself, talked little. On rare occasions, he spoke to me in English. Once in the American infirmary, I stood by the window and looked at the forest, which was situated not far away to the east of the infirmary. Dr. Amrich came up to me and said, "Tell me, Doctor, is it true that in Kiev at Babi Yar the Germans shot 90,000 Jews?" I answered that this was a fact, that I personally in September, 1941, talked with people who were there. Amrich burst into tears and I could not get him to calm down. Oh no, I thought, now I am in trouble. Amrich will tell the Germans and I'll get a bullet in the head. But everything turned out all right. Amrich calmed down. He was a Jew.

N. Aseyev
1 September, 1949.

I did my best to deliver Dr. Aseyev's message of gratitude and remembrance to all those on his list. I found that some have died, among them the brave brothers Wowczuk. One or two find the memory of

Stalag 3-B so painful that they refuse to discuss it, even now, even on the telephone. In spite of a diligent search by the Military Field Branch of the Department of Defense and by the Center of Military History in Washington, several remain unaccounted for. By recent act of Congress, World War II prisoners of war have been awarded decorations, years after their imprisonment. So far as I know, none of the heroes of Stalag 3-B has ever been honored for what he did there, except in the memory of an aging Russian dentist.

"It was a terrific operation," William Jarema said. "Terrific. We were repaid many times by our feeling of satisfaction, knowing we helped people in need.

"See, when you're starving, it is an awful feeling, your stomach tightens up on you. People don't know how it feels. If you've ever been starving yourself, you can't just walk away from a person who's starving. We were all in trouble in that camp, and we did everything we could to help one another."

He thought about it for a minute and said, "There ought to be more of that in the world today."

25

REGRETS

I knew it was going to be a long, lonely drive, and that's what it turned out to be. I rented a Peugeot in Lima, stowed a sack of meat pies and some water bottles in the backseat and half a dozen five-gallon cans of gas in the trunk and set out north along the coast road one afternoon in February, midsummer in Peru. After three or four hours, I turned off to the right into a side road and started climbing up into the Andes. The road turned into a dirt track about the time night came on.

I was headed for a primitive village hundreds of miles up in the mountains. Willard Van Dyke, the famous pioneer filmmaker, was up there working on a documentary for CBS about the life of the Quechua Indians, descendants of the proud Incas who were turned into serfs by the Spanish and who still live in thrall to faraway landowners. I was to spend a week or two helping out on interviews and working on the script, and I had been delayed by having to attend an attempted *coup d'état* in Bolivia or somewhere. Van Dyke, I knew, was waiting for me, and there was no way to send a message to him, so I figured it was better to drive all night than to keep him wondering for another day whatever the hell had become of his reporter.

At first, I passed through occasional little settlements of six or eight huts with the light of kerosene lanterns showing at the windows, but then the lights went out and there were no more signs of civilization at all except the winding dirt trail that I followed up and up toward the top of the cordillera. I was utterly alone up there in the dark, and driving carefully. There were no guardrails and my headlights showed me what I would have been able to do if I took any sharp curve a little too fast. I would have been able to whistle sixteen bars of the Peruvian national anthem in thin air on the way down. The stars came out, looking like headlights in the black sky. I'd have welcomed a pair of real headlights coming down the hill as a sign that other human beings coexisted in that starry night, but none ever came. I had heard stories of bandits, and half expected to find armed men in the road around every bend, but no bandits appeared. No animals crossed the road. I was the last creature on earth, driving a French car up a Peruvian mountain in the desolate darkness.

I kept checking my watch, so I know it was just after two A.M. when I heard the loud ping under the hood. The accelerator started flopping under my foot and the car slowed down and stopped in the middle of the narrow trail. I cursed and kicked the accelerator. It lay dead on the floor.

I set the hand brake and got out. A vertical slope rose a few feet to the left of the car and a chasm fell off a few feet to the right. I reached inside and turned off the car's lights. Whatever my other problems were, I knew I didn't need a dead battery. After that, I didn't know what to do. I stood there for a while in the dark beside the dead car, cold and scared. I thought after a while, well, lift the hood. That's what people do, isn't it? I fumbled around until I figured out how to lift the hood of a Peugeot and got it open. It was too dark to see anything in there. I remembered a battery penlight that I once had carried in my shaving kit and wondered if it might still be there. After another few minutes of groping in the dark—ridiculous thing to be doing, I thought to myself, throwing things out of your suitcase onto a dirt road in the Andes in the middle of the night—I found the shaving kit, and inside it, under the soap and the razor and the laxative pills and the bottle of paregoric and the aspirin and deodorant and Swiss Army knife and house keys and collar stays, my hand fell around the little flashlight. The battery will be gone, I thought. But it wasn't. I remember that tiny light coming on in that great darkness as one of the glad moments of my life.

I shined it around under the hood of the car until I found a broken wire hanging loose. When I jiggled the wire, I discovered that it went inside the car and made the gas pedal move. I am not much of a mechanic, but it didn't take much of a mechanic to figure out that this was the accelerator cable, and that it was busted in the middle. I found the other end up by the carburetor. I held the little flashlight in my teeth, took the broken ends of the wire in my hands and brought them together. How could I make them *stay* together?

I could think of only one way. I tied them together in
a knot.

I closed the hood, got back into the car and turned
the ignition key. In neutral, the engine raced with a
roar I had not heard from a motionless car since the
fifties, when the hot-rodders of my youth gunned their
motors before "scratching off" from the Central High
School parking lot. I shifted into low and the Peugeot
scratched off. The rear wheels spun, dug in, and drove
the car crazily toward the next steep curve. I jammed
on the brakes. The car slid to the edge of the precipice, cornered like a Maserati at Le Mans and roared
into the uphill straightaway. Another curve coming
up. Another hard, fast slide and another rocket ride
up the mountain. The accelerator, I calculate, was
tied down to about fifty miles per hour; on that road,
thirty was a suicidal speed. I drove with my foot on
the brake and one hand on the gearshift lever, dropping her back into neutral as we approached the most
perilous turns. Several times when I smelled the brake
lining beginning to burn I coasted to an uphill stop to
let the brakes cool off and my heartbeat slow down.
Then back into gear and back into orbit, skidding up
and around the mountain again.

I was so intent on the driving that I didn't notice
at first that I was beginning to see farther up the road
than the range of my headlights. Daylight was arriving. The curves became gentler and finally the road
straightened out. I had reached the top, the great high
plateau that divides the coastal range of the Andes
from the snowcapped Cordillera Blanca away to the
east. I could see in the early morning light the thin

line of the road stretching miles ahead to the north over a treeless, rolling plain dotted with small lakes. The meaning sank in: I wasn't going to drive over a cliff. The cliffs were all behind me. I had made it.

I stopped the car and turned off the damned roaring motor. The silence was the most profound I had ever known. I stepped out, feeling weak and dizzy from the thin air and the lack of sleep and the relief at having come through the crisis. I unwrapped a meat pie and ate it slowly, leaning against the car in the morning cold, looking around at the mountains. I uncorked a bottle of water and drank most of it down. Just as I was preparing to climb back into the car, dreading the thought of having to listen to that insane racing motor again, I heard another sound, a human sound, a faint and muffled shout.

I knew the altitude had made me light-headed. I could see nothing but the two mountain ranges and the vast, vacant plateau. But I heard it again, the same sound, a shout. I scanned the landscape more carefully—and saw him, a man running uphill toward me from the direction of a lake which lay below the road a mile or so ahead.

Good God, where had he come from? What was he doing in this barren place? I thought of bandits and of ambush. I thought of turning the car around and escaping the way I had come, but that would take me back into the hairpin turns of the mountain, downhill this time, with the car really out of control. He shouted again. He was scrambling and stumbling toward me over the rocks as fast as he could, but he still had a few hundred yards of hill to climb before he reached the road. I leapt into the car, started it, slammed it into gear and bolted straight ahead. He altered his course to intercept me on the road. As I grew closer, I could tell he was wearing a black woolen coat and an Indian balaclava hood pulled down over his face. He was carrying something in one hand—a club, a gun? He ran toward a point in the road ahead, waving his free hand at me. I drove for my life, terrified.

He reached the road an instant ahead of the car, lifted the hood from his face, raised the thing he was carrying high in the air and shouted at me at the top of his voice. As I roared past, I caught a glimpse of what it was he was holding.

It was a fish.

He was trying to sell me a fish.

The poor man had been fishing all night on the shore of that godforsaken lake, trying to stay warm in his black coat and his face mask, in the hope of catching a fish he could sell for a few *soles* at the roadside. My car, appearing so early in the morning, must have seemed sent from heaven. We were the only two souls in the wilderness. We met as if by destiny. But one of us was from another world, and wildly misunderstanding. I sped past him like a maniac, leaving him standing there in the dust. In the rearview mirror, I could see him put his fish down in the grass and sit down beside it to catch his breath.

I could have gone back. I could have apologized, and bought the fish. But I knew I couldn't explain to him. He was probably a Quechua speaker who did not understand Spanish. Anyway, there is no language for putting into words the embarrassment of acting foolishly out of fear. I drove on, using the brake and the gearshift until I came to a small settlement beside a river where I found a man with a length of strong wire who could help me replace the accelerator cable.

Sometimes at night before sleeping, little regrets come back to me. The guy with the fish comes back. The reporter's existence is one of perpetual motion. He wraps up one story, gets started on the next one and thinks he must be accomplishing something. But the good memories are all of stopping and staying a while. I realize I've always driven too fast through life, carrying in my baggage too much impatience and apprehension, missing too many chances, passing too many good people in the dust.

Nobody ever knew the Minnesota north woods better than Bill Magie. After he died, the other guides and outfitters put a plaque on a boulder in the middle of a lake in the Boundary Waters canoe country. It says on the plaque:

> *Think on this land of lakes and forests.*
> *It cannot survive man's greed*
> *without man's selfless dedication.*
> *William H. Magie,*
> *friend of the wilderness,*
> *devoted most of his life to this cause.*
> *Now, it is yours.*

I spent a day doing a story about Bill. He was already seventy-six. Every summer, he said good-bye to Lucille, his understanding wife, left her behind in Superior, Wisconsin, and went up into the Minnesota woods to camp alone beside a lake with his old dog, Murphy. He hired himself out guiding canoeists. Bill Magie remembered everything that had ever happened to him in a lifetime guiding in the Minnesota-Ontario wilderness. He told about the hunting trip he took Knute Rockne on back in the twenties and about the night he crawled inside a moose he had shot to keep from freezing and all about his mapping expeditions in winters past. "I'm the only man alive that's walked from Lake Superior to Lake of the Woods on the ice and carried a transit on his shoulder all the way," he said. Bill Magie was a wonderful man and such a good storyteller that we were able to finish up our story about him before the sun went down.

Over supper, he said to me earnestly, "You know, I want to take one more long canoe trip before I get too old to carry a canoe on the portages. I believe I like you well enough to invite you to come along with me."

I could tell he meant it. I felt honored and a little abashed.

"I don't know much about canoes," I said.

"I could teach you everything," he said. "You like fishing, hell, we'll catch our supper every night and listen to the loons and live off the land the way I used to. I'll promise you this: I can take you to some lakes that damn few people have ever seen. I'd like to see them one more time myself."

"How long a trip are you talking about?" I asked him.

"We could do the whole thing in six weeks, maybe eight," he said. "We'll leave the Fourth of July next summer and be back the end of August. How about it?"

I didn't know how to answer. I could never take that much time away from work, but his invitation was so eager and heartfelt that I hated to tell him so. I said, "Six or eight weeks is kind of a long time for me, Bill."

"The hell it is," he said. "It's six or eight weeks is all it is. What are you going to do for six or eight weeks that would be better than this?"

I told him I'd think about it and let him know.

He wrote me letters over the winter to make sure I was thinking about it. In one of them, he said if it was money I was worrying about, why of course he wasn't planning to charge me for guide service, he thought I understood that. "Just your grub is all you'd have to pay for," he said. "Write me soon."

But I never did write him, and after a while he gave up on me. I found later that he never made the long canoe trip. He spent the next summer around Moose Lake, guiding a few tourists on overnight camping outings, telling them some of his stories around the campfire and paddling them back the next day. A year or two later, Lucille Magie wrote to me from Superior to tell me that Bill had died.

I wish with all my heart I had made the long canoe trip with Bill Magie. I can't remember what I was doing from the Fourth of July to the end of August the summer he wanted to go fish every night and listen to the loons and see those distant lakes one more time. What could I have been doing that would have been better than that?

There was a flood one spring in West Virginia and the assignment desk sent me to meet a camera crew in Charleston. I got there late at night and drove around looking for a place to stay. Even the ma-and-pa motels and the tourist courts were all filled with people who had been flooded out of their houses. I wound up at the desk of a seedy hotel on a side street run by a burly tattooed night manager in shirt-sleeves and a mentally retarded bellboy in a dirty uniform. The bellboy slumbered in a lobby chair with a pornographic magazine open on his lap until, in a parody of Grand Hotel style, the manager tapped the bell on the desk.

"What?" said the startled sleeper.

"Room four twenty-six, that's what," the manager said.

The bellboy picked up my bag with a yawn and opened the door to the elevator, the old lever-operated variety. On the way up, he looked me over.

"You need anything?" he asked.

"Nope," I said. "Just some sleep."

By now, he had overshot the fourth floor. As he coaxed the lift back down in fits and jolts, he said, "You know what I mean. You *need* anything?"

"Nope," I said.

He got the elevator door open at last. "Where's my room?" I asked.

"I got a lot better room," he said with an idiot leer. He dug a key out of his pocket, opened a door across from the elevator and switched on the ceiling light with a flourish. There on the bed, uncovered by so much as a sheet, a young woman lay naked. She turned her head to the door and smiled.

"Hello, honey," she said to me.

"It's my cousin," the bellboy said proudly.

I stood there gaping. She had dirty blonde hair that fell to her shoulders. Her sleepy eyes were blue. She was pretty.

"Well, come on in," she said. She sat up in bed and pulled the sheet up around herself. A gesture of modesty for my sake.

"I'm Sally," she said.

"I can't come in," I stammered. "I mean, nice to meet you, Sally, but it's a mistake. It's the wrong room."

She looked back at me. "Well," she said. "All right."

She lay back down and turned to the wall. She said, "Turn the light out, Luther."

Luther did, and shut the door, and walked ahead of me down the hall. At the door of 426, he handed me the key and walked away disgustedly. He said over his shoulder, "You're crazy, man."

One of us is crazy, I thought. My room was tiny and stuffy. The window, painted shut, overlooked an air shaft. A spindly floor lamp tilted from its base beside a horsehide chair. There was a cheap veneer desk with nothing but a Western Union blank in the dusty drawer. Luther was right. Sally's *was* a better room. I sat down on the edge of the lumpy bed, a little shaken, and started to take off my shoes. Outside in the hall, a bell started ringing.

"Forget it, it's nothing," the manager said on the phone. I could hear his switchboard buzzing like crazy.

"Yeah, but what is it?" I asked him.

"It's the fire alarm," he said. "It'll go off. It happens all the time. It's nothing."

I undressed, got into bed and waited for the bell to stop ringing. Pretty soon, there was a commotion in the hall, somebody banging on the doors and shouting, "Get up! Get up! Get out of here!" I got up and cracked the door. It was Sally. She was barefoot and wrapped in a chenille bedspread.

"The guy downstairs says it's nothing," I said.

"It's not nothing!" she hollered. "I smell smoke. Get out of here!" She went on down the hall pounding on doors and shouting.

I put on my shirt and pants, went out and found a stairway and made it down to the lobby. The lobby was full of smoke, so I went out onto the street. Luther and the tattooed desk clerk were already safely there, I noticed. Other people kept coming down the stairs and out of the smoky lobby until there were maybe fifty of us standing on the sidewalk. After a while, the fire trucks came and the first firemen jumped off and went running into the hotel while the others hooked up hoses. It turned out to be a fire in a storeroom in the back of the fleabag hotel, and the firemen had it out in a few minutes. But they wouldn't let us back into the building until the smoke was aired out, so we stood out there half dressed in the dark for another couple of hours with the red and white lights of the fire trucks flashing over our heads and the truck radios crackling. A little shower came past, and we all flattened ourselves against the buildings to try to stay dry. I found myself standing next to Sally. She was still wrapped in her bedspread. She was perfectly calm.

"Well, thanks for saving my life," I said.

"That's all right," she said.

"And I'm sorry for barging in on you like that before."

"That's all right," she said.

"Well," I said, "I guess now we're going to get rained on."

She looked up at the sky.

"Yeah," she said.

Her blonde hair was all wet and matted and shining in the lights of the fire trucks. She lifted a corner of the bedspread off her shoulder.

She smiled. She said, "Are you still sure you don't want to get under here with me?"

It was five o'clock in the morning. The first light was appearing in the gray sky. People were going back into the hotel and trudging up the stairs. I was weary and lonely. She was still smiling. She touched my hand. . . .

I kissed her chastely on the cheek, went up and got my bag and walked down the street in the drizzle, looking for breakfast.

This was about thirty years ago. Harry Golden, the old editor and author who lived in my hometown, told me when I was a young newspaper reporter, "When

you get to be my age, sonny, all you ever think about
are the women you could have gone to bed with and
didn't.''

I laughed then.

26

A PLACE TO COME HOME TO

There is a cabin in a grove of cottonwoods beside a western river. The cabin, and a timber bridge across a creek to give access to the cabin, are the only disturbances of nature along the river. The river runs, as it has for centuries, between deep-cut banks, leaving gravel bars on the insides of its frequent bends. When Lewis and Clark passed a few miles away in 1805, they sent one of their sergeants to explore westward up the river. He reported tough going through thickets of wild roses on the banks. The roses are still there, a few steps from where the cabin now stands. They still discourage travel along the river.

Ring-necked pheasants and sharp-tailed grouse, however, find cover in the briars the year round and nourishment in the rose hips of late summer. Hundreds of smaller birds chortle and tweet unseen in the heart of the thicket, protected there from the marsh hawk who appears in the afternoons to hang in the thermals overhead.

Upriver, the roses give way to young willows, which crowd the banks. Deer have made paths through the willows, and follow these paths to drink from the river in late afternoon before they retreat to

335

the tall grass of the river bottom meadow to bed down for the night.

Every few hundred yards, a creek enters the main stream. These creeks are the homes of beavers, whose broad tooth marks girdle every cottonwood within falling distance of water. The beavers are notoriously busy, and also very patient. They may wait for many seasons for a huge and ancient tree to fall, wait until the bright, deep indentation of their gnawing and the yellow wood chips they have left at the base of the tree have been turned gray by weather. They know one winter a storm will come and seize the tree by its spreading upper branches and wrench it down across the creek, and the giant will be theirs. Beavers like their cottonwoods horizontal. Nobody traps beavers here any longer, so they proliferate. When it comes to dam-building, they could give lessons to the U.S. Army Corps of Engineers. Their dams are built to last, and if breached, are quickly repaired. In these creeks, the beavers reveal their instinctive intention: to turn all the flowing waters this side of the Continental Divide into a series of placid ponds stretching downstream to the Gulf of Mexico.

Late in spring, if there has been much snow in the mountains, the quiet river rises, becomes a torrent, forces the beavers into a flurry of dam-mending, and robs them of their patiently felled and stripped cottonwood trunks. These are hurtled down the river into great logjams in the bends, where they may remain through many drier springs when the river has not the force to propel them farther. Under these piles of wreckage, in the quiet currents and eddies, live the

largest brown trout of the river. They venture out at
dusk to sip mayflies, caddis flies, drowned ants or
grasshoppers, according to the season, their rises from
the depths creating awesome circles on the dark surface of the water. In the faster current below the logjams the rainbow trout feed on such insects as have
floated past the marauding browns. The rainbows rise
more exuberantly, sometimes arching unexpectedly
out of the water and falling back with a splash, disturbing the grave peace of the river after sundown.

Elk, migrating moose and wandering brown bears
are visitors to this place, but always move on after a
few days. Sandhill cranes arrive in spring to spend
the short summer in the meadows, and Canada geese
claim the shallows of the river for a month or two.
The year-round residents are the less spectacular
common creatures of the west, the white-tailed and
mule deer, the raccoon, muskrat, porcupine and
skunk, gray turkey and blue heron. All, by instinct,
are shy of human beings, yet so unchanged is this
place from its ancient state of nature, altered to human
purpose only by the presence of the cabin and the
bridge, that one or another of these animals or birds
is almost always visible from the cabin porch, sometimes a number of them at once. It is naive and sen-
timental for a man to think he can live as one with
the creatures of river, wood and thicket, but in this
one place, almost, he can. At the moment, I am irritated only by the beavers.

I am in this place now. I have been watching a pair
of barn swallows. Every few daylight minutes for a
week, they have been feeding their chirping young in

their mud nest on a porch beam, and today I watched the chicks leave the nest one by one, clumsily trying to learn to swoop and dart in the air like swallows. It is getting late in the year for them. They have to find their wings quickly because they have a long trip south ahead of them, all the way to Mexico.

The sun will be going down soon, and the big brown trout will soon be swimming out from beneath the logjam on the river to sip their supper. A male pheasant in full plumage just strutted past the window without his harem. A white-tailed doe and her two fawns have been passing every evening, and I expect them presently.

I hear an owl hooting from the top of a not-yet-fallen, beaver-girdled cottonwood. A coyote is moaning somewhere in the dry hills that look down on this small, green, river bottom Eden. The moon is rising.

I love this place. When I am here, I think I would be happy never to leave it. Every trip has to end.

About the Author

Charles Kuralt appears regularly on the *CBS Evening News* and anchors the CBS News broadcast *Sunday Morning*. He and his crew have logged more than a million miles "On the Road" alone and in the process have won a host of honors, including nine Emmys and three Peabody Awards. Kuralt is the author of four previous books, *To the Top of the World*, *Dateline: America*, *On the Road with Charles Kuralt*, and *North Carolina Is My Home*. He makes his home in New York City—when not "on the road."

KILLJOY

Books by Julie Garwood

JULIE GARWOOD
KILLJOY

A Novel

BALLANTINE BOOKS • NEW YORK

2018 Ballantine Books Mass Market Edition

Copyright © 2002 by Julie Garwood

All rights reserved.

Published in the United States by Ballantine Books, an imprint of Random House, a division of Penguin Random House LLC, New York.

BALLANTINE BOOKS and the HOUSE colophon are registered trademarks of Penguin Random House LLC.

Originally published in hardcover in the United States by Ballantine Books, an imprint of Random House, a division of Penguin Random House LLC, in 2002.

ISBN 978-0-525-61884-3
Ebook ISBN 978-0-345-45859-9

Cover design: Lynn Andreozzi
Cover photograph: PeopleImages/Getty Images

Printed in the United States of America

randomhousebooks.com

9 8 7 6 5 4 3 2 1

Ballantine mass market edition: March 2018

For Mary K. Wahlstedt Murphy, my sister and my friend.

With your steady strength, your quiet grace, and your wonderful sense of humor, you make the world a better place.

PROLOGUE

AVERY ELIZABETH DELANEY'S mother was a frickin' maniac.

Fortunately her mother, Jilly, left for parts unknown just three days after Avery was born.

Avery was raised by her grandmother Lola and her aunt Carrie. The three generations of females lived quietly and modestly in a two-story frame house on Barnett Street just two blocks from the city square in Sheldon Beach, Florida. The atmosphere on Barnett Street was vastly different after Jilly left home. The household, which had once been in a constant uproar, was now peaceful. Carrie even learned to laugh again, and for five wonderful years, life was very nearly idyllic.

The previous years with Jilly had taken their toll on Grandma Lola, however. She hadn't become a mother until she was almost old enough to begin the change of life, and she was an old, tired woman now. The day Avery turned five, Lola began having chest pains. She could barely get the icing on the child's birthday cake without having to sit down and rest a spell.

Lola didn't tell anyone about her problem, and she didn't

see her regular doctor in Sheldon Beach because she didn't trust him to keep quiet about his findings. He might just take it upon himself to tell Carrie about her illness. She made an appointment with a cardiologist in Savannah and drove all the way there to see him. After giving her a complete physical, his diagnosis was grim. He prescribed medication that would ease the pain and help her heart, told her she had to slow down, and also, as gently as he could, suggested that she get her affairs in order.

Lola disregarded his advice. What did that quack of a doctor know about anything? She may have one foot in the grave but, by God, she was going to keep the other firmly planted on the ground. She had a granddaughter to raise, and she wasn't going anywhere until she got the job done.

Lola was an expert at pretending everything was fine. She'd perfected the art during the turbulent years trying to control Jilly. By the time she got home from Savannah, she had convinced herself that she was as healthy as an ox.

And that was that.

Grandma Lola refused to talk about Jilly, but Avery wanted to know everything she could about the woman. Whenever she asked a question about her mother, her grandmother would pucker her lips and always answer the same way. "We wish her well. We wish her well away." Then, before Avery could try again, her grandmother would change the subject. And that, of course, wasn't a satisfactory answer, especially for a curious five-year-old.

The only way Avery could find out anything about her mother was to ask her aunt. Carrie loved to talk about Jilly, and she never forgot a single one of the bad things her sister had ever done, which, as it turned out, added up to a considerable number.

Avery idolized her aunt. She thought she was the most beautiful woman in the whole world, and she wished more than anything that she looked like her instead of her no-good mama. Carrie had hair the exact color of Grandma's homemade peach jam and eyes more gray than blue, like the furry white cat Avery had seen colored pictures of in one of her storybooks. Carrie was constantly on a diet to lose twenty pounds, but Avery thought she was perfect just the way she was. At five feet six inches, Carrie was tall and glamorous, and when she put on one of her glittery bar-rettes to keep her hair out of her eyes while she was study-ing or working around the house, she looked just like a princess. Avery loved the way her aunt smelled too, like gar-denias. Carrie told Avery it was her signature fragrance, which Avery knew had to be special. When Carrie was away from home and Avery was feeling lonely, she would sneak into her bedroom and squirt some of the special perfume on her arms and legs and pretend her aunt was there in the next room.

What Avery loved most about Carrie, though, was that she talked to her like she was a big person. She didn't treat her like a baby the way Grandma Lola did. When Carrie spoke about Avery's no-good mama, Jilly, she always began by saying in her no-nonsense tone of voice, "I'm not going to sugarcoat the truth just because you're little. You've got a right to know."

One week before Carrie moved to California, Avery went into her bedroom to help her pack. She kept getting in the way, and when Carrie had had enough, she sat her niece down at her vanity table and placed a shoe box filled with cheap costume jewelry in front of her. She'd collected the baubles at neighborhood garage sales as a present to give to Avery before she left. The little girl was thrilled with the sparkling treasures and immediately began to primp in front of the oval mirror.

"How come you got to go all the way to California, Carrie? You're supposed to stay home with Grandma and me."

Carrie laughed. "I'm 'supposed to'?"

"That's what Peyton says her mama says. Peyton says her mama says you already went to college and now you're supposed to stay home and help take care of me 'cause I'm a handful."

Peyton was Avery's best friend, and because she was a year older, Avery believed everything she said. In Carrie's opinion, Peyton's mother, Harriet, was a busybody, but she was nice to Avery, and so Carrie put up with her occasionally butting into family business.

After folding her favorite, baby blue, angora sweater and placing it inside the suitcase, Carrie once again tried to explain why she was leaving.

"I've gotten that grant, remember? I'm going to get my master's, and I know I already explained at least five times why the extra schooling is important. I have to go, Avery. It's a wonderful opportunity for me, and after I've started my own company and I've become rich and famous, then you and Grandma will come and live with me. We'll have a big house in Beverly Hills with servants and a swimming pool."

"But then I can't take my piano lessons, and Mrs. Burns says I have to 'cause I've got ears."

Since her niece sounded so serious, Carrie didn't dare laugh. "She said you've got the ear, and that means that if you practice, you could be good, but you can take piano lessons in California. You could take karate lessons there too."

"But I like taking karate here. Sammy says I'm getting stronger with my kicking, but you know what, Carrie? I heard Grandma tell Peyton's mama she doesn't like me taking karate. She says it isn't ladylike."

"Too bad," Carrie said. "I'm paying for the lessons, and I want you to grow up knowing how to defend yourself."

"But how come?" Avery asked. "Peyton's mama asked Grandma how come too."

"Because I don't want anyone to be able to push you around the way Jilly used to push me," she said. "You're not going to grow up being afraid. And I'm sure there are wonderful self-defense schools in California with teachers just as nice as Sammy."

"Peyton's mama says that Grandma said Jilly went away to be a movie star. Do you want to be a movie star too, Carrie?"

"No, I want to build a company and make tons of money. I'll make other people stars."

Avery turned back to the mirror and clipped on a pair of fat green rhinestone earrings. Then she untangled the matching necklace and put it around her neck. "You know what else Peyton said?" She didn't wait for a reply. "She says her mama says when Jilly had me, she was old enough to know better."

"That's right," Carrie answered. She pulled out her sock drawer, dumped the contents on the bed, and began to match the pairs. "Jilly was eighteen."

"But what did Peyton's mama mean? How come she should know better?"

"She meant that Jilly should have taken precautions."

The drawer fell on the floor. Carrie picked it up and slid it into the dresser, then went back to the chore of sorting through the pile of socks.

"But what does that mean?" Avery asked. She was making faces at herself in the mirror as she put on the second necklace.

Carrie ignored the question. She didn't want to get into a long-winded discussion about sex and birth control.

Avery was too young to hear about all that now. Hoping to turn her niece's attention, she said, "You know, you're very lucky."

"'Cause I have you and Grandma to look after me 'cause I'm a handful?"

"That's right," she agreed. "But you're also lucky because Jilly wasn't drinking like a fish or taking feel-good pills by the fistful when she was carrying you. If she had put all that garbage inside her, you would have been born with serious problems."

"Peyton says her mama says I'm lucky I got borned at all."

Exasperated, Carrie said, "Peyton's mother sure likes to talk about Jilly, doesn't she?"

"Uh-huh," she said. "Are 'feel-good pills' bad?"

"Yes, they are," Carrie said. "They'll kill you."

"Then how come people take them?"

"Because they're stupid. Put that jewelry away and come sit on this suitcase so I can get it closed."

Avery carefully put the earrings and the necklaces back in the shoe box. She climbed up on the canopy bed.

"Can I have this?" she asked as she picked up a small book with a blue vinyl cover.

"No, you can't. That's my diary," Carrie answered. She snatched the book from Avery's hand and tucked it into one of the side pockets. She closed the suitcase and Avery scooted on top. Leaning on it with all her weight, Carrie finally got the latches to lock.

She was helping Avery off the bed when her niece asked, "How come you're packing now and not next week? Grandma says you're doing it backwards."

"Packing before I paint the room for you isn't backwards. This way, my things will be out of the way, and we can get you all set up in your new room before I leave. Tomorrow, you and I will go to the paint store and pick out the color."

"I know. You already told me I could pick the color. Carrie?"

"Yes?" she asked as she set the suitcase by the door.

"Did my no-good mama hate me when she saw me?"

Carrie turned around, saw the worry in Avery's eyes, and was instantly furious. Even though Jilly wasn't there, she was still causing pain. Would it never end?

Carrie remembered, as though it had happened yesterday, the night she found out her sister was going to have a baby.

Jilly had graduated from high school on a balmy Friday evening in May. She then came home and ruined the celebration by announcing that she was almost six months pregnant. She was just barely showing.

Reeling from the shock, Lola at first thought about the embarrassment and shame the family would have to endure, then came to her senses. "We're a family," she said. "We'll work this out. We'll figure a way to get through this. Isn't that right, Carrie?"

Standing at the dining room table, Carrie picked up the knife and cut herself a piece of the sheet cake Lola had spent all morning decorating. "In this day and age you've got to be really dumb to get pregnant. Haven't you ever heard of birth control, Jilly, or are you a complete moron?"

Jilly was leaning against the wall, her arms folded, glaring at Carrie. Lola, hoping to avoid a screaming match between the two daughters, hastily interjected, "There isn't any need to be snide, Carrie. We don't want to get Jilly upset."

"You mean *you* don't want to get her upset," Carrie corrected.

"Carrie, you will not take that tone with me."

Contrite, she bowed her head and scooped the piece of cake onto a plate. "Yes, ma'am."

"I did think about birth control," Jilly snapped. "I went to the doctor over in Jacksonville to get rid of it, but he refused to do it because he said I was too far along."

Lola slumped into a chair and covered her face with one hand. "You went to a doctor . . ."

Jilly had already lost interest in the subject. She went into the living room, plopped down on the sofa, grabbed the channel changer, and turned on the television.

"She causes the trauma and then she walks away," Carrie muttered. "Leaving us to clean up the mess. How typical."

"Don't start, Carrie," Lola pleaded. She rubbed her brow as though to ease a headache and then said, "Jilly just doesn't always take the time to think things through."

"Why should she? She has you to clean up her mistakes. You've let her get away with everything but murder just because you can't stand her fits. I think you're afraid of her."

"That's ridiculous," Lola blustered. She got up from the table and went into the kitchen to do the dishes. "We're a family and we're going to get through this," she called out. "And you're going to help, Carrie. Your sister needs our moral support."

Carrie clenched her fists in frustration. What was it going to take to get her mother to open her eyes and see the selfish bitch she'd raised? Why wouldn't she see the truth?

The rest of that summer was an awful memory. Jilly was her usual demanding nightmare, and their mother was run ragged waiting on her hand and foot. Fortunately, Carrie had a summer job at Sammy's Bar and Grille, and she did her best to get as much overtime as possible so she wouldn't have to go home.

Jilly went into labor at the end of August. After she gave birth in the county hospital, she took one look at the squirming, blotchy-faced infant who had caused her so much pain and decided that she didn't want to be a mother. Not now, not ever. If the doctors had agreed, she would have had her uterus yanked out or her tubes tied that very day.

Lola dragged Carrie to the hospital to see her sister. They hadn't even walked into the room before Jilly announced that she was too young and pretty to be saddled with a baby. There was a big world outside of Sheldon Beach, Florida, just waiting to pay her some attention, but no man with any money would ever notice her if she was lugging a baby around on her hip. No, motherhood wasn't for her. Besides, she had her heart set on becoming a famous movie star. She would get her start by being crowned Miss America. She had it all figured out, she told them. Boasting that she was much prettier than those cows she had seen on television last year marching around the stage in their swimsuits, she was positive that, as soon as the judges got a good look at her, they would give her the crown.

"God, you're ignorant," Carrie muttered. "They don't give the crown to girls who have had babies."

"You're the ignorant one, Carrie."

"Hush, you two," Lola ordered. "Do you want the nurses to hear you?"

"I don't care if they hear me or not," Jilly said.

"I told you to hush," Lola snapped. "Use your head, Jilly. You're a mother now."

"I don't want to be a mother. I want to be a star," Jilly screamed.

Mortified, Lola pulled Carrie into the room and told her to shut the door. Gripping the potted plant she'd brought Jilly in one hand, Lola held on to Carrie's arm with the other so she wouldn't bolt.

Carrie was annoyed that she was being forced to be supportive. She leaned against the door and glared at her sister.

"Now, Jilly, I don't care what you want," Lola said in a low, furious whisper.

Her mother didn't usually use that tone with Jilly. Carrie perked up and began to pay attention to the conversation.

"You're going to be responsible," Lola said. Her voice turned earnest as she moved toward the bed. "You will be a good mother, and Carrie and I will help you raise the baby. It will all work out. You'll see. I do think you should call the baby's father—" Jilly's laugh stopped her. "What's so funny?"

"You," Jilly replied. "You've got my life all mapped out, don't you? Always trying to make me behave and act the way you think I should act. Really, Mother. I'm a grown-up now. I'm eighteen," she reminded her. "And I'll do whatever I want to do."

"But, Jilly, the father has a right to know he has a daughter."

Fluffing her pillow behind her head, Jilly yawned loudly. "I don't know who the father is. It could be the college boy from Savannah, but I can't be sure."

Lola let go of Carrie. "What do you mean, you can't be sure? You told me—"

"I lied. You want me to tell you the truth? Fine, I will. The father could have been a dozen other men."

Lola shook her head. She refused to believe her daughter. "Stop talking like that. Tell me the truth."

Carrie's head came up. "Oh, my God, Jilly."

Jilly loved shocking people and being the center of attention. "I am telling the truth. I really have lost count of the men I've been with. I couldn't possibly know who the father might be." She saw the disgust on her mother's face.

"Have I upset you?" Jilly asked, inordinately pleased by the possibility. "Men love me," she boasted. "They'll do anything I want just to please me. They give me expensive gifts and cash too, which I've had to hide from you and Carrie so you wouldn't get jealous and act like you are now, so holier than everybody else. You would have taken the money and the jewelry away from me, wouldn't you? Only, I wouldn't give you the chance. I'm smarter than you think, Mother."

Lola closed her eyes, battling the waves of nausea. "How many men have there been?"

"How would I know? Weren't you listening? I just told you I lost count. All I had to do was let them use my body for a little while. They adore me and I let them. I'm much more beautiful than all the actresses in Hollywood put together, and I'm going to be more famous. You just wait and see. Besides, I like sex. It feels good when they do it just right. You just don't understand the modern woman. You're old, Mother, and all dried up inside. You probably don't remember what sex is."

"Taking money for sex? Do you know what that makes you?"

"Liberated," Jilly snarled.

Carrie stepped away from the door. "No, it doesn't. It makes you a dirty little whore, Jilly. That's all you'll ever be."

"You don't know what you're talking about," Jilly shouted. "Men don't want you the way they want me. I can drive them crazy, and they don't give you the time of day. I am liberated and you're just jealous."

"Come on, Mother. Let's leave." Carrie touched her mother's shoulder.

Turning her head into the pillow, Jilly muttered, "Yes, leave. I'm sleepy now. Go away and let me rest."

Carrie had to help Lola to the car. She had never seen her mother so distraught, and it scared her.

As they drove away from the hospital, Lola stared blankly out the window. "You've always known what she was like, and you tried to tell me, but I wouldn't listen to you. I've been living in a fog, haven't I?"

Carrie nodded. "Something's wrong with Jilly. The mean streak inside of her goes beyond . . . it isn't normal."

"Did I do that to her?" Lola asked, sounding bewildered. "Your father spoiled her, and after he left us, I spoiled her too so she wouldn't feel abandoned. Did I make her the monster she's become?"

"I don't know."

Neither one of them said another word until they reached home. Carrie pulled the car into the driveway, parked it in front of the garage, and turned the motor off. She was opening the door when Lola grabbed her arm.

"I'm so sorry for the way I've treated you." She began to weep then. "You're such a good girl, and I've taken you for granted all these years. Our lives have revolved around Jilly, haven't they? It seems I've spent the better part of her eighteen years keeping her calm . . . happy. I just want you to know that I'm proud of you. I've never told you so, have I? I guess it took this nightmare to make me realize what a treasure you are. I love you, Carrie."

Carrie didn't know how to respond. She couldn't remember if or when her mother had ever told her she loved her before. She felt as though she'd just won some kind of a contest, but by default. The golden child was tarnished, and because she was the only one left, she got the prize.

It wasn't enough. "What are you going to do about Jilly?" she asked.

"I'm going to make her do the right thing, of course."

Carrie pulled away. "You still don't get it. She won't do the right thing. Maybe she can't. I don't know. She's sick, Mother."

Lola shook her head. "She's spoiled, but I can work on—"

Carrie stopped her. "You're still living in dreamland," she muttered. She slammed the door when she got out of the car and went into the house.

Lola followed her into the kitchen, took an apron from the wooden peg on the wall, and tied it around her waist.

"Do you remember what happened on my eighth birthday?" Carrie asked as she pulled a chair from the kitchen table and dropped into it.

Hoping to avoid the unpleasant remembrance, Lola didn't turn around. "Not now, dear. Why don't you set the table and I'll start dinner."

"You gave me that Barbie doll I wanted."

"Carrie, I don't want to talk about this now."

"Sit down. We need to discuss this."

"It happened a long time ago. Why do you need to go over it again?"

Carrie wasn't going to back down this time. "I came into your bedroom that night."

"Carrie, I don't—"

"Sit down, damn it. You can't keep living this way. You have to face the facts. Sit, Mother." She wanted to grab her by the shoulders and shake some sense into her.

Lola gave in. She took the chair across from her daughter, and primly folded her hands in her lap. "I remember your father was very upset by your accusations," she said. "And Jilly was crying. You woke the whole household that night carrying on."

"She wanted my doll," Carrie said. "When I wouldn't give it to her, she told me she was going to cut my eyes out with scissors. I woke up around midnight and she was standing over me with your shears in her hand. She had this sick smile on her face. She was opening and closing the scissors making this horrible clicking sound. Then she held up my new Barbie doll and I saw what she'd done to it. She'd stabbed the eyes out, Mother, and that smile on her face . . . it was so awful. As I was about to scream, she leaned down and whispered, 'Now it's your turn.' "

"You were too young to remember exactly what happened. You've blown this little incident way out of proportion."

"Oh, no, I haven't," she said. "That's exactly how it happened. You didn't see the look in her eyes, but I'm telling you she wanted to kill me. If I had been alone in the house with her, she would have done exactly what she wanted to do."

"No, no, she was just trying to scare you," Lola insisted. "She never would have hurt you. Jilly loves you."

"If you and Dad hadn't been there, she would have hurt me. She's crazy, Mother. I don't care what happens to her, but there's an innocent baby now." She took a deep breath, and then blurted out, "I think we should encourage Jilly to give the baby up for adoption."

Lola was outraged by the suggestion. "Absolutely not," she said, and slammed her hand down on the table. "That baby is your niece and my granddaughter, and I'm not going to let strangers raise her."

"It's her only hope for a decent future," Carrie argued. "She's already got one huge strike against her with Jilly as her mother. I only hope whatever is broken inside of Jilly isn't genetic."

"Oh, for heaven's sake. The only thing wrong with Jilly is that she's used to getting her way. Lots of young women are fooling around with men these days. It's wrong," she hastily added, "but I understand why Jilly wanted men to love her. Her father left her, and she's been trying to—"

"Will you listen to yourself?" Carrie shouted. "For a little while, I thought you were finally seeing what Jilly was, but I guess I was wrong. You're never going to open your eyes. You asked me if you had made her the monster she's become, remember?"

"I meant to say that her behavior was monstrous, but Jilly's a mother now. When I go back to the hospital to bring her and the baby home, you'll see. She'll be all right."

It was like talking to a brick wall. "You think the maternal instincts are going to kick in?"

"Yes, I do," Lola said. "You'll see," she repeated. "Jilly will want to do the right thing."

Carrie gave up. Sickened, she went to her room and stayed there the rest of the night. When she came down the following morning, there was a note on the kitchen table. Her mother had gone to Sears to purchase a crib, baby clothes, and an infant car seat.

"Dreamland," Carrie muttered.

On Monday morning, Lola went to the hospital to bring Jilly and the still unnamed baby home. Carrie refused to go with her mother. She told her she had to work an early shift at Sammy's and left the house before Lola could question her.

Jilly was waiting for her mother. She was dressed and standing in front of the bathroom mirror brushing her hair. She waved her hand toward the screaming infant she'd dropped in the middle of the unmade bed seconds after the nurse had left the room and told Lola she could either keep her, sell her, or give her away—she didn't much care what she did with her. She then picked up her overnight bag and walked out of the hospital with the money she'd stolen from her sister's college fund tucked into her bra.

The withdrawal didn't appear on the bank statement until two weeks later. Carrie was outraged. She'd worked hard to save the money, and she was determined to get it back. She tried to report the theft to the police, but Lola wouldn't let her.

"Family business stays in the family," she decreed.

Carrie graduated from high school the following spring and worked two jobs that summer. Lola used some of her savings to help with Carrie's college tuition, and Carrie found part-time work on campus to help with expenses. When she came home for Christmas break, she could barely look at Jilly's baby.

However, Avery wasn't the kind of child who put up with being ignored. It only took a couple of drooling smiles, and Carrie was smiling back. Each time she returned home, the bond grew stronger. The child adored her, and the feeling, though never openly stated, was reciprocated.

Avery was the sweetest, most intelligent little girl, and Carrie in every way possible had become her substitute mother. She certainly had all the protective instincts of a mother. She would do anything to keep Avery safe.

Yet here they were, five years later, and Jilly was still able to cause the family pain.

"Did she, Carrie? Did she hate me?"

Carrie forced herself to concentrate on the child's question. Planting her hands on her hips, she took a deep breath and then asked, "What do you care what Jilly thought about you?"

Avery lifted her shoulders. "I don't know."

"Now, you listen to me. Your no-good mama probably did hate you, but not because of who you are or what you looked like when you were born. You were a perfect baby. Jilly just didn't want responsibility." She pointed to the chair adjacent to the bed. "I'm going to tell you something important, and I want you to pay attention, so sit down."

Avery hurried to do as she was told.

"You're probably too young to hear this, but I'm going to tell you anyway. Your mother's a frickin' maniac."

Avery was disappointed. She thought she was going to hear something new. "You already told me that, Carrie. Lots of times."

"That was just another reminder," she said. "Jilly has never been normal. Fact is, she should have been locked up in a loony bin a long time ago."

Avery was intrigued by the thought of her mother being locked away. "What's a loony bin?"

"It's a place where sick people go."

"Is Jilly sick?"

"Yes," she answered. "But not the kind of sick where we feel sorry for her. She's mean and hateful and just plain crazy. She'd have to be crazy to walk away from someone as wonderful as you," Carrie added. Leaning forward, she brushed the hair out of Avery's eyes. "Your mother grew up with something important missing from inside her head. She might not be a pure sociopath, but she's damn close."

Avery's eyes widened. In a hushed voice she said, "Carrie, you just said '*damn*.'"

"I know what I said, and I know what I'm talking about."

Avery got out of her chair and went to sit beside Carrie on the bed. She latched on to her hand and said, "But *I* don't know what you're talking about."

"I'm going to explain. A sociopath is a person who doesn't have a conscience, and before you ask, I'll tell you what a conscience is. That's what's inside your head that tells you when you've done something wrong. Your conscience makes you feel . . . bad."

"Like when I told Grandma I already practiced on the piano, but I didn't, and then she told me I was a good girl, but I wasn't 'cause I lied, and then I felt bad?"

"Yes, just like that," she said. "Your mother doesn't have any heart or soul, and that's the truth."

"Like the song you like to sing? Is it that kind of heart and soul?"

"Yes, just like the song," Carrie assured her. "Jilly doesn't have room in her heart to feel any emotion that doesn't directly involve or benefit her."

Avery was leaning into her side, looking up at her with those wonderful violet blue eyes that were so much more beautiful than her mother's. Carrie could almost see the purity and goodness behind them. "Jilly's too busy loving herself to love anyone else, but you can't waste your time feeling bad about that. None of it is your fault. You believe me, don't you?"

Avery solemnly nodded. "It's my no-good mama's fault, all right."

Carrie smiled. "That's right."

"Do I have a soul?"

"Yes, you do. Everyone but your no-good mama has a soul."

"Before Jilly hurt Whiskers and made him die, did he have a soul?"

"Maybe," she allowed, thinking of the kitten Jilly had cruelly taken from her.

"Where is it?"

"Your soul?" Carrie had to think about the question for a few seconds before answering. "It's inside you, wrapped around your heart. Your soul is as pure as an angel's, and I mean to help you keep it that way. You're nothing like Jilly, Avery."

"But I look like her. You said so."

"It's not what you look like that's important. It's what's inside you that matters."

"Does Jilly love you and Grandma and just not me?"

Carrie was exasperated. "I thought you understood what I was telling you. Jilly doesn't love anyone but herself. She doesn't love Grandma, she doesn't love me, and she doesn't love you. Now do you understand?"

Avery nodded. "Can I play with the jewelry now, Carrie?"

Carrie smiled. The child, it seemed, had moved on to more important matters. She watched her sit at the vanity and begin to dig through the box again. "You know what's the best thing that ever happened to you?"

Avery didn't look around when she answered. "Having you for my aunt Carrie."

"Is that what you think is the best thing?" she asked, surprised and pleased. "How come?"

" 'Cause that's what you told me is the best thing."

Carrie laughed. "Yeah, well, there's something even better."

"What?"

"You aren't growing up afraid all the time the way I was. Jilly's never going to come back. You won't ever have to see her . . . not ever. That's definitely the best thing."

A shiver ran down Carrie's back the second the words were out of her mouth. Was she tempting fate by making such a boast? Could one summon up a demon simply by proclaiming that it didn't exist? The chill felt like a premonition. But of course it wasn't. She was just a worrier, that was all. Shaking off her grim feeling, she went back to work.

The following week was busy. Avery chose pink for her walls, and Carrie added white trim. She thought the bedroom looked like an explosion of Pepto-Bismol, but Avery loved it. She was all settled in the big front bedroom by Sunday afternoon. Carrie's suitcases had been packed in the trunk of the car. Carrie was going to sleep in Avery's old bedroom on the grossly uncomfortable daybed her last night.

They had all of Carrie's favorite foods for dinner that night—forbidden food on her perpetual diet—fried chicken, mashed potatoes and gravy, and green beans simmering in bacon fat. Lola had made a fresh salad, using the vegetables she'd grown in her backyard, but Carrie barely touched it. Since she'd already decided to take a day off from her diet—one wonderful, guilt-free day—she ate two helpings of everything else with unbridled gusto.

After Grandma Lola had read Avery a story and tucked her into bed, Carrie went in to kiss her good night. She turned on the nightlight, shut the bedroom door, and then went back downstairs to put some last-minute paperwork in her carry-on.

One task led to another, and she didn't get back upstairs until after eleven. Lola was already asleep in her room at the back of the house. Carrie checked on Avery—oh, how she was going to miss the pip-squeak—and she almost burst into laughter when she spotted her niece in the big bed. The child was wearing at least five necklaces and four bracelets. The tarnished tiara with most of its glass diamonds missing was tangled in strands of her hair and tilted to the side of her head. She was sleeping on her back clutching a worn-out teddy bear in her arm. Carrie sat down on the bed and tried not to disturb her niece as she gently removed the jewelry.

After she put the trinkets back in the box, she walked quietly to the door. She was pulling it closed when Avery whispered, "Good night, Carrie."

She'd already closed her eyes by the time Carrie turned around to look at her. In the soft glow from the streetlight the little girl looked like a cherub. Carrie didn't think she could love her any more if she were her very own child. The instinct to protect was overwhelming. She hated the thought of going away, felt as though she were abandoning her.

She had to leave, she reminded herself. Avery's future depended on her. When she was financially secure, she would be able to support her mother and her niece in the style she felt they both deserved. Guilt was a powerful deterrent, but Carrie wasn't about to let it interfere with her plans. She had her goals and her dreams, and Avery and Lola were tied to both.

"I'm doing the right thing," she whispered as she walked down the hall to the bathroom. She was still trying to convince herself when she stepped into the shower.

Carrie had just turned on the water full blast when the slamming of the car doors awakened Avery. She heard a deep laugh and got out of bed to see who was making the noise. She saw a man and a woman. They were standing by the side of an old, beat-up car, their heads together, laughing and talking.

The woman had golden hair. The man was as dark as she was fair. He had something in his hand. Avery peeked around the side of the window so they wouldn't see her and maybe shout at her to stop being nosy. The man raised a bottle and took a big drink. Then he offered the bottle to the woman, and she tilted her head back and took a drink too.

What were they doing in front of Grandma's house? Avery got down on her knees and hid behind the lace curtains. She ducked when the woman turned and started up the sidewalk. The mean-looking man didn't follow her. He leaned against the fender of the car, one ankle crossed over the other. He took another drink, then threw the empty bottle into the street. The sound of the glass shattering was almost as loud as Avery's gasp. It was bad to litter. Grandma Lola told her so.

The man wasn't looking at the house. He was watching the street, so Avery thought it was safe to straighten up and get a better look. She saw something sticking out of his back pocket when he turned toward the car. What was it? Maybe another bottle?

The mean-looking man wearing the dirty T-shirt must be awful thirsty 'cause he reached behind and pulled the bottle out. Only it wasn't a bottle after all. She gasped again. The bad man was holding a shiny black gun. Just like the kind she'd seen on television.

She was too excited to be scared. Just wait until she told Peyton what she was seeing. Should she wake up Grandma and Carrie and tell them about the gun? Maybe they'd call Officer Friendly at the police station and then he would come and take the bad man away.

Avery jumped when the banging started at the front door. It was the lady, she thought, calling on Grandma in the middle of the night.

The lady was shouting terrible bad words. Avery ran back to bed and hid under the covers in case her grandmother checked on her before she went downstairs to tell the lady to stop making so much noise. She knew what her grandma would say to the woman. "Are you trying to wake the dead?" That's what she'd say, all right. It was the same thing she always said to Carrie when she had the television or the stereo up too loud. But if Grandma looked in and saw that Avery was out of bed before she went downstairs, then Avery would never know what was going on.

Sometimes you had to do bad things to find out anything important. Peyton had told her that it wasn't awful bad to listen to other people talking as long as you didn't ever tell anyone what you heard.

The banging turned into pounding as the lady demanded that Grandma let her in.

Grandma opened the door, and Avery heard the lady shouting some more. She understood every word she said. Avery suddenly wasn't curious any longer. She was terrified. Throwing the sheet off and jumping to the floor, she dropped to her belly and crawled underneath the bed. She scooted up to the headboard and rolled into a ball with her knees tucked under her chin. She was a big girl, too big to cry. The tears streaming down her cheeks were just there because she was squeezing her eyes shut so tight. She cupped her hands over her ears to block out the terrible yelling.

Avery knew who the bad lady was. She was her no-good mama, Jilly, and she had come back to take her away.

CHAPTER 1

THE WAIT WAS making Avery crazy. She sat in her little square cubicle, her back against the wall, one leg crossed over the other, drumming her fingertips against the desktop with one hand and holding an icepack against her wounded knee with the other. What was taking so long? Why hadn't Andrews called? She stared hard at the phone, willing it to ring. Nothing. Not a sound. Turning in her swivel chair, she checked the digital clock for the hundredth time. It was now 10:05, same as it was ten seconds ago. For Pete's sake, she should have heard something by now.

Mel Gibson stood up and leaned over the partition separating his workspace from Avery's and gave her a sympathetic look. That was his honest-to-goodness, real name, but Mel thought it was holding him back because no one in the law enforcement agency would ever take him seriously. Yet, he refused to have it legally changed to "Brad Pitt," as his supportive coworkers had suggested.

"Hi, Brad," Avery said. She and the others were still trying out the new name to see if it fit. Last week it was "George Clooney," and that name got about the same reaction "Brad" was getting now, a glare and a reminder that his name wasn't "George," it wasn't "Brad," and it wasn't "Mel." It was "Melvin."

"You probably should have heard by now," he said.

She refused to let him rile her. Tall, geeky-looking, with an extremely prominent Adam's apple, Mel had the annoying habit of using his third finger to push his thick wire-rimmed glasses back up on his ski nose. Margo, another coworker, told Avery that Mel did it on purpose. It was his way of letting the other three know how superior he felt he was.

Avery disagreed. Mel wouldn't do anything improper. He lived by a code of ethics he believed personified the FBI. He was dedicated, responsible, hardworking, ambitious, and he dressed for the job he wanted . . . with one little glitch. Although he was only twenty-seven years old, his clothing resembled the attire agents wore back in the fifties. Black suits, white long-sleeved shirts with button-down collars, skinny black ties, black wingtip shoes with a perfect shine, and a crew cut she knew he got trimmed once every two weeks.

For all of his strange habits—he could quote any line from *The FBI Story,* starring Jimmy Stewart—he had an incredibly sharp mind and was the ultimate team player. He just needed to lighten up a bit. That was all.

"I mean, don't you think you should have heard by now?" He sounded as worried as she felt.

"It's still early." Then, less than five seconds later, she said, "You're right. We should have heard by now."

"No," he corrected. "I said that *you* should have heard. Lou and Margo and I didn't have anything to do with your decision to call in the SWAT team."

Oh, God, what had she been thinking? "In other words, you don't want to take the flak if I'm wrong?"

"Not flak," he said. "The fall. I need this job. It's the

closest I'm going to get to being an agent. With my eye-sight . . ."

"I know, Mel."

"Melvin," he automatically corrected. "And the benefits are great."

Margo stood so she could join the conversation. "The pay sucks, though."

Mel shrugged. "So does the work environment," he said. "But still . . . it's the FBI."

"What's wrong with our work environment?" Lou asked as he too stood. His workstation was on Avery's left. Mel's was directly in front of hers, and Margo's cubicle was adjacent to Lou's. The pen—as they lovingly called their hell-hole office space—was located behind the mechanical room with its noisy water heaters and compressors. "I mean, really, what's wrong with it?" he asked again, sounding bewildered.

Lou was as clueless as ever, but also endearing, Avery thought. Whenever she looked at him, she was reminded of Pig-Pen in the old *Peanuts* cartoon. Lou always looked disheveled. He was absolutely brilliant, yet he couldn't seem to find his mouth when he was eating, and his short-sleeved shirt usually had at least one stain. This morning there were two. One was jelly from the raspberry-filled dough-nuts Margo had brought in. The big red spot was just above the black ink stain from the cartridge pen in his white shirt pocket.

Lou tucked in his shirttail for the third time that morn-ing and said, "I like being down here. It's cozy."

"We work in the corner of the basement without any windows," Margo pointed out.

"So what?" Lou asked. "Where we work doesn't make us any less important. We're all part of a team."

"I'd like to be a part of the team that has windows," Margo said.

"Can't have everything. Say, Avery, how's the knee?" he asked, suddenly changing subjects.

She gingerly lifted the icepack and surveyed the damage. "The swelling's gone down."

"How'd it happen?" Mel asked. He was the only one who hadn't heard the grisly details.

Margo ran her fingers through her short dark curls and said, "An old lady nearly killed her."

"With her Cadillac," Lou said. "It happened in her parking garage. The woman obviously didn't see her. There really ought to be an age restriction on renewing a driver's license."

"Did she hit you?" Mel asked.

"No," Avery answered. "I dove to get out of her way when she came roaring around the corner. I ended up flying across the hood of a Mercedes and whacked my knee on the hood ornament. I recognized the Cadillac. It belongs to Mrs. Speigel, who lives in my building. I think she's about ninety. She's not supposed to drive anymore, but every once in a while I'll see her taking the car out to do errands."

"Did she stop?" Mel asked.

She shook her head. "I don't think she had a clue I was there. She was accelerating so fast I was just glad there weren't any other people in her way."

"You're right, Lou," Margo said. She disappeared behind her cubicle wall, bent down to push the box of copy paper into the corner, and then stood on top of it. She was suddenly as tall as Mel. "There should be an age limit on keeping a license. Avery told us the woman was so little she couldn't see her head over the back of the seat. Just a puff of gray hair."

"Our bodies shrink as we age," Mel said. "Just think, Margo. When you're ninety, no one will be able to see you."

Margo, a petite five feet two inches, wasn't offended. "I'll just wear higher heels."

The phone rang, interrupting the conversation. Avery jumped at the sound, then checked the time. It was 10:14.

"This is it," she whispered as it rang a second time.

"Answer it," Margo anxiously demanded.

Avery picked up the phone on the third ring. "Avery Delaney."

"Mr. Carter would like to see you in his office at ten-thirty, Miss Delaney."

She recognized the voice. Carter's secretary had a distinct Maine accent. "I'll be there."

Three pairs of eyes watched her as she hung up the phone. "Oh, boy," she whispered.

"What?" Margo, the most impatient of the group, demanded.

"Carter wants to see me."

"Uh-oh. That can't be good." Mel made the remark, and then, as if he realized he'd said something he shouldn't have, added, "You want us to go with you?"

"You'd do that?" Avery asked, surprised by the offer.

"I don't want to, but I would."

"It's okay. I'll take the bullet alone."

"I think we should all go," Margo said. "A mass firing. I mean, we're all in this together, right?"

"Yes," Avery agreed. "But you three tried to talk me out of going to Andrews. Remember? I'm the only one who screwed up." She stood, put the icepack on top of the file cabinet, and reached for her jacket.

"This can't be good," Mel repeated. "They're breaking the chain of command. It must be really bad to get the boss's boss involved. Carter was just promoted to head of in-house operations."

"Which means he's now the boss's boss's boss," Margo pointed out.

"I wonder if all the bosses will be there," Lou said.

"Right," Avery muttered. "Maybe all three of them want to take a turn firing me." She buttoned her suit jacket and then said, "How do I look?"

"Like someone tried to run over you," Mel said.

"Your hose are shredded," Margo told her.

"I know. I thought I had another pair in my drawer, but I didn't."

"I've got an extra pair."

"Thanks, Margo, but you're a petite, and I'm not. Mel, Lou, turn around or sit down."

As soon as they turned their backs, she reached up under her skirt and pulled off her panty hose. Then she put her heels back on.

She was sorry now she'd worn the suit. She usually wore pants and a blouse, but she was going to a luncheon today and so she'd pulled out all the stops and put on the Armani suit her aunt Carrie had sent as a present two years ago. The color was a wonderful taupe gray and had a matching sleeveless V-neck shell. At one time there had been an obscene slit up the side, but Avery had sewn it together. It was a great-looking suit. Now it would be remembered as the suit she wore the day she got fired.

"Catch," Margo said as she threw the new package of panty hose at Avery. "These are the one-size-fits-all kind. They'll work just fine. You have to wear hose. You know the dress code."

Avery read the label. It did say the hose would fit every size. "Thanks," she said as she sat down again. Her legs were long, and she was afraid of tearing the hose when she pulled them up over her hips, but they seemed to fit.

"You're going to be late," Mel told her when she stood up again and adjusted her skirt. Why hadn't she noticed how short it was? The hem barely touched the top of her knees.

"I've got four minutes left." After she'd put on some lip gloss and clipped her hair back behind her neck with a barrette, she slipped the heels back on. Only then did she notice how loose the right heel was. She must have broken it when she slammed into the hood of the car.

Can't do anything about it now, she thought. She took a deep breath, straightened her shoulders, and limped toward the aisle. With every step, her left knee throbbed.

"Wish me luck."

"Avery," Mel shouted. He waited until she turned around, then hurled her clip-on ID. "You should probably wear this."

"Yeah, right. They'll want to take it from me before they escort me out of the building."

Margo called after her. "Hey, Avery, think of it this way—if you get fired, you won't have to worry about all the work piling up while you and your aunt chill out at that fancy spa."

"I haven't decided if I'm going to meet my aunt or not. She still thinks I'm chaperoning those kids around D.C."

"But now that that got canceled, you ought to go get pampered," Margo argued.

"That's right, you should go," Lou said. "You could stay at Utopia a whole month and work on your résumé."

"Not helping, guys," Avery said without looking back.

Carter's office was four flights up. On any other day she would have taken the stairs as aerobic exercise, but her left knee ached too much, and the heel on her right shoe was too wobbly. She was exhausted by the time she reached the elevator. While she waited for it, she rehearsed what she would say when Carter asked what in God's name she thought she was doing.

The doors parted. She took a step forward and felt something snap. Glancing down, she spotted the heel of her shoe lodged in the seam between the elevator and the floor. Since she was alone, she hiked her skirt up and bent down on her good knee to pry the heel loose. It was then that the elevator doors closed on her head.

Muttering an expletive, Avery fell back. The car began to move and she grabbed the railing. She clutched the broken heel in her hand and pulled herself to her feet just as the doors opened on the first floor. By the time she reached the fourth floor, the elevator was full of passengers, and she was squeezed to the back of the car. Feeling like an idiot, she excused her way to the front and limped off.

Unfortunately, Carter's office was located at the end of a long corridor. The glass doors were so far away she couldn't even read the name etched above the brass handle.

Suck it up, she thought as she started walking. She was halfway there when she stopped to check the time and give her leg a rest. She had one minute. She could make it, she thought as she started walking again. Her barrette slipped out of her hair, but she caught it before it fell to the floor. She clipped it back in place and continued on. She was beginning to wish Mrs. Speigel's car had actually struck her. Then she wouldn't have to come up with any excuses, and Carter could call her at the hospital and fire her over the phone.

Suck it up, she repeated. Could it get any worse?

Of course it could. At precisely the second she was pulling the door open, her panty hose began to slip. By the time she'd limped over to the receptionist, the waistband was down around her hips.

The stately brunette woman wearing a knockoff Chanel suit looked a bit startled as she watched Avery approach.

"Miss Delaney?"

"Yes," she answered.

The woman smiled. "You're right on time. Mr. Carter will appreciate that. He keeps a tight schedule."

Avery leaned forward as the woman picked up the phone to announce her. "Is there a ladies' room close by?"

"It's down the hall, past the bank of elevators, on your left."

Avery glanced behind her and considered her options. She could be late for the appointment, try to run like hell down the mile-long hallway and rip off the damn panty-hose, or she could—

The receptionist interrupted her frantic thoughts. "Mr. Carter will see you now."

She didn't move.

"You may go inside," she said.

"The thing is . . ."

"Yes?"

Avery slowly straightened. The panty hose stayed put. Smiling, she said, "I'll go on in then."

She pivoted and held her smile as she grabbed the edge of the desk, and then tried to walk as though her shoe still had a heel. With any luck, Carter wouldn't even notice her condition.

Who was she kidding? The man was trained to be observant.

Tall, distinguished-looking, with a thick head of silver-tipped hair and a square chin, Tom Carter stood when she entered. She hobbled forward. When she reached the chair in front of his desk, she wanted to throw herself into it, but waited for him to give her permission.

Carter reached across the desk to shake her hand, and it was then, as she was stretching forward, that her panty hose gave up the fight. The crotch was now down around her knees. In a panic, she grabbed his hand and shook it vigorously. Too late she realized she was clutching the heel of her shoe in her right hand. She hadn't sweated this much since she took the graduate record exam.

"It's a pleasure to meet you, sir. An honor, really. You wanted to see me? My, it's warm in here. Would you mind if I removed my jacket?"

She was rambling but couldn't seem to stop. The remark about the temperature had gotten his attention, though. Thank God, the rumors were right. Carter did have his own thermostat and liked to keep his office just below freezing. It was like an Alaskan tomb. Avery was surprised she couldn't see her breath when she exhaled. That's when she realized she wasn't breathing.

Calm down, she told herself. Take a deep breath.

Carter enthusiastically nodded. He didn't mention the heel that had dropped on top of a stack of files on his desk. "I thought it was warm, but my assistant keeps telling me it's cold in here. Let me just turn down the thermostat a notch."

She didn't wait for him to give her permission to sit. The second he turned his back, she snatched the heel off the files—which she noticed were labeled with her name and the names of the other members of the pen—and then fell into the chair. Her panty hose were in a wad around her knees. She frantically unbuttoned her jacket, removed it, and draped it over her lap.

Her arms and shoulders were covered in goose bumps seconds later.

Suck it up, she thought. It was going to be okay. Once he sat down behind his desk, she could slowly work the hose down her legs and get rid of them. Carter would never be the wiser.

It was a great plan, and it would have worked if Carter had cooperated, but he didn't return to his chair. He walked over to her side, then leaned back to sit on the edge of his desk. She wasn't short by Margo's standards, but she still had to tilt her head back in order to look into his eyes. There seemed to be a twinkle, which she thought was quite odd, unless, of course, he enjoyed firing people. God, maybe that rumor was true too.

"I noticed you were limping. How did you hurt your knee?" he asked. He bent down to pick up the barrette that had fallen to the floor.

"An accident," she said, taking the barrette and dropping it in her lap.

She could tell from the quizzical look in his eyes she hadn't given him a satisfactory answer.

"An elderly lady . . . quite elderly, as a matter of fact, driving a rather large vehicle, didn't see me when I was walking toward my car in my parking garage. I had to jump out of the way so she wouldn't hit me. I ended up on top of a Mercedes, and I think that's when I broke my heel and bruised my knee." Then, before he could make a comment about the unfortunate incident, she plunged on. "Actually, I only loosened the heel then. It broke off in the elevator as the doors were closing on my head." He was staring at her as though she had just turned into a babbling fool. "Sir, it hasn't been a good morning."

"Then I'd brace myself if I were you," he said, his voice suddenly grim. "It's going to get worse."

Her shoulders slumped. Carter finally went behind his desk and sat down. She seized the opportunity. Slipping her hands under her jacket and skirt, she worked the panty hose down her legs. It was awkward but doable, and, other than appearing to be squirming in the hot seat, she managed the feat. While he opened her file and began to read the notes he or someone else had compiled against her, she grabbed the hose and wadded them into a ball. She had her shoes back on by the time he looked up at her again.

"I received a call from Mike Andrews," he began. There it was again, that grim, you're-gonna-get-your-ass-fired tone of voice.

Her stomach felt as though it had just dropped to her ankles. "Yes, sir?"

"I believe you know him?"

"Yes, sir. Not well," she hastened to add. "I found his number and called him before I left the office."

"And during that phone call you convinced him to deploy a SWAT team to First National Bank on . . ." He looked down again, searching the file for the location.

She rattled off the address, adding, "The branch is near the state line."

He leaned back, crossed his arms, and said, "Tell me what you know about these robberies."

She took a deep breath and tried to relax. She was on safe ground now, in control. Since she had typed all the agents' reports into the computer and looked at the bank tapes, she'd learned, and pretty much memorized, every little detail.

"The robbers call themselves the Politicians," she said. "There are three of them."

"Continue," he urged.

"There have been three robberies in the past three months. The men, all wearing white clothes, entered the first bank, First National Bank and Trust on Twelfth Street, on March fifteenth, exactly three minutes after the bank had opened for business. The men used guns to subdue the personnel and one customer, but they didn't fire those weapons. The man shouting the orders held a knife against the security guard's neck. When the other two were running toward the door, the leader stabbed the guard, dropped the knife, and then left. The guard had done nothing to provoke the man. There was absolutely no reason to kill him."

"No, there wasn't," Carter agreed.

"The second robbery took place on April thirteenth at the Bank of America in Maryland. A bank manager, a woman, was killed during that robbery. The leader was on his way out the door. He suddenly turned around and fired point-blank. Once again, there didn't seem to be a reason, because the personnel had been desperately trying to cooperate."

"And the third robbery?"

"That one took place on May fifteenth at Goldman's Bank and Trust in Maryland," she said. "As you know, the violence escalated. Two people were killed, and a third was left for dead but has miraculously recovered."

"Okay, you've got your facts down," he said. "Now, tell me. What made you think a little branch of the First National Bank in Virginia would be the next target?"

His stare was unnerving. She glanced down at her lap while she gathered her thoughts and then looked up again. She knew how she had arrived at the conclusion, but explaining it to the head of in-house operations was going to be difficult.

"I guess you could say it's all in how I look at things. It was all there . . . most of it anyway, in the file."

"No one else saw it in the file," he pointed out. "They hit different banks with the three robberies, but you convinced Andrews that they were going to hit another branch of First National again."

"Yes, sir, I did."

"It's . . . remarkable how you talked him into it."

"Not really," she said, hoping Andrews hadn't told Carter every word she'd said.

"You used my name."

She inwardly cringed. "Yes, sir. I did."

"You told Andrews the order came from me. Is that correct, Delaney?"

Here it comes, she thought. The you're-getting-your-ass-fired part. "Yes, sir."

"Let's get back to the facts, shall we? Here's what I want to know. The Politicians had struck on March fifteenth, April thirteenth, then May fifteenth. We didn't know why they were hitting on those specific days, but you did, didn't you? That's what you told Andrews," he reminded her. "But you didn't go into an explanation."

"There wasn't time."

"There's time now. How did you arrive at your conclusion?"

"Shakespeare, sir," she answered.

"Shakespeare?"

"Yes, sir. The robberies all followed the same pattern, almost like a ritual of some kind. I got a printout of the first bank's records for the week prior to the robbery. I did the same with the other two banks. I thought something might show up that would link them," she said.

She paused to shake her head. "I had reams and reams of printouts all over the office, and I did find something a little curious. Fortunately, I had the discs from the banks, and I was able to cross-check with the computer."

Carter rubbed his jaw, distracting her. She could see a hint of impatience in his eyes. "Sir, bear with me another minute. Now, the first bank was robbed on March fifteenth. Does that date trigger anything in your mind?"

Before he could answer, she plunged ahead. "The ides of March? Julius Caesar?"

He nodded.

"That must have been in the back of my mind last night while I was reading all the printouts, and I noticed an ATM withdrawal was made by a man named Nate Cassius. I still hadn't quite put it together," she admitted. "But I realized, if I was right, and I was hoping to heaven I was, that the leader of the Politicians was leaving us clues. Maybe he was playing some twisted game. Maybe he was waiting to see how long it would take us to catch on."

She had his full attention now. "Continue," he said.

"As I mentioned before, the dates frustrated me until I did my research. I looked up the Roman calendar and found that when the Romans were calculating the length of the months, they also figured the date of the ides. We know from Shakespeare's play *Julius Caesar* that the ides of March falls on the fifteenth. But not all the months. Some fall on the thirteenth. So, using that logic, I went back over the ATM withdrawals the week prior to the second and third robberies, and guess what I found?"

"Did Nate Cassius make a withdrawal from those banks?"

"No, sir," she answered. "But a William Brutus did in one bank, and Mario Casca did in the other . . . and the withdrawals happened just two days before the robberies. I think they were sizing up the layout of the banks."

"Go on," he said, leaning forward now.

"I didn't put it together until the last minute. I had to pull up the transaction records for all of the banks in the tri-state area from the eleventh on."

"Because the other two withdrawals were made exactly two days before the actual robberies."

"Yes," she said. "I spent most of the night cross-checking

with the data I had in the computer for the eleventh, and by gosh, there it was. Mr. John Ligarius had made a withdrawal from that little branch of First National at three-forty-five in the morning. All of these names—Cassius, Brutus, Casca, Ligarius—they were conspirators against Caesar. I didn't have time to run a check on the people who owned these cards, but I did find out that the cards were issued from banks in Arlington. It added up. Ligarius made a withdrawal from the First National Bank. So, the First National Bank was the next target.

"I thought that time was critical, and my superior, Mr. Douglas, wasn't available. He had already left to catch a four-hour flight, and it wasn't possible for me to talk to him. I used initiative," she stressed. "And I would rather have been wrong and lose my job than keep silent and find out after the fact that I was right. Sir, my conclusions and subsequent actions will be in the report I'm typing up, and when you read it, you will note that I take full responsibility for my actions. My coworkers had nothing to do with my decision to call Andrews. But in my defense," she hastened to add, "I, like the others in my department, have a master's degree, and we're all very good at what we do. We aren't simply typists transferring agents' notes into the database. We analyze the information we're given."

"So does the computer program."

"Yes, but the computer doesn't have heart or instincts. We do. And, sir, now that we're on the subject of job descriptions, I would like to mention that the minimum wage has gone up, but our salaries have not."

He blinked. "Are you hitting me up for a raise?"

She winced. Maybe she had said too much, but at least if she was going to lose her job, Lou and Mel and Margo might benefit. She felt a sudden burst of anger because she and her coworkers were so undervalued. She folded her arms and looked directly into his eyes. "As I've reviewed the facts for you, I've become more convinced than ever that I was right. I had no other choice than to notify Andrews, and he wouldn't move until I used your name. I know I overstepped my authority, but there simply was no time and I had to—"

"They got them, Avery."

She stopped short and then said, "Excuse me, sir?"

"I said Andrews and his men got them."

She didn't know why she was so shocked by the news, but she was. "All of them?" she asked.

He nodded. "Andrews and his team were waiting, and at precisely three minutes after ten, the three men stormed the bank."

"Was anyone hurt?"

"No."

She sighed. "Thank heavens."

Carter nodded. "They were wearing white. Did you figure out the significance of the color?"

"Sure. The Roman senators wore white robes."

"The three men are being interrogated now, but I imagine you have already figured out what their game was."

"They probably consider themselves anarchists trying to bring down the government. They'll tell you they're trying to kill Caesar and probably even hail themselves as martyrs for the cause, but you know what? When you cut through all the phony baloney, it's the same old same old. Greed was the real motivator. They were trying to be clever about it. That's all."

She was smiling, feeling quite pleased with herself, when a sudden thought occurred to her. "Sir, you said my morning was going to get worse," she reminded him. "What did you mean?"

"There's going to be a press conference in . . ." He paused

to glance at the clock. ". . . ten minutes, and you're the star attraction. I understand you have an aversion to being in the spotlight. I don't like press conferences either, but we do what we have to do."

Avery could feel the panic building. "Mike Andrews and his team should do the press conference. They apprehended the suspects. I was simply doing my job."

"Are you being modest, or—"

She leaned forward as she interrupted him. "Sir, I'd rather have a root canal."

He caught himself before he smiled, but the twinkle had returned to his eyes. "So this aversion is deep-rooted then?"

"Yes, sir. It is." She appreciated his attempt to lighten the mood, but she couldn't get rid of her growing apprehension. "May I ask you a question?"

"Yes?"

"Why is my file on your desk? I did follow procedure . . . as best I could," she pointed out. "And if you didn't plan to fire me . . ."

"I wanted to familiarize myself with your department," he said as he picked up the file.

"May I ask why?"

"You're getting a new superior."

She didn't like hearing that. She and the others got along well with Douglas, and change was difficult.

"Is Mr. Douglas retiring, then? He's been talking about it for as long as I've been here."

"Yes," Carter answered.

Bummer, she thought. "May I ask who my new boss is?"

He glanced up from the folder in his hand. "Me," he answered. He let her absorb the information before continuing. "The four of you will be moved into my department."

She perked up. "We're getting new office space?"

Her excitement was quickly squelched. "No, you'll stay where you are, but starting Monday morning, you'll report directly to me."

She tried to look happy. "So, we'll be running up and down four flights of stairs every time we need to talk to you?" She knew she sounded like a whiner, but it was too late to take the words back.

"We do have elevators, and most of our employees are able to ride them without getting their heads caught between the doors."

The sarcasm didn't faze her. "Yes, sir. May I ask if we'll be getting raises? We're all way past due for our evaluations."

"Your evaluation is taking place right now."

"Oh." She wished he'd mentioned that fact starting out. "How am I doing?"

"This is the interview portion of the evaluation, and during an interview I ask the questions, and you answer them. That's pretty much how it works."

He opened her file and began to read. He started with the personal statement she'd written when she'd applied, then scanned her background information.

"You lived with your grandmother, Lola Delaney, until the age of eleven."

"That's correct."

She watched him flip through the pages, obviously checking facts and dates. She wanted to ask him why he felt the need to go over her history, but she knew that if she did, she'd sound defensive and maybe even antagonistic, and so she gripped her hands together and kept quiet. Carter was her new superior, and she wanted to start off on the right foot.

"Lola Delaney was murdered on the night of . . ."

"February fourteenth," she said without emotion. "Valentine's Day."

He glanced up. "You saw it happen."

"Yes."

He began to peruse the notes once again. "Dale Skarrett, the man who killed your grandmother, was already a wanted man. There was a warrant for his arrest in connection with a jewelry heist where the storeowner was murdered, and over four million in uncut stones were stolen. The diamonds weren't recovered, and Skarrett was never formally charged."

Avery nodded. "The evidence against him was circumstantial, and it's doubtful they would have gotten a conviction."

"True," Carter agreed. "Jill Delaney was also wanted for questioning in connection with the robbery."

"Yes."

"She wasn't at the house the night your grandmother was murdered."

"No, but I'm sure she sent Skarrett to kidnap me."

"But you didn't cooperate."

Her stomach began to tighten. "No, I didn't."

"No one knew what had happened until the next morning, and by the time the police arrived, Skarrett was long gone and you were in critical condition."

"He thought I was dead," she interjected.

"You were airlifted to Children's Hospital in Jacksonville. One month later, when you had recovered from your injuries—a remarkable feat given the extent of the damage—your aunt Carolyn took you to her home in Bel Air, California." He leaned back in his chair. "That's where Skarrett came after you again, didn't he?"

She could feel the tension building inside her. "Yes," she said. "I was the only eyewitness who could put him away for life. Fortunately, I had a guardian angel. The FBI was protecting me without my knowing it. Skarrett showed up at school just as it was letting out."

"He was unarmed and later told the authorities he only wanted to talk to you. Skarrett was arrested and charged with second degree murder," he said. "He was convicted and is currently serving his sentence in Florida. He was up for parole a couple of years ago and was denied. His next hearing should be coming up sometime this year."

"Yes, sir," she said. "I regularly check with the prosecutor's office, and I will be sent notification once the date for the hearing is set."

"You'll need to go."

"I wouldn't miss it, sir."

"What about the new trial?" he asked. He tapped the papers with his knuckles and said, "I was curious to know why his attorney thinks he has grounds."

"I'm afraid he does have grounds," she said. "The brief that was filed accused the prosecutor of withholding vital information. My grandmother had a heart condition, and the physician who treated her came forward after he read about her death. That information wasn't handed over to Skarrett's attorney."

"But you haven't heard yet if, in fact, there will be a new trial?"

"No, sir, I haven't."

"Now let's get back to you," he said.

She couldn't be cooperative a second longer. "Sir, may I ask why you're so interested in my background?"

"You're being evaluated," he reminded her. "Two weeks after Skarrett was convicted, Jill Delaney was killed in an automobile accident."

"Yes."

Avery had forgotten much of her childhood, but she re-

membered that phone call clearly. She had just celebrated
Carrie's birthday, a belated event since Avery had been in
the hospital on the actual date, and was helping the housekeeper put the vegetables on the table before they all sat
down to dinner. Avery had placed the mashed potatoes
next to Uncle Tony's plate when Aunt Carrie answered the
phone. A funeral director was calling to tell her that Jilly
had been cremated in a fiery car crash, but there were
enough of her remains left to put in an urn. He wanted
to know what Carrie wanted done with the ashes and the
personal effects, which included a charred driver's license.
Avery was standing in front of the bay window staring out
at some frantic hummingbirds when she overheard Carrie
tell the man to throw them in the nearest Dumpster. She
could recall every second of that moment.

Carter drew her attention back to their discussion when
he suddenly switched subjects.

"You did your undergraduate work at Santa Clara University, graduated with honors with a major in psychology
and a minor in political science and another minor in history. You then went to Stanford and received a master's in
criminal justice." Having said that, he closed her file. "In
your personal statement you said you made up your mind
to become an FBI agent when you were twelve years old.
Why?"

She knew he'd already read her answer. It was there in
the personal statement she'd made when she'd applied to
the Bureau. "An FBI agent named John Cross saved my life.
If he hadn't been watching out for me . . . if Skarrett had
taken me from school, my life would have been over."

Carter nodded. "And you believed you could make a difference working for the Bureau."

"Yes."

"Then why didn't you become a field agent?"

"Bureaucracy," she said. "I ended up in my current position. I was going to put in another six months and then request a transfer."

His assistant interrupted. "Mr. Carter, they're waiting for you."

The panic grabbed her again. "Sir, Mike Andrews really should handle the press conference. Any credit should go to him and his team."

"Look, none of us likes doing this," he snapped. "But this was such a high-profile case, and frankly, most people would appreciate receiving some recognition."

"My coworkers and I would rather have raises . . . and windows, sir. We'd like windows too. Are you aware that our offices are located behind the mechanical room?"

"Space is at a premium," he said. "And when did you get the idea we were negotiating?"

Her back stiffened. "Sir, in an evaluation—"

He cut her off. "You told me you acted alone when you called Andrews."

"Yes, that's correct, but the others were . . . integral. Yes, sir, they were integral in helping me go through those files for names."

One eyelid dropped. "You do realize that lying won't get you a raise, don't you?"

"Sir, Mel and Lou and Margo and I are a team. They did help. They just weren't as convinced as I was . . ."

The buzzer sounded on his intercom. Carter impatiently hit the button and said, "I'll be right there."

Then he reached for his suit jacket and put it on, frowning at her all the while.

"Relax, Delaney," he finally said. "You're off the hook. I'm not going to make you do the press conference."

Her relief made her weak. "Thank you, sir."

She stood when he walked around the desk, the wadded

panty hose hidden under the jacket draped over her arm. Carter stopped at the door and then turned back with the frown still creasing his brow.

"Don't ever use my name again without my permission, Delaney."

"Yes, sir."

"One more thing," he said.

"Yes, sir?"

"Good work."

CHAPTER 2

Marriage isn't for the squeamish. Both husband and wife must be willing to let their inner children play dirty if they want their marriage to survive and flourish. They must let their inner children roll around in the mud. Mistakes will be inevitable, of course, but a shower of love and forgiveness will cleanse the union, and the healing will then begin.

What a crock. Carolyn Delaney Salvetti sat in wide-eyed disbelief as she listened to the garbage the marriage counselor pontificated from his self-help, self-published manual, aptly and ludicrously titled *Let Your Inner Child Get Dirty.* Was the moron talking about marriage or mud wrestling? Carrie didn't know, and at the moment she didn't particularly care.

Without being too obvious about it, she pushed the sleeve of her silk blouse up over her wrist and glanced down at her Cartier watch. Ten minutes to go. God, could she last that long?

She took a deep breath, let go of her sleeve, and leaned back in the plush chair, nodding ever so sagely so her husband and the moron would think she was paying attention.

Marriage isn't for the squeamish, he repeated in his slow, nasal, baritone drawl. His voice was like a loofah made of steel wool, irritating every nerve in her body.

The counselor was a pompous, fat, flatulent fraud who insisted on being called Dr. Pierce because he felt his full name, Dr. Pierce Ebricht, was too formal for such an intimate discussion. After all, he was supposed to be helping them bare their guts. After the first session, Carrie had dubbed him Dr. Prick. Her husband, Tony, had chosen him because he was "in" at the moment. The counselor, with his drive-through-window degree, was the newest guru whom everyone who was anyone flocked to for marriage rejuvenation. Dr. Pierce was the Dr. Phil for the rich and famous, but unlike Dr. Phil, the prick was a complete buffoon.

But then, so was Tony. He sat beside Carrie, his sweaty palms held together as though in prayer, looking so earnest and engaged, like a wooden Howdy Doody the counselor manually manipulated, nodding in quick agreement whenever Dr. Prick paused from reading his bible to look up expectantly.

Chewing on her lip was the only way she could keep from laughing . . . or screaming. Oh, how she wanted to scream. She didn't dare, though. She had made a bargain with her faithless sleazebag of a husband, and if she didn't behave and pretend that she was really trying to save their *Titanic* marriage, she would be paying alimony for the rest of her life. It was a chilling possibility.

The odds were against her. Tony came from a long line of centenarians. His uncle Enzo was still chugging wine out on his postage-stamp piece of land on the good side of Napa at the ripe old age of eighty-six and didn't seem to be slowing down at all. His only concession to living healthy was, at the age of eighty-five, to quit smoking his unfiltered Camels—a three-pack-a-day habit—and increase the amount of garlic he put on everything he ate, including his morning wheat toast. If Tony turned out to be as healthy and fit as Enzo was, by the time Carrie croaked, she would be drained dry financially, and there would be nothing left in the coffers to leave to the only person she had ever loved, her niece, Avery. If, on the other hand, she cooperated with Tony and attended all ten sessions with Dr. Prick, and the marriage still ended—a foregone conclusion, in her opinion—then, Tony promised, he would give up his interest in the business and not ask for a dime in alimony.

Carrie wasn't a fool. Cynical to the bone, she wasn't about to accept the word of a man she considered a habitual liar and a thief. There was a hundred and twenty-three thousand dollars missing from one of their business accounts. She couldn't prove that Tony had helped himself to the money, but she knew he had taken it, most likely to buy expensive trinkets for his mistress. The bastard. And so, to ensure he couldn't change his mind and come after her for alimony, she had made him put his promise in writing, then had called in her assistant to witness her husband signing the document. The paper was now safely locked away in her safe-deposit box at First Commerce Bank.

How had they come to this? she wondered. Tony used to be a loving and thoughtful man.

Carrie remembered the night she'd awakened in excruciating pain. She was sure her agony was due to food poisoning—they had eaten dinner at a new Thai restaurant all of her friends had been raving about. She refused to go to the hospital, and Tony was beside himself with worry. He finally picked her up, carried her to the car, and drove her to the hospital. He saved her life that night. After treatment in the emergency room, she was admitted, and Tony sat in a chair the rest of the night watching over her. He

charmed the hospital staff into putting up with her com-
plaints and demands, and filled the room with gerbera daisies, her favorite flowers.

Tony was so charismatic then. He still was, damn it,
which was probably why all the young wanna-be starlets
flocked around him. Was the temptation too much to resist? After all, she was getting older, and the years were
beginning to show. Was that the reason he'd decided to be
unfaithful?

Surreptitiously checking her watch again, she suppressed
a heartfelt sigh. In just five minutes the last session would
be over and she wouldn't have to pretend to be nice to Dr.
Prick. Then, like it or not, she was going away for a little
rejuvenation of her own. Her Prada workout clothes were
stuffed into her Gucci bags, along with her state-of-the-art
laptop computer, three battery packs, and two cell phones
with chargers. The luggage waited in the trunk of the limo
that would take her from Dr. Prick's office to the airport.

The forced vacation was the first time she would be away
from her company, Star Catcher, in over eight years, and
she was filled with trepidation. She had a good staff, and she
knew they could handle any problems that came up while
she was away, but she was admittedly a control freak and
couldn't stand the idea of letting anyone else make decisions, if only for fourteen days. According to Avery, Carrie
was a Type A personality. She couldn't abide being idle or
bored. She hadn't even taken time off for a honeymoon
when she'd married Tony. The short weekend in Baja had
felt like a year away from her fledgling company, which was
damned ironic considering she had allegedly been in the
throes of love at the time.

The gold embossed reservation from the posh Utopia
Spa had arrived three weeks ago—just after their second
session with Dr. Prick, and Carrie, after taking one look at

the invitation, had been certain that Tony was behind the scheme to get her out of L.A. Her husband had feigned surprise, but she hadn't been fooled. He'd been urging her to take some time off for months now and use the hiatus to work on their struggling marriage.

No matter how she nagged him to admit it, Tony wouldn't 'fess up. He insisted he hadn't made the reservation or paid the outrageous fee, and because he was even more stubborn than she was, she finally gave up trying to pry the truth out of him.

The reservation was accompanied by an elaborate brochure displaying the luxurious facility and outlining the treatments available at Utopia. There was also a letter attached with a list of testimonials from famous men and women who were regular clients.

She had heard of the spa—everyone in Hollywood knew about it—but she hadn't known how obviously popular it was with the rich and famous. Because the cost was so exorbitant, she hadn't ever considered it.

Carrie was torn. How important was it for her to go? Where one was seated at the "in at the moment" restaurants in L.A. was of paramount importance because one was seen and noticed, but a spa? It was so elegantly quiet and hush-hush, who would ever know besides the people attending that she had been there? Would the owner ask her to give a testimonial? God, wouldn't that be wonderful? If her name went on the list of the rich and famous, what an incredible boost that would be for her company. In her line of work, the only reason for doing anything these days was with the singular goal of impressing others and making them squirm with envy. Only the high rollers who didn't need to work got work in Hollywood.

What guarantee did she have that her name would go on that list, though? Carrie did the math, figured out to the penny how much each day would cost, and decided to stay home. She wasn't about to let Tony spend so much of her money. She would call the spa in the morning and request a refund. No way in hell was she going to fork over that much. She must have shouted those very words to Tony at least five times before he began to read aloud the names of those who regularly attended the rejuvenation spa and sang Utopia's praises. She stopped shouting when she heard the name Barbara Rolands. Everyone referred to the aging actress with three Oscars under her belt as the best face-lift on the coast. Barbara had disappeared for three weeks just last year, and when she next made a public appearance at a trendy fund-raiser, she looked incredible. Had she had the work done at the spa?

Carrie snatched the papers out of Tony's hands. She read the names of the personnel on call to attend to the client's every need. Two world-renowned plastic surgeons topped the list.

Would she be getting evaluated by the same physicians who had worked on some of the most influential men and women of the century? God only knew she could use some freshening up. Not a face-lift—she wasn't even forty-five yet—but the bags under her eyes were getting more and more pronounced, and she really did need to do something about that. Lack of sleep, long hours of work, and twenty cups of strong coffee every day without ever taking time to work out had definitely taken their toll.

According to the letter, she would fly from L.A. to Denver, then go by smaller plane to Aspen. Utopia was located in the mountains, fifteen minutes away from the closest ski resort. She would arrive in the shank of the evening, and the following morning she would be evaluated by the physicians there. Liposuction, she noticed, was offered as one of the choices available. The procedure was listed just below full body massage.

How could she refuse? How could she, indeed, especially after Tony mentioned that the anonymous gift was nonrefundable. She just knew he'd used company money to pay for the trip. The man couldn't keep a dime in savings. Since they had merged their two companies and she had brought in their first multimillion-dollar account, he had been living high off the hog. He had absolutely no business sense.

Tony said it didn't matter where it came from and suggested she take the vacation as an early birthday present. He firmly believed one should never look a gift horse in the mouth. He told her he hoped she would use the time to reflect on all the wonderful words of wisdom Dr. Prick had spoken about the sanctity of marriage. She knew Tony was hoping that, once she slowed down, as one was wont to do on a vacation, she would realize how she had wronged him with her accusations and she would know in her heart that she still loved him.

Carrie had her own agenda. While she was being "redone," she would work on coming up with a killer commercial that would land her company another Clio. It had been too long since she'd received the last award, almost four years now, and she was becoming more and more anxious. Advertising was a cutthroat business, and her competition, based mostly in Manhattan, was fierce. The twenty-year-old set was taking over. Some executives wouldn't even speak to a man or woman over the age of thirty, which was why Carrie had added three young, with-it, business majors to her staff. She called the Nintendo fanatics her babies.

It was imperative that Carrie stay in the moment, every moment. In her work, it didn't matter how many past

achievements there had been. With all the new movers and
shakers pushing their way into her circle of influence, Star
Catcher had to be out there as much as possible. Hollywood was a fickle town. Those with the power were only
interested in who was creating the buzz that day. If Carrie
didn't keep pushing her staff to grab bigger and bigger accounts, she would find herself in the has-been category
overnight.

She owed her first Clio to her niece. She'd begged Avery
to step in when the temperamental teen actress she'd hired
threw a tantrum and demanded double her fee at the last
moment. The silly girl thought she had Star Catcher by the
balls because of the time crunch, and if Avery hadn't come
to the set with Carrie that day, Carrie would have had
to pay the little bitch. Avery had been mortified by what
Carrie wanted her to do, but she had a good voice and a
great body, and that was all that was required. The soap
commercial was a resounding success, and Carrie, acting as
Avery's agent, could have gotten her at least a year's work.
Avery wasn't interested, though. As soon as spring break
was over, she went back to finish high school and then went
on to college.

Her niece did continue to work with Carrie every summer, but she hated leaving the office to meet with company
executives. Carrie couldn't understand her reserve. Avery
didn't seem to know—or if she did know, she didn't particularly care—that she was, as Tony often remarked, a
knockout.

The problem with her niece was that she wasn't the least
bit superficial. She was sweet and wholesome and had a
firm grasp on what was important in life, and what wasn't.
But what could Carrie expect? After all, she'd raised her to
sort out such things. Ironic, Carrie thought, that she herself
should end up working in a field consumed with the super-

ficial. What a hypocrite she had turned out to be. When would she learn to practice what she had constantly preached to Avery? Maybe after she made another couple of million?

Carrie had eventually become excited about the spa. Once she had made the decision to go, she called Avery and begged her niece to join her at Utopia for one week. She knew Avery was using part of her vacation to chaperone teenagers around D.C., and Carrie tried to guilt-trip her into giving her family equal time. Carrie was feeling confident that Avery would come for at least a few days, but knew she would have heart failure if she ever found out how much the stay would cost her aunt. Carrie didn't have any qualms about paying the fee for Avery. She would do anything for her, anything at all. Probably because Avery never asked her for anything. Carrie didn't know how her niece could live on the tiny salary she made, and though she offered her money every time she talked to her, Avery always declined. She was doing just fine, or so she said.

Avery kept her grounded, and in the back of her mind, she knew that her niece wouldn't let her get swept up in the moment at Utopia and sign up for every treatment available.

Avery was going to pitch a fit when she found out that Carrie was thinking about booking an appointment for liposuction. She smiled as she thought about the argument her niece would give. Avery would shake her head when she saw her workout clothes too. Everything matched and had designer labels. Oh, yes, Avery would roll her eyes, no doubt, and then launch into her favorite lecture about getting fit and healthy.

God, how she missed the brat.

"What are you smiling about, honey?" Tony asked.

Jarred back to the present, she realized both her husband and their marriage counselor were staring at her. She shrugged to cover her embarrassment. "I was thinking about all the things I need to think about." That nonsense was the best she could come up with on the spur of the moment.

Dr. Prick looked pleased enough to roll around in the mud with his inner child. He nodded agreement and then stood, indicating the session was finally over.

Tony towered over her as he walked by her side to the waiting limo.

"You sure you don't want me to ride to the airport with you?"

"I'm sure."

"Did you remember to bring the reservation?"

"Yes." She pulled away from her husband when the driver opened the back door for her. "I still haven't heard from Avery, and I've left three messages for her. I was hoping to talk to her before I left L.A."

"You know how busy she is at work. She probably just hasn't had time to call you."

"But what if there's an emergency while I'm away?"

"Then she'll call me or try to get you on your cell phone."

"I don't like the idea of her working with children. It's too hard for her. She—"

"She wouldn't do it if she didn't love it," he pointed out. "You've got to stop worrying. Avery's a big girl now."

"Check my e-mails when you get home," she said then. "Maybe she sent me a message."

"Yes, I'll check and call you."

"The parole hearing is the sixteenth. I wonder if Avery was notified yet. I just got my—"

"Of course she knows. Why are you worrying about that now?"

"I can't miss it," she snapped. "I always go with Avery. Both of us speak before the board decides . . ."

"Honey, you aren't going to miss the hearing, and neither will Avery. It's a month away, for Pete's sake. You didn't miss the last one, and you won't miss this one. Now try to relax. I want you to enjoy yourself."

She nodded. "Yes, okay."

She hadn't sounded sincere. Frowning, he said, "You're tense because you haven't had any time off in such a long time. It's just last-minute jitters."

She nodded again, then tried to get into the car, but Tony grabbed her by the shoulders and kissed her. "I love you," he whispered. "I've always loved you. From the moment we met. I want this marriage to work again."

"Yes, I know," she answered, her tone dismissive.

The second the car pulled away from the curb, Carrie reached for her laptop. She had just turned it on when her cell phone rang. Assuming that it was Tony calling to once again nag her about their marriage, she answered curtly.

"What is it now?"

"Guess what?" Avery said.

"Hi, sweetie. I thought you were Tony. Are you enjoying your vacation?"

"Not yet," she answered. "I'm finishing up some last-minute details at the office. I had a big meeting with my new boss a couple of days ago, and I can't wait to tell you about the case I helped solve. How about sharing a late dinner in Aspen?"

Carrie screeched. "You're going to join me? All my nagging and browbeating worked?"

"If I say yes, then you'll just get worse. Guilt worked this time, Carrie, but don't think—"

"What happened to the kids you were going to drag around Washington?"

"The trip got rescheduled."

"Ah. So I win by default."

"Do you want me to come or not?"

"Of course I want you to come. I'll call Utopia right away. Have you got your flight yet?"

"I'm looking at the computer screen right now. I can get a connecting flight in Denver, but I won't get in until late," she warned.

"Now I'm excited. We're going to have such fun. Let me know your arrival time. As soon as you've booked it, call me back. See you soon, Avery. Love you."

Carrie's frame of mind vastly improved. She disconnected; then she called Utopia. After that, she went to work. She made notes until the limo pulled up to the airport. The lines through security moved at a snail's pace. Carrie, shifting the strap of her carry-on from one shoulder to the other, took a palm recorder from her purse and dictated instructions for her office staff. When the plane had taken off and she was comfortably seated in business class with a chilled glass of Chardonnay, she opened her laptop and went to work again.

Her thoughts kept going back to Avery. She could call her now, she decided, and find out what time her flight was. She reached for the phone hooked into the armrest, then changed her mind. Better to wait. If she used the plane phone, she'd have to shout to be heard over the drum of the engines and the static, and then the other passengers around her would hear every word.

As soon as she got off the plane in Aspen, she moved out of the main traffic stream and sat down to dig through her carry-on for her cell phone. She'd pulled everything out before she remembered she'd stuck the phone in her purse. It wasn't like her to be so disorganized, she thought as she closed the carry-on. She happened to glance up and see the man holding a sign with her name on it. Another limo driver, she assumed, dressed in a dark navy business suit. He was quite distinguished looking and handsome, a younger version of Sean Connery. She quickly stood as she tucked the phone in the pocket of her blazer. Adjusting the collar of her blouse, she called out, "I'm Carolyn Salvetti."

His smile was dazzling. "Good afternoon, Mrs. Salvetti." He had a charming British accent. The name tag pinned to his lapel read "Mr. M. Edwards."

"Are you with Utopia? . . . The spa?" she asked.

"Yes, I am," he said. "Do you have your reservation with you?"

She reached for her travel bag. "It's right here."

"Oh, I don't need to see it, Mrs. Salvetti. I was to make certain you had the papers with you. Shall we go get your luggage?"

She felt ridiculous, all but running in her Manolo Blahnik slingbacks, trying to keep pace with her long-legged escort. She slipped once, and if he hadn't grabbed her arm to steady her, she would have fallen on her face. She'd meant to change her shoes before she got on the plane, but then she'd gotten caught up in work and had forgotten about it.

They passed a phone bank that reminded her she still needed to know Avery's flight itinerary. Damn it, she'd told her to call as soon as she'd booked her flight. Carrie knew what had happened. Avery had gotten waylaid with work and then had to run to get everything done.

It was probably too late to catch her at work or at home. She was probably already at the airport or perhaps on the plane now. Still, Carrie wanted to try. Maybe Avery would check her phone messages when she got to Denver. Yes, she would call as soon as they reached the baggage claim area.

"Will any other guests be going with us to the spa?" she asked.

"Yes," he said. "There are two other guests. They're waiting in the lounge. As soon as I pick up your luggage, we'll head out."

"Do you have anyone scheduled for pickup this after-noon or this evening?"

"No, this is my last trip. Why do you ask?"

"My niece, Avery Delaney, is joining me at the spa."

Her comment so surprised him he stopped in the middle of the corridor. "You were expecting Miss Delaney to join you?"

Hadn't she said so? "Yes," she said. "But she's flying out of D.C. If you aren't scheduled to come back and pick her up, the spa must be sending another escort."

They continued walking. "Yes, that must be so," he said, sounding somewhat preoccupied.

"I don't have Avery's flight information, but she might have called the spa to tell them so someone would pick her up. Could you call Utopia and find out? It would be lovely if we could wait for her. I do know she's coming through Denver," she thought to add.

"I'll be happy to call the spa," he said. Glancing around, he nodded toward a line of empty chairs in front of a de-serted gate. "Why don't you have a seat."

He was placing her carry-on at her feet when she asked, "What does the 'M' stand for?"

"Pardon me?"

"Your name. 'Mr. M. Edwards.' What does the 'M' stand for?"

He saw no reason to lie. "Monk. The 'M' stands for Monk."

"How delightfully different."

"I prefer that all clients call me Mr. Edwards."

What a stiff-neck, she thought. "Yes, of course."

"If you'll excuse me . . ." He moved to the window as he pulled out his cell phone. Carrie grabbed her bag and went after him. She wanted to ask him to find out if there were any messages waiting for her at the spa.

His back was to her as she approached. She tapped him on the shoulder. "Mr. Edwards."

Startled, he whirled around. "Hold on," he said into the phone. Then, "Yes?"

"Would you ask the receptionist if I have any messages?"

He repeated the question, waited a moment, and then shook his head. Carrie felt foolish standing there and so she went back to the chair and sat down.

He wasn't on the phone long, and when he returned to her side, he picked up her bag and apologized for the delay.

"There is another escort assigned to Miss Delaney."

"Couldn't we just wait?"

"I'm sorry. Did you say something?" he asked.

His preoccupation was irritating. "I asked if we could wait for my niece."

"I'm afraid not," he replied. "The other two clients have been waiting for you. I couldn't ask them to wait even longer. I hope you understand."

"Yes, of course."

"Thank you," he said. "The others will, no doubt, appreciate your cooperation."

"Who are they?" she bluntly asked.

"I'm sorry?"

"I was asking, Mr. Edwards, who the other clients are."

"Mrs. Trapp is from Cleveland, and Judge Collins's plane arrived from Miami."

Carrie hadn't heard either name before and wondered if they were famous. She certainly hoped so. She could use as many influential connections as she could get. Maybe the judge was one of those celebrities on television. Wouldn't that be something?

They finally reached the baggage claim area and joined the hordes of passengers pushing their way to the front. "How long will the drive to the spa take?"

"Not long," he answered. "You won't be going directly to Utopia this evening, however," he added. "There was a problem with the water main, but it will be repaired by midnight. So that you won't be inconvenienced, the director has made arrangements for you and Mrs. Trapp and Judge Collins to spend the night at a private retreat."

Carrie was about to protest that, yes, it was an inconvenience. She would have to unpack and then pack again, but then Mr. Edwards said in a casual, off-handed way, "I believe Mr. Cruise and a companion were the last guests."

Her eyes widened. "Tom Cruise?"

"That's right. Then tomorrow morning," he continued smoothly, "you'll be taken to the spa."

"Will my niece be staying at the retreat too?"

"I'm not certain. If the problem has been solved by the time her flight arrives, then she'll be taken directly to the spa."

"Is the retreat near Aspen?"

"Just outside, high up in the mountains in an area called Land Between the Lakes. It's quite beautiful there. Cold nights and warm, mostly sunny days this time of year. Great climate for hiking and camping."

"I'm not the outdoor type, but you certainly look like you are," she said, noticing the thickness in his shoulders and the bulging muscles straining the fabric of his obviously custom-made suit. What were they paying chauffeurs these days?

They must have stood side by side for a good ten minutes before the bags began to roll along the conveyor belt.

"That one's mine," she said, pointing to an overstuffed, black Gucci bag moving along the conveyor. "Be careful," she warned. "It's heavy."

"Is this the only one?"

Surely he was joking. "No, there are three more."

"How long are you going to be at the spa?" he asked.

"Two weeks. How long have you worked there?" she asked, making idle chitchat to pass the time while she waited for the rest of the luggage. If they lost any of her bags, she was up a creek because her extra batteries for her laptop and her other cell phone were packed inside.

"A year," he answered.

"That's nice," she remarked, not really interested. Where the hell were her other suitcases? She could feel herself getting anxious and took a deep breath. Relax, she told herself. You're on vacation.

She glanced around the luggage area, spotted a ladies' room, and said, "Before we leave, I'd like to splash some cold water on my face."

"If you could wait until we get to—"

"Actually, I can't wait," she interrupted. She handed him her carry-on but kept her purse. "Don't let go of that bag. It's got my laptop and my cell phone inside."

Then she hurried into the rest room. As she was washing her hands, she remembered she'd put the other cell phone in her pocket and decided to call Avery right then.

Carrie went into the last stall so she would have some privacy, prayed the signal wouldn't get blocked, then hit speed dial. She called Avery's apartment first, listened to the answering machine, and told her to call her as soon as she got this message. Then, thinking she might have left for the airport, Carrie hit speed dial again. The number was a direct line to Avery's desk. Her voice mail picked up on the second ring.

"Damn it, Avery, you were supposed to call me back with your flight information, but you forgot, didn't you? I hope to heaven you're on the plane now and will check your messages from Denver. I think I'm obsessing because I don't want you to bail on me. I know how that job of yours sucks you in. If I find out you've missed your plane because you got stuck in one of those horrid meetings, I'll pitch such a fit your ears will be ringing for a month. Honestly, Avery, when I think about all the things you could be doing and all the money you could be making, and here you are, stuck in that windowless dungeon analyzing God only knows what. It's a waste of your talents. Surely you realize that. I wish you'd let me help you change careers."

Carrie realized what she was doing and laughed. "Listen to me going on and on. You've heard it all before, haven't you? Anyway, I called to tell you I'm in Aspen now. I wanted to wait until you landed so we could ride to the spa together, but there are other guests here, and it would be too much of an inconvenience to make them sit and wait. I won't be going to the spa tonight. They had some kind of plumbing problem, which my escort tells me should be fixed by the time you get there. I'll be sound asleep by then. The other two women and I will be spending a luxurious night at a posh mountain retreat. I've already forgotten the other women's names, but one of them is a judge. I'll bet she's famous. Then tomorrow," she continued, "I'll check in at Utopia and find you."

Carrie felt another burst of excitement. "The retreat is called The Land Between the Lakes. How quaint is that? Tom Cruise was their last guest, so you know it has to be incredibly beautiful. I mean, he's on top of the A list, and they wouldn't put him in anything shabby. I better hang up now before my escort comes looking for me in the ladies' room. I can't wait to see you. We're going to have such fun.

Oops, I hear my escort calling my name. The spa sent a real hunk to carry my luggage. He's kind of stiff and formal, and he has the faintest British accent. And, oh, is he sexy. His name's Monk Edwards, but trust me, he doesn't look like any monk I've ever seen. Maybe they'll send another hunk to pick you up. Bye, brat. See you soon."

CHAPTER 3

THE TRAIL LED to Utopia. John Paul Renard had been tracking the professional killer for over a year now, but he hadn't had much success. The last known hit had taken place on the Riviera, an execution of a wanted man named John Russell, but since then, the killer calling himself Monk seemed to have vanished off the face of the earth. There had been a hint of his work in Paris and in Cannes, but nothing substantial enough to be considered a real lead.

Until now.

When John Paul had been in the Marines and then, for a short time, had worked for the Agency, he'd learned patience. He figured that eventually the killer would return to the United States. It had been a hunch, nothing more, but lo and behold, he'd been right. Just three weeks ago, Monk had finally resurfaced. He'd actually messed up too. He'd used one of his old credit cards. It was such a sloppy thing to do and so out of character for a man who, up until now, had been pretty damned flawless in his executions. John Paul wondered if Monk had thrown the card away and someone else had found it and used it.

It was worth checking out. A charge had been made at a

spa in Colorado called Utopia for a woman named Carolyn Salvetti. John Paul ran a credit check on her and discovered that she had more than enough money tucked away in her IRAs and her pension plans to buy a couple of spas. Was there a connection to Monk here? Had she hired him to kill someone? Or was she his next victim?

John Paul also ran her name through the government database. He used his old code to get access, knowing full well that as soon as he logged on, the men who had run him would immediately know it and would leap to the incorrect assumption that he was ready to come back. For that reason he didn't stay on the computer long. In less than two minutes he found out what he needed to know. Salvetti was clean as a whistle. No warrants outstanding, no parking tickets, no illegal activities of any kind. Her husband was also clean. Carolyn Salvetti was president of a company called Star Catcher. Tony Salvetti was vice president.

The database hadn't given him any answers. If Carolyn Salvetti was Monk's next target, then who had hired him? Who wanted the woman dead?

John Paul was determined to find out. Since his brother, Remy, lived in Colorado Springs, he decided to drive there to see him. Known in his hometown, Bowen, Louisiana, as a surly recluse, John Paul shocked his family and few friends when he purchased an old Ford SUV. He made a few alterations, souped up the engine, packed it with a couple of kitchen chairs he'd made for Remy, and headed out.

He spent two days with his brother, but on June sixteenth, the day Salvetti was scheduled to arrive at the spa, John Paul was there waiting for her. His hope was that Monk was right behind her, and he could nail the bastard.

Carolyn Salvetti didn't show. The desk clerk, an uptight, exceedingly nervous young man with weird, oversized, capped teeth, told John Paul that Mrs. Salvetti had canceled her reservation at the last minute. "But it's noted right here, under her old reservation, that her niece, Avery Delaney, will be staying at the spa. Miss Delaney will only be here one week," he thought to add. "Is that at all helpful?"

Instead of answering the question, he asked to speak to the manager. The clerk tripped when he hastily pivoted, then went running to fetch his employer.

Tim Cannon showed up a minute later, with the clerk half hiding behind his back. Since John Paul had left the Agency, he didn't have any credentials to threaten the tight-lipped, sweaty little man, and so he used intimidation. As usual, it worked like a charm. For some reason he couldn't quite understand, people tended to be afraid of him. His sister, Michelle, told him it was because of his size and the fact that he rarely smiled. Though he thought it was peculiar that strangers backed away from him, he used their fear to his advantage. Cannon, operating under the false assumption that John Paul worked for the government—an assumption John Paul had hinted at but hadn't actually stated—and obviously embarrassed to admit that he was afraid of John Paul, didn't call security or ask to see identification. The fact was, the manager couldn't have been more helpful. He invited him into his office, offered him the use of his desk and phone, and then, stammering about an emergency errand he simply had to complete, he left his office and pulled the door closed behind him.

The second he was alone, John Paul turned on Cannon's computer, found the site, and typed in his access code. How he hated the technology, but it was the only way he could get the information he needed. He wanted to see if an alert had been posted regarding Monk and was pleasantly surprised that there hadn't been. The spa wasn't swarming with agents yet—in John Paul's estimation, they were as easy to spot as nuns in black habits—which could only mean that the Bureau didn't know that Monk was back in the States. John Paul wasn't inclined to tell them. The FBI would only screw it up. Monk would spot the agents, get spooked, and vanish into thin air again.

John Paul wasn't about to let that happen. He was one step in front of the Bureau, and that was all he needed. He had a personal reason for going after the killer, and he wasn't going to let anyone get in his way.

A little over a year ago, Monk had tried to kill John Paul's sister, Michelle, and had it not been for her husband and a friend, he would have succeeded. Monk got away, which, in John Paul's estimation, was unforgivable. He vowed he wouldn't rest until he had hunted the bastard down and sent him to hell where he belonged.

Once he started doing the research, John Paul's need for vengeance intensified. One case in particular had really shaken him up. A father had hired Monk to kill his teenage daughter so that he could collect the insurance money and pay his gambling debts. The FBI knew Monk had murdered the girl because the killer always left behind a rose, and though the father had removed the evidence, a thorn was found in the girl's bedspread. There wasn't any other family to mourn or seek justice for the young girl. John Paul knew there were other victims the FBI didn't even know about yet. How many more innocents would die before the killer was stopped?

CHAPTER 4

MONK KEPT THE three women entertained while he drove them to their destination. Carrie thought he was charming and oh so terribly correct. He was her idea of the perfect English butler.

He had transferred their luggage into the back of a brand-new, fully equipped Land Rover, explaining that the SUV was suited for the mountain roads, and for that reason he hadn't driven one of the spa's limos. Anne Trapp sat in the front, and Carolyn sat next to Judge Sara Collins in the back. The seats were plush beige leather and very comfortable.

All of them were excited and nervous, but there was little conversation among them. Monk told them a brief history of the spa and then regaled them with several fascinating stories about some of the famous people who had stayed at the mountain house he was taking them to.

Carrie wasn't sure how long they had been driving. She hadn't checked the time when they'd left the airport, but it seemed that at least an hour had passed, maybe even more. Monk's stories so intrigued her she didn't mind the long drive or the slight case of car sickness. While Sara ooh'd and ah'd over the scenery as they climbed higher and higher up the mountain and Anne sat in stony silence, Carrie questioned Monk about the previous guests he'd served. She wasn't particularly interested in hearing about politicians. She wanted to hear all about the peculiarities of the movie stars.

"Russell Crowe was a guest? What was he like?"

Monk replied with an amusing tidbit about the Australian actor. "He was quite fond of the house," he added, "and wanted to purchase it."

"It must really be nice," Sara remarked.

Monk assured them that the house had all the amenities and that he would be acting as their butler until they checked into Utopia.

"I certainly hope there won't be any more screwups," Anne said irritably.

"Was there a screwup?" Sara asked her.

"There certainly was," Anne said. She turned in her seat so she could look at Sara while she explained. "No one from the spa was waiting for me at my gate to help me with my carry-on, and if I hadn't seen Mr. Edwards holding up the sign at your gate as I was walking toward the baggage claim area, I would have been left to fend for myself. I was quite weary," she added. "And the thought of carrying my luggage to a taxi stand was more than I could bear."

"There were skycaps around who could have assisted you," Carrie told her.

"That isn't the point," Anne snapped. "I shouldn't have been inconvenienced."

What a bitch, Carrie thought. The look on Anne's face was almost comical. She was pouting like an eight-year-old.

"I assure you, Mrs. Trapp, your every need will be taken care of by an excellent staff, and I once again apologize for the inconvenience."

"Will there be servants at the retreat?" she asked.

"Yes, of course."

"How many?"

"Four," he answered. "They'll be arriving from the spa shortly."

"I wish to have one of them assigned to me," Anne demanded. "Will you see to it?"

"Yes, of course."

Anne nodded. "Good," she said, and she sounded mollified.

Sara and Carrie exchanged a look that spoke volumes. Then Anne said, "I'm pleased to know we won't be alone tonight . . . in the event something should happen . . . or break. You just never know."

"The house is getting a new alarm system. The wires haven't been properly hidden yet, but it's workable," he promised. "Once it's turned on, you won't be able to open your windows or outside doors, of course, but it does get quite chilly up here at night, so I can't imagine you would want to keep any windows open."

Carrie studied her traveling companions. They both looked vaguely familiar to her, but she couldn't pinpoint where they might have met.

She stared at the back of Anne's head and then finally tapped her on her shoulder and asked. The blond woman with deep-set brown eyes half turned in her seat and smiled slightly.

"I don't believe we've ever met," she said. "Have you ever been to Cleveland?"

"No," Carrie answered.

Up close, she noticed how sallow the woman's complexion was. She didn't think Anne was at all well. Her eyes were dull and lifeless, and her skin was almost waxy, but that could have been due to the heavy makeup she was wearing. Perhaps Anne had paid her fee for some kind of miracle cure for her waiflike, nearly anorexic body. Carrie judged her to be around her own age, give or take a few.

Judge Sara Collins had just the opposite problem. She could have stood to loose a good sixty or seventy pounds. Perhaps she was going to have liposuction or stomach staples. She looked old, around seventy or so, and her face definitely showed her age. Maybe she was there to have a face-lift. Carrie was dying to ask but didn't dare.

Where could she have recognized her from? Maybe she'd seen her on television. Court shows were the rave now. Did Sara have her own program like Judge Judy?

She would have asked, but their chauffeur had turned into a tour guide and was keeping up a steady monologue about Colorado. One story led to another and another, but they were interesting tidbits, and Carrie thought it would be rude to interrupt. Still, he wasn't giving them time to get to know each other. She decided she'd ask Sara if she was a celebrity when they were settled in the house.

Then she began to wonder what the other women thought about her. She knew she looked older than her actual age. An old hag, she thought. Yes, that's what they probably thought.

They'd been on private roads now for quite a while, and it was getting steeper. Winding around and around was making Carrie more carsick. Great, she thought. I'm going to throw up on our proper English butler. Wouldn't that be a wonderful way to impress the other houseguests?

"Does the company own all this land?" Sara asked Monk.

"Yes, madam," he answered.

"Is the house much farther?" Carrie asked.

"It's just around the next bend."

They were in the middle of nowhere. A wilderness, Carrie thought, and she began to feel uneasy . . . nervous. She suddenly realized she hadn't seen a house or even a cabin in quite a long time. Then it occurred to her that an alarm system wouldn't do any of them any good. If the alarm went off, who would hear it? Was it tied into the nearest police station, and if so, where in God's name was that? An hour away? Two hours? Or would the alarm sound at the spa?

Yes, that was surely how it worked. And that meant that the spa was close by. Having figured it out, Carrie leaned back in the leather seat and tried to relax.

The house suddenly came into view. It was incredible. Massive gables of natural cedar rose into the sky, and two-story panes of glass reflected the mountain peaks behind them, as if the magnificent structure were placed there with no other purpose than to pay tribute to the grandeur that surrounded it. A circle drive curved toward the wide porch that stretched across the front of the house. Waist-high stone walls were built as protective barriers from the sheer drop at the back.

Sara gasped. "Look at that wonderful porch and those lovely rocking chairs. I simply must try one of them out."

Monk parked the Land Rover in the center of the stone circle drive and rushed to open the doors for his passengers.

"If you stand on the porch and look in the window, you can see through the house to the vista beyond," he pointed out.

"Oh, it is lovely," Anne said. "It looks brand-new," she added as she walked to the wall on the side of the drive and looked down at the trees below.

"It was built four years ago."

"How in heaven's name did they get all the glass up these mountains?" Sara asked.

"Very carefully, I would imagine," Carrie replied.

"I believe you ladies will be very comfortable here," Monk said.

"Oh, yes, we will be." Sara was so enthusiastic that Carrie wouldn't have been surprised if she'd started clapping her hands.

Wasn't Sara used to such ambience? She was a judge, for heaven's sake. Surely she had money. And obviously so did Anne. Neither one of them would have been able to afford the spa if they weren't well-off.

"If you ladies would like to go inside, there's champagne chilling for you. I'll bring the luggage in."

Carrie opened the door and led the way inside. She noticed the thin wires up against the house and assumed they were part of the alarm system.

"Watch your step," she said. "Don't trip over the wires."

The floor plan was open, very spacious. To the left of the huge marble entry was a magnificent spiral staircase that reached up three stories. Light flooded the room, and when they raised their eyes higher, they could see the golden clouds through a long rectangular skylight.

"Isn't the staircase beautiful?" Sara said. "The wood . . . the steps, they're twice the length and depth of any I've ever seen. It must have cost a fortune to build it," she added. "Look at the railing. The craftsmanship is exceptional."

Carrie agreed. Then Anne called to them. "The mountains look like they're on fire with the sunset. Come see." Even Anne, a difficult woman to please, couldn't contain her enthusiasm.

Carrie stood in the foyer taking in the view. Colorful oriental rugs—high-quality rugs—were scattered across the living room's pale brown, marble floor. In harmony with the mountains, the furnishings were done in soft browns and beiges. The stone fireplace was at least sixteen feet high and similar, she thought, to the fireplace in the villain's house she'd admired when she'd watched one of her favorite movies, *North by Northwest*. The room was square like the living room in the movie too. No, this one was much better, the furniture updated and more exquisite.

Directly ahead, the sun was setting, and the burst from the fiery ball filled the room with a soft orange hue.

"I feel like I'm in heaven," Sara said.

"If you go to the top of that spiral staircase, you will be in heaven," Carrie joked.

Anne spotted the silver bucket with a bottle of champagne on the sideboard. There was a beautiful crystal vase with three long-stemmed, bloodred roses next to it. The petals were just beginning to open. "Shall we have a glass of champagne?"

"But of course," Sara answered.

The three women stood in front of the window overlooking the panorama as Anne struggled to get the bottle uncorked. She laughed nervously when the cork popped and the liquid bubbled over, then carefully filled each Waterford crystal flute.

"We should have a toast," Carrie said.

"Good idea," Sara agreed.

She and Anne lifted their glasses and waited for Carrie to do the honors.

"To us," she said. "May all our dreams come true."

"That's lovely," Anne said.

They sank down onto the plush, down-filled sofas and sipped their champagne, making idle chitchat, carefully avoiding any personal topics, while Monk carried their luggage upstairs to their suites. Carrie was still feeling a little nauseous, so she didn't drink more than one tiny sip.

Monk joined them ten minutes later with a tray of

canapés. As he was placing the linen napkins next to the tray on the coffee table, Carrie heard a door close. She looked toward the hallway leading from the dining room and saw a woman wearing a black dress walk into the kitchen.

"Maids have arrived," she remarked to Sara.

"Do have one of these cucumber canapés," Anne suggested. She'd just finished eating the bite-size treat. "They're quite tasty."

Carrie didn't want to tell either woman she wasn't feeling well, and she certainly wasn't going to admit she'd gotten carsick.

"Yes, I will," she said. She popped the little sandwich into her mouth, barely chewing it before swallowing it down. "It is good," she said.

She couldn't make herself eat another and became even more queasy watching Anne eat two salmon puffs as well as the cucumber sandwiches, and Sara devour twice as many.

Within minutes they were all yawning. Monk noticed. "If you ladies will follow me, I'll show you to your rooms," he said as he leaned down to turn on one of the table lamps. Now that the sun was going down, the room was filled with shadows.

"I am so sleepy," Anne said.

"It must be the mountain air," Sara suggested. "I'm feeling lethargic myself."

They followed Monk to the spiral staircase. Carrie looked up and remarked, "Who would have thought stairs could be a work of art."

"I hate stairs," Anne said. "The next house I build will be a sprawling ranch."

Sara and Carrie ignored her comment. Monk drew their attention when he said, "I've unpacked your overnight bags. Mrs. Trapp, you and Judge Collins will be in suites on the second level on opposite ends of the floor. Mrs. Salvetti, you're one floor up. I hope you'll all find the accommodations satisfactory."

Anne followed Monk, then came Carrie, and Sara, gripping the banister for support, was the last in line.

"I feel like I've been in this house before," Sara said. "Yet I've never seen a spiral staircase like this, so I don't know why I feel that way."

"I think it's the fireplace," Carrie said. She paused on a step to look down into the living room once again. "Did you ever see the movie *North by Northwest*? It starred Cary Grant and Eva Marie Saint, and in the climax, they had to climb out on the presidents' faces?"

"I do remember. The stone fireplace is very like the one in the movie. That must be why it seems so familiar to me."

"I never saw the movie," Anne said.

Carrie was floored. "You've got to be kidding. It was one of Hitchcock's best."

Anne shrugged. "I was busy running my business," she said. "I didn't have time to go to movies."

"But it's a classic. It's been on television at least a hundred times," Sara said.

"Oh, I never watch television."

Carrie didn't know how to relate to the woman. Anne sounded as though she were boasting about the fact that she didn't watch television. Carrie's life revolved around networks and sponsors. She looked up at Anne now as if she were an alien. Not watch television or go to the movies? Amazing. No wonder the woman was so dull.

She didn't feel at all guilty about her snap judgment. Anne, unknowingly, had just insulted everything that Carrie worked for or believed in.

Monk showed Sara into her suite first.

"I think I'm going to call it a night," Sara said. "I'll see you in the morning."

"Good night," Carrie called as she followed Monk down the long hallway.

He opened Anne's door for her, and then turned to Carrie. "Your suite is directly above Judge Collins's," he said. He led her up the staircase to the next level.

"So there are four full suites?" Carrie asked.

"Yes," he answered.

They reached her door, and Monk stepped back to let her go inside. The large bedroom with an adjoining sitting room was a soothing amber color. Two overstuffed chairs flanked a fireplace, and the four-poster bed made of light, burled pine was covered with a thick down comforter.

She yawned loudly. Monk or one of the maids had laid out her robe and gown on the bed. She spotted her carry-on on the luggage rack. It was open and empty, and she was going to ask where her laptop was, but then a wave of nausea and dizziness struck, and she had to sit down. She took several deep breaths as she held on to the bedpost.

"Is everything all right, Mrs. Salvetti?"

She didn't want to be difficult or complain the way Anne did, and so she simply said that she was weary from the long day. "I'm usually a night owl, and I don't go to bed until two or three in the morning, but tonight I can barely keep my eyes open."

Monk's expression was sympathetic. "It takes a while to get used to the mountain air, and the staff from the spa did suggest that all of you have an early night. Tomorrow promises to be quite busy."

"Yes, I'm sure it will be."

"I'll be the last to retire," he said as he walked to the door. "I'll set the alarm then. Please remember not to open any windows."

"What happens if the alarm goes off? Who will hear it?" she asked. "We're out in the middle of nowhere."

"The alarm is electronically connected to the spa. I thought I had mentioned that before. Should we need it, help will arrive in less than three minutes."

"The spa's that close?"

He nodded. "If it weren't for the trees, you'd be able to see the domes from your window. Would you like me to close the drapes?"

"No. I prefer them open." She turned away, gripping the bedpost now as the bile came rushing up into her throat. She was going to ask him where the servant quarters were located, but her throat burned too much to get the question out.

"Good night," she said. "Close the door behind you, please."

The second she heard the door click shut, she bolted from the bed and ran into the bathroom, one hand covering her mouth. She barely got the lid up in time before she threw up the canapé she'd eaten. The damn car sickness. She'd had the problem since she was a child. She should have spoken up and explained she couldn't sit in the back-seat. Worried what the others would think of her, she hadn't said a word.

What the hell was the matter with her? What did she care what strangers thought about her? She would probably never see them again after breakfast.

Her stomach heaved at the thought of food. She hadn't felt this ill in years, not since that horrid case of food poisoning. Avery was fourteen at the time, and she'd stayed home from school to help take care of Carrie. Tony had been a real gem back then too. She remembered how he'd held her when the chills got so bad.

Carrie felt too weak to take a shower. She brushed her

teeth, washed her face, and put on her nightgown. She stumbled back into the bedroom, heard the clinking of glasses, and assumed that Monk was cleaning up. Then she heard a woman's laughter. Was the maid flirting with him? Might as well, she thought. There wasn't anything else for them to do, since she and Anne and Sara were already going to bed. My heavens, it wasn't even nine o'clock yet, and she was so exhausted, she could barely focus.

The room kept spinning. God, she felt awful. She fell into bed, struggled to get the covers up, and tried resting on her side. The nausea was still coming in waves. She slowly, carefully rolled onto her back. That was better, much better. She closed her eyes and fell asleep.

She didn't know how long she'd slept, but it was dark in the room when she heard someone faintly calling out to her. She couldn't respond. Then she heard a clicking sound over and over. No, the noise was snapping, like fingers coming together, or clinking, like knives being sharpened. Carrie couldn't understand why the noise wouldn't stop.

Someone nudged her shoulder, calling her name again.

She couldn't summon the strength to open her eyes. "Yes?" she whispered.

"Carrie."

"Yes?"

The noise made it difficult for her to concentrate. And, oh, she was so sleepy. She tried but couldn't even raise her hand to cover her eyes when a light went on.

"Go away," she said, her voice a croak.

"I heard your toast, Carrie. Do you remember what you said?"

"No . . ."

"May all your dreams come true. But what about your nightmares? Those come true too."

The words weren't making any sense. "What? Night-mares? No . . . no nightmares."

"Open your eyes, Carrie."

The sound was getting louder. "Come on. Look at me."

The voice floating above her became more demanding, more menacing. Carrie was finally able to open her eyes a little. She saw the scissors opening and closing in front of her face. They were shiny. That was the snapping noise, she realized. But why were there scissors?

And then the noise stopped, and the scissors vanished. A face appeared just inches above her own, and that smile, that hideous, gloating smile that was horrifically familiar.

She tried to scream. "No . . . no . . . no . . . oh, my God, help me . . . no . . . Jilly."

CHAPTER 5

Avery lost track of the time. She was frantic to get as much work done as possible before she had to leave for the airport. Her desk had been clear when she'd left the night before. She'd gotten to the office at six-thirty that morning just so everything would be caught up.

She was so bleary-eyed now she could barely focus on her computer screen. And doing a slow burn. Someone, she didn't know who the culprit was, had dumped twenty-two files on her desk, and she was expected to transfer all the information into the database. She also had at least sixty e-mails to read and answer, and she hadn't remembered to check her private voice mail in over twenty-four hours.

Her cubicle still looked like a cyclone had hit. The files seemed to be multiplying, and how was that possible?

"Aren't you supposed to be on a plane?" Margo asked. She was juggling a stack of files, her empty water bottle, and a doughnut box.

"I've got a little time left," Avery answered as she typed a reply to one of her e-mails.

Lou stood and stretched his arms. "Margo, are there any Krispy Kremes left?"

"One," she answered. "Avery didn't eat hers."

"Help yourself," Avery said.

Lou grabbed the box out of Margo's arms and opened it. "When are you leaving?"

"Soon."

"Flying?"

"Of course she's flying," Margo said.

"I've got it all figured out down to the minute. If I leave at four-fifteen on the dot, I'll have time to drive home, change clothes, and pick up my luggage, then take the interstate to the airport, park in long-term, and make it to the gate in plenty of time."

Margo took her purse from her drawer and came back around the corner. "Hey, Avery, did you have time to call Mrs. Speigel's caretaker and tell her to do a better job of hiding those car keys?"

"No, I forgot."

"You want me to look up her phone number and call her? She's got to do something to protect the public from that woman."

"I'd appreciate it if you would call," Avery said. "But don't be bossy, Margo. Mrs. Speigel's a sweetheart. She knows she shouldn't be driving, but sometimes she gets confused."

"Avery, she almost killed you." Margo sighed then. "Okay, I won't be bossy."

Mel joined the conversation. "Everyone in D.C. will be on the interstate. There's bound to be a pileup. You ought to take the Jefferson Davis, then cut over to ninety-five. It'll save you a good twenty minutes."

Margo disagreed. "She's leaving in rush hour. The interstate is much faster."

Avery was only half listening. Her fingers were flying over the keyboard as she replied to interoffice inquiries. "I feel terrible leaving you guys with my mess," she said to no one in particular.

"Don't worry about it," Lou said.

"We'll all split the work," Margo said. "Lou, you've got some powdered sugar on your belt."

She reached over Avery's head, grabbed a tissue from the box on the shelf, and handed it to Lou. Then she turned back to Avery. "I'm planning to dump all my work on all of you when I go to San Diego next month for my cousin's wedding."

"I think I'd better type up that route you should take to the airport," Mel said. "I'll hand you the printout as you're leaving the office."

"As long as I'm out of here by four-fifteen."

"I'll make sure you are," Mel promised. "Shall we synchronize our watches?"

"That's a nerdy thing to do," Margo told him. "Now, Brad Pitt would never—"

Her phone rang, interrupting her thought. While she hurried to her cubicle, Lou picked up where she'd left off. "Face it, you guys. We are nerds."

"So what's wrong with that?" Mel asked. "I mean, think about it. Bill Gates is a nerd, and he's doing all right."

"Maybe, but we aren't making his billions, now are we? And we're thought of as nerds by everyone in the Bureau."

"I don't believe that," Mel argued. "We're all important members of the team."

Margo interrupted. "Agent Andrews is on his way down here," she called out. "Douglas's secretary heard him ask where the pen was."

"He's probably coming down to thank you, Avery, for letting him have the glory," Lou said.

"He's late," Margo said. "He should have thanked her the other day, after the press conference."

"Andrews is going to cut into your time," Mel said. "Maybe I better go ahead and print out that alternate route. You can decide which way to go once you're in the car. Just be sure to turn the radio on and listen to the traffic updates."

Avery tried not to smile. Mel did tend to obsess over the tiniest details. "Thanks, Mel."

"We'll let Andrews talk for what? Four? Five minutes?"

"That'd be good."

"Then you interrupt," Mel told Lou. "You're good at that."

Andrews ruined the schedule. Although Avery had never met the agent, she had him all figured out in less than a minute. He thought he was a charmer. It was an incorrect assumption on his part. He got the "thank yous" over with quickly but then perched on the edge of her desk and invited her to have dinner with him. His stare wasn't quite a leer, but it was damned close. Lou and Mel immediately tried to get rid of him.

"Avery's leaving on vacation," Mel said. "She's got a plane to catch."

When Andrews didn't take the hint, Lou decided to be more blunt. "You better leave. She's on a tight schedule, and you're messing it up."

Andrews's response was to fold his arms and widen his goofy smile.

It didn't take investigative skill to know what was happening. Andrews was suffering from LAFS, "lust at first sight," but that didn't make him unusual. Most of the men who got close to Avery became temporarily afflicted by the debilitating condition. Mel theorized that the syndrome was brought on by her big, baby blue eyes. When she looked at a man and gave him her full attention, his brain simply shut down. Lou didn't agree with Mel's assessment. Blue

eyes might have had a little to do with catching a guy's interest, but it was Avery's killer body and long, silky blond
hair that turned him into a blithering idiot.

Andrews was blithering now. It was sad, really, to watch
a skilled professional sink so quickly into the quagmire.

Mel, the more protective of Avery, hoped Andrews
would hurry up and compliment her. They all did, sooner
or later, and then Avery would send him on his way.
Mel checked the time as he silently willed Andrews to
tell Avery how pretty she was. If he didn't hit on her soon,
Avery would miss her plane.

Come on, come on, Mel silently urged. Go for it. Tell
her what a knockout she is.

"I've got to ask you something," Andrews said.

"Yes?" Avery asked.

"How come such a beautiful woman like you is stuck
down here in the basement?" The agent all but crooned the
question like a country singer. "With your looks—" It was
as far as he got. Poor guy never knew what hit him.

Avery's voice sizzled as she curtly responded, "Agent Andrews, I had nothing to do with the way I look. Now, if
you'll excuse me, I have work to do, and I assume you do
too. Get off my desk and go away."

That having been said, she swiveled in her chair and
began typing again. Andrews had that *what'd-I-say?* look
of bewilderment on his face as he stood and slowly walked
away, blushing like a girl.

Mel didn't start laughing until he was out of earshot.
"So I guess you won't be going to dinner with Andrews
when you get back from vacation?"

"I'm trying to work here."

Lou put his hand out, and Mel, frowning as he pulled his
wallet from his back pocket, extracted a dollar bill and
handed it to his friend. The two men had a standing bet as

to the nature of the compliments given Avery. Since Andrews hadn't said anything about her legs, Lou won the dollar. Her legs were pretty amazing, and most men noticed them right away, but Andrews apparently wasn't a leg man.

"How come that never happens to me?" Margo asked. "I'm cute, aren't I?"

"Yeah, sure you are," Lou said.

"And I want to get married one day and have a family," she continued as though Lou hadn't answered. "Whereas Avery has made it perfectly clear on countless occasions that she's never going to get married. It's just not fair. I'd be perfect for Andrews. I really would. But he never even glanced my way."

"What makes you think you'd be perfect for him?" Lou asked.

"Because he's a hottie," she answered. "And no one appreciates a full-fledged hottie more than I. We'd be perfect for each other," she said over her shoulder as she went back to her workstation.

Mel shoved his wallet back into his pocket and went to work. At four-fifteen, he stood up and called, "It's time to leave, Avery."

"Just give me another ten minutes . . ."

The ten turned into forty-five, and she didn't get out of the office until after five. Fortunately, her knee was much better today, and she was able to run. Nevertheless, she still missed her flight. There was an accident on the interstate, blocking two lanes, and by the time she finally arrived at the airport and sprinted to the terminal, the plane was in the air.

Avery toyed with the idea of going back home and crashing in her own bed. She hadn't averaged more than four hours' sleep a night in over a week, and she was exhausted. She didn't dare give in to the urge, though. Carrie would kill her if she were a full day late.

Utopia wasn't her idea of a great vacation. She was going only to please her aunt. When she went someplace new, she wanted to see the sights, soak in the local color. She didn't relish the idea of being stuck in a spa for six days, but Avery had given her word, so she couldn't back out.

The next flight through Denver into Aspen was full, and she was forced to take a convoluted route from D.C. She ended up in Grand Junction, Colorado. She would have to wait until morning to board yet another flight. After she collected her luggage and checked into the hotel adjacent to the airport, she called Carrie on her cell phone. She got her voice mail on the first ring. She assumed her aunt was recharging her phone and had already gone to bed—it was midnight Aspen time. She left a message that she would arrive at the spa around noon tomorrow.

Then she called the spa to let them know she was delayed. Since she'd left a message on Carrie's cell phone, she didn't ask the receptionist to connect her to her aunt's suite.

That night Avery slept like the dead. The following morning, while she ate her continental breakfast of toast, juice, and milk, she called her office voice mail. There were over twenty messages in her mailbox, but fortunately none of them was urgent. She made notes as she listened and then erased each one. Carrie's message made her smile. She sounded so excited about staying in a mountain house where Tom Cruise had allegedly been a guest. How like her aunt to get stars in her eyes over such a silly little thing. Avery erased that message and continued on until she was finally finished.

She was downstairs and checking out by eight-fifteen. While the receptionist printed her bill, Avery looked over a map of Colorado. Aspen wasn't all that far from Grand Junction, just two and a half hours away by car. Then she heard an elderly couple talking about the lovely sights in the area, and on the spur of the moment, she decided to rent a car and drive to the spa. She took the shuttle back to the airport, rented a sedan, and headed out.

Avery was wearing her weekend uniform, a pair of old jeans, a plain white T-shirt, and a pair of scuffed tennis shoes. Carrie wouldn't approve of the outfit, but Avery opted for comfort over fashion.

Once she was on I-70 heading east toward Aspen, she felt as if she was really on vacation. It was a beautiful, crisp, summer morning. The sun was shining, and the sky was such a brilliant shade of blue it looked almost artificial. She rolled the window down and took a deep breath. It was wonderful. The air was so clean and light, as though she were breathing pure oxygen. It was a refreshing change after the smog of the big, overcrowded city.

She stopped at a McDonald's for a bottle of water and a Diet Coke. After she paid for her order, she sat down in one of the booths to look over the map. There might be an interesting side trip she could take on her way to the spa, maybe see something historical. She knew that once she checked in, Carrie wouldn't let her leave, and she did want to see a little of Colorado. What she'd already seen on her drive was beautiful, but she felt she was only glimpsing a tip of what the state had to offer. Besides, Carrie was going to be irritated anyway because Avery was late. What difference did it make if she was another hour or two behind schedule?

She spread the map on the table in front of her and, first of all, tried to find the spot where Carrie had told her she'd spent the night. What was it? Land of the Lakes? No, that wasn't it.

"Are you lost, darlin'?"

The deep baritone voice jarred her. Annoyed her too. She simply wasn't in the mood to get hit on. Suppressing a sigh, she frowned as she looked up, ready to tell whoever was trying to bother her to go away, but then she saw the gentleman standing before her and she smiled. He was at least eighty years old. Immaculately dressed in a freshly pressed denim shirt with a turquoise bolo tie, and Levi's tucked into tan cowboy boots with scrollwork around the tops, he held a tan Stetson in one hand and a cup of steaming coffee in the other. His face was full of character, from his sparkling golden brown eyes and his leathered complexion to the handlebar mustache that was perfectly waxed and groomed. Both his mustache and his hair were pure white.

"Excuse me?"

"I asked you if you were lost," he repeated. "I saw you looking over that map, and I figured I might be able to help you get where you're wanting to go since I know just about every little nook and cranny in Colorado. I've lived here all my eighty-four years, come September."

"I was just looking over places of interest," she said. "Actually, I could use your help. Would you care to join me?"

"I'd be delighted," he said. He put his coffee down, then scooted into the booth across from her and carefully placed his Stetson on the seat next to him. "Can't stay but a couple of minutes. My granddaughter will be swinging by to pick me up. She's got a nice little Western store, and I help her with the customers two days a week. That's why I'm duded up," he explained. "Now, where are you headed?"

"Aspen."

"You couldn't be lost then. There are signs all around you. Aspen's just a few miles away."

"Yes, I know," she said. "But I was trying to locate an area called Land of the Lakes or Around the Lakes. Have you ever heard of such a place?"

"If you're talking about Land Between the Lakes, then, yes, I sure have heard of it. My name's Walt Gentry, by the way."

"Avery Delaney," she said as she offered her hand to shake his.

"It's a pleasure to meet you," he said. He moved his coffee so he wouldn't knock it when he stacked his hands on the table and said, "You won't find the place on that map, so you might as well stop looking. Most folks outside of Colorado wouldn't even know about it. You see, people come in here from California and Washington and buy a couple of acres of land. Then they build themselves a big house, and they think they ought to name the place, like it was the Ponderosa or something. Now, a fella named Parnell, Dennis Parnell, purchased about forty acres of prime land up high above Aspen some time back. He shouldn't have been able to buy it, but he did," he added with a shrug. "Then, about six years ago, he decided to build his dream home up there. It took more than two and a half years to finish it, and Parnell made those environmentalists crazy tearing up that beautiful, untamed land the way he did. Big old semis going up and down the mountain, tearing out trees to make room for a road. It was a crying shame what he did, but Parnell got away with it because money talks, and he got every kind of permit he needed. Don't think that could happen today," he added. "In the last couple of years, we got stronger laws passed protecting our land. Anyway," he continued, "when Parnell's house was all finished, he put up a big fence all the way around it. I heard the house came in at eight million, but that was a few years ago, so I'm sure the price has more than doubled. It was rumored that Parnell paid cash and owns the house and the land free and clear. I didn't believe that gossip, but folks around here did, and then, of course, they had to speculate as to where he could have gotten his hands on so much money."

Avery was caught up in the story. "How did he?"

"Folks thought it must be drug money, but turns out Parnell owned a little computer company out in Silicon Valley. One of his engineers designed a new computer chip that revolutionized the business. Don't understand any of it," he admitted. "But since that engineer worked for Parnell, he got the patent. He made his fortune, sold the company before it went belly-up, and moved here."

"He doesn't still own the place, does he?" she asked, thinking that Parnell must have sold it to the owner of Utopia to use as a retreat for important visitors.

"He does and he doesn't," Walt replied. "This is where the story takes a sordid turn. Parnell got married at the church about a mile from here. It was quite an event too, and cost a fortune. Five hundred people were invited to the reception," he said. "I heard it took a year to plan the big party. They even had flowers flown in from Europe. I guess the flowers in the United States weren't good enough. Anyway, the planning of the marriage lasted longer than the union. Parnell was only married eighteen months when he filed for divorce."

He paused to shake his head. Then he got sidetracked. "I sure don't understand this modern world. Me and my wife, Ona May, have been married forty-seven years, and sure, there have been times when I wanted to leave and never come back. I imagine she felt the same way every now and again, but we stayed together because we said our vows and we meant them. Now I read in the papers about this new trend called 'starter marriages.' Have you ever heard of them?"

She smiled. "I've heard the term."

"I don't understand it," he said. "Those couples ought to just live together and leave the vows out of it. I think Parnell thought he was in a starter marriage, the way he filed so quick. It's been a real nasty divorce with lots of mudslinging, which of course hits the papers. People gobble that trash right up. He filed over a year ago, and it's still dragging on. Everyone's waiting to hear who's gonna end up owning that house. The soon-to-be-ex-wife swears he promised it to her, and she thinks she ought to be able to keep it. The judge is deciding now which one of them is going to get it. Pamela Parnell says she'll die before she lets him have it, and he says that's fine with him. They're both acting like five-year-olds, if you ask me. Just last week Parnell gave another interview and was quoted as saying that no matter what the judge ruled, he was never gonna let his ex have that house. Those two are quite a pair," he added. "But the folks around and in Aspen are just as bad. Do you know they got a lottery going?"

"You mean they're betting over which one gets the house?"

"That's right. The odds are ninety to ten in favor of Pamela Parnell getting it because of the shady way Dennis got himself those permits. There's talk he'll be indicted. And the judge who's deciding which one of those sorry characters will get the house is a real dedicated environmentalist. Time will tell, I suppose."

He leaned forward, tapped the map with his forefinger. "Right there," he said. "That's Land Between the Lakes. It was so named, you see, because it sits between two big, clear-water lakes. Have you got a pen on you? I could circle it for you."

Avery dug through her backpack, found a ballpoint pen, and handed it to Walt. His fingers were crippled with arthritis. He had trouble holding the pen as he made the circle.

"From where we're sitting, it's about a two-hour drive away. There are some other fancy homes up there, but you won't get near any of them because all the roads are privately owned and gated."

"I thought my aunt was staying at a retreat called Land Between the Lakes, but I must have been mistaken. Maybe I didn't hear her correctly. There was a lot of static on the line."

"Could she have said Twin Lakes?" he asked. "Now, Land Between the Lakes is up north, but Twin Lakes is south of here, and it is marked on the map."

He pointed to the location. Avery nodded, then folded the map and put it in her backpack. She shook his hand again as she stood. "Thank you for helping me," she said.

"It was my pleasure," he replied. "You be sure to buckle up, darlin'. There are some crazy drivers out there, taking those winding roads at seventy miles an hour. They're begging for death. Don't you let them take you with them."

She got back in the car and started out again. Guilt prevented her from taking any side trips. Besides, she had soaked up a little local color when she'd visited with Walt. He was a genteel old man, and she'd thoroughly enjoyed listening to him.

Maybe she could talk Carrie into doing a little hiking. That thought was so absurd, she laughed. Avery had heard that her aunt actually had been quite a jock in high school. She'd played volleyball, basketball, and just about every other sport that was offered. Avery remembered playing with Carrie's tennis trophies. Did her aunt still have them, or had she thrown them away? Oh, well, no matter. Carrie definitely wasn't an outdoors girl now. She detested exercise.

Carrie's goal for her stay at Utopia was to be pampered, not whipped into shape. Avery sighed loudly. She hoped to heaven Carrie didn't make her do all that girly stuff with her, like mud baths and seaweed wraps. It wasn't that she had anything against being pampered, but she didn't have all that much time to have fun, and she would rather get muddy exploring the countryside.

Avery drove through Aspen and continued on. An hour later she was certain she was lost. She was about to pull over and check the map again when she spotted the sign for Utopia. The road curved sharply, then climbed and narrowed to a gravel driveway. Then the gate came into view. She stopped to give her name to the guard on duty.

"Your name isn't on the list for today's check-ins."

"I have a reservation," she insisted. "My name should be there."

He moved closer to the car and smiled. "I'm sure it's just a mix-up. You can straighten it out at the front desk."

"Thanks," she called out as she drove through.

They certainly were friendly at the spa if the guard was an indicator. She glanced in her rearview mirror and saw him standing in the middle of the road watching her drive away.

His salt-and-pepper hair reminded her of her uncle Tony. Oh, Lord, she forgot to call him last night. As soon as she checked into her room, she'd do just that. Tony was such a worrier. Avery knew that he and Carrie were having problems, but she hoped that they would be able to work them out. Carrie was probably the reason they weren't getting along. Although Avery loved her aunt with all her heart, she wasn't blind to her faults. Carrie could be a real pain sometimes. Marrying Tony was the best thing she had ever done, and maybe, while she was relaxing at the spa, she would take the time to think about her priorities. She had always taken Tony for granted, and no marriage could survive long that way. Fortunately, her uncle had the patience of a saint. He'd hung in there longer than any other man would have.

She went around another sharp curve. For Pete's sake, where was the spa? Since passing through the gate, she had to have driven halfway up the mountain, and she was completely surrounded by wilderness. Then, when she was sure she must have taken a service road by mistake at the last fork, Utopia came into view.

It was aptly named. "My goodness," she whispered. The place was gorgeous and seemed to radiate tranquillity. The buff-colored stucco buildings were nestled in the lush landscape of towering evergreens. The main structure looked as though it were part of the sloping mountain. Small bungalows dotted the hillside with stone paths winding in and around the thick pines. There were wildflowers everywhere. She could hear the sound of rushing water. She turned and saw a fountain of steps built into the side of the lower hill. The bubbling water rolled down the slate and splashed over a golden sphere suspended in a circular pool.

A maintenance truck pulled out in front of Avery's car from a service road. She braked and waited as the crew quickly unloaded some barrels, her gaze taking in the beauty and serenity of her surroundings. A young couple, obviously in love, caught her attention. They were holding hands as they strolled down the path parallel to the fountain. They stopped halfway, turned to each other, and kissed passionately.

Avery felt a pang of envy and forced herself to look away. And then she couldn't stop herself from glancing back at the couple and noticing the way they looked into each other's eyes. They were probably newlyweds, she thought.

The truck moved out of her path, and with a sigh, she drove up the steep incline. At the crest was a cobblestone circle drive. Huge clay pots overflowing with ivy and pink and yellow flowers were placed like sentinels in front of the marble steps leading up to the entrance.

People were coming and going, all at a sedate pace. Like the lovey-dovey couple on the hillside, the guests were dressed in identical navy blue jogging suits. On the jacket, above the breast pocket, was a little logo of a sphere with the name of the spa printed in gold thread.

Avery put the car in park as the doorman rushed forward. He opened her door, put his hand out to assist her, and said, "Welcome to Utopia."

CHAPTER 6

Monk was in love. Though he hadn't believed such a miracle could happen, he had met the woman of his dreams, and since then he had been acting like a crazy, ridiculous fool. Jilly was his soul mate. No doubt about it. They were absolutely perfect for each other, for they shared the same dreams, the same fantasies, the same goals, and most important of all, the same sense of unfair play.

She had hypnotized him from the moment they'd met in that dirty nameless little bar and grill on the outskirts of Savannah. His breath had caught in his throat when she walked in, a vision in a silky red dress and red stiletto heels. She was simply . . . magnificent. As he had instructed over the phone, he was waiting in the corner booth with a blue folder in his hands. When she saw him, she smiled, and in that instant, he knew he was lost.

The bloom of first love hadn't worn off. He still ached with his love for her. Even when he was supposed to be working, he couldn't stop smiling. These days his mind only had room for thoughts of her. While he was doing the necessary drudge work of surveillance, one of his favorite ways to pass the time was to recall, to the most intimate detail, the first time they had made love. It had happened exactly three hours after they had met. Jilly had taken him back to her hotel room, stripped him of his clothes and his inhibitions, and had made passionate love to him. He closed his eyes in bliss as the memory flooded his senses. The sweet taste of her in his mouth, the musky scent of her perfume, the heat of her silky body pressed against his, the deep, almost animal sounds she made when he touched her just so. She had been wild, forceful, and rough—just the way he liked it—and yet, at the same time, she had been exquisitely vulnerable.

Monk marveled over his lack of discipline when it came to Jilly. Never in his wildest imagination would he have believed he was capable of silly romantic behavior, or that he would ever marry. Yet, two months ago he had proposed—down on one knee, no less—and she had thrilled him with her acceptance. He told her he would do anything for her, anything at all, and then set about proving it. Desperate to please her, he knew he was putty in her hands, yet he couldn't seem to mind.

Jilly was the first person in the world whom he completely trusted to keep his secrets. He knew all of hers too. They had been living together for four months when, late one night, after they had made love and were cuddling together on the sofa in their silk robes and sipping chilled champagne, he opened up to her and told her all about his bleak life on the dried-up patch of farmland in Nebraska with his dried-up, stern, joyless parents. His father hadn't believed in sparing the rod, and his mother, a weakling who was afraid of her own shadow and who never went anywhere or did anything outside of the home except church on Sunday mornings, would stand with her hands folded behind her back and watch as her husband tried to whip the wanderlust out of their only child. Monk learned early in life never to complain to her because she always told his father what he had said. By the time he was ten, he hated both of them and would fall asleep at night dreaming of new ways to torture them.

His life had been claustrophobic. He stole money from the church safe—just a little here and there on Sundays. After he graduated from high school, he packed up his bag, a grocery sack actually, and left the farm. He went to college in Omaha. He had enough saved to pay for the first semester and received government loans to pay the rest of the tuition, loans he never intended to repay. Four years later, he left the state of Nebraska, vowing never to return.

To this day, he didn't know if his parents were dead or alive, and he didn't particularly care.

He'd never really cared about anyone—until now.

He told Jilly everything about himself. He told her he had committed his first murder at the ripe old age of twenty-two. He also told her he had once had dreams of working in the theater. He loved getting into costume and taking on different roles. And he was a good actor, he boasted, so good that he tried out for a major part in a summer stock play. Another actor mocked his performance and humiliated him in front of the director. Monk became so rattled by the heckling that he made a mess of his audition and, of course, didn't get the part. Vowing to get even, he bided his time, and two years later he went after the boy. He'd used his knife that time and had found the experience both exciting and liberating.

"When did you change your name?" she asked.

"The day I enrolled in college," he said. "I had a fake birth certificate, and I managed to make it look real enough to fool the administrator's office. It was really quite crude, but it got the job done."

"I didn't get to go to college," she told him. "I wanted

to, but my mother didn't think I was smart enough. She took the money I'd saved and used it to pay for Carrie's education."

"What was your life like growing up?"

Jilly's eyes welled up with tears. "Loveless," she said. "I don't remember my father. He left when I was little. It was because of her."

"Your mother?"

"Yes," she said. "She drove him away. He ran off with another woman, but looking back, I can't blame him. Mama was a cold and bitter woman. She never showed me any affection, and I think that's why I got into trouble . . . you know . . . got pregnant. I was looking for someone to love me. I shamed the family. I can't tell you the number of times my sister and mother shouted those very words at me." She shook her head and then whispered, "I was such an innocent fool. I was so sure that, once I had the baby, my mother and my sister, the golden girl, would forgive me and help me raise her. I wanted to do the right thing by my child."

"But that didn't happen, did it?"

She gripped his hand. "No, it didn't. It was so awful. Mama and Carrie came to the hospital. I thought they were going to take me and my daughter home."

"What happened, my love?" he asked when she was too overcome to continue. He leaned forward to pour more champagne into her glass.

"Carrie left the hospital room with my daughter. She never said a word to me. She just went to the bassinet, picked her up, and left. Mama grabbed my arm when I tried to go after my sister. I asked her where Carrie was going with my beautiful baby, and she said that she was taking little Avery home. 'Avery.' That's the stupid name my mama came up with for my daughter." She wiped the tears away from her face with her fingertips. "They wouldn't even let me name my own child. Carrie was making all the decisions, telling Mama what she ought to do, and Mama went along with whatever her golden girl decreed."

"And then what happened?"

"Mama told me I had to leave town and that I could never come home again. She said I had humiliated her and Carrie for the last time. I couldn't get through to her, and even though I begged her to forgive me, she wouldn't. I can still see that ugly, pinched look on her face. It was just like Carrie's. She called me terrible names, and then she opened her pocketbook and pulled out a hundred-dollar bill. She threw it in my face and walked out of the room."

"Wasn't there anyone who would help you?"

She shook her head. "Mama was real tight with the chief of police. She had him wound around her little finger. He used to drop by late every other night when Carrie and I were supposed to be sleeping, but one night I heard all this groaning and grunting going on, and I snuck down to see what was happening. I peeked in the living room, and there was the chief sprawled out as pretty as you please on our sofa with his pants down around his ankles. Mama was kneeling between his legs, servicing him. The fat pig was a married man," she added. "And he'd do anything to keep Mama from telling his wife about their sordid affair. Mama told me that the chief would lock me up in jail if I didn't leave town right away. I knew she had the power to make him do it."

She was sobbing uncontrollably now. He put his arm around her and held her close until she was able to calm down. Then he asked, "What happened to your daughter?"

"Carrie raised her and brainwashed her against me. My sister has always hated me. She wasn't . . . pretty the way I was, and she was eaten up with jealousy. Stealing my baby was her way of getting even with me, I suppose."

"How did you meet Dale Skarrett?" he asked.

"After I left Sheldon Beach, I worked odd jobs to support myself. I was trying to save up enough money to hire a lawyer and get my baby back. I didn't have any training to do much of anything, so I worked in bars and restaurants. I stole money a couple of times to help pay the rent, and I slept with men too. Twelve in all," she admitted. "I kept count . . . I don't know why, but I did, and I took every precaution so I wouldn't get any disgusting diseases. I hated doing it, but I needed the money. I was so desperate to get my daughter back." She turned away as she recalled the anguish. "Then, one night when I was working at a flea-infested bar down in Savannah, I met Dale Skarrett. God, he disgusted me," she said. "But he had money. He made sure I saw the wad of bills, and he wanted me. We lived together off and on for what seemed an eternity. I tried to move on with my life, but he kept coming back. And then one night he told me about this jewelry store he and his buddies, Frank and Larry, were going to rob. Larry was shacking up with the daughter of the owner of the store, and she liked to talk about her family's money. Dale pretty much planned the robbery, but I helped with all the details."

"So you were an accomplice."

"Yes," she said. "The robbery went off without a hitch, but Frank had a big mouth, and he started talking about all the money he was going to get when Dale sold the diamonds. Dale had hid the uncut stones, and we had all agreed to wait at least six months before fencing them."

"But things went wrong, didn't they?"

"Oh, yes. An informant told the police about Frank's bragging. They picked him up for questioning, and he ended up making a deal with them. He gave them Larry's name, but he didn't give them Dale's or my name until later. He was holding out for a better deal, I guess. Larry called us and warned us in time, and we were able to get out of town. Larry didn't make it, though. There was a shootout, and Larry killed a policeman before he was killed."

Jilly started crying again. "I didn't care about the diamonds. Dale promised me that he'd help me get my daughter back. That was going to be my cut for helping him with the robbery. We drove back to Sheldon Beach, and he went to Mama's house to get Avery. I didn't look at it as kidnapping. I was simply taking back what my sister had stolen from me. I didn't know Carrie had made Mama go to court to have Carrie named Avery's legal guardian. The court took away all my rights as a mother and gave them to my sister. She stole my baby from me, Monk. She stole her . . ."

"I know your heart's breaking, my love."

"Avery was just a little girl when Dale went to get her, but Carrie had already turned her against me. Dale told me he tried to calm Avery down by telling her how much I loved her and that she would be happy with me. Avery became hysterical. God only knows what horrid lies Carrie had told her. She fought him like a tigress, kicking and trying to scratch his eyes out. He said he took off his belt to tie her hands together and that he gave her a couple of swats to get her to stop her tantrum."

Monk handed her another Kleenex so she could wipe her tears away. "Go on. You'll feel better after you get all that poison out."

She nodded. "Yes, you're right. Avery's screams woke Mama. She came running out with a gun in her hand. The chief of police had given it to her for protection. She tried to kill Dale. He told me he was backing away with Avery

when she fired the gun. She shot my daughter by mistake."
She shuddered. "Dale didn't tell me about that for a long
time, so I didn't go to the hospital to see her."

"What happened with your mother?"

"When she saw what she had done, Dale said she
screamed, then suddenly clutched her chest and fell down.
She was dead before she hit the floor . . . according to
Dale."

"Heart attack?"

"Yes, but I didn't cry about her dying. She had turned
against me, and I pretty much did the same to her. I didn't
shed a single tear," she said proudly.

"I understand."

"Dale tried to keep his promise to me. He followed
Avery when she went to live with my sister in California.
He watched her school, thinking he could grab her when
she came outside. She had a bodyguard, though, an FBI
agent looking out for her. Carrie obviously convinced them
that Dale would come after Avery. My sister is very clever,"
she added with a sneer. "She must have alerted the principal
because he told the security guards that Dale was dangerous. There was always someone watching her. Dale tried to
grab her as she was crossing the campus, but the FBI agent
spotted him and tackled him to the ground. Dale wasn't
armed," she added. "He was arrested and sent back to Florida to stand trial for my mother's death."

"And he was convicted."

"Yes. The autopsy report proved Mama had a heart attack, but the jury still believed Dale was responsible."

"And you don't?"

"I really don't care if he was responsible or not, but
Mama did have a bad heart. I have something to confess
now, darling. Please don't be angry. Let me explain before
you react."

"I could never become angry with you. I promise," he said.

"Do you remember the money you gave me to pay off all my debts?"

"The thirty thousand?"

"Yes," she whispered. Her hand slid under his robe, and she began to caress his chest. "I gave most of the money to an attorney as a retainer."

"Why?" he asked. "Why did you need an attorney?"

"I hired him to help Dale. I want to get him out of prison, and now it looks like that might happen. When the attorney was going through the boxes of evidence, he found a bill from a cardiologist in Savannah. He went to see him," she continued. "And the doctor told him my mother's condition was fatal. More important, he said that he had come forward and told the prosecutor that he had treated Mama, but the prosecutors withheld that information from the public defender who had been assigned to represent Dale."

Monk was suddenly feeling insecure and angry, but he contained his emotions.

"Go on," he said.

"The attorney I hired did it," she said. "Dale's getting a new trial, and it's going to be soon. The judge was outraged when he heard that the prosecutor had suppressed evidence to help him win. It seems there's bad blood between the two men, and this was the last straw. Dale's attorney told me another case was postponed, and the judge gave Dale that opening. Carrie and Avery can't testify. Dale will stay in prison if they do."

"What about the parole hearing? Is that still scheduled?"

"Yes, but the trial should be over by then. If Dale doesn't get out of prison, I'll never get those diamonds. After all I've been through, I think I deserve them. Of course, whatever I get belongs to you too. Am I being too greedy?"

"No, I don't think so," he said. "But you must be honest with me now. Do you have feelings for Dale?"

"Oh, God, no," she cried. "I've always hated him, and I know how I can prove it to you."

"How?" he asked, intrigued by the sly smile of hers he found so titillating.

"As soon as Dale leads us to the diamonds, I'll let you watch me kill him."

All of his insecurities faded with that promise. She kissed him then and whispered, "I love you with all my heart. I would die rather than hurt you. Killing Dale will prove my love, but I want proof from you as well."

"What can I do?" he asked. He wasn't a man given to poetry, but he tried to be romantic as he vowed, "If you wish me to walk on water, I swear I'll find a way to do it. I'll do anything for you, dearest Jilly. Anything at all."

She snuggled up against him. "My sister and Avery both spoke at the last parole hearing," she said. "They're the reason he didn't get out then."

"And you want me to find a way to keep your sister and your daughter away from the trial and the parole hearing this time? Is that what you want?"

"Darling, I don't want you to just keep them away. I want you to make it impossible for them to testify. I want you to kill them."

CHAPTER 7

CARRIE WOKE UP in a cold sweat. The nightmare had consumed her, terrified her. Trembling like a child, she wrapped herself in the down comforter and tried to calm her racing heartbeat. She felt as if she were having a heart attack. She put her hand to her chest and took a couple of deep breaths. The nightmare had been so real. My God, what had brought that on? She hadn't thought about Jilly in years. Why was her sister suddenly tormenting her sleep again?

Maybe she was just overly tired. Yes, that was it, she thought, latching onto the possibility. It made sense, didn't it? She had been working seventy-, eighty-hour weeks for the past two months, firming up and then nailing the incredibly lucrative Bliss account. The contracts were all signed and delivered, and now that she could finally slow the pace, her overloaded brain had simply had a minor meltdown.

Rolling onto her back, she closed her eyes against the piercing sunlight streaming in between the partially opened drapes and tried to remember some of the yoga exercises Avery had taught her. Take deep, cleansing breaths. She remembered that much. Clear the mind and concentrate on relaxing every muscle of the body. Okay, it was coming back to her. First the toes. Then the legs. That's it, she thought. Now relax, damn it.

It wasn't working. Anxiety, like the boogeyman hiding in the closet, was still lurking, waiting to pounce.

For heaven's sake, it was just a nightmare. Vivid as hell, but still not real, so stop freaking out.

Carrie wished Valium were still in vogue. She would have taken a couple to soothe her nerves. Then she realized she was calming down. Her heart no longer felt as though it were trying to leap out of her chest like one of those creatures in *Alien*.

What she needed was a good long shower. Carrie threw the covers off and sat up. What time was it? Did the sun come up brighter here in the mountains than in L.A.? Of course it did, because there wasn't any smog.

Coffee, she thought. I'll ring for coffee. The caffeine will clear the fog in my head, and I'll be able to start thinking like a human being again.

Carrie was swinging her legs over the side of the bed when she saw them. There, pointed toward her on the night-stand, was a pair of shiny steel-bladed scissors. She froze, the scream lodged in her throat. She couldn't make herself look away, couldn't make the scissors disappear.

Her heart was slamming against her rib cage again. Could a person die of fright? Was this some kind of a sick joke? No. Whoever had put the scissors there couldn't possibly know about her nightmare. Think, damn it. Try to think.

Were they real? Carrie tentatively reached out to touch them, thinking she was having some kind of hallucination. When her fingers touched the hard, cold steel handle, she whimpered. Son of a bitch, they were real.

There had to be a reasonable explanation. Maybe the

scissors had been there on the nightstand the night before, and while she hadn't consciously noticed, her subconscious had picked up on them. The possibility sounded desperate, but she clung to it. Then she spotted the yellow, invitation-sized envelope with her name handwritten in beautiful script propped up against the lamp. She was positive it hadn't been there the night before. Her hand trembled as she picked it up and opened it. The stationery was expensive, but there wasn't a Utopia seal or logo printed on it, or a return address.

"What the hell is going on?" she whispered. And then she pulled the two sheets out, unfolded them, and read the note.

Carrie:

Did you mourn me when you heard I died in that car crash so many years ago? Or did you celebrate? You always believed you were so superior. I was just a stupid girl. Do you remember how you called me that? I've never forgotten. Your biggest problem was that you always underestimated me. Always. Surely you recall how I so loved to get even. That glorious day has finally arrived, and now you're right where I want you to be.

The house is wired, Carrie, and there isn't any way out. If you open a window or an outside door . . . boom. A simple push of a button and the house will disintegrate. Do you wonder how long I'll wait?

Tick. Tick. Are you scared?

Shall I tell you how I plotted and planned? I began by finding the man of my dreams. He loves me, of

course, but then they all do, don't they? This one is
very special. A perfectionist, actually. His name is
Monk, and when I first seduced him, I must say he
was terribly set in his ways. He's a hit man, my hit
man, though he prefers to be called a professional.

He does whatever I ask him to do, and in return
I've taught him how to have fun with his job. He's a
proud man, proud of what he does, and he's careful
and methodical, and so he won't let me make any
mistakes. In the past, he only took on one job at a
time, but I've convinced him to reach for bigger and
better. He'd already contracted to blow up the house.
It just took a little more planning to kill a few incon-
sequential women at the same time.

You know why you must die. You stole my dream
from me and gave it away. You took my child from
me too, and you turned her against me. Those are
just two reasons, Carrie, but when all is said and
done, your biggest sin is that you have made me un-
happy.

Jilly

P.S. Don't worry about Avery. I'm going to take
care of her too.

Carrie screamed once and began to sob. She was terrified. Shaking, she leapt from the bed and ran to the sliding
glass doors. She grabbed a fistful of the drapes, ripped them
out of her way, and looked outside. Then down. She saw
the blinking red light protruding from the explosives, as
evil and horrific as the devil's eye, and shouted, "Oh, God,
oh, God . . ."

She ran for the bedroom door, tripped over her shoes,
and slammed her right foot into the bedpost. Pain shot up

her calf. Cursing, she continued on. She stopped short in the hallway just outside her door and called out, "Is anyone there?"

Nothing. Not a sound. Too late, she realized she should have grabbed the scissors to use as a weapon just in case someone had been waiting, but Jilly had touched those scissors. Jilly, who had written the horrific, gleeful letter. Jilly, the psycho.

God help them all.

She edged along the wall to the spiral staircase. She was afraid to look down, afraid not to. It took her a good minute to get up the courage, and then relief, sweet, sweet relief, made her weak because no one was looking up at her. Maybe Carrie and Sara and Anne were all alone in the house. No, not a house now. A bomb.

She ran down the stairs, then raced to the judge's suite. She didn't bother to knock, but threw the door open and rushed inside.

The room was pitch black. Carrie couldn't even see her hand in front of her face. She felt her way across the sitting room, nearly knocking over a lamp when her elbow bumped into the shade. She grabbed it, and finally got it turned on.

Sara was in bed. Carrie could see a form huddled under the blanket, but she couldn't see her face. The drapes were tightly drawn. Carrie opened them and looked down. "Son of a bitch," she muttered. There it was, another blinking red light.

Turning, she slowly approached the side of the bed as she strained to hear the sound of Sara's breathing. She couldn't hear anything but the noise of the air conditioner as it kicked on.

Carrie gently shook her. "Wake up, Sara," she ordered.

She didn't move. She shook her again, much harder this time. "Come on, Sara. You have to wake up." Sara groaned.

She put her hand on Sara's wrist, feeling for a pulse with her fingertips. When she finally found it, she felt like shouting with relief.

Carrie knew what had happened. The food they'd eaten last night had been drugged, but because she had thrown up, she'd gotten rid of most of the poison. How much had Sara and Anne eaten?

She grabbed Sara by her shoulders and started shaking her. "Open your eyes, damn it. Wake up, Sara."

Another groan was her only response. Carrie looked at the clock on the bureau and saw that it was already one in the afternoon. Then she turned to the nightstand, and just as she expected, there was another envelope propped against the lamp with Sara's name written on it. The handwriting was identical.

Should she open it?

"Go away."

Carrie jumped at the sound of Sara's gruff voice. She was struggling to open her eyes. Carrie stepped back as Sara rolled onto her back and told her once again to go away.

"No," she said. "Keep your eyes open. You have to wake up."

Sara heard her. She struggled to sit up but only made it halfway before she collapsed against the pillows. She focused on Carrie, awareness slow to penetrate.

"What . . . what are you doing here?"

"Listen to me," Carrie ordered. "You've been drugged. Do you understand what I'm saying? Please, try to pay attention. We're in trouble."

"Drugged?" She shook her head. "No, I don't take drugs."

In her frustration, she shouted at the woman. "They

put it in the food, Sara. Can you understand what I'm saying?"

"Yes. You're telling me the food was drugged?"

"Yes, that's right," Carrie said. "Keep your eyes open. I'm going to get a cold wet cloth. Come on, Sara," she coaxed. "Sit up."

By the time Carrie returned from the adjoining bath with a washcloth dripping with cold water, Sara had managed to pull herself up. Her shoulders were pressed against the headboard.

She looked at Carrie as though she was only just now seeing her. "Why are you in my room?"

Carrie tried to put the wet cloth on Sara's face, but the woman knocked it away.

"We're in trouble," she repeated. "I have to go wake Anne. So you have to listen to what I'm going to tell you. Okay? Can you concentrate yet?"

"Will you stop shouting at me? I'm awake now. What kind of trouble are you talking about?"

"The house is wired."

Sara blinked. "I don't understand."

"We're prisoners," Carrie said. "If one of us opens a door or a window, the house will blow up. Look at the glass door," she urged. "See the red blinking light?"

Sara wouldn't believe her. "This is just some kind of sick prank."

"No, it isn't," she said. Then she grabbed the envelope from the nightstand. "Open it," she said. "I got one too. Bring the letter with you down to the living room, and I'll bring mine. Even if you can't believe it, don't open any windows or doors. Okay? Now I've got to get to Anne before she wakes up and decides to open a window."

Sara nodded. "All right. I'll meet you downstairs."

She was opening the envelope when Carrie rushed out of

the room. Anne's suite was at the opposite end on the same level. She ran to it.

Anne wasn't in bed. Carrie could hear her in the bathroom. She was throwing up. Carrie went to the door and knocked. "Anne, do you need help?"

She didn't answer her. Carrie tried again and again. She didn't know how long she stood there pounding on the door. Finally, Anne opened it.

The frail woman looked green. "What do you want?" she asked. She was swaying on her feet.

"Let me help," Carrie said. She put her arm around her waist, thinking it was the size of a pencil, and helped her back to bed.

"You should stay away from me," Anne said, her voice weak. "I've got some kind of a bug. Now you'll get it."

"No," Carrie said. "You don't have a bug." She was all but carrying the woman across the room. When she reached the bed, she pulled the sheet back and helped Anne sit down.

"I was up half the night, throwing up," she said. "Of course I have a bug. It's probably just one of those twenty-four-hour viruses."

There wasn't an envelope on Anne's nightstand. "You were up all night?" she asked as she helped the woman into bed. "Did you hear anyone . . . see anyone?"

"No, I didn't," she answered. "Let go of me. I don't want to lie down." She adjusted the pillows and slowly leaned back on one elbow.

"We were all drugged," Carrie explained. "The stuff had to have been in the food we ate."

"That's ridiculous. It was spoiled food, that's what it was. Am I going to give them an earful when I get to the spa. I could sue," she said. "And I just might. First, the inconvenience at the airport and now food poisoning. It's simply unforgivable."

Carrie didn't argue. She plodded ahead, telling about the envelopes she and Sara had received.

"The most important thing you need to know is that there are detonators on every window and door in this house. If we open one of them, the house will blow up."

Anne was looking at her as though she'd lost her mind. "Oh, for heaven's sake. What's the matter with you, trying to scare me like this?"

"I'm not trying to scare you. I'm telling you the truth. Did you find an envelope with your name on it?"

"No, I did not."

The answer was too quick, too angry. Carrie knew she was lying, but for the life of her, she couldn't understand why.

"Anne, we're all in this together. You have to tell the truth."

Indignant, she responded, "I am telling you the truth. Now get out of here and leave me alone."

"No," Carrie said. "I don't know how much time we have, and we have to find a way to get out of here without triggering the explosives."

Anne's pinched face was rapidly turning red. "I asked you to leave."

Carrie tried a different approach. "Sara and I . . . we need you, Anne. We have to work together to figure out what is going on."

Anne glared at her. "Why do you need me?"

"Because you're smart."

"You couldn't possibly know if I'm smart or not."

"You ran your own company, didn't you? That's what you told me."

Anne's chin came up a notch. As she smoothed the

sheets around her waist, she said, "I started on a shoestring and turned my little hobby—that's what my father called my shipping company—into a forty-million-dollar operation. By next January, I'll have increased my profit margin to quadruple the amount my accountants anticipated."

Carrie didn't have time for this. To be forced to pander to the stupid woman's ego just to gain her cooperation was outrageous. Didn't Anne realize what they were all up against?

With effort, Carrie was able to control her temper. "Do you think you could join Sara and me downstairs in the living room to talk about our situation? We could sure use your . . . advice on how to proceed."

Anne tilted her head to the side and stared at Carrie for a long minute without saying a word. Then she shook her head. "You're really serious about this story of yours, aren't you? You believe—"

"It's true," she snapped.

Anne nodded. "What is your name? I've forgotten."

"Carolyn," she answered, trying not to shout at the obtuse woman. "You may call me Carrie if you like."

"All right, Carrie. I'll join you and Sara downstairs."

"If you don't feel strong enough, Sara and I could come in here—"

"What makes you think I'm not strong enough?" She sounded angry again.

"I heard you in the bathroom. You were throwing up."

"You said the food was poisoned."

"Yes."

"That's why I was throwing up. I'm not sick."

Who gives a damn if you're sick or not, she longed to ask. She took a deep breath, nodded, and said, "All right. Come downstairs."

"I still don't see what all the fuss is about."

Carrie completely lost it then. "Fuss?" she roared. "We're sitting inside a time bomb. Did you just not listen to a word I've been saying?"

"Yes, I listened. But isn't the answer right in front of you? Simply pick up the phone and call Utopia. Have them send someone to disarm the thing."

The phone. My God, why hadn't she thought to try calling for help? Carrie ran around to the other side of the bed and picked up the phone. Her excitement and hope were short-lived. The line was dead.

"It doesn't work," she said. She didn't bother to hang up the phone but dropped it on the bed.

"What about the cell phones?" Anne asked. "Do you think we'll be able to get a signal up here?" Glancing at the table beside her, she frowned and said, "Where's my cell phone? I had it sitting in the charger right over there, but now it's gone. Did you move it?"

"They took it," Carrie cried out. She ran to the sliding glass doors that opened to Anne's balcony, drew the drapes back, and said, "See that light, Anne? See it?"

"Stop yelling at me."

"See all the wires? The house is rigged," she said. "Do you understand yet?"

"Yes, all right," Anne said. She looked sullen now.

Maybe Sara could get through to the woman. Carrie took a breath and then said, "I'm going back to my room to see if they took my cell phones. Please hurry downstairs," she added, "and remember, don't open any doors or windows."

"I get it."

Carrie wasn't so sure about that. She didn't want to antagonize the woman, and so she pretended to agree. She paused in the open doorway and said, "Bring the letter with you . . . please. Sara and I are bringing ours."

"There wasn't any letter on my nightstand," Anne snapped.

Carrie turned around. "I never said anything about a nightstand."

Anne turned her head away from Carrie. "Shut the door after you."

What in God's name was the matter with Anne? Why was she lying? What could she possibly have to gain?

Carrie didn't have any answers. She went back to her suite but stopped short just inside the door. Her beautiful Gucci bags had been ripped open with a knife, and all of her clothes were strewn about the sofa and chair. Why hadn't she noticed the mess before? Just as she suspected, one of her two cell phones, her chargers, and the laptop were all missing.

She sprinted for the closet. "Please, God," she whispered as she threw the double doors open. Maybe Jilly hadn't been that thorough. Maybe she hadn't found the cell phone in her pocket.

Carrie started to cry when she saw her blazer on the floor. Her sister had found the phone. She looked away, sobbing now as the magnitude of her situation overwhelmed her.

She let herself weep for a couple of minutes, then struggled to get her emotions under control. "I'm losing it," she said out loud. Wiping her face with the backs of her hands, she staggered to her feet and went into the bathroom. She stared at herself in the mirror. God, she was a mess. Her eyes were swollen, and her face looked haggard.

Carrie took the time to brush her teeth and wash her face. She lifted her robe off the hook behind the bathroom door and put it on. She felt better now, more in control.

After she picked up the letter and the envelope her dear, demented sister had left for her, she went downstairs.

Neither Sara nor Anne was waiting for her. Carrie went into the kitchen and was surprised to find the pantry hadn't been stripped. There were boxes of unopened cereal, canned vegetables, and fruit. She noticed the tops had dust on them, indicating they'd been there quite awhile. The refrigerator was empty, but there was a full container of Folgers coffee in the freezer.

Carrie kept going to the hallway to see if Sara or Anne had come down yet. What the hell was taking them so long? She went back into the kitchen, made a pot of coffee, and then carried a mug of the steaming brew into the living room. She deliberately kept away from the windows, just in case someone was out there watching.

She sat down in one of the easy chairs near the dining room and waited tensely. Her hand trembled, and hot coffee spilled over the rim, burning her fingers. Five minutes later, she saw Sara slowly making her way down the winding staircase. She was dressed in a royal blue floral silk robe. From the way she clung to the railing, she appeared to be woozy still.

"Do you need help?" Carrie called out when Sara stopped for the fifth time. She had a white-knuckle grip on the railing.

"No, I can make it. I'm a little dizzy. What in heaven's name was in that food?"

"I don't know what it was," Carrie said. "But it was powerful."

"It could have killed us."

Wouldn't that have been something? Carrie thought. To die from a canapé and never know about all the trouble Jilly had gone to. Her sister would have been enraged. Carrie smiled at the thought, as sick as it was.

"Would you like some coffee?"

"I don't think I can handle it just yet. How do you know that it wasn't poisoned?"

"It isn't," she assured her. "My letter was from my sister. She's gone to a lot of trouble to terrify me. She obviously wants me to suffer before I die, and poison would act too quickly."

"Then why did she drug the food?"

"To knock us all out," Carrie answered. She waited until Sara had taken a seat across from her, and then said, "She came into our rooms last night."

"Someone was here," Sara agreed. "He or she went through all my things. My cell phone and Palm Pilot are both missing."

"The phone line's dead too."

"Yes," Sara said. "I checked."

It suddenly occurred to Carrie that the judge was awfully calm. She asked her why.

"I don't see any reason to become hysterical. What would it solve? I'd rather exert my energy figuring out a way to get out of here . . . in one piece."

Carrie took another long drink of her coffee. It was tepid now and bitter, but she drank it anyway.

"My sister came back from her grave."

"Excuse me?"

"My sister . . . I thought she was killed in a car accident years ago," Carrie said. "My husband and I celebrated after my niece went to bed. I was told that her body was cremated in the inferno, but there were items from her purse that had been thrown clear during the impact, and those items convinced the police that the victim was my sister. I was a fool to believe it. Jilly was wanted for questioning by the police at the time."

"So she feigned her own death," Sara said, nodding. "Clever."

"Oh, yes," Carrie agreed. "Jilly was always sneaky and clever." She got up and handed the letter to Sara. "She's hired a hit man. That's what she called him. Her hit man."

"Your own sister did this to you."

Sara didn't sound surprised, just intrigued. Carrie wondered at her reaction. In normal families, if there really was such a thing, sisters certainly squabbled. Some might even hate each other, but how many would go to the extreme of hiring someone to kill a sibling?

"You're not shocked," she said.

"No, I'm not."

Carrie shook her head. "Jilly isn't like anyone you've ever known."

"Want to bet?" Sara said dryly. "I've put away hundreds of men and women who committed heinous crimes. I believe I've heard and seen it all in the twenty-two years I've sat on the bench. Nothing can shock me now."

Carrie scoffed. "I wouldn't count on that. So tell me, Sara. Who wants you dead?"

Sara carefully adjusted the belt on her robe so that the bow was perfect, then folded her hands in her lap. "Who wants me dead? Oh, quite a few people, I would imagine."

She handed the letter to Carrie and watched as she unfolded the note and read it. It was short and to the point.

Judge Collins:

> *I told you I would get even, and I'm a man of my word. Now it's your turn to suffer. I wish I could be there to watch . . . from a safe distance, of course. You're going to die very soon now.*
>
> *Rot in hell, bitch.*

Carrie dropped the letter on the coffee table. Then she handed Jilly's letter to Sara.

"While you read her short but not-so-sweet note, I'm going to get another cup of coffee."

"I'd love a cup now," Sara said.

Carrie went back into the kitchen, and when she returned a minute later with two mugs, Sara had placed the note on the coffee table next to the one she'd received. Carrie handed her a mug, warned her the coffee was very hot, and sat down.

"Your sister hates you."

"Oh, yes."

"She accused you of stealing her child and turning her against her."

"That didn't happen."

"She seems to believe that all of her failures were your fault and that your success was stolen from her."

Carrie nodded. "Jilly always had the unique ability to rewrite history. Once she said it, in her mind it was real."

"She sounds like a psychopath."

"She is," Carrie said. "It was never officially diagnosed, but I'm sure that's what she is."

Sara began to trace the worry line in her forehead with her fingertip as she listened to Carrie. Back and forth, back and forth. She was so deep in thought she probably wasn't even aware of what she was doing. "What happened with the child?"

"Avery," she said. "Her name is Avery, and she's an adult now, not a child. Jilly left her in the hospital. She told my mother and me that we could keep her, sell her, or give her away. She didn't care what happened to her." Tears sprang into Carrie's eyes. She hated herself for showing such weakness in front of a virtual stranger, but she was powerless to do anything about it. "Jilly's going after Avery too. Oh, God, she could already have her locked away somewhere now. My niece was going to join me at the spa . . ." She covered her face with her hand. "We've got to get out of here soon. We have to find a way."

"Your sister has gone to quite a lot of trouble to hurt you," Sara said.

Carrie told her about Jilly coming into her room during the night and how she had believed she was having a nightmare. Sara was a good listener and so calm Carrie was actually comforted.

"Jilly could be very patient when she really wanted something, and, oh, how she loved complicated plans. Nothing could ever be simple."

Sara put her coffee cup down and leaned forward. "How much time do you think we have?"

"She's gone to a lot of trouble setting this up. She'll want to prolong my agony."

Both of them kept glancing at the spiral staircase, expecting to see Anne coming down the stairs.

"I've already checked every window I could reach. They're all wired."

"Yes, I would expect so."

"I wish I could be calm like you."

"I'm not calm," Sara protested. "I'm quite . . . discombobulated."

Her choice of words made Carrie smile. "So am I," she said.

"I'm thinking . . ."

"Yes?"

"How curious it is that the three of us are in this house together. What is it that we have in common?"

"I don't know," Carrie said. "And I don't know that we'll have the time to find out."

"We will get out of here."

Her resolve bolstered Carrie. "Yes, we must, and we will."

"I wonder what's keeping Anne."

"She's going to be a problem."

"Oh?"

Carrie nodded. "She won't admit she received a letter."

"Perhaps she's in shock."

Carrie thought Sara might be right about that. "And denial," she said.

"We're going to all have to work together, but I don't know how much help I can be. I'll do whatever I can. I'm sixty-eight years old." Sara shrugged. "And I'm terribly out of shape. When I received the invitation for a free two-week stay at the spa as a promotion, I thought to myself, why not? The experts say it's never too late to turn your life around. I decided to get into better shape. As you can see, I'm overweight, and once we get outside—and we will find a way to do that," she said with conviction, "I won't be able to walk far. I should have had both of my knees replaced several years ago. I'm walking with bone on bone now."

"Then Anne and I will hide you somewhere . . . somewhere safe in the woods while we go get help."

They heard a door close and both looked up. Anne had finally decided to join them. Carrie's mouth dropped open when the frail woman started down the stairs. She couldn't believe what she was seeing. Anne was all dressed up in a hot pink St. John pants suit. Her gold earrings matched the buttons. She had taken the time to put on makeup and curl her hair. When she reached the bottom of the stairs, she smiled, and then crossed the living room to join them. Her high heels clicked against the marble floor. Where in heaven's name did she think she was going? A formal brunch?

"Oh, dear," Sara whispered.

"Good morning, ladies," Anne said. "Or rather, good afternoon."

She sounded so cheerful. Had her mind snapped? Carrie wondered. She was about to ask the woman what the hell was the matter with her when Sara suggested Anne sit down.

"Did you sleep well?" Anne asked Sara. Then, before she could answer, Anne continued on. "I can't believe I slept so long. It must be this wonderful mountain air. Coming from Cleveland, it's a delightful change."

"Would you care for some coffee?" Sara asked. She was watching her closely, as though she was trying to interpret the woman's bizarre behavior.

"Not just yet. I'll ring when I'm ready."

Carrie turned to Sara. "I told you she was going to be a problem."

"I'm sorry. What did you say?" Anne asked. She carefully sat down and crossed one ankle over the other.

Carrie turned to her. "It wasn't the wonderful mountain air that made you sleep so long, Anne. We were all drugged."

"That's nonsense. Look where we are," she said. "Who would do such a thing in this beautiful—"

Carrie cut her off. "Did you bring your letter down?"

"I don't know what you're talking about."

"See what I mean?" Carrie asked Sara.

The judge took over. "Anne, Carrie and I each received a letter. They're there on the coffee table. Please read them."

Carrie noticed that Anne's hand was violently shaking as she reached for the letters. She picked them up and then quickly placed them back on the table. "I don't need to read these."

"Yes, you do," Sara gently asserted. "You'll see that we're in trouble here. Someone has wired this place to kill us."

"What rubbish," Anne muttered. "I will not have my day ruined with this ridiculous game you two are playing."

"We're locked inside this house," Sara told her.

"We are not."

"It's no use," Carrie said. "I tried to tell her all of this upstairs."

"You're lying," Anne said.

Carrie considered punching the woman. She thought she'd probably kill her if she did because Anne was so painfully thin and sickly. A good wind could have done her in.

"If any of us opens a window or door, the house will blow up," Sara patiently explained.

Neither she nor Carrie anticipated Anne's reaction. The woman bolted from her chair and ran across the living room. "You're only lying to get me upset. The house isn't wired, and I'm going to prove it to you."

She was headed for the front door.

CHAPTER 8

JOHN PAUL HAD to hang around Utopia longer than he'd anticipated, but the wait was worth it. He was sitting, or rather sprawling, in an easy chair half hidden behind a couple of limp palm trees inside the lobby's bar when Avery Delaney walked inside. One hard look and he had her all figured out. She was a typical California blonde. No, maybe not typical. She was unique, he'd give her that. But she was definitely all about her body. Why else would she want to spend a week at a spa? Why would anyone?

The Delaney woman wore a short white T-shirt that fit snugly across her full breasts, and tight jeans, obviously intending to show off her long legs and her tight ass. Her long, straight, blond hair shimmered in the light. It looked natural, but he doubted that it was. Probably came from a bleach bottle. Her sunglasses hid her eyes, but he figured she was probably wearing colored contact lenses. Her T-shirt hid her belly button, but he wouldn't have been surprised to find that she'd had it pierced. Wasn't that the fashion these days?

She was hot, all right. In fact, Avery Delaney was a beautiful woman, but she wasn't his type. She was a little too perfect for his tastes. Sexy as sin, though. As he watched her stop and take in her surroundings—pretending she didn't notice how the other guests had stopped to stare at her—John Paul wondered how much of her was real and how much had been cosmetically "enhanced." The breasts, definitely. And maybe even the ass.

She wasn't the kind of woman he'd want to have a lasting relationship with, but then he didn't want a lasting relationship with any woman. One night with her, however, sounded like a damned good idea. Hell, the woman probably had the IQ of a tsetse fly, but in bed, brainpower really didn't matter.

Miss Airhead couldn't seem to figure out where check-in was. Was she waiting for someone to take her hand and lead her across the lobby? She was looking up at the golden sphere slowly rotating like one of those old disco balls. Had the thing hypnotized her?

Avery knew she was gawking like a tourist. She couldn't help it; Utopia was incredible. The lobby was gigantic, the floors a shiny, ebony marble. Above her, hanging from the gilded dome was a glistening orb. She couldn't take her gaze off it. Was it real gold? It must have cost the owners a fortune, she thought.

She turned to her right and stopped again. One entire wall was a waterfall, and in the center of the gathering pool was a statue of Atlas. Another smaller sphere was perched on his shoulder. Both the sculpture and the bubbling waterfall were meant to impress the guests willing to pay a fortune to be pampered in such an environment, and in Avery's estimation, the owners got the job done.

Shaking her head over the expense of it all, she pulled up the strap of the old, hand-me-down Gucci backpack Carrie had given her, and crossed the lobby to the reception desk. A man about her age wearing a name tag labeled

"Oliver" stood behind the granite counter waiting to welcome her. His smile was dazzling, his teeth astonishingly white. Freakishly so. He or his dentist had obviously overdone the bleach job, and his artificially tanned face only made his teeth more prominent. She tried not to stare as she gave him her name and leaned against the cool counter while he pulled up her reservation on the built-in computer screen.

Oliver's smile blessedly vanished. "Oh, dear."

"Excuse me?"

He wasn't looking at her now, but stared intently at the screen when he said, "Your reservation was canceled, Miss Delaney."

"No, that has to be a mistake. I didn't cancel."

"According to my computer, you canceled. It's noted right here," he added, pointing to his screen, which she couldn't possibly see unless she pole-vaulted over the countertop.

"That's wrong."

"The computer's never wrong. You called Utopia at . . ." He was trying to pull up the exact time she called in.

"Oliver," she said. Her impatience was brimming in her voice. "I didn't cancel. In fact, I called to tell reception I would be a day late."

"Yes, you did," he agreed, pointing to the screen once again. "But then you called again and canceled."

"No, I didn't," she insisted.

"But my computer—"

She interrupted him before he could tell her his computer was infallible again. "Why don't you just book me into another room. Anything will do."

She lifted her backpack and placed it on the counter. She began to dig through it looking for her billfold so she could give Oliver her credit card. Against her wishes, the week had been paid for by her aunt, but Avery wanted the charges transferred to her card.

Oliver, she noticed, had stopped typing. "Is something wrong?" she asked.

He coughed delicately and finally looked at her. "I'm afraid it won't be possible to book you into another room, and unfortunately, the room you canceled has already been assigned to another guest. We're at a hundred percent occupancy," he continued. "I'll be happy to put you on our waiting list, but I must warn you. There's little chance of an opening. Our guests book months in advance."

"I'm certain my aunt was able to reserve a room for me here," she protested. "If there had been a problem I'm sure she would have told me."

He was frantically typing again. Then he stopped and nodded. "Yes, we were able to accommodate you because of another cancellation. That is peculiar," he added. "Our guests rarely cancel at the last minute."

He frowned as he said the last, as though by canceling, he thought she had committed a terrible breach in etiquette.

"But I didn't cancel," she said. Lord, this was frustrating. "I'm joining my aunt here," she explained. "She checked in yesterday afternoon or early evening. Could you give me her room number? Her name's Carolyn Salvetti."

"I'm sorry, but we aren't allowed to give out the room numbers of our guests."

Of course he couldn't. She knew that. "Please call her room. I'm sure she'll be able to clear up this misunderstanding. She might have decided that I should stay with her."

Oliver looked relieved that the problem would be solved and he could get rid of her. Fortunately, there weren't any other guests waiting in line to check in. He flashed her another startling smile and said, "I'm sure that's what must

have happened. Guests simply do not cancel at the last minute the way you did."

She had the sudden urge to grab him by his shoulders
and shake him until he admitted the spa had screwed up.
Gritting her teeth to keep from saying something she would
regret, she spelled the name Salvetti and waited.

"I know that name," he said.

"You do?"

He nodded. "A gentleman was in here yesterday asking
for your aunt. He was very disappointed she wasn't here."
He started typing, but a couple of seconds later, he was
frowning again.

"Is there a problem?" she asked, knowing full well there
was.

"There are no problems at Utopia," he said, and it was
such a quick, automatic response she thought he'd been
programmed to say those very words. "We do occasionally
have minor inconveniences."

Give me a break. "All right. Explain the minor inconvenience."

"Mrs. Salvetti canceled."

"No, she didn't."

Oliver's shoulders slumped. She knew what he was
thinking. Here we go again.

"I'm afraid Mrs. Salvetti did cancel. It is odd, I'll agree.
It's so rare to get two last-minute cancellations like this. Of
course, you're both members of the same family, so I guess
we could say it was really only one last-minute cancellation
for two rooms."

"Listen to me. My aunt didn't cancel. She called me
from the Aspen airport yesterday."

"Perhaps something came up at the last minute and she
had to return home," he suggested.

"Something's very wrong."

"It's right here in my computer, Miss Delaney. Your aunt called yesterday afternoon."

What in the world was going on? As much as Avery wanted to continue to argue with Oliver, she knew it wouldn't solve anything. She wasn't sure what to do now. If an emergency had come up at work and Carrie had had to return to Los Angeles, she would have called. She wouldn't have left Avery hanging like this. Oh, God, what if something had happened to her or Uncle Tony? What if there had been an accident?

Calm down, she told herself. If anything bad had happened to either Carrie or Tony, one or the other would have called her.

Avery began searching her backpack for her phone. She would get hold of Carrie on her cell phone right this minute and find out what was going on.

She pulled out her Day-Timer and her billfold, clutched them in her right hand, and kept searching for her phone with her other hand. The damned thing always ended up on the bottom. "My aunt didn't cancel," she muttered. Then, more to herself than Oliver, she added, "There must have been a crisis at work. That's all I can think of to make Carrie turn around and go back home."

"Oh, your friend's back." Oliver didn't sound very cheerful.

"I'm sorry?"

"Your friend . . . he's coming this way. Maybe he can clear up this misunderstanding."

She didn't know what he was talking about. She didn't have any friends meeting her here. She turned around to see whom Oliver was watching, but there was only a man striding toward the counter, a big man, she corrected. Odd, but he seemed to be staring at her. And he didn't look happy.

"Are you referring to the gentleman coming this way?"

"Yes," he answered. "He was the one I was telling you about. He was here yesterday, looking for your aunt." In a low voice he added, "If anyone could benefit from our aroma stress-relief massage therapy, it's definitely your friend. I suggested the treatment to him, but he was quite . . ."

"Quite what?"

"Resistant to the idea. Actually, he was quite difficult about everything. I know I shouldn't say anything negative about a potential guest, but your boyfriend is wound tight inside. He should be practicing yoga on a daily basis. I mean, the man growled at me. He really did. Can you imagine? I told him you were scheduled to check in. It was noted in the computer under Mrs. Salvetti's reservation, and that's who he asked for when he came up to the counter. Your aunt called in and canceled. I had the unfortunate duty of telling him. Let me tell you, he wasn't happy about that news. He told me he'd come back today to see you, and he's been here since early morning. I noticed him when I came on duty. I hope he's in a better mood today."

She wasn't paying much attention to Oliver's prattling. She was busy watching the man crossing the lobby. He was something else. She'd never seen anyone like him, except maybe in the movies. The closer he came, the bigger he got. Tall and muscular, with dark hair and a weathered complexion. She guessed that he spent a good deal of his time outdoors or in a gym somewhere working on his abs. He was ruggedly good-looking, but he was too into the physical to appeal to her. She much preferred brains over muscle.

The man had great bone structure. That thought led to another, and she suddenly thought she knew who he was and what he wanted.

"You do know the gentleman, don't you?"

"It's okay. I'm sure he's a friend of my aunt's."

Carrie had probably used him in one of her commercials, and maybe, since he was in the area and had found out she was staying at the spa, he'd decided to stop by and say hello. It was either that, or muscle man was out of work and hoping that Carrie would take a liking to him and offer him a job.

Avery had great sympathy for actors because it was such a competitive field and so much of the decision-making process was out of their control. The odds against making it in Hollywood were astronomical. She made up her mind to do what she could to help. She waited until he was about three feet away, then put her hand out and introduced herself. "My name's Avery Delaney." Oh, yes, he was definitely an actor. He had the dark, brooding look down cold.

He grasped her hand in his. "My name's John Paul Renard." His voice was deep and wonderfully southern.

Lordy, he had great eyes. The color of a gray dawn. She couldn't imagine him holding up a roll of paper towels in a commercial. Explosives, maybe, but not paper towels.

His body language intrigued her. He turned so that his back was to the counter; then his gaze slowly scanned the lobby. She got the odd feeling he was memorizing every face.

"You're a friend of my aunt Carrie's?"

"Yes."

No further explanation, no embellishment whatsoever.

"You're an actor, right?"

The question so surprised him he smiled. "No."

"Oh . . . I thought . . . then what do you do for a living?" God, she hated it when people asked her that question, and it was really none of her business how the hunk, who couldn't even bother to look at her when she spoke to him, paid his rent.

"I'm a carpenter."

No way. "A carpenter?"

"Uh-huh." He drawled out the answer and stared into her eyes. She could feel the heat rush to her face and hoped to heaven she wasn't blushing. The man did have the strangest way about him.

Carrie was right. She really needed to start dating again. It had obviously been way too long. If a brute of a man like this one could affect her . . . way too long.

"A carpenter," she repeated. Then, "Okay." She'd go along. "And you've done some work for my aunt?"

"No." He was back to watching the people strolling into the lobby as he answered. "I need to talk to her," he said impatiently. "It's important. Where is she?"

"I'm not sure," she said. "But I'm about to find out." She turned around to search through her backpack again when a sudden, horrid thought occurred to her. She almost groaned out loud. "Did my aunt want you to meet me here?"

Carrie was up to her old tricks again, Avery decided, trying to play matchmaker. She was a little surprised at her aunt's nerve. She thought that her last talk with Carrie had done the trick. Her aunt had promised—vowed, actually—never to try to fix her up again.

Avery's voice was curt when she said, "Carrie isn't here today. If you're in the area, you could try back tomorrow."

He didn't take the hint and go away. Deciding to ignore him—no small feat considering his size—she continued to hunt for her phone. She finally found it on the very bottom and pulled it out. Oliver began to shake his head. "Is there a problem?" she asked.

"There are no problems at Utopia, but the use of cell phones on the premises is frowned upon." Having said that, he pointed to a black-and-gold sign propped on the counter near the corner.

She flipped open the phone's cover, pushed the speed dial to Carrie's cell phone, and said, "Then I guess you better start frowning."

John Paul liked her response. Spunk, he thought. What a surprise. The plastic California girl with the too-blue-to-be-true eyes had a backbone.

Carrie's voice mail came on after the first ring, which meant the phone was either still being recharged or she was out of signal range. She called Uncle Tony next. He answered, and the second he heard her voice, he proceeded to give her hell because she hadn't called before her aunt left for the spa.

"You know how she worries when she doesn't hear from you."

"I'm sorry," she said. "Have you talked to Carrie since she left L.A.? Has she called you?"

"No, but I don't expect to hear from her. We said good-bye in L.A. She wouldn't let me ride to the airport with her," he said. "And I promised her I wouldn't bug her at the spa. She's there to relax and think about her . . . priorities. I'm sure she'll want to talk to you, though. Give her a call and be sure to tell her I send my love."

Her uncle didn't know she was at Utopia. Avery was about to explain her last-minute decision to join her aunt but then changed her mind. She didn't want to get Tony upset over what she still hoped was just a colossal screwup.

"If she doesn't answer her phone, don't fret. She's probably just getting a massage or something."

The lobby was becoming crowded. A raucous and loud group of twelve came into the hotel. Avery put her hand over her ear as she asked, "Tony, were there any problems at work? Has the office called you?"

"No," he said. "Are you expecting trouble? I talked to Jeanie this morning. Everything's good," he said. "Star

Catcher isn't going to fall apart in two weeks. When you talk to Carrie, tell her to stop worrying."

"Yes, I'll tell her," she said. "I'll call you later, Tony. Love you."

She ended the call and looked at Oliver. "I'd like to speak to your manager."

Oliver looked offended by the request. He stiffened and his voice turned snippy. "I assure you Mr. Cannon will tell you the same thing I just did. We're booked to capacity. It's a misconception to think that we hold back rooms. I'll be happy to assist you in finding suitable lodging in Aspen. Nothing will compare to Utopia, of course, but you could take advantage of our day spa treatments. I'm sure you'd enjoy our stress-relief hot-stone massage. It's quite invigorating."

His tone was grossly condescending. She wasn't interested in his damn massage. She wanted to find her aunt. Keeping her irritation in check was difficult, but she managed it. She had never used her job to get around obstacles before, and she wasn't about to start now, but the urge was nearly irresistible. Oh, how she would have loved to pull out her ID and flash it in front of Oliver's face. He'd sure as certain stop being so snippy then, wouldn't he? She couldn't do it, though, because it wouldn't be honest, acting like a full-fledged agent when she actually worked in the basement keyboarding all day. Besides, it wasn't a real FBI badge, and anyone with half a brain would know it.

She suddenly realized she was projecting her frustration and anger on the innocent clerk. Oliver was simply doing his job. Maybe Carrie had lost track of the time. She might have met a famous movie star at the mountain retreat and didn't want to leave.

That had to be it. Her aunt was busy networking and had forgotten to call. Avery clung to the possibility because it was all she had. Her anxiety didn't go away, though. Why had Carrie canceled her reservation at the spa?

"I really need to talk to your manager."

Oliver didn't move.

John Paul said quietly, "Do as the lady asks."

"Mr. Cannon went downstairs to the mail room to see about a package."

"Go get him and tell him that John Paul Renard is back and wants to talk to him again. We'll wait in his office."

It wasn't what John Paul said but how he said it that got Oliver moving. He stepped back from the computer, turned, and jogged down the corridor.

John Paul didn't give Avery time to ask questions or argue. He started shoving her things back in her backpack, then grabbed her hand and pulled her along. "Come on. I know the way."

"I can handle this, Mr. Renard. You don't need to—"

"Call me John Paul." He led her behind the counter, then down a long, red-carpeted hall.

She jerked away from him and dug in her heels at the door to the manager's office.

"All right. I want some answers," she demanded. "First of all, exactly how do you know my aunt?"

He had his own question. "Why didn't you tell your uncle that your aunt is missing?"

"I don't want him to worry. I'm not certain she is missing."

"Then where is she?"

Good point. Carrie was probably drinking mimosas on top of a mountain somewhere having a fine old time. And making Avery nuts worrying about her. No, Carrie would never be so thoughtless. Something was wrong.

"I don't know where she is, but I'm going to make some calls and find her."

"Why would she cancel?" he asked. "The clerk said a woman called—"

"The hotel must have screwed up our reservations. You don't need to hang around. If you'd like to leave your phone number, I'll make sure Carrie gets it. She'll probably come strolling into the lobby any second now with some outrageous excuse."

She didn't believe a word of what she'd just told him, but she hoped he would buy it and go away.

"Then I'll wait with you until she gets here."

She gave up. The man was more tenacious than she was. She would find out what his agenda was after she located her aunt.

Ten minutes later, she was sitting behind Mr. Cannon's art deco desk in his spacious wind tunnel of an office overlooking the serenity pool. The overhead ceiling fan was on low and making a clicking sound with each rotation. The noise reminded her of Mrs. Speigel. The sweet old woman made the same sound when she spoke because of her ill-fitting false teeth.

Cannon also had another fan perched on top of his black lacquered filing cabinet, but that one was going full speed. All the papers on his desk were weighted down with gold sphere-shaped paperweights.

"Cannon's taking too damned long. While you make your phone calls, I'll go find him," John Paul said. "You stay put."

Avery waited until he'd left the office and closed the door before she dialed her home answering machine. She hoped Carrie had left her a message explaining her absence, but that wasn't the case. Then Avery tried her office voice mail, and there wasn't a message from her aunt there either.

Now what? In desperation she called the pen. Maybe, just maybe, Carrie had talked to Margo or Lou or Mel.

Margo answered the main line. "I'm so glad you called, Avery. You're not going to believe this. I called your neighbor's caretaker like I told you I would—"

"Margo," Avery interrupted. "You can tell me later. I've got a problem here, and I need your help."

"You need to hear what I found out," her friend insisted. "Mrs. Speigel broke her hip."

Avery's nerves were nearing the breaking point, but she knew that she was going to have to wait until Margo finished talking about Mrs. Speigel before she'd let her get a word in.

"I'm sorry to hear that."

"She broke her hip two weeks ago, and then she got pneumonia. She almost died," she added. "But Marilyn, the lady who takes care of her, told me the antibiotics are finally working, and it looks like she's going to recover. That's pretty amazing considering the fact that Mrs. Speigel is in her nineties."

"Why are you telling me this?" She rubbed her brow as she asked the question.

"Don't you get it? Mrs. Speigel couldn't have snuck her car out. She was in the hospital. Someone stole her car, and whoever it was was in such a hurry to get out of the parking garage, he or she almost hit you." Before Avery could comment, Margo enthusiastically continued. "The car was abandoned on M Street. It was illegally parked, so they towed it. Marilyn told me that it would break Mrs. Speigel's heart if the family sold her car. Even though she never drives it, she feels independent having it in the garage. Marilyn uses it to take the old lady on errands. Aren't you happy to know Mrs. Speigel wasn't trying to kill you?" she added with a laugh.

"Margo, I need help. Stop talking for a minute and listen. My aunt's missing."

She filled her in on the information she had, then said, "There's a man here waiting to talk to Carrie. He won't tell me how he knows her or what he wants. He's the strong, silent type. Run his name through the computer, will you? There's something about him. His name is John Paul Renard."

"What do you mean, 'There's something about him'?"

"He says he's a carpenter, but he doesn't look like one."

"What's a carpenter supposed to look like?"

"Come on, Margo. See if there's anything in the system."

"I'm typing in the name right now. Are you looking for parking tickets or something?"

"I don't know what I'm looking for," she admitted. "He's got this air about him. When I first saw him across the lobby, I was sure he must be an actor, but later, I noticed the way he was watching the people coming and going. He might be . . . dangerous. I think he could be." She sighed dismissively. "I'm probably overreacting because I'm so worried about Carrie. It isn't like her to take off like this. Just look up the name, okay?"

"Jeez, Avery. You think he's a criminal?"

"I don't know . . ."

"Whoa."

"What? You found something?"

"Oh, boy, did I. Your John Paul isn't a criminal."

"He's not my John Paul."

"He used to work for the government. Wait, I'm scrolling down. Whoa. Get this. His file is classified."

"Classified?" She wasn't prepared to hear that.

"I'm trying to access . . . ah, here we go. I could lose my job for this, and so could you."

"I know. Just tell me what you see, okay?"

"Renard was in the Marines. Honorable discharge," she

added. "He was recruited while he was still a Marine, according to the file."

"Recruited for what?"

"I don't know. It just says 'special branch operations.' There's a bunch of numbers and initials, but I don't know what any of it stands for." She read the information to Avery as she scrolled down. She stopped suddenly, then said, "He's taken a leave of absence." Then, a few seconds later, she sighed loudly into the phone. "It won't give me any more information. That's all I can get because I don't have the necessary clearance. Hold on. I'm pulling up an old photo ID. Ah, here we go." She whistled.

"What?"

"I think I'm in love."

"Get serious," Avery said. She described John Paul to verify.

"I think it's the same guy. He's from Louisiana. He has family there. His brother-in-law is an attorney for the Justice Department." She read a few more personal facts and then said, "It looks like he went on quite a few missions when he was a Marine. Wait a minute, here's something interesting. It says one of the missions involved rescuing some hostages in the Middle East, but get this, Renard carried out the assignment despite the fact that he'd suffered a compound fracture of his left arm." Margo was silent as she scrolled through the rest of his record; then she said, "Beyond the Marine duty, it won't tell me anything. Do you want me to go to Carter? The man intimidates me, but I'll do it if you want me to. I'm sure he could get into Renard's file."

"No, don't ask him. At least, not until I think about it."

"What's going on?" Margo asked. "What does this Renard want with your aunt Carrie?"

"I don't know. Listen, Margo, when Carrie called me

from the Aspen airport, she said there was a driver there from the spa waiting to take her and two other women to a mountain retreat for the night. Carrie said the spa had trouble with a broken water pipe or something. The driver's name was Monk Edwards . . . or Edward Monk. I'm not sure which. I know it's not much, but it's all I've got. I remember Carrie also said the driver had a British accent. Run the name through, and if you find anything, call me on my cell phone."

"Do you have any idea how many Edwardses there are in the United States?"

"Monk isn't such a common name, though . . . unless it's just a nickname."

"Okay," Margo said. "Give me your room number at the spa in case I can't reach you on your cell phone."

"I'm not staying at Utopia because my reservation was canceled. I'm leaving anyway," she added. "Carrie said she was staying in a house owned by the spa. I'm hoping she's still there. If she's not . . ."

"Don't borrow trouble. Your aunt probably lucked into something much cooler than the spa. She'll get in touch with you. You'll see. And I'll get right on that search for a Monk Edwards or an Edward Monk."

Margo had just hung up the phone when it rang again. The call was from the department head reminding her that she still hadn't turned in her vacation forms. She spent ten minutes finding and then filling out the forms between interoffice business calls, then had to hand deliver the papers to Human Resources. She didn't get a chance to run the search for Avery until midafternoon.

After she typed the first name Avery had given her and hit the search key, she called out to Lou and Mel as they were heading to lunch and told them about Carrie. Each man had a theory as to what had happened to Avery's aunt.

Lou was sure she went back to L.A.—they all knew the woman was a workaholic and obsessive to boot—but Mel thought she had probably hooked up with a business associate out in Colorado and called the hotel and left a message for Avery, but the spa had misplaced or erased the call.

"I never get my messages when I stay in a big hotel," he said.

"She probably found something better to do than sit in a mud bath all day and forgot about Avery," Lou suggested.

"Carrie wouldn't be so thoughtless," Margo argued. "She and Avery are really close." She happened to turn back to her computer screen and noticed the alert flashing. "What the . . ." Scrolling down, she saw in big, bold letters, the priority code. She shouted to Mel and Lou again as she frantically read the information.

"Oh, my God."

Margo jumped up and started running to Carter's office.

CHAPTER 9

M̲R̲. T̲IMOTHY̲ C̲ANNON̲, dressed for the tropics in a white Palm Beach business suit, stepped into the office and introduced himself. He was a dapper gentleman with a soft, prissy voice.

"Have you been able to locate your aunt yet?"

Just then John Paul walked inside. Avery watched him shut the door and then lean against it. When he folded his arms, she noticed the faint scar, about two inches long, on his left forearm. How could she have thought he was an actor? How could her instincts be that off base?

She forced herself to focus on the manager. "No, not yet," she said. "May I ask you a few questions?"

"Yes, of course."

Cannon sat down in the chair facing his desk, crossed one leg over the other, and began to straighten the crease in his pants with his thumb and forefinger.

"Do you always send a staff member to the airport to pick up your guests?"

"Yes, we certainly do. We don't want our guests to be inconvenienced by having to find transportation on their own or carry their luggage."

"Did you send a staff member to the airport yesterday?"

Cannon smiled. "I see where you're heading. You're wondering about the rash of cancellations, aren't you? It's so unusual, you see, to have a last-minute cancellation at Utopia. The rooms are booked months in advance, but some of our more prominent guests do have last-minute schedule conflicts, and we try to be accommodating."

"What do you mean by a 'rash of cancellations'?"

He looked surprised by the question. He obviously thought she already knew about them. "I had scheduled three separate pickups at the airport yesterday afternoon," he said. "The guests were all ladies," he thought to add. "One flight, as I recall, arrived at three-fifty. Another came in at four-twenty, and the last was coming in at five-fifteen. I could check and tell you which time your aunt was sched-uled to arrive."

"I'd like the flight information, credit card numbers, and anything else you've got on all three women."

"I couldn't give you that information."

Oh, yes, he could. And would, she thought. She didn't want to put the manager on the defensive yet. She had too many other questions she needed answered first, and Can-non was doing his best to be cooperative.

"If all three women were coming in within an hour or so of one another, why would you send three separate cars?"

"Because this is Utopia," he answered. "We pride our-selves on excellent service. None of our guests should be expected to wait for another. That would be an inconve-nience. So, you see, I was going to send three separate cars, but when all three guests canceled at the last minute, I noti-fied the staff members not to make the trip. As it turned out, we had unexpected guests arrive at our desk last night, and they were thrilled that we had openings for them."

She filed the information away and immediately asked

another question. "Did you have a problem with a water main yesterday? Or a broken pipe?"

"Water pipe problems? At Utopia?" He scoffed at the notion. "There weren't any problems. We have an excellent maintenance crew here, and they anticipate problems before they arise."

"You have to get your water from outside the spa. Did one of those pipes break?"

"No."

"What about a mountain house . . . a retreat?" she asked. "Does Utopia own such a place in the mountains for guests to use when there is a problem?"

His jaw clenched. "We don't have problems at Utopia," he insisted. "And the owners of Utopia don't have a mountain retreat. Clients who come to us stay with us. We don't parcel them out to other locations."

After he finished his explanation, he made a point of letting her see that he was checking his watch, then said, "If you don't have any other questions, I really must get back to work. Most of our clients who come for a week's stay are checking in today. It's going to become hectic. I wouldn't worry about your aunt," he added as he stood. "I'm certain she'll turn up soon."

He was blowing her off. Avery didn't budge from her chair. "May I have a list of your employees? All of your employees?"

"What do you want with it?"

"I'm looking for a specific name."

"I pride myself on knowing every one of my employees. Give me the name and I'll tell you if he or she works for Utopia."

"Edwards," she said. "The name is either Monk Edwards or Edward Monk."

Cannon didn't show any reaction to the name. He simply shook his head. John Paul, however, reacted as though she'd just thrown a fiery torch at him. He jerked away from the door and moved to the desk with the speed of light. Planting his hands on the blotter, he leaned toward her and demanded, "How do you know that name?"

The look on his face gave her goose bumps. They weren't the good kind.

A chill of dread settled around her heart. "How do *you* know the name?" she countered.

"Answer me."

"My aunt called me from the Aspen airport. She left the message that she and two other women were being driven to a mountain house by a staff member from Utopia. She said his name was Monk Edwards. She also said the man had a British accent." Turning to Cannon, she asked, "Are there any employees—"

"With a British accent? No, I'm afraid not. Someone is playing a cruel trick," he said. "I did not dispatch a driver to the airport yesterday. Perhaps your aunt was . . . misinformed."

John Paul picked up the phone on Cannon's desk and began dialing. He turned away from Avery and spoke in a low voice, but she still heard every word.

"Noah, it's John Paul. Yeah, well, what can I tell you. Stop trying to interrupt and listen. I'm at a spa called Utopia just outside of Aspen. Monk's back. Looks like he's taken on three this time. Must be going for some kind of a record."

Avery pushed the chair back and stood. She was reaching into her backpack when John Paul said, "You better call in the troops. We both know they won't find anything, but you should probably go through the routine anyway. It's too late," he added, his tone antagonistic now. "He's already got them."

He hung up and started for the door but stopped when she called out, "Where are you going?"

He kept walking. "I've called in some people who will help you."

"What people? The police?"

"No, the FBI." He paused at the door. "Noah's a friend of my brother-in-law's. He knows Monk real well. I'll let him explain it to you when he gets here."

"Do you think the FBI will be able to locate my aunt?"

He didn't tell her that he thought her aunt was already dead and that the agents would eventually, with luck, be able to find the body . . . unless Monk had left her for the wild animals to dine on.

"Yeah, sure."

"Tell me the truth."

"Okay," he said. "I think they'll mess it up."

She was taken aback by the venom in his voice. "Why?"

" 'Cause they're FBI."

She left it alone. "Where are you going?" she repeated.

"I'll check out a couple of possibilities, but I doubt I'll find anything."

"And then?"

"Home. I'm going home."

If she had a gun, she would have considered shooting him in the foot. He was such a jerk. "You aren't leaving until you tell me what you know about Monk."

"Look, lady. There isn't anything I can do to help you now. I thought I had a head start, but I was still too late. I've called in help for you, so just hold tight and let them try to do their job."

As he left the office, Avery turned to Cannon. "I want the names, addresses, phone numbers, and any other pertinent information you have on those two other women traveling with my aunt . . . the two who canceled. If I don't get this information in the next two minutes, I swear to heaven I'll tear this place apart, and I'll make sure you're arrested for obstruction. Now get me that information."

She pulled out her FBI credentials and waved them in front of his face. Cannon blinked twice, then rushed to his computer to get what she demanded.

"This is highly irregular," he muttered as she grabbed her backpack, slung it over her shoulder, and went running after John Paul. "Highly irregular."

Avery caught up with John Paul as he was walking past reception. The lobby was crowded with incoming guests now, and she had to cut around three separate groups to get to him. When she finally reached him, she grabbed hold of his upper arm and tried to make him stop.

The creep didn't even slow down. He just kept going, pulling her along as she held tight. She noticed he didn't walk around people. They got out of his way. She dug in and tightened her hold. If she'd had long nails, she would have broken every one of them. His skin was warm, indicating he was human, but his muscle felt like rock.

"Will you stop? I need to talk to you." Then, when he still didn't slow down, she added, "Please, John Paul. I need your help."

Ah, hell. She sounded as if she was going to cry. There wasn't a damned thing he could do for her, but she was too naive to know that. She'd probably been sheltered from the real world all her life and couldn't possibly know how to cope. Like it or not, she was about to find out that life didn't always end happily ever after.

He felt sorry for her. Cursing under his breath, he finally turned to her. He thought about trying to soft-pedal the truth, but then decided she was going to have to deal with reality sooner or later.

"I can't help you."

"What did you mean when you said it was already too late? I heard you on the phone."

"I'll let the FBI explain. Do you have someone you could call to come and sit with you? Some family member or close friend who could take care of you?"

Avery stopped abruptly. God, he was callous. "You think my aunt is dead, don't you?"

He didn't immediately answer her, but the way he was looking made her think he was trying to judge if she was strong enough before he said anything. Was he worried she'd become hysterical?

"I'm not going to fall apart. Just answer me."

He took a step closer. "Yes," he said. "I do think your aunt and the other two women are already dead."

She let go of his arm and stepped back. "Why? Why do you think that?"

"Isn't there anyone you could . . ."

"Call?" she snapped. "Aunt Carrie and Uncle Tony are my only family, and I'm not going to scare my uncle half to death the way you're trying to scare me until I have all the facts. Tell me how you know this Monk."

"Miss Delaney?"

Oliver was calling to her. She turned and saw the clerk holding up a house phone and beckoning her.

It couldn't be Margo, she thought. Her friend would have called her on her cell phone. Who then? Carrie . . . Maybe Carrie was on the line. Avery was suddenly so frightened, she couldn't catch her breath. Please, let it be Carrie.

She dropped her backpack as she sidestepped a couple. She was in too much of a hurry to pick it up. As she neared the counter, Oliver said, "The caller says it's urgent."

John Paul followed with her backpack. He saw her grab the receiver, then heard her say, "Carrie?"

"Sorry, darling girl. It isn't Carrie."

Jarred by the endearment and the whisper-soft voice of the woman on the line, Avery asked, "Who is this?"

"Who I am isn't important at the moment, but your Carrie is, isn't she? We have her. Would you like to see her again?"

The voice was muffled. Avery didn't think she had ever heard it before.

"What have you done with her? Is she all right? If you hurt her . . ."

"Stupid girl, be quiet and listen," the woman ordered. "I'm only going to say this once, so pay attention. Three lives depend upon your cooperation. I've left a manila envelope on the counter with your name on it. It's right there, on your left. Ah, don't turn around," she said in a hushed croon that made Avery's skin crawl. "If you see me, all the rules will change and your poor, poor Carrie and her new best friends will have to pay the price."

Avery stiffened. "Where are you?" she whispered.

"Here," the voice answered. "I'm watching you. You want to look, don't you?" She laughed. "Don't be a killjoy and ruin my game. Pick up the map, Avery. That's my girl. See the nice watch? Put it on. Now."

Avery picked up the man's Swatch athlete's watch and quickly slipped the band over her hand.

"That's it," the woman said. "Now open the map and find the little red X I've marked for you. Hurry now."

Avery propped the phone on her shoulder, opened the map, and began to search for the mark. She dropped the phone as she leaned forward, trying to see a glimpse of a face in the reflection of the shiny granite wall behind the counter.

John Paul reached around her and picked up the phone. She grabbed it from him.

"Clumsy girl," the voice chided.

"I'm sorry."

John Paul watched Avery closely. The color had drained from her face, and she had a white-knuckle grip on the phone. He couldn't stop himself from putting his arm around her, concerned now that whatever she was hearing was going to be too much for her. He wasn't any good at comforting women—he'd actually never attempted it before—but he felt obligated to try.

"Oh, isn't that sweet," the voice was syrupy now. "Is he your lover?"

She was so rattled she couldn't think. "Yes . . . no."

The woman laughed. "Who is he?"

"No one."

"Oh?"

Avery said the first thing that popped into her head. "He's an actor. He worked . . . works for Carrie in commercials. I'll send him away."

"No, no, don't do that. He's in the game now, darling girl. By now he knows you're having trouble finding Carrie. We don't want him asking questions or calling the police. Besides, he'll have more fun on the treasure hunt with you. But no one else. You say one word to anyone, and we'll know it. From the time you hang up this phone, we'll be monitoring your progress. You're going to tell the manager Carrie called and everything's fine. Then you're going to take your cell phone out of your purse and drop it in the fountain on your way out of the hotel. Do you understand?"

"Yes."

"Take your boyfriend's cell phone. Let me see you do it."

She turned to John Paul. "Give me your cell phone."

"I don't have one."

She repeated what he'd said into the phone.

"We'll know if you're lying. It really doesn't matter,

though. You won't be able to get a signal where you're going, but I still want to see you get rid of your phone."

"Yes, I will. Is Carrie all right? Is she—"

"She's fine . . . for the moment. Do what I tell you to do if you want her to stay that way." The tone of her voice turned hard and brittle, yet there was an underlying edge of excitement there as well. "Have you found the red X?"

"Yes, I see it."

"Follow the directions I've written at the bottom. You've got exactly two hours to get there."

"But it's at least a three-hour drive from here. It isn't possible. It doesn't look like there are any roads once we get—"

"I said two hours," the woman interrupted. "One hundred and twenty minutes, Avery, and not one minute more. Didn't you hear me?"

"Yes, but what if we don't make it in time? What if we're late?"

The woman laughed. "Boom."

CHAPTER 10

THE WOMAN SOUNDED demented. She was laughing as she disconnected the line. Avery, shaken to the core, handed the receiver to Oliver, and as she did so, she leaned into the counter and, slipping her hand into her backpack, pushed the speed dial number that would connect her to the pen. She waited a second, then pushed the star to signal an alert. Cannon hurried toward her and dropped the printout of information she'd demanded on the counter.

"You were right," she said, her voice strained with what she hoped sounded like good cheer. "That was Carrie on the phone. It was all just a crazy mix-up. Now, if you'll excuse us, John Paul and I are going for a ride."

She was trying not to let them see how frantic she was. She shoved the papers Cannon had placed on the counter into her backpack before he could snatch them back, grabbed her cell phone and the map, and sprinted for the entrance.

She glanced at each face she passed, but there were so many people loitering in the massive lobby, it was impossible to get a good look at all the women. Where were the phone banks? There were palms and huge ficus trees everywhere. The caller could be hiding as she watched Avery now.

"Let's go," she shouted to John Paul before she realized he was right behind her.

"What's going on?"

She didn't answer. She rushed to the fountain, dropped her cell phone into the water, and then ran out the front doors and bumped into the bellman.

"Miss Delaney, if you'll give me your room number, I'll take your luggage up—"

Ignoring him, she ran down the stairs and stopped in the middle of the circle drive as she tried to locate her rental car. Where was it?

John Paul lifted the black duffel bag from the luggage rack. "This one hers?" he asked the bellman.

"Yes, sir. See, her name's on it. Has she checked in yet?"

"What have you done with my car?" she shouted at the same time.

She was running toward the valet stand when John Paul intercepted her. She wasn't going to go anywhere until he let her, and he wasn't going to do that until she told him what the hell was going on. She was shaking violently.

"Take a deep breath and calm down. You aren't going to faint, are you?" he asked.

"No."

"Okay, tell me what happened. Talk to me, damn it. Who was on the phone?"

"It was a woman. I didn't recognize her voice. She said they have my aunt."

"They?" he demanded. "You're sure she said they?"

"Yes," she said. She was growing more frantic with each passing second. "Carrie's in trouble, and I have to get to her before it's too late."

"Did the woman tell you to get rid of your cell phone?"

Struggling to get away from him, she whispered, "Yes. Look, this isn't a prank. I could tell. She said that they would kill Carrie and two other women who are with her if we don't get moving. Please," she pleaded in desperation. "You have to go with me. She said you're in the game now. We have to hurry. She's given us two hours to get to a place she marked on the map, and I don't know how we'll make it in time. It's so far away . . ."

"You know this is probably a trap, don't you? You've got to know—"

"Yes," she shouted, no longer caring who heard her. "And once we're on our way, I'm going to try to think of a way to stay alive and help Carrie. Listen to me. I don't have a choice. If it were your mother or your daughter, would you stand here analyzing the situation? I know you wouldn't. You'd do exactly what I'm going to do. Play along and seize whatever chance you can. Now move it, Renard. Time's running out."

She was right. He would have paid the ransom or done anything humanly possible to keep someone he loved alive a little longer.

"Come on," he said. "We'll take my car."

Weak with relief because he wasn't arguing, she whispered, "Thank you."

He grabbed her hand and ran to the parking lot, with her stumbling along behind him. His SUV was illegally parked in front of a walkway. There was a security guard standing beside the hood shaking his head.

"Are you the owner of this—" He stopped when he saw the expression on John Paul's face, then quickly backed away, stepping into a bed of pansies.

John Paul ignored him. He pushed the security button on his key chain to unlock the doors and tossed Avery's bag into the back with his gear while she ran around to the front passenger seat.

She had the map out and was pointing to the red X by the time he slid behind the wheel. "We've got exactly two hours. No, one hour and fifty-seven minutes now, to get to this spot. Let's go."

John Paul studied the map for about ten seconds. "It's going to be close," he said as he started the ignition.

"But we can make it?"

"Maybe," was all he would allow. "You navigate. Put your seat belt on."

He couldn't floor it until they were out of the parking area, but by the time they'd reached the gate at the end of the long, winding road, he was going fifty.

Avery was leaning forward, rocking, as though that motion would help them get closer to their destination. She realized what she was doing and forced herself to sit back while she concentrated for the moment on giving him directions.

He sped down the highway. "There," she shouted when she saw the sign. "Take the cutoff up ahead. It should be about a mile or so. You can stay on that two-lane for at least twenty miles, maybe thirty." Gripping her hands together, she watched the road until the turnoff came into view. "Slow down. There it is. You'll miss it."

"I see it," he said calmly.

He took the blacktop road on two wheels. Avery braced herself with her hand against the dashboard. Didn't these things turn over all the time? That was all they needed, for John Paul to wreck the car. Carrie would be doomed.

Calm down, she told herself. We'll make it. We have to.

She looked down, saw the masculine Swatch watch half on top of her little Timex, and quickly removed it. After she examined the front and the back, she carefully placed it in the cup holder between them.

The road straightened ahead, and he glanced over. "Now you start talking," he said. "Tell me exactly what she said."

She told him what she could remember, and then she said, "She was there watching us. I tried to find her on my way outside, but there were so many people milling around."

"She might not have been inside. Didn't you notice all the security cameras?"

She shook her head. "No."

"All she had to do was hook into their system. She didn't have to be there to watch you at the counter. Was there anything to distinguish her voice?"

"No, nothing. She just sounded . . ."

"What?"

"Creepy. She told me not to be a killjoy, called what she was doing a game. She didn't want me to spoil her fun."

Avery remembered the papers she'd shoved in her backpack and pulled them out.

"What's that?"

"I asked Cannon to give me all the information he had on the other two women who canceled at the last minute. She told me there were two women with Carrie now. They have to be the same ones. The first name is Anne Trapp. She lives in Cleveland and owns Trapp Shipping Company. Then there's Judge Sara Collins from Miami. It appears that all three reservations were made on credit cards. Each with a different name on it." She read the names to him.

"Do the names mean anything to you?"

"No," she answered. "I don't think Carrie's ever mentioned any of them, and I don't know how she would know them. Carrie and my uncle live in Bel Air."

"I figured that was where you were from."

"For a while I was," she said. "I live in Virginia now." She picked up the watch and checked the time again. "Can't we go any faster?"

"I'm going close to eighty now. The speed limit is fifty-five. I just hope the highway patrol isn't around."

Oh, God, she hadn't thought about that. They would be delayed indefinitely if they were stopped.

"Slow down then."

"Make up your mind, sweetheart. Fast or slow? It's your call."

"We'll make up the speed on the access road. Slow down for now."

He did. "You're sure the woman on the phone said, 'We have her'?" stressing the plural.

"You already asked me that, and, yes, I'm still sure she said *they* have her. Why is that important?"

He could barely contain his excitement. "Because just maybe Monk is waiting for you at that spot on the map, and that gives me a unique opportunity to kill the bastard. If I can figure out a way to get ahead of him . . ."

He didn't go on, but she noticed he increased their speed again. "I think it's time for you to answer some questions," she said.

"Like what?"

"Why were you looking for Carrie? How do you know her?"

He had to confess. "I don't know her."

"But you said . . ."

"I lied," he said curtly. "I know the man who . . ."

"Who what?"

He was going to say *the man who killed her* because, if Monk was continuing with his pattern, those three women were already dead and buried. He had changed one thing,

John Paul acknowledged. He was obviously now working with a partner.

". . . who is after the women," he said. "The man calling himself Monk. I doubt that's the name on his birth certificate."

"Tell me what you know about him. Who is he?"

"A professional killer."

"A what?" she asked sharply.

He repeated himself, and then he glanced at her face to see how she was taking the news. Not well, he decided. Not well at all. She was rapidly turning green.

"Are you gonna get sick?" He asked the question without a bit of sympathy in his voice.

"No."

He didn't believe her. "Roll down the window and lean out if you think—"

"I'm okay," she said, even as she hit the button to automatically lower the window. She took a couple of deep breaths. The air was heavy with an earthy, musty scent. It made her want to gag. No, fresh air wasn't helping.

A professional killer. My God, she thought.

She exhaled and tried to clear her thoughts. Deal with what you know as fact, she told herself. Think it through.

Anne Trapp. Sara Collins. Those two women were throwing a wrench in her analysis. What was the common denominator?

"There has to be a connection," she said, and as soon as the words were out of her mouth, she shook her head. "No, I can't assume that."

He concentrated on the road. He had increased the speed once again because there weren't any other cars around, and he was betting the highway patrol was busy monitoring the more congested areas. He eased up on the gas pedal when the needle hit seventy.

"Road ends in five miles."

She grabbed the map. "How do you know?"

"I just read the sign."

"We're supposed to take the access road."

"I'm looking," he said.

She glanced at the watch for what had to be the hundredth time and saw that a full twenty minutes had passed. Then she measured the distance in her mind to the red X.

He glanced over at her. "Without good roads, it's going to be close. We might not make it, Avery."

"We'll make it," she insisted. "We have to make it."

"Ah, here we go," he said as he swerved off the road onto an access. Gravel spit up over the tires and hit the windshield as he fishtailed up the winding road. It was only wide enough for a single car, and the branches of the evergreens scraped the sides of the SUV as it zoomed past.

"We're headed in the right direction, and that's all that matters," he said.

"If we're lucky, maybe farther up we'll hook into a better road."

"Or no road at all."

"How exactly do you know Monk?"

"I've never met him, if that's what you're asking. He's become a hobby of mine. He went after someone close to me."

"Someone hired him to kill this friend of yours?"

"No," he answered. "But she got in the way. It was my sister. He was hired to get some information she had, and he tried to kill her to get it. Fortunately, his plans got all screwed up, and he ended up going to ground."

"So you've been tracking him for some time."

"Yes," he answered. "The man I called from Cannon's office also has a vested interest in Monk."

"Who is he?"

"Clayborne," he answered. "Noah Clayborne. He's FBI," he added with a note of disdain.

"But he's a friend of yours?"

"I wouldn't call him that."

She tilted her head as she studied him. What was his problem? He turned her attention then when he said, "Like I said, Monk went underground for over a year. Couldn't find more than a hint of his work . . . until now."

"How did you know he was in Colorado?"

"He used a bogus credit card he'd used before in Bowen . . . that's where I live," he said. "Bowen, Louisiana."

"Then the FBI knows he's in Colorado too," she said.

"No, they don't."

"But if you tracked him with the credit card receipt, surely the FBI—"

"They don't know about the credit card receipt."

"You didn't notify them?"

"Hell, no."

There it was again, that surly edge of hostility.

"Why not?"

"Because I didn't want them to screw it up."

"The FBI does not screw up investigations. They're experts and extremely efficient in their—"

He cut her off. "Spare me the platitudes. I've heard all the propaganda before. I didn't buy it then, and I don't buy it now. The Bureau has become too glutted with bosses all trying to break the backs of the agents working under them so they can get to the top. There isn't any loyalty these days. It's just dog eat dog. They're . . . bureaucratic," he added with a shudder.

"You're cynical."

"Damn right."

She looked out the side window. "Thank you anyway."

"What are you thanking me for?"

"Coming with me. You could have refused."

"Just so you understand. I'm not doing this for you or your aunt. I want to get Monk before he kills anyone else."

"In other words, you have your own agenda, and you aren't doing me any favors. I understand," she said.

She didn't understand, though. How could anyone be that hardened? She found herself wondering if he ever went out of his way to help anyone in trouble. Probably not. He was the type of man who drove past accidents and stepped over heart attack victims.

They rode in silence for several minutes, and then Avery said, "Tell me what you've learned about Monk. He must have a pattern. They all do."

He thought it was odd she'd know about such things. "Actually he did have a pattern, but it's obviously changed."

"How has it changed?"

"Monk always kept a low profile. In and out as fast and as clean as possible."

"You sound like you admire him."

"No, I don't admire him," he said. "I'm just saying his pattern never varied much before. In the beginning, the murders he committed all took place within a two-week span every year. That didn't change for seven years. I have a theory about that."

"You think he holds down a full-time job somewhere? That he's living two separate lives."

"I think he used to," he corrected. "Murder obviously pays a hell of a lot more, so I'm guessing he probably quit his other job. Couldn't you just picture him sitting at his desk, diligently working. He would have been the nice guy. You know, the one who draws the chart for the football pools, and because he was so well liked, people would tell him their troubles. I'll bet you this, Avery. When he gets caught, the people he worked with will be shocked. They'll all say the same thing. Bob was such a sweet, charming man."

"So was Ted Bundy."

"Exactly my point."

"How do you know the early murders were his work? Did he leave a card or something so he'd get credit?"

"Sort of," he answered. "He likes roses. He leaves a long-stemmed red rose."

"That's eerie," she said. "So he used to be a nine-to-fiver, and killing people was his idea of a great vacation, but now he's strictly a professional killer . . . any time of the year. What else is different about him these days? You seem to have studied his work closely."

He nodded. "He's never tried anything like this . . . taking three victims. He isn't a showman. And he's always acted alone before. Now it appears that he's hooked up with a woman. Maybe he's showboating to impress her."

They struck a bump in the road. Avery grabbed the dashboard again as the top of her head hit the roof.

"Are we still headed north?" It was impossible to tell. The trees hid the sky, and it was ominously dark in this stretch of forest.

"Northwest," he said.

She heard a scream in the distance. No, it was more like an animal's screech. The sound gave her chills.

"How does he get his contracts? Do you know?"

"No, but I'm guessing the Internet," he answered. "It's easy. It's anonymous, and up until now, he's been careful and discriminating in selecting his targets. He probably has enough work to keep busy for the next fifty years. You'd be surprised how many husbands want their wives dead and how many wives would pay through the nose to get rid of their husbands."

"My uncle Tony had nothing to do with this."

"You're sure?"

"I'm sure," she answered emphatically.

He let it go for the moment. "You said there had to be a connection between the women . . ."

"I was analyzing what we know, trying to put it together. I made the assumption that one man or woman hired Monk to kill all three women, so that's why I was trying to think of something they all had in common. But my premise might not be valid."

"Meaning?"

"We have to allow for the possibility that three different people hired Monk, and that, for whatever reason, he decided to kill the victims all at the same time."

He had to admit she was right. "One thing is certain. Monk was paid a hell of a lot of money to kill these women. He doesn't come cheap. If he has lumped them together, the real question is, who wants your aunt dead?"

He expected her to immediately tell him what a sweet, lovable woman her aunt was and that she didn't have an enemy in the world.

"Lots of people dislike my aunt. Some, I would imagine, hate her."

He wasn't prepared for that. He actually smiled. "Yeah?"

"Carrie can sometimes be . . . abrasive."

"Is that right?"

Avery nodded. "She's in a cutthroat business."

"Oh? What business is that?"

"Commercials."

"Excuse me?"

"She makes commercials."

He laughed, the sound harsh in the confines of the car.

"However," she continued, ignoring his reaction, "none of her business associates would go to such extremes to get rid of her."

"How can you be so sure?"

"I just am," she said.

"Okay, then that brings us back to your uncle Tony. How strong is their marriage? Any problems you know about?"

She was suddenly feeling sick to her stomach. "Carrie thinks Tony's cheating on her."

"Ah."

"They've been seeing a marriage counselor."

"Is that right?"

"Tony loves Carrie," she said.

"How well do you know your uncle?"

"Not as well as I should," she admitted. "I went away to boarding school and was only home during the summer, and then I worked in Carrie's office. Still, I think I'm a good judge of character. Tony would never be unfaithful."

"Wives usually know."

"Carrie isn't your typical wife. She's got a very suspicious nature. I think, deep down, she can't believe any man could love her. She's . . . insecure, and that's why she's often abrasive. She doesn't want anyone to see her vulnerability."

"So that leads us right back to . . ."

"If they are separate contracts, and one person hired Monk to kill Carrie and me, then . . ."

"Then what?"

"I know who he is."

CHAPTER 11

THE FIRST HOUR was a nightmare, and then it got worse.

The crazy woman had almost blown them to kingdom come. Anne's hand was on the doorknob when Carrie tackled her to the floor. She was so skinny she went down hard, and Carrie landed with a thud on top of her. Both of them were screaming. Carrie had her hands full, and it was impossible to get the woman to listen to reason. Twisting and turning, Anne tried to claw Carrie's eyes with her long, tapered, acrylic nails. She made it to her knees and nearly got away from Carrie when Sara grabbed her by her ankles and dragged her from the door.

As thin and frail as Anne appeared, her rage gave her almost superhuman strength, but fortunately it was quickly spent. Panting from exertion, Carrie kept the woman pinned to the marble floor by sitting on her spine. She held Anne's head down with both her hands pressed against the back of her neck.

"Find something we can tie her up with," Carrie shouted to Sara so she could be heard over Anne's screeching.

Ten minutes later Anne was sitting in a chair at the

round table in the breakfast nook. Her wrists were tied to the arms of the chair with two phone wires.

"How dare you treat me this way. You're not going to get away with this. You just wait and see. I'm going to report you."

Carrie, exhausted, fell into the chair adjacent to Anne's. She covered her brow with her hand, her elbow propped on the table, and calmly asked, "How do you plan to do that, Anne?"

"You bitch," Anne railed. "I'll call the police."

"Be my guest. Use the phone. Oh, wait. You can't because the damn phone's dead."

"You're lying."

Carrie turned to Sara, who was leaning against the counter, watching. "Is she just on another planet? I think her mind's completely snapped."

"Perhaps," Sara said. "Shock will sometimes make a person . . . irrational."

"What in God's name are we going to do?" Carrie whispered.

Sara pulled out a chair and sat down across from Anne. She folded her hands on the tabletop. "Now, Anne, it won't do for you to continue to pretend that everything is all right. We're all in trouble here, and we need your cooperation."

Anne's immediate response was a glare. "Leave me alone, you fat pig."

"Charming," Carrie muttered.

"Bitch," Anne shouted at the top of her voice.

"If you continue to scream every word, Anne, I'm afraid I'm going to have to gag you," Sara warned. "Are you going to calm down?"

Anne's glare grew even stronger.

"Anne, where's the letter that was left for you?" When

Anne turned her head away, Sara asked, "Are you giving us the silent treatment now?"

"Wouldn't that be a blessing?" Carrie scoffed.

Sara leaned back in her chair, adjusted her silk robe to cover her gown, and said, "You know, Anne, if you didn't get a letter . . ."

"I didn't," Anne snapped.

"Then you could be an innocent bystander who just got caught up in our . . . dilemma."

Dilemma? Carrie was about to take issue with Sara's poor choice of words. For God's sake, they were sitting inside a bomb. But then she caught Sara's eye and decided to keep quiet when the older woman gave a quick shake of her head.

"You see, Anne," she continued in a calm tone. "As a judge, I put away a good number of hardened criminals over the years. I had a reputation for giving harsh sentences, but in all of those cases, the men and women who came before me were career criminals. I don't have any regrets."

Anne finally looked at Sara with icy disdain. "Why are you telling me this?"

"Because it's important. Over the years there have been numerous threats against my life, but I've never given any of them a second thought."

She went into the living room to get the letters she and Carrie had received. She returned to her seat at the table and read her letter to Anne. When she was finished, she held the paper up in front of Anne's eyes so she could see she was telling the truth.

"And you think one of those criminals is making good on his threat?"

"Yes, that's exactly what I think. Either there's an ex-con behind this, or someone still in jail has gotten outside help."

"Where would an ex-con or a prisoner get the money to hire a killer?"

"Who cares where he got the money," Carrie interjected.

"I'm not talking to you, bitch," Anne hissed.

Sara raised her hand for silence. She didn't want Carrie's temper to trigger another tantrum.

"It's a valid question," Sara said. "I don't know how he got the money. Perhaps a relative came into an inheritance or . . ."

"And maybe you put away an innocent man, and those relatives know it."

"Yes, that might be how it happened."

Carrie was gritting her teeth to keep from interrupting. She wanted to tell both women that right now they needed to find a way to get out of the house, and then, once they were safe, they could speculate on the who, how, and why until the cows came home.

"Carrie's letter wasn't like mine," Sara said. "Hers was signed."

Anne looked intrigued. "So he wanted you to know how much he hated you before you died?"

"Not 'he,' " Sara corrected. "She."

Carrie nodded. Anne still wouldn't look at her, but Carrie didn't care about that. "My letter was written by my sister, Jilly."

The announcement so shocked Anne she couldn't continue her stony silence with Carrie any longer. "Your own flesh and blood wants you dead?"

"Yes."

Appalled, she asked, "What kind of a family do you come from?"

Carrie held her temper. "Dysfunctional, Anne. I come from a very dysfunctional family. My sister's crazy."

"Good heavens," Anne said. "Wait a minute. Are you

lying? I mean, if your sister is really crazy, why hasn't she
been locked away?"

"I was told years ago that Jilly died in a car accident.
The funeral home wanted to send me her ashes. Jilly, it
turns out, was much smarter than I thought. She's waited
and planned all these years to get even with me."

"Why? What did you do to her?"

"She thinks I stole her child."

"Did you?"

"No, Jilly abandoned her when she was a baby. My
mother and I raised her."

"And your sister never came back?"

"Oh, yes, when Avery was five, Jilly came back with a
sleazebag of a boyfriend named Dale Skarrett. She thought
she could just waltz in and take Avery away. She'd already
used extortion to get money out of my mother. That's
true," she said when Anne looked so appalled. "My mother
had to pay to keep Avery. I was home when they came, and
while I physically tried to shove Jilly out of the house, my
mother called the police. When Dale Skarrett heard the sirens, he grabbed Jilly and took off. I moved to California
the following morning. While I was off building a career,
Avery stayed with my mother. Then, when Avery was
eleven, Jilly sent Skarrett to the house to kidnap her. Avery
wasn't going to go quietly. She fought him tooth and nail,
and he used his belt to beat her within an inch of her life.
She was so young . . . and helpless. I guess I sort of thought
of myself as her mother, but when it mattered, really mattered, I wasn't there to protect her the way a mother
should."

"What about your mother? Didn't she do anything?"

Carrie looked down as she continued. "The police chief
was a friend, and he had given mother a gun, taught her
how to use it too. She was in the backyard and didn't hear

the screaming until she came into the house. My mother had become hard-of-hearing," she added. "From what the police were able to ascertain, mother tried to shoot Skarrett. She must have given him warning because he grabbed Avery just as she fired. The bullet struck my niece."

The words came out in a monotone, but there were tears in her eyes. "I left an old woman to take care of my niece, knowing that Jilly was out there."

"But surely you couldn't have anticipated . . ."

"Oh, but I did know what Jilly was capable of," Carrie said.

"What happened to your mother?" Sara asked.

"She suffered a massive heart attack. She was dead by the time the police got to the house, and Avery was hanging on by a thread. I caught a flight from L.A. to Jacksonville. By the time I got there, Avery had already had surgery and was in ICU. The first thing the doctor told me was that Avery would recover, but he didn't give me time to rejoice because he said she wouldn't be able to have children. A hysterectomy at age eleven. That has to be some kind of record," she said bitterly.

Sara looked startled, and Carrie assumed she was reacting to her morbid account of that awful day.

"That poor child," Anne said. She sounded genuinely compassionate.

"I remember her," Sara whispered.

"What?" Carrie all but shouted.

Sara nodded. "The names . . . there were so many over the years; it isn't possible to remember all of them. And I didn't remember Avery until you mentioned the hysterectomy at age eleven. I'll never forget reading the transcripts of the trial."

"I don't understand," Carrie said. "Why would you read the transcripts? Judge Hamilton was the judge at the trial."

"Yes, but Hamilton died before the sentencing date. He had a massive stroke, and the case was given to me. I'm the judge who sentenced Skarrett, and he has every reason to want me dead. I gave him the maximum."

Astounded, Carrie sat back. "So *there's* the connection between the two of us. Dale Skarrett . . . and Jilly."

"Jilly was never charged with any of it, was she?" Sara asked.

"There wasn't any proof to go after her. Besides, she had vanished," she explained. "It was Avery's sole testimony that got Skarrett convicted of second-degree murder. A few weeks after his sentencing, I got a call from a funeral home in Key West asking me what I wanted done with Jilly's ashes. That's how I found out she was dead."

"Except she isn't dead," Anne said.

"No, she definitely isn't. I saw her in living color last night," Carrie said emphatically. "She hasn't aged much at all. She's still beautiful . . . and still frickin' nuts."

Sara went to the kitchen cabinet and took down a cup and saucer.

"I always wanted to have a daughter, but my husband didn't want children. He convinced me that it would cramp our lifestyle," Anne said.

"What was your lifestyle?" Sara asked as she poured the hot coffee.

"Work. Just work. I felt guilty about that," she confessed. "And so I gave in to my husband on all the little things."

Anne considered having children a little thing? "I see," Carrie remarked.

"Eric is ten years younger than I am," Anne continued. "But age never mattered to him. He loves me very much."

"I'm sure he does."

"He's taken over operations. You know, the mundane office managerial tasks, and he's so clever. He found a new health insurance carrier with a group rate that was less than half of what we had been paying."

Carrie couldn't understand why Anne wanted to talk about this now. Sara untied Anne's left hand and placed the cup of coffee in front of her. "There isn't any milk," she said. "But I found some sugar if you want it sweetened."

"No, thank you."

Carrie couldn't put up with the nonsense a second longer. The two were acting as if they were at a tea party. "What the hell are we going to do?"

"Find a way to get out," Sara said. "We're three smart women. We should be able to think of something."

Anne didn't seem at all interested in that topic. "Sara? What did you mean when you said I could have been an innocent bystander?"

Sara refilled her cup and sat down. "If you didn't have a letter on your nightstand . . ."

"I didn't," Anne rushed to assure her.

"Then I think I know what happened. Your plane landed just a few minutes before mine did, remember?"

"Yes."

"And didn't you tell us that you were irritated because the driver from the spa was waiting for me at my gate, but there wasn't anyone waiting for you? In the car you said that if you hadn't seen the man holding up the sign for Utopia, you would have had to carry your own luggage and get a taxi."

Anne nodded. "Yes, I certainly do remember, and I was extremely put out. I'm still going to register a complaint with the manager. There should have been a driver waiting for me at my gate."

"Therefore," Sara continued as though Anne hadn't gotten sidetracked, "perhaps you weren't meant to be part of this. However," she hastened to add before Anne could interrupt, "the fact remains that you are going to die when this house blows up."

"But why? I didn't do anything wrong."

"And we did?" Carrie asked.

Anne shrugged.

"Answer me," Carrie demanded. "Do you honestly think we deserve to die like this?"

"I don't know," Anne said. "You must have done something pretty awful to make your sister so mad, and, Sara, you might have sent an innocent man to prison."

Carrie had thought that Anne was going to be sensible, but her comments indicated she was still in Lala Land.

"I still don't understand why he brought me here," she said.

"Because you saw his face," Carrie muttered. "How could you have run a business? You ask such stupid questions."

"I don't like you." Anne took a dainty sip of her coffee after making the childish remark.

"I don't give a damn if you like me or not."

"Ladies, this isn't getting us anywhere," Sara interjected. "Anne, the killer couldn't leave you behind. You had also met me, and if you had gone to the spa, you would have complained to the management, and that would have signaled an alarm . . . since they obviously didn't send a driver to the airport."

"You also could have given a description of the man to the police. It was much too risky for him to leave you behind," Carrie explained. "And you could have told the police where he was taking us," Sara added.

"Oh, I'm sure he lied about where we were going. He lied about everything else, didn't he?" Sara asked. She suddenly looked weary, and her voice trailed off.

"No, he didn't lie about that."

Both Sara and Carrie frowned at Anne. "How do you know?" Carrie asked.

"Because I saw the sign. It was a tarnished brass plaque in the center of the iron gate. The driver pushed the button on that remote control gadget, and I read the sign as the gate was swinging open. Land Between the Lakes. So he didn't lie about that."

"That was very observant of you," Sara said.

"For all the good that does us," Anne said. "We can't tell anyone."

Carrie's head snapped up. "Oh, my God, I did tell."

"What did you say?" Sara asked.

"I called my niece from the airport. I was in the ladies' room, and I remembered I had my cell phone in the pocket of my blazer, so I called her. Her voice mail picked up and I left a message telling her where we were going to be spending the night. What a fool I am. I went on and on about the famous guests who had stayed here before. Monk—if that is his real name—must have done his research." Tears flooded her eyes as she whispered, "That's why he was telling those stupid stories about movie stars. He knew I'd be impressed. I'm such a shallow fool."

"He played all of us," Sara said. "Did you tell your niece the name of the property?"

"Yes," Carrie answered. "I don't know if she got the message because she might have already left for the airport. What if he was there waiting for her?" Her voice broke on a sob.

Sara reached across the table and patted Carrie's hand. "If he had been waiting for her, wouldn't he have driven her here? Maybe that's what they're waiting for," she added. "Maybe that's why they haven't . . ."

"Haven't what?" Anne asked.

"Killed us," Sara said bluntly.

"But you said they left us food in the pantry and in the freezer, so they obviously want to keep us alive a little while longer," Anne argued.

Sara disagreed. "The food . . . that's what's so alarming. Doesn't it seem more frightening to you that they didn't empty the cabinets?"

Carrie hadn't thought of it that way, but now she agreed with Sara. "I think that means they're going to blow the house soon. They're not going to let us sit in here until it's all gone. They left the water on too," she pointed out. "We have to get out of here." She buried her face in her hands and whispered, "I've got to get to Avery. If that monster has her . . ."

"Concentrate on finding a way out, Carrie, so that you can help your niece."

Anne straightened in her chair and nodded. "As long as you both agree I'm innocent, I'll help and I won't do anything crazy, like opening a door. I promise, but you have to say it."

Carrie lifted her head. "Say what?"

Anne straightened in her chair. "That I'm innocent."

She was, of course, implying that Sara and Carrie weren't. It was infuriating, her holier-than-thou attitude, but Carrie caught Sara's nod and decided she had to get along with Anne if she wanted her cooperation. "Yes, you are innocent," she said.

After Sara concurred, Anne turned to Carrie. "You should try to make amends with your sister, fix the wrong you did."

Oh, how Carrie hated the woman. She held her tongue as Anne preached on. "Family is the most important thing of all. I recently learned that truth. Being able to lean on someone . . . like my husband when times get difficult . . . that's very important. I'm very fortunate," she continued. "My husband adores me."

She was excited when she turned to Sara. "He'll sound the alarm. My husband calls every single day. He's never missed. I told him not to bother while I was at the spa because I'd be doing all those treatments, and it would be difficult for him to get hold of me, but he wouldn't listen. He said he couldn't go to sleep at night unless he talked to me. So don't you see? If we can just wait it out, my husband will have the police tearing Colorado apart looking for me."

"We can't wait," Carrie objected.

Sara shook her head at her for losing her cool. "You sound like you have a wonderful marriage," she told Anne.

"Yes, I do. We're blissfully happy." There was a note of defiance. "And he will search for me."

"Yes, I'm sure he will," Sara placated. "But we might not have time to wait for the police to find us. Colorado's a big state."

Anne nodded. "Yes, you're right. We have to help ourselves. All right," she said as she untied the cord around her right arm. "What can I do? I don't know that I can be much help because I'm just getting over a long bout of illness. I've lost weight, and I don't have my strength back yet. I'm an excellent cook, though. I could fix us something to eat."

"That would be wonderful," Sara said. "Thank you, Anne."

Carrie wasn't as trusting. Maybe Anne had come to her senses. Then again, maybe she was simply playing them. The stakes were too high to trust her. Carrie decided that either she or Sara had to keep an eye on the woman at all times.

"Is anyone hungry now?" Anne asked as she stood.

"I am," Sara said.

Anne didn't seize the opportunity to make a sarcastic

remark about Sara's weight this time. In fact, she apologized for what she had said earlier, and damn if she didn't sound sincere.

"I never should have called you a fat pig. I was overwrought, but that is a poor excuse for hurting your feelings."

"Sara, why don't you stay here and keep Anne company while I search the house again," Carrie said. "I'll start at the top and work my way down. I've got to be missing something."

She was actually beginning to feel a little optimistic as she ran up the stairs. She hurriedly dressed in her designer sweats and then methodically rechecked each opening. There was a tiny window high up in the corner of her bedroom. It took her a long time to move the bureau over to the wall and then climb up, but she still wasn't tall enough. She ran downstairs to get one of the dining room chairs. She noticed Sara was standing on a chair in front of the double-pane living room windows. She had a lipstick and was printing the word "help" across the glass.

Carrie stopped her. "If Monk, or whatever the hell the bastard's name is, has put a triggering device outside . . ." She didn't have to finish her thought.

"The house will blow when help arrives."

"It's a possibility," Carrie said as she lifted the chair and started back up the stairs.

"I'll stop," Sara said. She got off the chair and went to get a towel to wipe off the letters she'd just written.

"What about trying to cut through the glass?" Carrie heard Anne ask as she continued on up the spiral staircase.

Carrie's arms ached from the exertion of lifting the chair on top of the bureau. It took her three tries, and she was panting because she was so terribly out of shape. She fell trying to climb to the top, but fortunately, she landed on the bed. She propped the chair against the wall and tried again. When she was finally able to reach the window, she burst into tears. The son of a bitch had wired that tiny little egress too.

She wouldn't give up, no matter how hopeless their situation was. Maybe Anne's suggestion would work. Maybe they could cut through the glass without disturbing the wires. Wiping the tears from her eyes, she gingerly scraped her diamond ring against the sliding glass door. Fifteen minutes later she stopped. All she had managed to do in that time was make a small scratch on the glass.

Carrie walked down a flight to the next level and proceeded to examine Anne's room and then Sara's. She spent hours trying one thing and then another before she finally gave up. She'd wasted the afternoon and part of the evening on the impossible.

CHAPTER 12

JILLY WALKED AROUND the stone bench nestled in the grotto facing the serenity pool. She paused to watch an instructor dressed in white tai chi clothing lead his students in an ancient exercise. The teacher was quite graceful, but his students were obviously novices, and their movements were stiff and awkward.

She continued on to where Monk had parked the all-terrain Mercedes. Flowers were in full bloom wherever she looked. There were even large patches of flowers along the back parking lot. Utopia was enchanting, and perhaps when this business was concluded, she could come back here for a full week of pampering.

Her phone rang just as she slid behind the wheel of the new car. She had been waiting for Monk to call from his satellite phone, and she answered before the first ring ended.

"Hello, darling."

Monk smiled. He loved the sound of her throaty voice and the way she whispered the endearment. "Has she arrived yet?" he asked.

"Yes, I've just sent her on her way, and I'm leaving now.

I'll take the shortcut you found for me, and I'll be there a good forty minutes ahead of her."

"Did you enjoy talking to your daughter?"

"Oh, it was lovely," she gushed. "She's afraid. Thank you, darling, for letting me do this. There is one little worry, however."

"Yes?"

"Avery wasn't alone."

"What?" he asked sharply. "Who was with her?"

"A man," she answered. Adjusting her phone against her ear, she started the car and pulled out of the parking lot. "Her lover, no doubt," she speculated. "I had to include him because he knows that Carrie is missing. He went into the manager's office with Avery. Did I do the right thing? Did I?"

He knew she needed reassurance. "Yes, of course you did the right thing. Did you happen to get his name? Do you know anything about him?"

"No," she answered. "I thought about asking the clerk or the manager, but then I decided to wait and talk to you first. Do you want me to go back and find out who he is?"

"No, no, don't do that," he said. "You'd only draw attention to yourself. You're so beautiful, people will remember you . . . and you do look like Avery. I'll find out who he is."

"Yes, all right. Are you ready for both of them?"

"The plan's changed."

"Oh?"

"The river store is open, and business, I'm afraid, is booming. It's been busier than a 7-Eleven since early morning."

"How can that be?" she cried. "You checked. The owner was mauled by a bear and won't get out of the hospital for at least another week. You checked," she repeated.

She was becoming upset. He hurriedly tried to quiet her fears. "It's going to be okay."

She wouldn't let it go. "But how can the store be open?"

"The owner's cousin from Arkansas opened the store this morning. The owner must have called him. It doesn't matter," he stressed. "We're simply going to plan B. You remember, I told you I always have a contingency plan in mind whenever I take on a new assignment."

"I remember," she said, relieved. "You're so clever, darling."

The least little praise made him want to please her all the more.

"Wait," she said urgently. "The package with Carrie's red scarf. Is it still there on the counter?"

"No, but that doesn't matter now," he said. He had already thought the matter through. The original plan had been to lure Avery into the store by placing a large manila envelope with her name on it on the counter by the window so she would see it when she looked inside. She would be desperate and break in. Monk would be waiting for her, and after he had killed her, he would bury her in the forest about a hundred yards behind the store. He'd already gone to the trouble of digging her grave. The hole was deep enough to accommodate her lover as well, he supposed, but now that the store was open and there was a steady stream of customers coming and going, Monk knew he couldn't kill them there.

"Do you have Carrie's wallet with you?" he asked.

"Yes, it's in my purse."

"Good," he praised. "We'll use it, then."

"Do I get to help? You promised me," she reminded him.

How could he deny her? It would have been so much easier if she'd agreed to stay at the spa and let him do his job. Jilly complicated his life, made him scramble to get everything done the way she wanted it done, but she was such a joy to be with, he didn't mind. He had tried to talk her into blowing up the house before they left it last night, but she wouldn't hear of it. She wanted her sister to wake up and know who was killing her and why.

Monk didn't like leaving the women, but he couldn't be in two places at once, and Avery's unexpected arrival had thrown him a curve. He hadn't let Jilly know how unsettling and worrisome those last-minute changes were, but now that he'd worked it all out in his mind, he was feeling in control again. He wished he had more time to go over the plan, but that wasn't possible.

"Darling, did you hear me? I get to help, don't I?"

He pushed his concerns aside.

"Yes, of course you can help. How would you like to talk to Avery again?"

She laughed. "Oh, I'd love to," she said. "I'm hurrying to you. I'm already turning onto that little road you found. I won't be long. When I get there, you have to tell me exactly what you want me to say to her. I don't want to mess up again like I did in Virginia when I took that old woman's car."

"Hush now. Don't fret about that. It's water under the bridge. Besides, you're a rookie," he said with a chuckle. "You were bound to make a few mistakes."

"I only wanted to please you, and I thought that, if I could immobilize her, I would make your job so much easier for you. You could have broken into her apartment and killed her there. I thought you could make it look like a robbery."

They had been over this topic at least ten times, and each time he tried to reassure her that he had forgiven her misjudgment. She never should have gone after Avery with that car, not only because of the danger to herself, but also because she very well might have killed her. Jilly had been so proud of her careful research. She'd done her own surveillance, discovered the dusty old Cadillac was owned by a woman who never drove it, and had been so clever in the way she'd gotten into the apartment and stolen the keys. She'd had fun too, dressing up as a policewoman collecting for the widows' fund.

Still, Jilly hadn't thought the plan through. When he gently pointed out that if she had killed Avery, Carrie certainly would have canceled her vacation plans, Jilly was mortified. Now she always checked with him first so that she wouldn't do anything rash. He liked the way she looked up to him, trusted him to know what was best.

"I'll meet you at our designated spot. Now, here's what I want you to do," he began.

She listened, growing more excited as he explained the details. When he was finished, she giggled. "It's perfect, darling. Absolutely perfect."

CHAPTER 13

H<small>IS NAME IS</small> Dale Skarrett," Avery said, "and he's in prison now."

"Where?" John Paul asked.

"Florida," she answered. "He came up for parole a couple of years ago, and Carrie and I went to the hearing. We each spoke to the board, and they listened to what we had to say. We're the reason he didn't get out."

"So he has a real good reason for wanting both of you dead."

"Yes."

"What'd he do?"

She hated bringing those memories back to the surface. It made the wounds fester again.

"I'll explain later," she said, buying herself time.

"What'd he do?" he calmly repeated.

She turned away from him to stare out the window. "He murdered my grandmother," she answered. She anxiously looked at the watch. "We have twenty-three minutes left to get to God only knows where. What should we be looking for?"

He knew she was trying to make him focus on the problem at hand so that he wouldn't ask her any more questions. Eventually she would tell him what he wanted and needed to know if they were going to get through this alive, but he didn't press her now for the grim details. Like she said, they had only twenty-three minutes to go.

"We look for anything that doesn't belong."

They were still climbing higher and higher as they wound around the mountain. Avery had lost her sense of direction, but thankfully, John Paul hadn't.

Sunlight was streaming in through the branches again, and the area wasn't quite as thick with evergreens. She thought they were getting closer to an open area or a summit. Would they be sitting ducks?

"We're going to get nosebleeds if we keep climbing. Are you cold?" she asked.

"No."

He knew she was. He'd noticed her rubbing her arms a minute ago. He reached over and flipped on the heater. Avery immediately adjusted the vents so the hot air would blow on her arms.

"What do you think she meant?"

"What?"

"When the woman said 'boom.' I keep picturing those women tied to chairs with explosives."

"Maybe," he said. "Or maybe they're inside something that's wired."

"There are caves and old shafts around here, aren't there?"

"Yes," he said. "There are hundreds of them."

She checked the time again. "Twenty-one minutes."

"I'm aware of the time," he snapped.

"Can't you go any faster?"

"You want to drive?"

"No," she said. She realized her frustration and fear were misdirected. "Sorry, I didn't mean to criticize. I know you're doing the best you can."

It occurred to her then that she didn't know much about the man she had so eagerly jumped into the car with. No, that wasn't true. She knew enough to trust his ability. He had proven himself capable when he was in the military. Hopefully, the skills he'd learned would come in handy, if he still remembered them.

She decided to find out. "Were you any good at what you used to do before you took a leave of absence?"

The question jarred him. "What are you talking about?"

"You were in the military."

He gave her a sharp look. "How do you know that?"

"I had a friend look you up in the computer where she works."

She waited for a reaction. She was ready with a good reason for invading his private life if he asked. He didn't, though. In fact he didn't say anything for a while.

"When did you do that?"

"Look you up? When I was in the manager's office at the spa. You had left to go find Cannon."

"You did a background check on me." He seemed to be having trouble believing her.

"Yes, I did."

The glare he cast her should have scalded her face. "Where does this friend of yours work?"

"Quantico."

Uh-oh. He didn't take the news well at all.

"Son of a . . ." he began.

"You were a Marine," she blurted.

She watched him take a breath and knew he was trying

to keep his temper under control. Oh, yes, he was angry; his neck had turned pink. It didn't matter to her, though. She had done what she had to do, and he was going to have to deal with it.

The muscle in his jaw flinched. Lord, he was good-looking. The thought came out of nowhere. Jeez, Avery, get a grip. For all she knew, the man could be paying alimony to eight ex-wives. She quickly discounted the Henry VIII notion right away. There couldn't possibly be eight women in the United States willing to marry him. No way.

"You were a Marine," she repeated.

"So?"

She had to grab hold again when he swerved to avoid a tree trunk. There were deep ruts in the dirt from other cars or trucks that had ventured up this road, but it was so isolated, so . . . quiet she was a little unnerved. She felt completely out of her element. She was a big-city girl who fell asleep to the music of car horns and police sirens. The silence now seemed almost deafening.

Swarms of gnats scattered as they hit the windshield. Avery picked up the watch and checked the time again. Seventeen minutes left.

John Paul kept glancing over at her. She thought he expected her to finish what she'd started.

"So that was good to know," she said.

"Why?"

"Marines are trained in combat, and that could be helpful." He didn't respond to her observation. "I also found out you were recruited by covert—"

He didn't let her finish. "Look, I know what I was. You don't have to go into it."

Damn. She had been hoping he would finish for her and tell her what she didn't know. Had he been in special ops or covert operations? And what exactly had his expertise been?

She looked at the map while she gathered her gumption. She couldn't find out unless she asked, could she?

"So what exactly did you do?"

"Don't you know?"

"Your file was classified."

"I would bet so."

There it was, that snide tone of voice again. "Did they teach you to be obnoxious, or were you born that way? You've got that alienation thing down pat."

"Avery, leave it alone."

"You don't scare me."

His eyes narrowed as he looked over at her again. "Yeah, I do."

"Oh, brother."

He smiled in spite of his bad mood. Maybe he didn't scare her. Interesting, he thought. And different.

"Do you think the two of them are together? Monk and the woman who called me?"

"I don't know. If the missing women are still alive and if he's tied them up or hidden them somewhere that's really isolated, then he could be with her. He's got a lot going on," he said. "If the women are still alive."

"He has to keep his eye on them. And he has to follow us."

"I don't think he's following us."

"But he's tracking us, isn't he?"

He almost smiled. "How?" he asked. He already knew the answer, but he was curious to know if she had figured it out.

"There's some kind of device inside the watch."

"Yes," he said. "He knows exactly where we are."

She shivered. The killer was monitoring their progress. "Shouldn't we get rid of it?"

"No, I don't want to do that. I think we should use it to our advantage. Let's wait and see what happens when we get near the X."

Avery picked up the watch and looked at it carefully. "There isn't a single scratch or mark on it to indicate someone's tampered with it."

"Monk's a professional. He wouldn't leave any marks."

"So he knows all about transmitters? He understands that technology?"

"Yes, he does."

"How do you know so much about him?"

"I read his file."

"The FBI file?" Her eyes widened. "If you're on leave, that's got to be illegal."

"I'm sure it is."

"John Paul, you could get into serious trouble."

She sounded worried about him. She was just chock full of surprises, and what a piece of work she was turning out to be. If he didn't watch out, he would start to like her.

"I've got connections who could bail me out," he said.

"Like your brother-in-law?"

"How'd you know about Theo?" he asked.

"When my friend pulled up your file for me, she told me."

"Having a relative working in the Justice Department comes in handy."

"You don't like your brother-in-law?"

What an odd question. "Sure I do. My sister loves him, and they're happy together. Why would you ask me that?"

"You sneered the words 'Justice Department.'"

He smiled. She was a quick study. "I didn't sneer."

She decided not to argue with him. "Do you think the woman who called me hired Monk?"

"Could be," he said, "but I don't think so. From what you said about her, he's letting her call the shots. I think she might be more like a partner. It's so damn odd. Monk never played games before. So why the treasure hunt?"

"I don't know."

"We might catch a break if the woman is making some decisions. Maybe she isn't quite the perfectionist he is."

"She's someone who knows Carrie and me."

"Because?"

"The way she talked. Her tone was mocking when she said Carrie's name. She doesn't like her."

"That's a given."

"Which means she's interacted with her."

"What about you?"

"She called me stupid. I've got to assume she doesn't like me either," she said dryly.

"No kidding."

"Maybe it's just that Skarrett has told her about us. But the way she talked . . . it sure sounded like this was personal to her."

Avery picked up the Swatch watch again and then gingerly placed it back in the cup holder. She could almost visualize a red light inside, pulsating like a heart. The image creeped her out.

John Paul was a good driver. She decided to let him worry about getting stuck in the mud and nicking a tire on a rock. Closing her eyes, she leaned back and let her mind move from one possibility to another. What was she missing? She felt as though she had the answer to this crazy puzzle in the back of her mind, but she couldn't quite reach it.

"How much time's left?" As soon as she told him, he said, "I don't know what we're going to barrel into, so listen up. You do whatever I tell you. If I tell you to get down, don't argue. Just do it. Once I figure out where the X is, I'm gonna try to bypass it some way and then circle around. You'll stay in the car."

"I have to show."

"No, you don't."

"Are you crazy? Of course I have to," she argued. "The woman said they would kill Carrie and the others if we're late. If I don't show my face . . ."

"Did this woman offer you any proof that they're still alive? Did you ask for any?"

"No," she said. "I should have, but I didn't. The conversation was short, and she wouldn't let me ask questions."

"Then you should have said no."

"Tell her I wouldn't play her game?"

"Yeah," he said. "That's what I would have done."

She shook her head. "I don't believe you. But, I'm sorry I didn't ask for proof. I should have."

"Should have, could have . . . it's too late now. I figure we've got a ninety percent chance of walking into a trap, so I want—"

She wouldn't let him finish. "I told you, I don't have a choice. I have to show. I'm hoping I can figure out a way to placate the madwoman."

"Placate a madwoman? That's a contradiction, isn't it?"

"Don't be a smart . . ."

He raised an eyebrow. "Smart-ass? Is that what you were going to say?"

"No."

"Then what?" he challenged.

She became defensive. "Look, if you want to bail, that's fine with me. Just get me to the X and take off."

"I'm not going to bail."

"Okay, then," she replied, irritated she'd sounded so relieved. "I know there's a good chance Monk has already dug our graves, but if you think I'm going to hide in the woods and hope for the best, then you're out of your mind."

"All I'm trying to say is that, if I'm lucky, maybe I'll spot him and be able to get close."

"And you don't want to worry about me. You want blind obedience."

"Exactly."

"Two heads are better than one."

"How much survival training have you had?"

Point taken. "None, but I could still help."

"Yeah, sure."

"Get rid of the attitude, John Paul. I can help. I have a few moves of my own."

"I'll bet you do."

"What's that supposed to mean?"

"Never mind."

She was doing a slow burn. Out of all the people in the world, she had to get stuck with the most obnoxious one. "You think you've got me all figured out, don't you?"

"Just about," he drawled.

Avery concentrated on the road. Thankfully, Jungle Boy didn't have any other sarcastic remarks to make. His scowl could have been chiseled in stone.

She thought she heard something, quickly rolled her window down, and strained to listen. "Do you hear that?"

John Paul flipped off the heater blower, rolled his window down, and then nodded. The sound of running water was faint, but there. "We went farther than I thought if we're close to the river. Maybe it's a tributary. It sounds like a waterfall."

They came to yet another crossroad. This one was traveled more than the last. And there was a sign nailed to a tree: *Last Chance Country Store. Beer and Raft Rentals.* Below the sign was an arrow pointing to the west.

The road curved downward. They hit a deep rut and lurched forward as they once again broke through the trees.

"The store's got to be around the bend down there," he said as he shot across the road and up into the trees on the other side. There was just enough room to turn the car around. Satisfied that they were concealed from the road, he put it in park and turned the motor off.

"How much time do we have left?"

"Twelve minutes," she said. "You think that's the spot?"

"It's gotta be the place. It sticks out, doesn't it?"

He was right. Please, God, let him be right. She could just make out a small rustic building through the trees. It sat on the bank of a river and was a place where river travelers could stop for supplies.

He unhooked his seat belt, reached under the seat, and pulled out a SIG Sauer. When she saw the gun, her mouth dropped open.

"I'm leaving the keys," he said, ignoring her reaction to the gun. "If you hear gunshots, you get the hell out of here. You hear me?"

She wasn't about to leave him, but she thought he'd want to argue if she told him the truth, and so she simply nodded.

"Is it loaded?" she asked as he opened the door.

"Hell, yes."

Stupid question, she thought. Of course it was loaded. "Be careful." She moved into the driver's seat.

"Hand me the watch."

"You're taking it?" she asked.

"You think I'm going to leave it here with you and let Monk know exactly where you are? Give it to me."

"What are you going to do?"

"Go hunting."

CHAPTER 14

TIME HAD RUN out. Avery had just decided to go after John Paul when he opened her door. She never heard him coming. "Monk isn't close. He could be on his way, but he isn't here now."

"Are we driving down or walking?"

"I'll drive."

She scrambled back into the passenger seat, bumping her knee on the dashboard. He slid in and started the engine.

"How do you know he isn't hiding behind a tree or a bush somewhere?"

"Because I looked. There weren't any signs."

"You would have seen them?"

"Of course I would have seen them."

She was reassured by his arrogance. "Okay, then."

"There's a trailer behind the store about thirty yards to the south, and next to it is an old beat-up truck. No one was inside the trailer."

"You went in?"

He didn't answer. "There's a man and a woman inside the store. The woman's in the back office using the phone,

and the man's in front, working the counter. He keeps looking out the window like he's expecting company. While I
was there, a milk truck pulled out and another guy was unloading cases of beer. There are three or four customers."

He drove onto the road and continued down the slope.
His gun was in his lap.

"Do you see that man looking at us?" he asked. "He's on
the right by the door."

They watched a young couple herd their two little boys
out the front door, then saw the man inside slam the door.

"What the hell?" John Paul muttered when the man
turned the sign over in the window. "Closed, my ass."

He parked close to the side of the building so that she
would be protected when she stepped out. He turned the
motor off, slipped the keys into his jeans, and as he sprinted
around the hood of the car, she saw him tuck the gun into
his waistband.

They heard rap music blaring as a car pulled into the
parking lot. John Paul went to the corner of the building
and looked out front. Four young men in their late teens
piled out and stood laughing and guzzling their beers. On
top of the old Chevy were two kayaks roped to the roof.

John Paul motioned to Avery to stay put, retraced his
steps, and said, "I'm gonna check out the back again."

He let the man at the window watch him walk into the
woods, then circled around, swung over the railing at the
back door, and looked inside. The woman was hunched
over the desk, still talking on the phone.

Even though she was much too young, she reminded him
of Ma Kettle from the old movies he used to watch on television when he was a kid. Dressed in dirty overalls and a
muted plaid flannel shirt with the sleeves rolled up, she was
rattling off numbers into the phone as she turned the pages
of a Sharper Image catalog. She didn't notice him watching

her. He stepped back as the swinging door opened. A man poked his head in the room and braced the door with his hand to keep it from hitting him.

"Chrystal, we got us a problem," he said in a thick hillbilly accent. "There's two cars out front now. Four drunks just got out of one car. They're most likely stoppin' to stock up on more beer, I expect, but I'm most worried about that gal in the other car. She's gonna be knockin' on the front door any second now. I think maybe she spotted me peekin' out the window at her 'cause that car she was in is parked on the side of the building now. Think she's the one?"

"Can you hang on a minute, hon?" Chrystal said into the phone. She turned in the swivel chair and frowned at the dark-haired man. "Most likely she is, but I'm not finished with this catalog yet, and you promised me I could—"

He interrupted. "Maybe she ain't the one. Maybe she just needs to use the facilities. There was a big fella with her, but he went off into the woods to find his own facilities, I expect, like those four drunken boys. One of them is peein' on the petunias."

"Can't you see I'm busy here, Kenny? If that gal wants to use our facilities, you make her buy something first, and don't let her wander back here. I've still got a good ten pages to go."

"Don't know why you didn't think about doin' that earlier. Had to wait till the last minute, didn't you?"

John Paul went back to the entrance and was on the porch by the time Kenny unbolted the door.

Avery slipped around the corner of the building and ran to stand next to him. He pushed her behind him. He was being protective, and she didn't mind. She was so worried that they might not be in the right place, she couldn't think about anything else.

"Can't you read the sign? We're closed," the man said.

Avery stepped to John Paul's side. "It's an emergency," she blurted.

"Then you got to buy something first."

"Excuse me?"

"You heard me. You got to buy something, and after you pay, I'll let you use the facilities."

Kenny was snarling at her like an attack dog. He was a thoroughly unpleasant-looking man with blue-black dyed hair and bushy brown eyebrows. He wore a dark plaid shirt tucked into his faded black jeans. His gut hung down over his belt.

"Did you hear me?" he asked when she didn't respond. "I ain't gonna budge until you agree."

He changed his mind when John Paul stepped forward. If Kenny hadn't gotten out of the way, he was sure the big man would have walked right over him.

Up close, Kenny was much younger than John Paul had estimated. He couldn't have been more than thirty-five or forty years old. He was also agile. He warily kept his eye on John Paul and hurried around the counter as though the barrier would protect him.

Planting his big hands on the counter, he leaned toward Avery and smiled. One of his eyeteeth had a gold cap that gleamed in the sunlight streaming in through the dirty window. "All right, little lady. I'll tell you what I'm gonna do. Since you're so pretty, I'm gonna break the rules for you. You don't have to buy nothin'. Nothin' at all. The bathroom's right over there," he said, pointing to the door in the far corner.

She shook her head. "My name's Avery Delaney, and this is John Paul Renard. Has anyone come in here asking for us?"

"No," he answered, a little too quickly.

He was lying. All the telltale signs were there. He couldn't look her in the eye, and he was becoming more and more agitated by the second. Hostile too. He kept glancing up at John Paul as he shifted his weight from foot to foot.

The door crashed into the wall when it was thrown open. Avery and Kenny turned to see who was coming inside, but John Paul kept his attention on Kenny. He wasn't going to trust the bastard for as much as a second.

Three of the four boys sauntered in and staggered to a stop when they spotted Avery. She could hear the fourth boy. He was leaning over the porch railing throwing up.

"Hi there," one of them called out. Another tried to whistle, but he couldn't get his lips to work. Spit sprayed out of his mouth instead.

Two of the boys were obviously brothers, for they looked alike and sported identical eagle tattoos on their forearms. The oldest-looking one of the group had a scraggly goatee and a pierced eyebrow with a silver ring.

"The store's closed," Kenny shouted.

"No, it ain't," Goatee said. "You let *them* in," he added, pointing to Avery and John Paul. "We only want some beer."

"Yeah, beer," one of the brothers parroted.

They staggered toward the cooler against the back wall. One of them tripped into a display of cans and sent them careening everywhere. Goatee thought that was hilarious.

Kenny wasn't amused. He looked as if he wanted to kill someone. "You pick up every damned one of them cans and put them back like I had them. You hear me?"

A brother snickered while Goatee gave Kenny the finger.

"Get the hell out of my store," Kenny bellowed. He turned his wrath on Avery next. "If you ain't gonna use my facilities, and you ain't gonna buy nothin', then maybe you folks ought to leave."

"What about phone calls?" she asked, sounding as desperate as she was feeling. "Have you gotten any calls for me?"

"No."

One of the brothers was standing about three feet away from Avery and was fixated on her as he swayed on his feet. His stare was unnerving.

"Stop staring at me."

He grinned stupidly at her, then lunged with both arms outstretched with the obvious intent of hugging her.

John Paul was about to pull Avery into his side, but she was already moving. She lashed out at the drunk with a kick that was quick and effortless. Her foot struck him square in the stomach and sent him flying into the wall. He hit with a loud thud, slid down, and landed on his butt.

She pointed a finger at him. "You stay there."

And still the stupid grin remained on the drunk's face. He was too far gone to feel any pain.

She turned her attention to Kenny again. "May I use your phone?" Out of the corner of her eye she spotted Goatee and the other brother coming around the corner. Each of them had two six-packs of beer and a bag of ice. She didn't mince words. "Over there, both of you. Sit down next to your friend and be quiet until I'm finished."

Goatee shook his head. "You can't tell me what to do, sweet cakes."

"We don't have a phone," Kenny muttered at the very same time.

"Sure you do," John Paul asserted as he stepped toward Kenny.

"What happened, Mark?" the other brother asked.

Goatee strode forward, thinking he could elbow his way between Avery and John Paul.

"My turn," John Paul drawled a scant second before he sent Goatee sailing headfirst into the wall. He dropped the beer and the ice on top of Mark, then fell down next to him.

They didn't have to tell the third drunk to join his friends. He staggered over, put the beer down, and sat. Leaning back, he opened one can and took a long swallow.

Kenny realized John Paul was looking at the phone on the counter. "What I meant to say is that we got a phone. Of course we do, but it ain't workin'. Line's down and it takes weeks and weeks to get a repairman to come all this way. In case you haven't noticed, we're sittin' out in the middle of nowhere." He was talking so fast the words were tripping over each other.

Kenny could see John Paul wasn't buying it, and so he turned to Avery. The phony smile was back. "Your mister have a problem?" As he continued to smile at Avery, he slowly reached underneath the counter.

He looked down and too late realized he never should have taken his eyes off John Paul. He heard a click and jerked up to find the barrel of John Paul's gun pointed at his forehead.

"Now hold on. No need for that," Kenny stammered.

"John Paul, we need this man's cooperation," Avery said.

"And this is how we get it," he replied. "Kenny, turn around and put your hands on the wall behind you. Avery, get his gun from under the counter."

She walked around the counter and immediately spotted the Magnum on the shelf underneath. She slowly picked it up and then checked it. The weapon was loaded and ready. She engaged the safety, noticed a box of cartridges, and grabbed that too. She put both in a plastic sack with a picture of a squirrel on it.

"What are you doing with a Magnum? Do you have a permit?" she asked Kenny.

"That's none of your damn, nosy business."

The good-old-boy façade was gone now. True colors were finally spewing out. Kenny's face twisted with rage as he snarled, "I can refuse service to anybody I want to, and if I want to keep a loaded gun on the premises, then that's what I'm gonna do. Can I turn around now? I'm getting a crick in my neck. You can use the phone. I was just . . . worried you was gonna make a long-distance call, and my cousin George, he's the man who owns this place, well, he would see the bill and then he'd say to me, 'Kenny, you're gonna pay for this.'"

"Where is George?" Avery asked.

"He got hisself attacked by an old brown bear. He didn't know she was there until he saw one of her cubs," Kenny said. "Can I turn around now and put my hands down? You can see I'm cooperatin' and you got hold of my gun."

"Yeah, sure," John Paul said.

Avery was heading for the phone when, out of the corner of her eye, she saw a lady's billfold sticking out between two sales slips in the trash can next to the cash register. She leaned down to pick it up. Then she caught her breath. It was a new, black Prada billfold. Carrie owned everything Prada made.

Kenny was watching John Paul. "If you're gonna rob me, you might as well know I don't have much cash. Maybe two one-hundred-dollar bills and forty some in change."

"Where'd you get the hundred-dollar bills?" John Paul asked.

"A customer."

"We didn't come here to rob you," Avery said. She opened the billfold, saw that it was empty, and held it up for John Paul to see. "I think this belongs to my aunt."

Kenny grabbed her from behind. He wrapped his big arms around her in a bear hug and lifted her up so he could use her as a shield. His arms were like bands of steel, but his chest was soft, almost mushy.

"Let go of me," she ordered. "I don't have time for this."

Kenny was trying to duck down behind her so John Paul couldn't get a clear shot. "Not till your mister puts that gun down."

John Paul was surprised Avery wasn't frightened. If anything, he thought she looked put out. "That's not gonna happen," he said. "Avery, you'll have to change your clothes."

That remark got her full attention. She stopped squirming and asked, "Why?"

"Because I'm gonna get blood all over you when I blow this mother—"

"No," she said. "Kenny, I know this billfold belongs to my aunt, and I don't care that you took the money. But you're going to have to tell me where you got it. Now let go of me."

"No way," he snarled close to her ear and tightened his hold.

His fingers were interlocked around her waist. She took hold of one of his little fingers and jerked it back hard. At the same instant, she lowered her chin, then slammed the back of her head into his face. She heard a crunch as he gasped in pain and let go.

"Ouch," she whispered. Damn it, that hurt. She stepped away from Kenny and rubbed the back of her head as she walked over to John Paul. Not as simple as it looked in the movies, she thought. Lesson learned.

She noticed the incredulous look on John Paul's face. "What?" she asked.

His smile was slow and easy. "Not bad."

She rolled her eyes in exasperation and looked at Kenny, who was leaning into the counter. "I need to know where you got that billfold."

"It belonged to my wife, Chrystal. She got tired of it and tossed it in the trash."

"Stop lying. This is a matter of life or death," she said, her voice hostile now. "I really don't care if you took any money out of the billfold," she repeated. "But I need to know where you got it."

"I just told you . . ."

He wasn't going to admit anthing. Avery's initial panic had dissipated as soon as she'd spotted the billfold because now she knew she was in the right place. The tightness was still in her chest, however, and she was becoming infuriated over the man's uncooperative attitude.

Kenny's nose was bleeding. He held a Kleenex against his nostril and squinted at her. "I'm gonna sue you, bitch. That's what I'm gonna do."

"John Paul, I think you're going to have to shoot him after all," she said.

Kenny didn't seem worried until John Paul asked Avery, "How about the kneecap?"

Fortunately, Kenny had become a true believer. "Okay, okay," he said. "When we opened up this morning, me and Chrystal found a package with her name on it." He pointed to Avery. "It was just sittin' there on the counter, so Chrystal decided to have a look inside."

"And?" Avery prodded.

"And it was just a red scarf. It had a perfume smell to it Chrystal didn't care for, so she stuffed it back in the envelope and tossed it in the trash."

"How did you get the billfold?" she asked.

"I was gettin' to that," he said, resentment brimming in his words. "A woman came in just a little bit ago. She held up a brand-new hundred-dollar bill in exchange for that package with the scarf, and we took it, of course. Then she grabbed another manila envelope from our shelf. Just helped herself to it. She turned around so we wouldn't see what she was doin' and put that billfold inside. After she sealed it, she wrote your name on it and told us she'd give us another hundred if we'd promise to tell you that she was gonna call and for you to stay here until she did."

"But you opened the envelope as soon as she left?" John Paul asked.

"No, not that second. It nagged at Chrystal, though. She just had to have herself a peek inside, and when she saw the billfold filled with money, she helped herself. Anybody would've done the same thing."

Avery didn't waste time arguing ethics with him. "What exactly did the woman with the hundred-dollar bills say?"

"I already told you what she said."

"Tell her again," John Paul ordered.

"She's gonna call you. That's what she said. She told me she knew just about the time you folks would be coming into the store and said you was supposed to wait until she called."

"But you weren't going to tell us any of that, were you?" John Paul said. "You were going to send us on our way and never mention the billfold or the woman."

Kenny didn't answer. He shrugged and then said, "There wasn't much money in the wallet. Just a bunch of twenty-dollar bills."

"Hardly worth getting your nose broken?" John Paul said.

"Look, I should have told you, and now I'm sorry I didn't," Kenny said. "When my wife gets off the phone, I'm sure that lady will call. You're just gonna have to wait."

"Where is your wife?" Avery asked.

John Paul answered. "In the back office."

He grabbed her arm when she started in that direction. "Do you know how to use a gun?"

She pulled away from him and hurried to the back of the store. "I'm not going to shoot anyone, John Paul."

"Be careful," he ordered.

She took the warning to heart. When she reached the swinging door, she slowly pushed it open and looked inside. A woman was sitting with her back to the door. She was bent over with the receiver to her ear as Avery quietly walked forward. She heard the woman say, "No, I want five of them. That's right. Five. Now the last item is number A3491. The silver stereo with all them CD holders. I want eight of them. No, make it ten. That's it, hon. Are you ready for my credit card number? What? Oh, my name's Salvetti. Carolyn Salvetti. I'll be using my American Express card to pay for all this merchandise, but I want them shipped to my Arkansas home."

Avery was furious. She came up behind the woman and snatched the phone from her hand. Chrystal lurched out of her chair, sending it crashing into the wall. "Who do you . . ." she sputtered.

Keeping her eye on Chrystal, Avery spoke into the phone. "Cancel the order. She's using a stolen credit card."

"No," Chrystal shouted as Avery hung up the phone. "You got no right to come barging in here. No right at all. This is my private office. Now give me that phone back."

"You and Kenny are going to jail."

"Hold on there a minute. We didn't do nothin' wrong."

Chrystal's eyes were set a little too close together and her moon-shaped face was twisted in anger. Not pretty, Avery thought as she watched her step forward threateningly. Her brown eyes darted back and forth like a cornered rat's as she considered her options. "There's no reason to call the police."

The woman towered over Avery and outweighed her by a good sixty pounds. When a sudden gleam came into her eyes, Avery knew what she was thinking, that her size gave her the advantage.

"Don't even think about it," Avery said.

"This is private property," Chrystal half shouted. And then she lunged.

Avery didn't need to defend herself. She simply stepped to the left and watched as the large woman fell on top of the desk. Her precious catalog ripped open and flew to the floor.

What a klutz. "Behave yourself," Avery scolded like a teacher disciplining a child with a harsh warning. "Now get up and go into the store. Move it," she shouted when Chrystal didn't move.

Carrie's driver's license and all of her credit cards were on the desk, except the American Express card. She saw Chrystal slip the card into her pocket. "You just don't give up, do you? Give me the damn card."

Chrystal threw it at her. Avery caught it in midair and then nodded toward the swinging door again.

Chrystal shoved the door open and hurried ahead. She tried to push the door back in Avery's face, but Avery used her foot to block it.

"Bitch," Chrystal growled. Then she saw Kenny and took her wrath out on him. "I told you we'd get into trouble, but you wouldn't listen to me."

John Paul slipped his gun into the back of his jeans and then looked at Avery, waiting for an explanation. She took a step closer to him as she said, "Chrystal was doing a little early Christmas shopping with my aunt's American Express card."

"Aren't they a pair?"

"Yet another good reason I'm never going to get married," she said.

"I don't see any need to get the police involved," Chrystal muttered.

"Who said anything about the police, Chrystal?" Kenny demanded. "Why'd you have to go and bring them into this?"

"I didn't, you old goat. Blondie did," she added, pointing at Avery. "And all this is your fault, Kenny. If anyone's gonna go back to jail, it's gonna be you. I already got one strike against me. Didn't I tell you you shouldn't let me open that package? Didn't I?" she screeched like an irate hen. "You made me do it."

"Shut your trap," Kenny told her.

Chrystal finally noticed her husband's condition. He was sitting on the counter, swinging his legs back and forth while he held a torn Kleenex to his nose. She gave John Paul the once-over too. "Who's he?" she demanded. "And why are you pickin' at your nose?"

"I ain't pickin' nothin'. That gal behind you broke my fuckin' nose. I'm gonna get me a lawyer and sue her."

"From jail?" Chrystal bellowed. "You moron. You aren't gonna sue nobody."

John Paul had about had it with the happy couple. He went to the front door and stood to the side looking out. The teenager who had been throwing up was now curled up on the porch sound asleep.

"Stop arguing," Avery demanded. She was a little surprised that Kenny and Chrystal actually obeyed her.

"No reason to scream at us, missy. You can see we're cooperatin'," Chrystal said.

"Fine. You're cooperating. Where's the envelope?"

"You mean the one the billfold was in?" Chrystal asked.

"Yes."

"I threw it in the trash by the facilities," she said. "There was just the billfold, but I'll get it for you so you can see for yourself."

She took her sweet time crossing the store and returned a minute later with the yellow envelope. Thrusting it at Avery, she said, "See. It's empty."

Kenny's nose had stopped bleeding, and he tossed the Kleenex toward the wastebasket behind him but missed. "I told you everything that gal said to me, but she was pretty chatty with Chrystal."

"That's right. She sure was chatty. She told me you folks were goin' on a treasure hunt. Kinda old to be playin' games like that, aren't ya?"

Avery was close to pulling her hair out in frustration. These people were driving her crazy. "When she came in, did you see her car? Was there anyone waiting?"

"Had a nice new Mercedes," Kenny said. "But there wasn't nobody inside it. Just the gal."

"Did she tell you where she was sending us?"

Her obvious anxiety gave Chrystal a surge of power. She said snidely, "Depends."

"Depends on what?" Avery asked.

Chrystal rubbed her fingers together, the universal sign for money. Avery didn't have the patience to negotiate.

"The woman left instructions too, but Kenny and me aren't sayin' another word until you make it worth our while."

"Okay, John Paul. We're back to doing it your way. You may shoot one of them. That should get the other one talking."

He liked the way she thought. The gun was out, the safety off less than two seconds later.

"Got a preference?" he asked.

Chrystal put her hands up. "Hold on there. No need for violence. Kenny and me is peace-lovin' folks, aren't we, Kenny? We'll tell you what you want to know. The woman said a gal would be comin' in. Said the gal's name was Avery." Turning to her, she asked, "You're her, aren't ya? You got to be her."

"Yes. What else did she say?"

"That she'd be callin' and that you'd be leavin' in a hurry, but she was sure wrong about that, wasn't she? I mean, you're still here."

Kenny snorted. "They can't be leavin' in a hurry until after she calls, you twit."

"Avery, I really want to shoot these people. Put them out of their misery," John Paul said.

She understood how he felt. "Put the gun away, John Paul."

The second he lowered the gun, Chrystal cheered up and managed a smile. "Kenny, they'll need supplies for where they're headed. You carry what they want out to their car while I total it up in my head." Turning to Avery she asked, "You got cash on you, don't you?"

"We don't need supplies," she said.

"You want directions to where she's sendin' you?"

Avery understood. In other words, buy the damn supplies. "Yes," she answered.

"Don't you be givin' them no discounts, Chrystal. And no credit cards. These folks ain't gonna live long enough for the receipt to go through."

Chrystal nodded. "The woman's sending you to a fiver."

What in God's name were they talking about? Then Kenny said, "Don't know how you think you're gonna do the river. Since all the rain we've been having, only fools would try to raft it. You're gonna drown before you make it over the first rapids." The possibility so tickled him he chuckled. "Don't matter how experienced you are."

"That's right, hon," Chrystal said. "You're gonna get yourself drowned, all right. Now, that gal said you'd see a sign with writing on it and you'd find what you're lookin' for right by it."

"Did she tell you what's on the sign?"

"Coward's Crossing. All the locals use that name too, for that little area where you can look down at the river if you're too afraid to go in. Years ago, there used to be a rope bridge, which is why they called it a crossing."

"You'll have to hike to get there," Kenny said. "I know the lay of the land 'cause I've been comin' up here ever since I was a boy, and there ain't no path up there."

Chrystal didn't agree and began to argue with her husband.

Avery reached for the phone and then stopped. One quick call to Margo, she thought, to tell her where she was and what was going on. Should she chance it?

Kenny finally won the shouting match, and while Chrystal sulked, he gave Avery detailed instructions on getting to Coward's Crossing. She pulled the map from her pocket and asked Kenny to mark the area.

John Paul had two plastic sacks full of bottled water and food. He grabbed two more protein bars, shoved them into the smaller sack, and headed to the car. Kenny hopped off the counter to chase after him just to make sure he wasn't going to try to drive away without paying.

Avery grabbed a piece of paper and wrote down Margo's number. "Chrystal, I want you to drive to another phone and call this number. Tell whoever answers that I was here and where I'm headed. There's a lot of money in it if you make the call," she promised. "But don't use this phone."

"How much money?"

"Five thousand dollars." She said the first figure that popped into her head. "And when we capture the man we're after, there will be twice that amount, and you'll get all of it."

"How much exactly?"

"Ten thousand." The lies were getting easier.

Chrystal looked suspicious. "How do I know you aren't gonna help yourself to that money?"

"Because I'm FBI," she said. "My ID is in the car. Would you like me to go get it?"

"I should have guessed it," she snorted. "You bein' so bossy and all. You don't have to show me your badge. I believe you. You got that FBI look about you, and that fancy karate move you did on me in the office got my suspicions up. I should have paid attention to the warnin' bells goin' off in my head."

What fancy move was she prattling about? All Avery remembered doing was stepping out of the woman's way.

"That's very astute of you," she said dryly.

"Now, tell me again about that money. Would it be fifteen thousand in all?"

"Sure."

Chrystal squinted at Avery. "And you're saying all I got to do is make that call?"

"Yes, and will you—"

Chrystal cut her off. She'd glanced at the number on the paper and blurted, "Wait a minute. This here is a long-distance call. Can I reverse the charges?"

"Yes."

"Okay, I'll do it, but I got to tell you, I still don't get it. You could use the phone right there," she said, pointing to the counter. "What's the catch?"

She didn't waste time telling Chrystal she couldn't take

the chance the line might be tapped. "You just can't use this phone. Wait about twenty minutes, then get in your pickup and drive to the nearest phone."

"Will you pay for the gas?"

Avery felt like screaming. "Yes."

John Paul had just walked back inside the store when the phone rang. Avery flinched at the sound.

"That's probably her," Chrystal said. "We haven't gotten a single call since we reopened the store this morning, so that's got to be her. Want me to answer it?"

Avery grabbed the phone and answered on the second ring.

"You were late," the caller said.

"No, we weren't. We were right on time. The woman you left the package with was using the phone when we arrived."

"Yes, she was."

Avery then knew she had been monitoring the line. Thank God she hadn't tried to call Margo.

"Did you get the directions to where you're going?"

"Yes. I want to talk to Carrie."

"No, that isn't possible."

"Then how do I know she's still alive?"

"Carrie is alive . . . for now anyway. It's up to you to keep her and her friends that way, isn't it?"

"Why are you doing this?"

"No more questions," she hissed. "Or I'll hang up the phone right now. Do you understand me?"

"Yes."

"You're on a lovely treasure hunt, and you're winning points as you move along. The prize is Carrie. You do want to see her again, don't you?"

"Yes."

"That's good." She laughed. "You're so eager to please. You'd better hurry, Avery."

"How long—"

"Hurry now."

The woman disconnected the call. Avery's heart was pounding. She put the phone down as Chrystal asked, "Was it her?"

"Yes," she answered. "Chrystal, describe her to me."

"You mean you want to know what she looked like?"

"Yes."

"She was older than you, but not as old as me, and not as heavy as me. Kenny?" she shouted. "How old would you say that woman was?"

Kenny walked inside. He scratched his stubbly jaw while he considered his answer. "I don't know. Never could judge a person's age real good. She sure was a looker, though."

Chrystal nodded. "Had yellow-colored hair, and it's kind of funny really, you askin' me what she looked like."

"Why?" Avery asked.

"Well . . . 'cause . . ." Chrystal shrugged. "She kinda looked like you."

CHAPTER 15

CHRYSTAL TOLD KENNY they would receive a big reward if he drove to town and made a call for Avery. Kenny didn't believe his wife, and he didn't want to do it. Avery thought it might be because his nose had started bleeding again.

Unlike Avery, John Paul wasn't interested in trying to coax them into cooperating, because he understood how their twisted pea-sized brains worked. He had had enough of the Bonnie-and-Clod pair. He shoved Kenny into the wall and calmly told him that he would hunt him down and skin him alive if he didn't do what Avery asked. Simple as that. Kenny believed him, and so did Chrystal. The look in John Paul's eyes indicated he wasn't the type of man to make idle threats.

Chrystal jumped back when John Paul walked past. She knocked the phone off the counter and quickly picked it up. Instinctively putting the receiver to her ear to make sure no one else was on the line, she hung up and said to Kenny, "The phone isn't workin'."

"Are you sayin' the line's dead?" Kenny gasped the question, still trying to recover his breath.

"Didn't I just say it was broke?"

"She did it," Kenny decided, glaring at Avery. "She must have broke it after she finished talkin' to that woman and hung up. You saw her slam it down, didn't you, Chrystal? You're gonna have to pay for repairs," he told Avery.

Avery picked up the phone to see if Chrystal was telling the truth. The line was dead. That was quick, she thought. They must have been ready.

John Paul stood by the door waiting to get Avery's attention. "Avery . . ."

"Just a minute." She walked over to the teenagers sprawled out on the floor. Two of them were curled up like cats, sound asleep, but the droopy-eyed boy named Mark was still sitting upright and watching her every move with the stupid grin still plastered on his freckled face.

"Who's the driver?"

"Huh?"

She nudged his foot. "Who's driving the car?"

"Me."

"Give me the car keys."

The grin didn't falter. "I don't have to," he slurred even as he dug into his pocket and pulled out his key ring. He dangled the keys in front of his face. Then he giggled.

She snatched the keys out of his hand and tossed them on the counter. "Chrystal, you make sure those boys don't get into that car. You understand?"

"I'm not gonna be a baby-sitter. You expect me to stand here and watch them?"

"Make them sleep outside, but don't give them the keys." She turned to leave, but John Paul raised his hand for her to stop.

"More customers," he said. He glanced out the window and watched two older women, dressed in hiking clothes, get out of a Ford. He pushed Avery's hand away from the doorknob. "You're not going with me."

"Oh, yes, I am," she insisted.

"Listen to me," he ordered. "You go back to town with those women and get to a police station. Keep the gun just in case."

"While you go ahead to Coward's Crossing?"

"Yes. If I can get there quick, I might be able to find a good spot to ambush him."

She shook her head. "If you kill him, we won't be able to find Carrie and the others."

"The woman knows where they are."

"She'll disappear, and you know it. It's too risky. Besides, if Monk or the woman finds out I'm not with you—"

"They won't know."

"You have to take me with you."

"No. It's too dangerous for you, and you'll slow me down."

"Then I'm going to follow you. Kenny gave both of us the directions. I can find Coward's Crossing. I'll take the teenagers' car. Simple as that, John Paul." She poked him in his chest. "You need me to get him. Now get out of my way."

He didn't want to waste any more time arguing. He decided he'd have to find a place to dump her on the way. Someplace safe. Yeah, that's what he would do.

He opened the door. "You stay close," he whispered as he stepped back so the gray-haired women could come inside.

The ladies walked right past the teenagers and didn't seem to notice them when they headed for the facilities, as Kenny so quaintly called the bathroom.

Avery turned back to Chrystal, who, at this point, was the more agreeable of the two. "How long do you think it will take to get to Coward's Crossing?"

"You aren't gonna make it before nightfall," Chrystal answered. "What with all the rain, those little roads got all washed out."

John Paul was opening the door but paused when Kenny shouted, "Hey, wait a minute. You ain't gonna take my gun, are you? I've got to have something for protection, being out here with just the missus."

"Let it go, Kenny," Chrystal said. "George never got a permit for that thing."

Kenny's face turned red. "Why'd you have to open your big mouth and bring that up?"

"She would have wanted to see it," Chrystal argued. "They always do."

"Who's 'they'?"

"FBI." She pronounced each letter as though it were a profanity.

"What?" Kenny screeched. "You're saying that gal's FBI?" His eyes bulged at the news.

Mark groaned. "Ah, man, we're gonna get busted."

Ignoring the drunk, John Paul closed the door in Avery's face and asked softly, "You're an FBI agent?"

Uh-oh. One quick glance at his expression, and she inwardly cringed. He looked so offended that she didn't think it would be a good idea to explain it all to him now. Maybe later, she thought, when he was asleep.

"Answer me," he demanded. "Are you an FBI agent?"

He wasn't going to budge until she responded. She swallowed, then whispered, "Sort of."

Then Chrystal, who, Avery decided, really did have a big mouth, said, "She told me she left her ID in the car, but she'd go get it if I wanted to see it."

"I'm leaving," Avery announced. She used every ounce of strength she possessed to push John Paul out of her way so she could get out the door.

He didn't move an inch. "We'll be talking about this later."

She waited until he stepped back, then brushed past him. Childishly wanting to have the last word, she muttered, "No, we won't."

The SUV fantailed out of the lot onto the dirt road when John Paul floored it, the tires spitting up pebbles and dirt clumps. He headed toward the river and was driving like a lunatic.

"Slow down," she ordered.

He eased up on the pedal while Avery went over the directions. "I should have asked Chrystal to give me a guess as to how many miles Coward's Crossing was from the store."

"We're going to be hiking," he said.

"I'll keep up with whatever pace you set."

"We'll see. Tell me, what did the woman on the phone say?"

She repeated the conversation and added, "I demanded to talk to Carrie, but she said that wasn't possible."

He shook his head. "And yet you *still* believe your aunt's alive?"

"Yes, I do. I think the woman wants to keep Carrie around . . . for a little longer anyway." She didn't have a valid reason for why she felt that way. Maybe it was just desperate hope on her part. "You know what I don't understand?"

"What?"

"Why are they going to so much trouble if they want to kill me? Why make it complicated? There was ample opportunity to ambush me on the way to the spa, before you were even involved. It would have been so much simpler." She slapped her forehead. "Of course. They didn't know I was going to drive to the spa. When I missed my flight, they had to improvise. You were another complication. You were hanging around the spa asking questions. Now it makes sense."

She shook her head. She must be tired. It took so long for her to figure it out. She closed her eyes for a moment and thought about the phone call again.

"The woman . . . she's having fun."

"I'm sorry?"

"I could hear it in her voice. She was excited, even when she was hissing at me and calling me stupid. She doesn't want this to be over too soon. She wants to drag it out." She thought it over for a long minute and then said, "She likes giving orders, and as long as we play her little game, or treasure hunt, as she called it, she might prolong it even more."

He drove as fast as the dirt roads would allow while she gave him directions. Avery kept replaying the conversation in her mind, analyzing what little data she had. It was so frustrating.

John Paul interrupted her. "Okay, Avery. It's later."

"I'm sorry?"

"I said it's later, and we're going to talk about it now. Why the hell didn't you tell me you were an FBI agent?"

"You made it very apparent you didn't particularly like the Bureau."

"Yeah? When did I do that?"

"When we were in the manager's office at Utopia, you called your friend Noah. I heard you tell him to bring in the troops."

"And?"

"And then you told me they'd mess up the investigation. When I pressed you on your attitude, you became quite hostile. Besides . . ." She could feel herself blushing. "I'm not really an agent, not yet anyway."

He slowed the car. "Yeah? Then why are you telling people you are?" He shook his head and said, "Who in his right mind would want to impersonate an FBI agent?"

Avery hated being put on the defensive. God, he was such an obstinate, opinionated jerk. "I don't usually tell people I'm an agent. I just told Chrystal, in hopes of gaining her cooperation. Unlike you," she added, "I don't use coercion and brute force to get what I want."

John Paul ignored the criticism of his tactics. Why fix what wasn't broken? Brute force had always worked. "I do what I'm good at doing. That's my motto."

"Watch out," she warned as he turned the corner and nearly ran into a deer. John Paul hit the brakes and swerved off the road, narrowly avoiding the animal. The car rocked and bounced but held the ground.

It was too dangerous to try to maintain a high speed. He slowed the car and said, "Chrystal's right. We aren't going to make it before nightfall."

"Think positive."

"Why?" He sounded genuinely perplexed.

"Maybe we'll get a decent road soon," she said.

They drove around another sharp curve. Down below to the west was a road that looked well traveled. He decided to go for it.

"Hang on," he said as they started down the hill. The slope was steep, and he had to be mindful of jagged rocks.

Avery flattened her hands against the seat as they bounced along.

"So," he said, "were you lying about having a badge?"

"I have credentials in my backpack."

"But you're not an agent?"

"No."

"Then what the hell are you doing with credentials?"

"I do work for the Bureau. I'm just not a field agent."

"That's good."

"Why? Because you hate the Bureau?"

"No, because you're not any good at it."

"How would you know what I'm good at?" she said. Lord, he was irritating. Every time he opened his mouth, he said something that rubbed her the wrong way. No man had ever been able to get under her skin the way John Paul did.

"You don't have the instincts," he said. "And before you get all hot and bothered and argue, answer a question for me, and be honest."

She folded her arms and frowned at him. "What?"

"Did you anticipate that Kenny might have a loaded weapon under that counter? Did you even for a split second consider the possibility?"

"No."

"There you go."

"I haven't been trained to be a field agent. I didn't go through the academy."

"That's no excuse. You've either got it, or you don't. You've got some good moves," he added. "The way you kick-boxed that kid was impressive. But you'd still make a lousy field agent."

She refused to comment on his assessment.

"What exactly do you do for the Bureau?" he asked.

John Paul could see the blush was coming back. She was either embarrassed or so mad at him her face was turning a fire red. She sure was pretty. Ah, hell, where had that come from? He had no business thinking about such things, especially now that he knew she represented everything he detested.

"I type," she said. She heard how defensive she sounded

and quickly added, "There isn't anything wrong with being a typist."

"I didn't say there was."

"I'm part of a very important team."

"Ah, jeez."

"What?"

"You bought it all, didn't you? A team player. You're probably a damn liberal too, aren't you?"

"As a matter of fact I am," she said. "And I'm certainly not ashamed of being a typist . . . it's an honorable job, after all."

"Okay."

"Quit being so condescending. I wasn't hired to be a typist, but that's what I pretty much do anyway, all day, every day. I transfer information into the database. Now, can we let the matter drop?"

"Yeah, okay," he said.

He seemed preoccupied now. "What are you thinking?" she asked.

"This is a good road. Maybe we will get close to Coward's Crossing before it gets dark. We'll hike a couple of miles, find a secluded spot for you to hide, and then I can—"

That was as far as she'd let him get. "Not gonna happen," she said. "I'll tell you what. You drop me off, find another good road, and with any luck, you can make it back to Aspen before dark."

"And why would I want to drive back to Aspen?"

"I've been thinking . . ."

"Uh-oh."

She ignored the insult. "I think you should get out while you still can. You can tell the FBI where I'm going."

He blinked. "You're kidding. Right?"

She began to fold and unfold her hands. "No, I'm serious. What can they do if you leave? Nothing," she said, answering her own question. "Frankly, you don't need to be involved. You said it yourself. They want me, not you. Besides, you called Noah, and he's FBI. I'm sure he's alerted the local team, and they're most certainly on their way. When you get to a phone, you can call him again, and tell him exactly where I'm headed."

"I've got an opportunity to get Monk, and you think I'm gonna . . ." He was so angry he was sputtering. He shook his head. "Let me get this straight. You really believe I'll drop you off in the middle of nowhere and take off?"

"Wasn't that your plan?"

"Hell, no," he argued. "I was going to find a safe place for you to hide until I got back, someplace Monk would never find you."

"In other words, you'll drop me off in the middle of nowhere and take off." She didn't give him time to think about it. "You're not dropping me off anywhere, unless you plan to go back to Aspen."

"You're nuts, you know that? You're just plain nuts."

"I gather that's a no?"

He didn't respond to her sarcasm.

She brushed her hair away from her face with her fingers and laid her hands on top of her head. "I wish we could get out of this car. I need a quiet place to think."

"You can't think in a car?"

She knew he wouldn't understand. When she was in her cubicle at work, she felt the same way she felt when she was doing yoga. She'd perfected the technique of clearing her mind and then slowly entering data one clue at a time while her hands worked the keyboard. No, he couldn't possibly understand, and she couldn't explain.

"So who looks like you?"

"I'm sorry. What did you ask?"

"Back at the store," he said. "Chrystal said the woman looked like you. So I've gotta ask if you happen to have any crazy relatives trying to kill you."

"No. There's only my aunt Carrie and her husband, Tony. No other relatives."

"Parents dead?"

She turned in her seat and stared at his profile when she answered. "I don't know who my father was. I don't think the woman who had me knew who he was either," she said.

She watched him closely to see if she had shocked him. His expression didn't change.

"She died in a car crash quite a few years ago. There isn't anyone else."

"Chrystal said—"

"I heard what she said, John Paul. Do you know how many women her description fits?"

He glanced at her and asked, "So is it real?"

"Excuse me?"

"Your hair. Is it real?"

She blinked. "Are you asking me if I wear a wig?"

"No, I'm asking about the color. Are you a real blonde, or did you get that from a bottle?"

"Why do you care about the color of my hair?"

"I don't care," he said, growing irritated now. "But the woman looked like you, so I gotta wonder if you—"

"No, I don't color my hair."

He was surprised and didn't hide his reaction. "Yeah? What about your eyes?"

"What about them?"

"Colored contacts?"

She shook her head. "No."

"No kidding."

"Are you deliberately trying to be a jerk?"

"Look, I'm just trying to put it together, okay? Kenny said the woman was beautiful. A real knockout."

"And?" she pressed.

He shrugged. "Have you looked at yourself lately? You've got to know . . ."

"Know what?" she pressed when he didn't continue.

He frowned at her. "Hell, woman. You're pretty, damn it."

It was the most hostile, backhanded compliment she'd ever received, and the odd thing was, it didn't upset her. For the first time ever, she didn't feel the need to launch into her favorite lecture about how appearances weren't the least bit important.

She forced herself to consider the problem at hand. "The data isn't sufficient to form a conclusion."

"Jeez, you sound like a computer. A lot of things aren't adding up."

She agreed with a nod. Her stomach was hurting. She felt as though she had a hot coal lodged in her esophagus. She picked up her backpack, found her antacid, a bottle of water, and two energy bars. She opened the bottle, popped the pills, and swallowed. Then she handed the bottle to John Paul and opened one of the energy bars for him.

"Thanks," he said after he took a long swallow of the water. He took a bite of the bar and washed it down with another gulp. "It tastes like cardboard."

"You're welcome."

His smile lasted for half a second, but she still saw it and reacted. She surprised herself. She couldn't stand the man an hour ago, but now she didn't think he was so awful. He had a beautiful profile . . . and was sexy as hell. No reason for her to pretend she didn't notice, even though she wasn't going to do anything about it.

He was also protective. The way he tried to boss her

around in the store when she went running to the back office. He acted . . . worried. Worried about her safety. Nice,
she thought. He wasn't such a cold duck after all.

"It's gonna rain," he remarked.

"Rain will slow us down."

"It's still coming. The sun's going to be setting soon," he
said. "I'm going to plant the watch about a mile or two
from here. Then we'll go on for as long as we can."

He parked the car and picked up the watch. "What'd you
do with that gun we took?"

"It's in the sack on the floor."

"Get it out and keep it on your lap. Have you done any
target practice?"

"No."

He gave her a disgruntled sigh. "Keep the safety on." He
got the gun for her. "I won't be long."

He disappeared before she could tell him to be careful. A
fine drizzle began to fall, covering the windshield. It seemed
an hour had passed before he came sprinting down the hill
toward the car. When he opened the door, a blast of cold air
filled the interior.

The second he turned the motor on, she flipped on the
heater. "Where did you leave the watch?"

"I hooked it to a tree branch by a crossroad to the west.
If he's tracking us now, I'm hoping he'll think we took the
other road."

He drove on, thanking God he had a four-wheel drive.
He zigzagged up the side of the mountain, slowly weaving
in and out of the trees. When the terrain became too dense
to go any farther, he maneuvered the car into a cluster of
thick pines, turned it around, and then backed in until he
was assured the car couldn't be seen from the road below.

Night rushed in on them, closing them in together. The

drizzle had turned into rain. A booming clap of thunder sounded. She flinched.

"You've got a weapon just in case, food and water."

"What do you mean I've got food and water? You think you're going to leave me here?"

He reached for the door.

CHAPTER 16

By the time Carrie plopped down on the living room sofa, she felt doomed. Jilly and Monk had thought of every possible way out. Oh, yes, they'd wired every window . . . except, perhaps, one. She looked up at the skylight that loomed over the spiral staircase. The bubbled rectangle was over thirty feet above them. She shook her head. Even if they stacked table upon table upon wardrobes, they still wouldn't be able to hack their way through.

Anne had prepared a dinner from the contents of the pantry, and the three women ate in dejected silence. The sun had gone down and the house was dimly lit by the candles Anne had found. None of them wanted to turn on the lights, fearing Jilly and Monk were watching, and there weren't any drapes to cover the massive windows. Sara had brought up the possibility that Monk had hooked up a video camera to observe them. That so freaked out Carrie, she once again scoured the house, this time looking for a camera.

Anne was reclining on the sofa, and Sara sat in an easy chair waiting for her when she came back downstairs.

"I couldn't find anything," Carrie said. "I looked everywhere. I even searched the light sockets, the ones I could reach," she added. "I don't think anyone's watching us."

"What difference does it make if they can see or hear us?" Anne asked.

Carrie thought the question was stupid but didn't say so. "Because if we're digging our way out of the basement and they can see us, they'll push the button and kill us right then and there."

Digging through the basement was, of course, out of the question. The door to it was locked, and there was a big sign taped to it. One word, but quite enough to keep the three women from trying to break the lock. "Boom."

Exhausted and frightened, Sara and Carrie sat in silence as they stared out the windows at the deepening shadows on the beautiful landscape.

Anne struggled to sit up. Carrie noticed a stack of papers on the sofa next to her.

"What's all that?" she asked.

"Newspaper clippings I found in the chest in the foyer. One of the owners of the house must have saved them. Here they are," she said, handing Carrie a picture of a bride and groom on their wedding day.

"They look happy."

"I imagine they were," Anne said. "But now they're getting divorced and fighting over this house. Here, take all of the articles," she said, thrusting them at Carrie. "It's quite sordid. Is anyone ready for dessert?"

She sounded like a hostess of a party. Carrie found the question hilarious and laughed until tears came into her eyes. Sara was also tickled. She began to giggle.

"Oh, I don't know if I have room for dessert," Sara said. "After that gourmet dinner of baked beans and canned beets, I'm quite full."

"Don't forget the creamed corn," Anne reminded. "I worked hard to get just the right amount of pepper mixed in."

"It was very tasty," Sara said.

"I've taken inventory of the pantry," Anne said. "I thought we could have canned peaches for dessert. Shall we eat in the kitchen by candlelight? I've closed the blinds so no one can see in from the driveway."

Anne was sounding so chipper that Carrie became alarmed. Her own burst of laughter had been due to near hysteria, but Anne wasn't hysterical. She was acting as though she were having a lovely time getting together with old friends.

"After dessert, I have a surprise for you," Anne said. Her wry smile reminded Carrie of the cat who'd just eaten the canary.

"You aren't going to try to open the door to the garage, are you? That one is wired too," Sara said. "I checked it myself."

"In other words, you read the sign on the door?" Carrie said.

"Well, yes," Sara answered sheepishly.

Carrie put her hand out and helped pull Sara up from the easy chair.

"I'm a little stiff," Sara said.

Anne had already gone into the kitchen. They could hear her singing. Carrie, picturing Anne climbing up on the granite counter to open the window above the sink, rushed ahead of Sara. Blessedly, the image wasn't real. Anne was opening the can of peaches.

Carrie couldn't stop worrying. The woman had yet to grasp the futility of their situation. "Anne, you're not getting loopy on us again, are you?"

Anne laughed. It was a high-pitched noise, like china breaking. "I don't think so. Now sit down and relax."

At this point, Carrie knew she would have done anything Anne or Sara told her to do. She was feeling so beaten down. She was sick with worry for Avery, and though she was loath to admit it, she missed Tony.

"I miss my husband." She was surprised she'd said the thought out loud. "I guess I do love him."

"You don't know?" Anne asked. She placed the fluted ice cream bowls on the table and scooped peaches into each one.

"I thought he was cheating on me. He said he wasn't, but I didn't believe him. Some woman was calling at all hours of the night. The phone's on my side of the bed, and I always answered. She'd ask for Tony, but when he'd take the phone, he told me she hung up. What if it was Jilly calling?"

"You didn't trust your husband."

"No, I didn't."

The three women ate in silence while Carrie continued to wallow in self-pity. "You know what I hope?"

"What's that?" Sara asked.

"When it happens, I hope we're all sound asleep so we don't know it."

"That's grim," Sara said.

"Will the sound of the explosion wake us up before the pain of being incinerated—"

"Stop it, Carrie," Sara demanded. "We don't have time for such negative thoughts."

"Listen, if I want to—"

"Ladies, please," Anne interrupted. "Are you ready for my surprise?"

"You are loopy," Carrie muttered. "You found some Froot Loops?"

Anne didn't acknowledge her ridicule. "I've built two houses in the last ten years. The second one was over three thousand square feet. Cedar siding," she added. She nervously laughed as she qualified, "I hired a contractor, of course, but I was there every single day making sure everything was done the way I wanted it done. I drove the builder crazy."

"I'll bet you did," Carrie said.

"Why are you telling us this?" Sara wanted to know.

"I was leading up to my surprise," Anne said. She took a breath and then whispered, "I found it."

"Found what?" Carrie demanded.

Anne beamed with self-satisfaction. "A way out."

CHAPTER 17

Yᴏᴜ'ʟʟ ʙᴇ ᴏᴋᴀʏ here," John Paul told Avery.

"What do you mean, I'll be okay? You're thinking about hiking to Coward's Crossing now? In the dark . . . in a rainstorm? Are you nuts?"

"Avery," he began.

She grabbed his arm. "Okay, if your mind's made up, I'm going with you."

She knew he'd argue, and he did exactly that. He was almost civil as he told her she would slow him down, and he didn't want or need to have to worry about her out there. When that didn't work, he tried intimidation, even going so far as to threaten to tie her to the steering wheel.

She let him go on and on as she climbed into the backseat, found her black jogging jacket, and put it on, and then dug through her bag until she located her baseball cap.

Scooping her hair up under the black-and-orange Orioles cap, she adjusted the brim, sat back, and kicked off her tennis shoes. Her goal was to try to blend in with the night, and white tennis shoes would be seen.

Thank God she'd decided to bring her hiking shoes. She

knew he was watching her every move as she carefully re-packed her duffel bag.

"I think it's crazy to hike in the dark . . . only an idiot would try it, but if that's what you want to do, then I'm right behind you," she said.

"You're staying here," he said between gritted teeth.

She pretended she hadn't heard him. "We won't get far, and one of us might break an ankle or something walking into a hole we can't see. If I were making the decisions," she added as she carefully placed her tennis shoes, soles up, on top of her clothes and rezipped the bag, "I'd say we should stay in the car until dawn. Then we hike at a fast clip."

"Yeah, well, you're not making the decisions. I am."

She pushed the duffel bag to the floor, stacked her hands on the headrest, and leaned forward until she was just inches from his face. "Why?"

He couldn't hold on to his glare or his bad mood when she smiled. Hell, she even batted those big baby blue eyes at him.

"Are all the typists at the Bureau smart-asses like you?"

He was trying to put her on the defensive so she'd stop arguing with him and let him do what he was trained to do. It was a great plan, he thought, but unfortunately she was having none of it.

"Are all burnouts as obnoxious and stubborn as you are?"

He caught himself before he smiled. "Probably," he allowed.

"Are we going or not? Time's a-wasting, John Paul."

"We're going to wait until dawn," he said. "Don't give me that smug look, sugar. I had already decided to wait."

"Uh-huh."

He was smart enough to know it was time to stop arguing. Honest to God, she was more stubborn than he was, and in truth, that impressed the socks off him. She wasn't going to let him win this round, but he already had another plan in mind. He'd sneak away a little before dawn. When she woke up, she'd have to stay in the car and wait for him to come back.

And if he didn't make it back . . .

"I'm gonna leave the keys in the car."

"Okay."

"Get in the front seat so I can fold down the back. I've got a sleeping bag," he added. "You can use it."

"We'll both use it."

"Yeah?"

She rolled her eyes. "Don't get any fancy ideas, Renard."

"Fancy?" He laughed.

Avery had already found the latches and unhooked the seat backs. When they were flat, she spread out the sleeping bag. She tucked her hiking shoes under the seat, removed her jacket, and tossed it on the floor. John Paul stretched out on his back with his feet against the dashboard. He looked comfortable, his hands stacked on his chest, his eyes closed.

Shivering from the cold, she had to climb over his legs to get to the other side. Her teeth were chattering as she stretched out beside him. She couldn't reach her jacket. It was under the seat below him. A gentleman would have put his arms around her to warm the shivers away. He wasn't a gentleman, she decided, when he completely ignored her.

It had always been a point of pride with her never to complain. She was usually quite good at suffering minor and major ailments in silence. But John Paul brought out the worst in her. She really wanted to whine now, and she was more disgusted with herself than with him. He couldn't help being a jerk. She could.

Suck it up, she told herself. Then a minute later, when

she was sure her toes were frostbitten, she whispered, "Screw this."

"What?"

"I said it was cold."

"Huh."

"Huh, what?"

"I could have sworn I heard you say, 'Screw this.'"

He really liked being rude, she supposed, and no wonder, he was so very good at it. She smiled in spite of her misery. "Don't you think it's cold?"

"No."

Ignoring his answer, she said, "We should share our body heat." He didn't move a muscle. "Put your damn arms around me, Renard. I'm freezing. For God's sake, be a gentleman."

He still didn't move. She was half on top of him now, trying to steal some of the warmth his body generated. The man was like an electric blanket.

"Move it." She grimaced after giving the order. She sounded like a drill sergeant.

He was trying hard not to laugh at her. "If I put my arms around you, sugar, I might not remain a gentleman."

Oh, brother. "I'll take my chances, sugar," she drawled back.

She leaned up so he could put his arm out, and the second he did, she cuddled up against his side. John Paul rolled over and enveloped her with his arms.

He felt as if he were hugging an ice cube. The bottom of his chin rubbed the top of her head. Damn, she smelled good. Like peppermint, maybe, he thought as he began to rub her back.

"You're one big goose bump."

She didn't have the energy to talk. His warmth was so comforting, she closed her eyes and let him caress her. Her

T-shirt had ridden up above her navel, and too late, she felt his hands slip under the fabric. His fingers splayed wide across her back.

She lurched upward at the same instant he felt the scar tissue, her head slamming into his chin.

"Damn," he muttered as he dropped back. "What the hell did you do that for?" he asked, rubbing his jaw.

Avery frantically pulled her shirt down and rolled away from him. "Go to sleep."

She'd closed up on him quicker than he could snap his fingers. He rolled onto his back and closed his eyes. What in God's name had happened to her back? He knew what he'd touched was scar tissue. Who had done that to her?

"Leave me the hell alone," Avery whispered.

She was coiled for a fight. She waited tensely for the questions to start, holding her breath. She expelled it loudly. Why was he silent? Why wasn't he asking questions?

She told herself she had nothing to be ashamed of or embarrassed about, but very few men had ever seen or touched her back, and she had memorized their reactions. The look of shock, and in one instance, disgust. Mostly she remembered how one man she had actually believed wasn't superficial had visibly shuddered. Then, of course, the sympathy and the questions came . . . the hundreds of questions.

John Paul wasn't talking, though. She couldn't stand his silence long. She rolled toward him, propped herself up with her elbow, and glared down at him. The jerk's eyes were closed, and he looked as if he were sleeping. She knew better.

"Open your eyes, damn it."

"My name's John Paul, not Damn It."

What the hell was the matter with him? Why wasn't he

asking her questions . . . or flinching? She knew he'd felt the knotted scars. "Well?"

He sighed. "Well, what?"

She was getting angrier and angrier by the second. "What are you thinking?"

"Trust me, sugar, you don't want to know."

"Oh, yes, I do. Tell me."

"You sure?"

"Answer me," she demanded. "I want to know what you're thinking."

"Okay. I'm thinking that you're a real pain in the ass."

Her mouth dropped open. "What did you say?"

"You heard me. I said you're a real pain in the ass. You damn near broke my jaw when you jerked up. One second you're letting me warm you, and the next you're trying to kill me."

"I was not trying to kill you."

He rubbed his jaw. "I could have chipped a tooth."

Oh, brother. "Look . . . I'm sorry, okay? I was just startled, and I . . . Wait a minute. Why am I apologizing?"

He flashed a devilish grin. Her heartbeat immediately quickened. "'Cause you should," he drawled in his seductive southern accent.

The big jerk was so aloof and impassive, so why were her senses going berserk now? With the bursts of lightning, she could see his face clearly. The day's growth of whiskers should have made him look scruffy, but it didn't. She had to resist the urge to touch his cheek. His wonderful scent was driving her to distraction too. He smelled like wintergreen and musk and fresh wood shavings. And when he had held her in his arms to warm her, his body had felt like a smooth block of sculptor's marble. Everything about him was sexy, damn it. He was so masculine, so . . . Get a grip, she told herself. Remember, you're in charge.

Yeah, right. She put her forefinger and her thumb up in front of his eyes about a half-inch apart and said, "I'm this close to really hating you."

She'd used just the right amount of anger in her voice. She nodded too, just to let him know she meant every word.

He wasn't impressed or intimidated. He simply closed his eyes and lazily said, "I can live with that."

CHAPTER 18

WE GO THROUGH the wall." Anne made the announcement and then waited for the women's reaction to her suggestion. Sara looked incredulous; Carrie looked irritated.

"Yeah, right," Carrie muttered. "I'll use my superhuman karate kicks and my X-ray vision . . ."

"Now, Carrie, let's hear what Anne has to say," Sara chided.

"I'm telling you, it could work. When I got out of the car, I walked over to the stone wall and looked down. The mountain slopes on this side of the house. It's not a sheer drop like it is outside the living room windows."

"Go on," Sara urged.

"I also noticed the sides of the house are cedar boards, not stone like the front," she said. "There's an outside wall in the pantry that's just on the other side of the stone wall. I suggest we punch a big hole in the Sheetrock near the floor, so that when we do kick the cedar boards out, we won't be seen from the front."

"But Anne, there's more than just Sheetrock and cedar boards," Sara said.

"I know exactly what's between those walls," she boasted. "There's insulation, but that won't be difficult to tear out, and maybe wiring too, which we could work around, and a layer of sheathing . . ."

"And what else?" Sara asked. She leaned forward while she considered Anne's idea.

"Two-by-fours," Anne said. "Studs are usually about sixteen inches apart. We should all be able to squeeze through."

"How do we make a hole in the Sheetrock? With our fists?"

"We use the poker from the fireplace," Anne said. "And knives to widen the hole. I took inventory, and the kitchen knives are still in the drawers. If we started now, who knows? We might be out of here by morning."

"Time's running out," Carrie said. "I say we try to break a window and hope we don't . . ." She stopped when Sara shook her head.

"Too risky," Sara said. "I say we go with Anne's plan."

"What about the cedar boards?"

"It won't be as difficult as you think," Anne said. "They're nailed in, but if we hit them hard enough or kick them, they'll eventually pop right out."

"My goodness, we've got a plan," Sara said. She slapped her hand on the table and smiled. "I'm sure we won't be able to find any rope to use to climb down, but wouldn't sheets work?"

"In the movies, they always use sheets to get out," Carrie said.

"Really?" Anne asked.

Carrie nodded. "You honestly don't watch television, do you?"

Anne shook her head. "I could work on the sheets.

Maybe instead of tying knots, I could figure out a way to braid them together . . . or something."

"That's good," Sara said. "While you're doing that, Carrie and I will work on the wall. Anne, you're brilliant. I never would have thought to go out through a wall. I think this is doable."

"We have to leave during the night," Carrie said. "I don't relish the idea of tromping through the wilderness in the dark, but if we make our way downhill until we estimate we're past the fence, then we could get to the road and follow it back to town."

She'd made it all sound easy. Was she being naive, or could it be that simple?

"We should probably take a couple of sharp knives with us," Sara suggested. "Just in case we run into any wild animals."

"Or Monk," Carrie said. She shivered then. "I think I'd prefer fighting off a wild animal than running into him. Do you know . . ." She suddenly stopped, embarrassed at what she had almost confessed.

"What?" Sara asked.

"You'll think I'm gross, but I thought he was handsome."

Sara snorted with laughter. "I did too. I loved his accent. Do you think it was real?"

"I thought so," Carrie said. "I thought he was sexy."

Anne had been listening quietly to the conversation until Carrie made that comment. She couldn't keep silent any longer; her disapproval was evident. "Shame on you, Carrie. You're a married woman."

Carrie defended herself. "I'm married, yes, but I'm not blind, and there isn't anything wrong with appreciating a great-looking man. Surely you've—"

Anne cut her off. "Absolutely not," she insisted. "I would never insult my Eric by lusting after another man."

"Did I say I lusted after him?"

"Will you stop bickering," Sara begged. "You make me want to open a door."

CHAPTER 19

JOHN PAUL RETRIEVED the watch then hiked over twelve miles. He made a wide circle around the perimeter of the location marked on the map looking for signs—anything out of the ordinary, like a sniper hunkered down in the scrub. When he was satisfied he was alone, he planted the watch and backtracked four miles to Coward's Crossing.

There wasn't any doubt about being in the right place. There was a crude hand-painted sign nailed to a stake that had recently been pounded into the ground. The white paint with the words "Coward's Crossing" wasn't weathered and, therefore, couldn't have been more than a couple of days old. The arrow on top of the sign pointed to a boarded-up, abandoned mine shaft. There was a woman's bright red silk scarf nailed to another board above the entrance.

Dawn had arrived, and the mist was being burned by the rising sun. John Paul was safely concealed by the trees and bushes. From where he was positioned, he could see the entrance to the shaft. He didn't relish the idea of climbing down inside. Were the women there? Doubtful, he thought. Monk wouldn't have kidnapped them and then given Avery a map showing their location. No, Monk was isolating his prey. No doubt about that.

When would he take his shot? Maybe he thought they would want to go into the shaft. How had Monk planned to kill them? Explosives, he guessed. Yeah, that's what Monk would do. Clean and neat, an underground explosion no one would hear, and he wouldn't have to worry about burying what was left of their bodies.

Come on, John Paul urged. Show yourself. There was a good thirty yards of open space between the cover of the trees and the shaft. Check it out, Monk. Let me get one clear shot. He would try to immobilize him so he could question him and, hopefully, find out where the women were.

Someone was out there. The silence in the woods confirmed it. No birds singing, no squirrels scurrying about as they foraged for food. Nothing but the wind whistling a forlorn melody through the branches and an occasional rumble of thunder in the distance.

John Paul was patient. He could wait it out for as long as he needed. But what about Avery? How long would she sleep? And when she woke up and found him gone, would she try to come after him? The possibility sent chills down his back. He pictured her walking into a trap and had to force himself to block the image of her being gunned down.

He thought he heard something and tilted his head, straining to listen. The sound didn't come again.

What was Avery doing now? Was she still asleep? He'd left her snug as a bug in his sleeping bag with the gun next to her.

Damn, he'd hated leaving her. Knock it off, he told himself. She's fine. The car's well hidden and over ten miles away. Yeah, she was okay. Ah, hell, try as he did, he couldn't convince himself.

How in God's name had she worked her way under his skin so quickly? And what the hell was the matter with him to be attracted to her? She was a damn liberal, he reminded himself, one of those "Let's save the world" types. Worse, she was a team player, and the team she obviously loved playing for was the Bureau.

They were completely, thoroughly, absolutely unsuitable for each other. And yet here he was, worrying himself sick about her.

Monk could have tracked them . . . a twig snapped behind him. Without making a sound, he turned, trying to pinpoint the location. He thought it was maybe thirty or forty feet away, but with the rising wind it was impossible to be accurate.

For over five minutes he didn't move a muscle. Then he heard another sound, a faint rustling of leaves. Ever so slowly, he eased back on his haunches, zeroed in on the exact spot where the noise had come from, and took aim.

Then he saw those blue eyes staring at him between two little branches she had so painstakingly parted.

He was suddenly livid. He had damn near killed the woman. What could she have been thinking to sneak up on him like that? If she hadn't stayed perfectly still and let him see her face, if she had made one more little sound, he might have blown her away. Son of a bitch, he silently cursed as he eased up on the trigger. Son of a bitch.

Thank God he hadn't hurt her. An odd thought, given the fact that he was now contemplating wringing her neck.

He strained from the effort he exerted not to shout at her. He held up one hand, motioning for her to stay put. She slowly shook her head and held up one finger. Then she pointed behind her.

He moved through the brush toward her.

Avery knew he was furious. His jaw was clenched so

tight she thought it might shatter. She slowly got up on her knees, leaned into him until her mouth was touching his ear. Then she whispered, "He found the car."

John Paul heard movement and saw the glint of steel through the trees about fifty feet away. Like a lion, he sprang.

Avery didn't have time to react. One second she was whispering into his ear, and the next she was flat on her stomach on the ground, her face smashed into dead leaves with John Paul covering her as he fired. The dirt around her head was spitting up into her hair.

He rolled, fired again and again as he jerked her to her knees. "Move it," he ordered.

After the first shot, he knew Monk had a high-powered rifle. Probably with one of those fancy nightscopes too. All the bastard needed was one clear shot. No, make that two.

He figured Monk was trying to get them to run into the clearing by shooting at their only other way out.

Avery inadvertently cooperated. She veered to the right, away from the hail of bullets, but John Paul threw his arm around her and lifted her off the ground as he pushed her in front of him, using his body as a shield against the bullets flying around them.

"Go, go, go," he whispered, urging her on.

A branch came flying at her face. He blocked it like a football player with his forearm and shoved her ahead. She stumbled back against him, righted herself before he could try to jerk her arm out of its socket again, and kept going. They were running uphill now through a maze of trees. She heard a roaring in her ears, thought it was her heart pounding.

She was wrong about that. She reached a boulder. The surface was wet and slick. She scrambled up on her hands and knees, and then came to a hard stop. Good God, there was a sheer drop of at least fifty feet, and at the bottom was white, foaming water.

The hell with that. In her mind, they were out of options. The rapids were below them, but the killer was behind them and rushing toward them. As Avery peered over at the white water, she thought they had a better chance of surviving if they faced Monk head-on.

She unzipped her windbreaker pocket and pulled out the gun. John Paul emptied his gun, released the clip, and snapped another in. Then he flipped the safety on, glanced over the boulder to see what was below, and shoved his gun into Avery's pocket. After he zipped it up, he took her gun, put it in her other pocket, and zipped it closed.

She didn't like where this was leading. "We stay and fight," she said.

He shook his head. She frantically nodded. They could both hear Monk crashing through the brush. He was firing wild now, but nonstop. John Paul wrapped his arms around Avery's waist, holding her tightly in a bear hug. As he leapt from the rock ledge, he asked, "Can you swim?"

CHAPTER 20

COULD SHE SWIM? He had the gall to ask her that question after he'd lunged off the ledge with her locked in his arms. Avery didn't scream. Her life didn't pass before her eyes either on that endless flight down into the water below. She was too busy trying to punch him so he'd let go of her. And too scared to make a sound. Oh, Lord, don't let us drown.

They hit hard, plunging feetfirst into the icy water. It felt as if a thousand needles sliced through her feet and traveled at the speed of light all the way up into her brain. The impact was paralyzing.

He never let go of her. Not when they were sucked under by the raging water, and not during their frantic search for the surface as they were plummeting down the roaring rapids. Just when she was certain her lungs were going to burst, they finally clawed their way to air, but they had only enough time to fill their lungs before they were pulled under by the current.

She saw a brown bear watching them from the bank. She could have sworn he was grinning at them and didn't want that image to be her last before she died. She wanted to survive so she could give John Paul hell for trying to drown

her. As if something had hold of her ankles and was tugging her down, she sank again. She would damn well have
to fight harder to make it. She'd grown up swimming in the
ocean, first in Florida and then in California, and was a
stronger swimmer than most, but this wasn't swimming.
They were bobbing like corks.

They reached the surface again. Gasping to take in as
much air as possible, she spotted a big old gnarled tree
branch bouncing from one white-water crest to another.
With both hands, she grabbed hold when it came roaring
past.

The river zigged and zagged, but they were getting closer
to the bank. She started kicking with all her might. John
Paul hooked one arm over the branch and steered their lifeline in the same direction. When they finally reached shallow water, he stood and pulled her to the bank.

Sprawled out side by side on the grassy slope, they were
both too exhausted to move. Avery was gulping in air and
shivering so much her teeth were chattering.

"You okay, sugar?" he panted.

She suddenly bolted upright and gagged. She thought
she might have swallowed half the river.

"Can you swim?" she said between gasps. "Is that what
you asked me after you shoved me off that ledge?"

"So you heard me, huh?" He reached over and gently
pushed her dripping hair out of her eyes.

She looked back at the raging river. God surely had a
hand in their survival, she thought. There simply wasn't
any other explanation possible.

"Okay, so now we know what a fiver is," she said.

He sat up. "Yeah?"

She smiled. "They obviously rate the rapids," she explained. "This one was the big mother. A fiver."

He shook his head. They had just been through hell together, and all she wanted to do was tell him how they rate rapids?

"Did you hit your head or something?"

"No, I just figured out the rating system. That's all."

"Want to go again?"

"Been there, done that," she said. Squinting up at the cliffs above them, she said, "I think we lost him."

"I'm not sure," he said. Reluctant as he was to move, he forced himself to get up. He shook himself like a dog who'd just had a bath, then offered her his hand.

She made the mistake of clasping hold. He yanked her to her feet, pulling on her socket again. The man didn't know his own strength. Now what was he doing? He'd turned and was surveying the area they'd just vacated.

"What?"

"Grab some brush and throw it over our imprints. No, never mind. You'll only make it worse. I'll do it."

She walked into the protection of the trees and watched him pull several small branches over the soft earth. "Why is it that you automatically assume I'm incompetent? Is it just me you have a problem with, or are you that way with every woman?"

"Just you."

She saw him grin before he turned away. He got a kick out of irritating her, she decided, but she was too weary from near heart failure in the rapids to rise to his bait.

"Do you have any idea where we are?" she asked. Her words sounded slurred, and she was shaking almost violently now.

"No."

It wasn't the answer she was hoping for. "So I guess you weren't a Boy Scout?"

"I can get us where we need to go."

"Back to the car?"

"No. It would take too long trying to find a place to cross over the water."

"We need to get to a phone." And a hot shower and dry clothes, she silently added.

He finished covering their footprints, stepped back to survey his handiwork, and nodded with satisfaction.

"A phone's a given," he said as he walked closer to her. "Damn, babe, you're freezing, aren't you?"

"You're not?" she asked as he took her into his embrace and began to vigorously rub her arms.

"I'm okay," he answered. "I've got ice water in my veins, or so I've been told."

"Who would say such a thing?" she asked.

"My sister."

"Oh." Then, "She ought to know."

"Do you have any strength left?" He was unzipping her windbreaker so he could get to his gun. His weapon was just a little damp. He shoved it into the back of his jeans and zipped her pocket closed again.

"I have as much strength as you do."

"Then start jogging. You'll get warm in no time."

"Which way?"

"We have to go up before we can go down."

She looked at the mountains surrounding them. "It would be easier to follow the river, but Monk would antici-pate that."

She turned around and started jogging at a fast clip through the woods. Water sloshed between her toes as she ran. The sensation of ice cubes melting around her feet wasn't pleasant.

John Paul kept pace with her for over an hour. They nei-ther stopped nor spoke to each other.

He was impressed with her stamina. Once she had es-tablished the rhythm, she didn't slow down. She didn't complain either, and she wasn't clutching her side. He already knew she was in shape. One look at her body and he could tell she worked out. Still, the way she kept moving, so steady and sure, was proof that she did more than take a one-hour aerobics class once a week at some little spa back home.

He spotted the clear-water creek ahead and thought they should stop to catch their breath.

"Let's stop for a minute."

Thank God, thank God. "Are you sure you don't want to keep going?"

If he had said yes, she thought she would either burst into tears or keel over from exhaustion. The stitch in her side felt like someone was holding a hot coal against her ribs, and it had taken all she had not to grab hold and double over.

She noticed he didn't appear to be the least winded. Avery stretched her legs so they wouldn't cramp on her before she collapsed to the ground. Scooping up water with cupped hands, she greedily drank.

"Do you think he's tracking us?" she asked a minute later.

"Probably," he answered. "But he'll have to find a place to cross over those rapids, so we have some time. Tell me what happened at the car." He had been silently cursing himself for leaving her.

She sat down in the grass and leaned back against the tree. "I woke up and you were gone," she said. "So I decided to follow you."

His shoulder rubbed against hers as he sat beside her.

"I didn't get far," she admitted. "I had just started up the hill when I saw the headlights through the mist. Honest to Pete, I almost ran out to flag it down, but thankfully, I came to my senses and decided to wait until the car came closer."

"Ah, man," he whispered. "You could have walked right up to him before you . . ." He couldn't go on. The thought of what could have happened to her made him sick.

"He parked his car down below, then got out. He had a flashlight and a rifle tucked under his arm as he climbed the hill to where your car was hidden. He must have pinpointed the location before you moved the watch. I knew it was Monk, of course, so I stayed hidden."

"Then what happened?"

"He checked out the car."

"Did you see his face?"

"No. I could have if I'd moved, but I was afraid I'd make a noise, and he'd know I was there, watching. He opened the hood of your car, pulled something out, and threw it into that gully on the side of the hill. I could find it if we go back. He had the hood of his windbreaker up, so I couldn't see his face or the color of his hair, but he was at least six feet. He wasn't thin, though. He was quite muscular, not heavyset. He reminded me of a bodybuilder."

"He's good with disguises," he said. "Noah's description is what the FBI is using, but he didn't get a clear look at him either. From what I've heard about Monk, he could be in the same room with Noah today, and I doubt he would be recognized."

"I don't know if he was alone or not. He was driving a Land Rover, but when he opened the door and got out, the light didn't go on, and he parked it a good distance away. I couldn't see inside. Do you think the woman was with him?"

"I don't know."

"He's very good at what he does, isn't he?" She sounded disheartened.

"Yes, he is," he said.

"He stood there a long time, maybe five minutes," she said. "He didn't move a muscle. It was creepy."

"He was probably listening to the sound of the forest, hoping to hear something."

"Like me."

"Yes." He put his arm around her and pulled her close. "Thank God you didn't try to run."

"I thought about trying to get my gun out of my pocket, but I was so close to him I worried he'd hear the sound of the zipper."

"If you had been asleep, Monk . . ."

Before he could finish his bleak thought, she interrupted. "He'd shoot me? I'll tell you what, John Paul. If you ever leave me behind again, that's exactly what I'm going to do to you."

Since she was all but clinging to him so that she could borrow some of his warmth, the threat didn't carry much weight.

"I won't leave you again," he promised in a gruff whisper. "I never should have left you. Hell, I guess I've been away from it too long. My instincts are all screwed up."

She homed in on what he'd just said. "You've been away from it too long? What exactly is *it*, John Paul?"

"Come on, sugar. We should get moving. Time's awasting."

In other words, leave it alone. She decided to accommodate him now and try again later. She was stiff and sore when she stood. Groaning, she rubbed her backside, not caring that she appeared less than ladylike.

"You know what I need?"

"Food, dry clothes . . ."

"Yes, that too," she said. "But what I also need is to get into my yoga position, relax, and do my free-association exercises."

"Your what?" He was sure he hadn't heard correctly.

She repeated. "You let the fragments drift in your mind; then when you're completely relaxed, you take hold of one at a time and you analyze it. You can't do it, though, until you reach total relaxation."

John Paul watched her stretch her long legs. "So how do you reach total relaxation?" he asked.

"Visualization," she said. "I go to a place where I feel completely safe and free, like a real home. You know, I go to my . . . happy place."

"You're kidding."

"No."

He laughed. "You do know you sound insane, don't you?"

She wasn't joking when she answered. "It runs in the family."

She clasped her hands behind her back and twisted her torso, then shook her arms and legs to loosen them and started running again, her pace slower this time, but just as determined. Once again, he fell in right behind her and stayed there until she was panting for breath. They'd been climbing steadily since they'd left the river, and so far they hadn't seen a single sign of civilization. Where in thunder were they? Were they even still in Colorado?

She suddenly stopped, doubled over, and took a couple of deep, gulping breaths. Then she put her hands on her hips and slowly straightened.

"You okay?" he asked.

Why wasn't he winded? He was human, wasn't he? She made up her mind that, no matter what, she wouldn't utter one word of complaint. Not one frickin' word.

"Can't see the forest for the trees." She tried to sound flip. Cheerful was simply too much to ask for.

John Paul was sympathetic. "Do you want to rest?"

Is the Pope Catholic? Does it always rain on picnics? Hell, yes, she wanted to rest.

"No," she said weakly. Then, more forcefully, "I'm good to go . . . unless you want to . . ."

"No," he said. "Let's keep moving."

"Are we still heading north?" she asked, stalling for another minute to catch her breath. The air was so thin, she felt light-headed. "I can't seem to get my bearings. If the sun were out . . ."

"We're going northeast."

One foot in front of the other, she told herself. Steady as you go. Come on, Delaney, pick up the pace. Time's a-wasting. Suck it up.

She kept up the steady barrage of psychological nagging as she ran through the forest. She tried not to think about her soggy underwear sticking to her skin or the fact that she was lugging around at least a pound of mud on each of her hiking boots.

She didn't quite clear the dead branch she tried to jump over, tripped, and would have gone headfirst into a tree trunk if John Paul hadn't grabbed her. The terrain was getting steeper, more treacherous. As she raced along, the muscles of her calves began to burn, and she was finally forced to slow down when they broke through the trees.

She suddenly stopped. They had reached a shelf of rock that hung out over the side of the mountain. Spread out before them was a panoramic view of the lower hills. Lush green meadows were tucked in between towering peaks with hundreds and hundreds of trees, their branches stretching toward heaven. Everything was so green, so alive. And not a soul was around. People surely flocked to this paradise, didn't they? So where were they all hiding?

"Isn't it picturesque?"

"Yeah, yeah, it's picturesque," he mumbled.

Desperately trying to stay positive, she said, "Is your cup always half empty? Can't you appreciate—"

He cut her off. "Have you noticed where we are? It's going to take us a couple of days to get back to civilization." He studied the lay of the land below looking for roads, but he wasn't having any luck. He had, at least, gotten his bearings back.

"We don't have that much time," she said. Her shoulders slumped, and as she looked around her, the beauty suddenly turned menacing, and the realization of their predicament sank in. Could it get any more bleak? She wanted to cry, but she didn't give in to the urge. Suck it up, she told herself. "It'll be okay," she asserted.

"Yeah? What makes you think so?"

She had to think about it for a minute before she could come up with anything. "Because we're due for a break."

And that was when it started raining again.

CHAPTER 21

ANNE WAS ONE of the most uptight, rigid women Carrie had ever met. She was certain the woman wouldn't be at all helpful, but she was proven wrong. Anne more than held her own. After she finished tying together the sheets, she helped them with the wall. She was a hard worker, with surprising stamina. She didn't have any sense of humor, but then, there really wasn't anything to laugh about, was there? As long as Anne's sacred marriage wasn't discussed, she was almost pleasant to be around.

She was also the woman in charge, giving them orders as they worked side by side. Punching a large hole through the Sheetrock with a fireplace poker didn't take any time at all. The insulation was messy but not difficult to remove. They filled a leaf bag with the stuffing. Luckily, there weren't any wires or pipes in the area they uncovered. Next, they sliced through the sheathing with kitchen knives.

Then they got to work on the boards. That was a bitch. Carrie had to take a break when her thumb started bleeding. While Anne removed the splinter with her tweezers and bandaged the cut, Sara took over.

By three o'clock in the morning, they were all worn-out.

Sara and Carrie had Band-Aids on every finger. Anne still looked like a fashion plate. Her nails weren't even chipped.

"How's the sheet rope coming?" Sara asked. She pushed the sleeves of her striped blouse up to her elbows and fell into the chair.

"It's ready to use," Anne said. She placed a bowl of tomato soup in front of Sara and then went back to the stove to fill Carrie's bowl.

"I'm too tired to eat," Carrie said.

"You'll need to keep up your strength," Anne told her as she placed her bowl on the table.

Sara noticed Anne take two pills out of her pocket. She turned her back on them when she put them in her mouth and drank a glass of water.

"What did you just take?" Sara asked.

"Oh, nothing," Anne answered as she took her seat across from Carrie.

"Aspirin?" Carrie asked.

"Yes," Anne said just as Sara shook her head.

"Not aspirin. They were pink capsules."

"You're very observant," Anne remarked. "They're prescription medication for nausea. I'm just getting over a bout of illness."

Carrie was barely listening. She had one elbow propped on the table, resting her head in her hand. She was too beat to care about table etiquette.

"What kind of illness?" Sara asked. She was swirling the soup with her spoon.

"Nothing much," Anne said. "I found this tiny little bump about eighteen months ago, and I told Eric about it. He went with me to the doctor," she explained. "As it turned out, it was no big deal."

"Thank goodness," Carrie said.

Sara was watching Anne's eyes. "Where did you find this little bump?"

"In my right breast," she said. "I had the biopsy and then got on with my life. Like I said, it was no big deal."

"So it wasn't malignant," Sara said.

Carrie wondered why she was persisting with the subject. Hadn't Anne just told them everything was all right? She thought Sara was being nosy.

"She just said . . ." Carrie began.

Sara didn't look at Carrie as she nudged her under the table. "But it wasn't malignant?" She repeated the question.

Anne looked at her soup when she answered. "Just a little bit."

Carrie straightened. "Is that what the doctors said?"

"Oh, you know how doctors are," Anne said. She waved her hand as she added, "They're all alarmists. Eric said they only make money if they can do a lot of procedures . . . and surgeries . . . when it isn't at all necessary."

Carrie glanced at Sara before she asked, "Did they recommend surgery, then?"

"Of course, but Eric said they would, and of course he was right. They thought they could talk me into having my breast removed. Can you imagine what that would have done to our insurance premiums?"

"No, what would it have done?" Sara asked.

"The rate would have gone sky high. Besides, the insurance company wouldn't have paid for the little procedure anyway."

Removing a breast was a little procedure? Carrie was too stunned to speak. She picked up her spoon and pretended to eat.

"Eric had made some wonderful investments with our

cash surplus. He's so clever," she said. "They were good, sound investments that I, of course, approved when he told me about them."

"After he made the investments?" Sara asked. "He told you then?"

"Yes, of course," she said. "He has carte blanche. I mean, he is an equal partner in the business."

Carrie and Sara could see Anne's spine stiffening. She was becoming defensive. Sara took a taste of the soup and then said, "Good choice for dinner, Anne. I love tomato soup."

Anne smiled. "I do too."

"So why do you think the insurance company wouldn't pay?"

"Preexisting condition," Anne explained. "The old insurance policy had lapsed, and the new one Eric found that had a much more reasonable premium didn't begin for thirty days. I had the biopsy during that period where they could say it was preexisting. Eric told me to wait, but I was foolishly anxious. We had the money to pay for the procedure," she hastily added, "if we had believed it was necessary. He did a lot of research on the Internet, and we decided to explore alternative methods. Your soup is getting cold, Carrie."

"About this—" Carrie began. Sara kicked her under the table.

"Yes?" Anne asked. That guarded look was back in her eyes.

"Are there any crackers?"

"No, I'm afraid not."

"You're very lucky to have Eric," Sara said.

Carrie choked on her soup. "Yes, you are," she lied. "It's a shame he couldn't go to the spa with you."

"I tried to talk him into it," she said. "He gave me the week's stay as a surprise for my birthday. He wanted me to rest and relax, and when I got back home, we were going to go back to the doctors and see what needed to be done. I was worried about what all this would cost, but Eric wouldn't listen. He said that if we had to spend every penny to get me well, then that's what we would do."

That son of a bitch, Carrie thought to herself. He was getting rid of her, but Anne, perhaps still in shock, couldn't accept the truth, and so she painted this lovely picture of her adoring husband. Had he left her a letter, or did he want her to die without knowing he was responsible?

"We should be on our way before dawn," Sara said, interrupting Carrie's thoughts.

"My hands are raw, and so are yours. Getting down that rope . . ."

"We can manage it."

"Anne, did you bring any workout clothes?" Carrie asked. "You can't go tromping down the mountain in high heels or the slippers you're wearing now."

"No, I didn't."

"Between Sara and me, we'll be able to outfit you properly," Carrie said.

Her whole attitude toward Anne had undergone a radical change. She found herself feeling protective and hoping that Anne stayed in denial until they reached civilization.

"Why don't you pack us some food to take along," Carrie suggested to Anne. "And a first-aid kit."

"You could use my fanny pack," Sara said. "It's on my dresser, but I don't have the energy to go upstairs to get it."

"Oh, I'll get it. I love being useful. Don't touch those dishes," Anne ordered as she hurried out of the kitchen. "I'll wash them later."

The second Anne was out of earshot, Sara whispered, "That bastard."

Carrie nodded. "Now I've got another reason for wanting to get out of this alive. I'm going to kill that son of a bitch."

Sara nodded. "You hold the gun, and I'll pull the trigger."

CHAPTER 22

SOMETHING WAS GROWLING, and it definitely wasn't human. Avery scooted closer to John Paul. Promising her she could have twenty minutes to rest, he had found shelter for them under a jutting rock. The ground was dry, and the area was wide and deep enough for him to stretch his legs.

Avery had lobbied for finding a cave. John Paul had vetoed that idea because he didn't want any unexpected company, like mountain lions or bears, sharing the space.

She suggested a fire, but he vetoed that idea too. The smoke could be seen from miles away.

She heard the growl again. It seemed closer. She nudged John Paul and whispered, "Do you hear that?"

"Uh-huh."

He sounded half asleep. He was sitting up with his back against the rock, his long muscular legs stretched in front of him, one ankle crossed over the other. He put his arm around her and told her to relax.

Her head was down on his shoulder, and every now and then his chin would rub against the top of her head. She couldn't decide if he was being affectionate or if the day's growth of whiskers made his skin itch.

Another rustling noise came from below them. She tensed in reaction. Then she thought she heard something growl again. What in heaven's name was it? A bear? A mountain lion? What?

John Paul had his gun on the ground next to him, and his hand rested on the handle.

She took a deep breath and tried not to think about how uncomfortable she was. Think positive, she told herself. Keep that cup full. Be an optimist.

Oh, God, we're gonna die out here. She sighed then. So much for being an optimist. He must have felt her shivering because he began to rub her arm. She thought that was sweet. She really did try to relax, but anxiety was keeping her mind revved up. Could a body be too exhausted to rest? When she'd sat down, she had been close to collapsing, and she knew she had to rest if she wanted to be able to run again.

What would the woman do about Carrie and the others now? Was John Paul right? Were they already dead?

She forced the thought aside and once again tried to get comfortable. Every muscle in her body ached, and her toes throbbed. She tried to take her boots off, but John Paul stopped her. Her feet needed to acclimate to the wet boots, and all she had to do was walk off the cramps. He acted like an authority, and since she knew he'd had survival training while in the Marines, she acquiesced. Besides, she'd been too weary to argue.

Avery was determined that, no matter what, she wouldn't turn into a cynic like her aunt and John Paul. When the rain had begun and John Paul had teased her because she'd boasted that they were due for a break, she pointed out that the rain was a lovely, soft drizzle that brought with it a hazy fog, which, she insisted, was enchanting. Yep, that's what she'd said. She'd smiled too. Then the drizzle turned to a deluge. And still she tried to maintain her positive attitude. What more could happen? she reasoned. They were already wet.

And that's when the deluge turned into hail the size of golf balls, pelting their bodies as they ran into the protection of the trees.

More rustling noises pulled her back to the present. Had he heard the sound? She lifted her head from his shoulder and strained to hear. Fingers of gray light curled down through the branches as the rain continued.

His eyes were closed, but as she stared at him, they slowly opened. His gaze locked on hers. She was so thankful that he was there with her. She felt safe with him. She wasn't having to go through this nightmare alone, and his strength comforted her and gave her hope.

"I want . . ." She couldn't get the rest of the words out, couldn't tell him how much she appreciated his help. She couldn't stop looking at his mouth.

"Yeah, I do too."

Later, she wasn't so certain who initiated the kiss. She knew she'd leaned into him, and then his head had tilted down toward hers. Or had she pulled him close and had he merely accommodated her? She couldn't remember. Their mouths had just . . . merged.

And, oh, it felt wonderful. His mouth was so warm against hers, and, Lord, did he know how to get rid of a woman's defenses. He made her want much, much more. He was gentle and giving, yet rough and demanding at the same time. His hand cupped her chin, and he pressed it gently to let her know he wanted her to open her mouth for him.

She scooted up on his lap and wrapped her arms around

his neck. When he began to caress her, she let go of her inhibitions, and her bones felt like Jell-O. She got quivers in her stomach. His tongue was driving her wild, making her want to be bolder.

The warmth of his touch radiated through her body. When he ended the kiss, she realized his hands were under her T-shirt. She knew he was as affected by the kiss as she was, for she could feel his heart beating rapidly under her fingertips.

She tried to get off his lap then, to retreat, but he wouldn't let her. He held her tightly against him, then gently pushed her head down on his shoulder.

"You know what would be real nice now?" he whispered in that gruff, sexy tone of voice.

She was still trying to catch her breath. The taste of him lingered on her lips, and she was replaying every second of that powerful kiss in her mind.

The question suddenly penetrated. "For Pete's sake, John Paul."

"What?" he said.

"You want sex."

He didn't say a word for a long minute, acting as though he was taking his time to think it over. "Well, yeah. That would be nice too, I guess. Sugar, if you're offering, I'm not gonna turn you down." She wasn't looking at him, so he knew it was safe to smile. "But what I really want is a cheeseburger."

Her head snapped up. He got his chin out of her way in the nick of time. "What?"

"I was thinking a cheeseburger would be nice about now. And french fries and a cold beer," he added.

"The shrubs weren't enough for you?"

He laughed. "They weren't shrubs. Those were edible

leaves and berries I made you eat. They'll give us energy," he added. "But I still want a cheeseburger. My brother-in-law got me hooked on junk food."

"You were really thinking about food?"

He grinned. "Yeah, I was, but if you're desperate to have sex, I guess I could accommodate you."

"I do not want to have sex."

"You said you did."

He was exasperating. "No, I didn't."

"And you kissed me," he pointed out. "So I just assumed . . ."

"Oh, for Pete's sake."

"It's obvious you can't keep your hands off me, sugar."

No wonder love and hate were so closely linked. Right now, she wanted to strangle him. He enjoyed making her squirm, seemed to be getting a real kick out of it.

She really wanted to have the last word. "It was just a meaningless kiss."

"Then how come you got all hot and bothered?"

"I did not."

"Liar."

Only he could make the insult sound like a caress. "Did you get all hot and bothered?"

"Hell, no."

She laughed. "Now who's lying?"

"The first rule in any operation is to tell as few lies as possible. Now try to rest. Ten more minutes and we're moving."

She couldn't rest, not until she relaxed, and there was only one way to do that. She moved away from John Paul, assumed the lotus position she'd learned from her yoga instructor, put her hands on her knees, palms up, straightened her back, and closed her eyes. She concentrated on her breathing, deep cleansing breaths, forcing herself to block the noises of the forest and the thoughts rushing through her mind. It took a good five minutes before she could feel her muscles easing.

"What are you doing?"

His question pulled her back. "I'm doing my relaxation exercise."

"Yoga?"

"Sort of. I clear my mind, then I go . . ."

"What?"

She sighed. Home, she thought, I go to my imaginary perfect home. She answered, "I go to my happy place. Okay?"

He didn't laugh. "Yeah? So you were serious about that? I thought you were joking."

"I picture a place that makes me feel good. It's a porch," she said. "And I see myself sitting on this swing. I can smell lilacs, and I can hear water in the background. It's . . . soothing, and it frees my mind. Then I start filtering through the data I've collected."

"Whatever works," he drawled.

He didn't understand, but then she didn't expect him to. She closed her eyes again, ignoring him now, and once again concentrated on her breathing.

Another couple of minutes passed, and she began to let the bits and pieces of the puzzle come together. Ironically, it was something that John Paul had said that got her mind racing.

"What did you mean?" she asked.

"About what?"

She stretched her legs and then turned to him. "The first rule of an operation is not to lie?"

"No, I said tell as few lies as possible."

"Yes, that's what I meant. Why is that a rule?"

"Lies can come back to bite you . . . trip you up. So . . ."

She took it from there. "So, if you stick to the truth on all the little things that don't matter, you won't get tripped up. Oh, my God, of course."

She was suddenly as excited as a kid in a toy store. She unzipped her jacket pocket and pulled out a soggy map.

"I'm such an idiot. Monk could have read about the property in the paper, and when Carrie asked him where he was taking her, he came up with that name. I assumed he was lying. Why wouldn't I assume that? He'd lied about everything else, but John Paul, what if he was telling her the truth?"

Her babbling worried him. "Are you getting punchy?"

She smiled. "Yes," she said. "But it still all makes sense anyway."

"What are you trying to tell me?"

"I think I know where Carrie and those other women are."

Her announcement gained his full attention. "You think you know? How?"

"Carrie told me where Monk was taking her."

One eyelid dropped. "And you're only now mentioning that fact?"

"Hear me out," she said. "I thought he'd lied to her. I told you my aunt left me a message on my machine, and I erased it, and you heard my question to Cannon, didn't you?"

"I heard you ask him if there was a water problem."

"And Cannon said, no, not at Utopia. I also asked him if the spa owned a house in the mountains."

John Paul nodded. "I remember his answer was no."

"Because he said no, I didn't ask any other questions about the house. Carrie called it a retreat. I assumed that everything Monk told her was a lie. But what if it wasn't?"

"Why would you think he was telling the truth about their destination?"

"It's what you said. Why lie when you don't have to? Lies have a way of coming back to bite you." She repeated his very words. "Monk already had grabbed her, right? And he'd already told her his name. She was meekly going along, probably without a care in the world. But she called me on her cell phone from the ladies' room. And I doubt she would have told Monk she'd made the call. There wouldn't have been any reason."

"If Monk had told her where he was really taking her, he wouldn't have let her out of his sight."

"He couldn't go with her into the ladies' room," she pointed out. "And he might not have known she had one of her cell phones with her."

"One of her cell phones?"

Avery nodded. "She carries two at all times. Carrie's a workaholic, and it makes her crazy if the battery runs down. Besides, she uses one for personal and the other for business."

"She could just carry an extra battery."

"Oh, she does," she said. "So what do you think?"

"The truth? I think you're reaching."

"No, I'm analyzing the data, and I think we have at least a fifty percent chance I'm right. We have to check it out."

"You know where this house is?"

While he opened the map, she told him about the old gentleman who sat with her in McDonald's.

"Yeah, I see the circle he made."

Avery then told him about the couple who were fighting over ownership. "The judge is supposed to decide soon which one of the thoroughly unpleasant couple gets the house. He also told me the place has been vacant for weeks."

John Paul slowly nodded. "Okay, it's worth a look. Break's over. Time to move."

"We've got to get to a phone. That's the first order of business."

"No," he whispered. "The first order of business is staying alive so we can get to a phone."

And that, he knew, was easier said than done.

CHAPTER 23

Now that the three women were finally ready to leave, they were immobilized with fear.

It was four o'clock in the morning, and they estimated that they had approximately two hours before dawn. They huddled together at the kitchen table, dressed for the forest in layers of clothes, sipping hot tea to fortify them against the night air. A frigid breeze poured into the kitchen from the hole in the pantry wall.

"What if Monk put down trip wires or something?" Carrie asked. "What do we do then? We won't see them in the dark."

They all worried about the possibility, and then Sara said, "I don't think he'd take the time to climb up the side of the mountain. I'm sure he thinks he's got us locked in tight."

Carrie was so scared, she was trembling. "Listen," she whispered. "If I don't make it . . ."

"Don't talk like that. We're all going to make it," Sara said, but her voice lacked conviction.

"Let me say this," Carrie insisted. "If I die, I want you two to promise me you'll make the police find Avery and

protect her. Call my husband," she added. "Tony will want
to help keep Avery . . ." Her voice caught on a sob, and she
couldn't go on.

"Focus on one worry at a time," Sara suggested.

"That's right," Anne said. "Concentrate on climbing
down the rope."

Carrie nodded. "Yes, all right." She pushed her teacup
away and stood. "We should go now. No more stalling."

Anne grabbed Carrie's hand. "Everything is going to be
fine. You'll see."

Smiling, Carrie squeezed her hand. Uh-oh. Anne's eyes
were getting that glassy look. She had probably taken one
of her pain pills. When Carrie had searched the upstairs for
a way out, she'd noticed the bottles of medications lined up
on Anne's vanity. There were enough to start a small phar-
macy.

"Did you remember to put your medicines in your
jacket?" Carrie asked.

"Yes, of course I remembered."

"I could put some of the bottles in my jacket."

"No need," Anne assured her.

"What about the letters," Sara asked Carrie. "Did you
zip them in your pocket?"

"Yes, I've got them."

"Okay, then," Sara said. "Let's do it."

They had already decided that Sara should go first. One
end of the sheeted rope was anchored to the kitchen table,
which couldn't be pulled through the doorway, but Carrie
and Anne were still going to hold the rope while Sara lowered herself to the ground. Anne had tied big knots twelve
inches apart so they would have something to grab.

Carrie was the second one to go because Anne had argued that since she weighed the least of the three, she stood

the best chance of getting down on her own if the rope came loose from the table.

Carrie had wanted to go last, but Anne wouldn't hear of it. "If the rope doesn't hold or I fall, you and Sara could maybe catch me, but I couldn't help catch you or Sara. I have to go last."

"Oh, God, don't think about falling. You made a good, strong rope, Anne. It's going to hold."

"Yes, we'll all be just fine."

Anne sounded obscenely cheerful. Was she getting nuts again, or was the pain pill responsible?

Sara led the way into the pantry. Carrie and Anne watched as she picked up the end of the rope and tied it around her waist. "I hope this is long enough."

Sara got down on her knees, then scooted to the opening. "Get down on your stomach," Carrie whispered. "And go out slowly, feetfirst."

"Did you put the penlight in your pocket?" Anne asked.

"Yes, I've got it."

Carrie sat on the floor and braced herself with her feet against the two-by-fours. Anne got behind her to help hold the rope. Just when Carrie thought Sara was never going to reach the ground, the sheet went limp. Carrie fell back against Anne. Recovering her balance, she took a deep breath and said, "Guess it's my turn."

She rolled onto her stomach and scooted to the edge.

"Wait," Anne whispered. She grabbed Carrie's jacket, shoved a thick envelope in the pocket, and zipped it closed.

"What are you doing?"

"You're the strongest of the three of us, so if Sara and I don't make it, you make sure . . ."

"Yes?" Carrie prodded. "Come on. What?"

"Just make sure. Now go."

Carrie didn't waste time arguing. She would find out what Anne meant after they'd gotten away from the house.

Her hands were bleeding and raw, and she was too frightened to cry. She slowly lowered herself down. Anne tried to help, but when she tried to pull up on the rope so she could get a better grip, she almost went out the opening headfirst.

Carrie made it to the ground.

The rope went slack and Anne fell back. Quickly straightening, she looked down, trying to see the two women. She stayed on her hands and knees for a moment and listened to the soft calls from below.

Then she pulled the rope up. She backed away from the opening. *"Three blind mice, three blind mice,"* she sang. *"See how they run, See how they run . . ."*

She stood up, brushed the dirt off her borrowed sweatpants, and walked into the kitchen. *"See how they run,"* she sang. Odd, that that particular melody had popped into her head and wouldn't let go. She and Eric had decided never to have children, yet now she was singing a silly nursery rhyme. Her father used to sing that song to her. How did the rest of it go? Was it, "They all ran after the farmer's wife, she cut off their heads with a carving knife"? Or was it, "They all ran away from the farmer's wife"? And why couldn't she remember the rest of the song?

"Three blind mice," she sang softly as she knelt down and tried to get the knots out of the sheet. Realizing she could break a nail, she got up, went to the counter to get the scissors Carrie had brought down, and cut the rope from the table leg.

"Three blind mice." She stood again, paused to take a drink of her lukewarm tea, and then, because she knew that Carrie and Sara were anxiously waiting for her, she walked to the opening in the pantry and dropped the sheets

down. They surely couldn't misinterpret what that meant, for she'd tossed away her only lifeline. She heard one of them cry out, thought it must be Sara, for, of the two women, Sara seemed a tad more tenderhearted.

"*Three blind mice*. My goodness, I can't get that silly tune out of my head," she said as she shut the pantry door. Noticing the messy kitchen, she went to the sink, filled it with soapy, hot water, and did the dishes. When she was finished, she straightened the table and chairs, put fresh place mats in front of each chair, then blew out the candles and headed for the stairs.

She was feeling so tired and old and haggard. A good long nap would fix that, she thought. But first things first. She simply had to do something about her sorry appearance. She couldn't understand how fashion-minded women with money, like Carrie and Sara, could ever wear sweatpants. Why, even the name was offensive. Ladies shouldn't sweat. They shouldn't even perspire. Only common, coarse women did such disgusting things as sweating and belching and body piercing . . . or letting others, like doctors, mutilate their bodies for them. Hadn't her loving Eric told her that was how he felt? He adored her body and couldn't stand what the surgeon wanted to do.

Feeling a bit light-headed, Anne gripped the banister as she slowly made her way upstairs. After she took a long, hot shower, she curled her hair with her curling iron, then brushed it and lacquered it in place with hairspray. It seemed to take an hour to decide which of her new St. John knit suits to wear. The mint green with the adorable silver clasps won because she thought it was both elegant and chic. Slipping into her silver pearlized high heels, she picked up her favorite platinum-rimmed diamond earrings and put them on. The diamonds were a gift from Eric on their last anniversary.

She'd walked all the way down the hallway before she remembered she hadn't put on any perfume. Retracing her steps, she squirted a dab on each wrist. Sighing with contentment, she hurried downstairs but stopped on the bottom step. The rising sun had turned the living room into a golden temple. The color took her breath away. Eric should be here to see this, she thought. Yes, he should.

Anne didn't know how long she stood there. Ten minutes might have passed, or twenty, maybe more. The effects of the second prescription pain pill had finally caught up with her, and she zigzagged across the living room, giggling because she found it so amusing that she couldn't walk in a straight line. Was this what it felt like to be stoned? Was she stoned? Trying to focus, she reached the sofa and plopped down. She fell asleep seconds later.

Although she hadn't realized such a thing was possible, she knew she had wept while she slept because, when she awakened, her face was wet with tears. She struggled to sit up and wiped the dampness away with her fingertips. Noticing the makeup on her hands, she'd decided to go back upstairs to powder her face again when she thought she heard the sound of a car coming up the drive. Still somewhat disoriented, she staggered to her feet, adjusted the lapels of her jacket, and walked into the dining room to look out the window at the circle drive. Her gait was stiff and unsteady.

A silver Cadillac DeVille came screeching around the curve. "Now, who could that be calling at such an early hour?" Anne asked. She checked the time on her Bulgari watch—another gift from her beloved Eric—and was astonished to see that it was after nine in the morning.

Anne stepped back into the shadows as the car came to a rocking stop. The door opened and a woman with the most frightful look on her face leapt out. She slammed the door shut, then opened the back door.

The woman looked vaguely familiar, but Anne couldn't remember where she might have seen her before. Her face was contorted with rage, and though Anne couldn't hear what she was saying, she knew she was talking because her lips were moving.

Was she Jilly? The stranger did have blond hair, and she was tall and shapely, as Carrie had described, but she certainly wasn't what Anne would consider beautiful by any means. Perhaps, if her expression weren't so hostile and if she were smiling instead, she might be pretty. But not beautiful.

Her complexion was lovely. She'd give her that. From a distance it looked almost flawless, and Anne decided she really must find out what kind of facial cleanser the woman used to get such perfect skin. Or was it heavy makeup? Anne made a mental note to find out.

Her haircut was a little too short and spiky, but the color was wonderful. Highlights, Anne thought, and she wondered if the unpleasant woman would give her the name of her stylist. Why, she'd kill to have highlights like that. Suddenly feeling self-conscious about her own appearance, she patted her hair down, certain she'd gotten it mussed during her little nap.

"My goodness," Anne whispered when she saw what the woman was carrying. She had a red gasoline can in one hand and an ax in the other. "What does she think she's doing?"

The woman's head was down, and she hadn't spotted Anne yet, but as she strode to the steps, Anne remembered where she'd seen her before. She was pictured in one of the clippings she'd found in the chest. Oh, yes, she remembered now. The woman and her ex were fighting over ownership of this house.

Anne rushed to the foyer and stood in front of the elongated beveled glass panes that framed the door. She could hear what the woman was saying now. She was spewing filth. Anne's hand went to her throat. She was appalled by the vulgarity. The woman must have said the "F" word a good ten times, enraged at a judge for giving her house away.

Ah . . . now Anne understood. The house had been awarded to the husband. Anne didn't have any sympathy for the crude woman. She obviously hadn't been a good wife. Shouldn't the husband make all the important decisions? He'd paid for the house. He should keep it.

The woman rushed up the porch steps, screaming now. "That son of a bitch thinks he's going to take my house and leave me penniless? Screw the prenup. He thinks I'm bluffing. I told him he'd never live here. Surprise, surprise, bastard. When I'm finished redecorating . . ." She spotted Anne and came to a dead stop. Then she roared, "Who the hell are you, and what are you doing in my house?"

"Hello there," Anne called out. "What are you doing with that ax and that can?"

"None of your fucking business."

"I really would appreciate it if you wouldn't use obscenities in my presence. It offends me."

The woman put the can of gasoline down, dropped the ax, and reached into her pocket to get her key out.

"Did the bastard hire a housekeeper?" she yelled loudly enough so that Anne could hear through the door.

"I assure you I'm not a housekeeper."

"Open the fucking door."

"Oh, I don't think that's a good idea."

The woman shoved the key in the lock and tried to turn

it. When she realized it wouldn't work, she screamed, "Damn him to hell. How dare he change the lock. How dare he. He knew . . . He had that judge in his pocket. Well, fuck him."

She pulled the key out of the lock, threw it down, and glared at Anne. "If you don't open this door, I'm going to use this ax. You don't want to mess with me, bitch. Not today."

"Are you threatening me?"

"Open the damned door."

The sneer was the last straw. Tears flooded into Anne's eyes as she swung the door open and forced a smile. "Won't you come in?"

There was a second's delay, long enough for the woman to shove Anne back and step over the threshold.

The explosion blew half the mountain away.

CHAPTER 24

Keeping up with Jilly was a full-time job, but Monk found it thoroughly exhilarating. He hadn't felt this alive in years. He was the cautious one, of course, while she, with the enthusiasm of a novice, planned her grand schemes, never worrying about the little mundane things, like the FBI tracking one of the credit cards she'd used.

Monk couldn't fault her for making that mistake. He blamed himself because he should have destroyed the cards after he'd used them. He kept all of his credit cards under various names and addresses in his attaché case, and Jilly had simply helped herself to the first ones her hand touched.

The result hadn't been as bad as it could have been, though. John Paul Renard was now involved, and Monk was absolutely delighted about that turn of events. He'd known that Renard was trying to track his movements for over a year. He'd intercepted several inquiries Renard had made to various law enforcement agencies in Europe. Now Monk had the opportunity to get rid of the pest before he caused real trouble, and Monk could humor Jilly at the same time.

Before they'd settled on using Utopia to bring the women

to Aspen, his beautiful fiancée had had the time of her life, sitting at the table hour upon hour, poring over her notes. Oh, how she loved the intrigue, the excitement, and most of all, the danger, and she was trying to teach Monk how to have fun too. Whenever he did anything to please her, such as agreeing to last-minute changes in her complicated plans, she aptly rewarded him in creative ways. All of them of a sexual nature. Just thinking about some of the things she'd done to him and allowed him to do to her made him blush like a teenager.

She was turning him into a true romantic, but he didn't view that as a weakness, for his obsession was with Jilly and no other. He believed with all his heart that, if the erotic games they played in bed didn't kill him, they would grow old together.

Oh, yes, she was an obsession. His every waking minute was spent thinking about her, protecting her from harm. As long as he maintained his vigilance and cleaned up her mistakes, they would be safe.

Monk had had to talk Jilly out of one scheme. She had briefly toyed with the idea of kidnapping Avery and sitting down with her to tell her the truth about Carrie. Jilly was such an innocent. She believed she could convert her daughter. Monk gently explained that, after all the years of brainwashing by Carrie, Jilly would never be able to convince her daughter that she was, in reality, a loving mother.

Jilly wasn't perfect by any means. She had a twisted view of motherhood, for she believed that because she had brought Avery into this world, she owned her. She spoke of Avery as her possession, not a person, and Carrie had taken that precious treasure away from her. For years her anger at her sister had festered, but Jilly was patient when it came to vengeance. No matter how long it took, she would get even.

She insisted on being the one to push the button that

would blow the house apart. She promised Monk she wouldn't shed a tear over her sister's death. Carrie had brought this on herself. She was the reason Jilly hadn't succeeded in life; she was the reason Avery hated her. She was the reason for every one of Jilly's failures. And so it was only fair that Jilly get to watch her sister die.

Monk wasn't put off by Jilly's brutal honesty. How could he cast the first stone? She had accepted him with all his sins, and he could do no less for her.

Now he was trying to clean up the mistakes at the abandoned mine. Jilly had been sure they would climb down into the shaft to find the next clue as to Carrie's whereabouts, and then Monk could have dropped a couple of explosives into the hole, sealed it, and followed Jilly back to the retreat.

Monk hadn't believed Renard would go into the shaft, and he had been proven right. He had thought, however, that he could get a clear shot at the two and toss the bodies down the hole, but he missed his chance when they scrambled up the rocks and leapt into the river.

He was methodically tracking them now. He'd lost precious time backtracking to his vehicle and crossing the river, but with his car he'd been able to make up some time by speeding down the mountain road and cutting back to where he anticipated they'd be heading.

Renard hadn't left any tracks, but then Monk knew all about the ex-Marine and hadn't expected less. When he'd done his research on his stalker, he'd read his history, and he'd been impressed. He believed that under different circumstances they could have become friends. They were, after all, very much alike. They were both professional killers. Monk had murdered for money, while Renard killed for honor. That didn't make him superior, however. If anything, Monk believed it made him a fool.

Still, he would have liked to have had the opportunity to sit down with him, share some cold beers, and talk about their past exploits. But Renard would never go for that. The man was too honorable for his own good. According to his sealed file, which Monk had gotten unsealed, Renard was suffering from burnout. Monk didn't believe such nonsense. He thought Renard had left the job when he realized he was beginning to enjoy the power he felt every time he pulled the trigger. Honor be damned.

Was Renard as curious about him? Did he fantasize about sitting down to discuss the thrill of the hunt, the exhilaration of the kill? Monk wished he could find out. Maybe if he was able to wound him, paralyze him, then Monk could sit down beside him and chat it up like old friends until Renard bled out. Wouldn't that be something, to talk to an equal, to commiserate, to boast?

Monk chuckled. Now who was fantasizing? He checked the time and then shook his head. If he didn't spot the couple soon, he would have to get to his car and drive to where Jilly waited. She was anxious to get back to the little mountain retreat to see how her sister was holding up. By now, the three women had probably turned on one another like polecats, each one slowly going out of her mind with terror. That was what Jilly hoped anyway.

Stop daydreaming and get back to business, he told himself. He lifted his high-powered binoculars and scanned the terrain once again. He was turning toward the north when he saw the observation tower in the distance, maybe a mile away. Climbing down was a forest ranger. Monk watched until the man was standing on the ground.

"Well, well," he whispered as he calculated. "Just my size."

Exactly one hour later he was leaning over the rail at

the top of the tower, scanning the hills. Looking down at the bushes below he saw the white T-shirt of the forest ranger he'd shot in the temple and then stripped.

He was just about ready to give up the chase when he suddenly spotted the couple. Avery's blond hair, so like her mother's, shimmered gold in the sunlight. Monk couldn't believe his good fortune. There they were, all right, walking down the mountain as pretty as you please, looking as ragged and worn-out as any two people he'd ever seen. His burst of laughter echoed around him. Wait until he told Jilly. He knew what she would say. She'd tell him he was an exceedingly lucky man.

He'd agree, of course, even though he knew luck had very little to do with finding his prey. After poring over his map, he'd anticipated that if they survived the white water, they would get out before that tremendous drop below Coward's Crossing.

Monk decided to meet them head-on. He climbed down the ladder and walked around to the path, his head down, the bill of his cap concealing his face.

When he reached the wide-open space between the trees, he ever so slowly turned and pretended to notice them near the peak. He raised his hand to wave.

Avery heard John Paul behind her. "Fall down, Avery. Do it now."

She didn't hesitate. Pretending to stumble, she went down on one knee. John Paul caught up with her and dropped to put his arm around her shoulders to steady her.

"Act like you hurt yourself."

Rolling to her side, she clutched her ankle and gave an exaggerated grimace. She wanted to cry from disappointment. "He's not a forest ranger, is he?"

"No."

She kept rubbing her ankle. "How do you know?"

"I saw his rifle. Forest rangers don't have scopes on their rifles."

She looked up at him. "You saw the scope from this far away?"

"The sun caught it just right," he explained. "I think it's him. I'm not saying it's Monk, but . . ."

"Thinking he might be is enough for me," she said.

"Okay, I'm gonna help you stand. You lean against me, and we start down the hill again, but we'll angle toward the west. When we reach the trees, we run like hell."

"He'll come after us."

"Ready?"

He didn't give her a chance to answer, but hauled her up, lightly bracing her against his side.

"Limp," he ordered gruffly as they once again started down the hill. They were walking like two drunks, staggering toward the west as they moved along.

He was deliberately keeping them out of Monk's range. He was sure now that the man dressed as a forest ranger was the killer because he hadn't moved from his spot at the base of the trail. Rangers were helpful, weren't they?

"He's waiting for us to get within firing range."

"Oh, God."

"You scared?"

"Duh . . ."

Her response made him smile. "That's good," he said. "Okay, sugar. Start running."

She immediately bolted toward the safety of the trees. John Paul was right behind her, but he dared a quick look down below and saw Monk running toward them. They had a good head start. Avery led the way steadily downhill, hoping to intercept the road below Monk, all the way praying there would be campers or real forest rangers around who could help them.

Her ears were ringing. What was that sound? The wind whistling through the trees? Or was it the sound of gunfire sizzling? No, that wasn't it.

The noise stopped as suddenly as it had begun; then it started up again, but it was louder, shriller this time. It sounded like a whistle.

"Hear . . . that . . . ?" she panted.

"Yeah."

Then she heard a trumpet. Was she losing it? She kept running, her feet pounding into the soft earth as she raced along, still panting from her exertion.

The muscles in her legs were burning. Suddenly she lost her footing. She would have hurled headfirst into a gulley if John Paul hadn't reacted instinctively, lifting her off her feet as he kept stride.

He slowed as he let go of her, then kept pace just in case she went down again. All at once, they broke through the trees, crossed the road . . . and ran into the middle of Boy Scout Troop 183. Before he could stop, John Paul bowled over one pup tent and mowed down the troop master, who got the wind knocked out of him. The trumpet he was holding went flying into another tent.

"Cell phone," Avery shouted at the man sprawled on his back. "We need your cell phone."

"No signal up here," he answered as he came up on his elbows. His face was red with anger. "Who in thunder do you people think . . ."

John Paul was frantically searching the road ahead of them. Monk wouldn't have any qualms about taking a couple of kids out as long as he could get his primary targets. One of the boys shouted when he saw the gun tucked into the back of John Paul's jeans. One blistering look from John Paul shut the boy up.

Avery dropped down on her knees next to the leader. "Listen to me. We need help. There's a killer coming this way. Where's your transportation? Answer me, please," she begged.

Her terror got through to him. "We've got a camper here, but my Ford four-wheeler is parked about half a mile down the road. The keys are in my jacket in that tent over there, the one with the troop numbers painted on it."

John Paul was lifting Avery to her feet. "Get in that camper and get your boys out of here," he yelled back at the man as he pulled Avery toward the next slope, staying well hidden in the trees.

"Get to a phone and call for help," she shouted.

Her legs were trembling, and she didn't think she had it in her to run much longer. Concentrating on putting one foot in front of the other, her heart feeling as though it were lodged in her throat, she suddenly remembered they hadn't gotten the keys.

"We have to go back . . . the car keys."

"We don't need them," he said. "Now move it, sugar. You're starting to drag."

She fantasized about hiding somewhere and waiting for John Paul to come back with the car. She could find a spot where Monk wouldn't find her, couldn't she?

Suck it up. Damn it, I don't want to. I can do it. I can do it. She kept up the drill until the pain in her side became excruciating. She wondered if she could die upright. Sure she could.

Tears came into her eyes then, for she saw the old SUV parked in the gravel near the curve in the road. John Paul raced ahead of her. He broke the back window, reached in, and unlocked the front door.

Avery ran around to the other side as he unlocked the door for her. It took less than forty-five seconds for him to hot-wire the car, throw it into gear, and take off.

She was impressed. "Were you a juvenile delinquent growing up?"

The second they rounded the curve, she fell back against the seat and allowed herself to fall apart. A sob caught in her throat.

"Are you crying?"

"No."

"Sure sounded like you were." He gave her a sharp look.

"I'm joyful." She hastily wiped the tears of relief from her cheeks.

He grinned. He had the very same feeling, but it didn't last long. "Hell," he muttered.

"What hell?"

"The road's winding back around . . . he might be coming down, getting into position . . . ah, hell, that's what he's gonna do, and there isn't any way we can go off-road here."

He leaned forward, pulled his gun out, and dropped it into his lap. He rolled down his window, then picked up the gun.

She frantically got her weapon out and then rolled down her window. "What the hell are you doing?" he asked.

"Getting ready just like you."

"No. Get down and stay down. If he's coming at us, you'll be on his side."

She ignored his order. "Just tell me when to start shooting. We'll keep him down until we get past."

It sounded like a great plan, and she'd said it with gusto, but that was only because she didn't believe Monk could have gotten down the hills that quickly.

She was wrong about that. She spotted him before John Paul did.

"Get the hell down," John Paul shouted.

Her response was to flip the safety off. Leaning against the door, she put her arm out the window, steadied the barrel of the gun on the side mirror, and waited. She ducked down as much as she could.

When Monk crouched down and swung the rifle up, John Paul shouted, "Now!"

They fired simultaneously, again and again as they sped toward the killer. Monk dove for cover, then scrambled to roll over and get his weapon up. Avery kept firing, pinning him down as they flew past.

The road suddenly curved up the mountain. There was a dirt road that angled sharply to the south that would have taken them farther down the mountain, but John Paul knew that, at the speed he was going, the SUV would roll if he tried to make the turn.

"I'm out," he said as he emptied the magazine.

She was turning to look when John Paul grabbed the back of her neck and shoved her down. "Get on the floor," he ordered as the back window shattered.

They were still climbing and had reached another sharp curve when Monk blew out the left rear tire.

The car went into a spin. They careened off the road into the brush, narrowly missing a tree head-on, but finally stopping when they hit a rock.

"Move it," he shouted as he leapt out of the car and raced around to the other side. Avery had no sense of where they were, only knew they were once again climbing. Her heartbeat, like the turbulent white water, was roaring in her ears. She raced up the steep slope, then skidded to a stop.

"No," she cried.

John Paul stopped beside her. "Ah, hell."

She wanted to weep as she stared down at the swirling water below. No. Not again. Shaking her head, she said, "I won't do it. I can't. You can't make me."

He looked genuinely sorry when he grabbed her. "Sure I can."

CHAPTER 25

Picturesque, my ass. If Avery saw another white-water anything, she thought she just might start screaming and never stop. At the moment, she was feeling malevolent toward pine trees too. Hated every one of them. She wasn't real fond of John Paul either. He had tossed her over the cliff like a discarded candy wrapper, and on the way down she had vowed that, if he survived, she'd kill him, just for the sheer joy of it.

She knew she was being irrational. She didn't care. Her bad mood intensified when she cut her leg on a jagged rock. If they'd been in the ocean, the blood pouring from her cut would have sounded the lunch bell for the neighboring sharks. Trying to stay positive as she fought to stay afloat, she told herself to be thankful there weren't any sharks around. And her leg didn't hurt all that much compared to the searing charley horse in her calf that nearly caused her to drown. John Paul hauled her onto the bank, half carried her into the trees so they wouldn't be seen, and then dropped her. She landed with a thud on her backside.

He dropped beside her. "That wasn't so bad, was it?"

Since she'd taken in more than enough water to fill a

backyard swimming pool, she was too waterlogged to answer the absurd question. Shoving her hair out of her eyes, she glared at him.

"It wasn't as bad as the first jump, was it? I don't think that drop was more than twenty feet," he said.

"You pushed me over a cliff."

Actually, he hadn't pushed her. As he recalled, he'd thrown her so she wouldn't hit the rocks jutting out from the base of the cliff. He didn't think it would be a good idea to mention that now, though. "Did I have any other choice?"

She wasn't ready to admit that there really hadn't been any other alternative. Their guns were useless against a high-powered rifle, and Monk was hot on their trail.

"I don't want to talk about it."

He grinned. "Cup half empty, sugar? Where's that optimistic attitude?"

"At the bottom of the river."

He stood and offered her his hand. "Come on. Let's get out of here."

She didn't know if she had enough strength to even stand. She was so tired and cold and wet. Suck it up, she told herself.

"Right," she said as she grabbed hold. When he jerked her upright, she fell against him. He put his arm around her and held her tight while he made up his mind which direction they should go.

"Aren't you tired?" she asked.

"Yeah, I am."

She looked back toward the river. "Maybe he'll give up now."

John Paul shook his head. "That isn't gonna happen. He's a professional. He's taken the contract, and he won't stop coming after us until . . ."

"He succeeds?"

"Or until I kill him."

"I vote for the second option."

They both heard the sound of children's laughter. Avery pulled away from him and started running toward the noise. "I hope they have a phone."

"Doubt you can get a signal."

She actually smiled. "There's that negativity I so love. You had me worried, John Paul. For a minute there you were . . ."

"What?"

"Cheerful."

"The hell I was."

He sounded as though she'd just insulted him. She was laughing as she ran toward the sound. The reason for her sudden good humor was either joy or hysteria. A family of five was setting up tents near a little stream.

After a brief explanation, everyone piled into the father's minivan and headed toward a town the man remembered he'd driven through on the way up the mountain.

Thirty minutes later they reached the sleepy little community of Emerson. Downtown consisted of four streets. The father stopped the van in front of a two-story stone building. The second they got out of the van and closed the sliding door, the father sped away.

"I think maybe you scared him," Avery remarked.

"The faster he can get his family away from us, the safer they'll all be."

There was a police station, which was surprising, considering the size of the town. Sharing the same building, the police station was squeezed in between the volunteer fire department on one end of the building and Bud's Burgers on the other. There were three doors facing the street with signs above each one. They walked through the middle door into a wide hall. Swinging doors were on both sides.

One connected to the restaurant, and the other to the fire department. The police station was directly ahead.

The aroma of hamburgers and onions and french fries filled the air, but the smell didn't spur Avery's appetite. It actually made her nauseous. The lack of food, running for miles and miles, the cold, and the terror had taken their toll. She felt all used up. Getting from the door to the counter was suddenly more challenging than surviving the currents. Her feet felt as though they weighed a hundred pounds, and it took every ounce of stamina she had left to move at all.

John Paul could tell she was having trouble. She seemed to wilt before his eyes.

"You okay?" he asked as he put his arm around her waist.

"I feel like rigor mortis has set in," she said. "I'm not dead, am I?"

Smiling, he said, "You're still breathing."

He looked through the glass window and saw the police chief sitting behind his desk. There was a stack of papers on the blotter, and he was poring over them. Every couple of seconds he would glance up at a television mounted to the wall behind the counter. Dressed in navy pants and a white shirt with the name *Chief Tyler* on the pocket, the middle-aged man was frowning as he picked up a sheet of paper.

A woman in her late sixties stood behind the counter with her back to the door. Her hair was as white as Avery's face. She seemed mesmerized by the program on the television.

John Paul could hear her talking as he pushed the door open. "Didn't I tell you something bad was going to happen? Didn't I tell you, Bud?"

"Yes, Verna. You told me."

"And didn't I tell you he brought this on himself?" she asked. "Tearing out all those beautiful trees and digging away at the mountain just to build himself a fancy monument. It looks like Mother Nature decided to get even, didn't she?"

The chief wasn't paying much attention. "Yes," he drawled as he continued to scan the sheet of paper in his hand.

"If you ask me, he's the villain. I feel sorry for his wife."

"You mean ex-wife, don't you?"

"That's right. He got rid of her so he could move on to a younger model. It's criminal, if you ask me. Poor thing. He got her used to living the high life, and then he yanks the rug right out from under her."

The chief was clearly exasperated. He dropped the paper on the desk and looked at the television. "'Poor thing'? Didn't you see that interview they did with her last month? They had to bleep out every other word she said. I think he was crazy to ever marry her."

"But how is she going to get along now?"

"She can get a job and work like the rest of us. Nobody put a gun to her head when she signed that prenup," he pointed out.

John Paul and Avery had been listening from the doorway. They walked inside as Verna was telling the chief it was all a terrible shame. The chief spotted them, did a double take, and stood.

"What happened to you two?"

"It's a long story."

"I'll be happy to listen," he said.

Avery pulled away from John Paul and walked over to the counter. Verna gasped, and her brown eyes widened as she approached.

"My name's Avery Delaney," she said.

"You're soaking wet. What in heaven's name happened to you? You look like something my cat dragged in."

Avery didn't know where to begin. She saw John Paul shake the policeman's hand and sit in the chair he offered. She decided she'd let him do the explaining.

"May I use your phone?" she asked. "I need to call the FBI."

Verna's eyes now looked as if they were going to pop out of her face as she called over her shoulder, "Bud? The lady wants to call the FBI."

"Let her use the phone," the chief said. He was leaning into the desk, listening intently as John Paul explained the situation.

Verna placed an old-fashioned black phone on the counter. "There are showers on the second floor above the fire station and nice clean cots too. While you make your call, I'll go get a couple of blankets for you folks. Your lips are trembling. You're gonna get hypothermia if you aren't warmed up soon."

"Thank you," she said. "You're very kind."

Avery picked up the phone and then put it back down. Exhausted, she couldn't remember the phone number to the pen. She closed her eyes to think about it. Was it three-nine-one or nine-three-one?

Maybe she could call Carter. What was his private number? Then she heard John Paul ask the chief if he had ever heard of a property called Land Between the Lakes.

"Everyone in Colorado has heard about that property."

"How far away is it?"

"Quite a distance from here," he said. "And with all the Lookie-Lous out there, you won't be able to get close. By now, the police have the area sealed off. The best way to see it is on television."

John Paul didn't know what he was talking about. He glanced at the screen.

Nine-three-one. That was it. Avery picked up the phone and started dialing. The receiver was halfway to her ear when she happened to look up at the television. She froze, the phone number once again forgotten.

A local newscaster announced that they had new footage of the disaster from a hiker just outside of Aspen who had captured the explosion with his video camera.

"The judge's decision was announced at eight-fifteen this morning, granting ownership of the mansion to Dennis Parnell. For those of you who just tuned in, we repeat, late this morning, the Parnell mansion known as Land Between the Lakes was ripped apart by an explosion."

The phone crashed on the floor as Avery collapsed.

CHAPTER 26

Numb with shock and despair, Avery couldn't move. Carrie was dead. Carrie, who had given her unconditional love, always, no matter how crazy Avery made her with her career choices.

And Avery had failed her. Carrie would still be alive if Avery had been faster or more clever. All that time wasted running from point to point for the demented woman on the phone who taunted her with lies that Avery could save Carrie. She should have found a way to rescue Carrie and the other women. Now it was too late.

John Paul held her in his arms and let her ramble as she told him over and over how she was to blame.

Verna made soup and all but force-fed Avery, then led her upstairs and stood like a prison guard outside the bathroom while she showered. The old woman, hearing Avery's sobs, kept whispering, "The poor dear."

When she was finished, Verna handed her one of the chief's gray T-shirts to put on, then gathered up her clothes to wash.

She hovered over Avery like an anxious mother hen. She sat Avery down on one of the cots and knelt on the floor with her first-aid kit. The cut on her leg wasn't deep, but it needed to be cleaned. She applied a liberal amount of iodine and wrapped the wound in gauze.

When she was finished, she tucked Avery into bed and headed downstairs to fix a cup of hot tea for her. When she turned back at the doorway to ask her if she wanted a dab of milk in her tea, Avery was already fast asleep.

John Paul was waiting at the bottom of the stairs. "Is she okay?"

"She's sleeping, and that's the best thing for her now. She's all tuckered out."

Nodding agreement, John Paul went back into the station. The chief was on the phone verifying that John Paul was who he claimed he was. When he'd gotten the information he needed, his attitude became more open and friendly.

"The troops are on their way," he said. "I know you've got to be hungry, so I called over to the restaurant, and one of the employees is bringing some food for you."

"Thanks," John Paul said.

"I checked you out," he said then. "You were a Marine."

"Yes."

"I was in the army," he offered. "Went through West Point, then did some duty in Germany. My best friend was a Marine. He died last year, and I sure do miss him. He was a good man."

John Paul wasn't sure why he was telling him his history. "I hear you're good with a gun," Tyler continued. "Do you think trouble's coming this way? Until the FBI gets here, we're on our own."

"If Monk knows where we are, then maybe he'll try to end it here. I don't think he knows, though, and I'm guessing he's gone to ground to reorganize. That's what I'd do."

"We can't be taking any chances," Tyler countered as he stood and crossed to a cabinet on the other side of the room. He pulled a key from his pocket and unlocked the padlock. When he opened the doors, John Paul smiled. Chief Tyler had an arsenal at his disposal.

"You like to be prepared for just about anything, don't you?" he asked with approval.

The chief grinned. "Sometimes we get a cranky bear I have to go after."

"You go after them with an M1911?"

"No, that's just a leftover from my army days. Take your pick," he said. Turning to his assistant, he said, "Verna, you go on home to your daughter and stay there until this is finished."

"I don't want to leave that girl alone upstairs. She needs comfort now. I'm worried she might be going into shock."

"She's tougher than she looks," John Paul said. "I'll com— I'll watch out for her."

He'd damned near said he'd comfort the woman, but he'd caught himself in time. What was the matter with him? He didn't have a clue how he was supposed to make Avery feel better, only knew he didn't want her crying on anyone else's shoulder. None of this made any sense to him. She confused him, turned his thinking upside down, and put all sorts of crazy, impossible thoughts into his head. He couldn't understand how or why she had become so important to him, only knew he was driven to keep her safe from harm . . . at all costs.

Protect and serve. If he kept thinking like this, he would end up on the side of law and order again. He shuddered at the possibility.

The chief interrupted his thoughts. "I've got good strong doors with double-bolted locks. There's a back door out of this area, and that has a glass window, but I put in an alarm because of all the firepower I've collected, and the whole town will hear the noise if anyone tries to get in."

John Paul checked out the perimeter. Fifteen minutes later he and Tyler were satisfied with the lockdown. He ate, then went upstairs, showered, and put on the sweats and T-shirt Tyler had given him. When he stepped out of the bathroom, Verna was waiting with a plastic trash bag to collect his wet clothes.

"My son-in-law will drop these off with Avery's after they've been laundered," she said as she started down the stairs. "You take care of her. You hear?"

"I will," he promised.

She left a few minutes later with her daughter.

Tyler had insisted that he could hold down the fort while John Paul caught some shut-eye.

He hadn't argued. He tried not to make any noise as he walked into the dormitory where Avery slept. There were four cots, all with clean bedding, lined up against one wall. The chief had told him that when the building was constructed, the town believed they would have a full-time fire department, but when the town didn't develop the way the city planners thought it would, the budget couldn't afford salaried firefighters. It was volunteer now.

John Paul noticed the window was unlocked. It overlooked the alley behind the building, and there was a fire escape ladder just a couple of feet to the left. He locked the window and then sat down on the cot next to Avery's.

She was sleeping on her back. Her face was scrubbed clean; her hair was still damp from washing, and he thought she was the most beautiful woman he'd ever seen. She looked like an angel, but she had a little vinegar in her disposition, the way she tried to boss him around. He liked the fact that she stood up to him, held her own. He liked her attitude too. She viewed the world the way he used to when he had been naive.

He was tired, and surely his fatigue was the reason he

was thinking such foolish thoughts. When the FBI arrived, he'd leave. Simple as that. Avery was the ultimate team player, he reminded himself, so he'd let her team watch out for her.

"Hell," he muttered as he rolled onto the cot.

He got in two full hours of sleep before Tyler woke him. John Paul had heard him coming up the stairs and had the handgun aimed and ready when he opened the door.

The chief waited until John Paul put the gun down. Then he walked inside. "We've got company," he whispered. "The FBI's here, and the man in charge wants to see you."

Avery was still out cold. She'd kicked off the sheet, and one leg was hanging off the side of the bed. There was a bandage wrapped above her ankle. Spots of dark blood dotted the gauze. When had she hurt herself? he wondered as he carefully lifted her leg and tucked her back under the sheet. And why hadn't she told him?

He knew the answer to that one. She would never think to complain.

Fighting the urge to kiss her, he went into the bathroom to splash cold water on his face.

He became angry thinking about the interview he'd have to suffer through with the Feds. If the team leader turned out to be like so many others John Paul remembered, then he'd be an arrogant, opinionated, we-do-it-my-way-or-no-way prick.

By the time he'd dried his face and hands, he was ready for a fight. Fact was, he was looking forward to it. He found himself hoping the guy did turn out to be a prick because he was suddenly in the mood to kick some ass.

Unfortunately, Agent Knolte was neither a prick nor a know-it-all. The freckle-faced agent was intelligent, eager, and sincere, and seemed to know what he was talking about as far as strategy went. He'd certainly done his homework on Monk, knew almost as much about him as John Paul did.

There were only two problems with Agent Knolte. One, he looked like a twelve-year-old. And with a cowlick and braces, no less. What were they doing in the Bureau these days? Recruiting from grade school? The second problem was monumental. Knolte was a by-the-book agent.

"Mr. Renard, it's an honor to meet you," Knolte said, extending his hand as four other eager agents crowded around. "We all heard about the hostage rescue down in South America, and I want you to know we consider it a privilege to be able to work with you."

John Paul stared into Knolte's brown eyes. "I was never in South America."

"But I talked to—"

"I was never there."

"Yes, sir. If you say so," Knolte hastily agreed.

Another agent stepped forward. "Sir, we understand the Agency was elated to hear you decided to come back to work after your long leave of absence."

John Paul didn't look at the man when he responded. "I didn't take a leave of absence. I retired and I'm still retired." Then without missing a beat, he asked, "How old are you, Agent Knolte?"

The question didn't seem to faze the man. "Older than I look," he answered. "Let me introduce you to my team."

John Paul suddenly found himself surrounded by agents wanting to shake his hand. The attention didn't sit well. Chief Tyler observed the spectacle from the back hallway. When John Paul caught his eye, the middle-aged man shook his head and muttered something about a damn fan club.

"We'll need to question Miss Delaney," an agent named Brock said.

"Not until she's had some sleep," John Paul said. "You can talk to me."

The interview lasted an hour. There were constant interruptions as Knolte kept getting updates from another agent at the explosion site. He told John Paul that they'd brought in the dogs and were searching for bodies. Thus far, two had been found. From the remains of the vehicle near the site, they knew that one of the women was the former wife of Dennis Parnell, the owner of the house.

The wait for the discovery of the other bodies was grim and tense. Then Knolte got another call and thrust the phone at John Paul. "You'll want to hear this."

A minute later John Paul bounded up the stairs. Knolte could have sworn the brooding man actually smiled for a second there.

The door to the dormitory banged against the wall when he rushed inside, but the noise didn't disturb Avery.

He shook her awake. "Sweetheart, open your eyes. Come on, Avery, wake up."

She was slow to respond. She felt drugged and disoriented. She finally opened her eyes and struggled to sit up.

"Is it time to go?"

"Carrie's alive."

She squinted up at him, shaking her head as she tried to comprehend what he was saying. "Alive? How can she be alive? The house—"

"She got out before the explosion. I don't know how she managed it, but she's okay."

Avery burst into tears. John Paul sat down next to her and pulled her onto his lap. He held her while she cried all over him.

When she was finally able to calm down, she asked, "Did everyone get out? Where's Carrie now? Have they called Uncle Tony? The poor man will be beside himself. First, they tell him she's dead, and then they tell him she's alive. I hope to God he has a strong heart."

John Paul wasn't sure which question to answer first. "Carrie's in a hospital in Aspen."

She jerked away from him. "Why is she in the hospital? You told me she was okay."

"She is," he insisted. "But the other woman was hurt. The judge tore up one of her knees when they fell into a deep ravine," he explained. "Carrie twisted her ankle, and fractured her arm, but she was still able to drag some dead branches over them so they could hide the rest of the night. One of the police dogs found them," he added. "They were taken to the hospital, and the judge is in surgery."

"But what about the other woman? There were three . . . weren't there?"

"Anne Trapp. She stayed inside the house."

"Why? Why would she stay?"

"I don't know. You'll have to ask Carrie, or maybe Knolte knows the reason now."

Avery stood and nearly tripped over her backpack and duffel bag. "How did these get here?"

"The chief called a friend. He got my car working and drove it here."

Avery was so relieved and jubilant about Carrie, she felt limp and giddy. She wanted to laugh and cry, and kiss John Paul. Oh, she really wanted to kiss him, and a whole lot more. What was wrong with her? Maybe it was the endorphins. Yes, that's what it was.

She mentally shook herself. She needed to concentrate on Carrie now. And Uncle Tony. "Did anyone call my uncle?"

"Yes," he answered. "He's a happy man right now, but scared too. He wants to get on the next flight to Aspen."

She nodded approval. "Who's downstairs?" she asked as she knelt beside her duffel bag and unzipped it.

"FBI," he said. "There are five of them downstairs, all talking on their cell phones. They've taken over the police station, and Chief Tyler isn't real happy about that. Tyler's an okay guy," he added. "He doesn't much like the FBI either."

She rolled her eyes. "Your prejudice is juvenile, John Paul." She pulled out a pair of khakis. "I should go down and find out what they have so far. Any word on where Monk might be?"

"No," he answered. He was staring at her legs, noticing how long and shapely they were. One thought led to another, and another, and before he could stop himself, he was picturing her legs wrapped around his thighs.

He looked at the wall behind her head. "You can't go downstairs like that."

"Like what? I'm going to put on slacks," she said. "And since when do you care what I look like?"

"I don't care," he answered gruffly. "But I can see through that threadbare T-shirt."

She looked down, whispered, "Oh, God," and grabbed the sheet from the cot, tugging with all her might to get the end out from under John Paul. She dropped her slacks as she wrapped the sheet around her.

"Why didn't you say something sooner?" She was blushing.

"Now, why would I want to do that?"

His grin was lecherous. Shaking her head, she said, "I need to go to Carrie as soon as possible. She must be crazed after what she's been through."

His smile vanished. "Not a good idea," he said. "Sit down, Avery. We need to talk."

His tone of voice indicated it was serious. She sat down beside him. "You don't think I should go see Carrie?"

"No, I don't. Talk to her on the phone if you need proof she's okay, but don't go to her."

"Why not?"

"Because that's what the FBI wants you to do," he said. "The agent calling the shots from Aspen told Knolte—"

She interrupted. "Who's Knolte?"

"The kid agent downstairs running the show here," he explained. "He told me the game plan. They want to put you and Carrie and the judge together in protective custody until they get Monk, and that's not a good idea."

"John Paul, they're good at what they do."

"Yeah? Well, so is Monk," he said. "And staying together is gonna make it real easy for him."

Avery didn't say a word. She silently agreed, but she felt it would be disloyal to the Bureau to admit her reservations.

She tried to get up, but he put his hands on her shoulders.

"What are you doing?"

"Bracing you so you won't hit your head if you faint."

"Listen," she said. "Downstairs . . . when I lost it . . . that was the first time in my life I ever passed out. I'm not a weakling. I was sleep-deprived and stressed . . . really stressed out. I won't faint again. Now let go of me. I want to get dressed and go downstairs to talk to Agent Knolte."

"In a minute," he promised. He tightened his hold as he said, "There's something else you need to know."

"Yes?"

He was suddenly at a loss for words. He was searching for the best way to tell her. "It's going to be difficult . . ."

"I can handle it. Just tell me." She relaxed her shoulders then and said, "Sorry, I didn't mean to snap at you. What is it?"

"Carrie knows who the woman with Monk is."

She tilted her head. "She knows her?"

"Yes." He took a breath. "You know her too."

"Come on, John Paul. Stop fencing. Just tell me," she demanded.

"Jilly. Carrie said her name is Jilly."

Avery's reaction stunned John Paul. She didn't faint; she didn't cry; she didn't argue, and she didn't go into full-blown denial.

She roared.

CHAPTER 27

"GET ME A GUN, John Paul. I want a gun now. A big one."

She looked like an avenging angel as she paced around him. She stopped just inches in front of him, poked him in the chest, and made her demand again.

Chief Tyler stood just inside the doorway of the dormitory, shifting from foot to foot as he waited for one of them to notice him.

"She'll stay dead when I get finished with her," Avery railed. "I want a gun."

The chief couldn't stop himself from trying to reason with the distraught woman.

"Now, Miss Delaney, you shouldn't be talking crazy. What if someone does shoot your mother? With you making threats, who do you think the police will come looking for? I understand you're overwrought, but . . ."

She whirled around to confront the policeman. "Jilly is not my mother. She's the woman who gave birth to me, but she has never been nor will she ever be my mother. Are we clear on that?"

Tyler hastily nodded. Her wrath was blistering, and he was so surprised by the change that had come over her he didn't know how to proceed. She'd been such a sweet, appreciative little lady when he'd first met her, but now she was a spitfire.

The chief turned to John Paul for help. "This can't be the same woman I met downstairs. She wouldn't happen to have a twin, would she?"

"Sorry, no twin," he said. "She's just got a temper." He made that comment sound like a compliment.

The chief thought it was an understatement. "Can't you reason with her? She can't go running out of here with a gun, thinking she can shoot her moth . . ." He stopped himself in time. "If she isn't your mother—"

"She isn't."

"Then what should I call her?"

Avery didn't hesitate. "A frickin' maniac," she snapped. "A deviant sociopath, a psychopath. Take your pick. Just don't call her my mother."

"Yes, ma'am."

Mollified, she clutched the sheet to her neck, picked up her duffel bag, and walked with her head held high toward the bathroom.

"John Paul?"

"Yes?"

"Get me a damn gun."

The door shut before he could answer.

Tyler scratched his jaw and asked, "What are you going to do about her?"

He shrugged. "Get her a gun."

Tyler stepped into the room and shut the door behind him. "Are you going to let them take her to Aspen? You heard them talking. They want to put her, her aunt, and that judge in a safe house until they catch the man hired to kill them."

"Yes, I heard," he said.

"If you ask me, they're putting all their eggs in one basket, and I figure the reason must have something to do with their budget. Less manpower if they keep them together, but if this professional killer . . . what's his name?"

"Monk," John Paul said.

"If he's any good, he'll find them. All he'd have to do is wait around that hospital and follow the judge. That's what I'd do."

John Paul agreed. "I heard Knolte say they were going to keep them together."

"But you didn't hear the rest of their plans because you had already gone upstairs to tell Avery her aunt was alive. Did you know there's an important trial coming up?"

"No, I didn't know."

The chief lowered his voice as he continued. Even though he could hear the hair dryer humming in the bathroom and doubted Avery would hear them talking, he moved closer to John Paul.

"They're going to retry a man named Skarrett. You familiar with him?"

He tensed. "Yes," he said. "So he's getting a new trial? When is it?"

"It starts three weeks from today," he said. "Knolte was on the phone arguing with another agent who's giving them orders. Anyway, when he hung up, he noticed me watching him, and he closed up tight, until I told him I was coming up here to check on the girl." He smiled as he added, "Of course, I didn't come right up. I made a little noise going up a couple of steps, then snuck back down and lingered in the hall so I could hear what he was telling the others."

He glanced at the bathroom door before continuing. "If they haven't nabbed Monk by the time the trial starts, they aren't going to let Avery or her aunt testify, and from what

I could gather, the man in charge didn't think it would be so bad if Skarrett got off."

John Paul was astonished. "Are you serious?"

"Oh, yes," he drawled.

"Why in God's name would they—"

"They're hoping that Skarrett will lead them to a big stash he's got hidden away. It seems Skarrett robbed a jewelry store and stole several million in uncut stones. They're hoping to get them back."

"So they're going to make it easy for Skarrett to walk?"

"Avery's a key witness," Tyler pointed out. "And if she doesn't testify . . ." He left the sentence hanging. John Paul was staggered by the endless possibilities of what could and would go wrong. His voice reeked with sarcasm as he said, "Now, that's a plan guaranteed to get screwed up."

Tyler was in full agreement. "That's the way I see it too. Are you going to tell Avery? Once they've got her in that safe house, she won't be able to get out."

"I'll let Knolte tell her," he said. "Avery works for the FBI, so she's a believer in teamwork."

"An idealist, huh?"

"Afraid so."

"That's not good. What about you? What are you going to do?"

"I guess I'll take off," he said. "No reason to hang around here."

"You think this Monk has backed off?"

"Yeah, I do," he said. "But not for long. He's taken the contracts, and when he hears that Carrie and the judge are still alive, he'll hit again. He has to. His reputation is on the line. He's going to continue to go after Avery too."

Oh, yes, he'll strike again and again and again. Until he gets the job done.

It was as though Tyler had just read his mind. "So you

think it's okay to let those boys downstairs watch over Avery? You think she'll be all right?"

"She's a smart, tough woman. She can handle herself."

Tyler looked disappointed in him. "If you think that's the right thing to do, but if you don't and you decide you might want to do something on your own, I thought I'd mention I've got this nice little cabin tucked away in the mountains. I was going to go up there for a couple of weeks, and I just stocked the kitchen. Only needs the refrigerator foods, like milk and eggs, and you'd be all set. If you're heading toward Denver, it won't be much out of your way. It would be a good place to hide out until you and Avery decide what to do . . . about the trial and all."

John Paul tried to interrupt him, but Tyler rushed on. "There's a barn where I keep my car, and I'll write out directions for you and tell you where the key to the cabin is hidden . . . if you're interested. You think about it and let me know before you leave. I'll go down and write those instructions just in case."

Having had his say, he turned around and went back downstairs. John Paul didn't know what the hell he was going to do. He stood there thinking about the situation for several minutes, then muttered an expletive as he picked up his gear and carried it down to the car. The chief's assistant had dropped off his clean clothes. They were folded next to Avery's on the bottom step. He shoved his in the bag, ran back up the stairs, and placed hers on one of the cots, and then headed outside.

The chief's friend had parked Jean Paul's car in the alley between the buildings, just below the windows in the dorm. He threw the bags into the back of the SUV and then decided he should say good-bye to Avery. He couldn't just take off, could he? Saying good-bye and wishing her luck was the decent thing to do.

If she asks me to stay, then I will, he told himself. But if she doesn't ask, then I'm out of here. Simple as that. She doesn't need me. But if she asks . . .

He walked into the room and stopped cold. He nearly tripped over his own feet when he saw her. She was standing by the window with her arms folded, waiting for him.

"Why are you glaring at me?" he asked with a defensive scowl of his own.

"I saw you putting your bags in the car," she said, nodding toward the window. "Are you leaving, then?" She took a step toward him but stopped when she noticed his back stiffen. "I would appreciate an answer."

"Do you want me to stay?"

"Do you want to stay?"

"What kind of an answer is that? I'm not in the mood to play games, Avery." Then, before she could respond, he squinted at her and asked, "What happened to your face?"

Her hand went to her cheek. "What's wrong with my face?"

"Nothing. It just looks . . . different."

"I washed it, put on some moisturizer and a little makeup. That's all."

"Makeup? Why would you do that? Do you want to look nice for your FBI buddies?"

Oh, brother, was he in a mood. "What's the matter with you?"

He couldn't answer because he couldn't possibly put into words what was going on inside his head right now or how he was feeling. Why he was suddenly itching for a fight was beyond him. He only knew he was furious with her and with himself because she had been able to do to him what no other woman had done before. She had tied his stomach into knots. What was worse was that he had let her.

What was next? His heart? The hell with that.

"Have you talked to Agent Knolte yet?"

"No, I was waiting for you to come upstairs. Were you going to leave without saying good-bye?" The big jerk. She would not cry, no matter how angry he made her. She took a breath to steady her resolve, walked across the room, and thrust her hand out. "Thank you for all you've done."

He ignored her hand. "Avery . . . if you want—"

She interrupted. "Chief Tyler came upstairs looking for you. He wanted to talk to you, said it was important."

"I just talked to him not five minutes ago."

She shrugged. "He must have something else to say to you. He's waiting in the restaurant."

"Yeah, all right."

"Have a safe trip home," she said. She turned around and walked back to the window. "Good-bye, John Paul."

He couldn't believe she was blowing him off. He stared at her back for a minute, then abruptly turned and went downstairs. Her cold farewell had been that of a stranger, and he was too pissed off to try to figure out why her attitude had changed.

Fortunately, he didn't get swamped by agents as he walked through the police station. Knolte and a couple of other young hotshots were studying maps and talking on their cell phones. One agent did try to engage him in conversation, but he ignored him, shoved the swinging door open, and crossed over to the restaurant. The front was deserted, but he could hear whistling coming from the kitchen. He walked behind the red Formica counter and spotted the chief at the grill. The aroma of sizzling meat filled the air.

"You ready to take off?" the chief asked.

"Just about."

"You want to take a hamburger for the road?"

"No thanks. Where is everyone?"

"My restaurant crew? I sent them home a while back. If

Knolte and his friends want something to eat, they can fix it themselves."

"Did you want to see me about something?"

Tyler frowned. "I already said what I had to say. I went ahead and put that sheet of directions in your car just in case you change your mind and decide to take me up on my offer to use my cabin. You ought to think about it," he urged. "I can't get up there for another month, thanks to my wife's relatives. She informed me last night we have two weddings and a reunion to attend."

"Yeah, I'll think about it," he said. "Thanks for your help, Chief, and for the food and bed."

"Glad I could help," Tyler said. He unlocked the back door and stepped into the alley with John Paul.

"You take care of yourself."

"I will," he said as he opened the car door and slid behind the wheel. He noticed the folded paper the chief had placed on the seat next to him and picked it up with the intent of handing it back.

"You sure that little girl's gonna be all right?"

That was the third time the chief had asked him that question. John Paul gave him the same answer. "She'll be okay."

He didn't believe that nonsense, not for one second, and he could tell from Tyler's expression, he didn't believe it either.

"I'll be seeing you," Tyler called, raising the spatula he was holding in farewell.

John Paul put his key in the ignition, dropped the paper on the seat, and then sat there, brooding. His conscience wouldn't quiet down. Avery had made her choice, he reminded himself. Yeah, she had let him know in no uncertain terms that she didn't want or need him.

There was only one problem with her decision. He wanted and needed her.

He thought he'd gotten rid of his feelings years ago when disillusionment had taken root, but now he realized he'd only been fooling himself with his hate-everyone, don't-need-anyone attitude and that he was as human and flawed as everyone else. Who would have thought?

Did he even like Avery? Yeah, he did, he admitted. The woman was a real smart-ass. How could he not like her?

He shook his head and turned the key in the ignition. The engine purred like a well-fed kitten as he put the gear into drive.

God knows he tried, but he couldn't summon up the strength to drive away. Damn it, she was making him nuts. She was just like a chigger, itching and irritating. She wanted him to leave. Right? Hell, yes. She was sure she was going to be fine and dandy with that super-duper team watching out for her safety . . . God help her.

Avery was a fighter, and she could certainly handle anything that came her way. But could she control the actions of the agents assigned to protect her? Could she prevent them from screwing things up? And while she was watching them, who would be watching her?

He put the gear back in park and turned the motor off. What the hell was he going to do?

Let the FBI worry about her. Damn right. That was definitely what he was going to do. He started the motor again, but this time he didn't get the gearshift into drive. He sat there like a lump of ice, frozen with indecision, while the car idled.

What a game player he was turning out to be. He was now desperately trying to convince himself he didn't care what happened to her.

She made him laugh. She made him want things he thought he could never have.

Hell, she humanized him.

John Paul fought the good fight, but when all was said and done, he lost the battle. He bowed his head in submission as the truth sliced through him. Son of a bitch.

Face it, Renard. You aren't going anywhere without her.

He turned the motor off and reached for the door.

The voice stopped him. "Will you get going? Move it, Renard. I'm suffocating back here, and your sleeping bag smells like dead leaves."

He swung around. "What do you think you're doing?" he asked.

"Don't start with me, John Paul. Put the damn car into drive and get us out of here. Don't make me tell you again."

His smile was slow and easy. The tension eased out of his shoulders, and his stomach stopped aching. The world was suddenly right again. Avery was snarling at him like a mountain cat, definitely giving him attitude.

He started the engine and changed gears, but he didn't accelerate. "If you go with me, sugar, I'm calling the shots, and you're going to do what I tell you to do. Can you deal with that?"

She didn't hesitate in answering. "When I jumped off the fire escape ladder, I landed on the roof of your car and dented it. You deal with that."

He grinned as he drove down the alley. How could he not be crazy about her?

CHAPTER 28

J ILLY WAS ANXIOUSLY waiting to hear the body count. She paced around her hotel bungalow while the television, tuned in to a local Colorado station, droned on and on, but each time that wonderful film clip showing the explosion of the house came on, she hurriedly sat down on the edge of the bed. Enthusiastically and greedily, she devoured every second of the magnificent footage.

How fortuitous that a hiker just happened to be filming the landscape at the exact second the house disintegrated. His lens had captured every bit of the back of the house. Had Jilly not been able to watch it on television, she would have been irate. Admittedly, she was still a little irritated because she had been looking forward to pushing the button, but this clip that the station kept showing over and over again was almost as good.

The phone rang just as the clip ended. She hit the mute button before she answered.

"Hello, darling."

A second's pause followed. "Did you see it on television?"

He sounded so eager to please, yet nervous at the same time. "Yes, of course I saw it. Wasn't it marvelous?"

"Yes . . . yes," he replied. "Two bodies so far."

"One to go," she said. "You sound nervous, darling. What's wrong?"

"I was worried that, after the fact, you might feel bad. I'm glad to know you're okay."

"Feel bad about Carrie? She ruined my life and stole my daughter from me. I'm overjoyed," she said.

"I miss you," he said. "I want—"

Her voice dropped to a throaty whisper. "I know what you want. Are you in the car now?"

"Yes," he whispered back.

"You'd better pull over," she said. And then in the most erotic detail she told him what she would do to him when they were together. His breathing amused her. The rapid panting of a dog in heat, she thought. The power she had over men excited her.

"Will you like that?" she asked breathlessly so he would think she was as out of control as he was.

And then she gave him more until he was whimpering with his need. A sudden silence followed a low groan. She knew what was happening and smiled with satisfaction. She could have had a wonderful career doing phone sex, she thought, but she certainly wouldn't make the kind of money she wanted. Still, it was nice to know she had options.

"Are you feeling less lonely now, darling?"

"Yes," he answered with a sigh. "I'll be with you soon. I love you, Jilly."

"I know you do, darling. I love you too."

She hung up the phone and began to pace again. Would the police be able to tell who was who from what little was left of the bodies? She knew that skulls and teeth were one way of identifying victims, but what if those had also been blown to smithereens?

Umm. What would they do then?

The film came on the television again. Jilly rushed to the bed and sat down to watch. Oh, it was lovely, so lovely.

When the news bulletin ended, she went to her overnight bag and took out her precious videotape. She carried it with her wherever she went. She popped it into the VCR and knelt in front of the TV to watch. How many times had she seen it? A hundred? A thousand? And yet, she never grew tired of it . . . or the feelings it provoked.

"Now do you see why you have to die?" she whispered to the screen.

She happened to notice one of her nails was chipped and rushed into the bathroom to repair it. Checking the time, she realized that Monk would be arriving soon. She needed to get ready to greet him properly. And reward him, of course. Like a dog who'd performed a difficult trick, Monk would be anxious for his treat.

Virginal white, she decided as she pulled the negligee from her overnight bag. He'd like that. But then he liked everything she did to him, didn't he?

She mustn't forget to put on red lipstick. Oh, how men loved pouting red lips.

They loved her perfect body. They loved her angelic face.

They all loved her.

CHAPTER 29

THE PARAMEDICS TOLD Carrie she was in shock. She didn't agree, but she understood how they had reached their diagnosis. Granted, there was something a little peculiar about her behavior. When they'd lifted her out of the ravine, she had been sobbing uncontrollably and incoherently. She knew the words she wanted to say, yet she couldn't seem to get them out in the right order or at the right time. Still, their conclusion was a bunch of nonsense. They weren't doctors. What the hell did they know? Her mind was working just fine, thank you very much.

Camera lights glared in her face as she was carried on the stretcher and placed across from Sara in the waiting ambulance. Carrie struggled to sit up until she realized one of the paramedics had rudely strapped her down. She was able to move one of her arms, though. Reaching across the narrow aisle, she took hold of Sara's hand.

Her friend was in terrible pain. Both paramedics were working on her leg. "Is she going to be all right? Is she going to be all right?" The question became a chant she couldn't stop. Even though both men tried to assure her that yes, yes, she was going to be fine, Carrie felt compelled to keep asking.

One of them gave Sara an injection, and she closed her eyes seconds later. Her hand went limp in Carrie's. After they finished immobilizing her leg, one of them checked her blood pressure again while the other worked on Carrie.

"He's going to kill Avery. Make them stop him. Do you hear me? He's going to . . . going to . . ."

Carrie passed out. The terror of what she had been through, added to sleep deprivation, had finally caught up with her. Her body simply rebelled and shut down.

When she next opened her eyes, she was in a hospital bed. And, oh, how she ached. It seemed every muscle in her body throbbed. Had someone taken a stick to her?

She desperately tried to clear the fog in her mind. Avery. Oh, God, she had to find Avery before it was too late. She saw the call button pinned to the sheet on her left and tried to reach for it. Pain shot up through her elbow and she cried out. Looking down, she saw the cast on her arm and let out a low curse.

How had that happened?

The ravine, of course. She'd fallen headfirst into that deep pit, and she remembered putting her arm out to try to brace against the fall. She knew she'd injured her wrist, but she thought she'd just sprained it. It hadn't hurt all that much at the time, had it? She couldn't remember. Maybe it had gone numb, as numb as the rest of her at that point. She did remember landing on top of Sara, though. Her friend had been writhing in agony, and Carrie distinctly recalled putting her hand over her mouth to stifle her cries, terrified that Monk was lurking in the dark waiting to catch them.

Where was Sara? Carrie could hear men's voices in the hallway, and she couldn't reach the call button. She was about to shout when the door opened and a young doctor dressed in blue scrubs and a white lab coat came inside. He was holding a chart in his hand.

His name was Dr. Bridgeport, and he looked as if he hadn't had any sleep in a week. That can't be good, she thought. Then she noticed his hands. They were huge, as though he'd had them transplanted from a bigger body, along with the new row of dark hair plugs in his scalp.

"Are you my doctor?"

"I'm a neurologist. I've reviewed your X rays and CAT scan," he began.

"I had those tests?" she interrupted.

He nodded. "You suffered a mild concussion. I'm going to keep you overnight for observation. I didn't see anything alarming on the scan," he added.

"What about my arm?"

"You broke it."

"Obviously," she said.

He was writing in her chart and, without looking up, said, "Your primary physician will be in to check on you in a little while. Meanwhile, you've got quite a few eager law enforcement officers waiting to talk to you. I'm going to allow two in the room . . . if you're feeling up to it."

"My head hurts. May I have something for pain?"

"In a little while," he promised.

She knew what that meant. When Avery was little and wanted something Carrie didn't want her to have, she used the very same phrase. It hadn't worked on Avery then, and it wasn't working on Carrie now.

"I want something."

"You've suffered a concussion, Mrs. Salvetti, and I would rather—"

She cut him off. "Oh, never mind. Doctor, a friend of

mine rode with me in the ambulance. Her leg was all torn up. Where is she? Do you know?"

The doctor nodded. "Judge Collins is in surgery," he explained.

There was a hard rap on the door. The doctor closed the chart, smiled at her, and turned to leave. "You need to rest," he said as he opened the door and let two men in dark suits rush inside. "Ten minutes," he said to the agents, "then she needs to get some sleep."

They moved like soldiers on parade, arms stiff, heads high. They were also dressed alike, except for the choice of tie colors. One wore a gray-and-black-striped tie, and the other had on a muted plaid.

An agent named Hillman was in charge. There was a sharpness about his eyes she found comforting. She didn't think he would miss much.

The other, younger agent pushed the button to elevate her back, poured her a glass of water, and hovered at her side while Hillman questioned her. He led her through the sequence of events, rarely interrupting when she paused to collect her thoughts. She wanted to tell him everything at once, impatient to ask questions of her own, but Hillman was tenacious and made her keep to his agenda.

She turned to the more cooperative agent and asked him to find her jacket.

"The letters are in the pocket."

Hillman found the jacket hanging in the built-in closet. He pulled on a pair of gloves and dropped the envelopes into a Ziploc bag the other agent held out for him.

"Anne gave a letter to me. I want to read it."

"We'll let the lab dust it for prints," the sidekick told her.

She'd thought he was more malleable than Hillman, but now she realized he was just as tenacious.

"I want to know what that sick bastard of a husband

wrote to her. He hired Monk to kill her, you know. You have to arrest him."

Ignoring her demand, Hillman resumed his questions. Carrie had had enough. "No, it's my turn. I want to know where my niece is."

"We're searching for her . . ."

"Find her."

Seeing how distraught Carrie was, sidekick offered her a sip of water by holding the straw under her nose. She turned her head.

"Tell me what you know about . . ." Hillman once again tried to get her back on track.

"I want an update on Judge Collins, and I want it now."

The agents exchanged a glance, and then Hillman answered. "She's out of surgery and in ICU."

"So far, so good," the other man said.

She glared at him. "What's your name?"

"Bean, ma'am. Agent Peter Bean."

No wonder he hadn't introduced himself. Saddled with a name like that, she wouldn't have told anyone either. Bet they called him string bean in grade school, she thought.

Hillman started the questions all over again. For an hour he kept it up, grilling her, going over the same facts again and again until she began to feel as if she were the criminal they were trying to get to confess.

Her head was pounding. "That's it," she said. "I can't answer any more questions now."

Hillman looked disappointed, but he agreed to let her rest for a little while. She wasn't in the mood to be cordial. She told them not to come back until they had news about Avery. To calm her down—she was shouting now—Hillman let her call her husband. Bean dialed the number for her. The second she heard Tony's voice over the phone, she burst into tears.

"I need you, Tony. You have to come to Aspen."

His voice shook with emotion as he replied, "Sweetheart, they told me I couldn't. They said as soon as you're discharged from the hospital they're going to move you and the judge to a safe house somewhere. Carrie, love, are you all right? I wish I could be there with you. I wish . . . I'm sorry you're going through this alone."

"Have you heard from Avery?"

"No," he answered. "I didn't know she was planning to join you at the spa. One of the agents who came to talk to me told me she missed her flight."

"I don't know where she is," she sobbed.

"We'll find her," he promised. "Nothing's going to happen to her. I promise you. And I'm keeping the line open. She'll call. I know she'll call."

"Tony, I didn't realize . . . I'm so sorry about everything. You can have Star Catcher. You can run it any way you want. I don't care about any of that anymore. I should have trusted you. I've been such a fool."

She was sobbing now and angry because the agents were listening to every word.

"I love you," she whispered. "I do, Tony. I love you very much. Please . . . tell me it isn't too late."

"No, no, it isn't. I can . . . I love you too," he stammered. "I'll get on the next plane. We'll make our marriage work again. Anything is possible with your love. Anything."

CHAPTER 30

ANY HOPE THAT the FBI would be able to keep the names of the survivors out of the papers and off the television had been squelched when a news crew filmed Carrie and the judge being carried into the ambulance near the site of the explosion.

Avery heard about it on the radio as she and John Paul were driving through the mountains. As soon as they'd left the sleepy town, she'd climbed in front, clipping him on the shoulder with her left foot when she fell into the passenger seat. Her shoe fell in his lap. Shaking his head over her awkwardness, he handed her the shoe while she apologized.

They continued to listen to the broadcast until the signal faded. "Does everyone in the United States carry video cameras now?" he asked. He sounded disgusted. "Some people just love invading other people's privacy."

"Film crews from television stations usually carry cameras," she said.

"No need to be sarcastic, sugar."

"I wasn't being sarcastic. I was simply pointing out a fact. Carrie must have hated having a camera in her face.

Someone from the FBI should have grabbed the film. The crime-scene investigators must not have gotten there in time."

"Should've, could've," he drawled. "That's the Bureau's motto."

"You're not going to rile me."

He laughed. "I wasn't trying to."

She rolled the window down and let the cool night air in. "Yes, you were," she said. "I've finally gotten you all figured out."

"You think so?"

She smiled. "When I first met you, I thought you must have some kind of grudge against the FBI, but now that I know you better, I realize that isn't true at all. Your phobia is much bigger than that."

"Oh?"

She nodded. "You don't like any government agency."

"That's not true."

"When we talked about your brother-in-law working for the Justice Department, you sneered."

"Justice has too much power."

"What about the CIA? I know you worked for them."

He didn't argue or deny. "Their priorities change on a whim, leaving agents and civilians out there to hang."

"What about the IRS?"

"Everyone hates the IRS."

She'd give him that one. She kept on naming government agencies, and he continued to tell her what was wrong with each one of them.

"I think I've made my case. You know what your biggest problem is?"

"No, but you're going to enlighten me, aren't you?"

"Uh-huh," she said. "You don't like anyone in a position of authority."

He wasn't offended by her analysis. "You know what they say. Absolute power corrupts absolutely."

"The FBI doesn't have absolute power."

"They think they do."

"You know what I say?"

"What?"

"Therapy. You need intense therapy to help you get rid of your hostility."

Before he could tell her he hated therapy too, she changed the subject. "I need to get to a phone and call Carrie."

"Why didn't you call her from the police station?"

"Because you would have left without me. I still can't believe you were going to abandon me. I get mad every time I think about it."

Should he tell her the truth or not? He clenched his jaw while he thought about it. She'd sounded so disappointed in him, even hurt.

"Look . . ." he began, and then stopped.

"Yes?"

"Maybe I was going to stay."

"Maybe?" She poked him in his arm. "What does that mean?"

"It means I was gonna stay. Now it's your turn to squirm. How come you decided to leave your super team?"

"Stop calling them that. I'm sure Agent Knolte and the other agents are quite capable of doing a good job."

"Yeah? Then, I repeat, why did you decide to go with me?"

She shrugged. "I thought about what you said, and I agreed. It isn't smart to put all of us together in the same safe house."

"And?"

"And what? Are you waiting for a compliment?"

Before he could tell her the thought hadn't crossed his mind, she said, "Okay, fine. I think I have a better chance of surviving with you."

"What made you cross over to the dark side?" he asked, grinning. "Did Knolte say or do something that turned you into a rogue agent?"

"I'm not an agent. I'm an analyst, and he didn't say or do anything. I still have complete faith in the Bureau. No one is more loyal than I am."

"Uh-huh," he said. "So why'd you leave?"

She had to think about it for a while. "I'm taking initiative. We're taught to do that at the Bureau."

"Yeah, right," he scoffed. He nodded toward a sign on the side of the two-lane road. "There's a restaurant five miles ahead," he said. "I need to make a call too and get us some help."

Mr. Loner was going to ask someone for help? That was a shock.

"Then what?" she asked.

"You can call Carrie, but don't tell her where we're headed."

"How can I? I don't know where we're going."

He picked up the folded paper. "Chief Tyler has a cabin a couple of hours away. It's got a barn, and I can hide the car inside. We'll stay there tonight."

She glanced out the back window once again to make sure they weren't being followed. They hadn't seen another car in a long time, and she realized she was probably being a little paranoid, but she continued to stay on guard. One couldn't be too cautious, she reasoned.

"Do you have any guesses where Monk might be?"

"He's probably still in Colorado, and by now he's heard that your aunt and the judge are still alive."

"The FBI will be looking for us too," she said.

"Not us, sugar. You. They'll be looking for you."

"I turned the shower on in case one of the agents came upstairs, and I locked the dormitory door, but eventually Knolte will find out I'm gone, and he'll sound the alarm."

And then all hell was going to break loose. When Carter found out about the situation, he'd have her ass on a platter. She already had her argument rehearsed. She'd insist it wasn't insubordination. Carter was tough, but he was also a reasonable man. Surely he would see the merits of her taking initiative . . . again.

"Will the chief tell Knolte he offered you the use of his cabin?" she asked.

"No, he won't," he said. "Did he know you were going out the window?"

"No."

John Paul took the exit and pulled into the tarred parking lot adjacent to the restaurant. The neon letters were blinking *Open.*

"Are you going to tell me about Jilly?" He had avoided bringing up that subject until now because he had seen how Avery reacted when Tyler called the woman her mother. She didn't answer him. "You're going to have to tell me what I'm up against."

"What *we're* up against," she said. "Yes, I'll tell you what I know, but not on an empty stomach. Tomorrow," she promised, "I'll tell you everything."

"Okay."

He took her hand as they walked into the diner. The colors inside made both of them squint. The walls were painted a neon purple and orange as a backdrop to the white Formica countertops. A jukebox sat just inside the door. Elvis Presley was singing "All Shook Up" as they made their way down the narrow aisle.

John Paul chose a booth against the wall so he could watch the parking lot. He waited until Avery slid into the orange vinyl seat and then sat down across from her.

The waitress was a teenager, but she shuffled like a ninety-year-old. Her tongue was pierced, which gave her a speech impediment when she spoke.

"What can I git ya?"

They ordered turkey sandwiches and iced tea. As soon as the waitress went behind the counter, Avery dug some change out of her billfold and headed for the telephone she had spotted at the end of the aisle, between the men's and women's rest rooms.

The conversation with Carrie was mostly one-sided. Her aunt was in a state. "Where are you?" she demanded. "Why aren't you here? Are you all right? Did you hear? Jilly's alive. The demon faked her own death. I didn't think she was that smart. She's like a cat, Avery. Yeah, that's what she is. Do you realize, if you had shown up at the spa when you were supposed to, you'd have been inside that house with us?"

"Carrie, slow down," Avery said when her aunt finally paused.

Carrie took a deep breath and then told her some of what had happened from the moment she'd gotten into the car with Monk and the other women. Avery didn't say a word while she listened to the grisly highlights.

"When I see you, I'll tell you everything," Carrie promised. "How are you doing?"

"I'm fine."

"I was so scared and worried about you, but you're okay."

"Yes, I am," Avery said, her gaze locked on John Paul. "Carrie, who's the agent in charge of watching over you?"

Her aunt spoke at the same time that Avery asked the question. "They said they're going to put us in protective custody. I'm assuming they'll fly us to Florida."

"Why Florida?"

"Because of the trial."

"What trial?"

"Oh, Avery, you didn't know? That bastard Skarrett has a trial date set. Didn't anyone notify you? They sure as hell didn't call me."

Avery was stunned by the news. She had known that there was a possibility of a new trial, but she hadn't thought it would happen this soon.

"No, I wasn't notified."

Carrie was beside herself. "They told me this killer Jilly hired won't stop until we're dead."

"Or until we get him," she said. "And we will, Carrie. Now, please, try to calm down. Have you talked to Tony yet?"

Carrie's voice mellowed. Sniffling, she whispered, "He's beside himself with worry. He wants you to call him as soon as possible so he can hear your voice. I want to go home, Avery, and I want you to come with me, but they won't let us. I don't even know if they'll let Tony come stay with me. I'm trying to cooperate—"

Avery interrupted. "How is the judge doing?"

"What? Oh, Sara. Her name's Sara. She's hanging in there. She trashed her knee and had to go to surgery, but she's doing okay now. They're keeping her in ICU for another couple of hours because of her age, but that's just a precaution. The doctors already let me sit with her and talk to her for a few minutes. Oh, my God, I forgot to tell you. Sara Collins is the judge who sentenced Skarrett."

"No, that can't be right. I remember the judge. His name was Hamilton."

"Yes, Judge Hamilton heard the case and convicted Skarrett. We went back to Bel Air once the verdict was in, remember?"

"I remember."

"But Skarrett hadn't been sentenced yet. Anyway, Hamilton died, and when Skarrett came up for sentencing, Sara was the judge."

"So that's the connection," she said. "But what about the other woman?"

"Anne Trapp wouldn't go with us. It's a long story, and I'll tell you everything as soon as you get here. Are they going to bring you to the hospital, or will I meet you at the airport? If they want us to fly to Florida, I'm not going without you. We'll have three full weeks to catch up before they decide if they're going to let us testify or not. If Monk is still on the loose—"

Avery interrupted. "Three weeks? You're telling me the new trial will start in just three weeks?"

"Yes," she said. "I'm sure they'll put us in a safe house near the courthouse so that, if we do get to testify, it will be easier getting us there."

Avery couldn't compute the information in her head. "And you're saying there's a possibility we won't be allowed to testify?"

"Honey, what's the matter with you? Aren't you listening? Yes, there is that possibility that we won't get to testify. Okay? We'd be sitting ducks, and it would be a perfect opportunity for Monk to hurt us."

Avery gripped the phone. "No one is stopping me from testifying."

"Be reasonable."

"Do you want Skarrett to walk?" Her voice shook with her fury.

"Your safety is more important to me."

"I'm not letting him walk."

"We'll have plenty of time to talk about the trial," Carrie said. "Why aren't you asking me about Jilly?"

"I don't want to talk about her."

"I hope when they catch her, I get to have five minutes alone with her."

"She'd annihilate you."

"But not you, not with all that tai chi and karate stuff you learned." Carrie sighed. "Don't be afraid of her."

Avery felt like laughing. After all the hellacious stories she'd heard about Jilly over the years, she would have to be as crazy as Jilly not to be afraid.

"Did you see her? Was she inside the house?"

"Yes," Carrie answered. "I'll tell you everything when I see you."

"I want you to promise me that you'll do whatever the agents tell you to do. Okay, Carrie? Promise me."

"Yes, of course I will."

"Don't make their job . . . difficult. You know how you can get when you're upset or scared."

"I'm not scared; I'm angry. Very, very angry. Why the hell couldn't Jilly stay dead?"

"She never died," Avery pointed out.

"They better not put us in a flea-infested shack while they're protecting us. The house is in Florida, so I want something on the beach."

"Carrie, that isn't your decision."

"If it's not nice, you can pull some strings for us. I can't wait to see you."

Avery braced herself. Her aunt had a very short fuse when things weren't going her way, and Avery was about to ignite it.

"I'm not going to be joining you. I'm not going to the safe house with—"

That was as far as she got. Carrie's scream made her cringe, and she had to move the phone away from her ear.

From where John Paul was seated, he could hear the aunt shouting. The color left Avery's face as she listened. He got up, walked to the phone, and gently took it from her.

"Say good-bye, sugar."

"She's very upset."

"Uh-huh."

"I love you, Carrie, and I'll see you soon," she said. "Bye now."

She heard Carrie shouting, "Avery Elizabeth, don't you dare hang up this—"

John Paul placed the phone back in the cradle. "She sounds nice," he managed with a straight face.

The waitress was watching them as she placed their plates on the table. Avery pulled away from John Paul and went into the ladies' room to wash her hands. By the time she sat down in the booth, he had already devoured his sandwich and was finishing his iced tea.

"I don't want you to get the wrong idea about my aunt. Granted, she can be difficult, but I'm sure, once you got to know her, you'd love her as much as I do."

He grinned. "I don't see that happening."

She took a bite of her turkey sandwich, thought it tasted like pressed sawdust, and picked up her glass of iced tea to wash it down.

"You want this?" she asked as she pushed the plate toward him.

He pushed it back. "You need to eat that," he said as he helped himself to one of the limp potato chips.

She noticed him watching the highway beyond the parking lot. "They don't get much business here, do they?"

"They're closing in fifteen minutes. Maybe that's why we're the only customers. Tell me something, Avery. When you filled out your application to work for the Bureau, was it your goal to become an agent?"

"Yes."

"Then why didn't you?"

She was about to give him her standard answer, but then decided to be completely honest with him. Besides, she was pretty sure he'd cut through the bull and know she wasn't telling him the truth.

"I thought I should want to be an agent. An FBI agent saved my life, and I think that was when I got it into my head that I wanted to be just like him. You know, save people."

"So you were going to save the world. How old were you when you made this momentous decision?"

"Twelve. I'd just turned twelve."

"That's amazing."

"Why?"

"That you didn't change your mind, that you held on to that goal all through high school and college."

"Do you remember what you wanted to be when you were young?"

"I don't remember how old I was when I decided it would be pretty cool to be an astronaut. Maybe ten or eleven."

"That plan didn't work out?" she asked, teasing.

"Life got in the way," he said. "I ended up in engineering at Tulane, graduated, and joined the Marines."

"Why the Marines?"

"I was drunk."

She didn't buy it. "Tell me the real reason."

"I thought I could make a difference. I liked the discipline, and I wanted something different than Bowen, Louisiana."

"But you live in Bowen now, don't you?"

"Yeah, I do," he said. "I had to go away to realize what I really wanted in life. I actually live outside of Bowen, in the swamp."

"You really did drop out of life, didn't you?"

"I like solitude."

"Guess you don't get much company in the swamp."

"I like that too. Where did you go to college?" he asked.

"Santa Clara University," she answered. "Then Stanford." She took another bite of her sandwich and could barely get the horrible food down. The bread was soggy; the lettuce was wilted, and the turkey was dry.

"Neither one of us went very far away. We both stayed close to home. Carrie wanted me to go to college in L.A. so I could work part-time for her company."

"Doing what?"

She blushed. The instantaneous reaction made him all the more curious.

"She was pushing me to do more commercials. I got roped into doing one for her when she was in a bind."

"So what'd you have to do in this commercial?"

"Hold up a bar of soap, bat my eyelashes, and sing a silly jingle."

He didn't laugh but he came close. "Sing it for me."

"No," she said. "I was awful and I hated it. I guess I'm an introvert," she added with a shrug. "Since I'd had this dream of becoming an agent for so long, Carrie gave in and stopped nagging me. We both gave in actually."

She pushed her plate to the side, and John Paul reached over and took a couple more potato chips. "How did you give in?"

She folded her paper napkin just so and placed it on the table. "I did a project at a grade school in San Jose for one of my classes, and I really enjoyed working with the children, so much so that I considered becoming a teacher. I was good with them," she added, a hint of surprise in her voice. "I even went so far as to take a couple of the classes I would need to get a teaching certificate. I thought I could teach history. I didn't tell Carrie, though."

"Why not? What does she have against teachers?"

"Nothing. She just didn't want me to become one."

He leaned back and stared at her. "Avery, what aren't you telling me?"

Ignoring the question, she called out to the waitress to please bring them their bill.

"Come on, babe. Answer me. Why didn't she want you to teach?"

"The pay's terrible."

"What else?"

"Teachers don't get much respect. You know what they say. Those who can do, and those who can't teach. Carrie didn't think there was much . . . status in teaching. My aunt isn't a shrew," she said. "I know I've made her sound terrible, but she isn't like that. Honest."

"So was that all? That was your reason for not teaching? There wasn't enough status?"

"Carrie didn't think it would be a good idea for me to be around kids."

"Why not?"

He wasn't going to let it drop. "She thought it would be too difficult for me."

"Ah."

"What does that mean?"

He homed in like a pigeon. "You can't have kids, can you?"

She wanted to tell him. She felt an overwhelming need to tell him everything, to spill her guts, as her uncle Tony would say. She'd never felt this need before, but John Paul wasn't like any other man. He didn't give a hoot about silly things like status. He wasn't a game player, and he didn't have a hidden agenda. What you saw was what you got. Maybe that was the reason she was so attracted to him. And so comfortable.

"I don't know how you made that leap."

"You told me you weren't ever going to get married, which I thought was a little odd."

She jumped on his comment with a vengeance. "Why? Because all women should want to get married? You can't really believe that. Lots of women are very happy living the single life."

He put his hand up. "Whoa," he said. "I don't disagree, but when you told me you weren't going to get married, you were damned defensive about it. That's what I thought was odd. Now I understand why. You can't have children, and that's the reason Carrie doesn't want you working with them. I'm right, aren't I?"

"Yes."

She was primed for a fight. She'd let him see her vulnerability, and she knew that if he gave her an ounce of sympathy or was the least bit compassionate, she would lose it. She'd either pull his hair out or her own. Worse, in her estimation, she might cry. She knew her reaction was a defense mechanism, but she didn't care. Staring into his eyes, she waited, daring him to be nice to her.

He stared back. "Well?" she finally demanded when he didn't say a word.

"That's just damned stupid."

She blinked. "Excuse me?"

"You heard me, sugar. You love working with kids, so that's what you ought to do. Listening to your aunt and trying to please her is just damned stupid."

"But I'm good at my job in the Bureau."

"So what? You've got more than one talent, don't you? You can be good doing a lot of different things."

He got up to pay the bill and then made a phone call, but all the while, he never took his gaze off the parking lot. Avery looked over at the waitress who blew a bubble twice the size of her face and then leaned on the counter and stared at him.

Five minutes later he hung up the phone. "Come on. We need to get going."

She followed him to the car. He was about to open the door for her when she asked, "What are you good at doing?"

"Lots of things."

"I know you worked for the CIA. What was your talent then?"

He didn't deny it. "Shooting. I was a good shooter. No, that's not true. I wasn't just good. I was great. Eyesight of an eagle."

"Anything else you're good at doing?"

"Yeah," he drawled. He put his arm around her waist and began to slowly pull her toward him. "I'm real good at a couple of other things too."

"Like what?"

He drew her closer and put his lips to her ear. "If things go the way I plan, you'll get to see firsthand," he whispered.

"Oh, brother," she answered breathlessly.

Could he feel her goose bumps? Probably, she thought as she sighed and turned to look into his eyes.

Smiling gently, he kissed her warm, soft mouth, taking his time coaxing a response. She was becoming impossible to resist. The dazed look in her eyes made him feel arrogantly pleased with himself. "We'd better get out of here before I get carried away and show you right now."

He opened the door for her and then got behind the wheel. They drove out of the lot and once again headed toward Denver. "We need to put some distance between us and that diner," he told her. "The waitress will remember you."

"You think so?"

"Yeah. You're definitely memorable."

"News flash, sugar," she drawled, trying to imitate his sexy southern accent. "Bubble Gum was staring at *you*."

He shrugged. "It's going to take us at least another hour or more to get to Tyler's cabin. If I see a store on the way, we'll stop and get some supplies."

"I doubt anything will be open this late."

"And that's important because?"

"Shame on you. You're going to break in?"

"They'll never know I was there."

She didn't try to dissuade him. She was too busy thinking about his earlier remark. What would happen if things went the way he planned?

Thirty miles down the road, they found a fishing tackle/grocery store. It was dark inside.

John Paul's skills seemed endless. He got the door unlocked without making a scratch, charmed the black Doberman guard dog, and shopped to his heart's content. She helped him carry two gallons of milk and four grocery sacks to the car.

He calculated the expense as he sacked the items and left four twenty-dollar bills sticking out from under the cash register.

"How long are we going to be staying at Tyler's place?" she asked when they were once again on their way. "We've got enough food for a month."

"We'll stay at least one night, maybe two," he answered. "Tyler told me there's a little town about fifteen miles from the cabin. I've got Theo checking on a couple of things, and when I find out what is going on, we'll decide what to do."

"I'm not going to miss that trial."

"I understand. May I ask you something?"

"Yes?"

"Is Skarrett the reason you can't have children?"

"Yes," she said. "A bullet hit just right, but you know what? I would never have had children anyway. I wouldn't take the risk that what's wrong with Jilly is genetic. So, you see, it doesn't matter."

"Yeah, it does," he argued. "Skarrett took that choice away from you. That's what matters."

He couldn't keep the anger out of his voice, but she didn't become upset. What he'd said was true.

She changed the subject to a less stressful one, talking about silly things that had happened to her when she was growing up. He told her stories about his life and his family, and when he talked about his father, she laughed several times.

"People really call him Big Daddy?"

"Yeah, they do. You'll like him," he predicted.

He was assuming she would meet his father someday. She'd like that. She wanted to know about his family and his home and his work. She wanted to know everything about him. Before she could continue the conversation, they saw two pairs of headlights coming up the road toward them.

He swerved onto a side road and turned his lights off.

They silently waited until the cars passed by.

"When you asked your brother-in-law to help, were you worried he might tell the FBI where we're going?"

"Because he's with Justice?"

"Yes."

"Family comes first, sugar. Always."

"Still . . ."

"He won't tell, and he will help. I told him what I needed done, and he agreed."

"Good. I'm glad we can trust him."

They waited in the dark for a few minutes before he felt it was safe for them to go.

Avery's mind wandered and then circled around and around what he'd whispered in her ear. Maybe if she stopped staring at him, she could think about something else. It had been such a long time since she'd been intimate with a man, and she thought she had become an expert at blocking those thoughts and urges.

She *had* been an expert anyway, until he came into her life. Now the floodgates were wide open, and all she could think about was touching him. Everywhere.

For thirty more minutes she battled to think about something other than sex. She mentally balanced her checkbook, then calculated how long she could stay in her apartment without a paycheck coming in. Three months or four? If she got fired.

She started tapping her foot on the floor. Who was she kidding? Of course she was going to get fired. They couldn't arrest her for being insubordinate, but would Carter charge her with hindering an investigation?

John Paul put his hand on her knee. "How come you're so jittery?" Then, before she could come up with a good lie, he said, "There it is."

He pulled onto a dirt road. His night vision was better than hers. She hadn't even noticed the little curve. "You're sure?"

His hand was still on her leg, and she wasn't inclined to move it. She stared straight ahead, pretending to watch the road as she thought about ripping his clothes off him.

Was she turning into a slut? She shook her head. No, she was simply having normal urges, like any other woman, but because she hadn't had those urges in so long, she wasn't handling herself well.

"What are you thinking about?" he asked.

Sex, damn it. I'm thinking about sex. "Nothing much."

"Yeah?"

Even his voice was sexy. Threading her fingers through her hair, she realized how tense she was, and how horribly unsure of herself.

They drove around a bank of trees, and then the road flattened into what she thought might be a field. It was impossible to tell in the dark. She began tapping her foot on the floorboard again. She was nervous about being alone with him in the secluded cabin.

He pulled up to the steps in front. When he turned the motor and the lights off, it was pitch black. She couldn't even see her hand in front of her face.

"You stay put until I get the key from under the porch step."

She couldn't have moved if her life had depended on it. Her legs felt like rubber, and she thought she just might start hyperventilating. Fortunately, she had her wild thoughts under control by the time he'd unlocked the front door and turned the lights on inside the cabin. She got out and helped him carry in the bags.

The cabin was charming and smelled of pine and

Lysol. A stone fireplace faced the front door and was flanked by two wicker chairs with red-and-yellow-checked overstuffed cushions. The hunter green sofa had seen better days, for the arms were frayed, and the fabric was faded, but it looked very comfortable. To the right of the front door was a round pine table and four single ladder-back chairs.

Beyond the table was a narrow kitchen with a back door. She placed a bag of groceries on the counter, then walked through the living room to the other side of the cabin. There were two doors along the short hallway. The one on the left opened into a bathroom. At the end of the hall she opened the other door and stepped inside. Soft light spilled into the spacious room. A double bed with an old iron headboard was covered with a multicolored quilt.

The longer she stared at the bed, the faster her heart beat. She could hear John Paul putting the groceries away, knew she should probably help, but couldn't seem to make herself move.

"It's just a bed, for Pete's sake. What's the big deal?"

Disgusted with herself for being so nervous, she grabbed her duffel bag and went into the bathroom to take a shower.

She hadn't bothered to pack a pretty nightgown or a robe. After she dried her hair and brushed her teeth, she put on a pair of skimpy pink panties and her ratty old Santa Clara T-shirt. It was at least three sizes too big for her. It hung like a tent and ended just above her knees.

Staring into the mirror, she took inventory and decided she came up lacking in the feminine wiles department. For the first time in her life, she wanted to look pretty. Boy, wouldn't Carrie have a good laugh now? She was always criticizing the way Avery dressed, and for once, Avery had to agree.

There wasn't anything she could do about her appearance now. With a sigh, she put her bag in the corner of the bedroom so she wouldn't trip over it, then walked into the living room just as the front door opened and John Paul came inside. He shut the door, bolted it, then turned around and froze.

"What happened to you?" she asked. He didn't answer her. "You look like you showered in the dirt. What happened?" she repeated.

John Paul couldn't make himself stop staring at her legs. Fantasies were raging in his mind. "I put the car in the barn, and I thought . . . the oil . . . the tires . . ."

"Yes?"

"What?"

He finally forced himself to look into her eyes, knowing he probably resembled a buck caught in the headlights. When he'd noticed her standing in the doorway, his knees damned near buckled. That well-scrubbed look was intoxicating. She was simply gorgeous. Did she have any idea of the power she had over him?

"What about the oil and the tires?"

"That's right."

He was blathering like an idiot, and she was fully responsible for his radical drop in IQ. He strode past her, muttering incoherent words as he went into the bathroom and shut the door.

She took a bottled water out of the fridge, turned the lights off in the kitchen and the living room, and then went into the bedroom. She kept telling herself to relax as she folded the quilt. She found clean sheets on the closet shelf and put them on the bed with a lightweight blanket she pulled out of the cedar chest. She climbed on top, scooted to the middle. Straightening her back, she folded her legs in the lotus position. She tried to clear her mind and concentrate on her breathing. Just as she was about to sit down in her imaginary porch swing without a care in the world, she was interrupted.

"Going to your happy place?"

Her eyes flew open. John Paul was standing in the doorway watching her. He wore a pair of shorts and nothing else. He hadn't even bothered to button them. He had taken the time to shave, she noticed, and he'd washed his hair too. There were big drops of water glistening on his tanned neck and shoulders.

Sitting on the bed definitely put her at a distinct disadvantage. If they were going to approach their situation as adults, she wanted to be on equal footing. She scrambled to get off the bed.

"Yes, I was," she said. "I was trying to relax."

He yawned loudly. "Avery?"

"Yes?"

He leaned casually against the door frame, one ankle crossed over the other, his arms loosely folded across his chest. She tried not to stare at the dark swirl of hair around his navel.

"Am I sleeping on the sofa or in the bed?"

Did she have the courage to be completely honest with him, to tell him what she wanted? Put up or shut up time, she thought a little frantically. She cleared her throat, then whispered, "In bed . . . with me, if that's what you want."

Damn it, she sounded vulnerable, maybe even a little afraid. She couldn't quite manage to look into his eyes. "If you want," she repeated hoarsely.

"Yes, I want."

John Paul took a step toward her but stopped when she put her hand up. "Not so fast, Renard."

"What?" he warily asked.

"There are a couple of ground rules we need to go over first."

She wasn't kidding. He would have laughed if she hadn't looked so nervous. "Ground rules? Like no hitting below the belt? That kind of rule?" When she didn't immediately answer, he asked, "Are we going to box, or are you going to let me—"

"I'm keeping my T-shirt on. Agreed?"

"Okay, if you want to, but if you change your mind and want to take it off, that's fine too."

"If I want to, I will, but I don't want to, and I probably won't. Agreed?"

At this point he'd lost track of what she was negotiating. "Yeah, sure."

He took another step toward her. "I'm not finished."

He grinned. "I didn't think so. Okay, what else?"

"You have to use protection. I can't have children, but we haven't had blood tests, and we . . ."

"I planned on using protection," he said when she stammered to a halt.

"You planned?"

"Uh-huh." He pulled the condom out of his pocket and tossed it on the bed. "Anything else?"

"That was pretty presumptuous."

"Avery, if I don't touch you pretty soon, I'm gonna go nuts, so hurry up and finish the rules."

Her heart was racing. "If you're disappointed . . ."

"I won't be."

"But if you are, you keep it to yourself. Don't complain to me."

"Honey, are you always this uptight before sex?"

"Do you agree?"

"Okay. I won't complain."

"This isn't funny, John Paul. I'm serious."

He'd waited for as long as he could. "Now it's my turn," he said as he grabbed a wad of her T-shirt and pulled her toward him. "You are underneath here somewhere, aren't you?"

He let go and put his arms around her waist. His hand slipped up under the fabric and splayed wide across her back. She didn't try to wiggle away when his fingers touched her scars. He leaned down and kissed the side of her neck just below her ear.

Shivers raced down Avery's spine. Her hands had been balled into fists, but as he tickled her earlobe with the tip of his tongue, she began to relax. His sweet warm breath against her sensitive skin only made her shivers intensify. She could feel the strength, the power of those hard, steely muscles under her fingertips. How could anyone this strong be so very gentle? She sighed into his neck and dropped her head on his shoulder.

"Pay attention, sweetheart. I've got some ground rules too."

She lifted her head and stared into his eyes. Why hadn't she noticed how incredibly beautiful they were? When he smiled, they lit up.

"Yes?"

"Do you trust me?"

Trust him? She was falling utterly in love with him. Of course she trusted him. She was terrified of admitting it, though. "That's not a rule."

He wouldn't let her dodge the question, and when she tried to distract him by pressing against his groin and kissing him, he shook his head. "I already know the answer, but I want . . . no, I need to hear you say the words."

"You are the most opinionated, obstinate, exasperating man I've ever known, but almost from the moment we met, I felt this strange connection. It's as though I've waited all my life to feel so safe . . . and free. I can't explain it," she whispered.

He tilted her chin up, brushed his mouth over hers, and then whispered, "Then trust me. That's my rule. You have to trust me."

She thought she understood what he was asking. And he was right. Love and trust went hand in hand.

It was now or never. Please, God, don't let him be repulsed. She stepped back into the soft light from the bedside lamp, waited until he had let go of her, and then, before her courage completely deserted her, she pulled the T-shirt over her head and tossed it on the floor. She turned so that he could see her ravaged back.

Most of the damage had been done to her lower spine. The angry, ugly scars puckered her skin. She was afraid to turn around, to look into his eyes.

"Sugar?"

There was laughter in his voice. Confused by his reaction, she stood as stiff as a corpse with her hands at her sides, staring at the wall.

"Yes?" she whispered.

He put his hand on her shoulder. "I'm a little more interested in the front right now."

"What . . ."

He gently turned her around and pulled her up against him. Her soft breasts pressed against his chest. He squeezed his eyes shut and whispered, "Damn, I've been dreaming about this. It's better than the dream, though. Much better."

"But my back . . . You saw . . ."

"We'll get to that," he promised. "I've got a lot of territory to cover," he whispered as he kissed a tear away from her cheek. "But in my present condition, I've gotta prioritize."

Before she could argue, or worry, or cry, his mouth took absolute possession of hers in a kiss that was sinfully carnal. His tongue slid in and out of her mouth in a ritual of lovemaking until she was trembling with desire.

His hands were everywhere, caressing, stroking, teasing, as his mouth slanted over hers again and again. He rid her of her inhibitions, and she eagerly kissed him back. She stroked his chest, loving the feel of his coarse, dark hair under her fingertips.

He growled low in his throat with pleasure when she tweaked one of his nipples between her fingertips, and so she did it again.

They were both panting for breath when he ended the kiss and stepped back. He let his shorts drop to the floor, staring into her eyes, reveling in the passion he saw there.

Avery held his gaze as she slid her hand down to remove her panties. The look of surprise when she realized they were on the floor made him smile over his handiwork.

She let him have his moment. "You're good," she whispered shakily.

He followed her onto the bed. Bracing his arms on either side of her, he leaned up and said, "You haven't seen anything yet."

His face was taut with passion. The way he was looking at her made her feel bold. "Neither have you," she whispered back. She moved restlessly against him, her hands slowly easing down his sides. His body was as hot as his gaze.

John Paul loved the way she touched him. Hell, he loved everything about her. She made him crazy. She pulled him down for another kiss, and this time he let her be the aggressor. Their tongues dueled as their hands learned the secrets of each other's bodies.

When she touched his erection, he thought he might just lose it then and there, and he tried to get her to stop, but she wouldn't. He could barely breathe because of the ecstasy she evoked. His hand slipped down between her thighs, his fingers caressing her intimately until she arched off the bed and cried out.

He held off as long as he could until he was desperate to be inside of her. He hungrily kissed her soft, sweet mouth as his knee nudged her thighs apart. Gripping her derriere, he leaned up so that he could watch her. In one slow push, he entered her, then plunged deep.

She arched up against him at the same time, crying out in rapture as she wrapped her legs around his thighs and squeezed him tight.

Capturing the sides of her face with his hands, his mouth covered hers and his tongue sank into her warm sweet mouth. He took his time. Long, slow thrusts that cost him dearly. Beads of perspiration covered his brow, and as he made love to her, he realized it had never been this incredible before. Never.

Avery was overwhelmed by the sensations rushing through her. They were so intense, so new. She couldn't let him slow the pace any longer. She came undone in his arms, wild, more demanding, her nails scoring his shoulders as she met his thrusts with equal passion.

Driven to please her and give her fulfillment before he claimed his own, he tried to slow down, but she would have none of it. Their lovemaking turned uncontrolled, primitive, almost savage. He was consumed.

Avery could feel her control vanishing, but she wasn't

afraid. It was the most amazing feeling to be so uninhibited and to let herself go without fear or worry. She knew she was safe in his arms, and as she reached the precipice and her body began to shiver for release, she arched up against him. Wave after wave of undiluted pleasure coursed through her body as she clung to him.

Impossible to hold back, his orgasm was triggered by hers, and he climaxed deep inside of her, clenching his jaw in ecstasy.

They stayed joined together as one for long, blissful minutes. Their breathing was ragged, and neither one of them had the strength to move. Their hearts pounded in unison. He buried his face in her silky hair, closed his eyes as he inhaled her wonderful fragrance.

"Damn," he whispered. She'd taken every ounce of his strength. His bones felt like liquid as he tried to move so he wouldn't crush her.

She obviously didn't mind his weight because she squeezed him when he shifted his position, and whispered, "Not yet."

Had he been too rough with her? The thought popped into his head and anchored there. He could have been more gentle, but she'd been so wonderfully uninhibited, he'd gone a little crazy.

"Avery? You okay?"

She smiled because of the worry she heard in his voice. And then she whispered, "So that's what all the fuss was about."

And then she laughed with such delight, he smiled in spite of his exhaustion.

With a sigh, he rolled away, then got up and went into the bathroom.

She pulled the sheet up, adjusted her pillow, and fell

back. She was still a little overwhelmed by what she had just experienced. Sex, she decided, sex with John Paul anyway, could definitely become addictive.

The bed springs groaned when John Paul stretched out beside her. She opened her eyes and smiled. He looked so arrogantly proud of himself. He was on his side with his head propped up staring at her.

She looked thoroughly ravaged. Passion lingered in her eyes, and her lips were swollen from his kisses.

She knew she'd satisfied him, but she still needed him to tell her so. Silly how she could feel so powerful a minute ago and now the old insecurities were creeping back. No, she hadn't disappointed him. Why wasn't he telling her so?

He could see it happening. In her eyes. They were clouded. He didn't think she was regretting anything . . . just worried maybe.

He knew he'd guessed right when she said, "What are you thinking?"

He tugged on the sheet, pulling it down to the tips of her breasts. She pulled it back up.

"Bet I can get this off you faster than a prom dress," he drawled.

"Oh, brother. You're pretty happy with yourself right now, aren't you?"

"Damn right I am," he said as he leaned down and kissed her. His tongue slipped inside and tickled the roof of her mouth. When he pulled back, she was breathless. But then, so was he.

Oh, how she loved this man. He was so completely perfect for her. She reached up to brush his hair off his forehead, an excuse to keep touching him. She couldn't seem to get enough.

" 'Heavens to Betsy'?" he drawled. "That's what you

said, sugar, when you were coming apart in my arms. Actually, you screamed it."

She laughed. "I did not."

"Yeah, you did."

"I know what you shouted, but I'm not going to repeat it."

His grin was lecherous. "Guess what."

Her fingers trailed down the muscled cord on the side of his neck, then crossed his shoulder. She gently traced it with her fingertips.

"What?" she asked lazily.

"Prom dress is gone."

Startled, she lifted her head and looked down. The sheet was around her ankles. "You *are* good."

He leaned down and kissed each breast. His fingers slowly circled her navel. A jagged scar crisscrossed the lower part of her abdomen. The raised, puckered center indicated a bullet had done the damage. Probably a .38, he thought. Or maybe a .45.

Damn, it was a miracle she had survived. He leaned forward and took his time kissing every inch of her stomach, smiling as she inhaled sharply. He rolled back on his side so he could watch her face as his hand slid down into her soft curls.

Avery was having trouble catching her breath. "Do you want . . ."

"Oh, yeah. I want."

Moaning softly, she moved restlessly against him, her toes rubbing his lower legs.

She tried to touch him, but he grabbed her hand. "Relax, sugar. Let me . . ."

It was as far as he got. She was surprisingly strong. And bold. She pushed him onto his back and leaned over him.

"Relax? I don't think so, John Paul. This is a team sport, isn't it?"

He couldn't answer her. Her hands had captured his arousal, and she was slowly driving him wild with her caresses.

"And . . ." she whispered as she straddled his hips and kissed him passionately.

"And what?" he asked, his voice as coarse as sandpaper.

Her eyes sparkled when she answered. "I'm definitely a team player."

CHAPTER 31

THE MAN WAS insatiable. Avery woke up at noon. She didn't usually sleep so late, but John Paul hadn't let her get much rest during the night.

She was on her stomach with one arm hanging over the side of the bed. He was tickling her back. His fingers were as light as feathers. Was he trying to drive her crazy, or was he being so very gentle because of her scars?

Oh, God, her scars. Even Carrie, who loved her like a mother, couldn't stop herself from grimacing when she looked at her.

"You awake yet?" he asked. "Avery?"

She didn't say good morning. She blurted, "What do you think?"

"About what?'

"My back."

"Can you handle the truth?"

Uh-oh. She didn't like his tone one bit. She could feel her defenses building inside her. "Yes, I can handle it," she said tightly. "What are you thinking about?"

"Your sweet little ass."

She rolled over and looked up at him.

"It's the first thing I noticed about you when you came strutting inside the lobby of that spa."

Smiling, she said, "I didn't strut."

"Sure you did."

"You're a pervert."

"You're a liberal. I figure that makes us even. About the scars . . ."

She was still smiling when she asked, "Yes?"

"They're just scars. They don't define who you are. Now get up. Breakfast will be ready in ten minutes. Move it," he said as he rolled off the bed.

He was stark naked and seemed thoroughly happy about it. He was gorgeous. All muscle and male.

"Put some clothes on, for Pete's sake."

"Why?"

"Do you go around like that in the swamp?"

"I wish I could, but I can't, not with the gators and snakes."

He grabbed his jeans from the chair and went into the living room. Avery took a quick shower and put on a pair of navy shorts and a pale yellow blouse. Her hair was tucked behind her ears when she padded barefoot into the living room.

John Paul went into the kitchen to fix her plate and placed it in front of her. Then he handed her a bottle of Tabasco sauce.

He'd prepared scrambled eggs with lots of pepper. She took a bite and quickly washed it down with orange juice.

"You like spicy food," she said, smiling.

"In Louisiana, spicy food is a way of life."

"What was it like growing up in Bowen with a father everyone in town calls Big Daddy Jake?"

"Interesting," he answered. "My dad's quite a character,

always got something going, if you know what I mean. He's a bit of a con, but he's got a good heart."

He told her a couple of funny stories about the mischief that he and his brother, Remy, got into when they were boys. He mentioned his father and his younger sister often, and each time, she noticed, his voice softened.

"Mike's as bossy as you are." His smile indicated he thought that was a good thing. "She's a surgeon," he added proudly. "Her name's Michelle, but everyone calls her Mike, everyone but her husband. They're expecting their first baby in September."

"Theo," Avery said. "She's married to Theo, and he's an attorney with Justice."

"That's right."

He told her another story while she ate her breakfast, and then she helped him do the dishes.

"It rained hard early this morning. Thunder shook the rafters."

"I didn't hear a thing."

"I wore you out."

He sounded cocky. She decided to let him have his due. "Yes, you did," she agreed as she folded the tea towel and put it on the counter. "We have to make plans."

"I know," he agreed as he followed her into the living room. She curled up on the sofa. He sat down in a chair, kicked his shoes off, and propped his feet up on the opposite end of the sofa. He was such a big man he swallowed up the chair.

"But not today," he said. "Today we rest and talk. To-morrow we plan."

"What will we talk about?"

"Not what, but who," he said. "We need to talk about Jilly."

She had put it off as long as she could. Nodding, she said,

"Carrie kept a diary. She was very young, around eleven, when she started writing in it. The diary wasn't filled with her hopes and dreams and crushes, though. No, it was all about Jilly. Every single page was filled with one horrific incident after another involving her sick sister. Carrie told me she wanted to have some kind of record . . . proof, I guess, in hopes that one day Jilly would get caught, be put away. She thought that if the doctors read her diary, they would realize how dangerous Jilly was and make sure she stayed behind bars for the rest of her life, but I think there was more to it than that. I think that deep down Carrie believed that one day Jilly would kill her."

"That was a hell of a way to grow up," he said.

Avery agreed. "Carrie stopped writing in the diary when Jilly left town, but she always kept it, just in case Jilly came back. I knew where it was hidden, but Carrie wouldn't let me read it."

"But you did read it, didn't you?"

"Yes, I did. I wish to God I hadn't, though. I was old enough to think I could handle anything, but there was such scary, sick stuff in there . . ."

"How old were you?"

"Fourteen. I read every word, and I had nightmares for months. Carrie had put in a lot of details, and I learned all the twisted facts about Jilly."

She was hugging a throw pillow to her chest in a death grip. The sadness in her eyes was heartbreaking.

"I hate talking about her," she whispered.

"I know."

Her shoulders slumped. "There really are monsters in this world. Predators," she said. "Jilly's one of them. Do you know what scared me the most after I read that diary?"

"What?"

"That I would wake up one morning and be just like her.

You know, Dr. Jekyll–Mr. Hyde. Genetically, I'm forever linked to her."

"That isn't going to happen, Avery."

"How can you know that?"

"You have a conscience. That's not going to go away. You're nothing like her."

"That's what Dr. Hahn told me," she said.

"Who's Dr. Hahn?"

"A psychiatrist. I was waking up screaming every night, and in desperation, Carrie took me to Dr. Hahn." She added, "Carrie made me promise not to tell anyone because she didn't want people to think I was crazy."

"She was worried about what other people thought?" he asked, trying to keep the censure out of his voice.

"Dr. Hahn was wonderful, and he helped me . . . cope, I guess you could say. Carrie didn't know why I was having the nightmares because I hadn't told her I'd read the diaries, and I think it was the third or fourth session when Dr. Hahn asked her to come in and I told her then what I had done. She had a fit, of course, but when the doctor had gotten her to calm down, he asked her if he could read the diary, and she agreed. She would have done anything to help me get over what she called my night terrors."

She smiled at John Paul as she swung her legs down from the sofa. "I think the doctor had nightmares after he read them. I grew up knowing that Jilly was crazy, and Carrie did tell me stories, but they paled in comparison to what was in the diary."

"What did Hahn say about Jilly after he read it? What was his reaction?"

"He was excited."

"Excited?" he repeated, not understanding.

"He was sure Jilly was a pure sociopath, and he wished he'd had the opportunity to study her. Based on what he read, he concluded that Jilly was morally and emotionally stunted, which was why he believed she was incapable of feeling guilt or remorse. Other people's pain certainly didn't make her feel bad. On the contrary," she explained, "she enjoyed hurting people for no apparent reason. She just liked it. She was a master at blaming others and rewriting history, and she was very deceptive."

John Paul put his feet down on the floor and leaned forward, bracing his arms on his knees.

"She was . . . amazing, the way she could manipulate people. Everyone loved her, no matter what she did. She was so damned clever."

"Give me an example."

"When she was quite young, she started having fun with pets. She tortured and killed Carrie's cat with gasoline and a match. She told Carrie what she'd done, but in front of their mother, she cried because, she said, she so loved that cat. One of the neighbors took her to get an ice cream cone to make her feel better. By the time she was a senior in high school, she was into bigger and better. She was the most popular girl in school, of course. Everyone loved Jilly. A girl named Heather Mitchell was voted homecoming queen, and Jilly was voted first attendant. According to Carrie, Jilly was gracious about it at school, but when she came home that afternoon, she went into a rage that lasted for hours. She nearly destroyed the house. Carrie's bedroom suffered the most damage. Not Jilly's room, of course. Then, after dinner, she became real quiet and got that sly look in her eyes and pretended to accept it."

Avery took a breath. The muscles in her arms were aching, and she realized she was gripping the pillow. She let go.

"The next day a beaker of sulfuric acid was missing from the chemistry lab. After school, Jilly got Heather alone, but Carrie saw her take her arm and lead her down the street. Jilly told Heather that she'd better not show up for homecoming weekend or she'd be sorry. Heather was a sweet girl, and she was going through a terrible time. Her mother had died two weeks before of an aneurysm, and the poor girl was still reeling from the shock. When Jilly got through tormenting her, Heather locked herself in her bedroom, but her father finally got her to tell him what was wrong. He said that Jilly had admitted stealing the acid. She threatened to wait for Heather one day after school when she was all alone in her house and throw the acid in her face."

"Good God."

Avery nodded. "What Carrie wrote wasn't hearsay. She talked to Heather."

"What did Heather's father do?"

"He went to the principal the next morning and demanded that Jilly be expelled. He also went to the police."

"And what did they do?"

"Nothing," she said. "The chief of police was a close friend of my grandmother's, and he wasn't going to do anything that would upset her. Besides, it was one girl's word against the other's. Jilly, of course, denied the incident. My grandmother and Jilly were called into the principal's office that afternoon. Grandmother made Carrie go with them."

"Was Jilly expelled?"

"No," she said, scoffing at the notion. "Did I mention that the principal was a man? His name was Mr. Bennett, and he was a very unhappily married man. His wife was a cold woman and very difficult to get along with, or so Carrie wrote."

"What happened?" John Paul asked, bringing her back to the story.

"Carrie watched Jilly seduce Bennett. Jilly became hysterical. Lots of tears flowing, but it was all a calculated act. The principal rushed over to the sofa where Jilly was and sat down beside her. He put his arm around her to comfort her, but it was Jilly's body language that . . . fascinated Carrie . . . and Bennett's reaction."

She shook her head. "Have you ever seen a woman move like a cat? Carrie said Jilly was like that. When Bennett put his arm around her, she rubbed up against him in an obscene way."

"What did your grandmother do?"

"She was as clueless as ever, according to Carrie. She'd gone out to the front desk to get Jilly a glass of water, but even if she had stayed, she wouldn't have noticed anything because she didn't want to notice. Carrie wrote that Jilly was clinging to Bennett while she cried. She had her head on his shoulder, but she looked up at Carrie, who was standing behind the principal, and Jilly had this Cheshire cat smile on her face. When it was over, Bennett threatened to suspend Heather for making up the lie."

"Jeez."

"Like I said, Jilly had a way with men. Some of them became obsessed with her. They would call at all hours of the day and night. Every once in a while, Carrie would sneak upstairs into Grandmother Lola's bedroom and listen in on the extension. She wrote that the men cried and pleaded, and after Jilly hung up, she could hear her laughing. Oh, how she loved the power she had. She loved manipulating, and she used sex to get what she wanted. Her specialty was destroying married men. I'll bet you can guess who one of those men was," she said.

"Bennett."

"Yes."

"My God," he said. "And all this was going on while she

was in high school?" Before Avery could answer, he asked, "What happened to Heather?"

"She didn't go to homecoming, and Jilly was crowned queen, but that wasn't enough for Jilly. Heather had upset her, and so she had to be punished. Jilly tormented her. A month passed, and just as Heather was beginning to think Jilly had moved on, she came home from school one day and went up to her room. She had this old teddy bear she kept on her bed. Someone had poured acid all over it. That someone, of course, was Jilly."

John Paul rubbed his jaw and waited until Avery continued.

"Carrie heard about it at school the next day. She went to see Heather's father. He had to stay home with his daughter because she was so distraught, and Carrie told him Jilly wouldn't stop going after Heather and that he needed to get his daughter out of town and not tell anyone where she had gone. Heather was close to a nervous breakdown. She was seeing a therapist," she explained. "And the therapist thought it would be good for Heather to get away from Sheldon Beach. She left during Christmas vacation and didn't come back."

"Did it ever end?"

"Oh, no," she said. "Heather's father filed another report with the police two months later. He said that someone was stealing his mail. One Saturday afternoon, he happened to look outside and saw Jilly opening his mailbox. She was looking for letters from Heather so she could find out where she was."

"She doesn't give up, does she?"

"No, she doesn't. She never had sex with any of the boys in her high school. All her friends believed she was sweet and wholesome. Carrie heard a couple of rumors about

Jilly, but not from anyone at school. Heather was the one who was ostracized, not Jilly. She was that good at being bad."

She stood and stretched her arms above her head. "Do you want something to drink?"

After the story she'd just told him, hard liquor sounded good to him, but he settled on a Diet Coke instead. She got herself a bottle of Evian water and handed him his soda.

He opened the can, took a swig, and asked, "Did your grandparents try to get her some help when she was little, or did they know then that something was wrong with her?"

"Grandfather left when Carrie and Jilly were little girls, and Grandmother Lola lived in what Carrie called a fantasyland. She had an excuse for every atrocity Jilly committed."

"When did Jilly get pregnant with you?" he asked.

"Her senior year. Carrie thought her pregnancy saved Heather because Jilly had other things to think about. Jilly tried to get an abortion, but the doctor wouldn't do it because she was too far along. She gave birth and left town three days later. And that was the last entry in the diary," she added.

"Leaving me behind was the last straw for Grandmother. She dragged all of Jilly's things out to the curb for the trash collector. When she was packing up her things from the closet, she found a shoe box full of mail from Heather's house, and guess what else she found?"

"The acid."

Avery nodded. "The beaker was only half full, but it would have been more than enough to kill Heather. I think Jilly didn't forget about that girl. I think she was biding her time."

A clap of thunder jarred her. She flinched in reaction, then got up and walked to the window to look out. Dark angry clouds loomed overhead. Lightning sliced across the sky, and then there was another booming blast of thunder.

She didn't turn around as she said, "Carrie didn't think Jilly was very smart. She used her body to get what she wanted. She's obviously become more devious and clever over the years. Carrie said there wasn't a man alive who was immune to her charms."

"Do you believe that?"

"Skarrett obviously became obsessed with her, and look where he ended up. When I was five years old, Jilly and Skarrett came to the house. Jilly told Grandmother she had to pay to keep me. Fortunately, Carrie was home. She told Jilly she didn't have any legal rights to me and pushed her out the door. It was a horrible fight, but Skarrett kept his distance . . . then. Jilly kept screaming, 'You're dead, Carrie. You're dead.' "

"Where were you while all this was going on?"

She turned around and looked at him. "I don't remember any of it, but Carrie told me she found me hiding under my bed. After they left, Carrie promised me they would never come back."

She took a gulp of her water, put the lid back on, and stared down at her hand. There was a deep indentation in her palm from where she'd been gripping the bottle cap.

"But they did come back, didn't they?"

"Yes."

He watched her closely as she closed her eyes and told him what had happened on February fourteenth, all those years ago.

When she was finished, she said, "Skarrett's her puppet. And I think she's got Monk doing her bidding now too. She's playing both of them to get what she wants."

She put the bottle down on the table and took a step toward John Paul. "So now you know."

"Now I know . . ."

"So?" she demanded. "Tell me what you think."

He shrugged. "I think you're right. Jilly is a maniac."

She threaded her fingers through her hair and took another step toward him. "No, that's not what I was asking."

"Then what?"

She stopped a foot away from him. "Aren't you sorry?"

He felt as if he were playing twenty questions. In exasperation, he asked, "Sorry about what?"

"Getting involved with me. It's a temporary situation, but even so . . ."

"Hell, no."

She stepped back. "John Paul, you've got to be a little repulsed . . ."

"Afraid not."

She glared at him. "Why not? I don't come from a normal family. Genetically speaking, I'm a mess."

"Sugar, no need to be so melodramatic and no need to shout at me either. I can hear just fine."

"How can you smile after what you just heard? How can you—"

"Avery, you didn't do any of those things. Jilly did."

He thought he was being extremely logical, but she wasn't the least bit interested in being reasonable. "Now do you understand why I won't ever get married?"

Before she could take another step away from him, he reached for her. He put his hands on her hips and slowly pulled her toward him.

"No, I don't understand."

She tried to push his hands away, but they were cemented to her body.

"You're going to have to explain it to me. Are you afraid you'll sneeze and turn into a sociopath?"

"No, of course not, but I can't have children, and even if I could . . ."

"I know," he said softly. "You wouldn't risk it."

"Men want children."

She stood between his knees, frowning at him while she shifted from foot to foot.

"Some do," he agreed. "Some don't."

"Do you?"

He wasn't going to lie to her. "I always figured I'd settle down one day and have a couple of kids. I still might," he said. "But, Avery, there are a lot of children out there who need good homes."

"Do you think after doing a background check on my family that I would ever qualify?"

"Yes, I do."

"I won't get married."

The defiance was back in her voice. She was trying to hide her vulnerability, but it wasn't working. He knew she was hurting inside.

"Did I ask you to marry me?"

"No."

"Okay, then. I think we've had enough heavy talk for a little while. And I also think you need to lighten up a little."

It occurred to her that he was behaving the same way he had when she'd shown him her back. The scars hadn't seemed to faze him. Obviously, neither did the stories she'd told him about Jilly.

What the hell was the matter with him?

"You need to relax," he told her. He worked her blouse up over her navel and leaned forward to kiss her stomach.

"That's what yoga is for. It helps me relax."

"I've found a better way to unwind."

He unbuttoned her shorts and reached for the zipper. She grabbed his hand.

"What do you think you're doing?"

His smile made her heart race. Her hand dropped to her side, and she watched him unzip her shorts. As they fell to the floor, he finally answered her.

"It's simple, sugar. I'm going to *my* happy place."

CHAPTER 32

SECRETS WERE BEST shared in the bedroom. They made love, and after he had kissed and caressed every inch of her beautiful body, she was exhausted.

"I told you I'd get around to your back," he said as he rolled away from her.

She laughed because he'd sounded so smug. Still breathless from their lovemaking, she whispered, "You're insatiable."

He grinned arrogantly. "With you I am."

It was a lovely thing to say, almost a compliment, she thought. "Move over," she told him. "I'm falling off the bed."

The double bed didn't give him anyplace to go. "We're gonna need to buy a king-size bed."

Her mood changed as swiftly as the wind. "Why?" she asked tensely.

"Because I'm too big for a double bed," he answered. "My feet hang over. What's the big deal about a king-size bed?"

"We both know we can't have any kind of a lasting relationship."

"Did I ask?"

"No, but you implied . . ."

"Sugar, you worry too much."

She silently agreed. Of course, she worried . . . about everything. But what terrified her more than anything was ruining things. Admitting to herself that she loved John Paul had already put her in a mild panic. What was going to happen when they parted? Would she ever recover?

"I don't believe in marriage. Look what it does to some people."

"What people?"

"People like the Parnells . . ."

"Sugar, those aren't what you'd call typical people."

"What about the divorce rate?"

"What about couples who have stayed together?"

"I'd ruin things," she blurted out.

When he didn't respond, she propped herself up with her elbow, leaned over him, and waited. Had he fallen asleep?

"Did you hear what I just said?"

He was wearing an adorable smile and nothing else. He oozed self-confidence, probably because he didn't give a hoot what anyone else thought. She'd lived her life trying to please everyone. He was the complete antithesis. He didn't want to please anyone.

"You don't have much faith in yourself, do you? It's okay," he added before she could answer. "I've got enough for both of us."

She put her hand on his flat, hard stomach and circled his navel with her fingertips. He made everything sound so easy.

She couldn't stop touching him. She could almost see the strength radiating from his muscles, but she wasn't the least bit intimidated by him. When she was in his arms, she didn't feel overwhelmed or diminished. On the contrary, he made her feel powerful. It was the most incredible sensation, not worrying about pleasing him, just knowing that whatever she did was all right, being that free, that liberated. Her trust in him was absolute, and she realized what a wonderful gift he'd given her.

"John Paul?"

"Ummm?"

"Are you sleeping?"

"A little."

"I want . . ."

"Okay, sweetheart. Just give me a couple of minutes, and I'll be able—"

Her body was still tingling from the last time. She laughed. "Not that," she said. "I want you to tell me something."

He yawned. "You were perfect, Avery, but you've got to know—"

She pinched him. "I'm not asking for a review. I want to know why you walked away."

Before he could deliberately misinterpret, she said, "I've told you my secrets, most of them anyway, and now it's your turn. Why did you retire?"

"It's boring stuff."

She pinched him again. "Tell me."

He opened his eyes and looked at her. The determination he saw told him he wasn't going to be able to finesse his way out of this one. Besides, he figured he owed her.

"It wasn't any one big assignment that went wrong," he said. "Just a lot of little screwups that made me . . . reevaluate what I wanted out of life. I had a bad problem."

"What was it?"

"I started thinking too much. I had a lot of time to do that while I waited in hellholes for the next assignment. They were usually generals," he explained nonchalantly. "Little prick dictators who surrounded themselves with thugs. I didn't mind killing them, for the greater good," he added sarcastically. "And I liked going in after hostages. There was justice in that action, but one night, while I was freezing my ass off, I noticed I was getting a callus on my finger. My trigger finger," he added softly. "That really freaked me out."

"So what did you do?"

"I finished my assignment, told them I was done, and went home."

"Was it that easy? Didn't they try to change your mind?"

"Yes and no," he answered. "At the time, it was easy because I worked for a good, decent man. He knew I'd had it. I think the way he got around all the red tape was to give me an extended leave."

"But they're still trying to get you to come back?"

"Every once in a while," he agreed. "I won't, though." He closed his eyes again and said, "I did some badass things, Avery."

"I would imagine so," she whispered. "And you didn't believe that what you were doing made any difference, did you?"

She'd hit the mark dead center. "No, I didn't. Dictators are like weeds. You rip one out of the ground and two more pop up overnight."

He opened his eyes again and watched her as he recounted one of his bloodier assignments. When he was finished, he noticed she hadn't pulled her hand away. She was still stroking his chest. Her touch was soothing.

"So now you're a carpenter," she said.

"Yes."

"Are you any good?"

"Yeah, I am. I'm still using my hands, but now I build things that will last. I don't break necks. It's odd."

"What is?"

"The urge to kill. I never had that before. I do now."

Her eyes widened. He'd made the confession so casually. "Oh? Who do you want to kill?"

"Skarrett."

She shivered in reaction. "No," she said. "I don't want him to die."

"You've got to be kidding."

"I'm serious. I want him to live the rest of his life behind bars."

"Yeah, well, if I get the opportunity . . ."

"No," she said firmly.

"Okay," he said when he realized she was getting upset.

"I mean it."

"I said okay," he said.

"I won't mind if you kill Monk," she said then. "But I hope someone brings him in alive. Can you imagine the things he could tell them?"

He shook his head. "He won't talk. He's not the kind of man who likes to boast. Maybe, if the interrogators work him, treat him like a professional, he might give them a little insight, but I honestly don't see that happening." He shrugged and added, "I think they ought to squash him like a bug."

"And Jilly?"

"You call it."

"She needs to be locked up in an institution for the criminally insane, and she needs to stay there for the rest of her life."

"You don't want her dead?"

"No, I don't," she said. "I don't think she can help being the way she is. I just want to make sure she can't hurt anyone anymore."

He brushed his thumb across her lips. "You've got a gentle heart," he said.

"So do you."

"The hell I do," he grumbled. "But I've got great hands," he added as he reached for her.

She slapped his hand away. "I already know you're good with your hands," she said.

She got an impish gleam in her eyes as she rolled on top of him. He locked his legs around her to keep her from making a eunuch out of him.

"Now I'm going to show you how good I am," she cooed.

It wasn't an idle boast. Avery had a vivid imagination, and what she did to him with her hands and her mouth was magical, and probably illegal in some states, but of course he wasn't about to mention that to her.

That night they slept entwined in each other's arms even though both of them knew that the interlude would be over in the morning. They couldn't push reality away any longer.

Avery awakened before John Paul did and quickly showered and dressed in the bathroom so she wouldn't disturb him. Then she went into the living room, softly closing the bedroom door behind her, and checked the time. There was a digital clock on the wall above the table. She hoped it was accurate. Five forty-five Colorado time, which meant it was seven forty-five in Virginia.

She thought she heard the shower running as she reached for the phone. "Stay predictable, Margo," she whispered. "Don't get spontaneous now."

She dialed information, got the number she needed, then hung up and waited, her gaze locked on the time.

At exactly seven-fifty, Avery dialed. The phone was answered on the third ring.

Avery made up a name, told the employee it was an emergency and that he needed to put Margo on the phone. She described her friend and added, "She comes in every morning at seven-fifty."

"Yeah, the short lady, right?"

"Yes."

"She just left."

"Go after her," Avery shouted. "Hurry. Get her back. Go."

The phone clattered against the wall when the employee dropped it. She heard him shouting Margo's name, and then a minute later, she could hear Margo arguing.

"No one knows I'm here. What do you mean it's an emergency? Hello," she said.

"Margo, it's me, Avery."

"Oh, my God, Avery. How did you know I would be here . . . how did you . . ." She was rattled.

"You always pick up doughnuts on your way into the office."

"Do you have any idea how much trouble you're in?"

"I haven't done anything wrong," Avery countered.

"Why did you leave that police station in Colorado? The agents are there to protect you."

"I have protection."

"Renard?"

"Yes," she answered impatiently. "Tell me what you know."

The bedroom door opened, and John Paul stopped in the doorway, staring at her incredulously. She put her hand up when he started toward her.

"Hold on, Margo." Cupping the receiver with her hand, she said to John Paul, "Trust me." Then she raised the phone to her ear again. "Okay, Margo. Start talking."

"The trial begins July tenth," she said. "But Avery, the parole hearing is still on too. Skarrett might pull it off this time. He could get out."

"Over my dead body."

"Jeez, don't talk like that."

"Is the hearing still scheduled for the sixteenth?"

"I think so."

"Are you sure or not?"

"I'm sure," she said. "Don't get all hostile on me, Avery. They know about Jilly. Your aunt told them. That had to have been a hell of a shock. I'm so sorry—"

Avery interrupted. She didn't want sympathy. "Do they have any idea where Jilly and Monk might be?"

"Not a clue."

"What about my aunt? Have they moved her from the hospital yet?"

"No, not yet. Don't worry about her. A gnat couldn't get into that hospital. Security's unbelievable."

"I'm not worried," she said. "Monk can't be in two places at once."

"What does that mean?"

"I'm going to keep him busy. He's going to have to try and stop me from testifying at Skarrett's trial."

"What does he care about Skarrett?"

"He doesn't," she said. "But he's working for Jilly now, and she wants Skarrett out of prison. I'll bet, if you check the records at the prison for visitors over the past year, you'll find that Skarrett had a female visitor listed more than once. I think she's made some kind of deal with him."

"For the millions in uncut stones that he stole," Margo said.

"I'm sure Skarrett thinks they'll share the loot and that he'll live happily ever after with Jilly. But when they have what they want, Jilly will let Monk kill him."

"Avery, you're in over your head."

"Maybe," she whispered. "I can't stop now, though. About the trial . . ."

"Yes?"

"Find out who the prosecutor is, and make sure I'm on his witness list."

"Okay," she said. "Can I tell Carter I talked to you?"

You're going to tell him anyway, she thought. Margo was her friend, but Avery knew she would believe she was being helpful by filling Carter in.

"Yes, please do."

"Where are you now? He's going to ask."

"Alabama," she lied. "I've got to go now. Tell Carter I'll call him."

"Wait," Margo cried. "What are you going to do?"

Avery knew what she wanted to do. She just didn't know how yet. The conversation with Jilly popped into her head. What had she called her? Oh, yes, how could she forget?

"I'm going to be a killjoy."

John Paul trusted her. Otherwise he would have ripped the phone out of her hand and hung it up. He'd sat down on the sofa beside her and impatiently waited for her to finish her conversation. He looked relieved when she told him she'd caught Margo at the doughnut shop.

"Clever," he said with approval.

"She's a creature of habit."

She told him what Margo had said. "I promised I'd call Carter," she added, "when we get to Florida."

"But not before."

"You better think hard before you agree to go with me, John Paul. It could get . . ."

"Bloody?"

She nodded.

"I'm in," he said. "For the long haul."

He reached over, cupped the back of her neck with his hand, and drew her toward him. He kissed her possessively and said, "Did you hear me? I'm in it for the long haul. And like it or not, babe, so are you."

"Until we get Monk and Jilly."

He let go of her. "That's not what I mean, and you know it."

She pulled away and went into the kitchen. She fixed breakfast, cereal and toast, and then, because she was feeling restless, did the dishes while he looked over the map, figuring their route to Sheldon Beach.

She was putting the bowls back into the cabinet when he called out to her.

"We've got company."

She dropped the tea towel and ran into the living room. John Paul was standing by the front window, cautiously looking out. He held his gun at his side, pressed against his leg.

He saw the car when it came around the grove of trees and relaxed. "Better get packed," he said as he flipped the safety back on the gun and tucked it into the back of his jeans. "Our ride's here."

What ride? "You were expecting someone?"

He nodded. He couldn't see the driver yet because the sun bouncing off the windshield obstructed his view, but the make and model were right. It was a new, gray Honda.

"Who is it?"

He shrugged. "I told Theo I needed transportation. The police will be looking for my car, and I figured you didn't want them to hold us until the FBI took you into custody."

"The FBI wouldn't do that unless they had my permission."

He snorted. She assumed that meant he didn't agree. "They would not trample all over my rights as a citizen."

"Sure they would," he said. "And they'd tell you that they were only doing what they felt was best for you."

She wasn't going to get into a full-blown argument about the Bureau now. Besides, deep down, she was concerned that there was a kernel of truth in what he'd said. She wasn't willing to risk it.

"Theo drove all this way from Louisiana?" she asked.

"No," he answered. "He wanted to come, but I talked him out of it. I reminded him that he's going to be a father and that he's a lousy shot. If he gets himself killed, then I'll have to become the kid's father figure. Said I'd raise his son or daughter to be just like me."

"And that gave him chills?"

"Yep," he replied. "And like I said, he's a lousy shot. He'd probably shoot himself getting his gun out of its holster."

"And you don't want him to get hurt. You better watch it. You're beginning to sound nice."

He squinted against the sunlight trying to see the driver. "Theo said he knew someone who could keep quiet and help. Who wouldn't mind breaking some rules. Ah, hell," he groaned when he finally saw who was behind the wheel. "Not him. That son of a . . ."

"Who?"

"Theo. My brother-in-law has a sick sense of humor."

"John Paul, what are you talking about?"

"Theo sent him," he snapped, stabbing at the air with his finger.

"Who?" she demanded. She was beginning to feel like an owl.

"Clayborne. He sent Noah Clayborne." He spat the name out as though it left a foul taste in his mouth.

She was thoroughly confused by his attitude. "But you called Noah from the spa. I heard you on the phone. Why are you angry now?"

"Yes, I did call him, but I didn't think I'd have to see him," he muttered. He turned to her, gave her a quick once-over from head to toes, and barked, "Put some damn clothes on."

She looked down at herself. Yes, there were clothes. White tennis shoes, navy shorts, white T-shirt. "What's the matter with what I have on?"

"Too much skin showing. Ah, hell, it wouldn't matter if you were dressed like a nun. He's still gonna hit on you. Then I'm gonna have to shoot the bastard." He stomped to the door, all but pulled it off the hinges when he opened it, and went out onto the porch. "Just see if I don't."

Oh, brother. "He's bringing us a car." She called out the reminder. "Stop complaining about him."

"Yeah, you're right," he called back. "We'll make him stay here or take my car. He doesn't need to go with us."

Avery stepped back to the window. John Paul had made her curious about Theo's friend. She knew Noah couldn't possibly be as obnoxious as John Paul had implied. No one could be that awful.

The car stopped in front of the house, and Noah Clayborne opened the car door and emerged into the sunlight.

Avery felt like whistling. Tall, broad-shouldered, with sandy blond hair, the man was dressed casually in jeans and a gray T-shirt. He wore the old-fashioned shoulder holster and a pair of Ray-Ban sunglasses. John Paul scowled at him, but Clayborne smiled back, as though the joke were on Renard. The man had a dimple and definitely oozed sensuality.

She wasn't interested in him, of course, not in that way. John Paul was sexier—everything about him appealed to her—but Noah, in appearance anyway, could be a close runner-up. Of course, her analysis was strictly clinical. She had never taken the time to notice such things about a man before, or if she had, she hadn't been able to admit it to herself. Had finally having sex again turned her mind into mush?

"I'm going to need therapy when this is over," she whispered. "Big-time therapy."

Straightening her shoulders, she went outside to meet him. He'd reached the steps but stopped when she walked onto the porch.

John Paul's social graces definitely needed work. She waited a couple of seconds for him to introduce her, then realized he wasn't going to. She would have stepped forward, but John Paul put his arm around her shoulders and jerked her close to him.

Noah's response to the ridiculously possessive action was to widen his grin. He removed his sunglasses and looked directly at her. Blue eyes. The man had intense blue eyes. Bet he breaks a lot of hearts, she thought, as she felt John Paul tighten his hold.

Was he married? She hoped not because she could think of at least three friends to fix him up with, providing, of course, he wasn't just a body without a mind. Margo wouldn't be bothered by that, but Peyton, her childhood friend, would definitely want a man with a brain.

"What the hell are you staring at, Clayborne?" John Paul barked.

She put a stop to the pissing contest. She pushed his arm away and walked to the edge of the porch.

"Thank you for coming," she began. Extending her hand, she added, "My name's Avery Delaney."

Noah came up the stairs and shook her hand. He didn't let go as he introduced himself and then said, "I gotta know."

"Yes?"

He glanced at John Paul and said, "How'd a sweet thing like you get hooked up with him?"

"She's lucky," John Paul snapped. "Now let go of her."

Noah smiled at Avery and continued to hold on to her hand. He was enjoying himself by deliberately provoking John Paul. He seemed to know what buttons to push to get John Paul riled. Come to think of it, it didn't take much.

"We appreciate your help, don't we, John Paul?"

She had to elbow him to get him to answer. "Yeah, sure."

"Please, come inside. Are you thirsty?" she asked as she led the way into the cabin.

"If he's thirsty, he can get his own damned drink," John Paul said. "You don't have to play hostess, Avery."

She whirled around. "Stop being a jerk," she ordered. "I was being polite, something you know precious little about. Now stop acting like a rooster and get rid of the attitude."

He immediately backed down. "Yeah, all right."

Noah tried not to laugh.

John Paul looked a bit sheepish as he said to Noah, "She's got a temper."

"Uh-huh," Noah drawled.

"Look, it's not what you—"

"Yeah, it is. Never thought you'd fall. Hell, I never thought any woman would want—"

"Drop it, Noah."

"Hey, I'm just here to do Theo a favor," he explained. "Don't take your frustrations out on me." The fact was, he liked John Paul, and he respected him. Maybe even admired him a little because he'd had the guts to walk away from a job that usually broke a man.

Avery had gone into the kitchen to get a cold soda for Noah. She stopped in the kitchen doorway. The men had returned to the porch, and she couldn't hear what they were saying. She put the bottle back in the refrigerator and decided to pack her bag.

She heard a couple of crude and colorful expletives; then she heard laughter. They're nuts, she thought as she went into the bedroom and shut the door. The bed looked as though acrobats had practiced their act on it. She quickly stripped the sheets, put on fresh ones, and dropped the soiled linens in the hamper.

There wasn't much to pack. She changed into her khaki pants and searched through her bag for her pink blouse. The clothes the woman at the police station had taken home to launder for her were folded neatly on the side of the duffel bag.

It was such a sweet thing to do, washing her clothes. When this was over, she would have so many people to thank for their kindness. She'd have to do something especially nice for the police chief. Letting them use his cabin was above and beyond his duty.

She went into the bathroom to collect her toiletries. Glancing in the mirror, she was startled at how tired and pale she looked. She put on a little makeup to cover the dark circles under her eyes, added some blush and tinted pink lip gloss. Then she brushed her hair, gathered up her toothbrush and toothpaste, and put them in her makeup bag. She tossed John Paul's toothbrush on top.

She was ready to go when John Paul walked into the bedroom. He shut the door, leaned against it, and looked at her.

After she'd finished zipping her bag, she stood, then nervously brushed her hands against her slacks, as though she were trying to iron any wrinkles out.

"Is something wrong?"

"I don't want to leave." He was looking at the bed when he made the comment.

"I don't either," she admitted.

"Come here." His voice was low and urgent.

She didn't hesitate. She ran to him, threw her arms around his neck, and kissed him.

When at last they drew apart, there were tears in her eyes. She had never felt this kind of desperation before, and it was so wrenching, so heartbreaking she was afraid she would break down and sob.

How had she allowed herself to become so vulnerable? Love wasn't supposed to happen this quickly, was it? Why hadn't she protected herself? Love sucks, she decided then. All those stupid songs about how wonderful it was. All she felt was pain and fear, fear that something would happen to him. Damn it, she would not love him.

"You should go home," she said. She stepped back, nodded, and then repeated her decision, but this time she was more forceful. "I mean it. I want you to go home."

"Why?"

He had asked an obvious question, but she gave him an obscure answer. "You just should. I can drive myself to Florida. I don't need you or Noah to baby-sit me."

The more she explained, the more forceful her voice became. John Paul reacted to her outburst by simply grabbing his bag, dropping it on the bed, and then beginning to shove his clothes inside.

Noah was standing at the kitchen counter, drinking from a milk carton. He'd made himself a huge sandwich and was polishing it off as she carried her backpack to the door. John Paul was right behind her with her duffel bag and his.

"Let's go," he called to Noah.

"I'm right behind you."

She followed John Paul to the car. He opened the driver's door, popped the lid on the trunk; then, pausing to glare at her, he tossed their bags inside and slammed the trunk down.

"John Paul, I meant . . ."

He shook his head. "Don't."

"Don't what?" she asked.

"Don't insult me again. I told you at least three times I was in this for the long haul. Weren't you listening?"

She glanced at the door to make sure Noah wasn't there, then said, "I don't want you to get hurt. Okay? I couldn't stand it if anything happened to you . . . I don't think I could . . ."

"I love you too, Avery."

"It's too soon . . . you can't . . ."

"I do."

"How can you love me?" she whispered.

His left hand cupped the back of her neck, and as he slowly drew her toward him, he whispered, "Want me to count the ways?"

Tears stung her eyes. He wasn't going to be reasonable. "You're stubborn."

"So are you."

"It won't work."

"We'll make it work."

"I'm a liberal," she whispered in desperation.

He kissed her and then said, "I can live with that, but I can't live without you. Simple as that, sugar."

His wonderful mouth covered hers in a long, hot, thoroughly arousing kiss. He didn't overpower her with his strength, didn't have her chained to him. No, he was being extremely gentle as his mouth slanted over hers. She could have pulled back, but she didn't want to. She greedily kissed him back.

He growled low in his throat, which only encouraged her to be bolder. And when at last he lifted his head, she sagged against him.

She pushed away from him when the screen door opened.

Noah walked out onto the porch, pulled the door closed, and then tossed the keys to John Paul. "You drive while I catch up on some sleep."

He caught the keys without taking his gaze off Avery. "You're gonna marry me."

"No, I can't marry you."

"Did I ask?"

"You just said . . ."

"Did I ask?" he patiently repeated.

Noah glanced at both of them, shook his head, and then dove into the backseat. "Lover's spat?" he asked.

"No." They both snapped the word at the same time.

She grabbed the keys out of John Paul's hand. "I'm driving."

He didn't argue with her. The dynamics between the two fascinated Noah. Who would have thought the bear would ever fall? He guessed the old saying was true. There really was someone out there for everyone. A soul mate.

Wait until he told Theo about this. He wouldn't believe it either. The bear was in love.

He couldn't suppress his laughter. "What the hell's so funny?" John Paul grumbled.

"You. You're funny. Hey, Avery. Ever hear the one about the Marine . . ."

John Paul tilted his seat back and closed his eyes. It was going to be a long, long trip.

CHAPTER 33

The plans kept changing. Carrie didn't like change, any kind of change, unless, of course, she was the one in charge of making those changes. Agent Hillman was point man, and Agent Bean was his gofer. Hillman's first command when he was placed in charge of Carrie was to order Bean to tell her the decision had been made to keep her in Colorado.

After Bean informed Mrs. Salvetti of the Bureau's decision and suffered her reaction, he returned to Agent Hillman and threatened to hand in his resignation if Hillman ever made him do that again.

"I'm putting in for combat pay," Bean announced.

They could both hear Carrie screaming from the waiting room. "Doesn't she realize there are sick people in this hospital?" Hillman muttered, clearly appalled by the woman's conduct.

"She doesn't care," Bean countered. "She's demanding to go to Florida and stay in the safe house with her niece."

"I take it, then, you didn't tell her we can't find her niece?"

"No, sir. I thought I'd let you explain that to her."

"For God's sake, man. You're an agent with the FBI. Surely you can handle a cranky woman."

"With all due respect, sir, she isn't just a cranky woman. She's a . . ."

"A what?" Hillman snapped.

A she-devil, Bean wanted to say but didn't dare. Hillman wouldn't believe him. Besides, he would find out soon enough what the Salvetti woman was capable of when she wasn't happy. "Sir, she isn't what I would call a normal woman. Normal women don't have fire shooting out of their eyes."

Hillman was disgusted. "She'll do whatever we tell her to do."

Wanna bet? The ringing in his ears, he noticed, had subsided into a dull echo. "Yes, sir, I'm sure she'll listen to you." He said the last without breaking into a smile and was quite proud of his achievement.

"We have the woman's best interests at heart. Surely you explained our motives to her, didn't you, Bean?"

"She didn't give me the opportunity to explain our position."

"When she calms down—"

They both heard another shout. Bean grimaced as Hillman demanded, "Who's in there with her?"

"Gorman," he answered. "He must have told her we haven't been able to locate her niece."

The door to the waiting room opened and Gorman stepped out. Hillman and Bean stood at the end of the hallway and watched as Gorman hastily pulled the door closed. His face was as red as hot peppers.

Gorman spotted Hillman, drew himself up to his full six foot two height, and walked down the hall to join them.

"Is she giving you trouble too?" Hillman asked.

Bean tried not to snicker. Of course she'd given him trouble. Just look at his face.

"She's a . . . difficult woman," Gorman said, trying to be diplomatic. "She refuses to cooperate. Told me she's going to Florida with or without Hill of Beans."

"Hill of Beans?" Hillman asked.

Gorman cleared his throat. "That's what she's calling you and Agent Bean. Hill of Beans. She's also demanding a beach house."

"A beach house? She wants a beach house?" Hillman asked incredulously.

Bean cast him a smug I-told-you-so look. Now, perhaps, his superior would agree that the Salvetti woman was as difficult as he'd told him she was.

"And what did you say to her demands?"

"I told her that wasn't possible, that since her testimony isn't mandatory, she'll be staying in Colorado. I explained the defense attorney has the transcripts of Skarrett's first trial and he hasn't asked to depose Mrs. Salvetti again and that, for that reason, there wasn't any need for her to go to Florida."

"And her response?" Bean asked.

"She tried to grab my gun."

"I'm sure she was bluffing," Hillman said. "Let's give her a few minutes to cool off," he suggested.

It was going to take Carrie more than a few minutes to calm her temper. Blowing up was her response to the fear gnawing at her stomach. What the hell was Avery going to do? Did she think she could stroll into that courthouse and testify against Skarrett? Carrie kept picturing her niece being gunned down on the courthouse steps.

If Monk . . . or Jilly . . . got hold of her . . . Carrie rushed to the phone, got an outside line, and called Tony collect. She prayed he hadn't already left for the airport.

He must have been sitting by the phone, because he picked up on the first ring.

Carrie didn't waste time on preliminaries. "They're going to put me in a house and keep me here, in Colorado," she blurted.

"Where in Colorado?" he asked.

"They wouldn't tell me, but I heard one of them talking on his cell phone. He didn't know I was listening, and he mentioned a place called Wedgewood. It must be some kind of suburb."

"Aspen's too small to have suburbs," he countered.

"I don't know where the hell it is. Look it up on the Internet, for God's sake. Use your head. There can't be more than one Wedgewood suburb in Colorado." She burst into tears. "If I have to be in a safe house for a long time, what will happen to my company? I can't be away too long. I can't . . ."

"Honey, I can handle things here. I've run a company before."

"But I need you with me, Tony. You have to come."

"All right, I will," he promised. "I won't let you go through this alone. Do you want me to come to the hospital? Can they wait to move you until I get there?"

"I'll make them wait," she said. "Sara has already been moved into the new physical therapy wing. It hasn't even been opened yet, so security's easy. I'll stay there with her until they move both of us. I won't let them take me anywhere until you get here."

"Yes, okay," he said, sounding relieved.

"Do you know they can't find Avery? When she called me, she told me she wouldn't be joining me in protective custody. Have you talked to her?"

"No, not yet. I've been pacing by the phone, waiting. It's

not like Avery to make me worry. I don't understand why she hasn't called."

"She knows you'll give her hell for upsetting me," Carrie said. "She doesn't like to disappoint either one of us."

"I know, honey, but I'm worried sick about her."

"Me too. She'll call, and when she does, you tell her not to go to Sheldon Beach. Make her realize how dangerous it will be for her."

"Yes, I will," he promised. "I'm not going to let anything happen to her."

"What if Avery calls after you've left for the airport?"

"Honey, she knows my cell phone number."

Of course Avery did. Carrie was so rattled she couldn't think. "I'll see you soon."

Carrie hung up the phone and decided to call Avery's office to find out if her friends had heard from her, but she was prevented from making any more calls when Agent Hillman walked into the room and told her that Judge Collins wanted to talk to her.

"We'll be moving you into the new wing in a few minutes."

"Yes, all right. Whatever you say."

Hillman was surprised and pleased by her cooperation. He was feeling a bit smug too, for he'd been right. He'd told Bean and Gorman that once Mrs. Salvetti calmed down, she would cooperate, and she was doing exactly that now.

Maybe this wasn't going to be such a bad assignment after all.

CHAPTER 34

Jilly had just had a full body massage and was now wrapped in a four-hundred-count Egyptian cotton sheet with the logo of Utopia stamped on the hem. She lay on her back, her eyes closed, while the female technician applied an avocado facial mask. The stupid woman wouldn't stop talking. She gave Jilly one compliment after another about her flawless complexion and her oh, so perfect body.

Jilly never tired of hearing compliments from men, but she didn't care what women thought about her, and just when she was about to tell the technician to shut up, she finished applying the goo and said, "We'll just let this set for fifteen minutes."

She was finally alone. Loosening the sheet, she let the cool air caress her body. It felt good to relax, especially after she'd become so distraught over the news that Carrie and the judge had survived the explosion. Fortunately, Monk hadn't been in the bungalow when that horrid news came on the television, so she didn't have to try to behave. He had never seen her throw a full-blown tantrum, and she didn't know how he would react. She certainly didn't want to scare him, not yet anyway, because he was so terribly useful. There was still too much to be done, and it was imperative that Monk stay the loyal lapdog.

Carrie used to call her fits rages, but Jilly had learned control over the years. Not much, but some, she qualified. Admittedly, if one of the housekeeping staff had happened to walk into the bungalow just after Jilly had heard the news about Carrie, Jilly probably would have attacked her. And enjoyed every moment of it.

Jilly had never killed a person. She'd let her men take care of her problems. Wasn't that what they were for? She had often wondered, though, what it would feel like to kill someone with a gun or maybe even with her bare hands. If someone caused her to be unhappy, then watching her die did seem fitting. Why should she deny herself that joy and satisfaction? She realized now that Monk had been right all along. He had wanted to kill each woman separately and make the deaths look like accidents, but Jilly had pleaded and cajoled until he'd given in and done things her way. How could such a brilliant plan not work? It was so perfect, so simple, so . . . brilliant.

Carrie. Carrie was the reason the plan hadn't worked. That selfish bitch had ruined everything.

Jilly threw herself on the bed and pounded her fists into the pillows. She stopped suddenly. She heard the newscaster on CNN with the lead-in for the footage that was coming on the screen again. She bolted upright, impatiently wiping the tears from her eyes, and stared at the screen. The film was focusing on the judge, but Jilly wasn't interested in her, no matter how famous she was supposed to be. She waited, whimpering, until finally the camera turned to her bitch of a sister as she was being carried on a stretcher into the ambulance. Men, paramedics, no doubt, but still men, were actually fawning over her. How dare they give her any attention? How dare they? Jilly was more enraged by the men's behavior than by the fact that her sister was still very much alive.

The camera zoomed in on Carrie's face. Jilly thought she saw her smiling, and that proved to be the last straw. Screaming obscenities, she picked up a lamp and hurled it into the wall.

Carrie was ruining everything.

It took an hour for her to calm down. Then she called the spa and had a masseur come to the bungalow. The massage helped, and she was now able to think about a new plan. This one wouldn't be as complicated, she decided.

Why hadn't she given in to the urge and killed Carrie with her scissors? Because that wouldn't have been as much fun. After everything her sister had done to her, she deserved to suffer a long while before she died. It wasn't fair. Men worrying about her, taking care of her. Couldn't they see how ugly she was?

Jilly could feel herself getting worked up again. The mask on her face was beginning to itch. Her cell phone rang just as the technician came back into the suite.

"Go away," she said. "I'll wash this off. Shut the door behind you."

Jilly knocked over a stack of towels as she reached for the phone. "Yes?"

"I thought you would want to hear some good news. I found out where Carrie and the judge are."

She immediately perked up. "You know? Where, darling? Was I right?" she asked before he could answer. "Are they going to Sheldon Beach? Is that where they're going to hide Carrie until the trial?"

"Your sister isn't going to Florida because she isn't going to testify at the trial."

Jilly laughed with delight. "She's afraid."

"Yes."

The mask on her face cracked when she smiled. "That's wonderful news. Now tell me everything."

She listened carefully, and when he was finished, she told him not to worry, that she would come up with a new, even better plan. "But something less complicated this time," she promised. Then in a voice that sounded like a dove cooing, she said, "I miss you, darling."

"I'll see you soon?"

"Of course."

"I love you."

She smiled again. "Yes. I know."

She disconnected the call, dropped her towel, and went into the bathroom to shower. Wrapping herself in a terrycloth robe, she called housekeeping to come and clean up the mess she'd made. The cost of the damage would be put on her credit card.

Two hours later, when Monk walked into the room, she was ready for him. She wore a black chiffon dress and high heels, but had decided against undergarments. When she stood in the doorway with the light spilling out from the bedroom, she knew he could see through the filmy material. She'd checked to make sure.

Monk was weary by the time he got there, but as soon as he saw the love of his life, he was rejuvenated. He knew the trouble she'd gone to just to please him. She had instinctively known he would need to make love to her and had prepared the bedroom. There were candles burning to set the mood, and she was wearing his favorite dress. It was identical to the red one she used to have, until he'd torn it. As he strode toward her, he told himself not to ruin this one.

He watched her mouth. She was slowly rubbing her upper lip with the tip of her tongue. She knew he liked that too.

Their lovemaking was wild and crude. Like animals in heat, they tore at each other. Her dress fell to the floor in tatters. And when he was finally satisfied, he rolled off her, threw his arm back, and closed his eyes.

She had pleased him, and now it was his turn to please her. "I think we should wait a couple of days," Jilly said, "and then, after you're rested, you can take care of Carrie and the judge. They'll be all settled in and feeling safe by then. Don't you agree? It shouldn't be too difficult for you to get in and do what needs to be done."

"I need at least two weeks to organize and plan."

"Did I just make you happy, Monk?"

"You know you did, darling."

"Then make me happy. I could wait maybe a week, but I'd go crazy if I had to wait any longer. Carrie was smiling when they lifted her into the ambulance. I didn't like seeing her smile."

"I understand."

"She told the police about me. Now they know I'm alive, and they'll be looking for me. You were right," she whispered. "I shouldn't have insisted on the letters, and I shouldn't have let her see me. But I thought she would die in the explosion, and I wanted her to know . . ."

"Don't cry, Jilly," he said as he took her in his arms. "It's going to be all right."

"Yes," she said, cuddling up against him. "As soon as she's dead, everything will be all right. She's made me so unhappy for such a long time. Promise me you'll kill her soon."

"I promise," he answered. "You know I'll do anything for you."

She smiled against his neck. Her hands moved skillfully over his body. "Then we'll go to Sheldon Beach."

Monk's desperation to please her was making him frantic, but at the same time he felt he could do anything and succeed because of her faith in him. She often told him how brilliant she thought he was and how he underestimated and undervalued himself. He realized now that she was right. He could pull it off. He could get in and out without being noticed, no matter how many FBI agents were there.

He could even become invisible.

CHAPTER 35

THE DRIVE TO Florida took three days. They could have pushed it, but because they had the time, they took the more scenic back roads through Georgia.

They spent two nights in clean but no-frills motels tucked away in small towns. The first night they each had their own room. Avery hadn't invited John Paul to share her bed, and he hadn't asked or assumed. She was desperately trying to distance herself from him because she believed it would make their final parting less painful, but it wasn't working. She was only fooling herself. She loved him and didn't know what to do about it. She didn't sleep at all that first night, tossed and turned until she made herself dizzy, and by morning, her disposition was as charming as a rhino's. The second night, John Paul didn't ask. He simply paid for two rooms while Noah talked to one of his superiors on his cell phone.

John Paul followed Avery into her room and dropped his bag next to hers. She didn't argue but said, "We're just going to sleep. No sex."

Smiling, he stripped out of his clothes and headed for

the shower. "Did I ask?" he said before shutting the door in her face.

The air conditioner in the window was cranked up, the room was freezing, and around two in the morning she woke up in his arms, feeling toasty warm and amorous. He was simply irresistible. They made love, and it was even better than the last time because now each knew what the other liked, and within minutes they were perfectly attuned to each other's needs.

The wall separating their room from Noah's was paper thin. She tried to be quiet, but when she felt those first tremors of exquisite pleasure coursing through her body, the feeling was so intense she bit his shoulder to keep the shout of ecstasy from escaping.

It was so wonderful that when she awakened at six, she rolled into his arms and, as Margo would say, she jumped his bones again.

He went back to sleep. She went into the bathroom, and after she'd showered, she stood in front of the mirror looking at her face. Her cheeks were red from rubbing against his whiskers, and her lips were swollen from his kisses.

Sighing, she shook her head and whispered, "Hi. My name's Avery, and I'm a sexaholic."

She couldn't blame anyone but herself. Vowing to leave him the hell alone, she picked up her toothbrush and tried not to think about him as she got ready for the day.

John Paul was in a much better mood as they started out. He was almost pleasant to Noah. Not quite, but almost. Avery thought the two men acted like adversaries in some kind of contest, but it didn't take her long to realize they both got a kick out of trading insults.

After they had stopped for lunch, she got into the backseat, put on her baseball cap to block the sun from her eyes, and decided to take a nap.

The men lowered their voices so they wouldn't disturb her. Noah knew about Jilly. He'd read Avery's file, and he'd come prepared.

They speculated about how she had connected with Monk and what their relationship might be. Noah, of course, knew all about Skarrett too, and thought that maybe he was calling all the shots. John Paul disagreed, pointing out that once Monk had taken the contract, he did things his way.

One topic led to another. "Are you going to lose your job because you're helping us?" John Paul asked. "The FBI's looking for Avery."

"I don't work for the FBI. I'm what you might call an independent contractor."

John Paul was exasperated. "No, you work for the FBI. What the hell do you think that badge is for?"

"Better parking spots. It's the only reason I carry it."

"Get serious."

"Do you ever miss it?"

"Miss what?"

"The action."

"Hell, no."

"You still living in the swamp?"

"I live in Bowen."

"In the swamp."

"Yeah, I guess so."

"You think she'll want to live there?"

He pretended not to understand. "Who?"

He had forgotten how blunt Noah could be. "The woman you're sleeping with. The woman you can't take your eyes off even when you're driving. You've been looking in the rearview mirror every ten seconds since you got behind the wheel. You're gonna get us killed if you don't pay attention to the road."

John Paul was determined not to discuss Avery. "How far is it to that little town you picked out on the map for us to stay tonight? What was it called? Walden Point?"

"Now me, I don't think I'm ever gonna settle down. Too many fish in the sea," Noah said.

"And Walden Point is what? Twenty or thirty miles from Sheldon Beach?"

"I didn't think you'd ever find a woman who would put up with you, but I guess I was wrong."

John Paul couldn't pretend he wasn't listening any longer. "You don't even know me, Noah."

"Sure I do. I know all about you."

"Did you read my file?" He didn't give him time to respond but muttered, "Doesn't 'classified' mean anything anymore?"

"Guess not," Noah drawled. He hadn't had access to John Paul's file, but he had talked to Theo about his reclusive brother-in-law. Since it obviously upset John Paul to think that his file had been opened, Noah didn't tell him the truth. He liked annoying him.

"So, do you think she'll like living in Bowen?"

They had just come full circle. John Paul gripped the steering wheel as he tried to control his temper.

"We won't need to stop for gas."

Noah grinned. "Man, you've got it bad. Your face is getting red."

John Paul thought about punching him. "It's not like that."

"Oh? You two don't have any kind of arrangement?"

He wasn't about to discuss his and Avery's relationship. "No."

"No future plans?"

He glared at Noah. "No," he snapped. Turning back to

the road, he said, "Are you ready to talk about something else?"

"Sure," he said. "What do you want to talk about?"

"Stop hitting on Avery."

He was sorry the second the words were out of his mouth. Noah laughed. "Why would I want to stop doing that? You just said—"

"I know what the hell I said."

"And she is a beautiful woman."

Maybe he could reach over real quick, open Noah's door, and shove him out. That ought to shut him up.

"She's sexy as hell too."

"Yeah, well, you leave her the hell alone. Now, how far is it to Walden Point?"

"Beats me." Noah tilted the seat back, adjusted his sunglasses on the bridge of his nose, and closed his eyes.

"You're the damn navigator. Look at the map."

"Sure thing."

He was sound asleep seconds later.

The rest of the afternoon was blissfully quiet. They arrived in Walden Point around six that evening. The sleepy little town was exactly thirty-two miles from the bridge leading into Sheldon Beach.

If Avery had been in Walden Point as a child, she didn't remember it. The streets were lined with palm trees, the grass was brown from salt water and sun, and the houses along the side streets were ill kept and weather-beaten. It was a dismal, forgotten-looking place until they reached the older, more populated section of town. The houses along those avenues had been spruced up. The grass was lush and green, and flowers brimmed over terra-cotta pots on freshly painted porches. It was apparent there was a renovation in progress.

There were several pretty bed-and-breakfast homes

along the main street to the waterfront, but Noah wasn't interested in stopping there. He found a motel about twelve blocks away from the beach and told John Paul to pull into the lot.

Avery thought Noah was joking. Milt's Flamingo Motel had flaming pink concrete block walls and a red-tile roof in desperate need of repair. There were hand-painted flamingos in different colors on each lime green door. The U-shaped structure with twelve units had a gravel parking lot. Whoever had chosen the color scheme had to have been color-blind.

There weren't any other cars around. Avery thought Milt must have flown the coop, abandoning the dump.

"Are you sure this is open?"

"I saw a guy watching as we pulled in," Noah answered. "It's easy in and out. We park behind, and the car's out of sight from the street. What do you think?"

Since he was asking John Paul and not her, Avery kept her opinion of their lodgings to herself. After having passed the lovely bed-and-breakfast a couple of blocks away with the charming white picket fence and rockers on the wrap-around porch, she thought Noah's choice was awful. She waited for John Paul to protest.

"I like it," he said, dashing her hopes. "It kind of reminds me of my dad's bar. He's got a big flamingo on his roof."

"Yeah, I remember seeing it. I thought it was a pelican. I'll check us in."

"There's a bed-and-breakfast just down the road," she interjected. "It looked nice and clean. I noticed a vacancy sign in the yard."

"This is okay, isn't it?" John Paul asked.

If Noah hadn't been with them, she would have told him

no, it wasn't okay, but she didn't want to complain in front of an agent.

"Yes, it's fine."

He smiled because she sounded so disheartened. "Not as nice as Tyler's cabin?"

"It's fine," she repeated.

Noah had just gotten out of the car when his cell phone rang. John Paul walked ahead to the office, but Avery stayed with Noah. She stretched her arms and legs, stiff from the long ride.

Noah, his head down, walked away, obviously so that the conversation would be private. She saw his expression, knew something was wrong, and anxiously waited.

The conversation lasted a long time. John Paul came back with two keys, took one look at Avery, and said, "What's wrong?"

"Something," she said, leaning into his side.

Noah ended the call and walked back to the car. His gaze was on Avery. "Your aunt and the judge are fine."

"What happened?" John Paul asked.

"There was a delivery; some tanks to be installed behind the physical therapy wing."

"Ah, hell," John Paul whispered. He already knew what was coming. "They blew, didn't they?"

Noah nodded. "The fire took out most of the wing."

"How did Monk get past security?" Avery asked.

"He didn't," Noah said. "The delivery man was killed as he was unloading them. Monk got to those tanks before they were set."

"How many down?" John Paul asked.

"Two dead. An agent named Gorman was injured, but he's gonna make it. That's all I know."

"How the hell did this happen?" John Paul demanded.

"I'll tell you how it happened. Monk was there on the

hospital grounds all that time watching and waiting. He had to have known they couldn't move the judge so soon after her surgery. When the agents put those decoys in the car and drove off, he probably spotted something and knew the women weren't Carrie and the judge."

Noah led the way to their rooms. They were at the far end of the units and had a connecting door between them.

Their room was surprisingly clean. There was a double bed with a floral bedspread, two chairs by the window facing the gravel lot, with a small table and lamp in between. There wasn't a closet. On the far wall was a rack with hangers and built-in shelves next to it.

The second Noah stepped into their room, Avery asked, "Carrie and the judge weren't injured? You're telling me everything?"

"Yes," he said. "Your aunt had just wheeled the judge into the bathroom when it happened. The walls caved in on them and protected them from being incinerated."

Avery felt sick to her stomach. Noah's phone rang again, and he walked into his room. She waited until his back was turned and then went to John Paul, put her arms around his waist, and held him tight.

He could feel her trembling. "This nightmare will be over soon," he promised. Then, when she didn't answer, he asked, "Do you want to get out of here?"

"Yes."

"Where do you want to go?"

"I don't know," she whispered. "I can't think . . . I need to be able . . ."

He kissed her brow. "You need a porch swing, don't you?"

She nodded.

"With lilacs," he added.

She smiled because he remembered her happy place.

"I can't give you lilacs, and I can't drum up a porch swing for you, sugar, but water . . . I can give you lots of that."

Twenty minutes later she and John Paul walked hand in hand along the beach. Both of them had changed into shorts and had left their shoes on the steps where Noah sat.

Dark clouds were moving in, obscuring the sun. The beach was virtually deserted, and when Avery sat down and assumed the lotus position, John Paul didn't intrude. He walked back to the steps and sat down next to Noah.

"What the hell is she doing?" Noah asked when Avery hadn't moved for several minutes.

"Thinking," he answered.

"Okay."

When the sun was dropping, taking the light of the day, John Paul got up and went to Avery. Her eyes were closed. He squatted down in front of her and waited, knew she sensed he was there.

A moment passed before she acknowledged him. She opened her eyes and looked into his. A single tear slid down her cheek. She took a deep cleansing breath.

"I need to make a call."

CHAPTER 36

Monk was ready to make his move.

There was a "no vacancy" sign in the window of the manager's office, and nailed to the door was another sign. "Closed until further notice."

Monk knew the targets were inside. He had already canvassed the area, knew it like the back of his hand. Three cars were parked behind the motel. He was certain two of them belonged to federal agents assigned to protect Avery. The third vehicle was Renard's.

Monk drove Jilly past the motel so she could see where it was going to happen, and she could barely contain her excitement when she saw the light shimmering along the edge of the tightly drawn drapes in the unit Monk had pointed out to her.

"She's in there," she whispered, her excitement brimming in her voice.

Monk pulled into the parking lot up the street from Milt's Motel. The lot did double duty for patrons of the old Spanish-style movie theater, complete with bell tower, and the spillover from the Church of the Risen. He parked the car so that it faced the street, then handed Jilly his binoculars and took a drink of his iced tea.

"You're now officially on a stakeout."

She giggled. "This is wonderful."

Her excitement thrilled him. "You're having a good time, aren't you?"

"Oh, yes," she gushed. "It's better than I could ever have imagined. Much better."

A car pulled into the parking lot, and she quickly lowered the binoculars. "Are you sure we're safe here?"

"Of course we are. I'll always make it safe for you."

They shared a smile, and then Jilly lifted the binoculars again. She could just see the light framing the window, and she was trying to imagine what was happening inside the room.

Another car pulled in and parked three rows behind them. There was a revival going on inside the church, and it was also dollar night at the movie theater. The lot was nearly full now.

Jilly offered him the binoculars, but he didn't need to look. He had already spent one full night and day doing reconnaissance. It wasn't enough, but it would have to do. Normally, he would have spent at least two weeks following his subject, learning his routine, but this wasn't a normal situation. Time was running out, and Jilly was too impatient to wait much longer. Like a child, she wanted instant gratification.

"How many policemen are inside with them?" she asked.

"Agents," he corrected. "Not policemen. There are four."

"And you'll get them all?"

"Yes."

They were sitting ducks. His for the taking.

The night before, Monk had watched Renard sneak out the back door, get into his car, and drive away. Monk hadn't had a clear shot at him, but he wouldn't have taken it even if he had because he didn't want his primary targets moved once again. He had something special planned for them. Pity, they wouldn't know what hit them.

Renard had returned to the motel thirty minutes later carrying four big pizzas and a plastic bag Monk guessed was filled with beer or soft drinks.

He was disgusted with Renard's carelessness. He was certain the man didn't have any idea he was being observed. Smug complacency. That's what it was. He was disappointed in Renard. He'd expected better from his adversary and had made the mistake of believing that Renard was a professional. An equal. He realized now how foolish that hope had been. No one could ever equal or measure up to his standards. Jilly had been right all along. He was a legend.

"I think it might be a good idea to do it tonight," Jilly said.

"You're eager."

"Yes."

"Tomorrow," he promised.

"I don't want to wait too much longer."

"I know."

"I wonder if Carrie is feeling safe again. Can you imagine how claustrophobic she and Avery must be feeling now? Being cooped up in that flea-infested room night and day? They must be going crazy."

"I've deliberately waited," he explained, "so that the agents would be bored and . . . lethargic. Yes, that's the word. Lethargic."

"Hour upon hour of sitting in that tiny room, waiting

and worrying. They haven't let them out at all, have they?"

"Not while I was watching."

"I'm glad she didn't die in that hospital," she said. "This will be better because I'll get to watch."

Monk nodded. "Carrie demanded to come to Florida."

"She wants to die with Avery."

"She doesn't know she's going to die tomorrow," he said. "She thinks she's going to sit in that courtroom with Avery when the trial starts."

Jilly picked up the binoculars once again. Smiling, she said, "Third time's a charm."

Monk suppressed a yawn. He was exhausted, but he didn't dare complain. Jilly thought he was invincible, superhuman, and he was determined to maintain his knight-in-shining-armor image.

He knew he was taking risks he never would have considered before, but it was difficult to be cautious with Jilly constantly pushing him to his limits. She believed he could do anything, made him believe in himself.

Every once in a while a nagging doubt would surface in his mind. He had never walked away from a contract before. His word meant everything. If he wasn't reliable, his future would be in jeopardy, his reputation in tatters. The thought didn't repulse him, though. He had more than enough money to keep Jilly in the style she deserved. Maybe he could let this one go and walk away.

"You know, darling, we don't need the money," he said hesitantly.

Jilly knew where he was leading. "Do you know what I think?"

"What?"

"When we're finished here, let's sneak away to Mexico

and get married. The trial will go for at least a week. Dale isn't going anywhere. Shall we?"

She knew how much he wanted a wedding. His fatigue vanished, and he was suddenly smiling in anticipation. "Yes, yes," he said. He was embarrassed because he'd sounded so eager, but he added, "I know a perfect place . . . you'll love it, I promise."

"As long as I'm marrying you, nothing else matters."

She put her hand on his thigh, leaned across the console, and kissed him. Her hand moved upward to fondle him intimately.

He became aroused quickly. Satisfied with his reaction, she pulled away. "Why not put them out of their misery tonight?" she asked again, pouting now.

It took several seconds for Monk to understand what she was asking. He cleared his head and said, "You'll see it all tomorrow. Daylight's better. Besides, I have a few alterations to make, a few details before I'll be ready. You want it to be perfect, don't you, love?"

"Yes, of course. But why is daylight better?"

"No one expects to be hit with the sun shining, and in the past I've always tried to go in and get out during the night. Those agents believe they know my pattern."

"You think they've studied you?"

"Yes. When it's dark, their guard will be up."

She sighed then. "All right, I'll have to wait until tomorrow. Remember, you promised I could watch. You won't change your mind, will you?"

"No, I won't," he assured her. "You'll be safe, but in a wonderful spot where you can see everything. And I have a surprise for you. I was going to wait until tomorrow, but . . ."

"Tell me now," she pleaded. "Please."

"All right. I know how disappointed you were when you saw the house in Colorado blow. But this time will be different. I'm going to let you push the button."

She laughed with delight. "Are you going to dazzle me?"

He nodded. "Oh, yes. I'm a legend, remember? I'm going to dazzle everyone."

CHAPTER 37

AFTER MONK DROVE Jilly back to their hotel on the opposite side of Walden Point, he got back into the car and drove to a residential area a mile away from Milt's Motel.

He jogged a mile back to his hiding place and quietly climbed the stairs. He still had to put the finishing touches on the wiring. The job took much longer than he had anticipated, no doubt because he was weary, but when he was finally finished, he was content with his handiwork. Nothing was going to go wrong this time.

It was after three in the morning by the time he got ready for bed. Careful not to disturb Jilly, he eased down on the bed and sat next to her, watching her sleep. Oh, how he loved her. She was so beautiful, so exquisite . . . so perfect. He lay beside her thinking once again that he was the luckiest man in the world. He fell asleep with his arms around her, the scent of her perfume surrounding him, and dreamed of their honeymoon.

Fairy tales could come true. He and Jilly would live happily ever after.

* * *

Jilly dressed with care the following morning. She was going to church, after all, and so she wore a white skirt, white eyelet blouse, and strappy high-heel sandals. While she brushed her hair and curled it, Monk put their luggage in the car.

"Don't forget my tape," she reminded him.

"I would never forget that," he assured her, though, in fact, he had forgotten. She would have been beside herself if she'd lost it. She was so obsessed with what she called the evidence that she insisted on always carrying it with her. A peculiarity he put up with just as she put up with his odd little traits. That's what a solid relationship was all about, wasn't it? Give and take.

He removed the tape from the VCR, slipped it into the carrying case, and put it on the bed next to her straw purse.

She was primping in front of the mirror. He watched her put on her red lipstick and smiled because he knew she only wore that color to please him. She'd told him so.

Jilly put the lipstick in her purse with the tape, picked up her straw hat with the white ribbon, and then walked into the center of the room. Whirling around in a circle, she asked, "Do I look ready for church?"

Her face flushed with excitement. "You look beautiful," he whispered. "You always look beautiful."

She went to him, adjusted the knot in his tie just like an adoring wife would, and said, "You look wonderful in a suit. You should wear them more often."

"If it pleases you, I will."

She took hold of his hand and walked by his side to the car. He liked little things like that, he thought. Taking his hand. It was a sign of trust, wasn't it? The way she looked up at him with such admiration. He liked that too.

"I've already parked the other car down the street from

the church," he said. "Just as a precaution. The key's behind the visor."

"We won't need to use it," she said. "You've covered
every possibility."

He was certain that he had, and so he agreed, yet there
was still that nagging little worry about the wires. He'd
been so tired, he hadn't done more than one test, but that
was enough.

The wind had picked up as they drove. Monk glanced up
at the tower above the theater as he turned the corner. He
pulled into the lot, parked on the end in front so Jilly could
see everything. No one could block the front of his car,
and if he had to drive over the curb to get to the street, he
could do so without getting trapped.

He turned the motor off. "Are you ready?"

"Oh, yes."

"The remote's in the glove compartment."

She carefully lifted it out. "It looks like a garage door
opener."

"That's what it is," he said. "Modified, of course."

"When do I push the button?"

"I thought it would be nice to wait until the church bells
start."

Jilly turned in her seat to watch the men and women and
children hurry toward the church. They didn't want to be
late, she thought.

The show's outside. Too bad they wouldn't see it. "What
time is it now?"

"Five more minutes."

"I don't want to wait. I want to do it now."

Monk reached under the seat and handed her the binoculars. "Whenever you're ready."

Jilly wet her lips as she lifted the binoculars. She ad-

justed the lens until she was looking at the room that had
had the light on the night before.

"I'm taking my dream back," she whispered.

She pushed the button. Nothing happened, and so she
pushed it again. Then again, harder, holding it down.

"Damn," Monk muttered. "The wind must have knocked
loose one of the wires. Stop pushing that button, darling.
I'll have to go up there and fix it. You sit tight. All right?"

He gently removed the remote from her hand. "If anything goes wrong . . ."

"You worry too much. Fix the wire," she said, a bit more
sharply than she'd intended. "I'm sorry. I shouldn't be so
anxious. I can wait another few minutes."

"That's my girl," he said. "Just in case, you remember
what to do?"

"I go into the church, then out the side door, and get in
the other car."

"And drive away on the side street I showed you. Don't
drive in front of the motel."

"I won't leave without you."

Her loyalty was heartwarming. He patted her hand, put
the remote on the floor by his seat, and then got out of the
car. Slipping one hand into his pocket, he casually strolled
across the parking lot and up the stairs to the church.

The bells rang as he walked inside. Thirty seconds later,
he came out the side door, crossed the street, and walked
three blocks to the north before he was convinced he wasn't
being followed. He crossed the street and headed toward
the movie theater.

The back door was locked, of course. He used his tools
to undo the dead bolt, went inside, and quickly locked the
door behind him.

He was in the back hallway. The door leading upstairs to

the tower and the marquee was across the lobby. He stayed low and quiet.

He stood in the shadow behind the snack bar for several minutes, listening for any sounds, and when he was convinced he was all alone, he crept to the door. That, too, was locked, just as he had left it. He quickly unlocked it, opened the door, and looked up. The brown string he'd left on the third step hadn't been disturbed. No one had found his little hiding place. He stepped over the string and slowly, cautiously went up, aware that there was a squeak on the fifth step. He knew he was alone—the theater wouldn't open until the matinee at two—but he still avoided the step.

There was a trip wire at the top, much thinner than dental floss and all but invisible to the naked eye. Monk released the lever so that when he opened the door, he wouldn't be blown to kingdom come.

Good thing the owner didn't want to change the marquee today, he thought with a smile. He only changed the movies on Wednesdays, but Monk had set a trap anyway. Can't be too cautious, no matter what his darling Jilly believed.

He opened the door a crack and looked in. The rifle with the scope attached was still there in the corner, propped against the pillar.

His gaze went to the trigger mechanism below his homemade missile. Just as he had suspected, one of the wires had slipped down. It wasn't dangling free. The wind had loosened it just enough to break the connection.

He'd have it fixed in two seconds. He pushed the door open, stepped forward, and bent down on one knee. Then he froze. The voice came from his left on the other side of the bell. "Nice Roman candle you've got there."

Monk was too stunned to move. His mind was screaming, *No, no, no. The wire . . . the string . . . nothing had been disturbed. How did . . .*

Another voice came from his right. "I think he's having trouble getting it to work."

Monk lunged for his rifle. Neither man tried to stop him. He rolled, firing as he moved.

Nothing happened. The rifle was empty. Noah stepped into the sunlight. Monk saw him and coiled back. "You," he whispered. "I know you."

John Paul moved forward from the shadows.

"How did you know?" Monk's face twisted with fury, and his voice shook.

"Easy. I'm smarter than you."

Noah's gun was pointed at Monk's forehead. John Paul saw the look in Noah's eyes and knew exactly what he was thinking.

"Cuff him," he said. "Then read him his rights."

Noah shook his head. "I'm gonna kill him first. Then I'll cuff him and read him his rights."

"Yeah, well, you can't."

"Son of a bitch." Noah released the trigger and put the gun back into his holster. He had the cuffs out and was moving toward Monk when they heard an agent shouting.

Monk lashed out with his foot, knocking Noah off balance. He stumbled in front of the killer, making it impossible for John Paul to get a clear shot.

Agents were racing up the stairs as Monk tried to get his gun from his ankle holster, but John Paul anticipated that response. He slammed his foot down on Monk's leg, pinning him to the floor.

"Quit messing around," he shouted. "Get the hell off him so I can shoot him."

"I'm gonna shoot him," Noah shouted back. He hit Monk in the face, grunting from the sheer pleasure of hearing cartilage snap. He punched him again, trying to strike the exact spot so that it would hurt him more.

The door slammed into the pillar when the first agent came flying across the threshold. Monk seized the opportunity. With every ounce of strength he possessed, he shoved Noah off him and dove headfirst off the tower.

The killer landed on the slanted tin roof. He rolled to his hands and knees and crawled like a gorilla down to the marquee. When his right foot hit a bracket, he braced himself and went for his gun. He was swinging it up when John Paul and Noah, dropping down to the roof, fired simultaneously. Their bullets riddled Monk's body, sending him dancing backward like a marionette they were manipulating. He swung around and fell forward, his body draped across the marquee.

Panting, Noah put his gun away and then said, "You have the right to remain silent . . ."

"Damn right," John Paul muttered.

An agent leaning from the bell tower window called down to them. "Subject is on the move."

Noah pulled his walkie-talkie from his belt. He repeated what the agent had just told him.

"Roger."

"Was that Avery's voice? That was, wasn't it?" John Paul asked.

Noah spoke into the handset. "Avery? Is that you, sweetheart?"

He used the endearment just to piss off John Paul, and he grinned when he saw his reaction. If looks could kill, he'd be hanging over the marquee with Monk now.

John Paul snatched the handset. "What the hell are you doing, Avery? You were supposed to—"

"Are you all right?"

"Yeah, we're both fine. Where are you?"

"Roger. Over and out."

"Son of a bitch. She's in one of the tail cars."

They were both sprawled out on the roof. Noah laughed. "You could tell that from 'Roger, over and out'?"

John Paul ignored him and hit the button again. "Kelly?"

The agent in charge of the operation was quick to respond.

"Kelly here."

"Is Avery in one of the tail cars?" John Paul demanded. "Son of a bitch, I know she is. I told her to stay on that damn boat."

"Roger. Over and out."

Noah laughed. "Guess Avery's got a mind of her own." He leaned over the side of the building to judge the distance to the ground. "How the hell are we gonna get—"

John Paul shoved him off the roof. He followed him down and landed in a clump of dead shrubs beside the agent.

Kelly was on the handset again. "Do you have Monk in custody?"

"No, sir," John Paul answered.

"Where is he?"

He looked up at the marquee. "He's at the movies."

CHAPTER 38

JILLY HAD GROWN impatient waiting for Monk to return to the car. What was taking him so long? She picked up the binoculars from the floor and watched the tower. Where was he? He knew how much she hated waiting. "Fix the damn thing," she muttered. "Hurry up."

Monk suddenly came into view. Jilly gasped in disbelief as she watched him somersault onto the roof. She thought he was going to break his neck. He came flying down from the tower, but while he was still in the air, he twisted around and landed like a cat on his feet. He lost his balance, skated down the roof on his hands and knees. She thought he was going to flip down over the building, but he caught himself in time.

Two men leapt onto the roof above Monk. They were moving so fast their faces were a blur.

"Kill them," she whispered to Monk. "Kill them now. Do it."

Gunshots reverberated around her. She thought she heard Monk scream her name, and she watched with de-tached curiosity. He fell so ungracefully and draped over the marquee, blood pouring down over the lights. He died with his ass sticking up in the air. She cursed his incompetent soul.

How dare he do this to her? Her disappointment overwhelmed her, and her eyes stung with tears. The remote. She frantically grabbed it and pushed the button. Once, then again and again. Nothing happened.

Damn. How could Monk be so thoughtless? He knew how important her dreams were.

Stomping her feet on the floor, she cursed him because he had ruined everything. Worse, he had made her unhappy.

"Damn you to hell," she muttered.

He'd left the keys in the ignition. Ignoring his order to take the other car if there was trouble, she hiked her skirt up over her thighs, climbed over the console, and got behind the wheel. Men, FBI men, she knew, were running to the theater, and there were people flooding out of the church to see what all the commotion was about. No one would notice her leaving. She pulled out onto the street, and so that she wouldn't draw any undue attention to herself, she stayed below the speed limit as she cruised through town.

The second she reached the on-ramp to the highway, she slammed her foot on the gas pedal. Muttering curses, she slapped the steering wheel, trying to vent some of her rage.

She had someone else ready to help, of course. No one was going to steal her dreams again. No one. She knew Monk had weapons packed in his suitcases, and by God, if she had to kill Carrie and Avery herself to get her dreams back, then that's what she would do.

"Stupid Monk," she hissed. "Stupid, stupid man."

The tail car stayed well behind Jilly. There were three agents riding with Avery in the sedan. Kelly was driving, and she sat behind him. She tried not to let her anxiety show, but it was extremely difficult.

Her heart felt like it had stopped when she heard the gunshots, and she didn't take a breath until she heard John Paul's voice over the radio. She went weak with relief and then immediately started worrying again.

"Do you think she's spotted us?" she asked Kelly.

"I'm sure she doesn't know she's being followed," he replied.

Jilly was now so far ahead of them on the highway, Avery could barely see the back of her head.

"She's speeding, isn't she?"

"Yes," he answered. "She's going at least eighty."

"If there's a speed trap—"

"There isn't," he assured her.

"How do you know?"

"I know."

She moved on to another worry. "Shouldn't you get closer?"

"I'm not going to lose her, Delaney. Now sit back and relax."

"She's turning."

"I see her."

Avery forced herself to stop telling the agent in charge what to do. It would all be over in just a few minutes. If she could just stay calm that long, she could spend a month falling apart if that was her inclination. Stay cool, she told herself.

Jilly had almost missed the entrance to the Windjammer motel. Avery watched her slow her car, make the turn, and drive across the parking lot. She lost sight of her then as Kelly sped on. He pulled into the exit, circled around the motel, and parked next to the restaurant adjacent to the parking lot.

"She's parked in front of the steps," Kelly said.

Avery was looking up at the units. All the doors faced the street. Then she looked at Jilly. She wished they were closer so she could get a good look at her face.

"What's she doing?" she asked as she leaned forward.

"Brushing her hair," Kelly said.

Avery squinted against the sunlight. She saw Jilly pull down the vanity mirror.

"Is she putting lipstick on?"

"She sure is," Kelly said.

She sat back when the agent turned off the motor and rolled the window down. "You get out of this car, Delaney, and I swear—"

She didn't let him finish his threat. "I won't move."

Avery looked at Jilly again. She must have been satisfied with her appearance because she finally opened the car door and got out.

"Showtime," Kelly whispered.

Jilly ran up the first flight of stairs, raced along the outside corridor until she found the number she was looking for, and then stopped. Avery watched her spread the collar on her blouse so that cleavage would show. She smoothed her tight skirt, and then rapped on the door.

Avery's stomach lurched. She heard her voice calling out, "Darling, it's me, Jilly."

Tony Salvetti opened the door.

CHAPTER 39

THE TRIAL IN Sheldon Beach didn't drag on long. The attorney prosecuting the case was competent and effective, and with the evidence at hand, he was able to convince a second jury that Dale Skarrett had broken into Lola Delaney's home with the intent of kidnapping Avery Delaney. In the process of committing the felony, he had caused the premature death of Lola Delaney.

Skarrett insisted on testifying, which was a big mistake. He mumbled and squirmed, and by the time the prosecuting attorney got finished with him, the felon was screaming obscenities at him for twisting everything he said.

Skarrett insisted that he hadn't used Avery as a shield and that he was really only trying to assist the child to her feet when her grandmother fired the gun. He couldn't explain why he'd taken his belt off and beaten her nearly to death except to say that he was simply trying to coax her into going with him to see her mother.

The photos of Avery in the hospital proved beyond a reasonable doubt that Skarrett had left her in that hallway to die. Within an hour, the jury rendered its verdict, and Skarrett was led back to prison, where he belonged.

John Paul stayed in Sheldon Beach with Avery through the entire trial, and Carrie flew in the day before Avery was scheduled to testify. The aunt had been to hell and back, and he expected to meet a shattered woman. She wasn't, though. If she was devastated by her husband's betrayal, she didn't let it show.

In between her calls to her staff in Bel Air, John Paul told Carrie he was going to marry Avery. She didn't want to hear that. If her niece was going to marry, she should find a man with potential . . . and money. What kind of life would she have, married to a carpenter?

Oh, yes, Carrie was one tough cookie . . . and meaner than a crocodile when she didn't get her way.

He really liked her.

CHAPTER 40

"Mr. Carter will see you now."

"Thank you." Avery straightened her skirt and smiled at the receptionist as she walked to the door.

"You want me to go in with you?" John Paul asked.

She shook her head. "You'll wait here?"

"For as long as it takes."

She opened the door and stepped into the freezer. She'd come prepared this morning and was wearing a long-sleeved jacket.

"Good morning, sir."

"Have a seat, Delaney."

He didn't look happy, but then, she'd never seen Carter smile before, so she wasn't certain if he was still angry with her or not.

She sat in the chair facing his desk, folded her hands in her lap, and said, "Sir, if you're going to fire me, I'd like the opportunity to preempt and resign first."

"Why?" he asked.

He'd stood when she entered the room but now took his seat behind the massive desk.

"Resigning would look better on my résumé."

"No, I'm asking you why you think I'm going to fire you?"

"Because I didn't follow procedure," she said.

Her hands were trembling. She wasn't certain if it was due to the frigid air in the office or the fact that she was so nervous. He had the ability to turn her into an insecure twit simply by looking at her.

"I should have figured it all out much, much sooner, but in my defense, sir, I was busy jumping in and out of fivers and dodging bullets. I didn't have time to analyze the data, but I should have made the time," she hastily added so that he would know she was taking full responsibility for her mistakes. "I also used your name to force Agent Kelly to let me ride in the tail car, and you were very specific with your order that I should never do that again. I broke the chain of command. I didn't let the agents assigned to protect me do their job. Sir, I ran from them. I did. Oh, and I also bothered you during your monthly poker game when I called you that night from Walden Point, and everyone at the Bureau knows how sacred your poker games are to you."

She thought she noticed the corner of his mouth turn up just a little. Was he about to smile or sneer?

He leaned forward and stacked his hands on the desk. "Just so you know, I had a full house, Delaney, but you used the priority code, so I had to fold. Why did you call me instead of going through channels?"

She might as well tell him the truth. She didn't have anything to lose. "I knew you'd listen to me and tell me if I was right or wrong. I also knew you'd help me, and we had to move fast. Because you gave the okay, we could do that."

"Go on," he urged.

"While the agents were getting things set up in Florida, I called Aunt Carrie and told her that John Paul and I were staying at Milt's Motel in Walden Point and that she would be brought there to stay with us until Skarrett's trial. I knew she would call her husband, Tony, and tell him to come there. And, by the time she did that, agents were monitoring Tony's phone calls and e-mail."

"And if she hadn't called him?" Carter asked.

"Then I would have," she said. "But she did tell him, and just as I suspected, Tony contacted Jilly and gave her the news that Carrie and I would be together in Florida. Then he booked a flight there for himself."

She took a breath and continued. "By the time the agents pinpointed Jilly's location, she and Monk had vanished, but of course we knew where they were headed."

"Walden Point."

"Yes," she agreed. "I really hated using my aunt that way, blatantly lying to her, but it was the only thing I could do. After everything was in motion, thanks to the agent you put in charge, Tom Kelly, I called Carrie back and told her she'd be staying in Colorado for a while longer, and I told her why."

"How did she take the news about her husband?"

I broke her heart, Avery thought. "It was . . . difficult for her to accept. She's a strong woman," she added. "She'll survive."

"It was John Paul Renard who figured out how Monk would strike, wasn't it?"

"Yes. We moved to a houseboat while the trap was being set at the motel. The agents made it look like we were still there. It was John Paul who found the trip wire on the stairs leading to the tower, and he and Agent Clayborne got ready."

"Okay, I want to know. How did you put it together?"

"The Politicians, sir."

He raised an eyebrow. She nodded. "I was sitting on the beach . . . thinking about the situation, and that case came to mind. They had their own agenda, remember? They wanted everyone to think they were politically motivated, but it was really all about money. That got me thinking about agendas, I guess you could say. I realized I wasn't seeing the forest because of the trees. So I did the same thing I had done when I was working on the Politician case. I took it all apart and looked at each piece. Everyone had his own agenda," she added. "Monk and Jilly and Skarrett and Tony Salvetti." She couldn't bear to call the bastard her uncle now, not after what he had done. "They each wanted something desperately.

"It was what Jilly wanted that made everything fall into place. Carrie told me about the letter that Jilly had left for her. She said Jilly accused her of stealing her dream and giving it away. That kept nagging at me. I had read all of Carrie's diaries, and I knew what Jilly was capable of. I also knew how patient she was. She'd wait years to get even. I asked myself what she wanted most. Money? Revenge? Then it clicked. Jilly wanted to be a star. She craved adulation and attention. Carrie took her dream away from her. Carrie went to Hollywood and became successful and powerful. She made people stars. In Jilly's mind, Carrie had taken her dream. She blamed Carrie for all her failures. We found proof of her obsession when the agents confiscated her belongings."

Carter nodded. "Agent Kelly told me they found a tape in Jilly's purse. It was a copy of a commercial you starred in when you were a teenager."

"Yes," she said. "I think the commercial started it all. Jilly saw it on television, and I imagine became quite enraged. She began plotting and planning way back then. She knew who I was. Evidently Jilly felt Carrie had given her dream to me, and she was going to get even."

"She held on to that dream for over twenty years?" Carter asked.

"Oh, yes. She has a twisted, inflated opinion of herself," she said. "I asked myself, who did Jilly think could get her dream back? Who could make her a star?"

"Tony Salvetti."

"Yes," she said. "He was still co-owner of Star Catcher. I didn't want to believe Tony was involved with any of this. John Paul said that, on some level, I must have known all along because I never called to tell Tony where I was." She glanced down at her engagement ring and lovingly adjusted it on her finger.

"It was so easy for Jilly. When she met Tony, she found an angry, bitter man. Carrie and he had merged two companies. When they got married, they were supposed to run the business as equal partners, but Carrie started bringing in the accounts. She slowly squeezed Tony out of the operation until he didn't have any power at all. He told Agent Kelly that Carrie was trying to emasculate him. He knew he would lose everything when she divorced him, and that was inevitable because she was becoming more and more distrustful, especially after she discovered over a hundred thousand dollars was missing from their accounts. Tony told Carrie that the money was in the bank and that it was an accounting error, but she certainly would have had the company books audited.

"Jilly told Tony she had a connection that would solve the problem for them both. She knew a man serving a sentence in a Florida prison who could help them get a hit man."

"Dale Skarrett?"

"Yes. She went to Skarrett and promised to help him get out of prison. If he would give her the name of a killer for hire, she would get rid of Carrie and me, and there would be no one to testify against him. She told him that Tony Salvetti was willing to put up the money to get rid of his wife. Jilly also promised Skarrett that she would be waiting for him when he got out. He was still obsessed with her. I'm sure she would have found a way to keep him believing she loved him long enough to get the stolen diamonds. She also promised him she would get rid of the judge who had sentenced him.

"And that brings us to Monk. When Jilly met him, she found a killer for hire, but she also found a lonely man. It took nothing for her to win him over. As it turns out, she didn't even have to offer him the money that Tony had given her. He fell madly in love and was willing to do anything she asked. So, nobody was the wiser. She could keep the money for herself."

"Who came up with the idea of putting all those women in the Colorado house?"

"Jilly," she answered. "She does like to complicate things. The drama appealed to her, and making Carrie suffer was an added bonus. Monk had already taken the contract to kill Anne Trapp, and he'd also taken money from Dennis Parnell to blow up the mountain house. Parnell was convinced the judge would award the estate to his ex-wife," she explained. "And I can only imagine what he must have felt when he found out the judge had awarded the house to him."

"Monk was a busy boy."

"Oh, yes," she said.

"Did you see it on the news?" he asked. "Eric Trapp finally broke down and confessed. He's going to go away for a very long time. If your aunt hadn't given us that letter from Anne, we wouldn't have had the evidence we needed.

Trapp told the interrogator his wife was taking too long to die."

"Just like the Politicians," Avery said, "greed motivated all of them."

"Amazing," he said then, "the way Jilly manipulated Salvetti and Monk and Skarrett. She was the piper and they were dancing to her tune, none of them knowing what she was up to. I talked to Agent Kelly a little while ago," he said. "Skarrett still isn't admitting much, but Salvetti's talking. The odd thing is . . ."

"Yes?"

"Neither one of them will say a bad word about Jilly. They're still singing her praises."

That didn't surprise her. "I'll bet she's not talking, though."

"No, she's still stonewalling. You're going to make a great field agent, Delaney."

"Perhaps, with the proper training, I could be good, but sir, I don't want to, not anymore. If I've learned anything during the past weeks, it's that life is too short, and I don't want to waste another minute going after men and women who are beyond hope. I want to make a difference before it's too late."

She stood and waited until he walked around the desk. She shook his hand. "Thank you, sir."

"You're really going to resign? I can't talk you into staying?"

"I've made up my mind, sir. I need to leave."

"Have you decided what you're going to do?"

"Now that the trial and the parole hearing are over and Skarrett is back where he belongs, I'm going to spend a couple of weeks with my aunt, and then I'm moving to Louisiana and going back to school to get my teacher's certificate."

"I'm going to miss you," he said. "Good luck."

"Thank you, sir."

He opened the door for her, and as she walked past, he said, "One more thing, Delaney."

"Yes?"

"Good work."

CHAPTER 41

THE DETECTIVE LED Avery and John Paul down a long hallway to what he called their screening room.

"You'll be able to see her through the glass, but she won't be able to see you," he explained before he opened the door and stepped back.

Avery didn't move.

"She's in the interrogation room now with two detectives," he explained.

And still she didn't budge.

The detective glanced at John Paul. "I'll just let you take your time," he said before he turned and walked away.

"You don't have to do this," John Paul said.

"Yes, I do."

She stood on the threshold another long minute, and then she straightened her shoulders and walked in. The room was the size of a closet. She turned to the mirrored window, her hands fisted at her sides, and looked at the woman who had given her life and then had so desperately tried to take it away.

John Paul slipped his hand in hers and asked, "Do you remember her?"

"No. I was only five when she came to the house," she whispered. "So long ago."

Jilly sat on one side of the square metal table facing two detectives. Her back was straight, one leg crossed over the other, her hands folded on the table. The top three buttons of her eyelet blouse were undone, and the neckline opened a little wider each time she moved ever so slightly. She suddenly turned and looked directly at the mirror. Avery inhaled sharply and drew back as she felt the bile rising in her throat.

"Look," Avery whispered.

"I see her," John Paul said.

Avery shook her head. "Not her. Look at the detectives. Look how they're reacting to her."

Both detectives were leaning forward, as though they were unconsciously trying to get closer to her. One said something and then reached out and touched her hand.

"She's working them," Avery said.

A policeman opened the door to the interrogation room. Jilly looked up at him, then, like a languorous Persian cat, she stretched her lithe body and stood. As she followed him out the door, she paused to glance back over her shoulder and smile at the two men. Both detectives eagerly returned the smile. They watched her every movement until the door closed behind her.

Avery looked into John Paul's eyes. "I'm ready to move on now."

She led the way out of the police station. She didn't look back.

EPILOGUE

SUNSET WAS AVERY'S favorite time of day. She'd go outside and sit on the porch swing John Paul had built for her. She could hear the water lapping against the dock behind the house, and if she closed her eyes, she could almost smell the lilacs John Paul had planted.

The screen door opened and closed, and her husband sat down next to her. He put his arm around her, leaned back, and gave the swing a push.

"You ready for school tomorrow, sugar?"

"Yes."

"What were you thinking about?" he asked. "Were you going to your happy place?"

She put her head on his shoulder and smiled. "I'm already there."